JOEL WHITBURN'S
TOP *Adult* CONTEMPORARY

1961-1993

Billboard.

Compiled from *Billboard's* Easy Listening charts 1961-1979
and Adult Contemporary charts 1979-1993.

Record Research Inc.
P.O. Box 200
Menomonee Falls, Wisconsin 53052-0200 U.S.A.

ISBN 0-89820-099-7

Record Research Inc.
P.O. Box 200
Menomonee Falls, Wisconsin 53052-0200
U.S.A.

CONTENTS

    Most Charted Hits   Most Weeks At The #1 Position
    Most Top 40 Hits   Most Non-*Hot 100* Adult Contemporary Hits
    Most Top 10 Hits   Most Adult Contemporary Hits Only
    Most #1 Hits

Dedicated to...

...Bing Crosby, Frank Sinatra, Perry Como and Nat "King" Cole —
they set the stage for song stylists such as Frankie Laine, Tony
Bennett, Eddie Fisher and Al Martino.

...Dinah Shore, Jo Stafford, Margaret Whiting and Doris Day —
these songstresses paved the way for the likes of Patti Page,
Teresa Brewer, Rosemary Clooney and Joni James.

...And all of the timeless vocalists of days gone by.

AUTHOR'S NOTE

Before there was rock, before there was jazz, before there was country, R&B or big-band music, there was Adult Contemporary. Not always termed as such, Adult Contemporary has existed for generations as the serene side of the American popular music prism. A small sampling from the first 60 years of this century-old mellow music includes "After The Ball," "My Wild Irish Rose," "In The Good Old Summer Time," "For Me And My Gal," "My Blue Heaven," "Night And Day," "Sentimental Journey," "Some Enchanted Evening," "Because Of You," "Vaya Con Dios," "It's All In The Game" and "The Wayward Wind."

Billboard first distinguished the softer sounds of pop in July of 1961. Twenty titles from the *Hot 100* chart were identified as such and listed on the first *Easy Listening* chart. In July of 1965, *Billboard* further recognized these "middle-of-the-road" singles as an independent format by basing the chart not on *Hot 100* standing but on "national retail sales and radio station airplay." While the name and compilation of the chart has changed over the years, the popularity of Adult Contemporary as a separate format has continued to grow. Three decades later, it consistently remains at or near the top of each quarter's leading radio format ratings.

It endures because it endears. It is the pop music that is contemplative, pleasing to the ears and non-grating to the nerves. The broad umbrella of Adult Contemporary encompasses soft rock, bright jazz, sweeping instrumentals, slow melodies of love, longing and melancholy.

It is not generational. The Adult Contemporary chart hosts songs that appeal to the young and old set, whether it is a Def Leppard rock ballad or a standard by Linda Ronstadt. Adult Contemporary is not swept under by the latest trend and forgotten. A recent testimonial to this is the immense popularity of the classic-laden soundtrack to the film *Sleepless In Seattle*.

Its melodies are timeless. The many successful covers of Adult Contemporary classics — from Elvis Presley's to UB40's "Can't Help Falling In Love" — are evidence that it never goes out of style. Adult Contemporary will always be part of American popular music, no matter the trends to come.

JOEL WHITBURN

SYNOPSIS OF *BILLBOARD'S* ADULT CONTEMPORARY CHARTS 1961-1993

DATE	POSITIONS	CHART TITLE
7/17/61	20	**EASY LISTENING**
11/3/62	20	**MIDDLE-ROAD SINGLES**
5/2/64	20	**POP-STANDARD SINGLES**
10/24/64	15-25	**MIDDLE-ROAD SINGLES** (size varied from a top 15 to a top 25)
5/1/65	20-25	**POP-STANDARD SINGLES** (size varied from a top 20 to a top 25)
6/5/65	40	**EASY LISTENING**
7/7/73	50	**EASY LISTENING**
4/7/79	50	**ADULT CONTEMPORARY**
10/20/84	40	**HOT ADULT CONTEMPORARY**
9/19/87	50	**HOT ADULT CONTEMPORARY**
7/17/93	40	**HOT ADULT CONTEMPORARY**

USER'S GUIDE

The Artist Section lists by artist name, alphabetically, every record that charted on *Billboard's* Adult Contemporary charts from July 17, 1961 through July 17, 1993. (See page 6 for a chart synopsis.) Each artist's charted hits are listed in chronological order and are sequentially numbered. All Top 10 hits are highlighted in bold type.

EXPLANATION OF COLUMNAR HEADINGS

DEBUT DATE: Date first charted

PEAK POS: Highest charted position (highlighted in bold type)

WKS CHR: Total weeks charted

GOLD: Gold or Platinum record

POP POS: Peak position achieved on *Billboard's* "Hot 100" or "Bubbling Under The Hot 100" Pop charts

LABEL & NUMBER: Original record label and number

EXPLANATION OF SYMBOLS

★★21★★ Number to the left of an artist name denotes an artist's ranking among the Top 200 Adult Contemporary Artists of All Time

۞ Indicates that the artist never hit *Billboard's* "Hot 100" chart (appears to the right of the artist name)

1 Superior number to the right of the No. 1 or No. 2 peak position is the total weeks the single held that position. Also used in POP POS column.

↑ Beside peak position and/or weeks charted, indicates that the record was still on the charts as of the September 25, 1993 research cutoff date

● Gold record*

▲ Platinum record* (additional million units sold are indicated by a numeral following the symbol)

> *The primary source used to determine gold and platinum records is the *Recording Industry Association of America* (RIAA), which began certifying gold records in 1958 and platinum records in 1976. From 1958 through 1988, RIAA required sales of one million units for a gold single and two million units for a platinum single; however, as of January 1, 1989, RIAA lowered the certification requirements for gold singles to sales of 500,000 units and for platinum to one million units. Please keep in mind that some record labels have never requested RIAA certifications for their hits.

/ Divides a two-sided hit. Complete chart data (debut date, peak position, etc.) is shown for both sides if each side achieved its own peak position. If a title was shown only as the B-side, then only the weeks it was shown as a "tag along" are listed.

LETTER(S) IN BRACKETS AFTER TITLES

C - Comedy
F - Foreign language
I - Instrumental
N - Novelty

R - Re-entry, reissue, remix or re-release
  of a previously recorded single
S - Spoken
X - Christmas

TOP HITS AT A GLANCE

Listed in rank order below their artist biographies, in bold italic type, are the biggest charted hits of artists who meet the following requirements:

If an artist hit *Billboard's* Easy Listening/Adult Contemporary charts with:

♦ eight to nine hits, at least three of which were Top 10 hits, we show their <u>three</u> biggest hits;

♦ 10 to 19 hits, we list their <u>three</u> biggest hits;

♦ 20 or more hits, we list their <u>five</u> biggest hits.

> For an artist that charted 10 or more titles, their highest-charting single is blocked out in a thin-lined box.

For all of the above, these features allow a reader to see at a glance any of the top artists most successful chart hits. It reflects only chart status and may or may not relate to an artist's best seller over the years. Ties are broken based on total weeks at the peak position, total weeks in the Top 10, total weeks in the Top 40 and total weeks charted.

Big Bad John

"Big Bad John" by Jimmy Dean is shown as a #1 hit for 10 weeks in this book; however, it is shown as #1 for 11 weeks in our **Top 1000 x 5** book. Although <u>10 weeks is correct</u>, 11 weeks was initially determined due to a frozen chart and a change *Billboard* made during this record's reign at #1. The research inconsistencies began when *Billboard* did not publish an Easy Listening chart on 12/25/61; and, therefore, the chart was considered frozen for that week. "Big Bad John" was #1 for 10 weeks which included the frozen chart. Following the 12/25/61 issue, *Billboard* changed its issue date permanently from a Monday to a Saturday date; and, therefore, the next issue was dated 1/6/62. The difference between 12/25/61 and 1/6/62 is 12 days; and, due to this extended period of time between charts, our staff concluded that "Big Bad John" should receive one more week at #1, or a total of 11 weeks. In further analysis of the 12-day gap and the date change, we have determined that only 1 week, and not 2, should actually be considered frozen because the 12-day gap was due to a technical date change and not because of an unpublished issue.

ARTIST SECTION

Lists, alphabetically by artist name, every record that charted on *Billboard's* Easy Listening charts from 1961-1979 and Adult Contemporary charts from 1979-1993.

DEBUT DATE	PEAK POS	WKS CHR	GOLD	ARTIST — Record Title	POP POS	Label & Number

A

★★79★★ **ABBA**

Pop quartet formed in Stockholm, Sweden in 1970, using their first initials as an acronym. Consisted of Anni-Frid "Frida" Lyngstad and Agnetha Faltskog (vocals), Bjorn Ulvaeus (guitar) and Benny Andersson (keyboards). Benny and Bjorn recorded together in 1966. Bjorn and Agnetha married in 1971, divorced in 1979. Benny and Frida married in 1978, divorced in 1981. Disbanded in the early 1980s. Bjorn and Benny co-wrote the *Chess* musical with Tim Rice.

1)The Winner Takes It All 2)Fernando 3)Dancing Queen

9/28/74	**27**	7		1 Honey, Honey..	27	Atlantic 3209
11/1/75	**19**	8		2 SOS...	15	Atlantic 3265
2/14/76	**8**	13		3 I Do, I Do, I Do, I Do, I Do..........................	15	Atlantic 3310
6/5/76	**12**	10		4 Mamma Mia...	32	Atlantic 3315
9/4/76	**1²**	20		5 Fernando...	13	Atlantic 3346
12/11/76	**6**	18	●	6 Dancing Queen..	1¹	Atlantic 3372

ABBA:

5/14/77	**7**	16		7 Knowing Me, Knowing You..........................	14	Atlantic 3387
10/29/77	**38**	5		8 Money, Money, Money................................	56	Atlantic 3434
1/7/78	**9**	16		9 The Name Of The Game..............................	12	Atlantic 3449
4/29/78	**9**	16	●	10 Take A Chance On Me................................	3	Atlantic 3457
6/30/79	**41**	7		11 Does Your Mother Know.............................	19	Atlantic 3574
8/18/79	**40**	5		12 Voulez-Vous/	80	
9/29/79	**37**	15		13 Angeleyes..	64	Atlantic 3609
11/17/79	**15**	11		14 Chiquitita..	29	Atlantic 3629
11/29/80	**1²**	19		15 The Winner Takes It All.............................	8	Atlantic 3776
3/28/81	**14**	11		16 Super Trouper..	45	Atlantic 3806
1/16/82	**10**	15		17 When All Is Said And Done.........................	27	Atlantic 3889
3/12/83	**33**	7		18 One Of Us..	107	Atlantic 89881

ABBEY TAVERN SINGERS, The

Traditional Irish group.

9/24/66	**40**	1		Off To Dublin In The Green..........................	94	HBR 498

ABBOTT, Gregory

Soul singer/songwriter from New York. At age eight, member of St. Patrick's Cathedral Choir. Psychology major at Boston University and Stanford; taught English at Berkeley.

11/15/86	**2¹**	20	▲	1 Shake You Down...	1¹	Columbia 06191
3/21/87	**25**	7		2 I Got The Feelin' (It's Over).......................	56	Columbia 06632
5/28/88	**35**	6		3 I'll Prove It To You....................................		Columbia 07774

ABC

Electro-pop group from Sheffield, England. Formed as Vice Versa with Stephen Singleton and Mark White. Lead singer Martin Fry joined in 1980, group renamed ABC. Singleton left group in 1985.

10/5/85	**11**	15		1 Be Near Me..	9	Mercury 880626
8/15/87	**2¹**	17		2 When Smokey Sings....................................	5	Mercury 888604
				a tribute to Smokey Robinson		

ABDUL, Paula

Los Angeles singer/choreographer. Born on 6/19/62 of Brazilian and French Canadian parentage. While still a teen, was the choreographer and member of the Los Angeles Lakers cheerleaders. Choreographed Janet Jackson's *Control* videos and TV's *The Tracey Ullman Show*. Married actor Emilio Estevez on 4/29/92.

2/11/89	**39**	6	▲	1 Straight Up..	1³	Virgin 99256
4/22/89	**11**	17	●	2 Forever Your Girl.......................................	1²	Virgin 99230
2/24/90	**45**	4	●	3 Opposites Attract.......................................	1³	Virgin 99158
				PAULA ABDUL With The Wild Pair (Marv Gunn & Bruce Christian) Derrick Delite (rap)		
5/11/91	**1⁵**	27	●	4 Rush, Rush...	1⁵	Virgin 98828
8/3/91	**26**	13		5 The Promise Of A New Day.........................	1¹	Virgin 98752
10/26/91	**5**	18		6 Blowing Kisses In The Wind........................	6	Virgin 98683
4/11/92	**17**	11		7 Will You Marry Me?....................................	19	Virgin 98584
				Sandra St. Victor (backing vocal); Stevie Wonder (harmonica)		

ABRAMS, Miss, And The Strawberry Point School Third Grade Class

Rita Abrams was born on 8/30/43 in Cleveland, Ohio. Taught first grade but recorded with the third and fourth grade classes in Mill Valley, California.

7/25/70	**13**	6		1 Mill Valley...	90	Reprise 0928

DEBUT DATE	PEAK POS	WKS CHR	GOLD	ARTIST — Record Title	POP POS	Label & Number
				ABRAMS, Miss — Cont'd		
1/9/71	**39**	2		2 Buildin' A Heaven On Earth		Reprise 0971
				MISS ABRAHMS AND THE STRAWBERRY POINT FOURTH GRADE		
				written by Norman Greenbaum		
7/3/71	**37**	2		3 Wonder		A&M 1263
				MISS ABRAMS & THE STRAWBERRY POINT 4TH GRADE		
				ACE		
				Pub-rock quintet from Sheffield, England led by vocalist Paul Carrack. Disbanded in 1977. Carrack joined Squeeze in 1981, then Mike + The Mechanics in 1985.		
4/12/75	**24**	9		How Long	3	Anchor 21000
				ADAMS, Bryan		
				Rock singer/songwriter/guitarist based in Vancouver, Canada. Born on 11/5/59 in Kingston, Ontario. Lead singer of Sweeney Todd in 1976. Teamed with Jim Vallance in 1977 in songwriting partnership. Cameo appearance in the film *Pink Cadillac*.		
5/7/83	**29**	9		1 Straight From The Heart..	10	A&M 2536
5/11/85	**12**	19		2 Heaven	1²	A&M 2729
6/29/91	**1**⁸	34	▲³	3 (Everything I Do) I Do It For You	1⁷	A&M 1567
				from the film *Robin Hood: Prince Of Thieves*		
11/9/91	**40**	4	●	4 Can't Stop This Thing We Started	2¹	A&M 1576
5/2/92	**36**	11		5 Thought I'd Died And Gone To Heaven	13	A&M 1592
8/1/92	**5**	25		6 Do I Have To Say The Words?.................................	11	A&M 1611
				ADAMS, Oleta		
				Native of Yakima, Washington. Discovered by Tears For Fears in Kansas City; backing singer on their *Seeds Of Love* album and tour.		
8/4/90	**21**	11		1 Rhythm Of Life		Fontana 875018
11/17/90	**3**	27		2 Get Here	5	Fontana 878476
4/20/91	**17**	12		3 Circle Of One		Fontana 868162
				ADDRISI BROTHERS		
				Pop duo: Dick (b: 7/4/41) and Don (b: 12/14/38; d: 11/13/84) Addrisi. Both from Winthrop, Massachusetts.		
2/5/72	**10**	11		1 We've Got To Get It On Again	25	Columbia 45521
2/16/74	**42**	6		2 Somebody Found Her (Before I Lost Her)		Bell 45,434
5/21/77	**34**	8		3 Slow Dancin' Don't Turn Me On	20	Buddah 566
12/3/77	**28**	10		4 Never My Love	80	Buddah 587
9/1/79	**41**	4		5 Ghost Dancer	45	Scotti Br. 500
				AFTER 7		
				Indianapolis R&B vocal trio: Keith Mitchell with brothers Kevon and Melvin Edmonds. Keith is the cousin of L.A. Reid. Kevon and Melvin are the brothers of Babyface.		
5/19/90	**7**	23	●	1 Ready Or Not	7	Virgin 98995
9/22/90	**23**	16	●	2 Can't Stop	6	Virgin 98961
7/20/91	**36**	14		3 Nights Like This..	24	Virgin 98798
				from the film *The Five Heartbeats*		
				A-HA		
				Pop trio formed in Oslo, Norway: Morten Harket (vocals), Pal Waaktaar (guitar) and Magne "Mags" Furuholmen (keyboards).		
9/14/85	**4**	18		1 Take On Me	1¹	Warner 29011
2/16/91	**26**	10		2 Crying In The Rain		Warner 19547
				#6 Pop hit for The Everly Brothers in 1962		
★★64★★				**AIR SUPPLY**		
				Melbourne, Australia soft vocal duo: Russell Hitchcock (born on 6/15/49 in Melbourne) and Graham Russell (born on 6/1/50 in Nottingham, England). Disbanded in 1988. Both recorded solo. Reunited in 1991. Also see Russell Hitchcock.		
				1)Lost In Love 2)Even The Nights Are Better 3)Here I Am (Just When I Thought I Was Over You)		
2/16/80	**1**⁶	22		1 Lost In Love	3	Arista 0479
7/5/80	**5**	17	●	2 All Out Of Love	2⁴	Arista 0520
11/1/80	**2**²	18		3 Every Woman In The World	5	Arista 0564
5/23/81	**2**⁵	20	●	4 The One That You Love	1¹	Arista 0604
9/19/81	**1**³	19		5 Here I Am (Just When I Thought I Was Over You)	5	Arista 0626
12/19/81	**4**	18		6 Sweet Dreams	5	Arista 0655
6/12/82	**1**⁴	19		7 Even The Nights Are Better	5	Arista 0692
9/18/82	**13**	11		8 Young Love	38	Arista 1005
11/20/82	**4**	19		9 Two Less Lonely People In The World	38	Arista 1004
7/30/83	**2**¹	20	●	10 Making Love Out Of Nothing At All	2³	Arista 9056
6/1/85	**3**	16		11 Just As I Am	19	Arista 9353

DEBUT DATE	PEAK POS	WKS CHR	GOLD	ARTIST — Record Title	POP POS	Label & Number
				AIR SUPPLY — Cont'd		
8/24/85	**13**	13		12 The Power Of Love (You Are My Lady)	68	Arista 9391
8/16/86	**12**	11		13 Lonely Is The Night...	76	Arista 9521
8/17/91	**48**	2		14 Without You		Giant LP Cut
				from the album *The Earth Is...* on Giant 24426; #1 Pop hit for Nilsson in 1972		
7/10/93	**48**	1		15 Goodbye		Giant LP Cut
				from the album *The Vanishing Race* on Giant 24494		
★★**176**★★				**ALABAMA**		
				Country quartet from Fort Payne, Alabama: Randy Owen (vocals, guitar), Jeff Cook (keyboards, fiddle), Teddy Gentry (bass, vocals) and Mark Herndon (drums, vocals). Randy, Jeff and Teddy are cousins.		
				1)Love In The First Degree 2)Take Me Down 3)When We Make Love		
6/20/81	**9**	20		1 Feels So Right	20	RCA 12236
12/19/81	**5**	21		2 Love In The First Degree...................................	15	RCA 12288
5/22/82	**5**	21		3 Take Me Down	18	RCA 13210
5/14/83	**9**	16		4 The Closer You Get	38	RCA 13524
10/8/83	**18**	11		5 Lady Down On Love	76	RCA 13590
5/5/84	**8**	16		6 When We Make Love..	72	RCA 13763
3/23/85	**32**	7		7 There's No Way		RCA 13992
12/27/86	**28**	11		8 Deep River Woman..	71	Motown 1873
				LIONEL RICHIE with Alabama		
2/16/91	**14**	16		9 Forever's As Far As I'll Go		RCA 2706
11/23/91	**33**	9		10 Then Again		RCA 62059
				ALAIMO, Steve		
				Born on 12/6/39 in Rochester, New York. Star of TV's *Where The Action Is*, 1965-66. Member of The Unknowns. Appeared in the film *Stanley* and *Wild Rebels*. President of Vision Records in Miami since 1987. Cousin of Jimmy Alaimo of The Mojo Men.		
6/5/65	**22**	6		1 Cast Your Fate To The Wind.....................................	89	ABC-Para. 10680
7/10/71	**27**	6		2 When My Little Girl Is Smiling	72	Entrance 7501
				ALBERT, Morris		
				Brazilian singer/songwriter born Morris Albert Kaisermann.		
5/24/75	**2**[1]	18	●	1 Feelings	6	RCA 10279
12/27/75	**15**	12		2 Sweet Loving Man	93	RCA 10437
				ALBRIGHT, Gerald ☉		
				Prominent R&B session musician (saxophone/bass). Born and raised in Los Angeles. Attended Locke High School with Patrice Rushen and Ndugu.		
2/13/88	**42**	3		So Amazing		Atlantic 89163
				#94 R&B hit for Luther Vandross in 1987		
				AL B. SURE!		
				R&B singer born Al Brown in Boston and raised in Mt. Vernon, New York.		
6/11/88	**19**	12		1 Nite And Day	7	Warner 28192
3/31/90	**26**	10	●	2 The Secret Garden (Sweet Seduction Suite).....................	31	Qwest 19992
				QUINCY JONES/Al B. Sure!/James Ingram/El DeBarge/Barry White		
				ALIAS		
				Rock quintet formed in Los Angeles by former Sheriff bandmates Freddy Curci (vocals) and Steve DeMarchi (guitar), and Roger Fisher (ex-guitarist of Heart).		
10/6/90	**2**[1]	27		1 More Than Words Can Say..	**2**[1]	EMI 50324
2/16/91	**17**	17		2 Waiting For Love	13	EMI 50337
				ALLEN, Deborah		
				Born Deborah Lynn Thurmond on 9/30/53 in Memphis. Country singer/songwriter.		
10/1/83	**10**	24		Baby I Lied..	26	RCA 13600
				ALLEN, Michael ☉		
				New York-based singer.		
11/8/69	**37**	3		1 Early In The Morning..		London 20052
				#12 Pop hit for Vanity Fare in 1970		
8/25/73	**38**	6		2 Wait Until September..		MGM 14591
8/10/74	**19**	15		3 When Mabel Comes In The Room		Warner 7833
				from the Broadway show *Mack and Mabel*		
11/22/75	**23**	11		4 The Big Parade		Slipped Disc 45288
				written by Neil Sedaka and Howard Greenfield		

ALLEN, Peter

Born Peter Allen Woolnough on 2/10/44 in Tenterfield, Australia. Died on 6/18/92 of AIDS. Cabaret-style performer/songwriter. Married to Liza Minnelli from 1967-73. Oscar-winning, co-writer of "Arthur's Theme."

5/8/76	38	6		1 The More I See You	108	A&M 1813
				Herb Alpert (trumpet solo)		
1/24/81	45	4		2 Fly Away	55	A&M 2288
4/2/83	15	15		3 You Haven't Heard The Last Of Me........................		Arista 1052
10/8/83	26	8		4 Once Before I Go		Arista 9082
2/25/84	41	3		5 You And Me (We Wanted It All)...........................		Arista 9161

ALLEN, Rex Jr. ○

Born on 8/23/47 in Chicago; son of Rex Allen. Traveled with father from age six; played the rhythm guitar and worked as a rodeo clown. Moved to Nashville in the late '60s. Regular on *The Statler Brothers Show* on TNN from 1991.

6/22/74	34	7		Goodbye..		Warner 7788

ALLEN, Steve

Born on 12/26/21 in New York City. Comedian/actor/songwriter/author. In 1954, became the first host of TV's *Tonight Show*. Played title role in 1956 film *The Benny Goodman Story*. Hosted own variety and talk shows, 1956-80. Married to actress Jayne Meadows.

5/18/63	20	1		Gravy Waltz ....[I]	64	Dot 16457
				Don Trenner (orch.)		

ALLMAN BROTHERS BAND, The

Southern-rock band formed in Macon, Georgia in 1969. Consisted of brothers Duane (lead guitar) and Gregg Allman (keyboards), Dickey Betts (guitar), Berry Oakley (bass), and the drum duo of Butch Trucks and Jai Johnny Johanson (pronounced: Jay Johnny Johnson). Duane was killed in a motorcycle crash on 10/29/71 (age 24). Oakley died in another cycle accident on 11/11/72 (age 24); he was replaced by Lamar Williams. Chuck Leavell (keyboards) added in 1972.

9/22/73	12	9		1 Ramblin Man	2[1]	Capricorn 0027
2/2/74	29	7		2 Jessica...[I]	65	Capricorn 0036

★★9★★ ALPERT, Herb, & The Tijuana Brass

Herb was born on 3/31/35 in Los Angeles. Producer/composer/trumpeter/bandleader. Played trumpet since age eight. A&R for Keen Records. Produced first Jan & Dean session. Wrote "Wonderful World" hit for Sam Cooke. Formed A&M Records with Jerry Moss in 1962. Used studio musicians until early 1965, then formed own band.

1)This Guy's In Love With You 2)Taste Of Honey 3)Casino Royale 4)A Banda 5)Rise

HERB ALPERT'S TIJUANA BRASS:

4/18/64	19	1		1 Mexican Drummer Man	77	A&M 732
7/18/64	19	1		2 The Mexican Shuffle.....................................[I]	85	A&M 742
				tune used for a Teabury gum commercial		
3/27/65	13	7		3 Whipped Cream ....[I]	68	A&M 760

HERB ALPERT & THE TIJUANA BRASS:

6/26/65	26	4		4 Mae...[I]	116	A&M 767
				from the film *The Yellow Rolls Royce*		
9/4/65	7	9		5 3rd Man Theme/	[I] 47	
9/11/65	1[5]	21		6 Taste Of Honey ....[I]	7	A&M 775
12/25/65	2[3]	14		7 Zorba The Greek/	[I] 11	
				movie title song		
12/25/65	9	10		8 Tijuana Taxi ....[I]	38	A&M 787
3/12/66	4	10		9 Spanish Flea/	[I] 27	
				theme song from TV's *The Dating Game*		
3/19/66	2[1]	11		10 What Now My Love ....[I]	24	A&M 792
6/25/66	2[3]	12		11 The Work Song ....[I]	18	A&M 805
9/3/66	5	10		12 Flamingo ....[I]	28	A&M 813
11/26/66	2[1]	12		13 Mame	19	A&M 823
				Broadway show title song		
3/18/67	5	7		14 Wade In The Water ....[I]	37	A&M 840
4/15/67	1[2]	15		15 Casino Royale ....[I]	27	A&M 850
				movie title song		
7/15/67	4	10		16 The Happening...[I]	32	A&M 860
9/9/67	1[2]	13		17 A Banda (Ah Bahn-da)..............................[I]	35	A&M 870
1/20/68	3	9		18 Carmen ....[I]	51	A&M 890
				adaptation of the famous Bizet opera song		
4/13/68	13	7		19 Cabaret/	[I] 72	
				Broadway show title song		
5/4/68	36	3		20 Slick ....[I]	119	A&M 925
5/18/68	1[10]	17	●	21 This Guy's In Love With You	1[4]	A&M 929
				HERB ALPERT		

DEBUT DATE	PEAK POS	WKS CHR	GOLD	ARTIST — Record Title	POP POS	Label & Number
				ALPERT, Herb, & The Tijuana Brass — Cont'd		
8/24/68	**2**[3]	10		22 **To Wait For Love**	51	A&M 964
				HERB ALPERT		
12/7/68	**7**	11		23 **My Favorite Things** ....[X-I]	45	A&M 1001
3/29/69	**9**	7		24 **Zazueira (Za-zoo-wher-a)** ....[F]	78	A&M 1043
5/31/69	**5**	8		25 **Without Her**....................................	63	A&M 1065
				HERB ALPERT		
12/20/69	**34**	2		26 You Are My Life...............................	109	A&M 1143
1/24/70	**14**	7		27 The Maltese Melody ....[I]	108	A&M 1159
				written by Bert Kaempfert		
10/24/70	**6**	8		28 **Jerusalem** ....[I]	74	A&M 1225
6/5/71	**28**	5		29 Summertime	114	A&M 1261
				HERB ALPERT & THE T.J.B.:		
3/10/73	**22**	6		30 Last Tango In Paris ....[I]	77	A&M 1420
5/4/74	**14**	9		31 Fox Hunt ....[I]	84	A&M 1526
7/20/74	**13**	12		32 Save The Sunlight........................		A&M 1542
				Lani Hall (vocal)		
5/10/75	**19**	8		33 Coney Island ....[I]		A&M 1688
7/19/75	**28**	6		34 El Bimbo...................................[I]		A&M 1714
				#43 Pop hit for Bimbo Jet in 1975		
				HERB ALPERT:		
6/30/79	**1**[1]	23	●	35 Rise ....[I]	**1**[2]	A&M 2151
11/24/79	**23**	9		36 Rotation....................................[I]	30	A&M 2202
3/15/80	**41**	4		37 Street Life ....[I]	104	A&M 2221
7/26/80	**39**	5		38 Beyond ....[I]	50	A&M 2246
6/6/81	**43**	3		39 Come What May		A&M 2333
				LANI HALL Featuring Herb Alpert		
8/1/81	**22**	10		40 Magic Man ....[I]	79	A&M 2356
6/26/82	**4**	18		41 **Route 101** ....[I]	37	A&M 2422
10/2/82	**26**	9		42 Fandango ....[I]		A&M 2441
7/23/83	**14**	13		43 Garden Party ....[I]	81	A&M 2562
4/28/84	**32**	8		44 Come What May ....[R]		A&M 2632
				LANI HALL With Herb Alpert		
8/18/84	**22**	9		45 Bullish ....[I]	90	A&M 2655
				HERB ALPERT TIJUANA BRASS		
8/15/87	**21**	8		46 Making Love In The Rain..................	35	A&M 2949
				Lisa Keith (vocal)		

AMAZING RHYTHM ACES, The

Memphis country-rock group: Russell Smith (lead vocals, guitar), Barry "Byrd" Burton (guitar, dobro), Billy Earhart III (keyboards), Jeff Davis (bass) and Butch McDade (drums). Disbanded in 1980.

8/16/75	**33**	7		1 Third Rate Romance	14	ABC 12078
8/21/76	**23**	16		2 The End Is Not In Sight (The Cowboy Tune)	42	ABC 12202

AMBROSE, Stephen ⊙

4/7/73	**32**	4		Friend		Barnaby 5014

AMBROSIA

Los Angeles-based pop group. Lead singers David Pack and Joe Puerta with Burleigh Drummond and Christopher North (left in 1977).

8/30/75	**46**	4		1 Holdin' On To Yesterday...................	17	20th Century 2207
9/23/78	**11**	17		2 How Much I Feel	3	Warner 8640
4/12/80	**3**	18		3 **Biggest Part Of Me**......................	3	Warner 49225
7/19/80	**5**	21		4 **You're The Only Woman (You & I)**	13	Warner 49508

★★65★★ AMERICA

Trio formed in London in 1969. Consisted of Americans Dan Peek and Gerry Beckley, with Englishman Dewey Bunnell. All played guitars. Met at U.S. Air Force base. Members of Daze in 1970. Moved to the U.S. in February 1972. Won the 1972 Best New Artist Grammy Award. Peek left in 1976 and became a popular Contemporary Christian artist.

1)Today's The Day 2)Lonely People 3)Tin Man

3/11/72	**3**	11	●	1 **A Horse With No Name**	**1**[3]	Warner 7555
5/27/72	**7**	10		2 I Need You	9	Warner 7580
11/4/72	**3**	11		3 **Ventura Highway**	8	Warner 7641
2/10/73	**23**	7		4 Don't Cross The River	35	Warner 7670
8/11/73	**11**	10		5 Muskrat Love	67	Warner 7725
8/10/74	**1**[1]	16		6 **Tin Man**	4	Warner 7839

15

DEBUT DATE	PEAK POS	WKS CHR	GOLD	ARTIST — Record Title	POP POS	Label & Number
				AMERICA — Cont'd		
12/28/74	**1**[1]	15		7 **Lonely People**	5	Warner 8048
4/19/75	**5**	13		8 **Sister Golden Hair**	**1**[1]	Warner 8086
8/2/75	**4**	13		9 **Daisy Jane**	20	Warner 8118
12/13/75	**41**	7		10 Woman Tonight	44	Warner 8157
5/29/76	**1**[2]	11		11 **Today's The Day**	23	Warner 8212
8/7/76	**17**	9		12 **Amber Cascades**	75	Warner 8238
				Dan Peek left trio — duo hereon: Gerry Beckley and Dewey Bunnell		
11/17/79	**48**	1		13 All My Life		Capitol 4777
3/1/80	**45**	2		14 All Around		Capitol 4817
				above 9 produced by George Martin (Beatles' producer)		
7/31/82	**5**	25		15 **You Can Do Magic**	8	Capitol 5142
12/4/82	**16**	17		16 Right Before Your Eyes	45	Capitol 5177
6/25/83	**4**	16		17 **The Border**	33	Capitol 5236
9/22/84	**15**	10		18 Special Girl	106	Capitol 5398
12/22/84	**26**	8		19 (Can't Fall Asleep To a) Lullaby		Capitol 5430
				AMERICAN COMEDY NETWORK, The		
				Group of former D.J.s headed by Andy Goodman.		
2/25/84	**47**	2		Breaking Up Is Hard On You (a/k/a Don't Take Ma		
				Bell Away From Me) ....[N]	70	Critique 704
				parody of "Breaking Up Is Hard To Do"		
★★**88**★★				**AMES, Ed**		
				One of The Ames Brothers. Born Ed Urick on 7/9/27 in Malden, Massachusetts. Played the Indian "Mingo" on the *Daniel Boone* TV series.		
				1)My Cup Runneth Over 2)When The Snow Is On The Roses 3)Time, Time		
1/23/65	**17**	4		1 Try To Remember	73	RCA 8483
				from the musical *The Fantasticks*		
12/3/66	**1**[4]	23		2 **My Cup Runneth Over**	8	RCA 9002
				from the musical *I Do, I Do*		
5/6/67	**1**[1]	15		3 **Time, Time**	61	RCA 9178
8/5/67	**2**[1]	10		4 **Timeless Love**		RCA 9255
				written by Buffy Sainte-Marie		
9/30/67	**1**[4]	17		5 **When The Snow Is On The Roses**	98	RCA 9319
12/23/67	**6**	9		6 **Who Will Answer?**	19	RCA 9400
5/11/68	**10**	10		7 **Apologize**	79	RCA 9517
8/3/68	**12**	9		8 All My Love's Laughter	122	RCA 9589
11/9/68	**22**	4		9 Kiss Her Now		RCA 9647
				from the Broadway musical *Dear World*		
2/15/69	**11**	9		10 Changing, Changing	130	RCA 9726
5/17/69	**21**	9		11 Son Of A Travelin' Man	92	RCA 0156
7/19/69	**17**	8		12 Think Summer		RCA 9751
				ED & MARILYN (also see #16 below)		
10/25/69	**19**	5		13 Leave Them A Flower		RCA 0253
12/20/69	**21**	6		14 A Thing Called Love		RCA 0296
				#2 Country hit for Johnny Cash in 1972		
4/25/70	**28**	2		15 Three Good Reasons		RCA 0329
5/30/70	**38**	3		16 Think Summer ....[R]		RCA 9843
				ED AMES and MARILYN MAYE		
6/27/70	**36**	3		17 Chippewa Town		RCA 9864
				written by Neil Sedaka and Howard Greenfield		
				AMES, Nancy		
				Spanish/English vocalist born in Washington, D.C. Her grandfather was once president of Panama.		
9/10/66	**18**	10		Cry Softly	95	Epic 10056
				AMESBURY, Bill		
				Toronto-based singer/songwriter/guitarist.		
3/23/74	**37**	6		Virginia (Touch Me Like You Do)	59	Casablanca 0001
				ANDERSON, Bill		
				Born James William Anderson III on 11/1/37 in Columbia, South Carolina. Country singer/songwriter/ actor. Hosted Nashville Network's TV game show *Fandango*. Member of the *Grand Ole Opry* since 1961. Known as "Whispering Bill."		
5/4/63	**3**	12		1 **Still**	8	Decca 31458
8/24/63	**18**	4		2 8 X 10	53	Decca 31521

16

DEBUT DATE	PEAK POS	WKS CHR	GOLD	ARTIST — Record Title	POP POS	Label & Number
				ANDERSON, Carl — see LORING, Gloria		
				ANDERSON, Jon		
				Lead singer of Yes. Born on 10/25/44 in Lancashire, England. Also see Jon & Vangelis.		
1/18/86	38	2		Easier Said Than Done		Elektra 69580
				written by Vangelis; from Jon's Christmas album *3 Ships*		
				ANDERSON, Lynn		
				Born on 9/26/47 in Grand Forks, North Dakota; raised in Sacramento. Country singer; daughter of country singer Liz Anderson. An accomplished equestrian, she was the California Horse Show Queen in 1966.		
11/14/70	5	17	●	1 Rose Garden	3	Columbia 45252
5/1/71	6	9		2 You're My Man	63	Columbia 45356
8/28/71	30	6		3 How Can I Unlove You	63	Columbia 45429
1/29/72	16	6		4 Cry	71	Columbia 45529
7/21/73	34	5		5 Top Of The World	74	Columbia 45857
				ANDREWS, Julie		
				Born Julia Welles on 10/1/35 in Walton-on-Thames, England. Noted Broadway and film actress. Starred in the acclaimed Broadway productions of *My Fair Lady* and *Camelot*. Won 1964's Best Actress Oscar for *Mary Poppins*. Won an Emmy for her TV show *The Julie Andrews Hour*.		
4/24/65	14	5		1 Super-cali-fragil-istic- expi-ali-docious .... [N]	66	Vista 434
				JULIE ANDREWS - DICK VAN DYKE and THE PEARLIES		
				from the film *Mary Poppins*		
3/25/67	3	12		2 Thoroughly Modern Millie		Decca 32102
				movie title song starring Andrews		
				ANIMOTION		
				Pop group formed in 1984; several personnel changes. 1989 lineup included Paul Engemann (formerly of Device) and actress/dancer/singer Cynthia Rhodes (in films *Staying Alive* and *Dirty Dancing*; married Richard Marx on 1/8/89).		
5/6/89	46	2		Room To Move	9	Polydor 871418
				from the film *My Stepmother Is An Alien*		
★★63★★				**ANKA, Paul**		
				Born on 7/30/41 in Ottawa, Canada. Performer since age 12. Father financed first recording, "I Confess," on RPM 472 in 1956. Wrote "My Way" for Frank Sinatra, "She's A Lady" for Tom Jones. Also wrote theme for TV's *Tonight Show*. Own variety show in 1973. Cameo appearances in the 1962 film *The Longest Day* and the 1992 film *Captain Ron*. Longtime popular entertainer in Las Vegas.		
				1)*Times Of Your Life* 2)*Hold Me 'Til The Mornin' Comes* 3)*Anytime (I'll Be There)* 4)*Goodnight My Love* 5)*(I Believe) There's Nothing Stronger Than Our Love*		
1/4/69	2¹	12		1 Goodnight My Love	27	RCA Victor 9648
4/19/69	36	2		2 In The Still Of The Night	64	RCA Victor 0126
6/14/69	30	4		3 Sincerely	80	RCA Victor 0164
11/22/69	13	7		4 Happy	86	RCA Victor 9767
9/25/71	14	12		5 Do I Love You	53	Buddah 252
2/9/74	40	5		6 Let Me Get To Know You	80	Fame 345
7/6/74	5	15	●	7 (You're) Having My Baby	1³	United Art. 454
11/16/74	5	12		8 One Man Woman/One Woman Man	7	United Art. 569
				PAUL ANKA with ODIA COATES		
3/22/75	8	10		9 I Don't Like To Sleep Alone	8	United Art. 615
7/26/75	3	11		10 (I Believe) There's Nothing Stronger Than Our Love	15	United Art. 685
				PAUL ANKA with Odia Coates (Odia also has vocals on #7 & 9)		
11/22/75	1¹	13		11 Times Of Your Life	7	United Art. 737
4/3/76	2¹	10		12 Anytime (I'll Be There)	33	United Art. 789
11/13/76	20	9		13 Make It Up To Me In Love		Epic 50298
				ODIA COATES and PAUL ANKA		
12/11/76	10	12		14 Happier	60	United Art. 911
4/30/77	41	4		15 My Best Friend's Wife	80	United Art. 972
10/14/78	3	17		16 This Is Love	35	RCA 11395
7/28/79	29	9		17 As Long As We Keep Believing		RCA 11662
5/2/81	16	13		18 I've Been Waiting For You All Of My Life	48	RCA 12225
5/28/83	2³	24		19 Hold Me 'Til The Mornin' Comes	40	Columbia 03897
				Peter Cetera (backing vocal)		
6/30/84	14	13		20 Second Chance		Columbia 04407
				written by Paul Anka, David Foster and Michael McDonald		

DEBUT DATE	PEAK POS	WKS CHR	GOLD	ARTIST — Record Title	POP POS	Label & Number
				ANNA MARIE ○		
				Anna Marie Tumminia, native of southern New Jersey. Vocalist/keyboardist/oboist/songwriter.		
4/13/91	**35**	4		This Could Take All Night.....................................		MCA 53994
				ANN-MARGRET		
				Actress Ann-Margret Olsson. Born on 4/28/41 in Stockholm, Sweden. Moved to Wilmette, Illinois in 1946.		
4/7/62	**19**	1		What Am I Supposed To Do...............................	82	RCA Victor 7986
				ANTHONY, Ray		
				Big band leader/trumpeter. Born Raymond Antonini on 1/20/22 in Bentleyville, Pennsylvania and raised in Cleveland. Joined Al Donahue in 1939, then with Glenn Miller and Jimmy Dorsey from 1940-42. Led U.S. Army band. Own band in 1946. Own TV series in the '50s. Appeared in the film *Daddy Long Legs* with Fred Astaire in 1955. Wrote "Bunny Hop." Married for a time to actress Mamie Van Doren.		
7/14/62	**20**	2		1 Worried Mind .... [I]	74	Capitol 4742
3/26/66	**13**	6		2 It's Such A Happy Day .... [I]		Capitol 5589
				tune used for Jackie Gleason's monologue skits on his TV variety show		
				ANTON, Susan — see KNOBLOCK, Fred		
				APOLLO 100		
				English studio band featuring keyboardist Tom Parker.		
12/4/71	**2**[3]	17		1 Joy... [I]	6	Mega 0050
				adaptation of Bach's *Jesu, Joy of Man's Desiring*		
4/22/72	**24**	4		2 Mendelssohn's 4th (Second Movement) .... [I]	94	Mega 0069
7/15/72	**39**	2		3 Telstar... [I]		Mega 0080
				#1 Pop hit for The Tornadoes in 1962		
				ARBORS, The		
				Pop vocal group formed at the University of Michigan in Ann Arbor by two pairs of brothers: Edward and Fred Farran, and Scott and Tom Herrick.		
11/19/66	**18**	6		1 A Symphony For Susan	51	Date 1529
6/17/67	**19**	6		2 Graduation Day......................................	59	Date 1561
12/16/67	**26**	2		3 Valley Of The Dolls		Date 1581
				inspired by the book (and film) of the same title; not the same tune as Dionne Warwick's 1968 hit		
3/1/69	**26**	8		4 The Letter	20	Date 1638
				ARCHER, Tasmin		
				Female singer of Jamaican parentage. Native of Bradford, England.		
5/1/93	**24**	15		Sleeping Satellite...................................	32	SBK 50426
				ARCHIES, The		
				Studio group created by Don Kirshner; based on the Saturday morning cartoon television series. Lead vocalist Ron Dante (b: Carmine Granito on 8/22/45 in Staten Island, New York) was also the ghost voice of The Cuff Links. All tunes written and produced by Jeff Barry who was half of a prolific hit-writing partnership with his then-wife Ellie Greenwich.		
9/6/69	**22**	6	●	1 Sugar, Sugar	1[4]	Calendar 1008
1/17/70	**37**	2	●	2 Jingle Jangle.......................................	10	Kirshner 5002
				ARENA BRASS — see SHERMAN, Joe		
				ARKADE		
				Los Angeles-based pop trio.		
2/13/71	**16**	7		The Morning Of Our Lives	60	Dunhill 4268
				ARMAND, Renee ○		
				Prolific session vocalist. Member of The Coyote Sisters.		
7/29/78	**46**	4		(We're) Dancin' In The Dark		Windsong 11290
				ARMSTRONG, Louis		
				Born Daniel Louis Armstrong in New Orleans on 8/4/01 (not 7/4/1900, as Armstrong claimed). Died on 7/6/71 in New York. Nickname: "Satchmo." Joined the legendary band of Joe "King" Oliver in Chicago in 1922. By 1929, had become the most widely known black musician in the world. Influenced dozens of singers and trumpet players, both black and white. Numerous appearances on radio, TV and in films. Awarded a Lifetime Achievement Grammy in 1972. Inducted into the Rock and Roll Hall of Fame in 1990 as a forefather of rock music.		
2/22/64	**1**[9]	21		1 Hello, Dolly!	1[1]	Kapp 573
				Broadway musical title song (also #3 below)		
6/27/64	**7**	6		2 I Still Get Jealous...................................	45	Kapp 597
				LOUIS ARMSTRONG And The All Stars (above 2)		
10/10/64	**9**	3		3 So Long Dearie	56	Mercury 72338
5/7/66	**7**	13		4 Mame..	81	Mercury 72574
				Broadway musical title song		
10/14/67	**12**	21		5 What A Wonderful World	116	ABC 10982

DEBUT DATE	PEAK POS	WKS CHR	GOLD	ARTIST — Record Title	POP POS	Label & Number
				ARMSTRONG, Louis — Cont'd		
2/27/88	**7**	14		**6 What A Wonderful World**.............................[R]	32	A&M 3010
				featured in the film Good Morning Vietnam		
★★**84**★★				**ARNOLD, Eddy**		
				Born Richard Edward Arnold on 5/15/18 near Henderson, Tennessee. Ranked as the #1 artist in *Joel Whitburn's Top Country Singles 1944-1988* book. Became popular on Nashville's *Grand Ole Opry* as a singer with Pee Wee King (1940-43). Nicknamed "The Tennessee Plowboy" on all RCA recordings through 1954. Elected to the Country Music Hall of Fame in 1966. CMA award: Entertainer of the Year - 1967.		
				1)Make The World Go Away 2)I Want To Go With You 3)Turn The World Around		
5/29/65	**18**	7		**1** What's He Doing In My World..........................	60	RCA Victor 8516
8/14/65	**33**	3		**2** I'm Letting You Go............................	135	RCA Victor 8632
				written by Billy Grammer		
10/16/65	**1**⁴	18		**3 Make The World Go Away**	6	RCA Victor 8679
2/5/66	**1**³	14		**4 I Want To Go With You**..........................	36	RCA Victor 8749
5/7/66	**9**	11		**5 The Last Word In Lonesome Is Me**..................	40	RCA Victor 8818
7/23/66	**8**	10		**6 The Tip Of My Fingers**	43	RCA Victor 8869
10/15/66	**15**	9		**7** Somebody Like Me	53	RCA Victor 8965
3/25/67	**11**	10		**8** Lonely Again	87	RCA Victor 9080
5/6/67	**13**	9		**9** Misty Blue	57	RCA Victor 9182
8/19/67	**3**	14		**10 Turn The World Around**..........................	66	RCA Victor 9265
12/2/67	**15**	10		**11** Here Comes Heaven	91	RCA Victor 9368
2/17/68	**20**	6		**12** Here Comes The Rain, Baby	74	RCA Victor 9437
5/18/68	**15**	7		**13** It's Over	74	RCA Victor 9525
8/24/68	**6**	12		**14 Then You Can Tell Me Goodbye**	84	RCA Victor 9606
11/23/68	**19**	8		**15** They Don't Make Love Like They Used To........	99	RCA Victor 9667
3/29/69	**33**	3		**16** Please Don't Go	129	RCA Victor 0120
6/21/69	**31**	7		**17** But For Love	125	RCA Victor 0175
3/7/70	**28**	2		**18** Soul Deep		RCA Victor 9801
				ARTHUR, HURLEY & GOTTLIEB ☉		
				Country-rock trio.		
7/28/73	**25**	5		Sunshine Ship		Columbia 45881
				ARVON, Bobby		
				Born Robert Arvonio on 9/13/41 in Scranton, Pennsylvania. Singer/songwriter/pianist.		
12/17/77	**30**	9		**1** Until Now	72	1st Artists 41000
5/27/78	**42**	5		**2** From Now On	104	1st Artists 41003
				ASHFORD & SIMPSON		
				Husband-and-wife R&B vocal/songwriting duo: Nickolas Ashford (b: 5/4/42, Fairfield, South Carolina) and Valerie Simpson (b: 8/26/46, New York City).		
2/16/85	**34**	6		Solid	12	Capitol 5397
				ASSEMBLED MULTITUDE, The		
				Philadelphia-based studio group arranged and conducted by Tom Sellers (d: 3/9/88 in a fire in his hometown of Wayne, Pennsylvania at age 39).		
6/20/70	**8**	13		**1 Overture From Tommy (A Rock Opera)** ....[I]	16	Atlantic 2737
10/10/70	**23**	5		**2** Woodstock ....[I]	79	Atlantic 2764
1/9/71	**17**	7		**3** Medley From "Superstar" (A Rock Opera)...........[I]	95	Atlantic 2780
				ASSOCIATION, The		
				Group formed in Los Angeles in 1965. Consisted of Terry Kirkman (plays 23 wind, reed and percussion instruments), Gary "Jules" Alexander (guitar), Brian Cole (bass), Jim Yester (guitar), Ted Bluechel, Jr. (drums) and Russ Giguere (percussion). Larry Ramos, Jr. joined in early 1968. Richard Thompson (keyboards) replaced Giguere in 1970. Cole died on 8/2/72 of a heroin overdose. Thompson replaced by Rick Ulsky in 1974. Regrouped with original surviving members on 9/26/80.		
10/1/66	**38**	3	●	**1** Cherish............................	1³	Valiant 747
3/2/68	**22**	5		**2** Everything That Touches You	10	Warner 7163
5/25/68	**27**	5		**3** Time For Livin'	39	Warner 7195
3/15/69	**22**	6		**4** Goodbye Columbus	80	Warner 7267
				movie title song		
3/3/73	**27**	4		**5** Names, Tags, Numbers & Labels............	91	Mums 6016
2/7/81	**17**	10		**6** Dreamer	66	Elektra 47094
★★**149**★★				**ASTLEY, Rick**		
				Pop singer/guitarist born on 2/6/66 in Warrington and raised in Manchester, England.		
				1)Never Gonna Give You Up 2)Cry For Help 3)It Would Take A Strong Strong Man		
1/23/88	**1**³	20	●	**1 Never Gonna Give You Up**	1²	RCA 5347

19

DEBUT DATE	PEAK POS	WKS CHR	G O L D	ARTIST — Record Title	POP POS	Label & Number
				ASTLEY, Rick — Cont'd		
4/30/88	**2**²	18		**2 Together Forever**	1¹	RCA 8319
7/30/88	**1**¹	21		**3 It Would Take A Strong Strong Man**............	10	RCA 8663
12/24/88	**5**	19		**4 She Wants To Dance With Me**	6	RCA 8838
4/22/89	**11**	14		**5 Giving Up On Love**	38	RCA 8872
8/26/89	**16**	10		**6 Ain't Too Proud To Beg**	89	RCA 9030
2/9/91	**1**¹	30		**7 Cry For Help**	7	RCA 2774
6/15/91	**29**	7		**8 Move Right Out**	81	RCA 2839
				ATLANTA RHYTHM SECTION		
				Group formed of musicians from Studio One, Doraville, Georgia in 1971. Consisted of Rodney Justo (vocals), Barry Bailey and J.R. Cobb (guitars), Paul Goddard (bass), Dean Daughtry (keyboards) and Robert Nix (drums). Cobb, Daughtry and band manager/producer Buddy Buie had been with the Classics IV, others had been with Roy Orbison. Justo left after first album, replaced by Ronnie Hammond.		
3/12/77	**11**	14		**1 So In To You**	7	Polydor 14373
7/9/77	**39**	4		**2 Neon Nites**	42	Polydor 14397
3/25/78	**20**	12		**3 Imaginary Lover**	7	Polydor 14459
7/29/78	**43**	5		**4 I'm Not Gonna Let It Bother Me Tonight**......	14	Polydor 14484
6/9/79	**11**	13		**5 Do It Or Die**	19	Polydor 14568
9/1/79	**23**	10		**6 Spooky**	17	Polydor 2001
9/26/81	**16**	11		**7 Alien**...	29	Columbia 02471
				ATLANTIC & PACIFIC Featuring Peter Gormann ☉		
4/5/75	**44**	5		The Hands Of Time (Brian's song) .... #56 Pop hit for Michel LeGrand in 1972		P.I.P. 6501
				ATLANTIC STARR		
				Soul band formed in 1976 in White Plains, New York by brothers Wayne, David and Jonathan Lewis. Wayne and David on vocals with Sharon Bryant. In 1984, reduced to a quintet; Barbara Weathers replaced Bryant. Porscha Martin replaced Weathers in 1989. Rachel Oliver replaced Martin in 1991.		
2/1/86	**1**¹	18		**1 Secret Lovers**	3	A&M 2788
5/3/86	**11**	15		**2 If Your Heart Isn't In It**	57	A&M 2822
3/28/87	**1**²	23		**3 Always**	1¹	Warner 28455
2/8/92	**2**¹	30	●	**4 Masterpiece** .... written by Kenny Nolan	3	Reprise 19076
				AUSTIN, Patti		
				Born on 8/10/48 in New York City. R&B backing vocalist in New York. Goddaughter of Quincy Jones. Made Harlem's Apollo Theatre debut at age four. In the 1988 film *Tucker*.		
11/20/82	**1**³	23	●	**1 Baby, Come To Me** .... **PATTI AUSTIN with James Ingram**	1²	Qwest 50036
3/26/83	**24**	9		**2 Every Home Should Have One** ....[R] remix of song which originally made the *Hot 100* on 12/12/81 (POS 62)	69	Qwest 29727
5/14/83	**5**	20		**3 How Do You Keep The Music Playing**............ **JAMES INGRAM And PATTI AUSTIN** theme from the film *Best Friends*	45	Qwest 29618
12/1/84	**37**	3		**4 All Behind Us Now**..................................		Qwest 29136
11/25/89	**6**	31		**5 Any Other Fool** .... **SADAO WATANABE (Featuring Patti Austin)**		Elektra 69254
4/21/90	**9**	22		**6 Through The Test Of Time** .... background vocals: Jocelyn Brown, Robin Beck, Lani Groves, Rachele Cappelli, James "D-Train" Williams, Shelton Becton and Bill Eaton		GRP 3032
				AVALON, Frankie		
				Born Francis Avallone on 9/18/39 in Philadelphia. Teen idol managed by Bob Marcucci. Co-starred in many films with Annette. Appeared in films *Disc Jockey Jamboree* (1957), *Guns Of The Timberland* (1960) and *Back To The Beach* (1987).		
3/31/62	**7**	10		**1 You Are Mine**..	26	Chancellor 1107
1/24/76	**1**¹	13		**2 Venus**..[R] disco version of Avalon's #1 Pop hit from 1959	46	De-Lite 1578
				AWB (AVERAGE WHITE BAND)		
				Vocal/instrumental group formed in Scotland in 1972: Alan Gorrie, Hamish Stuart, Onnie McIntyre, Malcolm Duncan, Roger Ball and Robbie McIntosh (d: 9/23/74; replaced by Steve Ferrone).		
3/8/75	**45**	4	●	Pick Up The Pieces ....[I] **AWB**	1¹	Atlantic 3229

DEBUT DATE	PEAK POS	WKS CHR	GOLD	ARTIST — Record Title	POP POS	Label & Number
				AXTON, Hoyt		
				Born on 3/25/38 in Duncan, Oklahoma. Son of songwriter Mae Axton ("Heartbreak Hotel"). Appeared in the movies *The Black Stallion* and *Gremlins*.		
6/22/74	**31**	8		When The Morning Comes	54	A&M 1497
				Linda Ronstadt (harmony vocal)		
				AZNAVOUR, Charles ○		
				Born Charles Aznavurjan on 5/22/24 in France. Actor/singer.		
8/17/74	**44**	3		She..		RCA 10021
				theme from the TV series *Seven Faces of Woman*		

B

DEBUT DATE	PEAK POS	WKS CHR	GOLD	ARTIST — Record Title	POP POS	Label & Number
				BABYFACE ○		
				Rock band from Eau Claire, Wisconsin led by vocalist Edgar Riley and guitarist Bobby Barth. Group relocated to Florida in 1978 and charted on the *Hot 100* as Axe in 1982.		
11/13/76	**30**	9		1 Never In My Life		ASI 1009
3/26/77	**50**	1		2 Make Way Miami		ASI 1010
				BABYFACE		
				R&B vocalist/instrumentalist Kenneth Edmonds, formerly with Manchild and The Deele. Dubbed "Babyface" by Bootsy Collins. Brother of Kevon and Melvin Edmonds of After 7.		
4/21/90	**36**	9		Whip Appeal	6	Solar 74007
				BABYS, The		
				British rock group: John Waite (vocals), Walt Stocker, Mike Corby and Tony Brock. By 1980, keyboardist Jonathan Cain (later of Journey) had replaced Corby and bassist Ricky Phillips joined group. In 1989, Waite formed Bad English with Phillips and Cain.		
11/12/77	**49**	1		1 Isn't It Time	13	Chrysalis 2173
3/4/78	**39**	5		2 Silver Dreams	53	Chrysalis 2201
3/3/79	**36**	6		3 Every Time I Think Of You	13	Chrysalis 2279
				BACHARACH, Burt		
				Born on 5/12/28 in Kansas City. Conductor/arranger/composer. With lyricist Hal David wrote "Close To You," "What's New Pussycat" and most of Dionne Warwick's hits. Formerly married to actress Angie Dickinson. Now married to songwriter Carole Bayer Sager.		
11/25/67	**38**	2		1 Reach Out For Me		A&M 888
				#20 Pop hit for Dionne Warwick in 1964		
5/31/69	**18**	9		2 I'll Never Fall In Love Again	93	A&M 1064
				from the Broadway musical *Promises, Promises*		
1/30/71	**18**	7		3 All Kinds Of People..	116	A&M 1241
1/19/74	**50**	1		4 Something Big...		A&M 1489
★★169★★				**BACHELORS, The**		
				Pop vocal trio from Dublin, Ireland: brothers Declan and Con Cluskey, with John Stokes. Formed as a harmonica instrumental trio known as the Harmonichords.		
				1)Chapel In The Moonlight 2)Love Me With All Of Your Heart 3)Marie		
4/18/64	**3**	13		1 Diane..	10	London 9639
7/4/64	**7**	7		2 I Believe	33	London 9672
9/19/64	**13**	4		3 I Wouldn't Trade You For The World	69	London 9693
12/26/64	**3**	10		4 No Arms Can Ever Hold You.......................................	27	London 9724
6/5/65	**3**	12		5 Marie	15	London 9762
10/2/65	**2²**	10		6 Chapel In The Moonlight..	32	London 9793
4/2/66	**3**	14		7 Love Me With All Of Your Heart...................................	38	London 9828
7/2/66	**12**	7		8 Can I Trust You?...	49	London 20010
12/31/66	**26**	5		9 Walk With Faith In Your Heart	83	London 20018
12/16/67	**28**	2		10 Learn To Live Without You..		London 20033
				BACHMAN-TURNER OVERDRIVE		
				Hard-rock group formed in Vancouver, Canada in 1972. Brothers Randy and Robbie Bachman, with C. Fred Turner and Blair Thornton. Randy had been in The Guess Who and recorded solo.		
5/8/76	**15**	8		Lookin' Out For #1	65	Mercury 73784

DEBUT DATE	PEAK POS	WKS CHR	GOLD	ARTIST — Record Title	POP POS	Label & Number
				BAD ENGLISH		
				Rock supergroup: John Waite (vocals), Ricky Phillips (bass), Jonathan Cain (keyboards), Neal Schon (guitar) and Deen Castronovo (drums). Waite, Phillips and Cain were members of The Babys. Cain and Schon (ex-Santana) were members of Journey. Schon and Castronovo with Hardline in 1992.		
11/11/89	11	17	●	1 When I See You Smile	1²	Epic 69082
3/3/90	38	7		2 Price Of Love	5	Epic 73094
7/14/90	42	9		3 Possession	21	Epic 73398
				BADFINGER		
				Welsh rock quartet originally known as The Iveys. Consisted of Pete Ham (guitar), Tom Evans (bass), Joey Molland (guitar; joined in late 1968, after band's first hit single "Maybe Tomorrow") and Mike Gibbins (drums). All but Gibbins share vocals. Ham (b: 4/27/47) committed suicide on 4/23/75. Group disbanded from 1976-78. Molland and Evans re-grouped in 1979. Evans committed suicide on 11/23/83 (age 36).		
12/18/71	10	11	●	Day After Day	4	Apple 1841
				produced by George Harrison		
				BAEZ, Joan		
				Preeminent folk song stylist. Born Joan Chandos Baez in Staten Island, New York on 1/9/41 to a Mexican father and British mother. Became a political activist while attending Boston University in the late 1950s. Made her professional debut in July 1959 at the first Newport Folk Festival. Orientation changed from traditional to popular folk songs in the early '60s. Influential in fostering career of Bob Dylan.		
10/2/65	16	4		1 There But For Fortune	50	Vanguard 35031
8/7/71	1⁵	14	●	2 The Night They Drove Old Dixie Down	3	Vanguard 35138
				written by Robbie Robertson (leader of The Band)		
11/27/71	5	8		3 Let It Be	49	Vanguard 35145
7/29/72	22	6		4 In The Quiet Morning	69	A&M 1362
				written by Mimi Farina for Janis Joplin		
4/20/74	13	10		5 Forever Young		A&M 1516
				written by Bob Dylan		
7/12/75	46	5		6 Blue Sky	57	A&M 1703
9/13/75	5	12		7 Diamonds And Rust	35	A&M 1737
				BAHLER, John ✪		
				Singer/songwriter. Songwriting partnership with brother Tom in the mid-1970s.		
5/8/71	20	6		Love Looks So Good On You		Warner 7474
				BAILEY, Pearl ✪		
				Born on 3/29/18 in Newport News, Virginia. Died on 8/17/90 of heart disease. Band vocalist from 1933-45. Appeared in several films. Married drummer Louis Bellson in 1952. Long run in the Broadway musical *Hello, Dolly* in the '60s.		
4/4/70	37	2		Applause		Project 3 1376
				Broadway show title song		
				BAILEY, Philip		
				Born on 5/8/51 in Denver. R&B percussionist/co-lead vocalist with Earth, Wind & Fire since 1971.		
1/19/85	15	13	●	Easy Lover	2²	Columbia 04679
				PHILIP BAILEY with Phil Collins		
				BAILEY, Razzy		
				Born Rasie Michael Bailey on 2/14/39 in Five Points, Alabama. Country singer/songwriter. Big break came when Dickey Lee recorded Razzy's "9,999,999 Tears."		
5/30/81	41	4		Friends		RCA 12199
				BAJA MARIMBA BAND		
				Nine-man band led by marimbaist Julius Wechter (b: 5/10/35 in Chicago). Wechter was a member of Herb Alpert's Tijuana Brass.		
				1)Ghost Riders In The Sky 2)Fowl Play 3)I Say A Little Prayer		
10/1/66	15	9		1 The Portuguese Washerwomen .... [I]	126	A&M 816
11/26/66	4	10		2 Ghost Riders In The Sky......................... [I]	52	A&M 824
2/25/67	21	5		3 The Cry Of The Wild Goose...................... [I]	113	A&M 833
4/22/67	14	10		4 Georgy Girl .... [I]	98	A&M 843
				movie title song		
8/5/67	27	5		5 Along Comes Mary .... [I]	96	A&M 862
				JULIUS WECHTER & THE BAJA MARIMBA BAND:		
12/30/67	8	9		6 Fowl Play.................................... [I]		A&M 892
6/15/68	17	6		7 Yes Sir, That's My Baby .... [I]	109	A&M 937
9/14/68	10	7		8 I Say A Little Prayer .... [I]		A&M 975
12/21/68	15	9		9 Flyin' High .... [I]	125	A&M 1005
7/12/69	21	6		10 I Don't Want To Walk Without You	121	A&M 1078
				Julius Wechter (vocal)		
12/13/69	40	2		11 Can You Dig It? Part I ....[N]		A&M 1136

22

DEBUT DATE	PEAK POS	WKS CHR	G O L D	ARTIST — Record Title	POP POS	Label & Number
★★**137**★★				**BAKER, Anita**		
				Soul singer born on 1/26/58 in Toledo, Ohio and raised in Detroit. Female lead singer of Chapter 8 from 1976-84.		
				1)Giving You The Best That I Got 2)Sweet Love 3)Just Because		
7/26/86	**3**	22		1 Sweet Love	8	Elektra 69557
11/22/86	**9**	19		2 Caught Up In The Rapture...........................	37	Elektra 69511
3/28/87	**6**	17		3 Same Ole Love (365 Days A Year)..............	44	Elektra 69484
7/25/87	**9**	20		4 No One In The World	44	Elektra 69456
10/1/88	**1**¹	27		5 Giving You The Best That I Got	3	Elektra 69371
1/14/89	**4**	23		6 Just Because...	14	Elektra 69327
5/6/89	**32**	7		7 Lead Me Into Love......................................		Elektra 69299
6/23/90	**4**	20		8 Talk To Me..	44	Elektra 64964
9/22/90	**11**	15		9 Soul Inspiration	72	Elektra 64935
1/5/91	**27**	11		10 Fairy Tales..		Elektra 64910
				BAKER, Chet, And The Mariachi Brass ✪		
				Chet was born Chesney Baker on 12/23/29 in Yale, Oklahoma; died on 5/13/88. Flugelhorn/trumpeter/bandleader.		
2/19/66	**33**	5		Flowers On The Wall...................................... [I]	115	World Pac. 77815
				BAKER, George, Selection		
				Baker is Johannes Bouwens (b: 12/9/44). Pop vocalist/guitarist/keyboardist of Dutch group.		
12/13/75	**1**¹	15		**Paloma Blanca**	26	Warner 8115
				BALANCE		
				New York City-based rock trio led by Illinois native Peppy Castro (founder of the Blues Magoos).		
1/9/82	**43**	3		Falling In Love...	58	Portrait 02608
				BALIN, Marty		
				Born on 1/30/43 in Cincinnati. Co-founder of Jefferson Airplane/Jefferson Starship/KBC.		
6/13/81	**9**	15		1 Hearts	8	EMI America 8084
9/26/81	**11**	14		2 Atlanta Lady (Something About Your Love)	27	EMI America 8093
4/23/83	**17**	13		3 Do It For Love..	102	EMI America 8160
				BALL, Kenny, and his Jazzmen		
				Born on 5/22/30 in Ilford, England. Leader of English Dixieland jazz band formed in 1958.		
2/10/62	**1**³	13		**Midnight In Moscow** .... [I]	2¹	Kapp 442
				original Russian title: "Padmeskoveeye Vietchera"		
				BALTIMORE and OHIO MARCHING BAND, The		
				Studio group assembled by producers Joey Day and Alan Dischel.		
10/21/67	**28**	5		Lapland.. [I]	94	Jubilee 5592
				BAMA		
				Session band from Muscle Shoals, Alabama. Headed by songwriters Terry Skinner and J.L. Wallace.		
9/1/79	**42**	9		Touch Me When We're Dancing	86	Free Flight 11629
				BANANARAMA		
				Female pop-rock trio from London: Sarah Dallin, Keren Woodward and Siobhan Fahey. Group name is combination of the children's show *The Banana Splits* and the Roxy Music song "Pyjamarama." Fahey married Dave Stewart (Eurythmics) in early 1988, replaced by Jacqui O'Sullivan (who left in mid-1991). Fahey later formed duo Shakespear's Sister.		
9/22/84	**44**	4		1 Cruel Summer..	9	London 810127
8/16/86	**29**	6		2 Venus	1¹	London 886056
9/19/87	**32**	7		3 I Heard A Rumour	4	London 886165
				BAND OF GOLD		
				Dutch session vocalists and musicians assembled by producers Pete Wingfield and Paco Saval.		
10/20/84	**34**	6		Love Songs Are Back Again............................	64	RCA 13866
				Let's Put It All Together/Betcha By Golly Wow/Side Show/Have You Seen Her/ Reunited/You Make Me Feel Brand New/Kiss And Say Goodbye/ Love Songs Are Back Again		
				BAND OF THE BLACK WATCH, The		
				Scottish military unit.		
1/10/76	**22**	11		Scotch On The Rocks .... [I]	75	Private S. 45055

DEBUT DATE	PEAK POS	WKS CHR	GOLD	ARTIST — Record Title	POP POS	Label & Number
				BANGLES		
				Female pop-rock quartet formed in Los Angeles in January 1981. Consisted of sisters Vicki (lead guitar) and Debbi Peterson (drums), Michael Steele (bass) and Susanna Hoffs (guitar). Originally named The Bangs. Steele was previously in The Runaways. Hoffs starred in the 1987 film *The Allnighter*. Disbanded in October 1989. Hoffs recorded solo in 1991.		
3/22/86	**10**	12		1 Manic Monday	2[1]	Columbia 05757
				written by Prince under the pseudonym "Christopher"		
6/14/86	**24**	9		2 If She Knew What She Wants	29	Columbia 05886
4/11/87	**33**	5		3 Walking Down Your Street.............................	11	Columbia 06674
2/11/89	**1**[2]	21	●	4 Eternal Flame..	1[1]	Columbia 68533
				BARE, Bobby		
				Born Robert Joseph Bare on 4/7/35 in Ironton, Ohio. Country singer/songwriter.		
6/29/63	**4**	10		1 Detroit City	16	RCA Victor 8183
				written by Mel Tillis		
10/12/63	**4**	10		2 500 Miles Away From Home	10	RCA Victor 8238
2/22/64	**12**	3		3 Miller's Cave	33	RCA Victor 8294
11/14/64	**9**	4		4 Four Strong Winds	60	RCA Victor 8443
12/22/73	**14**	13		5 Daddy What If	41	RCA Victor 0197
				with 5-year-old son, Bobby, Jr.		
				BARRY, John, and His Orchestra		
				Born on 11/3/33 in York, England. Prolific movie soundtrack composer/conductor.		
3/13/65	**15**	2		Goldfinger..[I]	72	United Art. 791
				movie title song		
				BASIA		
				Britain-based, female pop-jazz singer/composer Basia Trzetrzelewska (pronounced: Basha Tshet-shel-ev-ska). Born on 9/30/59. Raised in Jaworzno, Poland. Former vocalist of the group Matt Bianco.		
4/30/88	**19**	20		1 Time And Tide	26	Epic 07730
11/19/88	**5**	18		2 New Day For You	53	Epic 08112
3/25/89	**8**	15		3 Promises		Epic 68608
3/10/90	**5**	18		4 Cruising For Bruising	29	Epic 73239
6/16/90	**18**	11		5 Baby You're Mine		Epic 73405
9/1/90	**33**	8		6 Until You Come Back To Me (That's What I'm		
				Gonna Do)		Epic 73485
				#3 Pop hit for Aretha Franklin in 1974		
				BASIE, Count		
				Born William Basie on 8/21/04 in Red Bank, New Jersey. Died on 4/26/84 of pancreatic cancer. World-renowned jazz, big-band leader/pianist/organist.		
8/20/66	**28**	6		Happiness Is		ABC 10830
				COUNT BASIE WITH THE ALAN COPELAND SINGERS		
				BASSEY, Shirley		
				Born on 1/8/37 in Cardiff, Wales. Soul songstress. Began professional career at age 16 as a member of touring show *Memories Of Al Jolson*. Became a popular club attraction in America in 1961.		
2/6/65	**2**[4]	12		1 Goldfinger..	8	United Art. 790
				a James Bond movie title song; John Barry (orch.)		
12/4/65	**38**	2		2 It's Yourself		United Art. 956
				from the musical *Maggie May*		
9/12/70	**6**	10		3 Something	55	United Art. 50698
1/1/72	**14**	13		4 Diamonds Are Forever	57	United Art. 50845
				a James Bond movie title song		
5/12/73	**8**	12		5 Never, Never, Never (Grande, Grande, Grande).............	48	United Art. 211
5/18/74	**44**	4		6 Davy		United Art. 387
				Bernard Ighner (male vocal)		
				BATDORF & RODNEY		
				John Batdorf and Mark Rodney. John formed the group Silver in 1976.		
8/23/75	**22**	10		1 You Are A Song	87	Arista 0132
11/29/75	**24**	10		2 Somewhere In The Night.............................	69	Arista 0159
				BAY CITY ROLLERS		
				Rock group formed in 1967 in Edinburgh, Scotland as the Saxons. Original members: brothers Alan and Derek Longmuir, Les McKeoun (lead singer), Eric Faulkner and Stuart "Woody" Wood.		
10/2/76	**27**	7		1 I Only Want To Be With You	12	Arista 0205
11/5/77	**16**	16		2 The Way I Feel Tonight	24	Arista 0272

★★134★★ BEACH BOYS, The

Group formed in Hawthorne, California in 1961. Consisted of brothers Brian (keyboards, bass), Carl (guitar), and Dennis Wilson (drums); their cousin Mike Love (lead vocals, saxophone), and Al Jardine (guitar). Brian quit touring with group in December 1964, replaced by Glen Campbell until Bruce Johnston (of Bruce & Terry) joined permanently in April 1965. Brian continued to write for and produce group, returned to stage in 1983. Daryl Dragon (of Captain & Tennille) was a keyboardist in their stage band. Dennis Wilson drowned on 12/28/83 (age 39). Lineup of Carl, Brian, Mike, Alan and Bruce continues to perform today. Carnie and Wendy Wilson, daughters of Brian Wilson, are members of Wilson Phillips. Group was inducted into the Rock and Roll Hall of Fame in 1988.

1)Getcha Back 2)Kokomo 3)California Dreamin'

DEBUT DATE	PEAK POS	WKS CHR	GOLD	ARTIST — Record Title	POP POS	Label & Number
9/4/76	33	5		1 It's O.K.	29	Brother 1368
				also released as the B-side of #8 below		
9/23/78	46	3		2 Peggy Sue	59	Brother 1394
5/12/79	12	9		3 Good Timin'.	40	Caribou 9029
9/22/79	39	5		4 Lady Lynda..		Caribou 9030
8/8/81	20	10		5 The Beach Boys Medley	12	Capitol 5030
				Good Vibrations/Help Me, Rhonda/I Get Around/Shut Down/Surfin' Safari/ Barbara Ann/Surfin' USA/Fun, Fun, Fun		
11/28/81	11	14		6 Come Go With Me	18	Caribou 02633
5/25/85	2¹	16		7 **Getcha Back**...	26	Caribou 04913
8/10/85	20	8		8 It's Gettin' Late	82	Caribou 05433
10/26/85	26	6		9 She Believes In Love		Caribou 05624
9/27/86	8	12		10 **California Dreamin'**....................................	57	Capitol 5630
				electric 12-string guitar solo by Roger McGuinn (The Byrds)		
12/12/87	45	6		11 Happy Endings		Critique 99392
				THE BEACH BOYS & LITTLE RICHARD from the film *The Telephone*		
7/23/88	5	30	▲	12 **Kokomo**..	1¹	Elektra 69385
				from the film *Cocktail*		
8/19/89	9	11		13 **Still Cruisin'**	93	Capitol 44445
				from the film *Lethal Weapon 2*		
8/11/90	38	5		14 Problem Child		RCA 2646
				movie title song		
7/18/92	17	11		15 Hot Fun In The Summertime........................		Brother 5247
				#2 Pop hit for Sly & The Family Stone in 1969		

BEATLES, The

The world's #1 rock group was formed in Liverpool, England in the late 1950s. Known in early forms as The Quarrymen, Johnny & the Moondogs, The Rainbows, and the Silver Beatles. Named The Beatles in 1960. Originally consisted of John Lennon, Paul McCartney, George Harrison (guitars), Stu Sutcliffe (bass) and Pete Best (drums). Sutcliffe left in April 1961 (died on 4/10/62 of a brain hemorrhage); McCartney moved to bass. Best replaced by Ringo Starr in August 1962. Group managed by Brian Epstein (died on 8/27/67 of sleeping-pill overdose) and produced by George Martin. First U.S. tour in February 1964. Won the 1964 Best New Artist Grammy Award. Group starred in films *A Hard Day's Night* (1964), *Help* (1965), *Magical Mystery Tour* (1967) and *Let It Be* (1970); contributed soundtrack to the animated film *Yellow Submarine* (1968). Own Apple label in 1968. McCartney publicly announced group's dissolution on 4/10/70. Won the Grammy's Trustees Award in 1972. Lennon was shot to death on 12/8/80. Inducted into the Rock and Roll Hall of Fame in 1988.

DEBUT DATE	PEAK POS	WKS CHR	GOLD	ARTIST — Record Title	POP POS	Label & Number
11/1/69	17	7	●	1 Something	3	Apple 2654
3/21/70	1⁴	10	●	2 **Let It Be**	1²	Apple 2764
5/30/70	2¹	7		3 **The Long And Winding Road**......................	1²	Apple 2832
				above 2 from The Beatles' documentary film Let It Be		
6/19/76	9	11		4 **Got To Get You Into My Life**	7	Capitol 4274
				from the 1966 Beatles album Revolver		
12/4/76	39	4		5 Ob-La-Di, Ob-La-Da	49	Capitol 4347
				from the 1968 white album The Beatles		
4/3/82	15	10		6 The Beatles' Movie Medley	12	Capitol 5107
				Magical Mystery Tour/All You Need Is Love/You've Got To Hide Your Love Away/ I Should Have Known Better/A Hard Day's Night/Ticket To Ride/Get Back		

★★52★★ BEE GEES

Trio of brothers from Manchester, England: Barry (b: 9/1/47) and twins Robin and Maurice Gibb (b: 12/22/49). First performed December 1955. To Australia in 1958, performed as the Gibbs, later as BG's, finally the Bee Gees. First recorded for Leedon/Festival in 1963. Returned to England in February 1967, with guitarist Vince Melouney and drummer Colin Peterson. Toured Europe and the U.S. in 1968. Melouney left in December 1968; Robin left for solo career in 1969. When Peterson left in August 1969, Barry and Maurice went solo. After eight months, the brothers reunited. Composed soundtracks of *Saturday Night Fever* and *Staying Alive*. Acted in film *Sgt. Pepper's Lonely Hearts Club Band*. Youngest brother Andy Gibb was a successful solo singer (d: 3/10/88).

1)How Deep Is Your Love 2)One 3)Too Much Heaven 4)How Can You Mend A Broken Heart 5)Run To Me

DEBUT DATE	PEAK POS	WKS CHR	GOLD	ARTIST — Record Title	POP POS	Label & Number
12/26/70	28	7	●	1 Lonely Days	3	Atco 6795
6/26/71	4	14	●	2 **How Can You Mend A Broken Heart**.............	1⁴	Atco 6824

DEBUG DATE	PEAK POS	WKS CHR	G O L D	ARTIST — Record Title	POP POS	Label & Number
				BEE GEES — Cont'd		
2/5/72	**19**	7		3 My World...	16	Atco 6871
8/5/72	**6**	9		**4 Run To Me**	16	Atco 6896
12/9/72	**20**	4		5 Alive	34	Atco 6909
7/7/73	**42**	3		6 Wouldn't I Be Someone...............................	115	RSO 404
11/9/74	**31**	8		7 Charade	103	RSO 501
6/21/75	**9**	12	●	**8 Jive Talkin'.**	1²	RSO 510
11/15/75	**16**	9		9 Nights On Broadway	7	RSO 515
1/10/76	**9**	11		**10 Fanny (Be Tender With My Love)**	12	RSO 519
7/31/76	**25**	10	●	**11 You Should Be Dancing**	1¹	RSO 853
10/9/76	**14**	15	●	**12 Love So Right**	3	RSO 859
8/27/77	**43**	4		13 Edge Of The Universe...............................	26	RSO 880
10/1/77	**1**⁶	26	●	**14 How Deep Is Your Love**............................	1³	RSO 882
1/7/78	**28**	13	▲	**15 Stayin' Alive**	1⁴	RSO 885
2/18/78	**19**	15	▲	**16 Night Fever**	1⁸	RSO 889
4/8/78	**39**	7		17 More Than A Woman..................................		RSO LP Cut
				above 4 from the film and album Saturday Night Fever on RSO 4001		
11/25/78	**4**	16	▲	**18 Too Much Heaven**	1²	RSO 913
2/17/79	**19**	10	▲	**19 Tragedy**	1²	RSO 918
4/28/79	**15**	14	●	20 Love You Inside Out.................................	1¹	RSO 925
6/18/83	**31**	6		21 The Woman In You....................................	24	RSO 813173
9/3/83	**22**	9		22 Someone Belonging To Someone	49	RSO 815235
				above 2 from the film Staying Alive		
9/26/87	**50**	1		23 You Win Again...	75	Warner 28351
8/5/89	**1**²	18		**24 One**	7	Warner 22899
2/10/90	**9**	16		**25 Bodyguard**		Warner 19997

BELAFONTE, Harry

Born Harold George Belafonte, Jr. on 3/1/27 in Harlem to a Jamaican mother and a West Indian father. Rode the crest of the calypso craze to worldwide stardom. Starred in eight films from 1953-74. Replaced Danny Kaye in 1987 as UNICEF goodwill ambassador. Father of actress Shari Belafonte.

9/16/67	**5**	14		1 A Strange Song.....................................		RCA Victor 9263
6/8/68	**38**	3		2 By The Time I Get To Phoenix		RCA Victor 9542
				#26 Pop hit for Glen Campbell in 1967		

BELL, Vincent

Veteran studio guitarist. Born Vincent Gambella. Formerly with the East Coast vocal group The Gallahads.

4/11/70	**2**³	11		Airport Love Theme (Gwen And Vern)..........................[I]	31	Decca 32659
				from the film Airport		

BELL, William

Born William Yarborough on 7/16/39 in Memphis. R&B singer. Own Peachtree and Wilbe labels. With Rufus Thomas band in 1953. In U.S. Army from 1962-66.

4/9/77	**25**	8	●	Tryin' To Love Two...................................	10	Mercury 73839

BELLAMY BROTHERS

Country duo from Darby, Florida: brothers Howard (b: 2/2/46; guitar) and David Bellamy (b: 9/16/50; guitar, keyboards). Made their professional debut in 1958. David wrote "Spiders And Snakes" hit for Jim Stafford. Moved to Los Angeles in 1973.

2/14/76	**2**¹	14		**1 Let Your Love Flow**	1¹	Warner 8169
4/9/77	**40**	2		2 Crossfire		Warner 8350

BELLE, Regina

Soul vocalist raised in Englewood, New Jersey. Featured female vocalist with The Manhattans, 1986-87. Married pro basketball player John Battle III of the Cleveland Cavaliers.

1/9/88	**8**	15		**1 Without You**..	89	Elektra 69426
				PEABO BRYSON & REGINA BELLE		
				from the film Leonard Pt. 6		
2/25/89	**34**	6		2 All I Want Is Forever...............................		Epic 68540
				JAMES "J.T." TAYLOR & REGINA BELLE		
				from the Gregory Hines film Tap		
2/17/90	**5**	20		**3 Make It Like It Was**..............................	43	Columbia 73022
6/23/90	**29**	9		4 This Is Love		Columbia 73346
11/21/92	**1**⁶	34	●	**5 A Whole New World (Aladdin's Theme)**	1¹	Columbia 74751
				PEABO BRYSON and REGINA BELLE		
				from the Walt Disney animated feature film Aladdin		
4/3/93	**12**	17		6 If I Could	52	Columbia 74864

BELLE STARS, The
English female band formed as The Bodysnatchers in 1981. Changed name to The Belle Stars in 1983. Features Jennie McKeown (vocals) and Sarah-Jane Owen (guitar).

5/6/89	41	5		Iko Iko	14	Capitol 44343
				from the film *Rain Man*		

BELLS, The
Canadian pop quintet — lead singers Jacki Ralph and Cliff Edwards.

3/27/71	8	10	●	1 Stay Awhile	7	Polydor 15023
6/26/71	26	5		2 I Love You Lady Dawn	64	Polydor 15027

BENATAR, Pat
Born Patricia Andrzejewski in Lindenhurst, Long Island, New York in 1952. Rock singer. Married her producer/guitarist Neil Giraldo on 2/20/82. Acted in the film *Union City* and the 1989 ABC afterschool TV special *Torn Between Two Fathers*.

11/17/84	34	10		We Belong	5	Chrysalis 42826

★★53★★ BENNETT, Tony
Born Anthony Dominick Benedetto on 8/13/26 in Queens, New York. One of the top jazz vocalists of the past 40 years. Worked local clubs while in high school, sang in U.S. Army bands. Break-through with Bob Hope in 1949 who suggested that he change his then-stage name, Joe Bari, to Tony Bennett. Audition record of "Boulevard Of Broken Dreams" earned a Columbia contract in 1950. Appeared in the film *The Oscar*.

1)*A Time For Love* 2)*Who Can I Turn To* 3)*I Wanna Be Around* 4)*Georgia Rose*
5)*I Left My Heart In San Francisco*

8/25/62	7	19		1 I Left My Heart In San Francisco	19	Columbia 42332
1/12/63	5	16		2 I Wanna Be Around	14	Columbia 42634
5/11/63	7	10		3 The Good Life	18	Columbia 42779
11/2/63	16	4		4 Don't Wait Too Long	54	Columbia 42886
8/29/64	19	2		5 A Taste Of Honey	94	Columbia 43073
10/3/64	3	10		6 Who Can I Turn To (When Nobody Needs Me)	33	Columbia 43141
2/13/65	8	6		7 If I Ruled The World	34	Columbia 43220
				from the musical *Pickwick*; with The Will Bronson Chorus		
7/10/65	17	10		8 Fly Me To The Moon (In Other Words)	84	Columbia 43331
				with The Ralph Sharon Trio		
11/6/65	8	13		9 Love Theme From "The Sandpiper" (The Shadow Of Your Smile)	95	Columbia 43431
2/26/66	10	10		10 Song From "The Oscar"/	104	
				from the film *The Oscar*		
4/9/66	27	4		11 Baby, Dream Your Dream		Columbia 43508
				from the Broadway musical *Sweet Charity*		
7/9/66	6	9		12 Georgia Rose	89	Columbia 43715
9/24/66	3	15		13 A Time For Love	119	Columbia 43768
				from the film *An American Dream*		
1/7/67	10	12		14 What Makes It Happen		Columbia 43954
				from the Broadway musical *Walking Happy*		
6/10/67	14	10	✓	15 Days Of Love (Theme from "Hombre")		Columbia 44154
9/9/67	8	19		16 For Once In My Life	91	Columbia 44258
3/16/68	12	6		17 A Fool Of Fools	119	Columbia 44443
4/20/68	10	11		18 Yesterday I Heard The Rain	130	Columbia 44510
2/22/69	27	3	✓	19 People (From "Funny Girl")		Columbia 44755
				#5 Pop hit for Barbra Streisand in 1964		
4/26/69	34	2		20 A Place Over The Sun		Columbia 44824
5/24/69	23	4		21 Play It Again, Sam		Columbia 44855
				Broadway show title song		
8/9/69	29	6		22 I've Gotta Be Me		Columbia 44947
				from the Broadway musical *Golden Rainbow*; #11 Pop hit for Sammy Davis, Jr. in 1969		
11/29/69	39	2		23 MacArthur Park		Columbia 45032
				#2 Pop hit for Richard Harris in 1968		
3/21/70	23	6	✓	24 Something		Columbia 45109
				#3 Pop hit for The Beatles in 1969		
5/5/73	38	3		25 Tell Her It's Snowing		MGM/Verve 10714
12/20/75	49	2		26 Life Is Beautiful		Improv 711
				written by Fred Astaire		
3/13/76	28	8		27 As Time Goes By		Improv 712
				#1 hit for Rudy Vallee in 1943		

DEBUT DATE	PEAK POS	WKS CHR	G O L D	ARTIST — Record Title	POP POS	Label & Number
				BENOIT, David ○ Contemporary jazz keyboardist from Hermosa Beach, California.		
7/30/88	**40**	5		The Key To You .... lead vocal by David Pack (of Ambrosia)		GRP 3025
★★**125**★★				**BENSON, George** Born on 3/22/43 in Pittsburgh. R&B-jazz guitarist. Played guitar from age eight. Played in Brother Jack McDuff's trio in 1963. House musician at CTI Records to early '70s. Influenced by Wes Montgomery. Member of Fuse One. *1)Lady Love Me (One More Time) 2)This Masquerade 3)I Just Wanna Hang Around You*		
7/10/76	**6**	12		1 **This Masquerade**	10	Warner 8209
10/23/76	**13**	13		2 Breezin' ....[I]	63	Warner 8268
8/20/77	**22**	11		3 The Greatest Love Of All .... from the film *The Greatest* starring Muhammad Ali	24	Arista 0251
4/29/78	**25**	9		4 On Broadway	7	Warner 8542
3/17/79	**12**	12		5 Love Ballad	18	Warner 8759
7/21/79	**27**	6		6 Unchained Melody		Warner 8843
8/2/80	**26**	14		7 Give Me The Night	4	Warner 49505
10/31/81	**9**	21		8 **Turn Your Love Around**	5	Warner 49846
3/6/82	**29**	10		9 Never Give Up On A Good Thing	52	Warner 50005
6/18/83	**35**	5		10 Inside Love (So Personal)	43	Warner 29649
8/13/83	**4**	18		11 **Lady Love Me (One More Time)**	30	Warner 29563
12/17/83	**30**	8		12 In Your Eyes		Warner 29442
12/22/84	**15**	14		13 20/20	48	Warner 29120
3/23/85	**7**	15		14 **I Just Wanna Hang Around You**	102	Warner 29042
8/16/86	**31**	9		15 Kisses In The Moonlight		Warner 28640
★★**83**★★				**BENTON, Brook** R&B singer/songwriter. Born Benjamin Franklin Peay on 9/19/31 in Camden, South Carolina; died on 4/9/88 of complications from spinal meningitis. In The Camden Jubilee Singers. To New York in 1948, joined Bill Langford's Langfordaires. With Jerusalem Stars in 1951. First recorded under own name for Okeh in 1953. Wrote "Looking Back," "A Lover's Question," "The Stroll," "It's Just A Matter Of Time" and "Endlessly." *1)The Boll Weevil Song 2)Rainy Night In Georgia 3)Don't It Make You Want To Go Home 4)Frankie And Johnny 5)Two Tickets To Paradise*		
7/17/61	**1**³	7		1 The Boll Weevil Song ....[N] The Mike Stewart Singers (backing vocals)	**2**³	Mercury 71820
8/21/61	**6**	8		2 **Frankie And Johnny/**	20	
10/2/61	**8**	5		3 **It's Just A House Without You**	45	Mercury 71859
3/30/63	**14**	6		4 I Got What I Wanted	28	Mercury 72099
7/6/63	**8**	6		5 **My True Confession**	22	Mercury 72135
9/21/63	**8**	8		6 **Two Tickets To Paradise**	32	Mercury 72177
2/8/64	**11**	4		7 Going Going Gone	35	Mercury 72230
5/23/64	**13**	4		8 Another Cup Of Coffee/	47	
6/6/64	**14**	4		9 Too Late To Turn Back Now	43	Mercury 72266
7/25/64	**13**	4		10 A House Is Not A Home .... movie title song	75	Mercury 72303
10/10/64	**15**	2		11 Lumberjack	53	Mercury 72333
7/3/65	**37**	2		12 Love Me Now	100	Mercury 72446
11/6/65	**9**	12		13 **Mother Nature, Father Time**	53	RCA Victor 8693
7/23/66	**37**	2		14 Break Her Heart		RCA Victor 8879
8/19/67	**37**	3		15 Laura (Tell Me What He's Got That I Ain't Got)	78	Reprise 0611
1/13/68	**36**	4		16 Weakness In A Man		Reprise 0649
10/12/68	**26**	5		17 Do Your Own Thing	99	Cotillion 44007
1/10/70	**2**³	15	●	18 **Rainy Night In Georgia**	4	Cotillion 44057
5/16/70	**35**	2		19 My Way	72	Cotillion 44072
6/6/70	**4**	8		20 **Don't It Make You Want To Go Home**	45	Cotillion 44078
1/2/71	**18**	8		21 Shoes .... The Dixie Flyers (backing vocals, above 2)	67	Cotillion 44093
				BERGER, Michel ○ French saxophonist.		
2/26/83	**23**	11		Innocent Eyes .... Rosanne Cash (vocal); available as a 7" promo single		Atlantic 477

DEBUT DATE	PEAK POS	WKS CHR	G O L D	ARTIST — Record Title	POP POS	Label & Number
				BERLIN Los Angeles electro-pop group. Went from a sextet to a trio in 1985 featuring Terri Nunn (vocals), John Crawford (bass) and Rob Brill (drums). Nunn, who as a teen acted on *Lou Grant* and several other TV shows, left band in 1987. Also see Paul Carrack.		
7/5/86	**3**	20	●	Take My Breath Away .... love theme from the film *Top Gun*	**1**[1]	Columbia 05903
				BERLIN PHILHARMONIC Symphony orchestra conducted by Karl Boehm.		
1/17/70	**40**	1		"2001" A Space Odyssey .... [I] theme for the film *2001* from *Also Sprach Zarathustra*	90	Polydor 15009
				BERNARDI, Herschel ◎ Born on 10/20/23 in New York City. Portrayed Tevye in Broadway's *Fiddler On The Roof*. Died on 5/9/86.		
2/27/71	**35**	3		Pencil Marks On The Wall	107	Columbia 45285
				BERTEI, Adele ◎ German singer/songwriter. Former lead singer of the punk-rock group the Contortions.		
11/12/88	**40**	4		Little Lives, Big Love		Chrysalis 43250
				BIDDU ORCHESTRA Biddu is an Indian-born songwriter/producer. To England, worked as a baker.		
9/13/75	**10**	11		1 Summer Of '42 .... [I] disco version of the movie theme	57	Epic 50139
1/24/76	**42**	4		2 I Could Have Danced All Night .... [I] from the musical *My Fair Lady*	72	Epic 50173
				BILK, Mr. Acker Clarinetist/composer. Born Bernard Stanley Bilk on 1/28/29 in Somerset, England.		
3/17/62	**1**[7]	21	●	1 Stranger On The Shore .... [I]	**1**[1]	Atco 6217
7/28/62	**19**	3		2 Above The Stars .... [I] from the film *The Wonderful World Of The Brothers Grimm*	59	Atco 6230
11/6/76	**41**	4		3 Aria .... [I] **ACKER BILK**		Pye 71078
				BIMBO JET French studio instrumentalists.		
5/24/75	**29**	7		El Bimbo .... [I] #1 song in 6 different European countries	43	Scepter 12406
★★158★★				**BISHOP, Stephen** Pop-rock singer/songwriter born in 1951 in San Diego. Wrote movie theme for *The China Syndrome*. Cameo role as the "Charming Guy With Guitar" in *National Lampoon's Animal House*. 1)It Might Be You 2)On And On 3)Unfaithfully Yours (One Love)		
12/25/76	**6**	15		1 Save It For A Rainy Day .... Eric Clapton (guitar solo); Chaka Khan (backing vocal)	22	ABC 12232
4/23/77	**2**[2]	32		2 On And On	11	ABC 12260
9/30/78	**5**	16		3 Everybody Needs Love	32	ABC 12406
12/13/80	**31**	10		4 Send A Little Love My Way (Like Always)............. "Bubbled Under" on 4/11/81 on Warner 49658	108	Warner 49595
9/25/82	**22**	11		5 If Love Takes You Away .... from the film *Summer Lovers*	108	Warner 29924
1/22/83	**1**[2]	25		6 It Might Be You .... theme from the film *Tootsie*	25	Warner 29791
2/25/84	**4**	17		7 Unfaithfully Yours (One Love) .... from the film *Unfaithfully Yours*	87	Warner 29345
5/3/86	**31**	4		8 The Heart Is So Willing .... theme from the film *The Money Pit*		MCA 52814
9/30/89	**13**	11		9 Walking On Air................................... produced by Phil Collins		Atlantic 88830
1/6/90	**42**	6		10 Mr. Heartbreak		Atlantic 88744
				BLACK, Cilla Born Priscilla White on 5/27/43 in Liverpool, England.		
7/18/64	**4**	5		1 You're My World	26	Capitol 5196
9/26/64	**15**	2		2 It's For You................................... written by John Lennon and Paul McCartney	79	Capitol 5258
				BLACKBYRDS, The Soul group founded in 1973 by Donald Byrd while teaching at Howard University in Washington, D.C.		
2/15/75	**5**	13		1 Walking In Rhythm	6	Fantasy 736
8/2/75	**25**	8		2 Flyin' High	70	Fantasy 747

DEBUT DATE	PEAK POS	WKS CHR	GOLD	ARTIST — Record Title	POP POS	Label & Number
				BLAKELEY, Peter ○		
				Native of Canberra, Australia. Briefly a member of the Rockmelons.		
5/12/90	**34**	6		Crying In The Chapel		Capitol 44517
				not the same song as Elvis Presley's 1965 hit		
				BLANCHARD, Jack, & Misty Morgan		
				Husband-and-wife country duo. Both born in Buffalo. Jack (b: 5/8/42) plays saxophone and keyboards. Misty (b: 5/23/45) plays keyboards. Met and married while working in Florida.		
3/28/70	**15**	8		1 Tennessee Bird Walk ....[N]	23	Wayside 010
7/18/70	**34**	2		2 Humphrey The Camel ....[N]	78	Wayside 013
				BLONDIE		
				New York City techno-pop sextet formed in 1975. Consisted of Debbie Harry (lead singer), Chris Stein, Frank Infante, Jimmy Destri, Gary Valentine and Clem Burke. Harry had been in the folk-rock group Wind In The Willows. She did solo work from 1980; appeared in several films. Group disbanded in 1983.		
5/12/79	**44**	3	●	1 Heart Of Glass	1[1]	Chrysalis 2295
12/13/80	**3**	16	●	2 The Tide Is High	1[1]	Chrysalis 2465
				BLOODSTONE		
				Soul group from Kansas City, Missouri. Formed in 1962 as the Sinceres. Consisted of Charles McCormick, Willis Draffen, Charles Love, Henry Williams and Roger Durham (d: 1973).		
6/23/73	**20**	8	●	Natural High	10	London 1046
				BLOOD, SWEAT & TEARS		
				Pop-jazz group formed by Al Kooper (The Royal Teens, The Blues Project) in 1968. Nucleus consisted of Kooper (keyboards), Steve Katz (guitar; The Blues Project), Bobby Colomby (drums) and Jim Fielder (bass). Kooper replaced by lead singer David Clayton-Thomas in 1969. Clayton-Thomas replaced by Jerry Fisher in 1972. Katz left in 1973. Clayton-Thomas rejoined in 1974. Colomby later worked as a television music reporter and an executive with Epic, Capitol, EMI and CBS.		
4/12/69	**18**	7	●	1 You've Made Me So Very Happy	2[3]	Columbia 44776
6/14/69	**1**[2]	11	●	2 Spinning Wheel	2[3]	Columbia 44871
11/1/69	**4**	10	●	3 And When I Die	2[1]	Columbia 45008
8/15/70	**14**	7		4 Hi-De-Ho	14	Columbia 45204
10/17/70	**39**	2		5 Lucretia Mac Evil	29	Columbia 45235
11/13/71	**33**	2		6 Lisa, Listen To Me	73	Columbia 45477
10/9/76	**6**	15		7 You're The One	106	Columbia 10400
				BLOOM, Bobby		
				Pop singer/songwriter, much session work in the '60s. Died from an accidental shooting on 2/28/74.		
10/10/70	**18**	10		Montego Bay	8	L&R/MGM 157
				BLUE HAZE		
				British male group.		
10/14/72	**5**	17		Smoke Gets In Your Eyes	27	A&M 1357
				BLUE MAGIC		
				Soul vocal group from Philadelphia. Consisted of Theodore Mills (lead vocals), Vernon Sawyer, Wendell Sawyer, Keith Beaton and Richard Pratt.		
7/6/74	**35**	6	●	1 Sideshow	8	Atco 6961
11/2/74	**26**	8		2 Three Ring Circus	36	Atco 7004
				BLUE RIDGE RANGERS — see FOGERTY, John		
				BLUE SWEDE		
				Swedish pop sextet — Bjorn Skifs, lead singer.		
3/16/74	**31**	7	●	Hooked On A Feeling	1[1]	EMI 3627
				BOFILL, Angela ○		
				Born in West Bronx, New York in 1954 to a French-Cuban father and Puerto Rican mother. Studied voice at Hartford Conservatory and at Manhattan School Of Music. Performed with Dizzy Gillespie and Cannonball Adderley. Featured vocalist for the Dance Theater of Harlem at age 22.		
4/28/79	**39**	7		This Time I'll Be Sweeter	104	Arista/GRP 2500
★★**40**★★				**BOLTON, Michael**		
				Born Michael Bolotin on 2/26/54 in New Haven, Connecticut. Lead singer of Blackjack in the late '70s. Began recording as Michael Bolton in 1983.		
				1)To Love Somebody 2)Love Is A Wonderful Thing 3)When A Man Loves A Woman		
9/19/87	**3**	24		1 That's What Love Is All About................................	19	Columbia 07322
1/30/88	**19**	13		2 (Sittin' On) The Dock Of The Bay	11	Columbia 07680
8/20/88	**14**	17		3 Walk Away		Columbia 07983
6/24/89	**3**	21		4 Soul Provider	17	Columbia 68909
10/28/89	**1**[2]	26		5 How Am I Supposed To Live Without You	1[3]	Columbia 73017

DEBUT DATE	PEAK POS	WKS CHR	G O L D	ARTIST — Record Title	POP POS	Label & Number
				BOLTON, Michael — Cont'd		
3/10/90	**3**	22		6 **How Can We Be Lovers**	3	Columbia 73318
5/26/90	**1**³	20		7 **When I'm Back On My Feet Again**	7	Columbia 73342
8/25/90	**6**	13		8 **Georgia On My Mind**................................	36	Columbia 73490
				sax solo by Kenny G on single version, Michael Brecker on album version		
4/20/91	**1**⁴	29		9 **Love Is A Wonderful Thing**......................	4	Columbia 73719
7/13/91	**1**²	27		10 **Time, Love And Tenderness**	7	Columbia 73889
8/31/91	**1**⁴	33		11 **When A Man Loves A Woman**	**1**¹	Columbia 74020
1/25/92	**1**³	30		12 **Missing You Now**................................	12	Columbia 74184
				MICHAEL BOLTON Featuring Kenny G		
5/9/92	**7**	25		13 **Steel Bars**		Columbia LP Cut
				written by Bolton and Bob Dylan; from the album *Time, Love & Tenderness* on Columbia 46771		
10/10/92	**1**⁵	29		14 **To Love Somebody**	11	Columbia 74733
12/12/92	**8**	20		15 **Reach Out (I'll Be There)**......................		Columbia 74798
				available as a 7" vinyl single; B-side "White Christmas" made the *Hot 100* Airplay charts (POS 73)		

BONEY M
Vocal group created in Germany by producer/composer Frank Farian. Farian sang solo on first recording in 1975, group formed later. Consisted of Marcia Barrett, Maizie Williams, Liz Mitchell and Bobby Farrell. All were from the West Indies. Farian created the Far Corporation in 1986 and Milli Vanilli in 1988.

| 7/1/78 | **35** | 11 | | Rivers Of Babylon .... | 30 | Sire 1027 |

BON JOVI
Hard-rock quintet formed in Sayreville, New Jersey: Jon Bon Jovi (b: 3/2/62; actual spelling: Bongiovi; lead vocals), Richie Sambora (b: 7/11/59; guitar), Dave Bryan (b: 2/7/62; keyboards), Alec John Such (b: 11/14/56; bass) and Tico Torres (b: 10/7/53; drums).

| 4/10/93 | **39** | 6 | | Bed Of Roses .... | 10 | Jambco 864852 |

BONOFF, Karla
Pop singer/songwriter/pianist. Born on 12/27/52 in Los Angeles.

3/8/80	**35**	9		1 Baby Don't Go	69	Columbia 11206
4/24/82	**3**	24		2 **Personally**...	19	Columbia 02805
9/11/82	**22**	12		3 Please Be The One	63	Columbia 03172
8/4/84	**16**	11		4 Somebody's Eyes	109	Columbia 04472
				from the film *Footloose*		

BOOKER T. & THE MG'S
Band formed by sessionmen from Stax Records, Memphis, in 1962. Consisted of Booker T. Jones (b: 11/12/44, Memphis), keyboards; Steve Cropper (b: 10/21/42, Ozark Mountains, Missouri.), guitar; Donald "Duck" Dunn (b: 11/24/41, Memphis), bass; and Al Jackson, Jr. (b: 11/27/34, Memphis; murdered on 10/1/75), drums. MG stands for Memphis Group. Jones received music degree from Indiana University; married Priscilla Coolidge (sister of Rita); and did production work for Rita Coolidge, Earl Klugh, Bill Withers and Willie Nelson (his *Stardust* album).

9/14/68	**32**	3		1 Soul-Limbo .... [I]	17	Stax 0001
12/21/68	**39**	2		2 Hang 'Em High .... [I]	9	Stax 0013
				movie title song		
4/19/69	**9**	8		3 **Time Is Tight**................................... [I]	6	Stax 0028
				from the soundtrack *Uptight*		
6/21/69	**20**	6		4 Mrs. Robinson .... [I]	37	Stax 0037
				from the film *The Graduate*		
8/8/70	**38**	3		5 Something .... [I]	76	Stax 0073
11/9/74	**25**	9		6 Evergreen .... [I]		Epic 50031
				BOOKER T		

BOONE, Daniel
English singer/songwriter. Real name: Peter Lee Stirling.

| 7/29/72 | **6** | 10 | | **Beautiful Sunday**................................ | 15 | Mercury 73281 |

BOONE, Debby
Born on 9/22/56 in Hackensack, New Jersey. Third daughter of Pat and Shirley Boone and granddaughter of Red Foley. Worked with the Boone Family from 1969, sang with sisters in the Boones' gospel quartet. Went solo in 1977. Winner of three Grammys including Best New Artist of 1977. Popular Contemporary Christian artist. Married Gabriel Ferrer, the son of Rosemary Clooney and Jose Ferrer, in 1982.

9/10/77	**1**¹	21	▲	1 **You Light Up My Life**	**1**¹⁰	Warner 8455
				movie title song; originally released on Warner 8446		
2/11/78	**20**	10		2 California..	50	Warner 8511
4/29/78	**14**	10		3 God Knows/	74	
4/22/78	**18**	11		4 Baby, I'm Yours	flip	Warner 8554
8/26/78	**48**	4		5 When You're Loved		Warner 8633
				from the film *The Magic Of Lassie*		

DEBUT DATE	PEAK POS	WKS CHR	G O L D	ARTIST — Record Title	POP POS	Label & Number
				BOONE, Debby — Cont'd		
9/1/79	45	6		6 See You In September		Warner 49042
5/10/80	31	8		7 Are You On The Road To Lovin' Me Again		Warner 49176
2/7/81	37	8		8 Perfect Fool		Warner 49652
				BOONE, Pat		
				Born Charles Eugene Boone on 6/1/34 in Jacksonville, Florida. To Tennessee in 1936. Direct descendant of Daniel Boone. Married country singer Red Foley's daughter, Shirley, on 11/7/53. Won on *Ted Mack's Amateur Hour* and *Arthur Godfrey's Talent Scouts* in 1954. First recorded for Republic Records in 1954. Graduated from New York's Columbia University in 1958. Hosted own TV show, *The Pat Boone-Chevy Showroom*, 1957-60. Appeared in 15 films. Toured with wife and daughters Cherry, Linda, Debby and Laura in the mid-1960s. Recording artist Nick Todd is his younger brother. Pat's trademark: white buck shoes.		
				1)Moody River 2)Big Cold Wind 3)I'll See You In My Dreams		
7/17/61	4	4		1 Moody River	1¹	Dot 16209
8/21/61	5	9		2 Big Cold Wind	19	Dot 16244
11/13/61	10	10		3 Johnny Will	35	Dot 16284
3/3/62	9	8		4 I'll See You In My Dreams/	32	
3/3/62	15	2		5 Pictures In The Fire	77	Dot 16312
10/13/62	14	4		6 Ten Lonely Guys	45	Dot 16391
10/22/66	12	9		7 Wish You Were Here, Buddy	49	Dot 16933
10/5/68	33	5		8 September Blue		Dot 17156
3/29/69	23	5		9 July You're A Woman	100	Tetragramm. 1516
				written by John Stewart (Kingston Trio)		
4/5/75	36	7		10 Indiana Girl		Melodyland 6005
				BOONES, The ○		
				Pat Boone's daughters: Debby (lead), Cherry, Lindy and Laury.		
4/12/75	25	10		1 When The Lovelight Starts Shining Through His Eyes......		Motown 1334
				#23 Pop hit for The Supremes in 1964		
5/14/77	32	9		2 Hasta Manana		Warner 8385
				written by Benny & Bjorn of Abba; re-issued as the B-side of Debby Boone's hit "You Light Up My Life" on Warner 8455		
				BORELLY, Jean-Claude, And His Orchestra ○		
				French trumpet player.		
1/31/76	15	11		Dolannes Melodie............................[I]	106	London 228
				BOSSA RIO ○		
				Latin sextet from Brazil. Led by female vocalist Gracinha. Discovered and produced by Sergio Mendes.		
11/29/69	22	8		1 Blackbird		Blue Thumb 107
				written by John Lennon and Paul McCartney		
6/13/70	15	6		2 With Your Love Now		Blue Thumb 113
				BOSTON		
				Rock group from Boston, spearheaded by Tom Scholz (guitars and keyboards) and Brad Delp (lead vocals).		
10/25/86	13	14		Amanda	1²	MCA 52756
				BOSTON POPS ORCHESTRA/ARTHUR FIEDLER		
				Conductor Arthur Fiedler was born in Boston on 12/17/1894; died on 7/10/79. Fiedler joined the Boston Pops Orchestra around 1915 as a viola player. Began his long reign as conductor in 1930, where he remained until his death. John Williams succeeded Fiedler as conductor in 1980.		
7/11/64	10	5		I Want To Hold Your Hand ....[I]	55	RCA Victor 8378
				a Richard Hayman arrangement of The Beatles' first U.S. hit		
				BOTKIN, Perry Jr. — see DeVORZON, Barry		
				BOURGEOIS, Brent		
				Former member of Bourgeois Tagg. Born in New Orleans, raised in New Jersey and Dallas.		
5/12/90	11	15		1 Dare To Fall In Love	32	Charisma 98971
9/29/90	46	3		2 Can't Feel The Pain		Charisma 98918
12/22/90	36	7		3 Time Of The Season		Charisma 98890
				#3 Pop hit for The Zombies in 1969		
				BOURGEOIS TAGG		
				West Coast rock quintet formed in 1984 and led by Brent Bourgeois and Larry Tagg.		
10/24/87	5	17		I Don't Mind At All	38	Island 99409
				produced by Todd Rundgren		
				BOYER, Charles ○		
				French romantic actor. Born on 8/28/1899; died on 8/26/78.		
7/31/65	40	2		Where Does Love Go ....[S]		Valiant 719
				written by the Addrisi Brothers; orchestra directed by Perry Botkin, Jr.		

DEBUT DATE	PEAK POS	WKS CHR	G O L D	ARTIST — Record Title	POP POS	Label & Number
				BOY GEORGE Born George O'Dowd on 6/14/61 in Bexleyheath, England. Former lead singer of Culture Club. Brief stint as Lieutenant Lush, a backing singer with Bow Wow Wow.		
3/20/93	**14**	15		The Crying Game .... movie title song; produced by the Pet Shop Boys	15	SBK 50437
				BOY KRAZY White female vocal quartet formed in New York: Kimberly Blake, Johnna Lee Cummings, Josselyne Jones and Ruth Ann Roberts (a former Miss Junior America).		
3/20/93	**19**	19		That's What Love Can Do	18	Next Plateau 857024
				BOY MEETS GIRL Seattle songwriting/recording duo: Shannon Rubicam and George Merrill. Wrote Whitney Houston's hits "How Will I Know" and "I Wanna Dance With Somebody." Married in 1988.		
9/17/88	**1**[1]	28		1 **Waiting For A Star To Fall**	5	RCA 8691
2/4/89	**28**	10		2 Bring Down The Moon	49	RCA 8807
				BOYS CLUB Duo formed in Minneapolis: vocalists Joe Pasquale and Gene Hunt (real name: Eugene Wolfgramm, formerly with his family group, The Jets).		
11/5/88	**4**	23		1 **I Remember Holding You**	8	MCA 53430
3/18/89	**39**	4		2 The Loneliest Heart		MCA 53507
				BOYZ II MEN R&B vocal quartet formed in 1988 at Philadelphia's High School of Creative and Performing Arts: Wanya Morris (age 17 in 1991), Michael McCary, Shawn Stockman and Nathan Morris. Discovered by Michael Bivins (New Edition, Bell Biv DeVoe). Appeared in 1992 TV mini-series *The Jacksons: An American Dream*.		
9/19/92	**35**	17	▲	1 End of the Road .... from the film *Boomerang*	1[13]	Motown 2178
12/12/92	**11**	23	▲	2 In The Still Of The Nite (I'll Remember) .... from the TV mini-series *The Jacksons: An American Dream*	3	Motown 2193
★★165★★				**BRANIGAN, Laura** Born on 7/3/57 in Brewster, New York. Former backing vocalist with Leonard Cohen. Acted in the TV show *CHiPS* and in the 1984 film *Mugsy's Girl*. *1)How Am I Supposed To Live Without You 2)Self Control 3)The Lucky One*		
11/20/82	**28**	11	●	1 Gloria..	2[3]	Atlantic 4048
4/2/83	**16**	16		2 Solitaire...	7	Atlantic 89868
7/16/83	**1**[3]	22		3 **How Am I Supposed To Live Without You**......................	12	Atlantic 89805
5/5/84	**5**	22		4 **Self Control**	4	Atlantic 89676
8/18/84	**13**	12		5 The Lucky One .... from the TV program *An Uncommon Love*	20	Atlantic 89636
11/10/84	**22**	10		6 Ti Amo	55	Atlantic 89608
8/10/85	**29**	6		7 Spanish Eddie	40	Atlantic 89531
3/1/86	**25**	6		8 I Found Someone	90	Atlantic 89451
8/8/87	**27**	7		9 Shattered Glass..	48	Atlantic 89245
10/24/87	**19**	11		10 Power Of Love	26	Atlantic 89191
9/22/90	**22**	13		11 Never In A Million Years		Atlantic 87865
				BRASS RING, The New York studio band headed by producer/arranger/saxophonist Phil Bodner (b: 6/13/21).		
4/30/66	**21**	4		1 The Phoenix Love Theme (Senza Fine)............................. [I] from the film *The Flight Of The Phoenix*	32	Dunhill 4023
7/9/66	**36**	4		2 Lara's Theme (From Dr. Zhivago)...................................... [I] tune also known as "Somewhere My Love"	126	Dunhill 4036
12/3/66	**25**	6		3 Samba De Orfeo (Black Orpheus)...................................... [I]		Dunhill 4047
1/28/67	**10**	12		4 **The Dis-Advantages Of You**... [I] melody taken from a Benson & Hedges cigarette jingle	36	Dunhill 4065
				BRAUN, Bob Born Robert Earl Brown on 4/20/29 in Ludlow, Kentucky. Hosted TV show in Cincinnati.		
8/11/62	**9**	7		**Till Death Do Us Part**.. [S]	26	Decca 31355
★★92★★				**BREAD** Formed in Los Angeles in 1969. Consisted of leader David Gates (vocals, guitar, keyboards), James Griffin (guitar), Robb Royer (guitar) and Jim Gordon (drums). Originally called Pleasure Faire. Griffin and Royer co-wrote award-winning "For All We Know" with Fred Karlin in 1969. Mike Botts replaced Gordon after first album. Royer replaced by Larry Knechtel (top sessionman, member of Duane Eddy's Rebels) in 1971. Disbanded in 1973, reunited briefly in 1976. All songs written and produced by David Gates. *1)If 2)Sweet Surrender 3)Baby I'm-A Want You*		
6/27/70	**4**	14	●	1 **Make It With You**	1[1]	Elektra 45686

DEBUT DATE	PEAK POS	WKS CHR	G O L D	ARTIST — Record Title	POP POS	Label & Number
				BREAD — Cont'd		
10/10/70	**2**¹	10		2 It Don't Matter To Me	10	Elektra 45701
3/27/71	**1**³	12		3 If	4	Elektra 45720
10/23/71	**1**¹	11	●	4 Baby I'm-A Want You	3	Elektra 45751
2/5/72	**3**	12		5 Everything I Own	5	Elektra 45765
4/29/72	**3**	10		6 Diary..	15	Elektra 45784
7/29/72	**1**¹	10		7 The Guitar Man	11	Elektra 45803
11/11/72	**1**²	11		8 Sweet Surrender	15	Elektra 45818
2/10/73	**4**	9		9 Aubrey	15	Elektra 45832
12/4/76	**3**	17		10 Lost Without Your Love	9	Elektra 45365
4/9/77	**2**³	15		11 Hooked On You	60	Elektra 45389

BREAKFAST CLUB
New York-based quartet. Madonna was with the group for a short time in the early '80s. Member Steve Bray co-produced Madonna's *True Blue* album.

9/19/87	**36**	3		Kiss And Tell	48	MCA 53128

BREATHE
Pop group from suburban London: David Glasper (b: 1/4/66; vocals), Ian "Spike" Spice, Marcus Lillington and Michael Delahunty (who left in 1988).

2/20/88	**2**¹	33		1 Hands To Heaven	**2**²	A&M 2991
9/3/88	**1**²	27		2 How Can I Fall?	3	A&M 1224
1/21/89	**5**	20		3 Don't Tell Me Lies	10	A&M 1267
5/13/89	**34**	6		4 All This I Should Have Known		A&M 1401
9/1/90	**3**	24		5 Say A Prayer..	21	A&M 1519
11/24/90	**17**	15		6 Does She Love That Man?	34	A&M 1535
				BREATHE featuring David Glasper		

BREMERS, Beverly
Chicago-born actress/singer.

6/5/71	**5**	20		1 Don't Say You Don't Remember..	15	Scepter 12315
5/13/72	**15**	12		2 We're Free	40	Scepter 12348
9/16/72	**18**	8		3 I'll Make You Music	63	Scepter 12363

BRENNAN, Walter
Beloved character actor born on 7/25/1894 in Swampscott, Massachusetts. Died on 9/21/74. First film role in 1924. Three-time Oscar winner. Played Grandpa on *The Real McCoys* TV series.

4/14/62	**2**³	10		1 Old Rivers ....[S]	5	Liberty 55436
11/3/62	**14**	6		2 Mama Sang A Song ....[S]	38	Liberty 55508
				The Johnny Mann Singers (backing vocals, above 2)		

BRESH, Tom ○
Country singer/actor born in Hollywood. Own TV series, *Nashville Swing*, in Canada.

10/9/76	**37**	5		Sad Country Love Song		Farr 009

BRICKELL, Edie, & New Bohemians
Vocalist Brickell (pronounced: BREE-kell) joined the Dallas-based band in 1985. Varying personnel since then. Married Paul Simon in June 1992.

1/28/89	**30**	7		What I Am	7	Geffen 27696

BRIDGES, Alicia
Atlanta-based disco singer/songwriter; originally from Lawndale, North Carolina. Born on 7/15/53.

11/25/78	**44**	3	●	I Love The Nightlife (Disco 'Round)	5	Polydor 14483

BRIGHTMAN, Sarah ○
Star of the 1987 Broadway musical *The Phantom Of The Opera*. Married to Broadway composer Andrew Lloyd Webber, divorced in 1990.

6/9/90	**45**	3		Love Changes Everything		Polydor 877352

BRISTOL, Johnny
Soul vocalist/composer/producer. Born on 2/3/39 in Morganton, North Carolina. Teamed with Jackie Beaver, recorded as Johnny & Jackie for Tri-Phi, 1961. Teamed with Harvey Fuqua as Motown producers until 1973.

11/23/74	**44**	4		You And I	48	MGM 14762

BRITTON, Vicki ○
Dallas-based singer/songwriter.

6/1/74	**36**	8		Flight 309 To Tennessee..		Bell 45,453

DEBUT DATE	PEAK POS	WKS CHR	G O L D	ARTIST — Record Title	POP POS	Label & Number
				BROOKLYN BRIDGE		
				Long Island, New York outfit led by vocalist Johnny Maestro (of The Crests). The Del-Satins, a vocal quartet led by Maestro, and The Rhythm Method, a seven-piece band, united as Brooklyn Bridge in 1967.		
3/14/70	**36**	2		Free As The Wind..	109	Buddah 162
				BROOKLYN DREAMS — see SUMMER, Donna		
				BROTHERHOOD OF MAN, The		
				British studio group featuring Tony Burrows, Johnny Goddison and Sunny (female singer). Burrows was lead singer of Edison Lighthouse, First Class, The Pipkins and White Plains. 1976 hit featured new members: Nicky Stevens, Sandra Stevens, Martin Lee and Lee Sheridan.		
5/16/70	**15**	10		1 United We Stand	13	Deram 85059
8/15/70	**11**	8		2 Where Are You Going To My Love......................................	61	Deram 85065
5/8/76	**1**[1]	11		**3 Save Your Kisses For Me**	27	Pye 71066
				BROTHERS FOUR, The		
				Folk-pop quartet: Dick Foley, Bob Flick, John Paine and Mike Kirkland. Formed while Phi Gamma Delta fraternity brothers at the University of Washington.		
2/24/62	**16**	3		1 Blue Water Line	68	Columbia 42256
10/16/65	**10**	10		**2 Try To Remember**	91	Columbia 43404
6/4/66	**30**	7		3 If I Fell		Columbia 43621
				#53 Pop hit for The Beatles in 1964		
10/29/66	**36**	4		4 Changes...		Columbia 43825
2/11/67	**32**	5		5 All I Need Is You...		Columbia 43984
5/13/67	**36**	2		6 Shenandoah		Columbia 44058
				traditional tune also known as "Across The Wide Missouri"		
				BROTHERS JOHNSON, The		
				Los Angeles R&B-funk duo of brothers George (b: 5/17/53) and Louis Johnson (b: 4/13/55). Own band, the Johnson Three + 1, with brother Tommy and cousin Alex Weir. With Billy Preston's band to 1975.		
8/27/77	**38**	6	●	Strawberry Letter 23..	5	A&M 1949
				BROWN, Bobby		
				Born on 2/5/69 in Boston. Former member of the teen R&B-pop group New Edition. Had a bit part in the film *Ghostbusters II*. Married Whitney Houston on 7/18/92.		
10/14/89	**28**	11	●	Rock Wit'cha	7	MCA 53652
				BROWN, Jim Ed		
				Born on 4/1/34 in Sparkman, Arkansas. Leader of The Browns. Had over 50 hits on the country charts. Hosted Nashville Network's TV talent show *You Can Be a Star!*. Member of *Grand Ole Opry* since 1963.		
11/28/70	**16**	9		1 Morning	47	RCA 9909
4/10/71	**29**	3		2 Angel's Sunday		RCA 9965
				BROWN, Polly		
				White soul singer. Born on 4/18/47 in Birmingham, England. Lead vocalist of Pickettywitch and Sweet Dreams.		
2/8/75	**29**	8		Up In A Puff Of Smoke	16	GTO 1002
				BROWNE, Jackson		
				Born on 10/9/48 in Heidelberg, Germany. Rock singer/guitarist/pianist/composer. To Los Angeles in 1951. With Tim Buckley and Nico in 1967 in New York City. Returned to Los Angeles, concentrated on songwriting. His songs were recorded by Linda Ronstadt, Tom Rush, Joe Cocker, The Byrds, Johnny Rivers, Bonnie Raitt, and many others. Worked with the Eagles. Produced Warren Zevon's first album. Wife Phyllis committed suicide on 3/25/76. Activist against nuclear power.		
				1)In The Shape Of A Heart 2)Somebody's Baby 3)Here Come Those Tears Again		
4/8/72	**18**	8		1 Doctor My Eyes..	8	Asylum 11004
2/26/77	**15**	8		2 Here Come Those Tears Again	23	Asylum 45379
				John Hall (Orleans - guitar solo); Bonnie Raitt (harmony vocal)		
8/19/78	**47**	3		3 Stay	20	Asylum 45485
8/14/82	**14**	16		4 Somebody's Baby..	7	Asylum 69982
				from the soundtrack *Fast Times At Ridgemont High*		
8/6/83	**24**	11		5 Lawyers In Love	13	Asylum 69826
10/22/83	**24**	14		6 Tender Is The Night	25	Asylum 69791
12/28/85	**21**	11		7 You're A Friend Of Mine	18	Columbia 05660
				CLARENCE CLEMONS and JACKSON BROWNE includes vocals by Daryl Hannah (Browne's then-girlfriend)		
3/22/86	**31**	5		8 For America..	30	Asylum 69566
6/14/86	**10**	13		**9 In The Shape Of A Heart**	70	Asylum 69543
9/2/89	**23**	8		10 Anything Can Happen..		Elektra 69284

DEBUT DATE	PEAK POS	WKS CHR	G O L D	ARTIST — Record Title	POP POS	Label & Number
				BROWNS, The		
				Family trio: Jim Ed Brown (b: 4/1/34, Sparkman, Arkansas) and his sisters Maxine (b: 4/27/32, Sampti, Louisiana) and Bonnie (b: 7/31/37, Sparkman, Arkansas).		
7/24/65	**35**	3		You Can't Grow Peaches On A Cherry Tree	120	RCA Victor 8603
				BRUBECK, Dave, Quartet		
				Born David Warren on 12/6/20 in Concord, California. Leader of jazz quartet consisting of Brubeck (piano), Paul Desmond (alto sax), Joe Morello (drums) and Eugene Wright (bass). One of America's all-time most popular jazz groups on college campuses.		
9/11/61	**5**	12		1 Take Five ....[I]	25	Columbia 41479
1/5/63	**20**	1		2 Bossa Nova U.S.A. ....[I]	69	Columbia 42651
				BRYANT, Anita		
				Born on 3/25/40 in Barnsdale, Oklahoma. As Miss Oklahoma, she was 2nd runner-up to Miss America in 1958.		
6/13/64	**17**	4		The World Of Lonely People	59	Columbia 43037
				BRYANT, Ray		
				Born Raphael Bryant on 12/24/31 in Philadelphia. R&B-jazz pianist/bandleader. Uncle of jazz guitarist Kevin Eubanks.		
9/30/67	**34**	6		Ode To Billy Joe ....[I]	89	Cadet 5575
				BRYDGE ○		
				Portland-based group led by Chicago singer/songwriters: M.J.S. Thompson, Kenn Berkley and Jack Cousens. Includes: Rich Gooch and Brian David Willis (both of Quarterflash), Cal Scott and Jim Fischer.		
12/5/87	**31**	8		Another Day Gone..		Avatar 6038
★★74★★				**BRYSON, Peabo**		
				Born Robert Peabo Bryson on 4/13/51 in Greenville, South Carolina. R&B singer/producer. First solo recording for Bang in 1970. Married Juanita Leonard, former wife of boxer Sugar Ray Leonard, in 1992.		
				1)A Whole New World (Aladdin's Theme) 2)If Ever You're In My Arms Again 3)By The Time This Night Is Over		
3/7/81	**25**	8		1 Lovers After All	54	Arista 0587
				MELISSA MANCHESTER AND PEABO BRYSON		
7/16/83	**4**	29		2 Tonight, I Celebrate My Love *	16	Capitol 5242
1/7/84	**5**	21		3 You're Looking Like Love To Me *	58	Capitol 5307
5/5/84	**15**	12		4 I Just Came Here To Dance *		Capitol 5353
				*PEABO BRYSON/ROBERTA FLACK		
5/19/84	**1⁴**	23		5 If Ever You're In My Arms Again	10	Elektra 69728
7/27/85	**37**	3		6 Take No Prisoners (In The Game Of Love)	78	Elektra 69632
1/18/86	**26**	6		7 Love Always Finds A Way		Elektra 69585
1/9/88	**8**	15		8 Without You...	89	Elektra 69426
				PEABO BRYSON & REGINA BELLE		
				from the film Leonard Pt. 6		
6/8/91	**11**	24		9 Can You Stop The Rain	52	Columbia 73745
11/16/91	**3**	34	●	10 Beauty And The Beast	9	Epic 74090
				CELINE DION and PEABO BRYSON		
				movie title song		
2/22/92	**45**	7		11 Lost In The Night		Columbia 73990
8/22/92	**34**	8		12 You Are My Home...		Angel LP Cut
				LINDA EDER & PEABO BRYSON		
				from the album The Scarlet Pimpernel on Angel 54397		
11/21/92	**1⁶**	34	●	13 A Whole New World (Aladdin's Theme)	1¹	Columbia 74751
				PEABO BRYSON and REGINA BELLE		
				from the Walt Disney animated feature film Aladdin		
5/15/93	**1²**	20↑		14 By The Time This Night Is Over	25	Arista 12565
				KENNY G with Peabo Bryson		
				BUCKINGHAM, Lindsey		
				Born on 10/3/47 in Palo Alto, California. Rock guitarist/vocalist/songwriter. In group Fritz from 1967-71; with Stevie Nicks (Fritz lead singer) formed duo, Buckingham Nicks, in early '70s. Both joined Fleetwood Mac in 1975. Lindsey left Fleetwood Mac in 1987. His grandfather founded Keystone Coffee; his father founded Alta Coffee. Lindsey's brother Gregg won a silver medal in swimming in the 1968 Olympics.		
11/7/81	**14**	15		1 Trouble	9	Asylum 47223
9/5/92	**32**	9		2 Countdown		Reprise 18860
12/12/92	**38**	10		3 Soul Drifter		Reprise 18675

DEBUT DATE	PEAK POS	WKS CHR	GOLD	ARTIST — Record Title	POP POS	Label & Number
★★154★★				**BUFFETT, Jimmy** Born on 12/25/46 in Mobile, Alabama. Has BS degree in history and journalism from the University of Southern Mississippi. After working in New Orleans, moved to Nashville in 1969. Staff reporter at *Billboard*, 1969-1970. Settled in Key West in 1971. Owns a store called Margaritaville and has his own line of tropical clothing.		
				1)Margaritaville 2)Come Monday 3)Changes In Latitudes, Changes In Attitudes		
9/1/73	23	7		1 Grapefruit - Juicy Fruit...		Dunhill 4359
5/4/74	3	17		2 **Come Monday**..	30	Dunhill 4385
10/19/74	44	4		3 Pencil Thin Mustache..	101	Dunhill 15011
4/2/77	1¹	23		4 **Margaritaville**	8	ABC 12254
9/24/77	11	13		5 Changes In Latitudes, Changes In Attitudes.......................	37	ABC 12305
11/3/79	42	2		6 Fins..	35	MCA 41109
12/15/79	43	8		7 Volcano..	66	MCA 41161
2/28/81	32	9		8 It's My Job...	57	MCA 51061
11/12/83	22	15		9 One Particular Harbour		MCA 52298
2/11/84	13	12	✓	10 Brown Eyed Girl..		MCA 52333
				#10 Pop hit for Van Morrison in 1967		
9/21/85	37	3		11 If The Phone Doesn't Ring, It's Me...................................		MCA 52664
9/24/88	24	7	✓	12 Bring Back The Magic...		MCA 53396
8/19/89	18	9		13 Take Another Road		MCA 53675
7/10/93	29	7		14 Another Saturday Night/		
				#10 Pop hit for Sam Cooke in 1963		
		1		15 Souvenirs		Margaritaville 54680
				BURKE, Solomon Soul singer. Born in 1936 in Philadelphia. Preached and broadcast from own church, "Solomon's Temple," in Philadelphia from 1945-55 as the "Wonder Boy Preacher." Church was founded for him by his grandmother. First recorded for Apollo in 1954. Left music to attend mortuary school, returned in 1960.		
10/9/61	6	14		1 **Just Out Of Reach (Of My Two Open Arms)**....................	24	Atlantic 2114
7/14/62	19	2		2 Down In The Valley	71	Atlantic 2147
3/14/64	16	2		3 He'll Have To Go...	51	Atlantic 2218
				BURNETTE, Rocky Born on 6/12/53 in Memphis. Son of Johnny Burnette, nephew of Dorsey Burnette and cousin of Billy Burnette (of Fleetwood Mac).		
6/14/80	39	7		Tired Of Toein' The Line..	8	EMI America 8043
				BURNS, George Born Nathan Birnbaum on 1/20/1896 in New York City. George and wife Gracie starred together in vaudeville, movies, radio and TV from the 1930s until Gracie's death in 1964. George went on to enjoy a remarkable second career, winning the Academy Award in 1975 for *The Sunshine Boys*. His only other charted record was back in 1933 — the all-time longest span between charted hits (47 years).		
1/26/80	25	10		I Wish I Was Eighteen Again	49	Mercury 57011
				BURNS SISTERS BAND, The ⊙ Five sisters: Jeannie, Annie, Teresa, Sheila and Marie Burns — of a family of 12 from Ithaca, New York. Featured on a 7/30/87 ABC-TV News *Closeup* News documentary.		
2/28/87	23	8		Listen To The Beat Of A Heart		Columbia 06641
				BURTON, Richard Born Richard Jenkins in Pontrhydfen, Wales on 11/10/25. Died on 8/5/84 of a cerebral hemorrhage. Leading actor from 1948-1983. Married actress Elizabeth Taylor, twice.		
2/6/65	15	3		Married Man .... [S]	64	MGM 13307
				from Broadway's *Baker Street*		
				BUTLER, Jerry R&B singer born on 12/8/39 in Sunflower, Mississippi. Dubbed "The Ice Man."		
10/9/61	3	17		**Moon River**	11	Vee-Jay 405
				from the film *Breakfast At Tiffany's*		
				BUTLER, Jonathan Born in Capetown, South Africa. Soul guitarist/singer/songwriter. Migrated to London, 1984 (at age 21).		
5/31/86	25	4		1 Baby Please Don't Take It (I Need Your Love) .... [I]		Jive 9500
5/30/87	16	17		2 Lies..	27	Jive 1038
2/6/88	24	9		3 Take Good Care Of Me...		Jive 1083
3/4/89	48	1		4 More Than Friends...		Jive 1174
				BYRD, Charlie Born on 9/16/25 in Chuckatuch, Virginia. Jazz and classical guitar virtuoso. Studied under classical master guitarist Segovia. With Woody Herman in 1959. Own tour of Latin America in 1961.		
10/20/62	4	13		1 **Desafinado** .... [I]	15	Verve 10260
				STAN GETZ/CHARLIE BYRD		

DEBUT DATE	PEAK POS	WKS CHR	GOLD	ARTIST — Record Title	POP POS	Label & Number
6/20/70	**40**	1		BYRD, Charlie — Cont'd 2 I'll Walk With The Rain ....[I]		Columbia 45099

C

CAFFERTY, John, And The Beaver Brown Band
Rock sextet from Narragansett, Rhode Island. Wrote and recorded the music for the soundtrack *Eddie And The Cruisers*. Band, led by singer/guitarist Cafferty, includes Bob Cotoia, Gary Gramolini, Kenny Jo Silva, Pat Lupo and Michael Antunes.

DEBUT DATE	PEAK POS	WKS CHR	GOLD	ARTIST — Record Title	POP POS	Label & Number
12/1/84	**30**	9		Tender Years ....[R] from the film *Eddie And The Cruisers*; originally made the *Hot 100* on 1/28/84 on Scotti Br. 04327 (POS 78)	31	Scotti Br. 04682

CALDWELL, Bobby
Born on 8/15/51 in New York City. Raised in Florida. Multi-instrumentalist/songwriter. Percussionist with Johnny Winter, Rick Derringer, Captain Beyond and Armageddon. Wrote tracks for *New Mickey Mouse Club* TV show, commercials, and Peter Cetera and Amy Grant's "The Next Time I Fall."

DEBUT DATE	PEAK POS	WKS CHR	GOLD	ARTIST — Record Title	POP POS	Label & Number
2/3/79	**10**	16		1 **What You Won't Do For Love**	9	Clouds 11
3/30/91	**41**	2		2 Real Thing .... from the album *Heart of Mine* on Sin-Drome 8888		Sin-Drome LP Cut

CALE, J.J.
Born Jean Jacques Cale on 12/5/38 in Oklahoma City. Rock singer/songwriter/guitarist. Wrote Eric Clapton's "After Midnight" and "Cocaine." In high school bands with Leon Russell. Worked with Phil Spector and Delaney & Bonnie. Session work with Art Garfunkel, Bob Seger and Neil Young.

DEBUT DATE	PEAK POS	WKS CHR	GOLD	ARTIST — Record Title	POP POS	Label & Number
3/11/72	**18**	7		1 Crazy Mama..	22	Shelter 7314
6/10/72	**26**	6		2 After Midnight	42	Shelter 7321
11/11/72	**33**	5		3 Lies	42	Shelter 7326

CALELLO, Charlie, Singers ○
New York-based singer/arranger/producer. Arranger and brief member of The Four Seasons in the mid-1960s.

DEBUT DATE	PEAK POS	WKS CHR	GOLD	ARTIST — Record Title	POP POS	Label & Number
4/8/67	**32**	4		When I Tell You That I Love You (Quando Dico Che Ti Amo)		Columbia 44064

CALLOWAY
Brother duo of Reggie and Cino-Vincent Calloway from Cincinnati. Both were members of Midnight Star. Duo's production work for The Whispers, Natalie Cole, Gladys Knight and Teddy Pendergrass.

DEBUT DATE	PEAK POS	WKS CHR	GOLD	ARTIST — Record Title	POP POS	Label & Number
4/28/90	**20**	12	●	I Wanna Be Rich	2[1]	Solar 74005

CAMPBELL, Debbie
Formerly the female lead vocalist with the group Buckwheat.

DEBUT DATE	PEAK POS	WKS CHR	GOLD	ARTIST — Record Title	POP POS	Label & Number
5/10/75	**12**	13		Please Tell Him That I Said Hello	84	Playboy 6037

★★15★★ CAMPBELL, Glen
Born on 4/22/36 in Billstown, Arkansas. Vocalist/guitarist/composer. With his uncle Dick Bills' band, 1954-58. To Los Angeles; recorded with The Champs in 1960. Became prolific studio musician; with The Beach Boys in 1965 and Sagittarius in 1967. Own TV show *The Glen Campbell Goodtime Hour*, 1968-72. In films *True Grit*, *Norwood* and *Strange Homecoming*; voice in animated film *Rock-A-Doodle*.

1)*Wichita Lineman* 2)*Galveston* 3)*Southern Nights* 4)*Try A Little Kindness* 5)*Rhinestone Cowboy*

DEBUT DATE	PEAK POS	WKS CHR	GOLD	ARTIST — Record Title	POP POS	Label & Number
1/13/62	**15**	2		1 Turn Around, Look At Me	62	Crest 1087
11/11/67	**12**	9		2 By The Time I Get To Phoenix	26	Capitol 2015
2/17/68	**20**	4		3 Hey Little One	54	Capitol 2076
4/13/68	**18**	8		4 I Wanna Live	36	Capitol 2146
7/6/68	**6**	11		5 **Dreams Of The Everyday Housewife**..........................	32	Capitol 2224
10/12/68	**8**	7		6 Gentle On My Mind...[R] originally made the *Hot 100* on 7/8/67 (POS 62)	39	Capitol 5939
11/2/68	**1**[6]	18	●	7 Wichita Lineman	3	Capitol 2302
11/9/68	**32**	6		8 Mornin' Glory .... BOBBIE GENTRY & GLEN CAMPBELL	74	Capitol 2314
2/8/69	**7**	9		9 **Let It Be Me** .... GLEN CAMPBELL AND BOBBIE GENTRY	36	Capitol 2387
3/1/69	**1**[6]	13	●	10 Galveston..	4	Capitol 2428
5/3/69	**10**	8		11 Where's The Playground Susie	26	Capitol 2494
7/26/69	**7**	10		12 True Grit.. movie title song (starring John Wayne and Campbell)	35	Capitol 2573
10/18/69	**1**[1]	11		13 Try A Little Kindness	23	Capitol 2659

DEBUT DATE	PEAK POS	WKS CHR	G O L D	ARTIST — Record Title	POP POS	Label & Number
				CAMPBELL, Glen — Cont'd		
1/17/70	4	9		14 Honey Come Back....................	19	Capitol 2718
2/21/70	4	9		15 All I Have To Do Is Dream.................	27	Capitol 2745
				BOBBIE GENTRY & GLEN CAMPBELL		
4/11/70	7	9		16 Oh Happy Day...............	40	Capitol 2787
7/4/70	3	9		17 Everything A Man Could Ever Need............	52	Capitol 2843
				written by Mac Davis		
9/12/70	2²	12		18 It's Only Make Believe.................	10	Capitol 2905
3/13/71	2²	10		19 Dream Baby (How Long Must I Dream)...........	31	Capitol 3062
6/26/71	12	9		20 The Last Time I Saw Her............	61	Capitol 3123
				written by Gordon Lightfoot		
10/23/71	13	5		21 I Say A Little Prayer/By The Time I Get To		
				Phoenix...............	81	Capitol 3200
				GLEN CAMPBELL/ANNE MURRAY		
1/15/72	36	2		22 Oklahoma Sunday Morning............	104	Capitol 3254
8/26/72	14	7		23 I Will Never Pass This Way Again...........	61	Capitol 3411
12/9/72	20	7		24 One Last Time............	78	Capitol 3483
				written by the Addrisi Brothers		
3/24/73	26	6		25 I Knew Jesus (Before He Was A Star)............	45	Capitol 3548
11/3/73	45	4		26 Wherefore And Why................	111	Capitol 3735
2/2/74	13	10		27 Houston (I'm Comin' To See You)...........	68	Capitol 3808
8/24/74	42	5		28 Bonaparte's Retreat............		Capitol 3926
				written in 1950 by Pee Wee King		
12/14/74	39	6		29 It's A Sin When You Love Somebody...........		Capitol 3988
6/14/75	1¹	15	●	30 Rhinestone Cowboy..............	1²	Capitol 4095
11/8/75	1¹	12		31 Country Boy (You Got Your Feet In L.A.)........	11	Capitol 4155
4/3/76	1¹	10		32 Don't Pull Your Love/Then You Can Tell Me Goodbye....	27	Capitol 4245
7/17/76	15	10		33 See You On Sunday............		Capitol 4288
2/5/77	1⁴	22	●	34 Southern Nights............	1¹	Capitol 4376
7/9/77	1¹	13		35 Sunflower............	39	Capitol 4445
				written by Neil Diamond		
6/10/78	38	10		36 Another Fine Mess/		
10/28/78	7	14		37 Can You Fool..............	38	Capitol 4584
3/10/79	38	3		38 I'm Gonna Love You..............		Capitol 4682
12/8/79	42	3		39 My Prayer............		Capitol 4799
5/17/80	39	9		40 Somethin' 'Bout You Baby I Like..............	42	Capitol 4865
				GLEN CAMPBELL and RITA COOLIDGE		
2/21/81	45	4		41 I Don't Want To Know Your Name.............	65	Capitol 4959
2/5/83	35	11		42 I Love How You Love Me..............		Atlantic A. 99930
				CAMPBELL, Jo Ann		
				Born on 7/20/38 in Jacksonville, Florida. First recorded for El Dorado in 1957. In the films *Johnny Melody, Go Johnny Go* and *Hey, Let's Twist*. Married singer Troy Seals in the early 1960s; recorded together as Jo Ann & Troy in 1964.		
9/22/62	10	2		(I'm The Girl On) Wolverton Mountain............	38	Cameo 223
				answer song to Claude King's "Wolverton Mountain"		
				CAMPBELL, Tevin		
				Texas native born in 1978. Won role in 1988 for the TV show *Wally & The Valentines*. Discovered by Quincy Jones. Appeared in the film *Graffiti Bridge*.		
2/15/92	43	5	●	Tell Me What You Want Me To Do............	6	Qwest 19131
				CANTRELL, Lana		
				Born on 8/7/43 in Sydney, Australia.		
9/28/68	36	2		1 Catch The Wind.............		RCA Victor 9619
				#23 Pop hit for Donovan in 1965		
11/8/69	29	4		2 Tomorrow Is The First Day Of The Rest Of My Life...........		RCA Victor 0268
				from the musical *Salvation*		
3/23/74	49	2		3 Remembering............		East Coast 1060
				theme from the film *England Made Me*		
12/7/74	8	17		4 Like A Sunday Morning..............	63	Polydor 14261
				CAPALDI, Jim		
				Born on 8/24/44 in Evesham, England. Drummer with Traffic, 1967-74.		
10/9/76	42	4		1 Good Night & Good Morning..............		Island 067
				written by Hall & Oates		
4/30/83	3	18		2 That's Love............	28	Atlantic 89849
				CAPPELLI, Rachele — see NATASHA'S BROTHER		

DEBUT DATE	PEAK POS	WKS CHR	GOLD	ARTIST — Record Title	POP POS	Label & Number
				CAPPS, Al ✪		
				Prolific arranger/conductor.		
5/19/73	**33**	5		Shangri-La	119	Bell 45347
★★**90**★★				**CAPTAIN & TENNILLE**		
				Daryl "The Captain" Dragon (b: 8/27/42, Los Angeles) and his wife, Toni Tennille (b: 5/8/43, Montgomery, Alabama). Dragon is the son of noted conductor Carmen Dragon. Keyboardist with The Beach Boys, nicknamed the "Captain" by Mike Love. Duo had own TV show on ABC from 1976-77.		
				1)Muskrat Love 2)The Way I Want To Touch You 3)Love Will Keep Us Together		
4/5/75	**1**[1]	17	●	1 **Love Will Keep Us Together**	1[4]	A&M 1672
				written by Neil Sedaka (also #3 and 10 below)		
10/4/75	**1**[2]	11	●	2 **The Way I Want To Touch You**	4	A&M 1725
				first released on Butterscotch Castle 001, then on Joyce 101, then on A&M 1624, all in 1974		
1/31/76	**1**[1]	13	●	3 **Lonely Night (Angel Face)**	3	A&M 1782
5/8/76	**1**[1]	11	●	4 **Shop Around**	4	A&M 1817
9/25/76	**1**[4]	19	●	5 **Muskrat Love**	4	A&M 1870
4/2/77	**12**	10		6 **Can't Stop Dancin'**	13	A&M 1912
				written by Ray Stevens		
6/11/77	**8**	11		7 **Come In From The Rain**	61	A&M 1944
9/10/77	**9**	14		8 **Circles**		A&M 1970
4/22/78	**6**	11		9 **I'm On My Way**	74	A&M 2027
8/5/78	**14**	14		10 You Never Done It Like That	10	A&M 2063
12/9/78	**17**	12		11 You Need A Woman Tonight	40	A&M 2106
11/3/79	**4**	17	●	12 **Do That To Me One More Time**	1[1]	Casablanca 2215
5/17/80	**27**	7		13 Happy Together (A Fantasy)	53	Casablanca 2264
				CARA, Irene		
				Vocalist/actress/dancer/pianist. Born on 3/18/59 in New York City. Professional debut at age seven. Won Obie Award for *The Me Nobody Knows* in 1970. Much TV work, including *Electric Company* and *Roots 2*; in films *Fame, D.C. Cab* and *The Cotton Club*.		
9/20/80	**20**	10		1 **Out Here On My Own**	19	RSO 1048
				from the film *Fame*		
4/30/83	**4**	24	●	2 **Flashdance...What A Feeling**	1[6]	Casablanca 811440
				from the film *Flashdance*		
8/4/84	**10**	13		3 **You Were Made For Me**	78	Geffen 29257
				CARAVELLES, The		
				English pop duo: Andrea Simpson and Lois Wilkinson.		
12/7/63	**2**[1]	8		**You Don't Have To Be A Baby To Cry**	3	Smash 1852
★★**112**★★				**CAREY, Mariah**		
				Born on 3/27/70 of Irish and Black/Venezuelan parentage. Her mother is Patricia Carey, former singer with the New York City Opera. Mariah sang backup for Brenda K. Starr. Won the 1990 Best New Artist Grammy Award. Married Tommy Mottola, president of Sony Music, on 6/5/93.		
				1)Can't Let Go 2)Vision Of Love 3)I'll Be There		
6/2/90	**1**[3]	28	●	1 **Vision Of Love**	1[4]	Columbia 73348
9/15/90	**1**[1]	38	●	2 **Love Takes Time**	1[3]	Columbia 73455
1/26/91	**5**	22	●	3 **Someday**	1[2]	Columbia 73561
4/6/91	**1**[1]	25		4 **I Don't Wanna Cry**	1[2]	Columbia 73743
8/31/91	**3**	18	●	5 **Emotions**	1[3]	Columbia 73977
11/16/91	**1**[3]	29		6 **Can't Let Go**	2[1]	Columbia 74088
3/7/92	**13**	17		7 **Make It Happen**	5	Columbia 74239
5/23/92	**1**[2]	21		8 **I'll Be There**	1[2]	Columbia 74330
				recorded on MTV's *Unplugged*; Trey Lorenz (male vocal)		
				CARLISLE, Belinda		
				Born on 8/17/58 in Hollywood. Lead singer of the Go-Go's, 1978-84. Married to Morgan Mason, son of late actor James Mason.		
8/9/86	**25**	7		1 **Mad About You**	3	I.R.S. 52815
11/7/87	**7**	15		2 **Heaven Is A Place On Earth**	1[1]	MCA 53181
2/6/88	**9**	16		3 **I Get Weak**	2[1]	MCA 53242
4/23/88	**5**	17		4 **Circle In The Sand**	7	MCA 53308
10/28/89	**8**	15		5 **Leave A Light On**	11	MCA 53706
2/17/90	**29**	8		6 **Summer Rain**	30	MCA 53783

DEBUT DATE	PEAK POS	WKS CHR	GOLD	ARTIST — Record Title	POP POS	Label & Number
				CARLISLE, Steve		
				Background and radio jingle vocalist.		
12/12/81	**29**	9		WKRP In Cincinnati	65	MCA 51205
				theme from the TV series of the same title		
				CARLTON, Carl		
				Soul singer. Born in 1952 in Detroit. Singing since age nine. First recorded for Lando Records in 1964.		
10/19/74	**15**	11		Everlasting Love	6	Back Beat 27001
				CARLTON, Larry		
				Born on 3/2/48 in Torrance, California. Top session guitarist. Member of The Crusaders, 1972-77. Fully recovered from a near-fatal gunshot wound suffered in a robbery attack in 1988. Married to Contemporary Christian artist Michelle Pillar.		
2/20/82	**13**	16		1 Sleepwalk .... [I]	74	Warner 50019
				#1 Pop hit for Santo & Johnny in 1959		
8/16/86	**35**	2		2 Smiles And Smiles To Go .... [I]		MCA 52844
7/11/87	**25**	7		3 Minute By Minute .... [I]		MCA 53119
				#14 Pop hit for The Doobie Brothers in 1979		
★★147★★				**CARMEN, Eric**		
				Born on 8/11/49 in Cleveland. Classical training at Cleveland Institute of Music from early years to mid-teens. Lead singer of the Raspberries from 1970-74.		
				1)Make Me Lose Control 2)Never Gonna Fall In Love Again 3)Hungry Eyes		
1/3/76	**6**	12	●	1 All By Myself	2³	Arista 0165
5/8/76	**1¹**	12		2 Never Gonna Fall In Love Again	11	Arista 0184
8/28/76	**33**	7		3 Sunrise	34	Arista 0200
9/24/77	**26**	9		4 She Did It	23	Arista 0266
9/30/78	**6**	21		5 Change Of Heart	19	Arista 0354
2/3/79	**30**	7		6 Baby, I Need Your Lovin'	62	Arista 0384
2/2/85	**10**	11		7 I Wanna Hear It From Your Lips	35	Geffen 29118
4/20/85	**16**	8		8 I'm Through With Love	87	Geffen 29032
12/5/87	**2¹**	24		9 Hungry Eyes	4	RCA 5315
				from the film *Dirty Dancing*		
5/28/88	**1³**	26		10 Make Me Lose Control	3	Arista 9686
★★139★★				**CARNES, Kim**		
				Vocalist/pianist/composer. Born on 7/20/45 in Los Angeles. Member of The New Christy Minstrels with husband/co-writer Dave Ellingson and Kenny Rogers, late 1960s. Wrote for and performed in commercials.		
				1)What About Me? 2)Don't Fall In Love With A Dreamer 3)You're A Part Of Me		
1/17/76	**32**	6		1 You're A Part Of Me		A&M 1767
6/17/78	**6**	15		2 You're A Part Of Me .... [R]	36	Ariola 7704
				GENE COTTON with Kim Carnes		
3/29/80	**2⁴**	19		3 Don't Fall In Love With A Dreamer	4	United Art. 1345
				KENNY ROGERS with Kim Carnes		
5/31/80	**6**	19		4 More Love	10	EMI America 8045
4/18/81	**15**	17	●	5 Bette Davis Eyes	1⁹	EMI America 8077
				written by Jackie DeShannon and Donna Weiss		
4/21/84	**9**	17		6 I Pretend	74	EMI America 8202
9/15/84	**1²**	19		7 What About Me?	15	RCA 13899
				KENNY ROGERS with KIM CARNES and JAMES INGRAM		
12/15/84	**8**	17		8 Make No Mistake, He's Mine	51	Columbia 04695
				BARBRA STREISAND (With KIM CARNES)		
2/9/85	**32**	5		9 Invitation To Dance	68	EMI America 8250
				from the anthology film *That's Dancing!*		
10/15/88	**13**	16	✓	10 Crazy In Love		MCA 53433
4/4/92	**23**	13		11 Hooked On The Memory Of You.....................		Columbia LP Cut
				NEIL DIAMOND with Kim Carnes		
				from the Neil Diamond album *Lovescape* on Columbia 48610		
				CARNIVAL ✪		
				Pop vocal quartet from Los Angeles.		
1/3/70	**40**	2		1 Laia Ladaia .... [F]		World Pac. 77932
3/20/71	**37**	2		2 Where There's A Heartache (There Must Be A Heart)		United Art. 50749
				CARPENTER, Mary-Chapin		
				Born on 2/21/58 in Princeton, New Jersey. Moved to Washington, D.C. in 1974. Graduated from Brown University with an American Civilization degree. Pursued folk music before she became a top country vocalist.		
1/30/93	**11**	20		Passionate Kisses	57	Columbia 74795

41

DEBUT DATE	PEAK POS	WKS CHR	GOLD	ARTIST — Record Title	POP POS	Label & Number
	★★11★★			**CARPENTERS**		
				Richard Carpenter (b: 10/15/46) and sister Karen (b: 3/2/50; d: 2/4/83 of heart failure due to anorexia nervosa). From New Haven, Connecticut. Richard played piano from age nine. To Downey, California in 1963. Karen played drums in group with Richard and bass player Wes Jacobs in 1965. The trio recorded for RCA in 1966. After a period with the band Spectrum, the Carpenters recorded as a duo for A&M in 1969. Won the 1970 Best New Artist Grammy Award. Hosts of the TV variety show *Make Your Own Kind Of Music* in 1971. 1988 TV movie *The Karen Carpenter Story* was based on Karen's life.		
				1)We've Only Just Begun 2)(They Long To Be) Close To You 3)Rainy Days And Mondays 4)Yesterday Once More 5)For All We Know		
12/27/69	19	8		1 Ticket To Ride	54	A&M 1142
6/13/70	1⁶	16	●	2 (They Long To Be) Close To You	1⁴	A&M 1183
9/19/70	1⁷	16	●	3 We've Only Just Begun........................	2⁴	A&M 1217
2/13/71	1³	11	●	4 For All We Know	3	A&M 1243
				from the film *Lovers And Other Strangers*		
5/15/71	1⁴	12	●	5 Rainy Days And Mondays	2²	A&M 1260
9/4/71	1²	13	●	6 Superstar/	2²	
				written by Leon Russell and Bonnie Bramlett		
12/11/71	26	6		7 Bless The Beasts And Children	67	A&M 1289
				movie title song		
1/15/72	1²	13	●	8 Hurting Each Other..........................	2²	A&M 1322
4/29/72	2⁴	12		9 It's Going To Take Some Time................	12	A&M 1351
				written by Carole King		
7/22/72	2¹	11		10 Goodbye To Love	7	A&M 1367
2/24/73	1²	12	●	11 Sing	3	A&M 1413
6/9/73	1³	12	●	12 Yesterday Once More	2¹	A&M 1446
10/6/73	2²	18	●	13 Top Of The World	1²	A&M 1468
4/13/74	1¹	14		14 I Won't Last A Day Without You	11	A&M 1521
11/30/74	1¹	13	●	15 Please Mr. Postman	1¹	A&M 1646
4/5/75	1¹	12		16 Only Yesterday	4	A&M 1677
8/9/75	1¹	11		17 Solitaire	17	A&M 1721
				written by Neil Sedaka		
3/6/76	1²	11		18 There's A Kind Of Hush (All Over The World)................	12	A&M 1800
6/12/76	1¹	11		19 I Need To Be In Love	25	A&M 1828
8/28/76	4	11		20 Goofus	56	A&M 1859
				there were 4 top 20 versions of this tune in 1932		
5/21/77	4	15		21 All You Get From Love Is A Love Song	35	A&M 1940
10/15/77	18	13		22 Calling Occupants Of Interplanetary Craft...........	32	A&M 1978
				(The Recognized Anthem of World Contact Day)		
1/14/78	7	18		23 Sweet, Sweet Smile	44	A&M 2008
				written by Juice Newton		
11/18/78	9	14		24 I Believe You	68	A&M 2097
				written by the Addrisi Brothers		
6/27/81	1²	16		25 Touch Me When We're Dancing	16	A&M 2344
9/19/81	14	12		26 (Want You) Back In My Life Again	72	A&M 2370
12/12/81	21	13		27 Those Good Old Dreams	63	A&M 2386
3/27/82	16	13		28 Beechwood 4-5789	74	A&M 2405
10/22/83	7	18		29 Make Believe It's Your First Time	101	A&M 2585
2/11/84	12	13		30 Your Baby Doesn't Love You Anymore		A&M 2620
10/3/87	12	14		31 Something In Your Eyes		A&M 2940
				RICHARD CARPENTER with Dusty Springfield		
11/25/89	18	13		32 If I Had You		A&M 1471
				KAREN CARPENTER recorded in 1979		
	★★109★★			**CARR, Vikki**		
				Born Florencia Martinez Cardona on 7/19/41 in El Paso, Texas. Regular on TV's *Ray Anthony Show*, 1962.		
				1)It Must Be Him 2)The Lesson 3)Eternity		
8/20/66	31	5		1 My Heart Reminds Me		Liberty 55897
				#9 Pop hit for Kay Starr in 1957 as "And That Reminds Me"		
10/15/66	32	4		2 So Nice (Summer Samba).....................		Liberty 55917
				#26 Pop hit for Walter Wanderley in 1966		
2/4/67	39	1		3 Until Today/		
				from the musical *A Joyful Noise*		
2/11/67	28	5		4 Now I Know The Feeling		Liberty 55937
8/12/67	1³	19		5 It Must Be Him	3	Liberty 55986
12/30/67	1¹	11		6 The Lesson	34	Liberty 56012

DEBUT DATE	PEAK POS	WKS CHR	GOLD	ARTIST — Record Title	POP POS	Label & Number
				CARR, Vikki — Cont'd		
3/23/68	**13**	6		7 She'll Be There/	99	
4/27/68	**32**	3		8　Your Heart Is Free Just Like The Wind	91	Liberty 56026
6/15/68	**7**	8		9 **Don't Break My Pretty Balloon**	114	Liberty 56039
9/14/68	**18**	7		10 A Dissatisfied Man		Liberty 56062
3/29/69	**6**	19		11 **With Pen In Hand**	35	Liberty 56092
9/20/69	**5**	9		12 **Eternity**	79	Liberty 56132
9/5/70	**30**	5	✓	13 Singing My Song		Liberty 56185
				#1 Country hit for Tammy Wynette in 1969		
1/23/71	**7**	9		14 **I'll Be Home**	96	Columbia 45296
6/19/71	**28**	6		15 Six Weeks Every Summer (Christmas Every Other Year)		Columbia 45403
12/25/71	**39**	3		16 I'd Do It All Again		Columbia 45510
7/1/72	**31**	7		17 Big Hurt	108	Columbia 45622
				#3 Pop hit for Miss Toni Fisher in 1959		
12/28/74	**45**	6		18 Wind Me Up		Columbia 10058
				CARRACK, Paul		
				Born on 4/22/51 in Sheffield, England. Lead singer of Ace (1973-76), Squeeze (1981, 1993) and Mike + The Mechanics (1985-1992). Keyboardist with Roxy Music (1978-80).		
10/9/82	**20**	9		1 I Need You	37	Epic 03146
1/30/88	**36**	8		2 Don't Shed A Tear	9	Chrysalis 43164
3/18/89	**14**	13		3 Romance		Columbia 68580
				PAUL CARRACK & TERRI NUNN (lead singer of Berlin)		
				love theme from the film *Sing*		
11/18/89	**22**	9		4 I Live By The Groove	31	Chrysalis 23427
				CARRADINE, Keith		
				Born on 8/8/49 in San Mateo, California. Leading actor in dozens of films including *Pretty Baby*, *Nashville*, *The Long Riders* and others. Son of actor John Carradine; half-brother of David Carradine.		
5/22/76	**1**¹	15		I'm Easy	17	ABC 12117
				from the film *Nashville* starring Carradine		
				CARROLL, David, And His Orchestra		
				Born Nook Schrier on 10/15/13 in Chicago. Arranger/conductor since 1951 for many top Mercury artists.		
3/17/62	**10**	5		The White Rose Of Athens	[I] 61	Mercury 71917
				from the film *Dreamland of Desire*		
				CARS, The		
				Rock group formed in Boston in 1976. Consisted of Ric Ocasek (lead vocals, guitar), Elliot Easton (guitar), Greg Hawkes (keyboards), Benjamin Orr (bass, vocals) and David Robinson (drums; formerly with the Modern Lovers). Ocasek, Orr and Hawkes had been in trio in the early 1970s. Group named by Robinson, got start at the Rat Club in Boston. All songs written by Ocasek. Disbanded in 1988.		
8/4/84	**1**³	19		1 **Drive**	3	Elektra 69706
3/9/85	**38**	2		2 Why Can't I Have You	33	Elektra 69657
12/21/85	**36**	6		3 Tonight She Comes	7	Elektra 69589
2/22/86	**24**	8		4 I'm Not The One	32	Elektra 69569
9/19/87	**12**	12		5 You Are The Girl	17	Elektra 69446
2/13/88	**37**	3		6 Coming Up You	74	Elektra 69432
				CARTER, Carlene		
				Daughter of June Carter Cash. Married for a time to Nick Lowe.		
11/17/79	**36**	6		Do It In A Heartbeat	108	Warner 49083
				CARTER, June — see CASH, Johnny		
				CARTER, Mel		
				Born on 4/22/39 in Cincinnati. Soul vocalist/actor. Sang on local radio from age four; with Lionel Hampton on stage show at age nine. With Paul Gayten, Jimmy Scott bands. Joined Raspberry Singers gospel group in the early '50s. With his mother's gospel group, The Carvetts, in the mid-1950s. Named Top Gospel Tenor in 1957. Recorded in late '50s for Tri-State, Arwin, then Mercury. With Gospel Pearls in the early '60s. Acted on TV's *Quincy*, *Sanford And Son*, *Marcus Welby, MD* and *Magnum P.I.*		
				1)*Band Of Gold* 2)*Hold Me, Thrill Me, Kiss Me* 3)*(All Of A Sudden) My Heart Sings*		
6/19/65	**1**¹	18		1 **Hold Me, Thrill Me, Kiss Me**	8	Imperial 66113
0/23/65	**3**	11		2 (All Of A Sudden) My Heart Sings	38	Imperial 66138
1/22/66	**21**	9		3 Love Is All We Need	50	Imperial 66148
4/9/66	**1**²	11		4 **Band Of Gold**	32	Imperial 66165
7/9/66	**11**	11		5 You You You	49	Imperial 66183
0/28/67	**23**	8		6 Be My Love	132	Liberty 56000
9/21/68	**38**	3		7 I Pretend		Bell 743
4/27/74	**39**	6		8 I Only Have Eyes For You	104	Romar 716

DEBUT DATE	PEAK POS	WKS CHR	GOLD	ARTIST — Record Title	POP POS	Label & Number
				CARTER, Mel — Cont'd		
7/10/76	47	2		9 My Coloring Book..		Private S. 45,087
				CARTER, Valerie — see WAGNER, Jack		
				CASCADES, The		
				Pop group from San Diego consisting of John Gummoe (lead vocals), Eddie Snyder, David Stevens, David Wilson and David Zabo.		
2/9/63	1²	12		**Rhythm Of The Rain**	3	Valiant 6026
				CASEY, Al — see EXOTIC GUITARS, The		
★★192★★				**CASH, Johnny**		
				Born on 2/26/32 in Kingsland, Arkansas. To Dyess, Arkansas at age three. Brother Roy led the Dixie Rhythm Ramblers band in late 1940s. In U.S. Air Force, 1950-54. Formed trio with Luther Perkins (guitar) and Marshall Grant (bass) in 1955. First recorded for Sun in 1955. On *Louisiana Hayride* and *Grand Ole Opry* in 1957. Own TV show for ABC from 1969-71. Worked with June Carter from 1961, married her in March 1968. Ranks within the top three male vocalists of the country charts. Daughter Rosanne Cash and stepdaughter Carlene Carter currently enjoying successful singing careers. Elected to the Country Music Hall of Fame in 1980. Won Grammy's Living Legends Award in 1990.		
				1)A Boy Named Sue 2)What Is Truth 3)One Piece At A Time		
11/2/63	13	6		1 The Matador	44	Columbia 42880
2/29/64	11	3		2 Understand Your Man	35	Columbia 42964
6/29/68	39	2		3 Folsom Prison Blues..[R]	32	Columbia 44513
				studio version recorded live at Folsom Prison; #4 Country hit in 1956 on Sun 232 (POS 4)		
8/9/69	1²	9	●	4 A Boy Named Sue ....[N]	2³	Columbia 44944
				recorded live at San Quentin prison		
1/24/70	9	8		5 If I Were A Carpenter......................................	36	Columbia 45064
				JOHNNY CASH & JUNE CARTER		
4/18/70	4	8		**6 What Is Truth**..	19	Columbia 45134
8/29/70	13	8		7 Sunday Morning Coming Down	46	Columbia 45211
				written by Kris Kristofferson		
12/12/70	19	7		8 Flesh And Blood	54	Columbia 45269
				from the film *I Walk The Line*		
3/27/71	28	5		9 Man In Black	58	Columbia 45339
2/12/72	37	3		10 A Thing Called Love	103	Columbia 45534
				The Evangel Temple Choir (backing vocals)		
5/1/76	6	8		**11 One Piece At A Time** ....[N]	29	Columbia 10321
				JOHNNY CASH And The Tennessee Three		
				CASH, Rosanne		
				Born on 5/24/55 in Memphis. Daughter of Johnny Cash and Vivian Liberto. Raised by her mother in California, then moved to Nashville after high school graduation. Worked in the Johnny Cash Road Show. Married Rodney Crowell in 1979 and divorced in April 1992. Also see Michel Berger.		
5/16/81	6	17		**1 Seven Year Ache**	22	Columbia 11426
1/30/82	37	8		2 Blue Moon With Heartache	104	Columbia 02659
6/22/85	16	12		3 I Don't Know Why You Don't Want Me		Columbia 04809
3/22/86	36	3		4 Hold On		Columbia 05794
6/26/93	45	3		5 The Wheel		Columbia 74973
				CASHMAN & WEST		
				Pop record producers/songwriters/singers Dennis "Terry Cashman" Minogue (b: 7/5/41) and Thomas "Tommy West" Picardo, Jr. (b: 8/17/42). Produced all of Jim Croce's recordings.		
10/14/72	28	6		1 American City Suite	27	Dunhill 4324
				Sweet City Song/All Around The Town/A Friend Is Dying		
12/30/72	16	7		2 Songman..	59	Dunhill 4333
4/13/74	43	5		3 Is It Raining In New York City		Dunhill 4380
2/5/77	30	6		4 I Know		Lifesong 45017
				TOMMY WEST		
5/9/81	28	8		5 Willie, Mickey And "The Duke" (Talkin' Baseball)............		Lifesong 45086
				TERRY CASHMAN		
				tribute to baseball's Willie Mays, Mickey Mantle and Duke Snider		
				CASSIDY, David		
				Son of actor Jack Cassidy and actress Evelyn Ward. Born on 4/12/50 in New York City. Played Keith Partridge, the lead singer of TV's *The Partridge Family*. Married for a time to actress Kay Lenz. Co-starred with his brother Shaun on Broadway's *Blood Brothers* in 1993.		
11/13/71	1¹	13	●	**1 Cherish**..	9	Bell 45150
2/26/72	13	8		2 Could It Be Forever	37	Bell 45187
5/20/72	3	10		**3 How Can I Be Sure**	25	Bell 45220

DEBUT DATE	PEAK POS	WKS CHR	GOLD	ARTIST — Record Title	POP POS	Label & Number
				CASSIDY, David — Cont'd		
10/20/90	**25**	11		4 Lyin' To Myself..	27	Enigma 75084
				CASSIDY, Shaun		
				Born on 9/27/59 in Los Angeles. Son of actor Jack Cassidy and actress Shirley Jones. Played Joe Hardy on TV's *The Hardy Boys*. Shaun and David Cassidy are half-brothers. Cast member of the TV soap *General Hospital* in 1987. Co-starred with his brother David in Broadway's *Blood Brothers* in 1993.		
7/2/77	**33**	7	●	Da Doo Ron Ron	1¹	Warner 8365
				CASTELLS, The		
				Santa Rosa, California quartet: Bob Ussery, Tom Hicks, Joe Kelly and Chuck Girard.		
6/23/62	**10**	3		**So This Is Love**	21	Era 3073
				CASTLE, David		
				Born on 11/28/52 in Overton, Texas. Staff songwriter with United Artists, 1973-77. Score work on film *Midnight Express*. Assistant music director since 1989 at Merv Griffin Enterprises.		
10/8/77	**45**	5		Ten To Eight	68	Parachute 501
				CATS, The ○		
				Soft-rock quintet from Holland.		
7/13/74	**18**	9		Be My Day		Fantasy 727
				CAVALIERE, Felix		
				Born on 11/29/43 in Pelham, New York. Lead singer of The Rascals after a stint with Joey Dee's band.		
2/16/80	**2**¹	14		1 Only A Lonely Heart Sees	36	Epic 50829
6/14/80	**41**	6		2 Good To Have Love Back	105	Epic 50880
★★89★★				**CETERA, Peter**		
				Born on 9/13/44 in Chicago. Lead singer/bass guitarist of Chicago for their first 17 albums.		
				1)Glory Of Love 2)After All 3)One Good Woman		
6/14/86	**1**⁵	19		1 Glory Of Love...	1²	Full Moon 28662
				theme from the film *The Karate Kid Part II*		
9/27/86	**1**²	22		2 **The Next Time I Fall**...................................	1¹	Full Moon 28597
				PETER CETERA w/AMY GRANT		
5/9/87	**24**	8		3 Only Love Knows Why		Full Moon 28383
3/26/88	**19**	12		4 I Wasn't The One (Who Said Goodbye)	93	Atlantic 89145
				AGNETHA FALTSKOG AND PETER CETERA		
7/23/88	**1**⁴	22		5 One Good Woman	4	Full Moon 27824
11/12/88	**22**	10		6 Best Of Times...	59	Full Moon 27712
3/11/89	**1**⁴	25	●	7 After All	6	Geffen 27529
				CHER and PETER CETERA		
				love theme from the film *Chances Are*		
6/27/92	**1**²	36		8 Restless Heart	35	Warner 18897
10/17/92	**5**	29		9 Feels Like Heaven	71	Warner 18651
				PETER CETERA with Chaka Khan		
4/24/93	**2**¹	23↑		10 Even A Fool Can See...	68	Warner 18561
				CHAD & JEREMY		
				Folk-rock duo formed in the early 1960s: Chad Stuart (b: 12/10/43, England) and Jeremy Clyde (b: 3/22/44, England). Broke up in 1967. Re-formed briefly in 1982.		
8/22/64	**2**⁶	13		1 A Summer Song *	7	World Art. 1027
11/14/64	**1**¹	13		2 Willow Weep For Me..	15	World Art. 1034
2/20/65	**6**	9		3 If I Loved You	23	World Art. 1041
				from the musical *Carousel*		
4/24/65	**9**	6		4 What Do You Want With Me *	51	World Art. 1052
				*CHAD STUART AND JEREMY CLYDE		
5/15/65	**4**	9		5 Before And After	17	Columbia 43277
10/16/65	**22**	6		6 I Have Dreamed	91	Columbia 43414
				from the musical *The King And I*		
				CHAMBERLAIN, Richard		
				Born on 3/31/35 in Los Angeles. Leading film, theater and TV actor. Played lead role in TV's *Dr. Kildare*, 1961-66.		
6/9/62	**4**	13		1 Theme From Dr. Kildare (Three Stars Will Shine Tonight)	10	MGM 13075
10/13/62	**7**	8		2 Love Me Tender	21	MGM 13097
3/2/63	**6**	8		3 All I Have To Do Is Dream/	14	
3/9/63	**18**	1		4 Hi-Lili, Hi-Lo	64	MGM 13121
				from the 1953 film *Lili* starring Leslie Caron		
10/26/63	**12**	4		5 Blue Guitar	42	MGM 13170

DEBUT DATE	PEAK POS	WKS CHR	GOLD	ARTIST — Record Title	POP POS	Label & Number
				CHAMPAIGN		
				Interracial sextet from Champaign, Illinois — Pauli Carman and Rena Jones, lead singers.		
3/14/81	**1**²	20		1 How 'Bout Us	12	Columbia 11433
6/4/83	**6**	18		2 Try Again	23	Columbia 03563
				CHAMPLIN, Bill		
				Leader of San Francisco's Sons Of Champlin for 13 years. Member of Chicago since 1982.		
7/10/82	**19**	15		1 Sara	61	Elektra 47456
4/25/87	**15**	11		2 The Last Unbroken Heart		MCA 53064
				PATTI LaBELLE AND BILL CHAMPLIN		
				from the TV series *Miami Vice*		
7/13/91	**40**	7		3 If You're Not The One For Me		GRP LP Cut
				TOM SCOTT with Brenda Russell & Bill Champlin		
				from the album *Keep This Love Alive* on GRP 9646		
				CHAMPS' BOYS ORCHESTRA, The		
				Instrumental group from France.		
6/5/76	**47**	2		Tubular Bells ....[I]	98	Janus 259
				theme from the film *The Exorcist*		
				CHANDLER, Karen		
				Sang with Benny Goodman under the name of Eve Young in 1946. Native of Rexburg, Idaho.		
11/25/67	**19**	9		I Get Along Without You Very Well....................		Dot 17049
				written by Hoagy Carmichael		
				CHAPIN, Harry		
				Folk-rock balladeer. Born on 12/7/42 in New York City. As a child, was a member of the Brooklyn Heights Boys Choir. Documentary filmmaker in the '60s. Signed to Elektra in 1971. Died in an auto accident on 7/16/81.		
11/11/72	**30**	4		1 Sunday Morning Sunshine	75	Elektra 45811
1/26/74	**37**	8		2 WOLD..	36	Elektra 45874
9/28/74	**6**	14	●	3 Cat's In The Cradle	**1**¹	Elektra 45203
2/22/75	**7**	9		4 I Wanna Learn A Love Song	44	Elektra 45236
8/16/75	**33**	9		5 Dreams Go By		Elektra 45264
11/15/80	**37**	11		6 Sequel	23	Boardwalk 5700
				sequel to Harry's 1972 Pop hit "Taxi"		
2/21/81	**47**	5		7 Remember When The Music		Boardwalk 5705
				CHAPMAN, Beth Nielsen ○		
				Singer/songwriter born in Harlington, Texas.		
3/9/91	**14**	18		1 Walk My Way		Reprise 19447
8/3/91	**12**	22		2 All I Have		Reprise 19214
12/21/91	**13**	15		3 I Keep Coming Back To You		Reprise LP Cut
6/6/92	**33**	6		4 Life Holds On..		Reprise LP Cut
				all of above from the album *Beth Nielsen Chapman* on Reprise 26172		
				CHAPMAN, Tracy		
				Boston-based singer/songwriter. Born in Cleveland. Graduated from Tufts University in 1986 with an anthropology degree. Won the 1988 Best New Artist Grammy Award.		
5/7/88	**7**	23		1 Fast Car	6	Elektra 69412
10/15/88	**45**	3		2 Talkin' Bout A Revolution	75	Elektra 69383
11/19/88	**19**	14		3 Baby Can I Hold You	48	Elektra 69356
11/4/89	**41**	4		4 Crossroads	90	Elektra 69273
				CHARLENE		
				Pop singer Charlene Duncan (nee: D'Angelo). Born on 6/1/50 in Hollywood.		
1/22/77	**23**	13		1 It Ain't Easy Comin' Down...............................	97	Prodigal 0632
				"Bubbled Under" on 7/24/82 on Motown 1621 (POS 109)		
5/7/77	**40**	6		2 Freddie..	96	Prodigal 0633
3/27/82	**7**	17		3 I've Never Been To Me ....[R]	3	Motown 1611
				originally made the *Hot 100* on 9/24/77 on Prodigal 0636 (POS 97)		
11/13/82	**31**	9		4 Used To Be	46	Motown 1650
				CHARLENE & STEVIE WONDER		

★★36★★ CHARLES, Ray

Born Ray Charles Robinson on 9/23/30 in Albany, Georgia. To Greenville, Florida while still an infant. Partially blind at age five, completely blind at seven (glaucoma). Studied classical piano and clarinet at State School for Deaf and Blind Children, St. Augustine, Florida, 1937-45. With local Florida bands; moved to Seattle in 1948. Formed the McSon Trio (also known as the Maxim Trio and the Maxine Trio) with Gossady McGhee (guitar) and Milton Garred (bass). First recordings were very much in the King Cole Trio style. Formed own band in 1954. The 1950s female vocal group, The Cookies, became his backing group The Raeletts. Inducted into the Rock and Roll Hall of Fame in 1986. Recipient of the Grammy Lifetime Achievement Award in 1987. Popular performer with many TV and film appearances.

1)I Can't Stop Loving You 2)Crying Time 3)You Don't Know Me 4)Together Again 5)Baby Grand

DEBUT DATE	PEAK POS	WKS CHR	GOLD	ARTIST — Record Title	POP POS	Label & Number
6/9/62	1^5	13	●	1 I Can't Stop Loving You/	1^5	
6/23/62	13	3		2 Born To Lose	41	ABC-Para. 10330
8/4/62	1^3	10		3 You Don't Know Me/	2^1	
8/11/62	19	1		4 Careless Love	60	ABC-Para. 10345
12/8/62	7	6		5 Your Cheating Heart	29	ABC-Para. 10375
5/11/63	3	7		6 Take These Chains From My Heart	8	ABC-Para. 10435
				Jack Halloran Singers (backing vocals)		
7/6/63	6	5		7 No One	21	ABC-Para. 10453
12/14/63	10	7		8 That Lucky Old Sun	20	ABC-Para. 10509
3/14/64	12	3		9 My Heart Cries For You	38	ABC-Para. 10530
7/25/64	8	5		10 No One To Cry To/	55	
8/1/64	6	5		11 A Tear Fell	50	ABC-Para. 10571
				Gene Lowell Singers (backing vocals, above 2)		
10/17/64	13	1		12 Smack Dab In The Middle	52	ABC-Para. 10588
12/12/64	11	7		13 Makin' Whoopee	46	ABC-Para. 10609
2/6/65	11	4		14 Cry	58	ABC-Para. 10615
7/17/65	22	5		15 I'm A Fool To Care	84	ABC-Para. 10700
10/9/65	19	7		16 The Cincinnati Kid	115	ABC-Para. 10720
				movie title song		
11/27/65	1^3	19		17 Crying Time	6	ABC-Para. 10739
3/26/66	1^3	11		18 Together Again	19	ABC-Para. 10785
				above 2 written by Buck Owens		
11/26/66	30	5		19 Please Say You're Fooling	64	ABC 10865
7/8/67	38	4		20 Here We Go Again	15	ABC 10938
7/27/68	33	2		21 Eleanor Rigby	35	ABC/TRC 11090
1/18/69	25	5		22 When I Stop Dreaming	112	ABC/TRC 11170
11/7/70	26	7		23 If You Were Mine	41	ABC/TRC 11271
4/10/71	22	6		24 Don't Change On Me	36	ABC/TRC 11291
1/15/72	20	5		25 What Am I Living For	54	ABC/TRC 11317
10/27/73	20	12		26 Come Live With Me	82	Crossover 973
3/21/87	3	15		27 Baby Grand	75	Columbia 06994
				BILLY JOEL Featuring Ray Charles		
1/6/90	30	9		28 I'll Be Good To You	18	Qwest 22697
				QUINCY JONES Featuring Ray Charles and Chaka Khan		
4/3/93	9	17		29 A Song For You	104	Warner 18611
				recorded by the Carpenters for their 1972 album *A Song For You*		

★★178★★ CHARLES, Ray, Singers

Born Charles Raymond Offenberg on 9/13/18 in Chicago. Arranger/conductor for many TV shows including the *Perry Como Show, Glen Campbell Goodtime Hour* and *Sha-Na-Na*. Winner of two Emmys.

1)Love Me With All Your Heart (Cuando Calienta El Sol) 2)Al-Di-La 3)Little By Little And Bit By Bit

DEBUT DATE	PEAK POS	WKS CHR	GOLD	ARTIST — Record Title	POP POS	Label & Number
4/25/64	1^4	13		1 Love Me With All Your Heart (Cuando Calienta El Sol)	3	Command 4046
7/18/64	4	5		2 Al-Di-La/	29	
9/26/64	18	1		3 Till The End Of Time	83	Command 4049
11/14/64	7	10		4 One More Time	32	Command 4057
3/13/65	15	1		5 This Is My Prayer	72	Command 4059
9/18/65	17	7		6 My Love, Forgive Me (Amore, Scusami)	124	Command 4073
1/29/66	13	10		7 One Of Those Songs	134	Command 4079
				one of Jimmy Durante's most performed songs		
9/3/66	39	3		8 Promises		Command 4085
3/4/67	31	4		9 Step By Step		Command 4092
4/15/67	6	16		10 Little By Little And Bit By Bit	135	Command 4096
3/23/68	39	2		11 I Can See It Now		Command 4115
5/30/70	26	5		12 Move Me, O Wondrous Music	99	Command 4135

DEBUT DATE	PEAK POS	WKS CHR	GOLD	ARTIST — Record Title	POP POS	Label & Number
				CHARLES & EDDIE		
				Soul vocal duo of Charles Pettigrew (from Philadelphia) and Eddie Chacon (from Oakland, California).		
8/22/92	**15**	30		Would I Lie To You?	13	Capitol 44809
				CHEAP TRICK		
				Rock quartet from Rockford, Illinois founded by Rick Nielsen (guitar) and Tom Petersson (bass), with Bun E. Carlos (real name: Brad Carlson; drums) and Robin Zander (vocals).		
6/25/88	**29**	16		1 The Flame	1²	Epic 07745
10/1/88	**32**	7		2 Don't Be Cruel	4	Epic 07965
★★49★★				**CHER**		
				Born Cherilyn LaPierre on 5/20/46 in El Centro, California. Worked as backup singer for Phil Spector. Recorded as "Bonnie Jo Mason" and "Cherilyn" in 1964. Recorded with Sonny Bono as "Caesar & Cleo" in 1963, then as Sonny & Cher from 1965-73. Married to Bono from 1963-74. Own TV series with Bono from 1971-77. Married to Gregg Allman from 1975-77. Member of the group Black Rose in 1980. Acclaimed film actress (won Best Actress Oscar in 1987 for *Moonstruck*).		
				1)After All 2)If I Could Turn Back Time 3)The Way Of Love 4)Living In A House Divided 5)Dark Lady		
9/25/71	**6**	12	●	1 Gypsys, Tramps & Thieves	1²	Kapp 2146
1/29/72	**2²**	13		2 The Way Of Love	7	Kapp 2158
5/20/72	**2¹**	10		3 Living In A House Divided	22	Kapp 2171
9/16/72	**19**	5		4 Don't Hide Your Love	46	Kapp 2184
				written by Neil Sedaka		
8/11/73	**3**	16	●	5 Half-Breed	1²	MCA 40102
1/26/74	**3**	14	●	6 Dark Lady	1¹	MCA 40161
6/1/74	**9**	11		7 Train Of Thought	27	MCA 40245
8/10/74	**3**	10		8 I Saw A Man And He Danced With His Wife	42	MCA 40273
11/16/74	**41**	5	✓	9 Carousel Man		MCA 40324
2/24/79	**19**	16	●	10 Take Me Home	8	Casablanca 965
2/27/88	**33**	9		11 I Found Someone..	10	Geffen 28191
				written and produced by Michael Bolton		
5/14/88	**11**	13		12 We All Sleep Alone	14	Geffen 27986
				co-written and co-produced by Jon Bon Jovi		
3/11/89	**1⁴**	25	●	13 After All	6	Geffen 27529
				CHER and PETER CETERA love theme from the film *Chances Are*		
7/29/89	**1¹**	20	●	14 If I Could Turn Back Time	3	Geffen 22886
11/25/89	**9**	15		15 Just Like Jesse James	8	Geffen 22844
3/31/90	**30**	8		16 Heart Of Stone	20	Geffen 19953
11/17/90	**7**	21		17 The Shoop Shoop Song (It's In His Kiss).....................	33	Geffen 19659
				from the film *Mermaids*		
6/22/91	**3**	22		18 Love And Understanding	17	Geffen 19023
10/26/91	**16**	19		19 Save Up All Your Tears	37	Geffen 19105
5/16/92	**15**	13		20 When Lovers Become Strangers		Geffen LP Cut
				from the album *Love Hurts* on Geffen 24369		
				CHERRY, Don		
				Born on 1/11/24 in Wichita Falls, Texas. Studied voice after the service in mid-1940s. Vocalist with Jan Garber band in the late '40s. Accomplished professional golfer.		
10/8/66	**30**	10		Married		Monument 971
				from the Broadway musical *Cabaret*		
				CHEVALIER, Maurice ✪		
				Born on 9/12/1888 in Paris; died on 1/1/72. Popular singer/actor.		
11/30/68	**30**	3		Dear World		Warner 7241
				MAURICE CHEVALIER & JIMMY DURANTE from the Broadway musical *Dear World*		
				CHIC		
				R&B-disco group formed in New York City by prolific producers Bernard Edwards (bass) and Nile Rodgers (guitar). Vocalists: Norma Jean Wright (replaced by Alfa Anderson) and Luci Martin; drums: Tony Thompson. Wright began solo career in 1978 as Norma Jean. Edwards recorded with the studio group Roundtree in 1978. Rodgers joined The Honeydrippers in 1984. Thompson joined the Power Station in 1985 and Edwards became their producer.		
1/20/79	**48**	2	▲	1 Le Freak	1⁶	Atlantic 3519
3/10/79	**9**	13	●	2 I Want Your Love	7	Atlantic 3557
7/21/79	**28**	10	●	3 Good Times	1¹	Atlantic 3584

DEBUT DATE	PEAK POS	WKS CHR	GOLD	ARTIST — Record Title	POP POS	Label & Number
	★★16★★			**CHICAGO** Jazz-oriented rock group formed in Chicago in 1967. Consisted of Robert Lamm (keyboards), James Pankow (trombone), Lee Loughnane (trumpet), Terry Kath (guitar; d: 1/23/78 [age 31] of accidental self-inflicted gunshot), Walt Parazaider (reeds), Peter Cetera (bass) and Danny Seraphine (drums). Originally called The Big Thing, later Chicago Transit Authority. To Los Angeles in the late '60s. Kath replaced by Donnie Dacus (left in 1979). Bill Champlin (keyboards) joined in 1982. Cetera left in 1985, replaced by Jason Scheff. Seraphine left in 1989, guitarist DaWayne Bailey added.		
				1)*Hard To Say I'm Sorry* 2)*You're The Inspiration* 3)*Look Away* 4)*If You Leave Me Now* 5)*Wishing You Were Here*		
11/21/70	5	11		1 **Does Anybody Really Know What Time It Is?**	7	Columbia 45264
7/10/71	1[1]	12		2 **Beginnings**	7	Columbia 45417
				originally released on Columbia 45011 in 1969		
11/13/71	34	4		3 Questions 67 And 68 ....[R]	24	Columbia 45467
				originally made the *Hot 100* on 8/9/69 on Columbia 44909 (POS 71)		
8/19/72	8	10	●	4 **Saturday In The Park**	3	Columbia 45657
10/6/73	7	19	●	5 **Just You 'N' Me**	4	Columbia 45933
4/20/74	8	10		6 **(I've Been) Searchin' So Long**	9	Columbia 46020
7/6/74	1[1]	13		7 **Call On Me**	6	Columbia 46062
10/26/74	1[1]	14		8 **Wishing You Were Here**	11	Columbia 10049
				The Beach Boys (backing vocals)		
3/8/75	23	7		9 Harry Truman	13	Columbia 10092
5/3/75	3	13		10 **Old Days**	5	Columbia 10131
9/13/75	27	6		11 Brand New Love Affair (Part I & II)	61	Columbia 10200
7/4/76	2[1]	10		12 **Another Rainy Day In New York City**	32	Columbia 10360
8/14/76	1[1]	18	●	13 **If You Leave Me Now**	1[2]	Columbia 10390
4/23/77	17	8		14 You Are On My Mind...	49	Columbia 10523
10/1/77	8	17		15 **Baby, What A Big Surprise**	4	Columbia 10620
3/11/78	40	6		16 Little One	44	Columbia 10683
5/27/78	39	3		17 Take Me Back To Chicago	63	Columbia 10737
11/18/78	39	4		18 Alive Again	14	Columbia 10845
1/13/79	5	15		19 **No Tell Lover**	14	Columbia 10879
9/13/80	46	5		20 Thunder And Lightning	56	Columbia 11345
6/12/82	1[3]	24	●	21 **Hard To Say I'm Sorry**	1[2]	Full Moon 29979
				from the film *Summer Lovers*		
10/2/82	8	19		22 **Love Me Tomorrow**..	22	Full Moon 29911
8/11/84	3	21		23 **Hard Habit To Break**	3	Full Moon 29214
11/24/84	1[2]	23		24 **You're The Inspiration**	3	Full Moon 29126
4/13/85	25	7		25 **Along Comes A Woman**	14	Full Moon 29082
11/29/86	2[3]	24		26 **Will You Still Love Me?**	3	Full Moon 28512
4/11/87	9	15		27 If She Would Have Been Faithful...	17	Warner 28424
6/11/88	5	22		28 **I Don't Wanna Live Without Your Love**	3	Reprise 27855
10/1/88	1[1]	24	●	29 **Look Away**	1[2]	Reprise 27766
2/4/89	9	19		30 **You're Not Alone**	10	Reprise 27757
5/27/89	12	16		31 We Can Last Forever	55	Reprise 22985
12/9/89	2[4]	21		32 **What Kind Of Man Would I Be?**...............................	5	Reprise 22741
1/26/91	13	14		33 Chasin' The Wind	39	Reprise 19466
7/13/91	11	18		34 You Come To My Senses		Reprise 19205
				CHILD, Desmond Prolific producer/songwriter. Born John Charles Barrett Jr. in Miami on 10/28/53 to a Cuban mother and a Hungarian father. Formed vocal group Rouge with Diane Grasselli, Myriam Valle and Maria Vidal in 1974. Wrote "We All Sleep Alone," "Livin' On A Prayer" and "Dude (Looks Like A Lady)."		
11/2/91	29	7		1 You're The Story Of My Life	74	Elektra 64850
2/22/92	19	13		2 Obsession		Elektra 64799
				Maria Vidal (guest vocals)		
				CHI-LITES, The R&B vocal group from Chicago. Consisted of Eugene Record (lead vocals), Robert "Squirrel" Lester (tenor), Marshall Thompson (baritone) and Creadel "Red" Jones (bass).		
6/3/72	34	4		Oh Girl	1[1]	Brunswick 55471
				CHINA CRISIS ✪ Liverpool, England rock quintet led by Garry Daly and Eddie Lundon.		
2/21/87	37	2		Arizona Sky..		A&M 2902

DEBUT DATE	PEAK POS	WKS CHR	G O L D	ARTIST — Record Title	POP POS	Label & Number
				CHIPMUNKS, The		
				Characters created by Ross Bagdasarian ("David Seville") who named Alvin, Simon and Theodore after Liberty executives Alvin Bennett, Simon Waronker and Theodore Keep. The Chipmunks starred in own prime-time animated TV show in the early 1960s and a Saturday morning cartoon series in the mid-1980s. Bagdasarian died on 1/16/72 (age 52). His son, Ross Jr., resurrected the act in 1980.		
				DAVID SEVILLE AND THE CHIPMUNKS:		
12/18/61	**12**	3	●	1 The Chipmunk Song (Christmas Don't Be Late) .... [X-R]	39	Liberty 55250
				originally made the *Hot 100* on 12/1/58 (POS 1) on Liberty 55168		
12/18/61	**15**	3		2 Rudolph The Red Nosed Reindeer .... [X-R]	47	Liberty 55289
				originally made the *Hot 100* on 12/19/60 (POS 21)		
12/15/62	**11**	3		3 The Chipmunk Song (Christmas Don't Be Late) .... [X-R]	40	Liberty 55250
				CHORDETTES, The		
				Female vocal group from Sheboygan, Wisconsin formed in 1946. Consisted of Janet Ertel (nee: Buschman; bass), her sister-in-law Carol Buschman (baritone), Lynn Evans (lead singer; replaced Dorothy Schwartz [nee: Hummitzsch], 1953) and Margie Needham (tenor; replaced Jinny Lockard, 1953). With Arthur Godfrey from 1949-53. Ertel married Cadence owner Archie Bleyer in 1954; her daughter Jackie was married to Phil Everly. Janet died of cancer on 11/22/88.		
7/17/61	**4**	8		**Never On Sunday**	13	Cadence 1402
				CHRISTIAN, Chris		
				Guitarist/songwriter/producer. With trio Cotton, Lloyd & Christian.		
10/10/81	**8**	16		1 I Want You, I Need You	37	Boardwalk 126
7/24/82	**21**	13		2 Ain't Nothing Like The Real Thing/You're All		
				I Need To Get By	88	Boardwalk 149
				vocal duet with Amy Holland		
				CHRISTIE		
				English rock trio: Jeff Christie, Vic Elms and Mike Blakely (brother of Alan Blakely of The Tremeloes).		
8/8/70	**22**	6		**Yellow River**	23	Epic 10626
				CHRISTIE, Lou		
				Born Lugee Sacco on 2/19/43 in Glen Willard, Pennsylvania. Joined vocal group the Classics; first recorded for Starr in 1960. Started long association with songwriter Twyla Herbert. Recorded as Lugee & The Lions for Robbee in 1961.		
11/14/70	**39**	3		1 Indian Lady	106	Buddah 192
1/5/74	**12**	16		2 Beyond The Blue Horizon	80	Three Bros. 402
				sung by Jeanette MacDonald in the 1930 film *Monte Carlo*		
				CHRISTY, Lauren ✪		
5/15/93	**17**	9		You Read Me Wrong		Mercury LP Cut
				from the album *Lauren Christy* on Mercury 512719		
				CISYK, Kacey		
				Studio singer based in New York.		
2/25/78	**33**	11		The One And Only		ABC 12333
				movie title song		
				CLAPTON, Eric		
				Prolific rock-blues guitarist/vocalist. Born Eric Patrick Clapp on 3/30/45 in Ripley, England. Eric's four-year-old son, Conor, died on 3/20/91 in a 53-floor fall in New York City. Nicknamed Slowhand in 1964 while with The Yardbirds.		
				1)Tears In Heaven 2)I've Got A Rock N' Roll Heart 3)Promises		
2/18/78	**25**	12	●	1 Lay Down Sally	3	RSO 886
5/27/78	**39**	9		2 Wonderful Tonight	16	RSO 895
10/21/78	**6**	22		3 **Promises**	9	RSO 910
				ERIC CLAPTON AND HIS BAND		
2/12/83	**6**	17		4 I've Got A Rock N' Roll Heart	18	Duck 29780
1/18/92	**1**³	30	▲	5 Tears In Heaven	2⁴	Reprise 19038
				from the film *Rush*; Eric wrote this for his late son, Conor		
7/4/92	**47**	3		6 It's Probably Me		A&M 2407
				STING with Eric Clapton		
				from the film *Lethal Weapon 3*; available only as a CD single		
9/12/92	**8**	21		7 Layla ....[R]	12	Duck 18787
				live accoustic version of Clapton's 1972 Derek And The Dominos #10 Pop hit		
4/10/93	**28**	11		8 Running On Faith		Duck LP Cut
				from the album *Unplugged* on Duck 45024		

DEBUT DATE	PEAK POS	WKS CHR	GOLD	ARTIST — Record Title	POP POS	Label & Number
	★★**47**★★			**CLARK, Petula**		

Born on 11/15/32 in Epsom, England. Pop singer/actress. On radio at age nine; own show *Pet's Parlour* at age 11. TV series in England in 1950. First U.S. record release for Coral in 1951. Appeared in over 20 British films from 1944-57; revived her film career in the late 1960s, starring in *Finian's Rainbow* and *Goodbye Mr. Chips.*

1)Don't Sleep In The Subway 2)I Couldn't Live Without Your Love 3)This Is My Song
4)Kiss Me Goodbye 5)A Sign Of The Times

DEBUT DATE	PEAK POS	WKS CHR	GOLD	ARTIST — Record Title	POP POS	Label & Number
6/5/65	**16**	1		1 I Know A Place	3	Warner 5612
7/10/65	**4**	11		2 **You'd Better Come Home**	22	Warner 5643
12/25/65	**4**	14		3 **My Love**	1²	Warner 5684
3/26/66	**2**¹	9		4 **A Sign Of The Times**	11	Warner 5802
7/16/66	**1**¹	12		5 **I Couldn't Live Without Your Love**	9	Warner 5835
11/12/66	**31**	4		6 Who Am I	21	Warner 5863
12/24/66	**10**	7		7 **Color My World**	16	Warner 5882
3/18/67	**2**⁴	13		8 **This Is My Song**	3	Warner 7002
				from the Charlie Chaplin film *A Countess From Hong Kong*		
6/17/67	**1**³	12		9 **Don't Sleep In The Subway**	5	Warner 7049
9/9/67	**9**	9		10 **The Cat In The Window (The Bird In The Sky)**	26	Warner 7073
12/9/67	**3**	11		11 **The Other Man's Grass Is Always Greener**	31	Warner 7097
2/24/68	**2**²	11		12 **Kiss Me Goodbye**	15	Warner 7170
7/20/68	**5**	14		13 **Don't Give Up**	37	Warner 7216
11/16/68	**18**	9		14 American Boys	59	Warner 7244
4/5/69	**12**	7		15 Happy Heart	62	Warner 7275
8/2/69	**14**	8		16 Look At Mine	89	Warner 7310
11/8/69	**18**	6		17 No One Better Than You	93	Warner 7343
9/26/70	**19**	7		18 The Song Is Love		Warner 7422
				written by Peter, Paul & Mary		
6/3/72	**12**	13		19 My Guy	70	MGM 14392
9/30/72	**9**	12		20 **Wedding Song (There Is Love)**	61	MGM 14431
5/25/74	**40**	6		21 The Old Fashioned Way (Les Plaisirs Demodes)		MGM 14708
11/30/74	**12**	11		22 Loving Arms		Dunhill 15019
1/30/82	**24**	12		23 Natural Love	66	Scotti Br. 02676

CLARK, Roy

Born on 4/15/33 in Meherrin, Virginia. Superb guitar, banjo and fiddle player. Acted in TV series *The Beverly Hillbillies*, appearing as both Cousin Roy and Roy's mother, Big Mama Halsey. With the TV series *Hee Haw* since the first show in 1969.

DEBUT DATE	PEAK POS	WKS CHR	GOLD	ARTIST — Record Title	POP POS	Label & Number
8/3/63	**19**	2		1 Tips Of My Fingers	45	Capitol 4956
6/7/69	**6**	13		2 **Yesterday, When I Was Young**	19	Dot 17246
				written by actor Charles Aznavour		
9/20/69	**12**	7		3 September Song	103	Dot 17299
1/24/70	**29**	4		4 Then She's A Lover	94	Dot 17335
6/2/73	**23**	6		5 Come Live With Me	89	Dot 17449
9/6/75	**47**	4		6 Heart To Heart		ABC/Dot 17565
6/19/76	**20**	9		7 Think Summer		ABC/Dot 17626

CLARKE, Stanley

Born on 6/30/51 in Philadelphia. R&B-jazz Bassist/violinist/cellist. With Chick Corea in Return To Forever in 1973. Much session work, solo debut in 1974. Member of Fuse One in 1982 and Animal Logic in 1989.

DEBUT DATE	PEAK POS	WKS CHR	GOLD	ARTIST — Record Title	POP POS	Label & Number
5/30/81	**16**	15		1 Sweet Baby	19	Epic 01052
				STANLEY CLARKE/GEORGE DUKE		
8/18/84	**36**	3		2 Heaven Sent You		Epic 04485
				Howard Hewett (vocal)		

CLASSICS, The

White vocal quartet from Brooklyn, formed in 1958. Consisted of Emil Stucchio (lead), Johnny Gambale, Tony Victor and Jamie Troy. First known as the Perennials. First recorded for Dart in 1959. Recorded as backup for Herb Lance on Promo in 1961.

DEBUT DATE	PEAK POS	WKS CHR	GOLD	ARTIST — Record Title	POP POS	Label & Number
7/13/63	**7**	6		Till Then	20	Musicnote 1116

CLASSICS IV

Quintet formed in Jacksonville, Florida. Consisted of Dennis Yost (vocals), J.R. Cobb (lead guitar), Wally Eaton (rhythm guitar), Joe Wilson (bass; replaced by Dean Daughtry) and Kim Venable (drums). Cobb, Daughtry and producer Buddy Buie joined the Atlanta Rhythm Section in 1974.

1)Traces 2)What Am I Crying For? 3)The Funniest Thing

CLASSICS IV Featuring Dennis Yost:

DEBUT DATE	PEAK POS	WKS CHR	GOLD	ARTIST — Record Title	POP POS	Label & Number
12/21/68	**26**	5	●	1 Stormy	5	Imperial 66328
2/22/69	**2**¹	10		2 **Traces**	2¹	Imperial 66352

DEBUT DATE	PEAK POS	WKS CHR	GOLD	ARTIST — Record Title	POP POS	Label & Number
				CLASSICS IV — Cont'd		
5/31/69	12	7		3 Everyday With You Girl..	19	Imperial 66378
				DENNIS YOST AND THE CLASSICS IV:		
8/16/69	25	6		4 Change Of Heart	49	Imperial 66393
12/6/69	23	5		5 Midnight	58	Imperial 66424
3/28/70	11	6		6 The Funniest Thing	59	Imperial 66439
10/31/70	14	8		7 Where Did All The Good Times Go.........................	69	Liberty 56200
5/8/71	31	4		8 It's Time For Love..		United Art. 50777
11/4/72	7	10		9 **What Am I Crying For?**	39	MGM South 7002
3/10/73	35	4		10 Rosanna	95	MGM South 7012
				DENNIS YOST:		
6/27/81	46	4		11 Going Through The Motions		Robox 7945

CLAYTON, Merry
Real name: Mary Clayton. Backup vocalist from Los Angeles. In The Raeletts, Ray Charles' backing group. Formed R&B vocal group, Sisters Love, in 1971. Acted in the 1987 film *Maid To Order*.

DEBUT DATE	PEAK POS	WKS CHR	GOLD	ARTIST — Record Title	POP POS	Label & Number
4/23/88	49	2		Yes	45	RCA 6989

from the film *Dirty Dancing*; B-side is "In The Still Of The Night" by The Five Satins

CLAYTON-THOMAS, David ○
Born David Thomsett on 9/13/41 in England. Lead singer of Blood, Sweat & Tears.

6/3/72	36	3		Magnificent Sanctuary Band................................		Columbia 45603

written by Dorsey Burnette; #39 Country hit for Roy Clark in 1971

CLEAN LIVING
Polka-country band.

11/25/72	31	5		In Heaven There Is No Beer ....[N]	49	Vanguard 35162

CLEMONS, Clarence — see BROWNE, Jackson

CLIFFORD, Mike
Born on 11/6/43 in Los Angeles. In the 1970s Broadway production of *Grease*.

9/29/62	4	11		**Close To Cathy**	12	United Art. 489

CLIMAX
Los Angeles-based pop quintet — Sonny Geraci, lead singer (formerly with The Outsiders).

1/22/72	6	11	●	1 **Precious And Few**	3	Rocky Road 30055
				originally released on Carousel 30055		
5/13/72	15	8		2 Life And Breath	52	Rocky Road 30061
				CLIMAX featuring Sonny Geraci		
10/27/73	38	8		3 Walking In The Georgia Rain		Rocky Road 30074
				SONNY GERACI AND CLIMAX		

CLIMAX BLUES BAND
Blues-rock band formed in Stafford, England. Nucleus consisted of Colin Cooper (sax, vocals), Peter Haycock (guitar, vocals), Derek Holt (bass) and John Cuffley (drums).

4/30/77	43	6		1 Couldn't Get It Right	3	Sire 736
4/4/81	20	11		2 I Love You	12	Warner 49669

CLIMIE FISHER
U.K.-based pop/rock duo: Simon Climie (vocals) and Rob Fisher (keyboards). Fisher was a member of Naked Eyes. Chrysalis songwriter Climie wrote Pat Benatar's "Invincible" and "I Knew You Were Waiting (For Me)" by Aretha Franklin and George Michael.

6/4/88	12	19		Love Changes (Everything)	23	Capitol 44137

CLINE, Patsy
Born Virginia Patterson Hensley on 9/8/32 in Winchester, Virginia. Killed in a plane crash with Cowboy Copas and Hawkshaw Hawkins on 3/5/63 near Camden, Tennessee. Elected to the Country Music Hall of Fame in 1973. Jessica Lange played Patsy in the 1985 biographical film *Sweet Dreams*.

8/21/61	6	7		1 I Fall To Pieces...	12	Decca 31205
				2 other Cline versions made the Country charts in 1980 and 1982		
10/23/61	2²	10		2 Crazy	9	Decca 31317
				written by Willie Nelson		
2/3/62	3	12		3 **She's Got You**..	14	Decca 31354
5/11/63	15	7		4 Sweet Dreams (Of You)	44	Decca 31483

CLOONEY, Rosemary
Born on 5/23/28 in Maysville, Kentucky. One of the most popular singers of the 1950s. Married for a time to actor Jose Ferrer; their son Gabriel married Debby Boone.

5/25/68	34	5		One Less Bell To Answer		Dot 17100
				#2 Pop hit for The 5th Dimension in 1970		

DEBUT DATE	PEAK POS	WKS CHR	GOLD	ARTIST — Record Title	POP POS	Label & Number
				CLOUT Four-woman, two-man band from Johannesburg, South Africa.		
9/23/78	35	8		Substitute	67	Epic 50591
				CLUB NOUVEAU Sacramento-based, dance-disco group formed and fronted by Jay King (producer/owner of King Jay Records; produced the Timex Social Club).		
4/4/87	31	6	●	Lean On Me .... King Jay/Warner 7" sold 600,000 units; Tommy Boy 12" sold 400,000	1²	King Jay/Warner 28430
				COATES, Odia Songstress from Berkeley, California. Sang with Paul Anka on four of his hits, 1974-75. Died of breast cancer on 5/19/91 (age 49).		
11/13/76	20	9		Make It Up To Me In Love .... ODIA COATES and PAUL ANKA		Epic 50298
				COCHRANE, Tom Toronto-based rock singer/songwriter. Born on 5/13/53 in Lynn Lake, Manitoba, Canada. Formed Red Rider in 1980. Nucleus of group included guitarist Ken Greer and keyboardist John Webster.		
8/8/92	45	7	●	Life Is A Highway	6	Capitol 44815
				COCKBURN, Bruce Cockburn (pronounced: Co-burn) was born on 5/27/45 in Canada. Pop-rock singer/songwriter.		
4/19/80	22	13		Wondering Where The Lions Are	21	Millennium 11786
				COCKER, Joe Born John Robert Cocker on 5/20/44 in Sheffield, England. Own skiffle band, the Cavaliers, late 1950s, later reorganized as Vance Arnold & The Avengers. Assembled the Grease Band in the mid-1960s. Performed at Woodstock in 1969. Successful tour with 43-piece revue, Mad Dogs & Englishmen, in 1970. Notable spastic stage antics were based on Ray Charles' movements at the piano.		
3/1/75	12	10		1 You Are So Beautiful	5	A&M 1641
8/21/82	3	25	▲	2 Up Where We Belong .... JOE COCKER and JENNIFER WARNES love theme from the film An Officer And A Gentleman	1³	Island 99996
11/3/84	31	5		3 Edge Of A Dream .... theme from the film Teachers	69	Capitol 5412
6/6/87	14	10		4 Love Lives On .... theme from the film Harry And The Hendersons		MCA 53077
7/2/88	32	7		5 A Woman Loves A Man .... from the film Bull Durham		Capitol 44182
12/16/89	12	16		6 When The Night Comes	11	Capitol 44437
				COFFEY, Dennis, And The Detroit Guitar Band Detroit native Coffey was a session guitarist for The Temptations, The Jackson 5 and others. Coffey later formed C.J. & Co.		
12/4/71	24	9	●	Scorpio .... [I]	6	Sussex 226
				COHN, Marc Cleveland-born singer/songwriter. Formed a 14-piece band in New York, the Supreme Court, which was discovered by Carly Simon and played at Caroline Kennedy's wedding. Won the 1991 Best New Artist Grammy Award.		
4/27/91	12	24		1 Walking In Memphis	13	Atlantic 87747
11/2/91	24	14		2 True Companion	80	Atlantic 87583
5/22/93	27	14		3 Walk Through The World	121	Atlantic 87350
				COLE, Bobby Singer/songwriter/organist.		
7/20/68	38	5		Mister Bo Jangles	79	Date 1613
				COLE, Jerry, & Trinity ✪ Guitarist Cole was a member of The Champs in the mid-1960s.		
5/17/75	20	11		Susanna's Song (In The California Morning)......................		Warner 8101
				COLE, Jude Native of East Moline, Illinois. Male guitarist/vocalist of Moon Martin's band. Touring guitarist with Billy Thorpe, Del Shannon and Dwight Twilley.		
4/28/90	19	23		1 Baby, It's Tonight	16	Reprise 19869
8/4/90	16	17		2 Time For Letting Go...	32	Reprise 19743
1/19/91	42	6		3 House Full Of Reasons	69	Reprise 19530
4/13/91	23	11		4 Compared To Nothing		Reprise 19340
12/26/92	19	16		5 Tell The Truth	57	Reprise 18673
7/17/93	37	4		6 Worlds Apart .... Tommy Shaw (Styx) and Jack Blades (Night Ranger), backing vocals	123	Reprise 18509

DEBUT DATE	PEAK POS	WKS CHR	GOLD	ARTIST — Record Title	POP POS	Label & Number
				★★85★★ COLE, Natalie		
				Born on 2/6/50 in Los Angeles. Daughter of Nat "King" Cole. Professional debut at age 11. Married for a time to her producer, Marvin Yancey, Jr. Later married Andre Fischer, former drummer of Rufus and producer for Brenda Russell, Michael Franks and Andrea Crouch, until 1992. Natalie won the 1975 Best New Artist Grammy Award. Hosted own syndicated variety TV show *Big Break* in 1990.		
				1)Miss You Like Crazy 2)I Live For Your Love 3)Someone That I Used To Love		
11/22/75	45	3		1 This Will Be	6	Capitol 4109
1/3/76	20	11		2 Inseparable	32	Capitol 4193
10/2/76	25	8		3 Mr. Melody	49	Capitol 4328
4/16/77	45	4	●	4 I've Got Love On My Mind	5	Capitol 4360
4/8/78	33	5	●	5 Our Love	10	Capitol 4509
7/12/80	3	22		6 Someone That I Used To Love	21	Capitol 4869
8/3/85	11	13		7 A Little Bit Of Heaven	81	Modern 99630
11/7/87	2¹	24		8 I Live For Your Love	13	Manhattan 50094
2/20/88	38	6		9 Over You		Geffen 28152
				RAY PARKER JR. with NATALIE COLE		
4/9/88	16	13		10 Pink Cadillac	5	EMI-Man. 50117
				written and recorded by Bruce Springsteen in 1984 (B-side of his Pop hit "Dancing In The Dark")		
8/6/88	14	15		11 When I Fall In Love..	95	EMI-Man. 50138
				recorded by Nat King Cole on his 1957 #1 Pop album *Love Is The Thing*		
4/8/89	1¹	24		12 Miss You Like Crazy	7	EMI 50185
8/19/89	15	11		13 I Do		EMI 50213
				NATALIE COLE with Freddie Jackson		
1/13/90	5	20		14 Starting Over Again		EMI 50235
6/15/91	3	20	●	15 Unforgettable	14	Elektra 64875
				NATALIE COLE with Nat "King" Cole		
				Nat's vocals are dubbed in from his original 1952 hit (POS 12)		
12/14/91	22	6		16 The Christmas Song (Chestnuts Roasting On An Open Fire) ....[X]		Elektra 64816
				#3 hit for Nat "King" Cole in 1946		
3/21/92	34	7		17 The Very Thought Of You		Elektra 64783
6/19/93	35	4		18 Take A Look		Elektra 64636
				★★95★★ COLE, Nat "King"		
				Born Nathaniel Adams Coles on 3/17/17 in Montgomery, Alabama and raised in Chicago. Died of lung cancer on 2/15/65 in Santa Monica, California. Own band, the Royal Dukes, at age 17. First recorded in 1936 in band led by brother Eddie. Toured with "Shuffle Along" musical revue, resided in Los Angeles. Formed King Cole Trio in 1939: Nat (piano), Oscar Moore (guitar; later joined brother's group, Johnny Moore's Three Blazers) and Wesley Prince (bass; replaced several years later by Johnny Miller). Long series of top-selling records led to his solo career in 1950. In films *St. Louis Blues*, *Cat Ballou*, and many other film and TV appearances. Stopped performing in 1964 due to ill health. His daughter Natalie is a recording star. Won Lifetime Achievement Grammy in 1990.		
				1)Ramblin' Rose 2)Dear Lonely Hearts 3)Those Lazy-Hazy-Crazy Days Of Summer		
7/17/61	14	4		1 Take A Fool's Advice	71	Capitol 4582
9/18/61	18	2		2 Let True Love Begin	73	Capitol 4623
8/18/62	1⁵	14	●	3 Ramblin' Rose	2²	Capitol 4804
11/17/62	2²	10		4 Dear Lonely Hearts	13	Capitol 4870
12/29/62	19	1		5 The Christmas Song (Merry Christmas To You) ....[X-R]	65	Capitol 3561
				Nat's original version hit the Pop chart on 11/30/46 (POS 3); holiday classic selected for NARAS Hall of Fame		
3/16/63	17	4		6 All Over The World	42	Capitol 4919
5/11/63	3	11		7 Those Lazy-Hazy-Crazy Days Of Summer......	6	Capitol 4965
9/21/63	3	10		8 That Sunday, That Summer............................	12	Capitol 5027
3/14/64	16	2		9 My True Carrie, Love......................................	49	Capitol 5125
5/2/64	6	8		10 I Don't Want To Be Hurt Anymore...............	22	Capitol 5155
				Merry Young Souls (backing vocals, above 2)		
9/19/64	6	9		11 I Don't Want To See Tomorrow/	34	
10/10/64	17	2		12 L-O-V-E	81	Capitol 5261
9/11/65	27	5		13 Wanderlust		Capitol 5486
12/11/65	27	7		14 Looking Back ....[R]	123	Capitol 5549
				originally made the *Top 100* on 4/14/58 on Capitol 3939 (POS 5)		
7/23/66	20	7		15 Let Me Tell You, Babe	90	Capitol 5683
6/15/91	3	20	●	16 Unforgettable	14	Elektra 64875
				NATALIE COLE with Nat "King" Cole		
				Nat's vocals are dubbed in from his original 1952 hit (POS 12)		

DEBUT DATE	PEAK POS	WKS CHR	G O L D	ARTIST — Record Title	POP POS	Label & Number
				COLEMAN, Cy ✪		
				Born on 6/14/29 in New York City. Songwriter/pianist. Composed numerous film and stage musicals.		
1/31/76	**29**	10		Chloe .... [I]		RCA 10440
				#7 hit for Paul Whiteman in 1928		
				COLEMAN, Durell ✪		
				Native of Roanoke, Virginia. R&B singer. Moved to Los Angeles in 1983. Was the 1985 winner of TV's *Star Search* (male vocalist category).		
9/14/85	**30**	5		Somebody Took My Love....................................		Island 99605
★★183★★				**COLLINS, Judy**		
				Contemporary folk singer/songwriter. Born on 5/1/39 in Seattle. Began studying classical piano at age five. Moved to Los Angeles, then to Denver at age nine, where her father, Chuck Collins, was a radio personality. Classical debut at 13, playing with the Denver Businessmen's Symphony Orchestra. Discovered folk music at 15. Signed to Elektra in 1961. Her cover versions gave exposure to then-unknown songwriters Leonard Cohen, Joni Mitchell, Randy Newman and Sandy Denny. Stephen Stills wrote "Suite: Judy Blue Eyes" for her. Appeared in the New York Shakespeare Festival's production of *Peer Gynt*. Nominated for a 1974 Academy Award for co-directing *Antonia: A Portrait of the Woman* — a documentary about Judy's former classical mentor and a pioneer female orchestra conductor, Dr. Antonia Brico.		
				1)Both Sides Now 2)Amazing Grace 3)Send In The Clowns		
11/16/68	**3**	13		1 **Both Sides Now**	8	Elektra 45639
2/22/69	**37**	2		2 Someday Soon	55	Elektra 45649
8/16/69	**25**	4		3 Chelsea Morning	78	Elektra 45657
12/13/69	**28**	7		4 Turn! Turn! Turn!/To Everything There Is A Season	69	Elektra 45680
				lyrics adapted by Pete Seeger from the *Book of Ecclesiastes*		
12/26/70	**5**	12		5 Amazing Grace	15	Elektra 45709
				recorded at St. Paul's Chapel, Columbia University; song attributed to hymn writer Rev. John Newton, 1779		
12/18/71	**23**	6		6 Open The Door (Song For Judith)	90	Elektra 45755
2/17/73	**10**	10		7 **Cook With Honey**	32	Elektra 45831
6/14/75	**8**	11		8 **Send In The Clowns**	36	Elektra 45253
				from the Broadway musical *A Little Night Music*		
10/15/77	**15**	14		9 Send In The Clowns .... [R]	19	Elektra 45253
3/24/79	**16**	9		10 Hard Times For Lovers	66	Elektra 46020
10/13/84	**42**	1		11 Home Again		Elektra 69697
				JUDY COLLINS with T.G. SHEPPARD		
10/20/90	**31**	11		12 Fires Of Eden		Columbia LP Cut
				from the album *Fires Of Eden* on Columbia 46102		
★★37★★				**COLLINS, Phil**		
				Born on 1/30/51 in London. Stage actor as a young child; played the Artful Dodger in the London production of *Oliver*. With group Flaming Youth in 1969. Joined Genesis as their drummer in 1970, became lead singer in 1975. Also with jazz-rock group Brand X. First solo album in 1981. Starred in the 1988 film *Buster* and appeared in *Hook* and *Frauds*.		
				1)Another Day In Paradise 2)Do You Remember? 3)Two Hearts		
11/27/82	**9**	19		1 **You Can't Hurry Love**	10	Atlantic 89933
3/3/84	**2**[6]	23	●	2 **Against All Odds (Take A Look At Me Now)**....................	1[3]	Atlantic 89700
				title song from the film *Against All Odds*		
1/19/85	**15**	13	●	3 Easy Lover...	2[2]	Columbia 04679
				PHILIP BAILEY with Phil Collins		
2/16/85	**1**[3]	21	●	4 **One More Night**	1[2]	Atlantic 89588
6/15/85	**30**	10	●	5 Sussudio	1[1]	Atlantic 89560
8/31/85	**25**	10		6 Don't Lose My Number	4	Atlantic 89536
10/12/85	**1**[3]	19		7 **Separate Lives**	1[1]	Atlantic 89498
				PHIL COLLINS and MARILYN MARTIN love theme from the film *White Nights*		
3/29/86	**2**[3]	17		8 **Take Me Home**	7	Atlantic 89472
4/2/88	**34**	15		9 We Said Hello Goodbye		Atlantic LP Cut
				from the album *No Jacket Required* on Atlantic 81240 (CD only) and the soundtrack album *Playing For Keeps* on Atlantic 81678; also the B-side of #6 above		
9/3/88	**1**[3]	22	●	10 Groovy Kind Of Love	1[2]	Atlantic 89017
11/19/88	**1**[5]	25		11 **Two Hearts**	1[2]	Atlantic 88980
				above 2 from the film *Buster* starring Collins		
11/4/89	**1**[5]	23	●	12 Another Day In Paradise...................................	1[4]	Atlantic 88774
				David Crosby (backing vocal)		
2/17/90	**3**	16		13 **I Wish It Would Rain Down**................................	3	Atlantic 88738
				Eric Clapton (guitar)		
4/28/90	**1**[5]	29		14 **Do You Remember?**...	4	Atlantic 87955
8/4/90	**2**[2]	29		15 **Something Happened On The Way To Heaven**	4	Atlantic 87885

55

DEBUT DATE	PEAK POS	WKS CHR	G O L D	ARTIST — Record Title	POP POS	Label & Number
				COLLINS, Phil — Cont'd		
11/24/90	**38**	8		16 Hang In Long Enough	23	Atlantic 87800
4/24/93	**3**	21		17 Hero..	44	Atlantic 87360
				DAVID CROSBY & PHIL COLLINS		
				COLOR ME BADD		
				New York City-based dance vocal quartet: Bryan Abrams, Sam Watters, Mark Calderon and Kevin Thornton. Formed while in high school in Oklahoma City.		
9/7/91	**38**	10	●	I Adore Mi Amor	1²	Giant 19204
				COLTER, Jessi		
				Born Miriam Johnson on 5/25/47 in Phoenix. Country singer/songwriter. Married to Duane Eddy from 1962-68. Married Waylon Jennings in October 1969.		
4/26/75	**16**	9		I'm Not Lisa	4	Capitol 4009
				COLVIN, Shawn ○		
				Female folk singer. Born on 1/10/56 in Vermillion, South Dakota. Backing vocalist for Suzanne Vega.		
1/27/90	**30**	9		1 Steady On		Columbia 73061
12/5/92	**44**	8		2 Round Of Blues		Columbia LP Cut
				from the album *Fat City* on Columbia 47122		
2/20/93	**16**	15		3 I Don't Know Why		Columbia 74861
				COMMANDER CODY And His Lost Planet Airmen		
				Group formed while Cody (George Frayne) attended the University of Michigan. To San Francisco in 1968.		
4/29/72	**28**	5		1 Hot Rod Lincoln ....[N]	9	Paramount 0146
7/7/73	**45**	2		2 Smoke! Smoke! Smoke! (That Cigarette) ....[N]	94	Paramount 0216
				COMMITMENTS, The		
				Band of Irish actors/musicians who starred in the film of the same name: Robert Arkin, Michael Aherne, Angeline Ball, Maria Doyle, Dave Finnegan, Bronagh Gallagher, Felim Gormley, Glen Hansard, Dick Massey, Kenneth McCluskey, Johnny Murphy and Andrew Strong. All did their own performing.		
10/12/91	**30**	7		Try A Little Tenderness	67	MCA 54128
				from the film *The Commitments*		
★★124★★				**COMMODORES**		
				R&B group formed in Tuskegee, Alabama in 1970. Consisted of Lionel Richie (vocals, saxophone), William King (trumpet), Thomas McClary (guitar), Milan Williams (keyboards), Ronald LaPread (bass) and Walter "Clyde" Orange (drums). First recorded for Motown in 1972. In film *Thank God It's Friday*. Richie began solo work in 1981, left in 1982.		
				1)*Three Times A Lady* 2)*Nightshift* 3)*Oh No*		
7/9/77	**14**	13		1 Easy	4	Motown 1418
7/1/78	**1³**	20		2 Three Times A Lady..	1²	Motown 1443
8/18/79	**9**	13		3 Sail On	4	Motown 1466
10/13/79	**6**	16		4 Still..	1¹	Motown 1474
2/2/80	**43**	5		5 Wonderland	25	Motown 1479
8/2/80	**47**	3		6 Old-Fashion Love	20	Motown 1489
10/11/80	**44**	3		7 Heroes	54	Motown 1495
7/11/81	**13**	15		8 Lady (You Bring Me Up)	8	Motown 1514
10/3/81	**5**	21		9 Oh No	4	Motown 1527
				Lionel Richie (lead singer on all of above)		
9/10/83	**8**	21		10 Only You	54	Motown 1694
1/26/85	**2¹**	23		11 Nightshift..	3	Motown 1773
				a tribute to Marvin Gaye and Jackie Wilson		
8/24/85	**8**	14		12 Janet	87	Motown 1802
6/6/87	**22**	9		13 United In Love		Polydor 8857607
★★44★★				**COMO, Perry**		
				Born Pierino Como on 5/18/12 in Canonsburg, Pennsylvania. Owned barbershop in hometown. With Freddy Carlone band in 1933; with Ted Weems, 1936-42. In the films *Something For The Boys, Doll Face, If I'm Lucky* and *Words And Music*, 1944-48. Own *Supper Club* radio series to late 1940s. Television shows (15 minutes) from 1948-55. Host of hourly TV shows from 1955-63. Winner of five Emmys.		
				1)*It's Impossible* 2)*Stop! And Think It Over* 3)*And I Love You So*		
				4)*You Made It That Way (Watermelon Summer)* 5)*Seattle*		
3/31/62	**6**	12		1 Caterina	23	RCA 8004
6/29/63	**16**	1		2 (I Love You) Don't You Forget It	39	RCA 8186
4/10/65	**3**	10		3 Dream On Little Dreamer..	25	RCA 8533
7/31/65	**18**	7		4 Oowee, Oowee	88	RCA 8636
				The Anita Kerr Quartet (backing vocals, above 2)		
5/21/66	**12**	9		5 Coo Coo Roo Coo Coo Paloma..................................	128	RCA 8823
4/22/67	**1¹**	16		6 Stop! And Think It Over..	92	RCA 9165

DEBUT DATE	PEAK POS	WKS CHR	G O L D	ARTIST — Record Title	POP POS	Label & Number
				COMO, Perry — Cont'd		
8/12/67	11	7	✔	7 I Looked Back		RCA 9262
11/18/67	2²	12	✔	**8 You Made It That Way (Watermelon Summer)**..................		RCA 9356
2/24/68	10	9		**9 The Father Of Girls**	92	RCA 9448
6/1/68	12	7		10 Happy Man	134	RCA 9533
2/15/69	18	5		11 Sunshine Wine/		
3/15/69	2¹	16		12 **Seattle**	38	RCA 9722
				from the TV series *Here Come The Brides*		
7/12/69	37	3		13 That's All This Old World Needs		RCA 0193
10/24/70	1⁴	19		14 It's Impossible	10	RCA 0387
3/13/71	5	11		15 I Think Of You...	53	RCA 0444
8/21/71	31	4		16 My Days Of Loving You......................................		RCA 0518
3/24/73	1¹	18		**17 And I Love You So**	29	RCA 0906
				written by Don McLean		
10/6/73	16	11		18 Love Don't Care (Where It Grows)	106	RCA 0096
5/11/74	8	15		**19 I Don't Know What He Told You/**		
5/18/74	5	14		**20 Weave Me The Sunshine**		RCA 0274
9/14/74	28	8		21 Temptation ....[R]		RCA 10045
				new version of Perry's #15 hit in 1945 on Victor 1658		
4/19/75	21	8		22 World Of Dreams		RCA 10257
10/11/75	24	13		23 Just Out Of Reach...		RCA 10402
				#24 Pop hit for Solomon Burke in 1961		
4/10/76	45	4		24 The Grass Keeps Right On Growin'		RCA 10604
12/13/80	44	11		25 When		RCA 12088
10/8/83	45	3		26 As My Love For You		RCA 13613
				CONCRETE BLONDE		
				Los Angeles alternative rock group formed in 1982 by female lead singer Johnette Napolitano and bassist James Mankey.		
11/10/90	42	3		Joey	19	I.R.S. 73014
				CONNICK, Harry Jr. ⊙		
				Jazz-pop pianist/vocalist from New Orleans. Born on 9/11/67. Studied jazz under Ellis Marsalis, the father of Wynton and Branford. Acted in the films *Memphis Belle* and *Little Man Tate*.		
1/16/93	46	6		Stardust...		Columbia LP Cut
				from the album *25* on Columbia 53172		
★★105★★				**CONNIFF, Ray**		
				Born on 11/6/16 in Attleboro, Massachusetts. Trombonist/arranger with Bunny Berigan, Bob Crosby, Harry James, Vaughn Monroe and Artie Shaw bands. Long string of hit albums beginning in 1957.		
				1)Somewhere, My Love 2)Lookin' For Love 3)Winds Of Change		
7/18/64	10	9		**1 Invisible Tears **	57	Columbia 43061
8/21/65	26	6		2 Happiness Is *		Columbia 43352
6/18/66	1⁴	18		**3 Somewhere, My Love **	9	Columbia 43626
				Lara's Theme from the film *Dr. Zhivago*		
10/1/66	2¹	12		**4 Lookin' For Love **	94	Columbia 43814
1/7/67	29	3		**5 Wednesday's Child**		Columbia 43939
				theme from the film *The Quiller Memorandum*		
2/11/67	13	9		**6 Cabaret**	118	Columbia 43975
				from the musical *Cabaret*		
4/29/67	15	10		7 "17"		Columbia 44055
				from the film *Seventeen*		
7/15/67	14	10		8 Wonderful Season Of Summer */		
8/12/67	24	8		9 Moonlight Brings Memories *		Columbia 44192
10/14/67	25	3		10 One Paddle Two Paddle		Columbia 44298
2/3/68	7	8		**11 Winds Of Change */**		
				from the film *How To Save A Marriage And Ruin Your Life*		
2/10/68	23	3		12 We're A Home *		Columbia 44422
				from the musical *Here's Where I Belong*		
6/1/68	34	2		13 Sounds Of Silence		Columbia 44536
9/28/68	12	13		14 Look Homeward Angel *		Columbia 44645
1/18/69	23	6	✔	15 I've Got My Eyes On You		Columbia 44724
1/2/71	35	2		16 Loss Of Love *		Columbia 45267
				love theme from the film *Sunflower*		
7/28/73	23	7	✔	17 Harmony...		Columbia 45893
3/19/77	48	4		18 Rain On		Columbia 10473
				*RAY CONNIFF AND THE SINGERS		

DEBUT DATE	PEAK POS	WKS CHR	GOLD	ARTIST — Record Title	POP POS	Label & Number
				CONTI, Bill		
				Born on 4/13/42 in Providence, Rhode Island. Composer/conductor for the first three *Rocky* films.		
3/12/77	**20**	16	●	1 Gonna Fly Now ....[I]	1¹	United Art. 940
				theme from the film *Rocky* starring Sylvester Stallone		
11/13/82	**18**	14		2 Theme From Dynasty ....[I]	52	Arista 1021
				from the TV series *Dynasty* starring Joan Collins and John Forsythe		
				CONTOURS, The		
				R&B vocal group formed in Detroit: Billy Gordon, Billy Hoggs, Joe Billingslea, Sylvester Potts, Huey Davis (guitar) and Hubert Johnson (d: 7/11/81).		
7/2/88	**24**	10		Do You Love Me...[R]	11	Motown Yest. 448
				originally made the *Hot 100* on 8/11/62 (POS 3); featured in the film *Dirty Dancing*		
				COOKE, Sam		
				Born on 1/2/31 in Clarksdale, Mississippi and raised in Chicago. Died from a gunshot wound on 12/11/64 in Los Angeles; shot by a female motel manager under mysterious circumstances. Son of a Baptist minister. Sang in choir from age six. Joined gospel group the Highway Q.C.'s. Lead singer of the Soul Stirrers from 1950-56. First recorded secular songs in 1956 as "Dale Cook" on Specialty. String of hits on Keen label led to contract with RCA. Nephew is singer R.B. Greaves. Inducted into the Rock and Roll Hall of Fame in 1986. Revered as the definitive soul singer.		
6/9/62	**12**	2		1 Having A Party	17	RCA 8036
10/6/62	**4**	10		2 Nothing Can Change This Love	12	RCA 8088
8/10/63	**2¹**	9		3 Frankie And Johnny	14	RCA 8215
10/17/64	**7**	1		4 Cousin Of Mine	31	RCA 8426
★★81★★				**COOLIDGE, Rita**		
				Born on 5/1/44 in Nashville. Had own group, R.C. and the Moonpies, at Florida State University. Moved to Los Angeles in the late '60s. Did backup work for Delaney & Bonnie, Leon Russell, Joe Cocker and Eric Clapton. With Kris Kristofferson from 1971, married to him from 1973-80. Known as "The Delta Lady," for whom Leon Russell wrote the song of the same name.		
				1)All Time High 2)We're All Alone 3)You		
2/17/73	**38**	2		1 My Crew	flip	A&M 1398
				made the *Hot 100* as the B-side of "Fever" (POS 76)		
11/10/73	**12**	13		2 A Song I'd Like To Sing *	49	A&M 1475
3/2/74	**25**	11		3 Loving Arms *	86	A&M 1498
12/21/74	**44**	5		4 Rain *		Monument 8630
2/15/75	**42**	4		5 Lover Please *		Monument 8636
				#7 Pop hit for Clyde McPhatter in 1962		
				***KRIS KRISTOFFERSON & RITA COOLIDGE**		
4/30/77	**5**	22	●	6 (Your Love Has Lifted Me) Higher And Higher................	2¹	A&M 1922
9/24/77	**1¹**	19	●	7 We're All Alone	7	A&M 1965
				written by Boz Scaggs		
1/21/78	**9**	13		8 The Way You Do The Things You Do.............................	20	A&M 2004
7/1/78	**3**	17		9 You...	25	A&M 2058
10/21/78	**20**	13		10 Love Me Again	68	A&M 2090
8/25/79	**15**	13		11 One Fine Day	66	A&M 2169
11/17/79	**3**	14		12 I'd Rather Leave While I'm In Love...............................	38	A&M 2199
5/17/80	**39**	9		13 Somethin' 'Bout You Baby I Like	42	Capitol 4865
				GLEN CAMPBELL and RITA COOLIDGE		
11/22/80	**15**	14		14 Fool That I Am	46	A&M 2281
6/25/83	**1⁴**	19		15 All Time High	36	A&M 2551
				from the James Bond film *Octopussy*		
10/22/83	**37**	3		16 Only You		A&M 2586
7/21/84	**15**	13		17 Something Said Love		A&M 2634
				COOPER, Alice		
				Born Vincent Furnier on 2/4/48 in Detroit. Formed rock group in Phoenix in 1965; changed name to Alice Cooper in 1966. To Los Angeles in 1968, then to Detroit in 1969. Known primarily for his bizarre stage antics. Appeared in the films *Prince Of Darkness* and *Wayne's World* among others.		
10/16/76	**24**	13	●	1 I Never Cry	12	Warner 8228
6/25/77	**23**	10		2 You And Me	9	Warner 8349
11/4/78	**22**	14		3 How You Gonna See Me Now	12	Warner 8695
				COOPER, Marty ○		
				Singer/songwriter/guitarist. Wrote Donna Fargo's #1 country hit "You Can't Be A Beacon."		
3/31/73	**22**	11		The Indiana Girl		Barnaby 5013
				COOPER BROTHERS		
				Richard and Brian Cooper and band.		
11/11/78	**26**	10		The Dream Never Dies	48	Capricorn 0308

58

DEBUT DATE	PEAK POS	WKS CHR	GOLD	ARTIST — Record Title	POP POS	Label & Number
				COPELAND, Alan, Singers ✪		
				Alan was born on 10/6/26 in Los Angeles. Composer/arranger for several TV shows and commercials.		
8/20/66	**28**	6		1 Happiness Is..		ABC 10830
				COUNT BASIE WITH THE ALAN COPELAND SINGERS		
9/14/68	**29**	4		2 Mission: Impossible Theme/Norwegian Wood.....................	120	ABC 11088
				medley of the TV series theme and The Beatles' tune		
1/25/69	**20**	3		3 Classical Gas/Scarborough Fair	123	A&M 988
				medley of the Mason Williams and Simon & Garfunkel tunes		
				COPPERFIELD BRASS ✪		
				Studio group assembled by producer Eddie Jason.		
3/6/71	**24**	6		Charlie.. [I]		RCA 0433
				theme from the Cinerama film *The Statue*		
				CORNELIUS BROTHERS & SISTER ROSE		
				Family group from Dania, Florida. Consisted of Edward, Carter and Rose. Billie Jo was added in 1973. All 15 Cornelius children play instruments or sing. Carter currently lives in Florida as Gideon Israel, the leader of a Muslim religious sect.		
6/24/72	**6**	8	●	1 Too Late To Turn Back Now	2²	United Art. 50910
9/23/72	**27**	6		2 Don't Ever Be Lonely (A Poor Little Fool Like Me).............	23	United Art. 50954
1/6/73	**10**	7		3 I'm Never Gonna Be Alone Anymore................................	37	United Art. 50996
				COSBY, Bill		
				Born on 7/12/38 in Philadelphia. Top comedian who has appeared in nightclubs, on film and on TV. His first seven comedy albums were all million sellers. Played Alexander Scott on TV series *I Spy*. Star of the highly-rated NBC-TV series *The Cosby Show*. Winner of five Emmys and nine Grammys.		
5/2/70	**17**	5		Grover Henson Feels Forgotten .... [S]	70	Uni 55223
				COSTA, Don		
				Born on 6/10/25 in Boston; died on 1/19/83. Arranger for Vaughn Monroe, Frank Sinatra, Vic Damone, The Ames Brothers and many more. A&R director of ABC-Paramount Records, then for United Artists Records.		
7/17/61	**16**	1		1 Never On Sunday .... [I]	19	United Art. 234
				movie title song		
4/29/67	**23**	7		2 Illya Darling.. [I]		Verve 10511
				from the musical *Illya Darling* (based on the film *Never On Sunday*)		
				COTTON, Gene		
				Born on 6/30/44 in Columbus, Ohio. Attended Ohio State University. Recording since 1967.		
10/12/74	**30**	9		1 Sunshine Roses	79	Myrrh 137
				also released on Myrrh 136 in 1974		
12/18/76	**7**	13		2 You've Got Me Runnin'	33	ABC 12227
1/21/78	**3**	18		3 Before My Heart Finds Out................................	23	Ariola 7675
6/17/78	**6**	15		4 You're A Part Of Me......................................	36	Ariola 7704
				GENE COTTON with Kim Carnes		
10/21/78	**35**	6		5 Like A Sunday In Salem (The Amos & Andy Song)	40	Ariola 7723
2/27/82	**22**	12		6 If I Could Get You (into my Life)...........................	76	Knoll 5002
				COTTON, LLOYD and CHRISTIAN		
				Darryl Cotton, Michael Lloyd and Chris Christian.		
8/23/75	**10**	12		1 I Go To Pieces	66	20th Century 2217
12/13/75	**19**	10		2 I Can Sing, I Can Dance		20th Century 2253
				COVEN		
				Pop quintet featuring the voice of Jinx Dawson.		
10/23/71	**16**	9		One Tin Soldier (The Legend of Billy Jack)....................	26	Warner 7509
				from the film *Billy Jack* starring Tom Laughlin		
				COWSILLS, The		
				Family pop group from Newport, Rhode Island. Consisted of five brothers (Bill, Bob, Paul, Barry and John), with their little sister (Susan) and mother (Barbara, d: 1/31/85 [age 56]). Bob, Paul, John and Susan reunited for touring in 1990. Susan married Peter Holsapple of The dB's on 4/18/93.		
2/3/68	**9**	7		1 We Can Fly	21	MGM 13886
6/22/68	**17**	9		2 Indian Lake	10	MGM 13944
10/5/68	**16**	5		3 Poor Baby	44	MGM 13981
5/3/69	**19**	4	●	4 Hair..	2²	MGM 14026
				from the rock musical *Hair*		
				COYOTE SISTERS, The		
				Female trio: Marty Gwinn, Leah Kunkel (sister of Mama Cass) and Renee Armand.		
7/21/84	**16**	13		1 Straight From The Heart (Into Your Life)........................	66	Morocco 1742
11/17/84	**39**	2		2 I've Got A Radio...		Morocco 1766

DEBUT DATE	PEAK POS	WKS CHR	GOLD	ARTIST — Record Title	POP POS	Label & Number
				CRADDOCK, Billy "Crash"		
				Country-rock singer. Born on 6/16/39 in Greensboro, North Carolina. First recorded for Colonial in 1957. Nickname "Crash" came from his stock car racing hobby.		
7/27/74	15	10		1 Rub It In	16	ABC 12013
12/7/74	23	10		2 Ruby, Baby	33	ABC 12036
1/31/76	44	4		3 Easy As Pie	54	ABC/Dot 17584
				CRAIG, Deran ○		
7/23/83	29	10		One Mind, Two Hearts		CBS Assoc. 03982
				CRAMER, Floyd		
				Nashville's top session pianist. Born on 10/27/33 in Samti, Louisiana and raised in Huttig, Arkansas. Played piano from age five. Moved to Nashville in 1955. Toured with Elvis Presley, Johnny Cash, Perry Como and Chet Atkins.		
7/17/61	3	6		1 **San Antonio Rose** [I]	8	RCA 7893
				written by Bob Wills in 1938		
1/27/62	9	7		2 **Chattanooga Choo Choo** [I]	36	RCA 7978
4/28/62	20	1		3 Lovesick Blues [I]	87	RCA 8013
1/12/63	12	4		4 Java [I]	49	RCA 8116
2/11/67	24	7		5 Stood Up [I]		RCA 9065
1/13/68	32	5		6 By The Time I Get To Phoenix [I]		RCA 9396
5/23/70	39	2		7 Theme From Two-Twenty-Two [I]		RCA 9841
				from the TV series *Room 222*		
5/10/80	34	6		8 Dallas [I]	104	RCA 11916
				TV series theme song		
				CRANE, Les		
				TV talkshow host from San Francisco.		
10/2/71	3	13		**Desiderata** [S]	8	Warner 7520
				originally a piece of prose, written in 1906 by Max Ehrmann		
				CRAVEN, Beverley ○		
				Born in Sri Lanka to British parents. Raised in England.		
12/21/91	30	9		Holding On		Epic LP Cut
				from the album *Beverley Craven.* on Epic 48543		
				CRAWFORD, Johnny		
				Born on 3/26/46 in Los Angeles. One of the original Mouseketeers. Played Chuck Connor's son (Mark McCain) in the TV series *The Rifleman,* 1958-63.		
11/17/62	2[1]	8		**Rumors**	12	Del-Fi 4188
				CRAWFORD, Randy — see SPRINGFIELD, Rick		
				CRAY, Robert, Band		
				Born on 8/1/53 in Columbus, Georgia. Blues guitarist/vocalist.		
10/8/88	35	6		Don't Be Afraid Of The Dark	74	Mercury 870569
				CREWE, Bob, Generation		
				Born on 11/12/37 in Newark, New Jersey. Wrote many hit songs beginning with "Silhouettes" in 1957. One of the top producers of the 1960s; worked with The 4 Seasons. Head of several labels, publishing and production companies. Assembled The Bob Crewe Generation, an aggregation of studio musicians.		
12/31/66	2[2]	14		1 **Music To Watch Girls By** [I]	15	DynoVoice 229
				tune used in a Diet Pepsi commercial		
4/29/67	29	6		2 Miniskirts In Moscow or [I]	129	DynoVoice 233
10/18/69	24	6		3 Where Do I Go		Crewe 335
				JULIUS LA ROSA with The Bob Crewe Generation		
				from the Broadway musical *Hair*; #86 Pop hit for Carla Thomas in 1968		
3/27/76	41	6		4 Street Talk [I]	56	20th Century 2271
				B.C.G. (B.C. Generation)		
★★170★★				**CROCE, Jim**		
				Born on 1/10/43 in Philadelphia; killed in a plane crash on 9/20/73 in Natchitoches, Louisiana. Vocalist/guitarist/composer. Recorded with wife Ingrid for Capitol in 1968. Lead guitarist on his hits, Maury Muehleisen, was killed in the same crash.		
				1)Time In A Bottle 2)I'll Have To Say I Love You In A Song 3)I Got A Name		
7/22/72	9	10		1 **You Don't Mess Around With Jim**	8	ABC 11328
10/28/72	11	10		2 Operator (That's Not the Way it Feels)	17	ABC 11335
2/10/73	8	9		3 **One Less Set Of Footsteps**	37	ABC 11346
4/21/73	9	19	●	4 **Bad, Bad Leroy Brown**	1[2]	ABC 11359
9/29/73	4	14		5 **I Got A Name**	10	ABC 11389
				from the film *The Last American Hero*		
11/24/73	1[2]	16	●	6 **Time In A Bottle**	1[2]	ABC 11405

DEBUT DATE	PEAK POS	WKS CHR	G O L D	ARTIST — Record Title	POP POS	Label & Number
				CROCE, Jim — Cont'd		
3/9/74	**1**[1]	14		7 I'll Have To Say I Love You In A Song	9	ABC 11424
6/15/74	**9**	13		8 Workin' At The Car Wash Blues	32	ABC 11447
12/27/75	**22**	11		9 Chain Gang Medley	63	Lifesong 45001
				Chain Gang/He Don't Love You/Searchin'; all of above produced by Terry Cashman & Tommy West		
				CROSBY, Bing		
				One of the most popular entertainers of the 20th century! Harry Lillis Crosby was born on 5/3/03 in Tacoma, Washington; died of a heart attack on 10/14/77 on a golf course near Madrid, Spain. Won the Lifetime Achievement Grammy in 1962. Ranked as the #1 artist in *Joel Whitburn's Pop Memories 1890-1954* book.		
12/11/61	**3**	4		1 White Christmas .... [X-R]	12	Decca 23778
				original version first charted on 10/3/42 (POS 1) on Decca 18429; the best-selling single of all-time		
12/22/62	**10**	2		2 White Christmas .... [X-R]	38	Decca 23778
1/6/68	**29**	2		3 Step To The Rear		Reprise 0645
				from the Broadway show *How Now, Dow Jones*		
11/22/75	**35**	7		4 That's What Life Is All About		United Art. 700
				CROSBY, Chris		
				Bing's nephew. Father is the late bandleader, Bob Crosby.		
3/14/64	**18**	2		Young And In Love...............................	53	MGM 13191
				from the TV series *Dr. Kildare*		
				CROSBY, David		
				Born David Van Cortland on 8/14/41 in Los Angeles. Vocalist/guitarist with The Byrds from 1964-68 and later Crosby, Stills & Nash. Frequent troubles with the law due to drug charges. Film cameos in *Backdraft*, *Hook* and *Thunderheart*; appeared on TV's *Roseanne*.		
4/24/93	**3**	21		Hero	44	Atlantic 87360
				DAVID CROSBY & PHIL COLLINS		
★★194★★				**CROSBY, STILLS & NASH (& YOUNG)**		
				Trio formed in Laurel Canyon, California in 1968. Consisted of David Crosby (guitar), Stephen Stills (guitar, keyboards, bass) and Graham Nash (guitar). Crosby had been in The Byrds, Stills had been in Buffalo Springfield, and Nash was with The Hollies. Won the 1969 Best New Artist Grammy Award. Neil Young (guitar), formerly with Buffalo Springfield, joined group in 1969, left in 1974. Reunion in 1988.		
				1)*Wasted On The Way* 2)*Just A Song Before I Go* 3)*Southern Cross*		
9/13/69	**28**	4		1 Marrakesh Express	28	Atlantic 2652
6/27/70	**28**	6		2 Teach Your Children *	16	Atlantic 2735
10/3/70	**20**	7		3 Our House *	30	Atlantic 2760
6/4/77	**5**	22		4 Just A Song Before I Go	7	Atlantic 3401
10/8/77	**21**	9		5 Fair Game	43	Atlantic 3432
6/26/82	**2**[5]	20		6 Wasted On The Way	9	Atlantic 4058
10/2/82	**6**	18		7 Southern Cross	18	Atlantic 89969
11/26/88	**49**	2	✔	8 American Dream *		Atlantic 89003
2/4/89	**11**	18		9 Got It Made *	69	Atlantic 88966
1/27/90	**45**	4		10 Chippin' Away		Atlantic 88732
				additional vocals by James Taylor *CROSBY, STILLS, NASH & YOUNG		
★★116★★				**CROSS, Christopher**		
				Born Christopher Geppert on 5/3/51 in San Antonio, Texas. Formed own group with Rob Meurer (keyboards), Andy Salmon (bass) and Tommy Taylor (drums) in 1973. Won the 1980 Best New Artist Grammy Award.		
				1)*Arthur's Theme (Best That You Can Do)* 2)*Think Of Laura* 3)*Never Be The Same*		
3/1/80	**24**	13		1 Ride Like The Wind	**2**[4]	Warner 49184
				Michael McDonald (backing vocal)		
6/28/80	**10**	19		2 Sailing	**1**[1]	Warner 49507
10/18/80	**1**[2]	18		3 Never Be The Same	15	Warner 49580
4/4/81	**15**	10		4 Say You'll Be Mine	20	Warner 49705
8/22/81	**1**[4]	23	●	5 Arthur's Theme (Best That You Can Do)	**1**[3]	Warner 49787
				from the Dudley Moore movie *Arthur*		
1/22/83	**3**	19		6 All Right	12	Warner 29843
5/14/83	**10**	14		7 No Time For Talk	33	Warner 29662
12/17/83	**1**[4]	20		8 Think Of Laura	9	Warner 29658
				popularized through play on TV's *General Hospital*		
6/23/84	**16**	12		9 A Chance For Heaven	76	Columbia 04492
				swimming theme from the Official Music of the XXIIIrd Olympiad Los Angeles 1984		
10/18/86	**27**	8		10 Loving Strangers		Arista 9530
				David's theme from the film *Nothing In Common*		

DEBUT DATE	PEAK POS	WKS CHR	GOLD	ARTIST — Record Title	POP POS	Label & Number
				CROSS, Christopher — Cont'd		
9/10/88	**41**	4		11 I Will (Take You Forever)...		Reprise 27795
				CHRISTOPHER CROSS with Frances Ruffelle		
				CROSS COUNTRY		
				Jay Siegel, Mitch and Phil Margo; all formerly with The Tokens.		
8/11/73	**6**	13		**In The Midnight Hour**...	30	Atco 6934
				CROWDED HOUSE		
				New Zealand/Australian trio founded by former Split Enz members Neil Finn (vocals, guitar, piano) and Paul Hester (drums), with Nick Seymour (bass). Neil's brother, Tim Finn (also of Split Enz) joined the band in 1991.		
3/21/87	**9**	18		1 **Don't Dream It's Over**...	2¹	Capitol 5614
6/20/87	**13**	17		2 Something So Strong	7	Capitol 5695
7/16/88	**26**	11		3 Better Be Home Soon...	42	Capitol 44164
				CROWELL, Rodney		
				Born on 8/7/50 in Houston. Country singer/songwriter/guitarist. Married Rosanne Cash in 1979 and divorced in April 1992. Wrote the Dirt Band's "American Dream" and many other country hits.		
7/26/80	**46**	2		1 Ashes By Now...	37	Warner 49224
7/4/92	**9**	20		2 **What Kind Of Love**		Columbia 74360
				co-written by Roy Orbison		
				CRUSADERS, The		
				Instrumental jazz-oriented group formed in Houston, as the Swingsters, in the early '50s. To California in the early '60s, name changed to Jazz Crusaders. Became The Crusaders in 1971. Included Joe Sample (keyboards), Wilton Felder (reeds), Nesbert "Stix" Hooper (drums) and Wayne Henderson (trombone).		
8/19/72	**35**	3		1 Put It Where You Want It ....[I]	52	Blue Thumb 208
11/4/72	**39**	3		2 So Far Away ....[I]	114	Blue Thumb 217
				CRYSTAL MANSION		
				Eight-man group — Johnny Caswell, lead singer.		
12/5/70	**34**	3		Carolina In My Mind...	73	Colossus 128
				CUFF LINKS, The		
				Group is actually the overdubbed voices of Ron Dante (The Archies).		
9/27/69	**5**	10		1 Tracy	9	Decca 32533
1/3/70	**30**	4		2 When Julie Comes Around	41	Decca 32592
6/13/70	**39**	2		3 Robin's World		Decca 32687
				CULTURE CLUB		
				Formed in London in 1981. Consisted of George "Boy George" O'Dowd (b: 6/14/61; vocals), Roy Hay (guitar, keyboards), Michael Craig (bass) and Jon Moss (drums). Designer Sue Clowes originated distinctive costuming for the group. Won the 1983 Best New Artist Grammy Award. Boy George went solo in 1987.		
				1)Karma Chameleon 2)Time (Clock Of The Heart) 3)Do You Really Want To Hurt Me		
12/25/82	**8**	20		1 **Do You Really Want To Hurt Me**	2³	Epic 03368
4/16/83	**6**	19		2 **Time (Clock Of The Heart)**	2²	Epic 03796
8/6/83	**33**	9		3 I'll Tumble 4 Ya	9	Epic 03912
12/10/83	**3**	18	●	4 **Karma Chameleon**...	1³	Virgin 04221
3/10/84	**12**	13		5 Miss Me Blind	5	Virgin 04388
				Jermaine Stewart (backing vocal)		
5/19/84	**8**	12		6 It's A Miracle...	13	Virgin 04457
1/5/85	**18**	10		7 Mistake No. 3...	33	Virgin 04727
4/19/86	**11**	13		8 Move Away	12	Virgin 05847
				CUMMINGS, Burton		
				Born on 12/31/47 in Winnipeg, Canada. Lead singer of The Guess Who.		
10/16/76	**2¹**	17	●	1 **Stand Tall**	10	Portrait 70001
2/26/77	**10**	9		2 I'm Scared...	61	Portrait 70002
6/18/77	**23**	8		3 Timeless Love...		Portrait 70003
1/20/79	**38**	3		4 I Will Play A Rhapsody		Portrait 70024
				B-side "Takes A Fool To Love A Fool" made the Country charts (POS 33)		
10/3/81	**22**	11		5 You Saved My Soul	37	Alfa 7008
				CUNHA, Rick		
				Los Angeles session guitarist/vocalist.		
5/18/74	**40**	5		(I'm A) YoYo Man	61	GRC 2016
				CUNICO, Gino ✪		
				Los Angeles-based singer/songwriter. Wrote Barry Manilow's "When I Wanted You."		
6/12/76	**43**	5		Daydreamer		Arista 0181

DEBUT DATE	PEAK POS	WKS CHR	G O L D	ARTIST — Record Title	POP POS	Label & Number
				CURB, Mike, Congregation		
				Mike was born on 12/24/44 in Savannah, Georgia. Pop music mogul and politician. President of MGM Records, 1969-73. Elected lieutenant governor of California in 1978. Formed own company, Curb Records.		
7/4/70	**16**	5		1 Sweet Gingerbread Man..		MGM 14140
				"Bubbled Under" on 8/14/71 on MGM 14265 (POS 115); from the film *The Magic Garden of Stanley Sweetheart*		
11/21/70	**16**	10		2 Burning Bridges...	34	MGM 14151
				from the film *Kelly's Heroes*		
6/17/72	**15**	8		3 See You In September	108	MGM 14391
7/28/73	**9**	10		4 **It's A Small Small World**	108	MGM 14494
				theme music used for an attraction at Walt Disney World		
				CURRENT		
				Five-man disco session band.		
2/12/77	**30**	8		Theme From "Rocky" (Gonna Fly Now) .... [I]	94	Playboy 6098
				CUTTING CREW		
				British rock group led by singer Nick Van Eede, with Kevin Scott MacMichael (guitar; from Canada), Colin Farley (bass) and Martin Beedle (drums).		
5/9/87	**24**	7		1 (I Just) Died In Your Arms..................................	1 [2]	Virgin 99481
9/5/87	**2** [1]	22		2 I've Been In Love Before	9	Virgin 99425
8/12/89	**4**	23		3 Everything But My Pride		Virgin 99184
12/23/89	**17**	14		4 The Last Thing..		Virgin 99133
				CYMARRON		
				Male pop vocal trio formed in Memphis: Richard Mainegra, Rick Yancey and Sherrill Parks.		
6/26/71	**6**	12		1 Rings	17	Entrance 7500
9/25/71	**19**	5		2 Valerie	96	Entrance 7502
				CYMBAL, Johnny		
				Singer/songwriter/producer. Born on 2/3/45 in Ochitree, Scotland. Died on 3/16/93 of a heart attack. Moved to Goderich, Ontario in 1952. Moved to Cleveland in 1960. Also recorded as Derek.		
6/8/63	**19**	2		Teenage Heaven .... [N]	58	Kapp 524
				CYRUS, Billy Ray		
				Born on 8/25/61 in Flatwoods, Kentucky.		
6/20/92	**23**	11	▲	1 Achy Breaky Heart..	4	Mercury 866522
10/3/92	**45**	10		2 Could've Been Me..	72	Mercury 866998

D

DEBUT DATE	PEAK POS	WKS CHR	G O L D	ARTIST — Record Title	POP POS	Label & Number
				DAHLSTROM, Patti ○		
				Born on 3/24/47 in Houston. Singer/songwriter. Wrote Helen Reddy's "Emotion."		
10/5/74	**46**	4		He Did Me Wrong, But He Did It Right..................................		20th Century 2113
				DAISY, Pat ○		
				Born Patricia Key Deasy on 10/10/44 in Gallatin, Tennessee. In girl trio while in high school. Moved to Huntsville, Alabama in 1966, worked in a folk group.		
3/18/72	**38**	3		Everybody's Reaching Out For Someone...........................	112	RCA 0637
				written by Dickey Lee; vocal accompaniment by The Jordanaires		
				DALE & GRACE		
				Pop vocal duo: Dale Houston (of Ferriday, Louisiana) and Grace Broussard (of Prairieville, Louisiana).		
10/12/63	**1** [2]	14		1 **I'm Leaving It Up To You**..	1 [2]	Montel 921
2/8/64	**3**	6		2 **Stop And Think It Over**	8	Montel 922
				DALTON, Kathy		
				Songstress from Memphis.		
8/31/74	**18**	10		1 Boogie Bands And One Night Stands..................................	72	DiscReet 1210
11/23/74	**44**	5		2 Justine		DiscReet 1313
				DALTREY, Roger		
				Born on 3/1/44 in London. Formed band the Detours, which later became The Who. Roger was The Who's lead singer and starred in the films *Tommy*, *Lisztomania*, *The Legacy* and *McVicar*.		
10/4/80	**4**	18		Without Your Love	20	Polydor 2121
				from the *McVicar* soundtrack		

DEBUT DATE	PEAK POS	WKS CHR	G O L D	ARTIST — Record Title	POP POS	Label & Number
				DAMIAN, Michael		
				Born Michael Weir on 4/26/62 in San Diego. Played Danny Romalotti on TV's *The Young & The Restless* since 1981 when discovered by the show's producers while performing on *American Bandstand*.		
9/23/89	7	28		1 **Was It Nothing At All**	24	Cypress 1451
5/19/90	47	3		2 Straight From My Heart		Cypress LP Cut
				from the album *Where Do We Go From Here?* on Cypress 0130		
2/15/92	26	12		3 (There'll Never Be) Another You		A&M LP Cut
				from the album *Dreams Of Summer* on A&M 5348		
				DAMON, Jimmy ☉		
1/11/69	39	3		Young Hearts, Young Hands		Decca 32412
				DAMON('S), Liz, Orient Express		
				Liz is the leader of the three-woman, six-man vocal/instrumental group from Hawaii.		
12/26/70	4	13		1 **1900 Yesterday**	33	White Whale 368
1/15/72	29	4		2 Loneliness Remembers (What Happiness Forgets)		Anthem 51005
				DAMONE, Vic		
				Born Vito Farinola on 6/12/28 in Brooklyn. Vic is among the most popular of postwar ballad singers. Appeared in several movies and hosted own TV series (1956-57). Married actress Diahann Carroll on 1/3/87.		
4/24/65	8	9		1 **You Were Only Fooling (While I Was Falling In Love)**	30	Warner 5616
7/10/65	25	5		2 Why Don't You Believe Me	127	Warner 5644
11/6/65	35	5		3 Tears (For Souvenirs)		Warner 5668
4/1/67	22	7		4 On The South Side Of Chicago		RCA 9145
8/12/67	12	7	✓	5 It Makes No Difference		RCA 9250
				written by Bert Kaempfert		
12/30/67	15	9	✓	6 The Glory Of Love and Theme from Guess Who's Coming To Dinner		RCA 9399
4/27/68	40	2		7 Nothing To Lose		RCA 9488
				from the film *The Party*; written by Henry Mancini		
9/14/68	21	8		8 Why Can't I Walk Away		RCA 9626
				from the Broadway musical *Maggie Flynn*		
4/26/69	31	3		9 To Make A Big Man Cry		RCA 0139
★★132★★				**DANA, Vic**		
				Born on 8/26/42 in Buffalo, New York. Moved to California as a teen.		
				1)Red Roses For A Blue Lady 2)Moonlight And Roses (Bring Mem'ries Of You) 3)Love Is All We Need		
3/31/62	12	9		1 I Will	47	Dolton 51
9/7/63	10	7		2 More	42	Dolton 81
4/11/64	8	8		3 Shangri-La	27	Dolton 92
7/18/64	7	6		4 Love Is All We Need	53	Dolton 95
10/17/64	13	2		5 Garden In The Rain	97	Dolton 99
2/6/65	2¹	12		6 Red Roses For A Blue Lady	10	Dolton 304
5/29/65	20	5		7 Bring A Little Sunshine (To My Heart)	66	Dolton 305
8/7/65	5	11		8 Moonlight And Roses (Bring Mem'ries Of You)	51	Dolton 309
				sung by Roy Rogers in the 1943 film *Song Of Texas*		
11/27/65	14	9		9 Crystal Chandelier	51	Dolton 313
5/28/66	20	6		10 I Love You Drops	30	Dolton 319
7/23/66	24	6		11 A Million And One	71	Dolton 322
11/12/66	33	4		12 Distant Drums	114	Dolton 324
1/31/70	14	9		13 If I Never Knew Your Name	47	Liberty 56150
5/30/70	30	5		14 Red Red Wine	72	Liberty 56163
				above 2 written by Neil Diamond		
12/25/76	14	12		15 Lay Me Down (Roll Me Out To Sea)		Casino 093
				DANIELS, Charlie, Band		
				Daniels (b: 10/28/36, Wilmington, North Carolina; vocals, guitar, fiddle) formed band in Nashville in 1971. Included Tom Crain (guitar), Joe "Taz" DiGregorio (keyboards), Charles Hayward (bass) and James W. Marshall (drums). Daniels led the Jaguars from 1958-67. Went solo in 1968 and worked as a session musician in Nashville. Played on Bob Dylan's *Nashville Skyline* hit album. In the film *Urban Cowboy*.		
8/4/73	37	5		1 Uneasy Rider [N] *CHARLIE DANIELS*	9	Kama Sutra 576
7/28/79	30	8	▲	2 The Devil Went Down To Georgia	3	Epic 50700
				DANNY WILSON		
				Trio from Dundee, Scotland: brothers Gary (lead vocals, guitar) and Kit Clark (keyboards, percussion), with Ged Grimes (bass). Group takes its name from a mid-1950s Frank Sinatra film. Disbanded in 1990.		
6/27/87	6	19		1 Mary's Prayer	23	Virgin 99465

DEBUT DATE	PEAK POS	WKS CHR	GOLD	ARTIST — Record Title	POP POS	Label & Number
				DANNY WILSON — Cont'd		
10/7/89	49	1		2 If Everything You Said Was True..................................		Virgin 99195
				D'ARBY, Terence Trent		
				England-based, soul-pop singer. Born on 3/15/62 in New York City. Last name originally spelled Darby. Was a member of U.S. Army boxing team.		
4/23/88	44	8	●	1 Wishing Well	1¹	Columbia 07675
6/25/88	13	17		2 Sign Your Name	4	Columbia 07911
				DARIN, Bobby		
				Vocalist/pianist/guitarist/drummer. Born Walden Robert Cassotto on 5/14/36 in the Bronx; died of heart failure on 12/20/73 in Los Angeles. First recorded in 1956 with The Jaybirds (Decca). First appeared on TV in March 1956 on *The Tommy Dorsey Show*. Won the 1959 Best New Artist Grammy Award. Married to actress Sandra Dee from 1960-67. Nominated for an Oscar for his performance in the film *Captain Newman, MD* (1963). Formed own record company, Direction. Inducted into the Rock and Roll Hall of Fame in 1990.		
5/25/63	5	7		1 18 Yellow Roses	10	Capitol 4970
9/21/63	11	5		2 Treat My Baby Good...	43	Capitol 5019
6/27/64	11	3		3 Milord ....[F]	45	Atco 6297
10/10/64	18	2		4 The Things In This House	86	Capitol 5257
2/6/65	18	3		5 Hello, Dolly!	79	Capitol 5359
4/16/66	3	14		6 Mame	53	Atlantic 2329
				Broadway show title song (above 2)		
2/4/67	17	8		7 Lovin' You	32	Atlantic 2376
12/30/72	32	7		8 Happy	67	Motown 1217
				love theme from the film *Lady Sings The Blues*		
				DARLIN, Florraine		
				Born Florraine Panza on 1/20/44 in Pittsburgh.		
9/8/62	15	3		Long As The Rose Is Red................................	62	Epic 9529
				answer song to Bobby Vinton's "Roses Are Red"		
				DARREN, James		
				Born James William Ercolani on 10/3/36 in Philadelphia. Singer/actor, studied acting in New York City. Moved to Hollywood in 1955. In films *Rumble On The Docks*, *The Brothers Rico*, *Operation Mad Ball*, *Gunman's Walk*, *The Guns Of Navarone*, *Because They're Young* and *Let No Man Write My Epitaph*. Played Moondoggie, Gidget's boyfriend, in *Gidget*, *Gidget Goes Hawaiian* and *Gidget Goes To Rome*. In *The Time Tunnel* TV series from 1966-67.		
8/21/65	30	4		1 Because You're Mine		Warner 5648
12/10/66	5	16		2 All..	35	Warner 5874
				from the film *Run For Your Wife*		
8/19/67	36	2		3 Didn't We		Warner 7053
				DAVE & SUGAR ✿		
				Country singer Dave Rowland with female duo of Vicki Hackeman and Jackie Frantz. Sue Powell replaced Frantz by the time of their second hit.		
3/12/77	32	8		1 Don't Throw It All Away...................................		RCA 10876
8/20/77	45	3		2 That's The Way Love Should Be		RCA 11034
				DAVID, F.R.		
				Born on 1/1/54 in Tunisia. Real name: R. Fitoussi. Moved to Paris in 1964.		
7/2/83	13	14		Words	62	Carrere 101
				DAVID & JONATHAN		
				Songwriting/producing/vocal duo from Bristol, England: Roger Greenaway (David) and Roger Cook (Jonathan). Both later were production team for White Plains. Cook founded Blue Mink.		
1/15/66	3	10		Michelle	18	Capitol 5563
				written by Lennon/McCartney; produced by George Martin		
				DAVIDSON, John ✿		
				Born on 12/13/41 in Pittsburgh. Singer/actor. Hosted own TV talk show, 1980-82. Co-hosted TV's *That's Incredible* and the new *Hollywood Squares*.		
6/18/66	13	10		1 Summer Love		Columbia 43635
4/1/67	36	2		2 I'll Always Remember		Columbia 44005
4/13/68	33	3		3 Visions Of Sugarplums		Columbia 44478
				written by Glen Campbell and Jerry Fuller		
3/8/69	38	2		4 The Wonder Of You		Columbia 44770
				#9 Pop hit for Elvis Presley in 1970		
6/19/76	7	11		5 Everytime I Sing A Love Song		20th Century 2293
11/20/76	34	6		6 Steal Her Away		20th Century 2313
2/12/77	22	8		7 Save The Last Dance For Me		20th Century 2326
				#1 Pop hit for The Drifters in 1960		

DEBUT DATE	PEAK POS	WKS CHR	G O L D	ARTIST — Record Title	POP POS	Label & Number
2/22/75	**9**	11		**DAVIS, Jan** ⊙		Ranwood 1015
				Hot Sauce... [I]		
				THE JAN DAVIS GUITAR		
★★**107**★★				**DAVIS, Mac**		
				Born on 1/21/42 in Lubbock, Texas. Vocalist/guitarist/composer. Worked as a regional rep for Vee-Jay and Liberty Records. Wrote "In The Ghetto," "Don't Cry Daddy," hits for Elvis Presley. Host of own musical variety TV series from 1974-76. Appearances in several films, including *North Dallas Forty* in 1979.		
				1)Baby Don't Get Hooked On Me 2)Stop And Smell The Roses		
				3)Rock N' Roll (I Gave You The Best Years Of My Life)		
4/25/70	**25**	7		1 Whoever Finds This, I Love You..............................	53	Columbia 45117
7/18/70	**14**	8		2 I'll Paint You A Song..	110	Columbia 45192
				from the film *Norwood*		
10/31/70	**25**	4		3 I Believe In Music	117	Columbia 45245
6/17/72	**1**³	21	●	**4 Baby Don't Get Hooked On Me**	**1**³	Columbia 45618
11/18/72	**13**	8		5 Everybody Loves A Love Song..............................	63	Columbia 45727
2/24/73	**32**	4		6 Dream Me Home	73	Columbia 45773
5/5/73	**28**	5		7 Your Side Of The Bed	88	Columbia 45839
3/16/74	**20**	18		8 One Hell Of A Woman..	11	Columbia 46004
8/24/74	**1**¹	14		**9 Stop And Smell The Roses**	9	Columbia 10018
12/21/74	**4**	11		**10 Rock N' Roll (I Gave You The Best Years Of My Life)**....	15	Columbia 10070
3/29/75	**31**	7		11 (If You Add) All The Love In The World....................	54	Columbia 10111
6/7/75	**20**	9		12 Burnin' Thing	53	Columbia 10148
9/27/75	**38**	6		13 I Still Love You (You Still Love Me).......................		Columbia 10187
4/3/76	**32**	7		14 Forever Lovers	76	Columbia 10304
10/16/76	**32**	7		15 Every Now And Then		Columbia 10418
6/11/77	**25**	11		16 Picking Up The Pieces Of My Life		Columbia 10535
6/3/78	**22**	12		17 Music In My Life		Columbia 10745
★★**143**★★				**DAVIS, Paul**		
				Born on 4/21/48 in Meridian, Mississippi. Singer/songwriter/producer. Pursued country music in the 1980s. Survived a shooting in Nashville in 1987.		
				1)Cool Night 2)Do Right 3)Ride 'Em Cowboy		
6/13/70	**27**	7		1 A Little Bit Of Soap	52	Bang 576
10/3/70	**34**	5		2 I Just Wanna Keep It Together..............................	51	Bang 579
10/26/74	**4**	14		**3 Ride 'Em Cowboy**	23	Bang 712
5/15/76	**31**	9		4 Thinking Of You	45	Bang 724
9/4/76	**31**	6		5 Superstar	35	Bang 726
				tribute to Elton John, Stevie Wonder, Linda Ronstadt and Joni Mitchell		
11/5/77	**25**	24		6 I Go Crazy	7	Bang 733
9/16/78	**7**	20		**7 Sweet Life**	17	Bang 738
				new version with Marie Osmond made the Country charts in 1988 (POS 47)		
3/15/80	**4**	16		**8 Do Right**...	23	Bang 4808
7/19/80	**36**	6		9 Cry Just A Little	78	Bang 4811
11/21/81	**2**³	21		**10 Cool Night**	11	Arista 0645
3/6/82	**5**	20		**11 '65 Love Affair**...	6	Arista 0661
7/17/82	**11**	16		12 Love Or Let Me Be Lonely	40	Arista 0697
★★**123**★★				**DAVIS, Sammy Jr.**		
				Born on 12/8/25 in New York City; died of throat cancer on 5/16/90. Vocalist/dancer/actor of Broadway, film and TV. With family dance act, the Will Mastin Trio, in the early 1940s.		
				1)I've Gotta Be Me 2)The Candy Man 3)What Kind Of Fool Am I		
9/22/62	**6**	12		**1 What Kind Of Fool Am I**	17	Reprise 20048
				from the musical *Stop The World-I Want To Get Off*		
12/29/62	**18**	2		2 Me And My Shadow ....[N]	64	Reprise 20128
				FRANK SINATRA and SAMMY DAVIS JR.		
3/9/63	**19**	1		3 As Long As She Needs Me	59	Reprise 20138
				from Broadway's *Oliver!*		
2/1/64	**7**	10		**4 The Shelter Of Your Arms**	17	Reprise 20216
6/5/65	**33**	4		5 No One Can Live Forever	117	Reprise 0370
4/27/68	**12**	11		6 Lonely Is The Name..	93	Reprise 0673
12/7/68	**1**⁷	20		**7 I've Gotta Be Me**	11	Reprise 0779
				from the Broadway musical *Golden Rainbow*		
3/4/72	**1**²	20	●	**8 The Candy Man**	**1**³	MGM 14320
				from the film *Willy Wonka And The Chocolate Factory*		
10/14/72	**16**	8		9 The People Tree	92	MGM 14426

DEBUT DATE	PEAK POS	WKS CHR	G O L D	ARTIST — Record Title	POP POS	Label & Number
				DAVIS, Sammy Jr. — Cont'd		
4/14/73	29	6		10 (I'd Be) A Legend In My Time................................ 116		MGM 14513
2/23/74	16	11		11 Singin' In The Rain		MGM 14685
				#1 hit for Cliff Edwards in 1929		
9/21/74	41	5		12 That's Entertainment		MGM 14736
1/18/75	24	8		13 Chico And The Man (Main Theme)............................		20th Century 2160
				from the TV series *Chico And The Man*; #96 Pop hit for Jose Feliciano in 1975		
11/15/75	32	7		14 Song And Dance Man..		20th Century 2236
4/24/76	42	4		15 Baretta's Theme (Keep Your Eye On The Sparrow)............ 101		20th Century 2282
				from the TV series *Baretta*		
				DAVIS, Skeeter		
				Country singer. Born Mary Penick on 12/30/31 in Dry Ridge, Kentucky. Recorded with friend Betty Davis as the Davis Sisters, until Betty was killed in a car accident on 8/2/53. Formerly married to TV's *Nashville Now* host, Ralph Emery. Later married Joey Spampinato, the bassist of jazz-rock band NRBQ.		
2/2/63	1⁴	16		1 **The End Of The World**.. 2¹		RCA 8098
5/11/63	13	7		2 I'm Saving My Love 41		RCA 8176
9/14/63	2¹	12		3 **I Can't Stay Mad At You**.. 7		RCA 8219
2/15/64	15	3		4 He Says The Same Things To Me 47		RCA 8288
5/23/64	15	4		5 Gonna Get Along Without You Now 48		RCA 8347
★★60★★				**DAWN**		
				Pop vocal trio formed in New York City: Tony Orlando (b: 4/3/44, New York City), Telma Hopkins (b: 10/28/48, Louisville) and Joyce Vincent (b: 12/14/46, Detroit). Orlando had recorded solo from 1961-63; Hopkins and Vincent had been backup singers. Orlando was manager for April-Blackwood Music at the time of their first hit. Own TV show from 1974-76. All of their hits produced by Hank Medress (The Tokens) and Dave Appell. Hopkins appeared on TV's *Bosom Buddies*, *Gimme A Break* and *Family Matters*. Also see Tony Orlando.		
				1)Say, Has Anybody Seen My Sweet Gypsy Rose 2)Tie A Yellow Ribbon Round The Ole Oak Tree 3)He Don't Love You (Like I Love You)		
8/29/70	8	9	●	1 **Candida** 3		Bell 903
11/28/70	2¹	13	●	2 **Knock Three Times**.. 1³		Bell 938
				Tony Orlando with Toni Wine and Ellie Greenwich (vocals, above 2)		
4/3/71	15	6		3 I Play And Sing 25		Bell 970
6/19/71	9	8		4 **Summer Sand** 33		Bell 45107
				DAWN featuring TONY ORLANDO:		
10/16/71	23	5		5 What Are You Doing Sunday 39		Bell 45141
7/1/72	37	4		6 Vaya Con Dios 95		Bell 45225
2/17/73	1²	16	●	7 **Tie A Yellow Ribbon Round The Ole Oak Tree**............ 1⁴		Bell 45318
7/14/73	1³	13	●	8 **Say, Has Anybody Seen My Sweet Gypsy Rose** 3		Bell 45374
				TONY ORLANDO & DAWN:		
11/10/73	3	14		9 **Who's In The Strawberry Patch With Sally** 27		Bell 45424
4/13/74	36	5		10 It Only Hurts When I Try To Smile........................ 81		Bell 45450
8/24/74	4	13		11 **Steppin' Out (Gonna Boogie Tonight)**........................ 7		Bell 45601
12/14/74	6	11		12 Look In My Eyes Pretty Woman 11		Bell 45620
3/15/75	1¹	12	●	13 **He Don't Love You (Like I Love You)** 1³		Elektra 45240
6/28/75	2¹	11		14 **Mornin' Beautiful** 14		Elektra 45260
9/13/75	13	7		15 You're All I Need To Get By 34		Elektra 45275
11/1/75	7	12		16 **Skybird** 49		Arista 0156
2/21/76	2²	11		17 **Cupid**.. 22		Elektra 45302
5/8/76	15	8		18 Midnight Love Affair		Elektra 45319
3/12/77	7	13		19 **Sing**.. 58		Elektra 45387
				DAWSON, Jim ☉		
				Singer/songwriter/guitarist. Former talent agent.		
8/31/74	44	5		Four Strong Winds..		RCA 10040
				#60 Pop hit for Bobby Bare in 1964		
				DAY, Arlan		
				Jazz pianist/vocalist from Manchester, England.		
10/10/81	27	9		I Surrender 71		Pasha 02480
				DAY, Doris		
				Born Doris Kappelhoff on 4/3/22 in Cincinnati. Star of own popular TV series from 1968-73. Her son, Terry Melcher, was a member of the Rip Chords and Bruce & Terry, and a prolific producer (The Beach Boys).		
6/24/67	19	8		Sorry..		Columbia 44150

DEBUT DATE	PEAK POS	WKS CHR	G O L D	ARTIST — Record Title	POP POS	Label & Number
				★★**179**★★ **DAYNE, Taylor**		
				Female pop singer born Leslie Wonderman on 7/3/62 in Long Island, New York.		
6/25/88	**2**²	30	●	1 **I'll Always Love You**	3	Arista 9700
12/10/88	**3**	21		2 **Don't Rush Me**	2¹	Arista 9722
11/18/89	**22**	14		3 With Every Beat Of My Heart	5	Arista 9895
1/27/90	**1**⁴	25	●	4 **Love Will Lead You Back**	1¹	Arista 9938
5/26/90	**15**	19		5 I'll Be Your Shelter	4	Arista 2005
8/11/90	**8**	19		6 **Heart Of Stone**	12	Arista 2057
6/5/93	**15**	17		7 Can't Get Enough Of Your Love	20	Arista 12582
				DEAN, Billy ☉		
				Born on 4/2/62 in Quincy, Florida. Country singer. Attended college in Decatur, Mississippi on a basketball scholarship.		
8/17/91	**18**	16		1 Somewhere In My Broken Heart		Capitol/SBK 44757
5/16/92	**48**	4		2 Only The Wind		Capitol/SBK 44803
11/21/92	**39**	9		3 If There Hadn't Been You		SBK/Liberty 57884
				★★**155**★★ **DEAN, Jimmy**		
				Born on 8/10/28 in Plainview, Texas. Country vocalist/pianist/guitarist/composer. With Tennessee Haymakers in Washington, D.C. in 1948. Own Texas Wildcats in 1952. Recorded for Four Star in 1952. Own CBS-TV series, 1957-58; ABC-TV series, 1963-66.		
				1)*Big Bad John* 2)*P.T. 109* 3)*The Cajun Queen*		
10/2/61	**1**¹⁰	16	●	1 **Big Bad John** ....[S]	1⁵	Columbia 42175
1/6/62	**6**	7		2 **Dear Ivan** ....[S]	24	Columbia 42259
				background music: "Battle Hymn Of The Republic"		
1/20/62	**6**	9		3 To A Sleeping Beauty/ [S]	26	
				background music: "Memories"; soliloquy first recorded by Jackie Gleason in 1957		
1/27/62	**4**	8		4 **The Cajun Queen** ....[S]	22	Columbia 42282
3/31/62	**2**²	11		5 **P.T. 109**	8	Columbia 42338
				based on the sinking of John F. Kennedy's torpedo boat in 1943		
6/30/62	**12**	7		6 Steel Men	41	Columbia 42483
9/15/62	**10**	9		7 **Little Black Book**	29	Columbia 42529
6/5/65	**19**	6		8 The First Thing Ev'ry Morning (And The Last Thing Ev'ry Night)	91	Columbia 43263
2/18/67	**13**	11		9 Sweet Misery		RCA 9091
5/22/76	**47**	2	●	10 I.O.U. ....[S]	35	Casino 052
				Jimmy Dean's ode of thanks to his mother		
				DEAN, Peter ☉		
11/16/74	**17**	10		Four Or Five Times		Buddah 434
				DE ANGELIS, Peter ☉		
				Born on 6/18/29 in Philadelphia. Managed Frankie Avalon in the late 1950s.		
11/5/66	**36**	6		Theme From "The Bible" ....[I]		20th Century 6646
				Bernie Leighton (piano); from the film *The Bible*		
				DEARDORFF & JOSEPH ☉		
				Danny Deardorff and Marcus Joseph.		
3/19/77	**22**	9		Never Have To Say Goodbye Again	109	Arista 0230
				★★**131**★★ **DeBARGE/El DeBARGE**		
				Family group from Grand Rapids, Michigan. Consisted of lead vocalist El (b: 6/4/61; keyboards), Mark (trumpet, saxophone), James (keyboards), Randy (bass) and Bunny DeBarge (vocals). Brothers Bobby and Tommy were in Switch. James was briefly married to Janet Jackson in 1984.		
				1)*Who's Holding Donna Now* 2)*All This Love* 3)*Rhythm Of The Night*		
				DeBARGE:		
5/21/83	**1**³	20		1 All This Love	17	Gordy 1660
10/15/83	**12**	19		2 Time Will Reveal	18	Gordy 1705
3/31/84	**21**	9		3 Love Me In A Special Way	45	Gordy 1723
3/2/85	**1**¹	19		4 **Rhythm Of The Night**	3	Gordy 1770
				from the film *The Last Dragon*		
6/1/85	**1**³	19		5 **Who's Holding Donna Now**	6	Gordy 1793
				EL DeBARGE with DeBARGE:		
12/7/85	**17**	12		6 The Heart Is Not So Smart	75	Gordy 1822
				EL DeBARGE:		
5/31/86	**18**	11		7 Who's Johnny	3	Gordy 1842
				theme from the film *Short Circuit*		

DEBUT DATE	PEAK POS	WKS CHR	G O L D	ARTIST — Record Title	POP POS	Label & Number
				DeBARGE/El DeBarge — Cont'd		
8/9/86	**8**	14		**8 Love Always**	43	Gordy 1857
12/13/86	**20**	13		**9** Someone...	70	Gordy 1867
4/4/87	**30**	6		**10** Starlight Express		MCA 53041
				theme song from Andrew Lloyd Webber's *Starlight Express*		
3/31/90	**26**	10	●	**11** The Secret Garden (Sweet Seduction Suite)........................	31	Qwest 19992
				QUINCY JONES/Al B. Sure!/James Ingram/El DeBarge/Barry White		
				DeBURGH, Chris		
				British pop-rock singer. Born Christopher John Davidson on 10/15/48 in Argentina of Irish parentage.		
10/4/86	**2**¹	31		**1 The Lady In Red**..	3	A&M 2848
7/11/87	**20**	11		**2** Fatal Hesitation...		A&M 2942
7/30/88	**36**	4		**3** Love Is My Decision.....................................		A&M 1220
				from the film *Arthur 2: On The Rocks*		
11/19/88	**38**	9		**4** Missing You..		A&M 1254
				DeCARO, Nick		
				Producer of albums for Mac Davis, Helen Reddy, Samantha Sang and others.		
11/30/68	**12**	13		**1** If I Only Had Time .... [I]	95	A&M 1000
3/15/69	**22**	7		**2** Happy Heart .... [I]		A&M 1037
7/13/74	**24**	9		**3** Canned Music .... [I]		Blue Thumb 251
				DEE, Kiki		
				Born Pauline Matthews on 3/6/47 in Yorkshire, England.		
3/20/71	**16**	7		**1** Love Makes The World Go Round	87	Rare Earth 5025
2/21/76	**25**	11		**2** Once A Fool	82	Rocket 40506
7/10/76	**1**¹	13	●	**3 Don't Go Breaking My Heart**	1⁴	Rocket 40585
				ELTON JOHN and KIKI DEE		
				DEELE, The		
				R&B funk sextet from Cincinnati, led by Darnell "Dee" Bristol. Included the songwriting/production team of Mark "L.A. Reid" Rooney and Kenneth "Babyface" Edmonds.		
4/23/88	**21**	14		Two Occasions	10	Solar 70015
				DEFFET, George ☺		
12/2/78	**46**	7		**1** European Nights (Nothin' Fits Me Like You, Babe)/		
4/28/79	**49**	2		**2** Star Crossed Lovers		GRR 103
				DeFRANCO FAMILY featuring TONY DeFRANCO		
				Family group from Ontario: Tony (age 13 in 1973), Merlina (16), Nino (17), Marisa (18) and Benny (19).		
10/13/73	**49**	1	●	Heartbeat - It's A Lovebeat	3	20th Century 2030
				DEL AMITRI		
				Rock quartet from Glasgow, Scotland led by vocalist Justin Currie and guitarist Iain Harvie.		
10/24/92	**42**	4		Always The Last To Know	30	A&M 1604
				DELANEY & BONNIE & FRIENDS		
				Delaney Bramlett (b: 7/1/39, Pontotoc County, Mississippi) and wife Bonnie Lynn Bramlett (b: 11/8/44, Acton, Illinois). Married in 1967. Friends — backing artists included, at various times, Leon Russell Rita Coolidge, Dave Mason, Eric Clapton, Duane Allman and many others. Delaney & Bonnie dissolved their marriage and group in 1972.		
6/12/71	**8**	12		**1 Never Ending Song Of Love**............................	13	Atco 6804
10/23/71	**32**	4		**2** Only You Know And I Know	20	Atco 6838
				DELANEY & BONNIE		
				DELEGATION		
				Soul-disco trio based in England: Jamaicans Ricky Bailey and Ray Patterson, with Texan Bruce Dunbar.		
3/3/79	**34**	10		Oh Honey..	45	Shady Brook 1048
				DELICATO, Paul ☺		
				Pop bassist from St. Louis.		
8/23/75	**7**	10		**1** Ice Cream Sodas And Lollipops And A Red Hot		
				Spinning Top		Art. of Amer. 101
				B-side "Lean On Me" made the Country charts (POS 91)		
11/15/75	**36**	10		**2** Those Were The Days		Art. of Amer. 105
				#2 Pop hit for Mary Hopkin in 1968		
2/7/76	**5**	12		**3** Cara Mia	108	Art. of Amer. 111
				#4 Pop hit for Jay & The Americans in 1965		
7/4/76	**46**	4		**4** I'll Be There		Art. of Amer. 122
				#1 Pop hit for The Jackson 5 in 1970		

DEBUT DATE	PEAK POS	WKS CHR	GOLD	ARTIST — Record Title	POP POS	Label & Number
				DELICATO, Paul — Cont'd		
10/2/76	**36**	10		5 I Take A Lot Of Pride In What I Am		Art. of Amer. 127
				#3 Country hit for Merle Haggard in 1969		
				DeLORY, Al		
				Producer/arranger/conductor for Glen Campbell, The Lettermen and other major artists.		
1/31/70	**33**	2		1 I Wasn't Born To Follow...		Capitol 2699
				theme from the film *Easy Rider*		
5/9/70	**7**	15		2 Song From M∗A∗S∗H ....[I]	70	Capitol 2811
				theme from the film and TV series *M∗A∗S∗H*; song title is actually "Suicide Is Painless"		
				DEL VIKINGS		
				Interracial R&B-rock group formed at the Air Force Serviceman's Club in Pittsburgh in 1955. Consisted of Norman Wright, Corinthian "Kripp" Johnson, Donald "Gus" Backus, David Lerchey and Clarence Quick. Backus and Lerchey are white, others black. Johnson died on 6/22/90 (age 57) of prostate cancer.		
2/10/73	**32**	2		Come Go With Me..[R]	112	Scepter 12367
				new version of The Dell-Vikings *Hot 100* hit on Dot 15538 (POS 4)		
				DENNIS, Cathy		
				Former lead singer of D-Mob. Born in 1970 in Norwich, England.		
4/27/91	**32**	12		1 Touch Me (All Night Long)	2²	Polydor 879466
7/27/91	**1²**	29		2 Too Many Walls	8	Polydor 867134
12/19/92	**6**	20		3 Irresistible...	61	Polydor 861210
5/1/93	**8**	14		4 Moments Of Love		Polydor 859054
				DENNY, Martin, and His Orchestra		
				Born on 4/10/11 in New York City. Composer/arranger/pianist. Originated the "Exotic Sounds of Martin Denny" in Hawaii, featuring Julius Wechter (Baja Marimba Band) on vibes and marimba.		
8/4/62	**13**	11		A Taste Of Honey..[I]	50	Liberty 55470
★★19★★				**DENVER, John**		
				Born John Henry Deutschendorf on 12/31/43 in Roswell, New Mexico. To Los Angeles in 1964. With the Chad Mitchell Trio from 1965-68. Wrote "Leaving On A Jet Plane." Starred in the 1978 film *Oh, God.* Won an Emmy in 1975 for the TV special *An Evening with John Denver.*		
				1)Annie's Song 2)Sunshine On My Shoulders 3)I'm Sorry 4)Fly Away 5)Back Home Again		
4/3/71	**3**	21	●	1 **Take Me Home, Country Roads**	2¹	RCA 0445
				backing vocals by Fat City (Bill Danoff & Taffy Nivert of Starland Vocal Band)		
11/20/71	**4**	12		2 **Friends With You**..	47	RCA 0567
2/26/72	**21**	6		3 Everyday	81	RCA 0647
				written by Buddy Holly		
7/22/72	**23**	9		4 Goodbye Again	88	RCA 0737
11/25/72	**3**	17		5 **Rocky Mountain High**	9	RCA 0829
6/9/73	**25**	8		6 I'd Rather Be A Cowboy	62	RCA 0955
9/8/73	**20**	7		7 Farewell Andromeda (Welcome To My Morning)	89	RCA 0067
2/2/74	**1²**	16	●	8 **Sunshine On My Shoulders**	1¹	RCA 0213
				also the B-side of "I'd Rather Be A Cowboy"		
6/1/74	**1³**	17	●	9 **Annie's Song**	1²	RCA 0295
				written by Denver for his wife Annie Martell (married 1967-83)		
9/21/74	**1²**	13	●	10 **Back Home Again**	5	RCA 10065
12/28/74	**1¹**	14		11 **Sweet Surrender**	13	RCA 10148
3/29/75	**5**	11	●	12 **Thank God I'm A Country Boy**	1¹	RCA 10239
				above 2 recorded live at Universal City Amphitheater, California		
8/16/75	**1²**	13	●	13 **I'm Sorry**	1¹	RCA 10353
12/6/75	**1²**	14		14 **Fly Away**..	13	RCA 10517
				Olivia Newton-John (backing vocal)		
3/6/76	**1¹**	10		15 **Looking For Space**	29	RCA 10586
5/22/76	**9**	7		16 **It Makes Me Giggle**	60	RCA 10687
9/4/76	**1¹**	12		17 **Like A Sad Song**	36	RCA 10774
12/25/76	**13**	11		18 Baby, You Look Good To Me Tonight...............................	65	RCA 10854
4/2/77	**13**	11		19 My Sweet Lady	32	RCA 10911
				also the B-side of "Thank God I'm A Country Boy"		
11/19/77	**2⁴**	15		20 **How Can I Leave You Again**	44	RCA 11036
2/18/78	**9**	11		21 **It Amazes Me**	59	RCA 11214
4/29/78	**10**	9		22 **I Want To Live**	55	RCA 11267
3/31/79	**10**	10		23 What's On Your Mind...	107	RCA 11535
				B-side "Sweet Melinda" made the Country charts		
7/7/79	**31**	8		24 Garden Song		RCA 11637
3/8/80	**20**	10		25 Autograph..	52	RCA 11915

DEBUT DATE	PEAK POS	WKS CHR	G O L D	ARTIST — Record Title	POP POS	Label & Number
				DENVER, John — Cont'd		
6/21/80	43	5		26 Dancing With The Mountains..............................	97	RCA 12017
6/27/81	12	18		27 Some Days Are Diamonds (Some Days Are Stone)	36	RCA 12246
1/16/82	22	7		28 Perhaps Love	59	Columbia 02679
				PLACIDO DOMINGO AND JOHN DENVER		
3/6/82	1[1]	21		29 Shanghai Breezes..	31	RCA 13071
7/24/82	23	12		30 Seasons Of The Heart	78	RCA 13270
7/23/83	26	9		31 Wild Montana Skies		RCA 13562
				JOHN DENVER & EMMYLOU HARRIS		
11/10/84	30	6		32 Love Again..	85	RCA 13931
				JOHN DENVER and SYLVIE VARTAN		
7/27/85	37	6		33 Don't Close Your Eyes, Tonight		RCA 14115
11/30/85	34	9		34 Dreamland Express		RCA 14227
				DEODATO		
				Born Eumir De Almeida Deodato on 6/21/42 in Rio de Janeiro, Brazil. Keyboardist/composer/producer/arranger. Kool & The Gang's producer from 1979-82.		
2/3/73	5	12		1 Also Sprach Zarathustra (2001)..................[I]	2[1]	CTI 12
				theme from the film *2001: A Space Odyssey*; written by classical composer Richard Strauss in 1896		
8/11/73	10	11		2 Rhapsody In Blue ....[I]	41	CTI 16
				the classic George Gershwin tune; a hit for Paul Whiteman in 1924		
6/22/74	18	10		3 Moonlight Serenade ....[I]		MCA 40252
				#3 hit for Glenn Miller in 1939		
7/10/76	27	7		4 Theme From Star Trek ....[I]		MCA 40578
				DeSARIO, Teri		
				Pop singer/songwriter from Miami.		
11/24/79	1[2]	20	●	Yes, I'm Ready	2[2]	Casablanca 2227
				TERI DeSARIO with K.C.		
				DeSHANNON, Jackie		
				Born Sharon Myers on 8/21/44 in Hazel, Kentucky. Vocalist/composer. On radio at age six. First recorded (as Sherry Myers) for Glenn in 1959. To Los Angeles in 1960. Attained prominence as a prolific songwriter (over 600 to date). Co-writer of mega-pop hit "Bette Davis Eyes." Toured with The Beatles for 26 concerts in 1964.		
7/19/69	2[1]	12	●	1 Put A Little Love In Your Heart................	4	Imperial 66385
11/1/69	11	9		2 Love Will Find A Way	40	Imperial 66419
2/28/70	9	7		3 Brighton Hill	82	Imperial 66438
5/20/72	21	8		4 Vanilla Olay/	76	
9/2/72	38	3		5 Only Love Can Break Your Heart....................		Atlantic 2871
				#33 Pop hit for Neil Young in 1970		
9/30/72	33	4		6 Paradise..	110	Atlantic 2895
11/12/77	20	9		7 Don't Let The Flame Burn Out	68	Amherst 725
3/11/78	44	4		8 To Love Somebody....................................		Amherst 728
				#17 Pop hit for the Bee Gees in 1967		
9/9/78	35	9		9 Things We Said Today		Amherst 737
				written by Lennon & McCartney (from The Beatles' album *Something New*)		
				DESMOND, Paul ○		
				Jazz alto saxophonist with Dave Brubeck. Born on 11/25/24 in San Francisco; died on 5/30/77.		
4/26/69	35	4		Ob-La-Di, Ob-La-Da ....[I]		A&M/CTI 1050
				written by Lennon & McCartney (from The Beatles' white album)		
				DeVAUGHN, William		
				R&B vocalist/songwriter/guitarist from Washington, D.C. Worked for the federal government.		
6/15/74	31	6	●	Be Thankful For What You Got	4	Roxbury 0236
				DeVOL, Frank		
				Born on 9/20/11 in Moundsville, West Virginia. Lead alto saxophonist/arranger with Horace Heidt and Alvino Rey. Composer/conductor/arranger for many top singers, radio and TV shows. Received several Academy Award nominations for film scores; composed the TV theme for *My Three Sons*.		
3/2/68	37	2		Theme from Guess Who's Coming To Dinner ....[I]		Colgems 1015
				ORCHESTRA CONDUCTED BY DeVOL		
				DeVORZON, Barry, and Perry Botkin, Jr.		
				Songwriting/producing/arranging duo based in California. Barry was born on 7/31/34 in New York City. Founded Valiant Records (The Cascades were on this label). Leader of Barry & The Tamerlanes. Began prolific songwriting career in the mid-1950s. Perry was born on 4/16/33 in New York City. Son of orchestra leader Perry Botkin, Sr.		
8/28/76	8	18	●	1 Nadia's Theme (The Young And The Restless) ....[I]	8	A&M 1856
				originally written as "Cotton's Dream" for the film *Bless The Beasts & Children*, then used as the theme song for TV's *The Young and The Restless*, and finally as the music for then Romanian olympic gymnast Nadia Comaneci		

DEBUT DATE	PEAK POS	WKS CHR	GOLD	ARTIST — Record Title	POP POS	Label & Number
				DeVORZON, Barry, and Perry Botkin, Jr. — Cont'd		
2/12/77	**24**	7		2 Bless The Beasts And Children ....[I]	82	A&M 1890
				movie title song		
				DEXYS MIDNIGHT RUNNERS		
				Kevin Rowland (b: 8/17/53, Wolverhampton, England), leader of eight-piece Birmingham, England band.		
4/9/83	**31**	9		Come On Eileen...	1¹	Mercury 76189
				DEY, Tracey		
				Also recorded as The Rag Dolls.		
5/23/64	**17**	4		Gonna' Get Along Without You Now	51	Amy 901
				DeYOUNG, Cliff		
				Born on 2/12/46 in Los Angeles. Actor in many films (*Harry & Tonto, Protocol, F/X, Glory* and others) and several made-for-TV movies (*Sunshine,* among them).		
12/15/73	**7**	18		My Sweet Lady...	17	MCA 40156
				written by John Denver; from the TV soundtrack *Sunshine*		
				DeYOUNG, Dennis		
				Lead singer/keyboardist of Styx. Born on 2/18/47 in Chicago.		
9/15/84	**4**	18		1 Desert Moon	10	A&M 2666
3/22/86	**5**	15		2 Call Me	54	A&M 2816
7/5/86	**32**	5		3 This Is The Time	93	A&M 2839
				from the film *The Karate Kid Part II*		
				DIABLOS — see LOS DIABLOS		
	★★**2**★★			**DIAMOND, Neil**		
				Born Noah Kaminsky on 1/24/41 in Brooklyn. Vocalist/guitarist/prolific composer. Worked as songplugger/staff writer in New York City. Wrote for *The Monkees* TV show. First recorded for Duel in 1961. Wrote score for the film *Jonathan Livingston Seagull.* Starred in and composed the music for *The Jazz Singer* in 1980.		
				1)Song Sung Blue 2)Yesterday's Songs 3)Heartlight 4)America 5)If You Know What I Mean		
7/5/69	**3**	15	●	1 Sweet Caroline (Good Times Never Seemed So Good) ...	4	Uni 55136
11/22/69	**5**	10	●	2 Holly Holy	6	Uni 55175
2/21/70	**11**	8		3 Until It's Time For You To Go	53	Uni 55204
3/7/70	**8**	10		4 Shilo	24	Bang 575
5/2/70	**5**	8		5 Soolaimon (African Trilogy II)	30	Uni 55224
7/18/70	**6**	10		6 Solitary Man ....[R]	21	Bang 578
				originally made the *Hot 100* on 5/21/66 on Bang 519 (POS 55)		
8/29/70	**2**¹	12	●	7 Cracklin' Rosie	1¹	Uni 55250
11/14/70	**4**	10		8 He Ain't Heavy...He's My Brother..................................	20	Uni 55264
11/21/70	**25**	6		9 Do It	36	Bang 580
				originally released as the B-side of Bang 519 "Solitary Man"		
3/27/71	**2**²	10		10 I Am...I Said/	4	
5/29/71	**30**	3		11 Done Too Soon	65	Uni 55278
7/31/71	**31**	3		12 I'm A Believer	51	Bang 586
11/13/71	**2**³	12		13 Stones	14	Uni 55310
5/6/72	**1**⁷	14	●	14 Song Sung Blue..	1¹	Uni 55326
8/12/72	**3**	11		15 Play Me	11	Uni 55346
11/11/72	**2**²	12		16 Walk On Water	17	Uni 55352
3/31/73	**19**	7		17 "Cherry Cherry" from Hot August Night ....[R]	31	MCA 40017
				live version of Neil's 1966 Pop hit (from *Hot August Night* LP)		
8/4/73	**41**	3		18 The Long Way Home	91	Bang 703
				originally released in 1967 on Bang 547		
8/25/73	**15**	7		19 The Last Thing On My Mind	56	MCA 40092
10/27/73	**11**	12		20 Be	34	Columbia 45942
3/9/74	**24**	9		21 Skybird	75	Columbia 45998
				above 2 from the film *Jonathan Livingston Seagull*		
10/12/74	**1**¹	13		22 Longfellow Serenade	5	Columbia 10043
2/1/75	**1**¹	11		23 I've Been This Way Before	34	Columbia 10084
5/24/75	**7**	11	✓	24 The Last Picasso		Columbia 10138
6/19/76	**1**²	13		25 If You Know What I Mean	11	Columbia 10366
9/18/76	**4**	13		26 Don't Think...Feel	43	Columbia 10405
12/11/76	**8**	11	✓	27 Beautiful Noise		Columbia 10452
12/3/77	**1**¹	18		28 Desiree	16	Columbia 10657
10/28/78	**3**	18	●	29 You Don't Bring Me Flowers	1²	Columbia 10840
				BARBRA & NEIL		
1/27/79	**2**²	16		30 Forever In Blue Jeans...	20	Columbia 10897

DEBUT DATE	PEAK POS	WKS CHR	GOLD	ARTIST — Record Title	POP POS	Label & Number
				DIAMOND, Neil — Cont'd		
5/19/79	**3**	12		31 **Say Maybe**	55	Columbia 10945
12/22/79	**2**[1]	16		32 **September Morn'**	17	Columbia 11175
4/5/80	**23**	7		33 **The Good Lord Loves You**	67	Columbia 11232
11/1/80	**3**	19		34 **Love On The Rocks**	**2**[3]	Capitol 4939
1/31/81	**3**	15		35 **Hello Again**	6	Capitol 4960
5/2/81	**1**[3]	18		36 **America**	8	Capitol 4994
				above 3 from the film *The Jazz Singer* starring Diamond		
11/7/81	**1**[6]	18		37 **Yesterday's Songs**	11	Columbia 02604
2/13/82	**4**	19		38 **On The Way To The Sky**	27	Columbia 02712
5/22/82	**2**[3]	17		39 **Be Mine Tonight**	35	Columbia 02928
9/11/82	**1**[4]	21		40 **Heartlight**	5	Columbia 03219
				inspired by the film *E.T.*		
1/15/83	**4**	17		41 **I'm Alive**	35	Columbia 03503
4/23/83	**5**	16		42 **Front Page Story**	65	Columbia 03801
8/4/84	**4**	14		43 **Turn Around**	62	Columbia 04541
10/27/84	**24**	10	✓	44 Sleep With Me Tonight		Columbia 04646
1/5/85	**28**	2		45 You Make It Feel Like Christmas ....[X]		Columbia 04719
5/10/86	**10**	14		46 **Headed For The Future**	53	Columbia 05889
8/9/86	**11**	13		47 The Story Of My Life		Columbia 06136
10/17/87	**13**	15		48 I Dreamed A Dream..........................		Columbia 07614
1/7/89	**9**	17		49 **This Time**		Columbia 08514
4/29/89	**7**	14		50 **The Best Years Of Our Lives**		Columbia 68741
8/19/89	**28**	6		51 Baby Can I Hold You		Columbia LP Cut
				written by Tracy Chapman; above 3 from the album *The Best Years of Our Lives* on Columbia 45025		
9/7/91	**14**	12		52 If There Were No Dreams......................		Columbia LP Cut
12/7/91	**19**	16		53 Don't Turn Around		Columbia LP Cut
4/4/92	**23**	13		54 Hooked On The Memory Of You..............		Columbia LP Cut
				NEIL DIAMOND with Kim Carnes		
				above 3 from the album *Lovescape* on Columbia 48610		
				DIBANGO, Manu		
				Jazz-R&B saxophonist/pianist. Born in 1934 in Cameroon, Africa.		
6/30/73	**29**	4		Soul Makossa ....[I]	35	Atlantic 2971
				DICK AND DEEDEE		
				Dick St. John Gosting and Deedee Sperling. Formed duo while students in high school at Santa Monica.		
3/30/63	**6**	9		1 Young And In Love.............................	17	Warner 5342
11/30/63	**15**	7		2 Turn Around	27	Warner 5396
				DICKENS, "Little" Jimmy		
				Born on 12/19/20 in Bolt, West Virginia. Country singer who stands only 4'11" tall.		
11/6/65	**8**	8		**May The Bird Of Paradise Fly Up Your Nose**.............[N]	15	Columbia 43388
				DIGGS, Joey — see KOZ, Dave		
				DILLMAN BAND, The		
				Country-rock quintet led by Steve Solmonson and Steve Seamans.		
5/23/81	**36**	7		Lovin' The Night Away	45	RCA 12206
				DION		
				Born Dion DiMucci on 7/18/39 in the Bronx. First recorded as Dion & The Timberlanes on Mohawk in 1957. Formed vocal group, Dion & The Belmonts, in the Bronx in 1958. Dion went solo in 1960. Moved to Miami in 1968. Brief reunion with the Belmonts in 1967 and 1972, periodically since then. Also records contemporary Christian songs. Inducted into the Rock and Roll Hall of Fame in 1989.		
7/13/63	**13**	6		1 Be Careful Of Stones That You Throw	31	Columbia 42810
11/23/68	**8**	10	●	2 Abraham, Martin And John....................	4	Laurie 3464
				a tribute to Lincoln, King and Kennedy		
8/5/89	**16**	10		3 And The Night Stood Still	75	Arista 9797
				Dave Edmunds, Patty Smyth and Mark Lennon (backing vocals)		
7/21/90	**28**	8		4 Sea Cruise		Elektra LP Cut
				from *The Adventures Of Ford Fairlane* soundtrack on Elektra 60952; #14 Pop hit for Frankie Ford in 1959		

DEBUT DATE	PEAK POS	WKS CHR	GOLD	ARTIST — Record Title	POP POS	Label & Number
★★119★★				**DION, Celine**		
				Born on 3/30/68 in Charlemagne, Quebec. Popular singer in France and Canada since her teen years. Youngest of 14 children.		
				1)If You Asked Me To 2)Nothing Broken But My Heart 3)Where Does My Heart Beat Now		
10/27/90	2¹	33		1 Where Does My Heart Beat Now	4	Epic 73536
3/30/91	8	20		2 (If There Was) Any Other Way..	35	Epic 73665
7/13/91	22	12		3 The Last To Know		Epic 73856
11/16/91	3	34	●	4 Beauty And The Beast	9	Epic 74090
				CELINE DION and PEABO BRYSON movie title song		
4/18/92	1³	33		5 If You Asked Me To..	4	Epic 74277
8/1/92	1¹	27		6 Nothing Broken But My Heart	29	Epic 74336
11/21/92	8	23		7 Love Can Move Mountains	36	Epic 74337
3/20/93	11	20		8 Water From The Moon		Epic 74809
7/3/93	6	13↑		9 When I Fall In Love	23	Epic 77021
				CELINE DION & CLIVE GRIFFIN from the film *Sleepless In Seattle*		
				DIRE STRAITS		
				Rock group formed in London by songwriter/producer Mark Knopfler (lead vocals, lead guitar) and his brother David (guitar), with John Illsley (bass) and Pick Withers (drums). David left in mid-1980, replaced by Hal Lindes (left in 1985). Added keyboardist Alan Clark in 1982. Terry Williams replaced drummer Pick Withers in 1983. Guitarist Guy Fletcher added in 1984.		
3/24/79	46	5		1 Sultans Of Swing	4	Warner 8736
11/23/85	4	17		2 Walk Of Life	7	Warner 28878
3/15/86	3	13		3 So Far Away	19	Warner 28789
				DIRKSEN, Senator Everett McKinley		
				U.S. senator from Illinois, 1950-69. Born in Pekin, Illinois in 1896; died on 9/7/69 (age 73).		
12/17/66	4	9		Gallant Men ....[S]	29	Capitol 5805
				John Cacavas (orch.)		
				DISTANT GALAXY, The ☉		
				Studio group led by Moog synthesizer player Don Sebesky.		
7/13/68	39	2		Elvira Madigan Theme/Honey ....[I]		Verve 10603
				"Elvira" is from a Mozart Piano Concerto; "Honey" was a #1 Pop hit for Bobby Goldsboro in 1968		
				DR. BUZZARD'S ORIGINAL "SAVANNAH" BAND		
				New York City 1930s-styled disco group formed by brothers Stony Browder and August Darnell (real name: Thomas August Darnell Browder), with Cory Daye, lead singer. Darnell left in 1980 to form Kid Creole & The Coconuts.		
12/11/76	22	13		Whispering/Cherchez La Femme/Se Si Bon	27	RCA 10827
★★173★★				**DR. HOOK**		
				Group formed in New Jersey in 1968. Fronted by vocalists/guitarists Ray Sawyer (dubbed "Dr. Hook" because of eye patch; b: 2/1/37) and Dennis Locorriere (b: 6/13/49). Appeared in and performed the music for the film *Who Is Harry Kellerman And Why Is He Saying Those Terrible Things About Me?*.		
				1)Better Love Next Time 2)When You're In Love With A Beautiful Woman 3)Sexy Eyes		
1/17/76	14	13	●	1 Only Sixteen	6	Capitol 4171
7/4/76	15	12		2 A Little Bit More	11	Capitol 4280
				B-side "A Couple More Years" made the Country charts (POS 51)		
12/18/76	21	9		3 If Not You...	55	Capitol 4364
7/16/77	39	5		4 Walk Right In...	46	Capitol 4423
9/30/78	18	19	●	5 Sharing The Night Together	6	Capitol 4621
3/3/79	41	4		6 All The Time In The World	54	Capitol 4677
4/28/79	5	22	●	7 When You're In Love With A Beautiful Woman	6	Capitol 4705
10/20/79	3	15		8 Better Love Next Time	12	Capitol 4785
2/23/80	6	17	●	9 Sexy Eyes	5	Capitol 4831
7/5/80	17	13		10 Years From Now	51	Capitol 4885
6/19/82	19	12		11 Loveline	60	Casablanca 2351
				DOHERTY, Denny ☉		
				Born on 11/29/41 in Halifax, Canada. Member of The Mamas & The Papas.		
5/25/74	13	12		You'll Never Know		Paramount 0286
				#1 hit for Dick Haymes in 1943		

DEBUT DATE	PEAK POS	WKS CHR	GOLD	ARTIST — Record Title	POP POS	Label & Number
				DOMINGO, Placido		
				Born on 1/21/41 in Madrid. One of the world's leading operatic tenors. Emigrated to Mexico in 1950. Debuted at the New York Metropolitan Opera in 1968.		
1/16/82	**22**	7		Perhaps Love..	59	Columbia 02679
				PLACIDO DOMINGO AND JOHN DENVER		
				DONALDSON, Bo, And The Heywoods		
				Cincinnati septet led by keyboardist Bo Donaldson (b: 6/13/54) and lead vocalist Michael Gibbons.		
5/18/74	**20**	9	●	1 Billy, Don't Be A Hero..	1²	ABC 11435
8/17/74	**19**	8		2 Who Do You Think You Are	15	ABC 12006
				DONNER, Ral		
				Born on 2/10/43 in Chicago; died of cancer on 4/6/84. Narrator for the film *This Is Elvis*.		
3/24/62	**18**	3		(What A Sad Way) To Love Someone........................	74	Gone 5125
				DONOVAN		
				Born Donovan Phillip Leitch on 5/10/46 near Glasgow, Scotland. Singer/songwriter/guitarist. Father of actress Ione Skye (*Say Anything*) and actor Donovan Leitch, Jr.		
5/15/65	**15**	3		Catch The Wind	23	Hickory 1309
				DOOBIE BROTHERS, The		
				Rock/R&B-styled group formed in San Jose, California in 1970: Pat Simmons (vocals, guitar), Tom Johnston (lead vocals, guitar, keyboards), John Hartman (percussion) and Dave Shogren (bass). First recorded for Warner in 1971. Shogren replaced by Tiran Porter (bass). Mike Hossack (percussion) added in 1972 (later replaced by Keith Knudsen). Jeff "Skunk" Baxter (slide guitar), formerly with Steely Dan, added in 1974. Michael McDonald (lead vocals, keyboards), added in 1975. Johnston left, 1978. Baxter, Hartman replaced by Cornelius Bumpus (keyboards, saxophone), John McFee (guitar) and Chet McCracken (drums) in 1979. Disbanded in 1983. Re-formed in early 1988 with Johnston, Simmons, Hartman, Porter, Hossack, and Bobby LaKind (percussion; d: 12/24/92 of cancer).		
2/22/75	**38**	7	●	1 Black Water..	1¹	Warner 8062
2/17/79	**22**	13	●	2 What A Fool Believes	1¹	Warner 8725
5/19/79	**13**	11		3 Minute By Minute	14	Warner 8828
9/22/79	**37**	7		4 Dependin' On You	25	Warner 49029
9/6/80	**10**	20		5 Real Love	5	Warner 49503
12/13/80	**21**	9		6 One Step Closer	24	Warner 49622
1/31/81	**31**	7		7 Wynken, Blynken And Nod	76	Sesame St. 49642
				from the various artists' album *In Harmony*		
6/17/89	**31**	12		8 The Doctor	9	Capitol 44376
9/16/89	**27**	6		9 Need A Little Taste Of Love	45	Capitol 44441
				DOODLETOWN PIPERS, The ❂		
				Nine-member folk group.		
8/12/67	**29**	5		A Summer Song		Epic 10200
				#7 Pop hit for Chad & Jeremy in 1964		
				DOORS, The		
				Rock group formed in Los Angeles in 1965. Consisted of Jim Morrison (b: 12/8/43, Melbourne, Florida; d: 7/3/71, Paris; lead singer), Ray Manzarek (keyboards), Robby Krieger (guitar) and John Densmore (drums). Group inducted into the Rock and Roll Hall of Fame in 1993.		
5/22/71	**29**	4		1 Love Her Madly	11	Elektra 45726
7/10/71	**11**	10		2 Riders On The Storm	14	Elektra 45738
				DORE, Charlie		
				British female vocalist.		
3/1/80	**4**	13		Pilot Of The Airwaves	13	Island 49166
				DORFF, Steve — see SPRINGFIELD, Dusty, and/or THOMAS, B.J.		
				DOUBLE		
				Swiss pop duo (pronounced: doo-BLAY) of Kurt Maloo and Felix Haug. Both were in jazz trio Ping Pong.		
6/14/86	**4**	20		1 The Captain Of Her Heart...............................	16	A&M 2838
10/11/86	**37**	3		2 Woman Of The World		A&M 2869
				DOUGLAS, Carol		
				Born on 4/7/48 in Brooklyn. Worked on commercials. Member of The Chantels vocal group in the early '70s.		
1/25/75	**42**	6		Doctor's Orders..	11	Midland I. 10113
				DOUGLAS, Mike		
				Born Michael Dowd, Jr. in Chicago on 8/11/25. Longtime syndicated TV talkshow host (1961-80). Singer with Kay Kyser's band, 1945-50 (vocalist on Kyser's #1 hit "Ole Buttermilk Sky" in 1946).		
12/25/65	**3**	11		1 The Men In My Little Girl's Life	6	Epic 9876
10/29/66	**25**	7		2 Cabaret..	129	Epic 10078
				Broadway show title song		

DEBUT DATE	PEAK POS	WKS CHR	GOLD	ARTIST — Record Title	POP POS	Label & Number
				DOUGLAS, Mike — Cont'd		
4/16/77	**49**	2		3 Sleep Well My Son..[S]		Image 3031
★★198★★				**DOVE, Ronnie**		
				Born on 9/7/40 in Herndon, Virginia. Discovered while singing in Baltimore. Nearly all of Ronnie's hits were produced by Phil Kahl (vice president of Diamond Records).		
				1)I'll Make All Your Dreams Come True 2)A Little Bit Of Heaven 3)Kiss Away		
6/12/65	**4**	10		1 A Little Bit Of Heaven	16	Diamond 184
8/28/65	**2**[1]	10		2 I'll Make All Your Dreams Come True	21	Diamond 188
10/30/65	**5**	10		3 Kiss Away	25	Diamond 191
1/22/66	**6**	10		4 When Liking Turns To Loving..................................	18	Diamond 195
5/14/66	**34**	4		5 Let's Start All Over Again	20	Diamond 198
6/18/66	**7**	10		6 Happy Summer Days	27	Diamond 205
9/3/66	**12**	8		7 I Really Don't Want To Know.................................	22	Diamond 208
12/17/66	**16**	6		8 Cry	18	Diamond 214
3/16/68	**37**	5		9 In Some Time	99	Diamond 240
9/14/68	**27**	5		10 Tomboy	96	Diamond 249
				DOWELL, Joe		
				Born on 1/23/40 in Bloomington, Indiana. Signed to Mercury's Smash label by Shelby Singleton, Jr.		
7/17/61	**1**[3]	13		1 Wooden Heart..	**1**[1]	Smash 1708
				based on the German folk song "Muss I Denn"; originally sung by Elvis Presley in the film *G.I. Blues*		
10/23/61	**10**	6		2 The Bridge Of Love	50	Smash 1717
				DRAKE, Pete, And His Talking Steel Guitar		
				Pete was born on 10/8/32 in Atlanta; died on 7/29/88. Was Nashville's top steel guitar sessionman.		
3/28/64	**5**	8		Forever	25	Smash 1867
				DRAPER, Rusty		
				Born Farrell H. Draper in Kirksville, Missouri. Began career at the age of 12, singing and playing guitar over the radio in Tulsa, Oklahoma.		
9/11/61	**20**	2		1 Signed, Sealed And Delivered	91	Mercury 71854
10/12/63	**17**	5		2 Night Life	57	Monument 823
				written by Willie Nelson		
				DREAM ACADEMY, The		
				English pop-rock trio: Nick Laird-Clowes (guitar, vocals), Gilbert Gabriel (keyboards) and Kate St. John (vocals).		
12/21/85	**2**[1]	17		1 Life In A Northern Town	7	Warner 28841
5/3/86	**13**	13		2 The Love Parade	36	Reprise 28750
				DRIFTERS, The		
				Vocal group featuring lead singers Rudy Lewis (1961-63) and Johnny Moore (1964-66). Rudy died of a heart attack in the summer of 1964. Many personnel changes throughout career and several groups have used the name in later years. Inducted into the Rock and Roll Hall of Fame in 1988.		
5/12/62	**19**	1		1 Stranger On The Shore	73	Atlantic 2143
4/23/66	**29**	3		2 Memories Are Made Of This..................................	48	Atlantic 2325
				DRUPI		
				Pop singer born in Pavia, Italy.		
9/15/73	**25**	8		Vado Via ....[F]	88	A&M 1460
				DUDLEY, Dave		
				Born David Pedruska on 5/3/28 in Spencer, Wisconsin. Country singer/guitarist/songwriter.		
6/22/63	**13**	9		Six Days On The Road..	32	Golden Wing 3020
				DUKE, George — see CLARKE, Stanley		
				DULFER, Candy — see STEWART, David A.		
				DUNDAS, David		
				Oxford, England-born singer/actor/commercial jingle writer.		
11/27/76	**37**	4		Jeans On..	17	Chrysalis 2094
				originally a jingle in England for Brutus Jeans		
				DUPREE, Robbie		
				Singer/songwriter. Born Robert Dupuis in Brooklyn in 1947.		
5/3/80	**5**	18		1 Steal Away	6	Elektra 46621
8/9/80	**24**	11		2 Hot Rod Hearts	15	Elektra 47005

DEBUT DATE	PEAK POS	WKS CHR	GOLD	ARTIST — Record Title	POP POS	Label & Number
				DUPREES, The		
				Italian-American vocal quintet from Jersey City: Joseph ("Joey Vann") Canzano (lead singer), Mike Arnone, Tom Bialablow, John Salvato and Joe Santollo. Joey Vann died on 2/28/84 (age 40).		
11/24/62	**2**[1]	5		1 My Own True Love	13	Coed 571
				Tara's Theme from *Gone With The Wind*		
9/21/63	**10**	3		2 Why Don't You Believe Me	37	Coed 584
11/30/63	**8**	5		3 Have You Heard..	18	Coed 585
				DURAN DURAN		
				Pop group formed in Birmingham, England in 1980. 1993 lineup: Simon LeBon (vocals), Nick Rhodes (keyboards), John Taylor (bass) and Warren Cuccurullo (guitar).		
1/23/93	**14**	19	●	1 Ordinary World	3	Capitol 44908
6/5/93	**19**	17↑		2 Come Undone..	7	Capitol 44918
				DURANTE, Jimmy		
				Born on 2/10/1893 in New York City; died on 1/29/80. Much-beloved comedian who started on vaudeville and became star of many Broadway shows and movies as well as his own TV show (1954-56).		
10/5/63	**13**	4		1 September Song..	51	Warner 5382
				song first popularized in 1939 by actor Walter Huston		
2/5/66	**26**	4		2 One Of Those Songs	135	Warner 5686
				with the Girls From The Folies Bergere		
11/30/68	**30**	3		3 Dear World		Warner 7241
				MAURICE CHEVALIER & JIMMY DURANTE		
				Broadway musical title song		
				DYLAN, Bob		
				Born Robert Allen Zimmerman on 5/24/41 in Duluth, Minnesota. Singer/songwriter/guitarist/harmonica player. Took stage name from poet Dylan Thomas. To New York City in December 1960. Worked Greenwich Village folk clubs. Signed to Columbia Records in October 1961. Innovator of folk-rock style. Motorcycle crash on 7/29/66 led to short retirement. Films *Don't Look Back* (1965), *Eat The Document* (1969) and *Pat Garrett And Billy The Kid* (1973). Made film *Renaldo And Clara* (1978). Member of the supergroup Traveling Wilburys. Inducted into the Rock and Roll Hall of Fame in 1988. Won Grammy's Lifetime Achievement Award in 1991.		
4/10/65	**6**	7		1 Subterranean Homesick Blues	39	Columbia 43242
8/23/69	**19**	7		2 Lay Lady Lay	7	Columbia 44926
8/8/70	**13**	6		3 Wigwam .... [I]	41	Columbia 45199
9/8/73	**5**	15		4 Knockin' On Heaven's Door	12	Columbia 45913
				DYSON, Ronnie		
				Soul singer. Born on 6/5/50 in Washington, D.C. and raised in Brooklyn. Leading role in the Broadway musical *Hair*. In the film *Putney Swope*. Died on 11/10/90 of heart failure complicated by chronic lung disease.		
3/17/73	**16**	8		1 One Man Band (Plays All Alone)	28	Columbia 45776
6/30/73	**30**	9		2 Just Don't Want To Be Lonely	60	Columbia 45867

E

★★121★★				**EAGLES**		
				Rock group formed in Los Angeles in 1971. Consisted of Glenn Frey (vocals, guitar), Bernie Leadon (guitar), Randy Meisner (bass) and Don Henley (drums). Meisner founded Poco; Leadon had been in the Flying Burrito Brothers; and Frey and Henley were with Linda Ronstadt. Debut album recorded in England in 1972. Don Felder (guitar) added in 1975. Leadon replaced by Joe Walsh in 1975. Meisner replaced by Timothy B. Schmit in 1977. Frey and Henley were the only members to play on all recordings. Disbanded in 1982.		
				1)Best Of My Love 2)New Kid In Town 3)Lyin' Eyes		
6/17/72	**12**	8		1 Take It Easy	12	Asylum 11005
1/20/73	**20**	9		2 Peaceful Easy Feeling	22	Asylum 11013
6/30/73	**26**	6		3 Tequila Sunrise	64	Asylum 11017
12/14/74	**1**[1]	17		4 Best Of My Love	**1**[1]	Asylum 45218
7/12/75	**20**	8		5 One Of These Nights	**1**[1]	Asylum 45257
9/27/75	**3**	12		6 Lyin' Eyes	**2**[2]	Asylum 45279
1/10/76	**4**	11		7 Take It To The Limit	4	Asylum 45293
12/25/76	**2**[3]	16	●	8 New Kid In Town	**1**[1]	Asylum 45373
3/12/77	**10**	16	●	9 Hotel California	**1**[1]	Asylum 45386
10/27/79	**38**	5	●	10 Heartache Tonight	**1**[1]	Asylum 46545
12/15/79	**34**	9		11 The Long Run	8	Asylum 46569
2/23/80	**3**	19		12 I Can't Tell You Why	8	Asylum 46608
1/17/81	**17**	10		13 Seven Bridges Road	21	Asylum 47100

DEBUT DATE	PEAK POS	WKS CHR	G O L D	ARTIST — Record Title	POP POS	Label & Number
				EARL, Stacy		
				Born on 12/28/62 in Boston.		
7/11/92	**32**	6		Slowly	52	RCA 62271
				EARTH, WIND & FIRE		
				Los Angeles-based R&B group formed by Chicago-bred producer/songwriter/vocalist/percussionist/kalimba player Maurice White. In 1969, White, former session drummer for Chess Records and member of The Ramsey Lewis Trio, formed the Salty Peppers; recorded for Capitol. Maurice's brother Verdine White was the group's bassist. Eighteen months later, the brothers hired a new band and recorded as Earth, Wind & Fire — named for the three elements of Maurice's astrological sign. Co-lead singer Philip Bailey joined as lead singer in 1971. Group generally contained eight to 10 members, with frequent personnel shuffling.		
9/1/73	**19**	5		1 Evil..	50	Columbia 45888
8/5/78	**30**	11	●	2 Got To Get You Into My Life	9	Columbia 10796
1/20/79	**41**	3	●	3 September	8	ARC 10854
7/14/79	**3**	21	●	4 After The Love Has Gone	2²	ARC 11033
12/13/80	**30**	9		5 You..	48	ARC 11407
2/18/84	**36**	4		6 Touch...	103	Columbia 04329
				EAST L.A. CAR POOL		
				Latin-disco group led by conga player Jack J. Gold.		
8/2/75	**10**	10		Like They Say In L.A.	72	GRC 2064
★★118★★				**EASTON, Sheena**		
				Born on 4/27/59 in Glasgow, Scotland. Real last name is Orr. Vocalist/actress. Portrayed a singer in the 1980 BBC-TV documentary *The Big Time*. Won the 1981 Best New Artist Grammy Award. Portrayed Sonny Crockett's wife in five episodes of TV's *Miami Vice*.		
				1)Morning Train (Nine To Five) 2)We've Got Tonight 3)Almost Over You		
2/21/81	**1²**	18	●	1 Morning Train (Nine To Five)	1²	EMI America 8071
6/6/81	**13**	13		2 Modern Girl	18	EMI America 8080
7/25/81	**6**	22		3 For Your Eyes Only	4	Liberty 1418
				movie title song		
12/12/81	**6**	20		4 You Could Have Been With Me.......................	15	EMI America 8101
4/10/82	**13**	18		5 When He Shines	30	EMI America 8113
10/30/82	**19**	12		6 I Wouldn't Beg For Water	64	EMI America 8142
1/29/83	**2⁵**	18		7 We've Got Tonight	6	Liberty 1492
				KENNY ROGERS and SHEENA EASTON		
9/10/83	**15**	14		8 Telefone (Long Distance Love Affair)	9	EMI America 8172
12/10/83	**4**	26		9 Almost Over You...	25	EMI America 8186
12/7/85	**39**	2		10 Do It For Love	29	EMI America 8295
8/23/86	**35**	5		11 So Far So Good..	43	EMI America 8332
				from the film *About Last Night*		
3/4/89	**43**	7		12 The Lover In Me...	2¹	MCA 53416
10/28/89	**21**	13		13 The Arms Of Orion	36	Warner 22757
				PRINCE with Sheena Easton		
				from the film *Batman*		
				EASTWOOD, Clint — see SHEPPARD, T.G.		
				EDDIE & DUTCH		
4/4/70	**24**	6		My Wife, The Dancer ....[N]	52	Ivanhoe 502
				EDDY, Duane		
				Born on 4/26/38 in Corning, New York. Duane originated the "twangy" guitar sound and is the all-time #1 rock and roll instrumentalist. Currently resides in the Nashville area.		
1/24/70	**24**	5		Freight Train..[I]	110	Congress 6010
				#6 Pop hit for Rusty Draper in 1957		
				EDELMAN, Randy		
				Singer/songwriter/pianist. Composed Barry Manilow's hit "Weekend In New England."		
2/22/75	**18**	9		1 Everybody Wants To Find A Bluebird................	92	20th Century 2155
3/6/76	**11**	10		2 Concrete And Clay	108	20th Century 2274
				#28 Pop hit for Unit Four plus Two in 1965		
				EDER, Linda ✪		
				Born in Brainerd, Minnesota to a Viennese father and a Norwegian mother. Seven-time winner on TV's *Star Search*. Made Broadway debut in *Jekyll & Hyde* in 1992. Eder rhymes with cheddar.		
8/22/92	**34**	8		You Are My Home		Angel LP Cut
				LINDA EDER & PEABO BRYSON		
				from the album *The Scarlet Pimpernel* on Angel 54397		

DEBUT DATE	PEAK POS	WKS CHR	GOLD	ARTIST — Record Title	POP POS	Label & Number
				EDISON LIGHTHOUSE		
				British studio group featuring lead singer Tony Burrows (also of The Brotherhood Of Man, First Class, The Pipkins and White Plains).		
3/14/70	20	4	●	Love Grows (Where My Rosemary Goes)	5	Bell 858
				EDWARD BEAR		
				Pop trio from Toronto — Larry Evoy, lead singer. Took name from a character in *Winnie The Pooh*.		
6/20/70	38	2		1 You, Me And Mexico	68	Capitol 2801
1/13/73	1²	12	●	2 **Last Song**	3	Capitol 3452
4/28/73	11	9		3 Close Your Eyes	37	Capitol 3581
				EDWARDS, Jonathan		
				Born on 7/28/46 in Minnesota. Formed bluegrass band Sugar Creek in 1965.		
12/11/71	7	11	●	**Sunshine**...	4	Capricorn 8021
				EDWARDS, Mark ○		
				Singer from the Detroit area. President of R&A Records.		
10/27/90	43	4		Just Having Touched..		R&A 10521
				EDWARDS, Vincent		
				Born Vincento Eduardo Zoine on 7/9/28 in New York City. Stage, film and TV actor. Best known as star of the TV series *Ben Casey*.		
6/12/65	39	1		No, Not Much	108	Colpix 771
				#2 Pop hit for The Four Lads in 1956		
				EGAN, Walter		
				Born on 7/12/48 in Jamaica, New York.		
8/12/78	18	8	●	Magnet And Steel	8	Columbia 10719
				ELBOW BONES & THE RACKETEERS ○		
				R&B group led by Ginchy Dan and Stephanie Fuller. Formed by August "Kid Creole" Darnell.		
3/17/84	34	10		A Night In New York..		EMI America 8184
				EL CHICANO		
				Mexican-American band formed in Los Angeles as the VIP's in 1965, featuring Jerry Salas (lead vocals).		
4/18/70	10	9		1 **Viva Tirado - Part I** ....[I]	28	Kapp 2085
				first released on Gordo 703 in 1970		
8/18/73	22	15		2 Tell Her She's Lovely	40	MCA 40104
				ELECTRIC INDIAN, The		
				Instrumental group assembled from top Philadelphia studio musicians. Some members later joined MFSB.		
8/16/69	6	11		1 **Keem-O-Sabe** ....[I]	16	United Art. 50563
				first released on Marmaduke 4001 in 1969		
12/20/69	30	3		2 Land Of 1000 Dances......................................[I]	95	United Art. 50613
				ELECTRIC LIGHT ORCHESTRA		
				Orchestral rock band formed in Birmingham, England in 1971, by Roy Wood, Bev Bevan and Jeff Lynne of The Move. Wood left after their first album, leaving Lynne as the group's leader. Much personnel shuffling from then on. From a group size of eight in 1971, the 1986 ELO consisted of three members: Lynne (vocals, guitar, keyboards), Bevan (drums) and Richard Tandy (keyboards, guitar). Bevan also recorded with Black Sabbath in 1987. Lynne is a member of the supergroup Traveling Wilburys.		
				1)*Xanadu* 2) *Calling America* 3)*Strange Magic*		
3/27/76	24	9		1 Strange Magic	14	United Art. 770
1/22/77	36	3		2 Livin' Thing	13	United Art. 888
6/30/79	40	7		3 Shine A Little Love	8	Jet 5057
11/10/79	41	3		4 Confusion	37	Jet 5064
6/28/80	48	2	●	5 I'm Alive...	16	MCA 41246
8/23/80	2²	22		6 Xanadu...	8	MCA 41285
				OLIVIA NEWTON-JOHN/ELECTRIC LIGHT ORCHESTRA		
10/11/80	46	3		7 All Over The World..	13	MCA 41289
				above 3 from the film *Xanadu*		
7/23/83	36	7		8 Rock 'N' Roll Is King *	19	Jet 03964
12/10/83	33	9		9 Stranger *	105	Jet 04208
				*ELO		
3/1/86	20	9		10 Calling America..	18	CBS Assoc. 05766
				ELGART, Larry, And His Manhattan Swing Orchestra		
				Larry was born on 3/20/22 in New London, Connecticut. Alto saxman in brother Les' band and his own band.		
6/19/82	20	12		Hooked On Swing ....[I]	31	RCA 13219
				In The Mood/Cherokee/American Patrol/Sing, Sing, Sing/Don't Be That Way/Little Brown Jug/Opus #1/Zing Went The Strings Of My Heart/String Of Pearls		

DEBUT DATE	PEAK POS	WKS CHR	G O L D	ARTIST — Record Title	POP POS	Label & Number
				ELLIMAN, Yvonne		
				Born on 12/29/51 in Honolulu. Portrayed Mary Magdalene on the concept LP and in the rock opera and film *Jesus Christ Superstar*. Joined with Eric Clapton during his 1974 comeback tour.		
				1)Hello Stranger 2)Love Me 3)If I Can't Have You		
5/8/71	**15**	6		1 I Don't Know How To Love Him	28	Decca 32785
10/9/71	**25**	4		2 Everything's Alright	92	Decca 32870
				above 2 from the rock opera *Jesus Christ Superstar*		
10/2/76	**5**	21		3 Love Me	14	RSO 858
3/26/77	**1**⁴	16		4 Hello Stranger	15	RSO 871
7/30/77	**19**	11	✓	5 I Can't Get You Outa My Mind		RSO 877
1/28/78	**9**	20	●	6 If I Can't Have You	**1**¹	RSO 884
				from the film *Saturday Night Fever*		
1/20/79	**32**	4		7 Moment By Moment	59	RSO 915
				movie title song starring John Travolta		
11/10/79	**33**	5		8 Love Pains	34	RSO 1007
				ELLIS, Ray		
				Born on 7/28/23 in Philadelphia. Saxophonist/conductor/arranger/producer.		
7/17/61	**18**	3		La Dolce Vita (The Sweet Life) ....[I]	81	RCA 7888
				from the film *La Dolce Vita* starring Marcello Mastroianni		
				EMMERSON, Les		
				Lead singer/guitarist of Five Man Electrical Band.		
2/3/73	**26**	6		Control Of Me	51	Lion 141
★★122★★				**ENGLAND DAN & JOHN FORD COLEY**		
				Pop duo from Austin, Texas: Dan Seals (b: 2/8/48) and Coley (b: 10/13/48). In the late '60s, both were members of Southwest F.O.B. Dan, the brother of Jim Seals of Seals & Crofts, charted solo pop hits and is currently a top country artist.		
				1)We'll Never Have To Say Goodbye Again 2)It's Sad To Belong 3)Love Is The Answer		
6/12/76	**1**¹	16	●	1 I'd Really Love To See You Tonight	**2**²	Big Tree 16069
10/16/76	**6**	17		2 Nights Are Forever Without You	10	Big Tree 16079
5/21/77	**1**⁵	17		3 It's Sad To Belong	21	Big Tree 16088
10/15/77	**8**	15		4 Gone Too Far	23	Big Tree 16102
3/4/78	**1**⁶	14		5 We'll Never Have To Say Goodbye Again	9	Big Tree 16110
6/10/78	**22**	8		6 You Can't Dance	49	Big Tree 16117
8/12/78	**41**	6		7 If The World Ran Out Of Love Tonight		Big Tree 16125
11/11/78	**31**	11		8 Westward Wind		Big Tree 16130
3/17/79	**1**²	21		9 Love Is The Answer	10	Big Tree 16131
10/20/79	**12**	8		10 What Can I Do With This Broken Heart	50	Big Tree 17000
3/15/80	**45**	3		11 In It For Love	75	Big Tree 17002
1/31/81	**42**	9		12 Part Of Me Part Of You		MCA 51027
				from the film *Just Tell Me You Love Me*		
				ENGLISH, Jackie		
11/22/80	**43**	10		Once A Night	94	Venture 135
				from the film *Hopscotch*		
				EN VOGUE		
				Black female vocal quartet from the San Francisco Bay area. Formed by the production team of Denzil Foster and Thomas McElroy. Consists of Dawn Robinson, Terry Ellis, Cindy Herron and Maxine Jones.		
7/25/92	**32**	9	●	Giving Him Something He Can Feel	6	EastWest 98560
				ENYA		
				Born Eithne Ni Bhraonain (Gaelic spelling of Brennan) in Donegal, Ireland. From 1980-82, she was a member of her siblings' folk-rock group Clannad.		
3/11/89	**7**	19		1 Orinoco Flow (Sail Away)	24	Geffen 27633
				Orinoco is a river in South America		
2/29/92	**29**	11		2 Caribbean Blue	79	Reprise 19089
				ERNIE — see HENSON, Jim		
				ESCAPE CLUB, The		
				London-based rock quartet formed in 1983: Trevor Steel (vocals), John Holliday (guitar), Johnnie Christo (bass) and Milan Zekavica (drums).		
6/8/91	**27**	19	●	I'll Be There	8	Atlantic 87683

DEBUT DATE	PEAK POS	WKS CHR	G O L D	ARTIST — Record Title	POP POS	Label & Number
				ESPOSITO, Joe "Bean"		
				Former lead singer of Brooklyn Dreams. Also see Brenda Russell.		
11/12/83	**36**	4		Lady, Lady, Lady	86	Casablanca 814430
				from the film *Flashdance*		
★★30★★				**ESTEFAN, Gloria/Miami Sound Machine**		
				Latin American-flavored pop music band based in Miami, led by singer Gloria Estefan with her husband, percussionist Emilio Estefan, Jr. Band formed in 1975. Gloria (b: Gloria Fajardo, 12/1/57) came to Miami in 1960 from Cuba where her father was a bodyguard for President Fulgencio Batista. Emilio emigrated in 1965. On 3/20/90, both were involved in a serious crash involving their tour bus, in which Gloria suffered a broken vertebra but fully recovered within a year.		
				1)Here We Are 2)Anything For You 3)Coming Out Of The Dark		
				MIAMI SOUND MACHINE:		
3/22/86	**8**	16	●	1 **Bad Boy**	8	Epic 05805
6/21/86	**1**²	25		2 **Words Get In The Way**	5	Epic 06120
11/8/86	**3**	19		3 **Falling In Love (Uh-Oh)**	25	Epic 06352
				GLORIA ESTEFAN and MIAMI SOUND MACHINE:		
7/18/87	**31**	7		4 **Rhythm Is Gonna Get You**	5	Epic 07059
9/19/87	**19**	11		5 **Betcha Say That**	36	Epic 07371
11/28/87	**1**¹	24		6 **Can't Stay Away From You**	6	Epic 07641
3/19/88	**1**³	22	●	7 **Anything For You**	1²	Epic 07759
6/11/88	**1**¹	19		8 **1-2-3**	3	Epic 07921
				GLORIA ESTEFAN:		
7/8/89	**2**⁵	23	●	9 **Don't Wanna Lose You**	1¹	Epic 68959
10/7/89	**5**	17		10 **Get On Your Feet**	11	Epic 69064
12/16/89	**1**⁵	27		11 **Here We Are**	6	Epic 73084
4/14/90	**31**	6		12 **Oye Mi Canto (Hear My Voice)**	48	Epic 73269
6/2/90	**1**¹	25		13 **Cuts Both Ways**	44	Epic 73395
1/26/91	**1**²	26		14 **Coming Out Of The Dark**	1²	Epic 73666
5/4/91	**44**	4		15 **Seal Our Fate**	53	Epic 73769
5/25/91	**2**³	25		16 **Can't Forget You**	43	Epic 73864
9/21/91	**2**²	26		17 **Live For Loving You**	22	Epic 73962
10/17/92	**5**	23		18 **Always Tomorrow**	81	Epic 74472
				all royalties Gloria receives from single will benefit the South Florida victims of hurricane Andrew		
2/6/93	**3**	34↑		19 **I See Your Smile**	48	Epic 74847
				ESTUS, Deon		
				Detroit-born black bassist. Formerly with George Michael, Wham!, Marvin Gaye and Brainstorm.		
3/11/89	**3**	18		1 **Heaven Help Me**	5	Mika 871538
				DEON ESTUS with George Michael		
6/24/89	**11**	13		2 Spell		Mika 889328
				ETHERIDGE, Melissa		
				Singer/guitarist born and raised in Leavenworth, Kansas. Studied guitar at Boston's Berklee College of Music. Discovered in Long Beach, California by Island Records' founder Chris Blackwell.		
10/24/92	**24**	11		Dance Without Sleeping		Island 864320
				EUROPE		
				Swedish rock quintet: Joey Tempest (vocals), Kee Marcello (guitar), John Leven (bass), Mic Michaeli (keyboards) and Ian Haugland (drums).		
10/10/87	**36**	4		Carrie	3	Epic 07282
				EURYTHMICS		
				Synth/pop duo: Annie Lennox (b: 12/25/54, Aberdeen, Scotland; vocals, keyboards, flute, composer) and David Stewart (b: 9/9/52, England; keyboards, guitar, synthesizer, composer). Both had been in the Tourists from 1977-80. First album recorded in Cologne, Germany, with drummer Clem Burke (formerly of Blondie). Stewart married Siobhan Fahey of Bananarama on 8/1/87. Lennox appeared in the TV film *The Room*. Also see Al Green (Annie Lennox).		
8/13/83	**36**	10	●	1 Sweet Dreams (Are Made of This)	1¹	RCA 13533
2/11/84	**6**	17		2 **Here Comes The Rain Again**	4	RCA 13725
8/25/84	**38**	6		3 Right By Your Side	29	RCA 13695
				EVERETT, Chad ✪		
				Born Raymon Lee Cramton on 6/11/37 in South Bend, Indiana. Starred on TV's *Medical Center*.		
7/16/77	**49**	2		I Got Love For You Ruby		Calliope 8006

DEBUT DATE	PEAK POS	WKS CHR	GOLD	ARTIST — Record Title	POP POS	Label & Number
				EVERLY, Phil ☯		
				Youngest of The Everly Brothers duo.		
1/24/81	**9**	16		1 **Dare To Dream Again**		Curb 5401
7/18/81	**42**	4		2 Sweet Southern Love		Curb 02116
				EVERLY BROTHERS, The		
				Donald (real name: Isaac Donald) was born on 2/1/37 in Brownie, Kentucky; Philip on 1/19/39 in Chicago. Vocal duo/guitarists/songwriters. Duo split up in July 1973 and reunited in September 1983. Inducted into the Rock and Roll Hall of Fame in 1986. Don's daughter Erin was married for a short time to Axl Rose of Guns N' Roses in 1990.		
5/12/62	**4**	11		1 **That's Old Fashioned (That's The Way Love Should Be)**	9	Warner 5273
11/10/62	**16**	3		2 Don't Ask Me To Be Friends	48	Warner 5297
9/8/84	**9**	12		3 **On The Wings Of A Nightingale**	50	Mercury 880213
				written by Paul McCartney; produced by Dave Edmunds		
2/15/86	**17**	9		4 Born Yesterday		Mercury 884428
				EVERYTHING BUT THE GIRL ☯		
				London-based duo: Tracey Thorn and Ben Watt. Group name taken from a furniture store on England's Hull University campus.		
5/12/90	**23**	10		1 Driving		Atlantic 87983
8/4/90	**30**	9		2 Take Me		Atlantic 87882
				EXILE		
				Band formed in Lexington, Kentucky in 1963 as The Exiles — J.P. Pennington, lead singer. Toured with Dick Clark in 1965. Changed name to Exile in 1973. Pennington left band in early 1989, replaced by Paul Martin. A top country act since 1983.		
8/12/78	**19**	10	●	1 Kiss You All Over	1⁴	Warner 8589
6/28/80	**44**	2		2 You're Good For Me	105	Warner 49245
				EXOTIC GUITARS, The ☯		
				Studio group featuring the lead guitar of Al Casey.		
9/7/68	**40**	1		Blueberry Hill .... [I]		Ranwood 811
				#2 Pop hit for Fats Domino in 1957		
				EXPOSÉ		
				Miami-based, vocal dance trio assembled by producer/songwriter Lewis Martinee. Consists of Miamian Ann Curless, Los Angeles native Jeanette Jurado and Italian-born, New York-raised Gioia Bruno (replaced by Fairbanks, Alaska native Kelly Moneymaker in 1992).		
12/12/87	**1**¹	22		1 **Seasons Change**	1¹	Arista 9640
9/23/89	**3**	20		2 **When I Looked At Him**	10	Arista 9868
4/14/90	**9**	20		3 **Your Baby Never Looked Good In Blue**	17	Arista 2011
2/27/93	**1**¹	31↑	●	4 **I'll Never Get Over You (Getting Over Me)**	8	Arista 12518
				EXTREME		
				Boston metal-funk band: Gary Cherone (vocals), Nuno Bettencourt (guitar; born in Portugal), Pat Badger (bass) and Paul Geary (drums).		
5/4/91	**2**³	25	●	1 **More Than Words**	1¹	A&M 1552
10/26/91	**32**	8		2 Hole Hearted	4	A&M 1564

F

DEBUT DATE	PEAK POS	WKS CHR	GOLD	ARTIST — Record Title	POP POS	Label & Number
				FABARES, Shelley		
				Born Michele Fabares on 1/19/44 in Santa Monica, California. Niece of actress Nanette Fabray. Starred with Elvis in three of his movies. Best known as Mary Stone on *The Donna Reed Show*. Married record producer Lou Adler in 1964; later divorced. Cast member of several TV series since 1972, among them *One Day At A Time* (1981-84) and *Coach*. Currently married to actor Mike Farrell.		
6/16/62	**7**	9		Johnny Loves Me	21	Colpix 636
				FABRIC, Bent, and His Piano		
				Born Bent Fabricius-Bjerre on 12/7/24 in Copenhagen. Head of Metronome Records in Denmark.		
9/8/62	**2**¹	12	●	1 Alley Cat .... [I]	7	Atco 6226
1/12/63	**16**	4		2 Chicken Feed .... [I]	63	Atco 6245

DEBUT DATE	PEAK POS	WKS CHR	G O L D	ARTIST — Record Title	POP POS	Label & Number
				FAGEN, Donald		
				Born on 1/10/48 in Passaic, New Jersey. Backup keyboardist/vocalist with Jay & The Americans. At New York's Bard College, formed band with Walter Becker and drummer-turned-comedic actor Chevy Chase. Fagen and Becker formed Steely Dan in 1972.		
10/23/82	**8**	18		1 I.G.Y. (What A Beautiful World)	26	Warner 29900
				I.G.Y.: International Geo-physical Year (Jul'57-Dec'58)		
2/26/83	**34**	5		2 New Frontier	70	Warner 29792
4/2/88	**30**	8		3 Century's End	83	Warner 27972
				from the film *Bright Lights, Big City*		
6/26/93	**32**	7		4 Tomorrow's Girls		Reprise 18502
				FAIRCHILD, Barbara		
				Born on 11/12/50 in Lafe, Arkansas and raised in Knobel, Arkansas. Country singer/songwriter.		
4/21/73	**9**	10		Teddy Bear Song	32	Columbia 45743
				FAIRGROUND ATTRACTION		
				English-Scottish quartet: female lead singer Eddi Reader with Mark Nevin, Simon Edwards and Roy Dodds.		
12/10/88	**31**	9		Perfect	80	RCA 8789
				FAITH, Percy, And His Orchestra		
				Born on 4/7/08 in Toronto; died of cancer on 2/9/76. Orchestra leader. Moved to the United States in 1940. Joined Columbia Records in 1950 as conductor/arranger for their leading singers (Tony Bennett, Doris Day, Rosemary Clooney, Johnny Mathis and others).		
8/5/67	**13**	9		1 Yellow Days		Columbia 44166
10/28/67	**24**	5		2 Can't Take My Eyes Off You		Columbia 44319
				#2 Pop hit for Frankie Valli in 1967		
2/1/69	**36**	4		3 Zorba .... [I]		Columbia 44734
				Broadway musical title song		
8/2/69	**26**	6	●	4 Theme From "A Summer Place" .... [R] 111		Columbia 44932
				vocal version of Percy's #1 Pop hit from 1960 (Columbia 41490)		
2/6/71	**31**	4		5 Everything's All Right		Columbia 45297
				from the rock opera *Jesus Christ, Superstar*		
10/27/73	**16**	14		6 Crunchy Granola Suite .... [I]		Columbia 45945
				charted as the B-side of Neil Diamond's *Hot 100* hit "Stones"		
3/30/74	**44**	4		7 Hill Where The Lord Hides .... [I]		Columbia 46013
				#76 Pop hit for Chuck Mangione in 1971		
9/21/74	**35**	6		8 Theme From "Chinatown" .... [I]		Columbia 10010
				from the film *Chinatown*		
11/8/75	**13**	10		9 Summer Place '76 (The Theme From "A Summer Place") .... [I-R]		Columbia 10233
				discofied instrumental of Percy's #1 Pop hit from 1960		
				FAITHFULL, Marianne		
				Born on 12/29/46 in Hampstead, London. Discovered by Rolling Stones' manager, Andrew Loog Oldham. Involved in a long, tumultuous relationship with Mick Jagger. Acted in several stage and screen productions. Married British art gallery owner John Dunbar, Vibrators bassist Ben Brierly and American playwright Giorgio Dellaterza.		
6/5/65	**7**	9		1 This Little Bird	32	London 9759
8/28/65	**4**	8		2 Summer Nights	24	London 9780
				FALTERMEYER, Harold		
				West German keyboardist/songwriter/arranger/producer. Arranged and played keyboards on the film scores of *Midnight Express* and *American Gigolo*.		
4/20/85	**1²**	21		Axel F .... [I]	3	MCA 52536
				from the film *Beverly Hills Cop*		
				FALTSKOG, Agnetha		
				Pronounced: Ag-nyet-ta Felts-kogue. Born on 4/5/50 in Sweden. Member of Abba.		
3/26/88	**19**	12		I Wasn't The One (Who Said Goodbye)	93	Atlantic 89145
				AGNETHA FALTSKOG AND PETER CETERA		
				FARAGHER BROTHERS		
				Danny, Jimmy, Tommy, Davey, Marty and Pammy Faragher.		
10/30/76	**46**	3		Never Get Your Love Behind Me		ABC 12210
				FARGO, Donna		
				Born Yvonne Vaughan on 11/10/49 in Mt. Airy, North Carolina. Recorded for Ramco in 1969. Worked as a high school teacher until June 1972. Donna was stricken with multiple sclerosis in 1979. Has own music publishing company.		
6/10/72	**7**	12	●	1 The Happiest Girl In The Whole U.S.A.	11	Dot 17409
10/21/72	**5**	15	●	2 Funny Face	5	Dot 17429
3/31/73	**35**	3		3 Superman	41	Dot 17444
7/14/73	**47**	3		4 You Were Always There	93	Dot 17460

DEBUT DATE	PEAK POS	WKS CHR	G O L D	ARTIST — Record Title	POP POS	Label & Number
				FARGO, Donna — Cont'd		
10/6/73	**43**	4		5 Little Girl Gone	57	Dot 17476
6/29/74	**14**	12		6 You Can't Be A Beacon (If Your Light Don't Shine)..........	57	Dot 17506
3/11/78	**45**	4		7 Do I Love You (Yes In Every Way)		Warner 8509
				FARNHAM, John		
				Popular Australian vocalist born in 1950. Lead singer of Little River Band from 1983-87.		
8/26/89	**38**	4		Two Strong Hearts		RCA 8915
				FARROW, Mia ○		
				Born on 2/9/45 in Los Angeles. Film actress. Daughter of actors Maureen O'Sullivan and the late John Farrow. Married to Frank Sinatra (7/19/66 to 1968) and to Andre Previn (9/10/70 to February 1979). Had a child with actor/director Woody Allen (never married; highly publicized breakup in 1992).		
8/10/68	**33**	2		Lullaby From "Rosemary's Baby" Part 1 ....[I] 111		Dot 17126
				from the film *Rosemary's Baby*, starring Farrow		
				FELICIANO, Jose		
				Born on 9/8/45 in Puerto Rico; raised in New York City. Blind since birth. Virtuoso acoustic guitarist. Composed score for TV's *Chico & The Man*. Won the 1968 Best New Artist Grammy Award.		
11/9/68	**31**	3		1 Hi-Heel Sneakers..............................	25	RCA 9641
5/3/69	**33**	3		2 Marley Purt Drive	70	RCA 9739
				written by the Bee Gees		
8/9/69	**19**	10		3 Rain...................................	76	RCA 9757
7/4/70	**15**	6		4 Destiny	83	RCA 0358
6/28/75	**45**	5		5 Twilight Time		RCA 10306
				#1 Pop hit for The Platters in 1958		
5/17/80	**44**	8		6 I'm Comin' Home Again		ALA 109
				FELLER, Dick		
				Born on 1/2/43 in Bronaugh, Missouri. Moved to Nashville in 1966, worked sessions with Mel Tillis, Warner Mack, Skeeter Davis and Stu Phillips. Staff writer for Johnny Cash in the early '70s.		
12/15/73	**36**	6		1 Biff, The Friendly Purple Bear ....[S] 101		United Art. 316
6/22/74	**33**	7		2 Makin' The Best Of A Bad Situation...............[N] 85		Asylum 11037
10/19/74	**40**	4		3 The Credit Card Song..........................[N] 105		United Art. 535
				FENDER, Freddy		
				Born Baldemar Huerta on 6/4/37 in San Benito, Texas. Mexican-American singer/guitarist. First recorded in Spanish under his real name for Falcon in 1956. In the film *The Milagro Beanfield War*. Joined the Texas Tornados in 1990.		
3/15/75	**19**	10	●	1 Before The Next Teardrop Falls	1[1]	ABC/Dot 17540
7/5/75	**9**	12	●	2 Wasted Days And Wasted Nights	8	ABC/Dot 17558
				originally recorded by Fender on the Duncan label in 1959		
10/25/75	**10**	11		3 Secret Love..................................	20	ABC/Dot 17585
2/28/76	**28**	10		4 You'll Lose A Good Thing	32	ABC/Dot 17607
7/10/76	**41**	3		5 Vaya Con Dios	59	ABC/Dot 17627
				FERGUSON, Maynard		
				Jazz trumpeter. Born on 5/4/28 in Verdun, Quebec, Canada. Moved to the U.S. in 1949. Played for Charlie Barnet and then Stan Kenton's Band (1950-56).		
5/7/77	**46**	4		Gonna Fly Now (Theme From "Rocky").............[I] 28		Columbia 10468
				from the film *Rocky*		
				FERRANTE & TEICHER		
				Piano duo: Arthur Ferrante (b: 9/7/21, New York City) and Louis Teicher (b: 8/24/24, Wilkes-Barre, Pennsylvania). Met as children while attending Manhattan's performing arts academy Juilliard School.		
				1)Tonight 2)Midnight Cowboy 3)Lay Lady Lay		
10/23/61	**2**⁴	12		1 Tonight ....[I] 8		United Art. 373
				from the musical *West Side Story*		
3/17/62	**18**	2		2 Smile...............................[I] 94		United Art. 431
				Charlie Chaplin wrote the music for this song in 1954		
7/16/66	**21**	11		3 Khartoum ....[I]		United Art. 50038
				main theme from the film *Khartoum*		
12/10/66	**24**	8		4 A Man And A Woman ....[I]		United Art. 50101
				movie title song		
12/2/67	**27**	6	✓	5 Live For Life (Vivre Pour Vivre) ....[I]		United Art. 50228
				from the film *Live For Life*		
11/8/69	**2**¹	15		6 Midnight Cowboy ....[I] 10		United Art. 50554
				movie title song starring Jon Voight/Dustin Hoffman; Vincent Bell ("water sound" guitar)		
3/14/70	**16**	6		7 Lay Lady Lay ....[I] 99		United Art. 50646

DEBUT DATE	PEAK POS	WKS CHR	G O L D	ARTIST — Record Title	POP POS	Label & Number
				FERRANTE & TEICHER — Cont'd		
10/17/70	**28**	4		**8** Pieces Of Dreams.. [I]		United Art. 50711
				movie title song		
3/6/71	**39**	2		**9** The Music Lovers (Main Title)..................... [I]		United Art. 50747
				from the film The Music Lovers; piano concerto in B flat minor		
4/8/72	**28**	4	✓	**10** Love Theme From "The Godfather" .... [I]		United Art. 50895
				from the film The Godfather		
				FERRELL, Rachelle ○		
				Pennsylvania-bred singer/songwriter/musician. After attending the Berklee School of Music, taught music for the New Jersey State Council on the Arts. Gained international popularity as a jazz singer.		
3/20/93	**25**	11		Welcome To My Love		Capitol 44892
				FERRY, Bryan		
				Lead singer of Roxy Music. Born on 9/26/45 in County Durham, England. Married socialite Lucy Helmore on 6/26/82.		
11/16/85	**26**	9		Don't Stop The Dance..		Warner 28887
				FIELD, Sally		
				Born on 11/6/46 in Pasadena, California. Leading television/film actress. Star of TV's *Gidget* and *The Flying Nun*. Oscar winner for *Norma Rae* and *Places In The Heart*. Emmy winner for TV's *Sybil*.		
12/9/67	**25**	3		Felicidad	94	Colgems 1008
★★**50**★★				**5TH DIMENSION, The**		
				Los Angeles-based R&B vocal group formed in 1966: Marilyn McCoo, Florence LaRue, Billy Davis, Jr., Lamont McLemore and Ron Townson. McLemore and McCoo had been in the Hi-Fi's; Townson and Davis had been with groups in St. Louis. First called the Versatiles. Davis and McCoo were married in 1969 and recorded as a duo since 1976.		
				1)Aquarius/Let The Sunshine In 2)Wedding Bell Blues 3)One Less Bell To Answer		
				4)If I Could Reach You 5)Never My Love		
6/17/67	**9**	10		**1** Up-Up And Away..	7	Soul City 756
3/22/69	**1**[2]	13	▲	**2** Aquarius/Let The Sunshine In	**1**[6]	Soul City 772
				from the Broadway rock musical Hair		
7/19/69	**9**	11		**3** Workin' On A Groovy Thing............................	20	Soul City 776
				written by Neil Sedaka (also #8 below)		
10/4/69	**1**[2]	12	▲	**4** Wedding Bell Blues	**1**[3]	Soul City 779
1/17/70	**7**	7		**5** Blowing Away	21	Soul City 780
3/14/70	**35**	1		**6** The Declaration	64	Bell 860
				from the play Bread, Beans & Things		
4/4/70	**6**	8		**7** The Girls' Song...	43	Soul City 781
5/9/70	**31**	5		**8** Puppet Man	24	Bell 880
6/20/70	**10**	8		**9** Save The Country	27	Bell 895
9/5/70	**12**	4		**10** On The Beach (In The Summertime)	54	Bell 913
10/24/70	**1**[1]	16	▲	**11** One Less Bell To Answer	**2**[2]	Bell 940
2/27/71	**6**	11		**12** Love's Lines, Angles And Rhymes	19	Bell 965
5/22/71	**12**	7		**13** Light Sings	44	Bell 999
				from the Broadway musical The Me Nobody Knows		
9/18/71	**1**[1]	12		**14** Never My Love...	12	Bell 45134
1/8/72	**8**	8		**15** Together Let's Find Love	37	Bell 45170
4/1/72	**2**[1]	14	▲	**16** (Last Night) I Didn't Get To Sleep At All	8	Bell 45195
9/9/72	**1**[1]	14		**17** If I Could Reach You	10	Bell 45261
1/13/73	**5**	9		**18** Living Together, Growing Together	32	Bell 45310
				from the film Lost Horizon		
4/7/73	**18**	7		**19** Everything's Been Changed	70	Bell 45338
				written by Paul Anka		
8/4/73	**7**	13		**20** Ashes To Ashes	52	Bell 45380
12/8/73	**30**	10		**21** Flashback	82	Bell 45425
2/15/75	**11**	10		**22** No Love In The Room...................................	105	Arista 0101
				FINE YOUNG CANNIBALS		
				Pop trio from Birmingham, England: Roland Gift (vocals) and English Beat members David Steele (bass) and Andy Cox (guitar). Group appeared in the film *Tin Men*; Gift was in the films *Sammy And Rosie Get Laid* and *Scandal*.		
6/24/89	**12**	19		**1** Good Thing...	**1**[1]	I.R.S. 53639
				from the 1987 film Tin Men		
12/2/89	**40**	3		**2** I'm Not The Man I Used To Be	54	I.R.S. 53686
				FINN, Mickie ○		
				Female banjo player. Mickie and her husband Fred co-hosted their own show on NBC-TV in 1966.		
8/27/66	**35**	5		King Of The Road..................................... [I]		Dunhill 4038
				#4 Pop hit for Roger Miller in 1965		

DEBUT DATE	PEAK POS	WKS CHR	GOLD	ARTIST — Record Title	POP POS	Label & Number
				FINN, Tim ○		
				Co-founder/vocalist of The Split Enz. Joined brother Neil Finn's band Crowded House in 1991. Married actress Greta Scacchi in 1985.		
6/24/89	17	12		1 How'm I Gonna Sleep		Capitol 44339
3/10/90	30	8		2 Not Even Close		Capitol 44512
				FINNIGAN, Michael — see STILLS, Stephen		
				FIRE AND RAIN		
				Patti McCarron and Manny Freiser.		
5/5/73	24	7		Hello Stranger	100	Mercury 73373
				FIREBALLS, The		
				Rock and roll band formed while high schoolers in Raton, New Mexico. Lead vocalist Jimmy Gilmer joined in 1960.		
5/4/68	33	3		Goin' Away	79	Atco 6569
				FIREFALL		
				Mellow rock group formed in Boulder, Colorado. Original lineup: Rick Roberts (lead singer), Larry Burnett (guitar), Jack Bartley (lead guitar), Mark Andes (Spirit, Jo Jo Gunne; bass) and Mike Clarke (drums). David Muse (keyboards) joined in 1977. Andes joined Heart in 1980. Roberts and Clarke were members of Flying Burrito Brothers.		
				1)Just Remember I Love You 2)You Are The Woman 3)Love That Got Away		
8/28/76	6	18		1 You Are The Woman	9	Atlantic 3335
4/2/77	35	8		2 Cinderella	34	Atlantic 3392
8/13/77	1²	22		3 Just Remember I Love You	11	Atlantic 3420
10/21/78	24	13		4 Strange Way	11	Atlantic 3518
1/20/79	10	14		5 Goodbye, I Love You	43	Atlantic 3544
7/5/80	9	14		6 Love That Got Away	50	Atlantic 3670
10/25/80	46	3		7 Only Time Will Tell		Atlantic 3763
2/21/81	46	5		8 Staying With It	37	Atlantic 3791
				Lisa Nemzo and Rick Roberts (lead vocals)		
1/22/83	24	12		9 Always	59	Atlantic 89916
				FIREFLY		
10/25/75	50	2		Hey There Little Firefly Part I	67	A&M 1736
				FIREHOUSE		
				Hard-rock quartet from North Carolina: C.J. Snare (vocals), Bill Leverty, Perry Richardson and Michael Foster.		
11/2/91	37	13	●	Love Of A Lifetime	5	Epic 73771
				FIRST CLASS		
				British studio quartet: Tony Burrows (vocals), John Carter, Del John and Chas Mills. Burrows was the vocalist on hits by The Brotherhood Of Man, Edison Lighthouse, The Pipkins and White Plains.		
9/7/74	38	5		Beach Baby	4	UK 49022
				FISCHER, Lisa		
				Native of Fort Greene, Brooklyn, New York. Session singer with Billy Ocean, Melba Moore and others. Touring vocalist with Luther Vandross.		
10/6/90	37	5		1 Glad To Be Alive		Elektra 64960
				TEDDY PENDERGRASS & LISA FISHER from the film *The Adventures of Ford Fairlane*		
4/27/91	16	19		2 How Can I Ease The Pain	11	Elektra 64897
6/5/93	18	12		3 Colors Of Love		Elektra 64633
				from the film *Made In America*		
★★185★★				**FISCHOFF, George**		
				Born on 8/3/38 in South Bend, Indiana. Pianist/songwriter. Wrote "98.6" for Keith.		
				1)Georgia Porcupine 2)Little Ballerina Blue 3)That Great Old Song		
4/27/74	10	16		1 Georgia Porcupine ....[I]	93	United Art. 410
12/14/74	19	12		2 That Great Old Song..[I]		GNP Cresc. 491
6/7/75	39	9		3 King Kingston ....[I]		PIP 6503
7/9/77	24	17		4 Piano Dancing ....[I]		Columbia 10533
				GEORGE FISCHOFF "SUPER-PIANO"		
12/2/78	28	11		5 The Piano Picker ....[I]		Drive 6273
3/21/81	19	13		6 Little Ballerina Blue */	[I]	
8/1/81	26	10		7 Foxy * ....[I]		Heritage 300
				*GEORGE FISCHOFF & The Luv Ensemble		
9/11/82	42	10		8 Pretty Kitty ....[I]		MMG 2
2/26/83	31	7		9 Carnival Island ....[I]		MMG 6

DEBUT DATE	PEAK POS	WKS CHR	GOLD	ARTIST — Record Title	POP POS	Label & Number
				FISCHOFF, George — Cont'd		
6/18/83	**23**	14		10 Summer Love/	[I]	
		14		11 Piano Power..	[I]	MMG 9
2/11/84	**45**	8		12 Boogie Piano Man	[I]	Reward 04354
8/18/84	**44**	7		13 Lovely Lady	[I]	Lisa 596
1/5/85	**32**	3		14 Starry Night	[I]	Lisa 02
				FISHER, Eddie Born Edwin Jack Fisher on 8/10/28 in Philadelphia. Married to Debbie Reynolds from 1955-59. Other marriages to Elizabeth Taylor and Connie Stevens. Daughter with Debbie is actress Carrie Fisher. Daughter with Connie is singer Tricia Leigh Fisher. Own *Coke Time* 15-minute TV series, 1953-57. In films *All About Eve* (1950), *Bundle Of Joy* (1956) and *Butterfield 8* (1960). Eddie was the #1 idol of bobbysoxers during the early 1950's.		
11/13/61	**12**	5		1 Tonight..	44	7 Arts 719
				from the musical *West Side Story*		
6/19/65	**22**	6		2 Sunrise, Sunset	119	Dot 16732
				from the musical *Fiddler On The Roof*; #84 Pop hit for Roger Williams in 1967		
11/20/65	**25**	9		3 Young And Foolish		Dot 16779
10/15/66	**2**¹	14		4 Games That Lovers Play	45	RCA 8956
1/28/67	**4**	13		5 People Like You	97	RCA 9070
5/20/67	**23**	8		6 Now I Know	131	RCA 9204
				FITZGERALD, Ella The most-honored jazz singer of all time. Born on 4/25/18 in Newport News, Virginia. Appeared in several films. Won the Lifetime Achievement Grammy in 1967. Winner of the Down Beat poll as top female vocalist more than 20 times and winner of 12 Grammys, she remains among the undisputed royalty of 20th century popular music.		
8/14/61	**20**	1		1 Mr. Paganini (You'll Have To Swing It).................	103	Verve 10237
2/24/68	**22**	5	✔	2 I Taught Him Everything He Knows......................		Capitol 2099
				FIVE FLIGHTS UP Five-man pop group.		
10/24/70	**35**	2		Do What You Wanna Do	37	T-A 202
				FIVE SATINS, The R&B group from New Haven, Connecticut. Consisted of Fred Parris (lead), Al Denby, Jim Freeman, Eddie Martin and Jessie Murphy (piano).		
3/6/82	**32**	6		Memories Of Days Gone By .... **FRED PARRIS & THE FIVE SATINS** 16 Candles/Earth Angel/Only You/A Thousand Miles Away/Tears On My Pillow/ Since I Don't Have You/In The Still Of The Night	71	Elektra 47411
★★**43**★★				**FLACK, Roberta** Born on 2/10/39 in Asheville, North Carolina and raised in Arlington, Virginia. Played piano from an early age. Music scholarship to Howard University at age 15; classmate of Donny Hathaway. Worked as a high school music teacher in North Carolina. Discovered by jazz musician Les McCann. Signed to Atlantic in 1969. *1)The First Time Ever I Saw Your Face 2)If Ever I See You Again 3)Feel Like Makin' Love* *4)Where Is The Love 5)Set The Night To Music*		
7/24/71	**36**	2		1 You've Got A Friend *	29	Atlantic 2808
1/22/72	**15**	6		2 Will You Still Love Me Tomorrow.........................	76	Atlantic 2851
3/11/72	**1**⁶	14	●	3 The First Time Ever I Saw Your Face	**1**⁶	Atlantic 2864
				popularized because of inclusion in the film *Play Misty For Me*		
6/10/72	**1**¹	12	●	4 Where Is The Love *	5	Atlantic 2879
2/3/73	**2**¹	11	●	5 Killing Me Softly With His Song	**1**⁵	Atlantic 2940
9/22/73	**3**	12		6 Jesse	30	Atlantic 2982
6/29/74	**1**²	17	●	7 Feel Like Makin' Love	**1**¹	Atlantic 3025
6/21/75	**38**	7		8 Feelin' That Glow	76	Atlantic 3271
12/3/77	**28**	8		9 25th Of Last December......................................		Atlantic 3441
2/25/78	**3**	19	●	10 The Closer I Get To You *	**2**²	Atlantic 3463
5/20/78	**1**³	19		11 If Ever I See You Again	24	Atlantic 3483
2/16/80	**46**	3		12 You Are My Heaven *	47	Atlantic 3627
				***ROBERTA FLACK & DONNY HATHAWAY**		
3/13/82	**7**	22		13 Making Love..	13	Atlantic 4005
				movie title song		
7/31/82	**10**	18		14 I'm The One	42	Atlantic 4068
11/6/82	**24**	11		15 In The Name Of Love......................................		Atlantic 89932
7/16/83	**4**	29		16 Tonight, I Celebrate My Love **	16	Capitol 5242
1/7/84	**5**	21		17 You're Looking Like Love To Me **	58	Capitol 5307
5/5/84	**15**	12		18 I Just Came Here To Dance **		Capitol 5353
				****PEABO BRYSON/ROBERTA FLACK**		

DEBUT DATE	PEAK POS	WKS CHR	GOLD	ARTIST — Record Title	POP POS	Label & Number
				FLACK, Roberta — Cont'd		
9/1/84	**31**	7		19 If I'm Still Around Tomorrow		Elektra 69700
				SADAO WATANABE with Roberta Flack		
11/5/88	**13**	18		20 Oasis		Atlantic 88996
9/28/91	**2**[1]	28		21 Set The Night To Music.......................	6	Atlantic 87607
				ROBERTA FLACK with MAXI PRIEST		
				FLATT & SCRUGGS		
				Influential bluegrass duo. Lester Flatt (guitar) was born on 6/28/14 in Overton County, Tennessee; died in Nashville on 5/11/79. Earl Scruggs (banjo) was born on 1/6/24 in Cleveland County, North Carolina. Duo formed in 1948 while both were members of Bill Monroe's band. Regulars on TV's *Beverly Hillbillies*. Separated in early 1969.		
2/9/63	**14**	2		The Ballad Of Jed Clampett	44	Columbia 42606
				from the TV series *The Beverly Hillbillies*		
★★58★★				**FLEETWOOD MAC**		
				Formed as a British blues band in 1967 by ex-John Mayall's Bluesbreakers Peter Green (guitar), Mick Fleetwood (drums) and John McVie (bass), along with guitarist Jeremy Spencer. Many lineup changes followed as group headed toward rock superstardom. Green and Spencer left in 1970. Christine McVie (keyboards) joined in August 1970. Bob Welch (guitar) joined in April 1971, stayed through 1974. Group relocated to California in 1974, whereupon Americans Lindsey Buckingham (guitar) and Stevie Nicks (vocals) joined in January 1975. Buckingham left in summer of 1987. Guitarists/vocalists Billy Burnette (son of Dorsey Burnette) and Rick Vito joined in July 1987. Christine McVie and Nicks quit touring with the band at the end of 1990. Vito left in 1991.		
				1)*Little Lies* 2)*Everywhere* 3)*As Long As You Follow* 4)*Save Me* 5)*Hold Me*		
1/3/76	**32**	7		1 Over My Head..	20	Reprise 1339
3/27/76	**33**	8		2 Rhiannon (Will You Ever Win)	11	Reprise 1345
7/24/76	**12**	12		3 Say You Love Me	11	Reprise 1356
2/19/77	**45**	3		4 Go Your Own Way	10	Warner 8304
4/30/77	**11**	15	●	5 Dreams	1[1]	Warner 8371
7/30/77	**22**	14		6 Don't Stop...	3	Warner 8413
11/5/77	**28**	8		7 You Make Loving Fun	9	Warner 8483
12/22/79	**13**	12		8 Sara...	7	Warner 49150
4/5/80	**39**	5		9 Think About Me......................................	20	Warner 49196
6/26/82	**7**	21		10 Hold Me...	4	Warner 29966
9/18/82	**9**	17		11 Gypsy..	12	Warner 29918
12/4/82	**11**	17		12 Love In Store	22	Warner 29848
4/9/83	**35**	6		13 Oh Diane...		Warner 29698
4/25/87	**23**	8		14 Big Love	5	Warner 28398
7/4/87	**13**	13		15 Seven Wonders	19	Warner 28317
9/5/87	**1**[4]	22		16 Little Lies	4	Warner 28291
12/5/87	**1**[3]	20		17 Everywhere	14	Warner 28143
4/9/88	**23**	7		18 Family Man	90	Warner 28114
11/26/88	**1**[1]	21		19 As Long As You Follow	43	Warner 27644
4/7/90	**6**	18		20 Save Me	33	Warner 19866
7/21/90	**10**	16	✓	21 Skies The Limit		Warner 19867
12/19/92	**32**	7		22 Paper Doll	108	Warner 18661
				FLEETWOODS, The		
				Pop trio formed while in high school in Olympia, Washington in 1958: Gary Troxel (b: 11/28/39), Gretchen Christopher (b: 2/29/40) and Barbara Ellis (b: 2/20/40).		
11/24/62	**14**	4		1 Lovers By Night, Strangers By Day	36	Dolton 62
6/15/63	**12**	8		2 Goodnight My Love.................................	32	Dolton 75
				FLINT, Shelby		
				Singer/songwriter. Born on 9/17/39 in North Hollywood, California.		
8/20/66	**11**	7		Cast Your Fate To The Wind	61	Valiant 743
				FLOWER ○		
12/3/77	**39**	8		Run To Me...		United Art. 1092
				#16 Pop hit for the Bee Gees in 1972		
				FLUEGEL KNIGHTS — see KING RICHARD'S FLUEGEL KNIGHTS		
				FLYING MACHINE, The		
				Studio project of British songwriters/producers Tony Macauley and Geoff Stevens. Touring group featured Tony Newman as lead vocalist.		
10/25/69	**6**	10	●	**Smile A Little Smile For Me**	5	Congress 6000

DEBUT DATE	PEAK POS	WKS CHR	GOLD	ARTIST — Record Title	POP POS	Label & Number
★★54★★				**FOGELBERG, Dan**		
				Born on 8/13/51 in Peoria, Illinois. Vocalist/composer. Worked as a folk singer in Los Angeles. With Van Morrison in the early '70s. Session work in Nashville.		
				1)Leader Of The Band 2)Make Love Stay 3)Believe In Me		
2/15/75	22	9		1 Part Of The Plan	31	Epic 50055
1/5/80	1¹	16		2 Longer	2²	Full Moon 50824
4/5/80	3	18		3 Heart Hotels	21	Full Moon 50862
12/20/80	8	15		4 Same Old Lang Syne	9	Full Moon 50961
8/29/81	2³	23		5 Hard To Say	7	Full Moon 02488
12/12/81	1²	22		6 Leader Of The Band	9	Full Moon 02647
4/3/82	3	19		7 Run For The Roses	18	Full Moon 02821
10/23/82	6	18		8 Missing You	23	Full Moon 03289
2/5/83	1¹	21		9 Make Love Stay	29	Full Moon 03525
2/11/84	14	15		10 The Language Of Love	13	Full Moon 04314
4/28/84	1¹	21		11 Believe In Me	48	Full Moon 04447
10/27/84	36	3		12 Sweet Magnolia And The Travelling Salesman		Full Moon 04660
3/30/85	6	14		13 Go Down Easy	85	Full Moon 04835
7/25/87	2¹	25		14 Lonely In Love		Full Moon 07275
11/21/87	15	14		15 Seeing You Again		Full Moon 07640
9/8/90	3	23		16 Rhythm Of The Rain/Rain		Full Moon 73513
				"Rhythm Of The Rain" was originally recorded by the Cascades and "Rain" was a Beatles' song written by Lennon and McCartney		
1/26/91	32	7		17 Anastasia's Eyes		Full Moon LP Cut
				from the album *The Wild Places* on Full Moon 45059		
				FOGERTY, John		
				Born on 5/28/45 in Berkeley, California. Multi-instrumentalist. With his brother Tom in the Blue Velvets in 1959. Group became the Golliwogs and recorded for Fantasy in 1964. Renamed Creedence Clearwater Revival in 1967. Wrote "Proud Mary," "Have You Ever Seen The Rain," "Bad Moon Rising," "Lookin' Out My Back Door" and many others. Went solo in 1972 and recorded as The Blue Ridge Rangers.		
1/20/73	11	8		1 Jambalaya (On the Bayou) *	16	Fantasy 689
4/28/73	31	5		2 Hearts Of Stone *	37	Fantasy 700
				***THE BLUE RIDGE RANGERS**		
2/16/85	33	3		3 The Old Man Down The Road	10	Warner 29100
5/25/85	17	10		4 Centerfield	44	Warner 29053
				FOOLS GOLD		
				Dan Fogelberg's backing group — Denny Henson, lead vocals, guitar.		
7/24/76	38	3		Rain, Oh Rain	76	Morning Sky 700
				FORBERT, Steve		
				Born in 1955 in Meridian, Mississippi. Moved to New York City in 1976.		
1/5/80	13	13		Romeo's Tune	11	Nemperor 7525
				FORCE M.D.'S		
				Staten Island-based, soul-rap quintet. Originally called Dr. Rock & The M.C.'s. M.D. stands for Musical Diversity.		
2/22/86	2²	16		1 Tender Love	10	Warner 28818
				from the film *Krush Groove*		
9/26/87	38	5		2 Love Is A House	78	Tommy Boy 28300
				FORDHAM, Julia ○		
				Singer from southern England. Member of Mari Wilson's eclectic Wilsations for two years. Also worked as a backing vocalist for Kim Wilde.		
3/11/89	24	10		1 Happy Ever After		Virgin 99294
7/15/89	40	4		2 Comfort Of Strangers		Virgin 99224
3/24/90	40	4		3 Manhattan Skyline		Virgin 99146
				FOREIGNER		
				British-American rock group formed in New York City in 1976. Consisted of Mick Jones (guitar), Lou Gramm (vocals), Rick Wills (bass) and Dennis Elliott (drums).		
10/17/81	5	20	●	1 Waiting For A Girl Like You	2¹⁰	Atlantic 3868
12/15/84	3	22	●	2 I Want To Know What Love Is	1²	Atlantic 89596
				vocal backing by the New Jersey Mass Choir and Jennifer Holiday		
3/30/85	24	10		3 That Was Yesterday	12	Atlantic 89571
1/30/88	41	4		4 Say You Will	6	Atlantic 89169
3/26/88	1¹	23		5 I Don't Want To Live Without You	5	Atlantic 89101

DEBUT DATE	PEAK POS	WKS CHR	GOLD	ARTIST — Record Title	POP POS	Label & Number
				FORTUNES, The		
				English pop quintet led by guitarists/vocalists Glen Dale (Garforth) and Barry Pritchard. Dale left in July 1966, replaced by Scotsman Shel MacRae.		
5/29/71	**8**	11		1 **Here Comes That Rainy Day Feeling Again**	15	Capitol 3086
9/25/71	**12**	7		2 **Freedom Comes, Freedom Goes**....................................	72	Capitol 3179
				FOSTER, David		
				Keyboardist/composer/arranger born in Victoria, British Columbia. Member of the groups Skylark and Attitudes. Wrote hits for Chicago, Barbra Streisand and others. Married to songwriter/actress Linda Thompson (formerly married to Olympic decathlete Bruce Jenner).		
9/7/85	**3**	21		1 **Love Theme From St. Elmo's Fire**................................ [I]	15	Atlantic 89528
				from the film *St. Elmo's Fire*		
5/31/86	**6**	16		2 **The Best Of Me**	80	Atlantic 89420
				DAVID FOSTER AND OLIVIA NEWTON-JOHN		
9/20/86	**38**	2		3 **Who's Gonna Love You Tonight**................................		Atlantic 89376
2/27/88	**28**	6		4 **Winter Games** .... [I]	85	Atlantic 89140
				theme song used during ABC's telecast of the 1988 Winter Olympics		
				FOUNTAIN, Pete		
				Born on 7/3/30 in New Orleans. Top jazz clarinetist. With Al Hirt, 1956-57. Performed on Lawrence Welk's weekly TV show, 1957-59. Own club in New Orleans, The French Quarter Inn.		
6/26/65	**27**	4		1 **Mae**.. [I]	129	Coral 62454
				from the film *The Yellow Rolls Royce*		
5/6/67	**28**	5		2 **Thoroughly Modern Millie** .... [I]		Coral 62516
				movie title song		
1/18/69	**24**	5		3 **Les Bicyclettes De Belsize** .... [I]		Coral 62557
				#31 Pop hit for Engelbert Humperdinck in 1968		
				FOUR FRESHMEN, The		
				Jazz-styled vocal and instrumental group formed in 1948 while at Arthur Jordan Conservatory of Music in Indianapolis. Consisted of brothers Ross and Don Barbour, their cousin Bob Flanigan and Ken Errair.		
8/21/65	**33**	4		**Old Cape Cod**		Capitol 5741
				#3 Pop hit for Patti Page in 1957		
				FOUR JACKS AND A JILL		
				South African quintet; Jill is Glenys Lynne (lead singer).		
3/23/68	**3**	16		1 **Master Jack**	18	RCA 9473
8/10/68	**25**	5		2 **Mister Nico**	96	RCA 9572
11/2/68	**34**	4		3 **Hey Mister**...	130	RCA 9655
				FOUR LADS, The		
				Vocal group from Toronto: Bernie Toorish (lead tenor), Jimmie Arnold (second tenor), Frankie Busseri (baritone) and Connie Codarini (bass). Sang in choir at St. Michael's Cathedral in Toronto. Worked local hotels and clubs. Worked Le Ruban Bleu in New York City. Signed as backup singers by Columbia in 1950. Backed Johnnie Ray on several of his hits, including his #1 hit "Cry."		
11/30/68	**26**	4		1 **A Woman**..		United Art. 50339
5/24/69	**38**	4		2 **My Heart's Symphony**...		United Art. 50517
				#13 Pop hit for Gary Lewis & The Playboys in 1966		
				FOUR PREPS, The		
				Vocal group formed while at Hollywood High School: Bruce Belland, Glen Larson, Ed Cobb and Marvin Ingraham. Belland, who was later in duo with Dave Somerville of the Diamonds, is the father of Tracey and Melissa Belland of Voice Of The Beehive.		
8/28/61	**4**	8		1 **More Money For You And Me** .... [N]	17	Capitol 4599
				Mr. Blue/Alley Oop/Smoke Gets In Your Eyes/In This Whole Wide World/ A Worried Man/Tom Dooley/A Teenager In Love		
4/7/62	**15**	5		2 **The Big Draft**.. [N]	61	Capitol 4716
				I'll Never Smile Again/Love Is A Many-Splendored Thing/The Mountain's High/ Heartaches/Anchors Aweigh/Michael/Runaround Sue		
				4 SEASONS, The		
				Vocal group formed in Newark, New Jersey. Lineup from 1975-77: Frankie Valli (vocals), John Paiva (guitar), Lee Shapiro (keyboards), Don Ciccone (bass) and Gerri Polci (drums, vocals).		
9/6/75	**7**	12		1 **Who Loves You**..	3	Warner 8122
1/17/76	**18**	11	●	2 **December, 1963 (Oh, What A Night)**	1³	Warner 8168
6/5/76	**24**	10		3 **Silver Star**...	38	Warner 8203
8/13/77	**40**	2		4 **Down The Hall**...	65	Warner 8407
				Gerri Polci (lead vocals, above 3)		

DEBUT DATE	PEAK POS	WKS CHR	G O L D	ARTIST — Record Title	POP POS	Label & Number
				FOUR TOPS		
				Detroit R&B vocal group formed in 1953 as the Four Aims. Consisted of Levi Stubbs (lead singer), Renaldo "Obie" Benson, Lawrence Payton and Abdul "Duke" Fakir. First recorded for Chess in 1956, then Red Top and Columbia, before signing with Motown in 1963. Group has had no personnel changes since its formation. Stubbs is the voice of Audrey II (the voracious vegetation) in the 1986 film *Little Shop of Horrors*. Group inducted into the Rock and Roll Hall of Fame in 1990.		
6/27/70	**39**	1		1 It's All In The Game	24	Motown 1164
3/3/73	**14**	8	●	2 Ain't No Woman (Like The One I've Got)	4	Dunhill 4339
11/3/73	**41**	6		3 Sweet Understanding Love	33	Dunhill 4366
9/12/81	**9**	16		**4 When She Was My Girl**	11	Casablanca 2338
10/29/83	**18**	15		5 I Just Can't Walk Away	71	Motown 1706
9/3/88	**20**	9		6 Indestructible	35	Arista 9706
				tune used by NBC-TV for the 1988 Summer Olympics		
11/12/88	**26**	10		7 If Ever A Love There Was		Arista 9766
				FOUR TOPS with ARETHA FRANKLIN Kenny G (sax solo)		
				FOX, Charles		
				Composer/pianist/conductor born on 10/30/40 in New York City. Composed many songs for TV and film.		
11/15/80	**20**	14		Seasons .... [I]	75	Handshake 5307
				based on the theme from the film *Ordinary People* (Pachelbel's Canon in D Major)		
				FRAMPTON, Peter		
				Born on 4/22/50 in Beckenham, England. Vocalist/guitarist/composer. Joined British band The Herd at age 16, before forming Humble Pie in 1969, which he left in 1971 to form Frampton's Camel. Went solo in 1974. Played Billy Shears in the 1978 film *Sgt. Pepper's Lonely Hearts Club Band*. Near-fatal car crash on 6/29/78 temporarily sidelined his career.		
8/21/76	**28**	7		1 Baby, I Love Your Way	12	A&M 1832
7/2/77	**26**	11		2 I'm In You	2³	A&M 1941
★★★42★★★				**FRANCIS, Connie**		
				Born Concetta Rosa Maria Franconero on 12/12/38 in Newark, New Jersey. First recorded for MGM in 1955. From 1961-65, appeared in films *Where The Boys Are, Follow The Boys, Looking For Love* and *When The Boys Meet The Girls*. Connie stopped performing after she was raped on 11/8/74. Began comeback with a performance on *Dick Clark's Live Wednesday* TV show in 1978. Pop music's #1 female vocalist from the late 1950s to the mid-1960s.		
				1)*Don't Break The Heart That Loves You* 2)*Together* 3)*When The Boy In Your Arms (Is The Boy In Your Heart)* 4)*Second Hand Love* 5)*Whose Heart Are You Breaking Tonight*		
7/17/61	**1¹**	8	●	1 **Together**	6	MGM 13019
11/27/61	**2²**	11		2 **When The Boy In Your Arms (Is The Boy In Your Heart)**	10	
12/11/61	**7**	4		3 **Baby's First Christmas** .... [X]	26	MGM 13051
2/10/62	**1⁴**	13		4 **Don't Break The Heart That Loves You**	1¹	MGM 13059
5/19/62	**3**	8		5 **Second Hand Love**	7	MGM 13074
10/20/62	**8**	7		6 **I Was Such A Fool (To Fall In Love With You)**/	24	
10/27/62	**18**	1		7 He Thinks I Still Care	57	MGM 13096
				#1 Country hit for George Jones as "She Thinks I Still Care"		
12/22/62	**19**	1		8 I'm Gonna Be Warm This Winter..	18	MGM 13116
3/9/63	**7**	9		9 **Follow The Boys**	17	MGM 13127
				movie title song		
10/19/63	**10**	7		10 **Your Other Love**	28	MGM 13176
2/29/64	**8**	4		11 **Blue Winter**	24	MGM 13214
5/23/64	**9**	6		12 **Be Anything (But Be Mine)**	25	MGM 13237
1/23/65	**7**	6		13 **Whose Heart Are You Breaking Tonight**......................	43	MGM 13303
3/13/65	**12**	4		14 **For Mama (La Mamma)**	48	MGM 13325
5/1/65	**14**	7		15 **Wishing It Was You**	57	MGM 13331
6/26/65	**16**	6		16 **Forget Domani**	79	MGM 13363
				from the film *The Yellow Rolls Royce*		
8/28/65	**10**	9		17 **Roundabout**	80	MGM 13389
11/20/65	**10**	12		18 **Jealous Heart**...	47	MGM 13420
4/2/66	**28**	4		19 Love Is Me, Love Is You	66	MGM 13470
9/10/66	**17**	8		20 So Nice (Summer Samba)		MGM 13578
				#26 Pop hit for Walter Wanderley in 1966		
11/19/66	**15**	8		21 Spanish Nights And You	99	MGM 13610
4/15/67	**14**	7		22 Time Alone Will Tell	94	MGM 13718
7/22/67	**12**	8		23 My Heart Cries For You	118	MGM 13773
10/14/67	**22**	7		24 Lonely Again		MGM 13814

DEBUT DATE	PEAK POS	WKS CHR	GOLD	ARTIST — Record Title	POP POS	Label & Number
				FRANCIS, Connie — Cont'd		
2/10/68	**35**	3		25 My World Is Slipping Away		MGM 13876
				written by Neil Sedaka		
4/20/68	**27**	4		26 Why Say Goodbye (A Comme Amour)	132	MGM 13923
11/30/68	**40**	2		27 I Don't Wanna Play House		MGM 14004
				#1 Country hit for Tammy Wynette in 1967		
2/22/69	**19**	9		28 The Wedding Cake	91	MGM 14034
1/31/81	**40**	6		29 I'm Me Again		MGM 14853
				FRANKE & THE KNOCKOUTS		
				Soft-rock quintet led by vocalist Franke Previte of New Brunswick, New Jersey.		
4/18/81	**40**	6		Sweetheart..	10	Millennium 11801
★★**126**★★				**FRANKLIN, Aretha**		

Born on 3/25/42 in Memphis and raised in Buffalo and Detroit. Daughter of Rev. Cecil L. Franklin, pastor of New Bethel Church in Detroit. Taught to sing gospel at age 9 by Rev. James Cleveland (d: 2/9/91, age 59). First recorded for JVB/Battle in 1956. Signed to Columbia Records in 1960 by John Hammond, then dramatic turn in style and success after signing with Atlantic and working with producer Jerry Wexler. Appeared in the 1980 film *The Blues Brothers*. Winner of 15 Grammy Awards. In 1987, became the first woman to be inducted into the Rock and Roll Hall of Fame. Won Grammy's Living Legends Award in 1990. The all-time Queen of Soul Music.

1)I Knew You Were Waiting (For Me) 2)Through The Storm 3)Spanish Harlem

DEBUT DATE	PEAK POS	WKS CHR	GOLD	ARTIST — Record Title	POP POS	Label & Number
8/21/65	**34**	1		1 (No, No) I'm Losing You	114	Columbia 43333
12/18/65	**32**	6		2 You Made Me Love You	109	Columbia 43442
				#1 hit for Al Jolson in 1913		
5/22/71	**40**	2	●	3 Bridge Over Troubled Water	6	Atlantic 2796
8/7/71	**6**	9	●	4 Spanish Harlem	2²	Atlantic 2817
4/1/72	**11**	11	●	5 Day Dreaming	5	Atlantic 2866
9/1/73	**44**	2		6 Angel	20	Atlantic 2969
1/12/74	**33**	9	●	7 Until You Come Back To Me (That's What I'm Gonna Do)	3	Atlantic 2995
7/6/85	**11**	16		8 Freeway Of Love	3	Arista 9354
10/19/85	**10**	14		9 Who's Zoomin' Who	7	Arista 9410
2/8/86	**21**	8		10 Another Night..	22	Arista 9453
12/13/86	**17**	12		11 Jimmy Lee	28	Arista 9546
3/7/87	**2³**	16		12 I Knew You Were Waiting (For Me)	1²	Arista 9559
				ARETHA FRANKLIN AND GEORGE MICHAEL		
11/12/88	**26**	10		13 If Ever A Love There Was		Arista 9766
				FOUR TOPS with ARETHA FRANKLIN		
				Kenny G (sax solo)		
4/15/89	**3**	18		14 Through The Storm..	16	Arista 9809
				ARETHA FRANKLIN AND ELTON JOHN		
2/15/92	**11**	22		15 Ever Changing Times		Arista 12394
				ARETHA FRANKLIN Featuring Michael McDonald		
				FRANKS, Michael		
				Born on 9/18/44 in La Jolla, California. Jazz-pop singer/songwriter.		
8/28/76	**45**	4		1 Popsicle Toes	43	Reprise 1360
8/3/85	**4**	17		2 Your Secret's Safe With Me		Warner 28928
12/28/85	**15**	12		3 When I Give My Love To You		Warner 28819
				MICHAEL FRANKS Featuring Brenda Russell		
				FRASER, Wendy — see SWAYZE, Patrick		
				FREE DESIGN, The ○		
				Mixed vocal quartet featuring Chuck and Ellen Dedrick.		
12/9/67	**33**	5		Kites Are Fun	114	Project 3 1324
				FREE MOVEMENT, The		
				Los Angeles-based vocal sextet. Several members formerly with gospel groups.		
9/18/71	**7**	11		1 I've Found Someone Of My Own	5	Decca 32818
12/25/71	**6**	10		2 The Harder I Try (The Bluer I Get)......................	50	Columbia 45512
★★**127**★★				**FREY, Glenn**		

Founding member of the Eagles. Born on 11/6/48 in Detroit. Singer/songwriter/guitarist. Appeared in episodes of TV's *Miami Vice* and *Wiseguy*; starred in the CBS series *South of Sunset* since 1993.

1)The One You Love 2)True Love 3)You Belong To The City

DEBUT DATE	PEAK POS	WKS CHR	GOLD	ARTIST — Record Title	POP POS	Label & Number
7/3/82	**27**	13		1 I Found Somebody	31	Asylum 47466
9/4/82	**2⁴**	22		2 The One You Love	15	Asylum 69974
1/15/83	**28**	6		3 All Those Lies	41	Asylum 69857
7/14/84	**23**	12		4 Sexy Girl	20	MCA 52413

DEBUT DATE	PEAK POS	WKS CHR	GOLD	ARTIST — Record Title	POP POS	Label & Number
				FREY, Glenn — Cont'd		
2/16/85	36	9		5 The Heat Is On	2¹	MCA 52512
				from the film *Beverly Hills Cop*		
10/12/85	2¹	17		6 You Belong To The City	2²	MCA 52651
				from TV's *Miami Vice* soundtrack		
8/20/88	2²	23		7 True Love	13	MCA 53363
12/3/88	5	18		8 Soul Searchin'		MCA 53452
4/8/89	22	7		9 Livin' Right	90	MCA 53497
5/4/91	7	21		10 Part Of Me, Part Of You	55	MCA 54060
				from the film *Thelma & Louise*		
7/4/92	12	15		11 I've Got Mine	91	MCA 54429
9/26/92	27	8		12 River Of Dreams		MCA 54461
				FRIENDS OF DISTINCTION, The		
				Los Angeles-based, soul-MOR group. Original lineup: Floyd Butler, Harry Elston, Jessica Cleaves and Barbara Jean Love. Butler and Elston were in the Hi-Fi's with LaMonte McLemore and Marilyn McCoo (later with The 5th Dimension).		
3/21/70	9	9		Love Or Let Me Be Lonely	6	RCA 0319
				FULLER, Jerry		
				Born Jerrell Lee Fuller in Fort Worth, Texas. Pop-country singer/songwriter.		
4/25/70	39	2		I Know We Can Make It............................		Columbia 45131
				FUNKY KINGS		
				Seven-man band led by Jack Tempchin and Jules Shear (of Jules & The Polar Bears).		
11/6/76	13	14		Slow Dancing	61	Arista 0209
				FURAY, Richie		
				Born on 5/9/44 in Yello Springs, Ohio. Member of Buffalo Springfield, Poco, and The Souther, Hillman, Furay Band.		
12/8/79	48	2		I Still Have Dreams	39	Asylum 46534

G

DEBUT DATE	PEAK POS	WKS CHR	GOLD	ARTIST — Record Title	POP POS	Label & Number
				GALLAGHER and LYLE		
				Scottish duo: Benny Gallagher & Graham Lyle — formerly with McGuiness Flint.		
6/12/76	27	8		1 I Wanna Stay With You	49	A&M 1778
9/4/76	17	10		2 Heart On My Sleeve	67	A&M 1850
3/19/77	46	3		3 Every Little Teardrop	106	A&M 1904
				GALLERY		
				Detroit pop group led by singer/guitarist Jim Gold (b: 1/12/47).		
3/25/72	5	17	●	1 Nice To Be With You	4	Sussex 232
8/19/72	12	13		2 I Believe In Music....................................	22	Sussex 239
				written by Mac Davis		
1/20/73	10	10		3 Big City Miss Ruth Ann	23	Sussex 248
7/14/73	40	2		4 Maybe Baby	118	Sussex 259
				GALLERY featuring Jim Gold		
				#17 Pop hit for The Crickets in 1958		
				GALLOP, Frank		
				Best known as the announcer on Perry Como's TV shows during the 1950s.		
4/16/66	2¹	10		1 The Ballad Of Irving ....[C]	34	Kapp 745
8/27/66	25	4		2 The Son Of Irving ....[C]		Musicor 1191
				ballad of Seymour, son of the 142nd fastest gun in the West		
★★94★★				**GARFUNKEL, Art**		
				Half of Simon & Garfunkel duo. Born on 10/13/42 in Queens, New York. Appeared in films *Catch 22*, *Carnal Knowledge* and *Bad Timing*. Has masters degree in mathematics from Columbia University.		
				1)(What A) Wonderful World 2)All I Know 3)I Only Have Eyes For You		
9/22/73	1⁴	14		1 All I Know *	9	Columbia 45926
12/29/73	4	13		2 I Shall Sing *	38	Columbia 45983
4/6/74	30	7		3 Traveling Boy *	102	Columbia 46030
9/14/74	6	11		4 Second Avenue *	34	Columbia 10020
				*GARFUNKEL		
8/23/75	1¹	15		5 I Only Have Eyes For You	18	Columbia 10190

DEBUT DATE	PEAK POS	WKS CHR	GOLD	ARTIST — Record Title	POP POS	Label & Number
				GARFUNKEL, Art — Cont'd		
1/10/76	**1**¹	13		6 **Break Away**................................	39	Columbia 10273
9/24/77	**25**	12	✓	7 Crying In My Sleep................................		Columbia 10608
1/28/78	**1**⁵	14		8 **(What A) Wonderful World**................	17	Columbia 10676
				ART GARFUNKEL with JAMES TAYLOR & PAUL SIMON		
4/7/79	**12**	12		9 **In A Little While (I'll Be On My Way)**........		Columbia 10933
6/2/79	**5**	11		10 **Since I Don't Have You**................	53	Columbia 10999
8/18/79	**29**	10		11 **Bright Eyes**................................		Columbia 11050
8/8/81	**10**	16		12 **A Heart In New York**................	66	Columbia 02307
3/26/88	**11**	14		13 **So Much In Love**................		Columbia 07711
				#1 Pop hit for The Tymes in 1963		

GARNER, Erroll ⊙

Jazz pianist/composer born on 6/15/21 in Pittsburgh; died on 1/2/77. No formal training on piano; could not read music. Composer of "Misty," later a hit for Johnny Mathis and others.

5/11/68	**40**	2		Watermelon Man................................[I]		MGM 13916
				#10 Pop hit for the Mongo Santamaria Band in 1963		

GARNETT, Gale

Born on 7/17/42 in Auckland, New Zealand. Came to the U.S. in 1951. Made singing debut in 1960. Worked as an actress from age 15. Appeared on many TV shows including *Hawaiian Eye* and *Bonanza*.

8/15/64	**1**⁷	17		**We'll Sing In The Sunshine**................	4	RCA 8388

GARRETT, Leif

Born on 11/8/61 in Hollywood. Began film career in 1969. Appeared in all three *Walking Tall* films, *Macon County Line*, *Bob and Carol and Ted and Alice* and *The Outsiders*.

12/10/77	**48**	3		1 Runaround Sue................................	13	Atlantic 3440
1/20/79	**38**	6		2 I Was Made For Dancin'................	10	Scotti Br. 403
9/8/79	**11**	13		3 When I Think Of You................	78	Scotti Br. 502

GARRETT, Siedah

Singer/songwriter from North Hollywood. Touring vocalist with Sergio Mendes; worked with Quincy Jones since 1983. Co-wrote Michael Jackson's "Man In The Mirror." Also see Dennis Edwards and Michael Jackson.

10/31/87	**30**	7		Everchanging Times................................		Qwest 28163
				theme from the film *Baby Boom*		

GARY, John

Born in Watertown, New York on 11/29/32. Singer on Don McNeill's radio program, *Breakfast Club*.

9/26/64	**19**	1		1 Soon I'll Wed My Love................	89	RCA 8413
9/25/65	**27**	7		2 Don't Throw The Roses Away................	132	RCA 8677
4/23/66	**24**	6		3 Don't Let The Music Play................		RCA 8806
6/10/67	**10**	11		4 Everybody Say Peace................		RCA 9213
11/11/67	**1**²	13		5 Cold................................		RCA 9361

GARY & DAVE

Canadian singing/songwriting duo: Gary Weeks and Dave Beckett.

11/17/73	**47**	4		Could You Ever Love Me Again................	92	London 200

★★199★★ GATES, David

Born on 12/11/40 in Tulsa, Oklahoma. Began career as a session musician, then a songwriter/producer before becoming the lead singer of Bread. Wrote The Murmaids' hit "Popsicles & Icicles."

1)Goodbye Girl 2)Clouds 3)Never Let Her Go

7/7/73	**3**	11		1 **Clouds**................................	47	Elektra 45857
10/20/73	**11**	10		2 **Sail Around The World**................	50	Elektra 45868
1/11/75	**3**	13		3 **Never Let Her Go**................	29	Elektra 45223
4/26/75	**34**	7		4 **Part-Time Love**................		Elektra 45245
12/10/77	**3**	25		5 **Goodbye Girl**................	15	Elektra 45450
				title song from the Neil Simon film		
8/5/78	**7**	20		6 **Took The Last Train**................	30	Elektra 45500
2/16/80	**9**	13		7 **Where Does The Lovin' Go**................	46	Elektra 46588
9/26/81	**15**	9		8 **Take Me Now**................	62	Arista 0615

GATLIN, Larry

Trio of brothers reared in several West Texas towns: Larry (b: 5/2/48, Seminole, Texas), Steve (b: 4/4/51) and Rudy (b: 8/20/52).

7/22/78	**50**	1		1 Night Time Magic................................		Monument 249
4/12/80	**36**	9		2 Taking Somebody With Me When I Fall................	108	Columbia 11219
				LARRY GATLIN AND THE GATLIN BROTHERS BAND		

DEBUT DATE	PEAK POS	WKS CHR	G O L D	ARTIST — Record Title	POP POS	Label & Number
				GAYE, Marvin		
				Born Marvin Pentz Gay, Jr. on 4/2/39 in Washington, D.C. Sang in his father's Apostolic church. In vocal groups the Rainbows and Marquees. Joined Harvey Fuqua in the re-formed Moonglows. To Detroit in 1960. Session work as a drummer at Motown; married to Berry Gordy's sister Anna, 1961-75. First recorded under own name for Tamla in 1961. In seclusion for several months following the death of Tammi Terrell, 1970. Problems with drugs and the IRS led to his moving to Europe for three years. Fatally shot by his father after a quarrel on 4/1/84 in Los Angeles. Inducted into the Rock and Roll Hall of Fame in 1987.		
10/7/67	37	2		1 Your Precious Love	5	Tamla 54156
				MARVIN GAYE & TAMMI TERRELL		
8/7/71	34	4		2 Mercy Mercy Me (The Ecology)	4	Tamla 54207
10/20/73	43	4		3 You're A Special Part Of Me	12	Motown 1280
				DIANA ROSS & MARVIN GAYE		
12/18/82	34	11	●	4 Sexual Healing	3	Columbia 03302
★★67★★				**GAYLE, Crystal**		
				Born Brenda Gail Webb on 1/9/51 in Paintsville, Kentucky and raised in Wabash, Indiana. Youngest sister of Loretta Lynn. First country artist to tour China (1979).		
				1)You And I 2)Ready For The Times To Get Better 3)Talking In Your Sleep		
6/26/76	40	5		1 I'll Get Over You	71	United Art. 781
8/20/77	4	24	●	2 **Don't It Make My Brown Eyes Blue**	2³	United Art. 1016
2/11/78	3	16		3 **Ready For The Times To Get Better**	52	United Art. 1136
6/24/78	3	22		4 **Talking In Your Sleep**	18	United Art. 1214
12/16/78	22	13		5 Why Have You Left The One You Left Me For..............		United Art. 1259
4/14/79	20	14		6 When I Dream	84	United Art. 1288
8/4/79	35	7		7 Your Kisses Will		United Art. 1306
9/22/79	9	17		8 **Half The Way**	15	Columbia 11087
2/9/80	17	9		9 It's Like We Never Said Goodbye	63	Columbia 11198
5/17/80	16	15		10 The Blue Side	81	Columbia 11270
10/11/80	18	15		11 If You Ever Change Your Mind		Columbia 11359
10/10/81	17	16		12 The Woman In Me	76	Columbia 02523
3/13/82	32	10		13 You Never Gave Up On Me		Columbia 02718
10/16/82	2⁵	28		14 **You And I**	7	Elektra 69936
				EDDIE RABBITT with CRYSTAL GAYLE		
5/28/83	23	12		15 Our Love Is On The Faultline		Warner 29719
7/30/83	9	18		16 **Baby, What About You**	83	Warner 29582
11/5/83	10	17		17 **The Sound Of Goodbye**	84	Warner 29452
3/3/84	15	17		18 I Don't Wanna Lose Your Love		Warner 29356
2/15/86	36	3		19 Makin' Up For Lost Time (The Dallas Lovers' Song)		Warner 28856
				CRYSTAL GAYLE & GARY MORRIS		
				GAYNOR, Gloria		
				Born on 9/7/49 in Newark, New Jersey. Disco singer. With the Soul Satisfiers in 1971.		
11/16/74	11	12		1 Never Can Say Goodbye	9	MGM 14748
1/27/79	9	16	▲	2 **I Will Survive**	1³	Polydor 14508
				GEDDES, David		
				While a teenager, formed the group Rock Garden, who recorded for Capitol.		
12/20/75	42	5		The Last Game Of The Season (A Blind Man In The Bleachers)	18	Big Tree 16052
				GEILS		
				Rock group formed in Boston in 1967 as J. Geils Band; named for guitarist Jerome Geils. Lead singer Peter "Wolf" Blankfield left in 1983.		
8/13/77	48	3		You're The Only One	83	Atlantic 3411
★★77★★				**GENESIS**		
				Formed as a progressive rock group in England in 1967. Consisted of Peter Gabriel (lead vocals), Anthony Phillips (guitar), Tony Banks (keyboards), Michael Rutherford (guitar, bass) and Chris Stewart (drums; replaced by John Silver in 1968, then John Mayhew in 1969). Phillips and Mayhew left in 1970, replaced by Steve Hackett (guitar) and Phil Collins (drums). Gabriel left in June 1975, with Collins replacing him as new lead singer. Hackett went solo in 1977, leaving group as a trio: Collins, Rutherford and Banks. Added regular members for touring with Americans Chester Thompson (drums), in 1977, and guitarist Daryl Stuermer, in 1978. Collins also recorded in jazz-fusion group Brand X. Rutherford also in own group, Mike + The Mechanics, formed in 1985. Hackett later formed group GTR.		
				1)Hold On My Heart 2)In Too Deep 3)Throwing It All Away		
5/20/78	21	11		1 Follow You Follow Me	23	Atlantic 3474
7/5/80	32	9		2 Misunderstanding	14	Atlantic 3662
12/17/83	7	23		3 **That's All!**	6	Atlantic 89724
6/23/84	11	16		4 Taking It All Too Hard	50	Atlantic 89656

DEBUT DATE	PEAK POS	WKS CHR	GOLD	ARTIST — Record Title	POP POS	Label & Number
				GENESIS — Cont'd		
6/7/86	**3**	17		5 **Invisible Touch**	1[1]	Atlantic 89407
8/23/86	**1**[2]	17		6 **Throwing It All Away**	4	Atlantic 89372
2/28/87	**8**	13		7 **Tonight, Tonight, Tonight**	3	Atlantic 89290
4/25/87	**1**[3]	22		8 **In Too Deep**	3	Atlantic 89316
11/2/91	**8**	24		9 **No Son Of Mine**	12	Atlantic 87571
3/14/92	**26**	14		10 **I Can't Dance**	7	Atlantic 87532
4/4/92	**1**[5]	36		11 **Hold On My Heart**	12	Atlantic 87481
8/15/92	**27**	15		12 **Jesus He Knows Me**	23	Atlantic 87454
10/31/92	**4**	35		13 **Never A Time**	21	Atlantic 87411

GENTRY, Bobbie
Born Roberta Streeter on 7/27/44 in Chickasaw County, Mississippi; raised in Greenwood, Mississippi. Singer/songwriter. Won the 1967 Best New Artist Grammy Award. Married singer Jim Stafford on 10/15/78.

9/2/67	**7**	11	●	1 **Ode To Billie Joe**	1[4]	Capitol 5950
11/9/68	**32**	6		2 **Mornin' Glory**	74	Capitol 2314
				BOBBIE GENTRY & GLEN CAMPBELL B-side "Less Of Me" made the Country charts (POS 44)		
2/8/69	**7**	9		3 **Let It Be Me**	36	Capitol 2387
				GLEN CAMPBELL & BOBBIE GENTRY		
11/29/69	**8**	11		4 **Fancy**	31	Capitol 2675
2/21/70	**4**	9		5 **All I Have To Do Is Dream**	27	Capitol 2745
				BOBBIE GENTRY & GLEN CAMPBELL		
7/11/70	**19**	6		6 **Apartment 21**	81	Capitol 2849
4/24/71	**37**	2		7 **But I Can't Get Back**		Capitol 3071

GENTRYS, The
Memphis-based rock band. Lead singer Jimmy Hart is currently a professional wrestling manager.

2/20/71	**28**	4		**Wild World**	97	Sun 1122

GEORGE, Susan ○
Born on 7/26/50 in England. Actress/singer. Appeared in such films as *Straw Dogs* and *Mandingo*.

6/12/76	**44**	4		**I'll Get Over You**		Chelsea 3044
				#1 Country hit for Crystal Gayle in 1976		

GERARD, Danyel
Folk-pop singer/songwriter from France.

5/27/72	**20**	9		**Butterfly**	78	MGM/Verve 10670

GERRARD, Donny
Lead singer of the Canadian group Skylark.

5/31/75	**42**	5		1 **(Baby) Don't Let It Mess Your Mind**	104	Rocket 40405
				written by Neil Sedaka		
4/3/76	**23**	9		2 **Words (Are Impossible)**	87	Greedy 101
2/5/77	**47**	4		3 **Stay Awhile With Me**		Greedy 109

GETZ, Stan
Born Stan Gayetsky on 2/2/27 in Philadelphia. Jazz tenor saxophonist. With Stan Kenton (1944-45), Jimmy Dorsey (1945-46), Benny Goodman (1946) and Woody Herman (1947-49). Seventeen-time winner of Down Beat polls as top tenor saxophonist. Leader of the bossa nova movement of the 1960s. Died of liver cancer on 6/6/91.

10/20/62	**4**	13		1 **Desafinado** ....[I]	15	Verve 10260
				STAN GETZ/CHARLIE BYRD		
6/27/64	**1**[2]	9		2 **The Girl From Ipanema**	5	Verve 10323
				STAN GETZ/ASTRUD GILBERTO above 2 written by Brazilian composer Antonio Carlos Jobim		

GIANT STEPS
English duo: vocalist Campsie and multi-instrumentalist George McFarlane. Both initially worked together as members of the British band Grand Hotel, then as Quick.

11/5/88	**25**	11		**Another Lover**	13	A&M 1226

★★177★★ **GIBB, Andy**
Born Andrew Roy Gibb on 3/5/58 in Manchester, England. Moved to Australia when six months old, then back to England at age nine. Youngest brother of Barry, Robin and Maurice Gibb — The Bee Gees. Hosted TV's *Solid Gold* from 1981-82. Died on 3/10/88 of an inflammatory heart virus in Oxford, England.

1)(Our Love) Don't Throw It All Away 2)An Everlasting Love 3)I Can't Help It

5/7/77	**8**	22	●	1 **I Just Want To Be Your Everything**	1[4]	RSO 872
11/26/77	**18**	19	●	2 **(Love Is) Thicker Than Water**	1[2]	RSO 883
4/22/78	**8**	17	▲	3 **Shadow Dancing**	1[7]	RSO 893
7/22/78	**8**	13	●	4 **An Everlasting Love**	5	RSO 904

DEBUT DATE	PEAK POS	WKS CHR	GOLD	ARTIST — Record Title	POP POS	Label & Number
				GIBB, Andy — Cont'd		
10/21/78	2²	19	●	5 (Our Love) Don't Throw It All Away	9	RSO 911
2/2/80	9	10		6 Desire............	4	RSO 1019
4/5/80	8	13		7 I Can't Help It............	12	RSO 1026
				ANDY GIBB AND OLIVIA NEWTON-JOHN		
12/27/80	29	8		8 Time Is Time	15	RSO 1059
3/28/81	45	3		9 Me (Without You)	40	RSO 1056
8/22/81	25	11		10 All I Have To Do Is Dream............	51	RSO 1065
				ANDY GIBB AND VICTORIA PRINCIPAL (Pamela Ewing on TV's *Dallas*)		
				GIBB, Barry Born on 9/1/46 in Manchester, England. Eldest brother of The Bee Gees. Appeared in *Sgt. Pepper's Lonely Hearts Club Band*.		
11/1/80	5	18	●	1 Guilty *	3	Columbia 11390
2/7/81	1⁴	17		2 What Kind Of Fool *	10	Columbia 11430
				*BARBRA STREISAND & BARRY GIBB		
9/8/84	8	10		3 Shine Shine............	37	MCA 52443
				GIBB, Robin Born on 12/22/49 in Manchester, England. Twin brother of The Bee Gees' Maurice Gibb.		
8/26/78	22	11		Oh! Darling............ from the film *Sgt. Pepper's Lonely Hearts Club Band*	15	RSO 907
				GIBBS, Georgia Born Fredda Gibbons on 8/17/20 in Worcester, Massachusetts. Sang on the *Lucky Strike* radio show from 1937-38. With Hudson-DeLange band, then with Frankie Trumbauer (1940) and Artie Shaw (1942). On the *Garry Moore-Jimmy Durante* radio show in the late '40s, where Moore dubbed her "Her Nibs, Miss Gibbs."		
2/19/66	37	3		Let Me Dream............ written and produced by Teddy Randazzo		Bell 635
				GIBBS, Terri Born on 6/15/54 in Augusta, Georgia. Country singer/pianist; blind since birth.		
1/31/81	3	19		1 Somebody's Knockin'............	13	MCA 41309
6/13/81	37	9		2 Rich Man	89	MCA 51119
				GIBSON, Debbie Singer/songwriter/pianist. Born on 8/31/70 in Long Island. Playing piano since age five and songwriting since age six. In 1991, played Eponine in *Les Miserables* on Broadway.		
9/5/87	31	9	●	1 Only In My Dreams	4	Atlantic 89322
2/20/88	16	13		2 Out Of The Blue	3	Atlantic 89129
5/21/88	8	17		3 Foolish Beat............	1¹	Atlantic 89109
1/28/89	3	21	●	4 Lost In Your Eyes	1³	Atlantic 88970
7/8/89	13	14		5 No More Rhyme	17	Atlantic 88885
1/12/91	48	3		6 Anything Is Possible	26	Atlantic 87793
2/13/93	49	3		7 Losin' Myself............	86	Atlantic 87392
				GIBSON, Don Born on 4/3/28 in Shelby, North Carolina. Country singer/songwriter/guitarist. Joined the *Grand Ole Opry* in 1958.		
12/4/61	15	3		Lonesome Number One	59	RCA 7959
				GILBERTO, Astrud Born on 3/30/40 in Salvador, Brazil. Wife of composer/guitarist Joao Gilberto.		
6/27/64	1²	9		1 The Girl From Ipanema............ STAN GETZ/ASTRUD GILBERTO	5	Verve 10323
9/30/67	31	4		2 I Had The Craziest Dream		Verve 10548
				GILL, Johnny Born on 5/22/66 in Washington, D.C. Sang in family gospel group, Wings Of Faith, from age five. Joined New Edition in 1988. His brother Randy and cousin Jermaine Mickey are members of II D Extreme.		
9/15/90	32	9		My, My, My	10	Motown 919
				GILL, Vince ☉ Country singer/guitarist. Born on 4/12/57 in Norman, Oklahoma. Member of Pure Prairie League from 1979-83. Married to Janis Oliver of the Sweethearts Of The Rodeo.		
9/19/92	30	9		I Still Believe In You		MCA 54406
				GILLEY, Mickey Born on 3/9/36 in Natchez, Louisiana. Raised in Ferriday, Louisiana. Country singer/pianist. First cousin to both Jerry Lee Lewis and Reverend Jimmy Swaggart. Owner of Gilleys nightclub in Pasadena, Texas. Gilley and the club were featured in the film *Urban Cowboy*. The club closed in 1989.		
8/7/76	37	4		1 Bring It On Home To Me	101	Playboy 6075

DEBUT DATE	PEAK POS	WKS CHR	GOLD	ARTIST — Record Title	POP POS	Label & Number
				GILLEY, Mickey — Cont'd		
5/31/80	**3**	22		2 Stand By Me	22	Full Moon 46640
				featured in the film *Urban Cowboy*		
9/6/80	**40**	4		3 True Love Ways	66	Epic 50876
7/25/81	**12**	15		4 You Don't Know Me.....................................	55	Epic 02172
				GLASS TIGER		
				Canadian rock quintet: Alan Frew (vocals), Sam Reid (keyboards), Al Connelly (guitar), Wayne Parker (bass) and Michael Hanson (drums).		
10/4/86	**30**	9		1 Don't Forget Me (When I'm Gone)................	2¹	Manhattan 50037
12/20/86	**4**	18		2 Someday...	7	Manhattan 50048
				GLAZER, Tom, And The Do-Re-Mi Children's Chorus		
				Tom (b: 9/3/14 in Philadelphia) is a novelty folk singer. Hosted own ABC radio program, 1945-47. Composed score for 1957 film *A Face In The Crowd*.		
6/8/63	**4**	8		On Top Of Spaghetti ....[N]	14	Kapp 526
				parody of the tune "On Top Of Old Smokey"		
				GLENCOVES, The		
				Teen folk trio formed at Chaminade High School in Mineola, Long Island, New York in 1961. Singers/guitarists Don Connors and Bill Byrne with singer Brian Bolger.		
7/6/63	**20**	1		Hootenanny	38	Select 724
				GODLEY & CREME		
				Kevin Godley (b: 10/7/45, Manchester, England) and Lol Creme (b: 9/19/47, Manchester, England) formed duo after leaving British group 10cc. Prior to 10cc, both were with Hotlegs.		
8/10/85	**5**	16		Cry	16	Polydor 881786
				GODSPELL		
				The original cast as featured in the Broadway rock musical *Godspell*.		
6/3/72	**8**	13		Day By Day	13	Bell 45210
				lead vocal by original cast member Robin Lamont		
				GOFFIN, Louise		
				Singer/songwriter. Daughter of Carole King and Gerry Goffin.		
5/28/88	**41**	5		Bridge Of Sighs..		Warner 27949
				GOLD, Andrew		
				Born on 8/2/51 in Burbank, California. Son of soundtrack composer Ernest Gold (*Exodus*) and singer Marni Nixon. Co-founder of the group Bryndle. Session and arranging work for Linda Ronstadt since early '70s. Member of pop duo Wax, 1986.		
6/11/77	**38**	7		1 Lonely Boy	7	Asylum 45384
3/4/78	**15**	11		2 Thank You For Being A Friend	25	Asylum 45456
6/24/78	**16**	13		3 Never Let Her Slip Away.............................	67	Asylum 45489
				GOLD, Jack, Sound ☉		
				Prolific producer for United Artists and Columbia. Born in 1921. Died on 12/26/92 (age 71) of a heart attack in Tujunga, California. Produced albums for Barbra Streisand, Johnny Mathis, Gladys Knight and many others. Later scored films and the TV soap opera *Santa Barbara*.		
4/26/69	**27**	7		1 It Hurts To Say Goodbye		Columbia 44808
				THE JACK GOLD ORCHESTRA & CHORUS		
8/1/70	**10**	9	✓	2 Summer Symphony.....................................		Columbia 45202
				written by Neil Sedaka		
7/24/71	**34**	4		3 Summer Symphony.................................[R]		Columbia 45397
				GOLDE, Frannie		
				Singer/songwriter from Chicago.		
7/21/79	**36**	6		Here I Go (Fallin' In Love Again)...................	76	Portrait 70031
★★**38**★★				**GOLDSBORO, Bobby**		
				Born on 1/18/41 in Marianna, Florida. Singer/songwriter/guitarist. To Dothan, Alabama in 1956. Toured with Roy Orbison, 1962-64. Own syndicated TV show from 1972-75, *The Bobby Goldsboro Show*.		
				1)*Watching Scotty Grow* 2)*Honey* 3)*Autumn Of My Life* 4)*See The Funny Little Clown* 5)*The Straight Life*		
1/19/63	**17**	2		1 Molly	70	Laurie 3148
2/8/64	**3**	9		2 See The Funny Little Clown	9	United Art. 672
4/18/64	**13**	8		3 Whenever He Holds You..............................	39	United Art. 710
8/22/64	**14**	3		4 Me Japanese Boy I Love You	74	United Art. 742
3/30/68	**1²**	15	●	5 Honey	1⁵	United Art. 50283
6/29/68	**2⁴**	13		6 Autumn Of My Life	19	United Art. 50318
10/26/68	**6**	9		7 The Straight Life	36	United Art. 50461
2/15/69	**7**	8		8 Glad She's A Woman	61	United Art. 50497

DEBUT DATE	PEAK POS	WKS CHR	GOLD	ARTIST — Record Title	POP POS	Label & Number
				GOLDSBORO, Bobby — Cont'd		
4/26/69	**14**	8		9 I'm A Drifter	46	United Art. 50525
8/16/69	**10**	10		**10 Muddy Mississippi Line**	53	United Art. 50565
12/27/69	**23**	7		11 Mornin Mornin	78	United Art. 50614
3/28/70	**8**	9		**12 Can You Feel It**	75	United Art. 50650
7/18/70	**38**	2		13 It's Gonna Change	108	United Art. 50696
12/19/70	**1**[6]	14		**14 Watching Scotty Grow**	11	United Art. 50727
5/8/71	**8**	7		**15 And I Love You So**	83	United Art. 50776
7/17/71	**15**	8		16 Come Back Home	69	United Art. 50807
11/27/71	**34**	4		17 Danny Is A Mirror To Me/	107	
1/22/72	**27**	2		18 A Poem For My Little Lady		United Art. 50846
4/1/72	**36**	4		19 California Wine	108	United Art. 50891
9/16/72	**28**	4		20 With Pen In Hand	94	United Art. 50938
2/17/73	**37**	3		21 Brand New Kind Of Love	116	United Art. 51107
6/16/73	**18**	17		22 Summer (The First Time)	21	United Art. 251
8/24/74	**8**	7		**23 Hello Summertime**		United Art. 529
4/26/75	**15**	10	✓	24 And Then There Was Gina..................		United Art. 633
8/9/75	**16**	9		25 I Wrote A Song (Sing Along)		United Art. 681
5/15/76	**7**	11		**26 A Butterfly For Bucky**	101	United Art. 793
2/26/77	**6**	12		**27 Me And The Elephants**	104	Epic 50342
11/1/80	**19**	15		28 Goodbye Marie		Curb 5400
3/14/81	**34**	5		29 Alice Doesn't Love Here Anymore		Curb 70052
				GOMM, Ian		
				Born on 3/17/47 in Ealing, England. Member of London band Brinsley Schwarz, 1972-75.		
10/6/79	**10**	7		**Hold On**..	18	Stiff/Epic 50747
				GOODRUM, Randy ♦		
				Country-pop singer/songwriter. Wrote Anne Murray's "You Needed Me" and "Broken Hearted Me."		
1/18/86	**28**	7		Silhouette		GRP 3013
				GOODWIN, Don		
				Singer discovered by Paul Anka while auditioning at a Las Vegas hotel.		
1/5/74	**44**	6		This Is Your Song	86	Silver Blue 806
				written and co-produced by Paul Anka		
				GORE, Lesley		
				Born on 5/2/46 in New York City; raised in Tenafly, New Jersey. Discovered by Quincy Jones while singing at a hotel in Manhattan. In films *Girls On The Beach*, *Ski Party* and *The T.A.M.I. Show*.		
5/30/64	**12**	4		1 I Don't Wanna Be A Loser	37	Mercury 72270
7/5/69	**36**	3		2 98.6/Lazy Day		Mercury 72931
				"98.6" was a #7 Pop hit for Keith in 1967; "Lazy Day" was a #14 Pop hit for Spanky & Our Gang in 1967		
2/28/70	**39**	2		3 Why Doesn't Love Make Me Happy		Crewe 338
				GORE, Michael		
				Brother of Lesley Gore. Songwriter — he and Lesley contributed tracks to the *Fame* soundtrack.		
3/24/84	**5**	21		**Theme from "Terms Of Endearment"**...........................[I]	84	Capitol 5334
				from the film *Terms Of Endearment*		
★★76★★				**GORME, Eydie**		
				Born on 8/16/31 in New York City. Vocalist with the big bands of Tommy Tucker and Tex Beneke in the late 1940s. Featured on Steve Allen's *Tonight Show* from 1953. Married Steve Lawrence on 12/29/57. They recorded as the duo Parker & Penny in 1979.		
				1)*If He Walked Into My Life* 2)*We Can Make It Together* 3)*I Want To Stay Here* 4)*Tonight I'll Say A Prayer* 5)*The Honeymoon Is Over*		
6/8/63	**18**	2		1 Don't Try To Fight It, Baby	53	Columbia 42790
8/29/64	**20**	2		2 Can't Get Over (The Bossa Nova).........	87	Columbia 43082
6/5/65	**39**	1		3 Just Dance On By	124	Columbia 43302
12/11/65	**36**	4	✓	4 Don't Go To Strangers		Columbia 43444
				#36 Pop hit for Etta James in 1960		
3/5/66	**17**	8		5 What Did I Have That I Don't Have?		Columbia 43542
				from the musical *On A Clear Day You Can See Forever*		
6/11/66	**5**	9		**6 If He Walked Into My Life**	120	Columbia 43660
				from the musical *Mame*		
12/17/66	**34**	3		7 What Is A Woman		Columbia 43906
				from the musical *I Do, I Do*		
2/4/67	**30**	6		8 Softly, As I Leave You	117	Columbia 43971

DEBUT DATE	PEAK POS	WKS CHR	G O L D	ARTIST — Record Title	POP POS	Label & Number
				GORME, Eydie — Cont'd		
12/30/67	**22**	7	9	How Could I Be So Wrong		Calendar 1002
				from the musical *Golden Rainbow*		
1/20/68	**35**	3	10	Life Is But A Moment (Canta Ragazzina)	115	Columbia 44299
8/3/68	**22**	6	11	This Girl's In Love With You		Calendar 1004
				#7 Pop hit for Dionne Warwick in 1969		
10/18/69	**8**	18	12	**Tonight I'll Say A Prayer**	45	RCA 0250
7/18/70	**24**	4	13	My World Keeps Getting Smaller Every Day		RCA 0360
				written by Neil Sedaka		
2/20/71	**23**	7	14	It Was A Good Time		MGM 14213
				Rosy's theme from the film *Ryan's Daughter*		
8/11/73	**47**	2	15	Take One Step		MGM 14563
12/22/73	**41**	5	16	Touch The Wind (Eres Tu)		MGM 14681
				#9 Pop hit for Mocedades in 1974		
9/4/76	**23**	8	17	What I Did For Love		United Art. 852
				from the Broadway musical *A Chorus Line*		
				STEVE LAWRENCE & EYDIE GORME:		
8/17/63	**8**	7	18	**I Want To Stay Here**	28	Columbia 42815
1/25/64	**14**	3	19	I Can't Stop Talking About You	35	Columbia 42932
2/4/67	**14**	8	20	The Honeymoon Is Over		Columbia 43930
				from the Broadway musical *I Do, I Do*		
6/15/68	**33**	6	21	The Two Of Us		Calendar 1003
4/5/69	**20**	7	22	Real True Lovin'	119	RCA 0123
4/25/70	**21**	5	23	(You're My) Soul And Inspiration		RCA 0334
2/13/71	**37**	3	24	Love Is Blue/Autumn Leaves		RCA 0420
				#1 Pop hits for Paul Mauriat in 1968 and Roger Williams in 1955		
8/26/72	**7**	14	25	**We Can Make It Together**	68	MGM 14383
				STEVE & EYDIE featuring The Osmonds		
2/24/73	**31**	5	26	Feelin'		MGM 14493
8/4/79	**46**	5	27	Hallelujah		Warner/Curb 8877
				PARKER & PENNY		
★★148★★				**GOULET, Robert**		
				Born on 11/26/33 in Lawrence, Massachusetts. Began concert career in Edmonton, Canada. Broadway/film/TV actor. Launched career as Sir Lancelot in the hit Broadway musical *Camelot*. Won the 1962 Best New Artist Grammy Award.		
				1)*My Love, Forgive Me (Amore, Scusami)* 2)*Come Back To Me, My Love* 3)*On A Clear Day You Can See Forever*		
10/24/64	**3**	15	1	**My Love, Forgive Me (Amore, Scusami)**	16	Columbia 43131
				B-side "I'd Rather Be Rich" Bubbled Under (POS 131)		
6/5/65	**14**	8	2	Summer Sounds	58	Columbia 43301
9/18/65	**5**	13	3	**Come Back To Me, My Love/**	118	
10/16/65	**13**	9	4	On A Clear Day You Can See Forever	119	Columbia 43394
				Broadway musical title song		
4/9/66	**37**	3	5	Young Only Yesterday/		
4/30/66	**28**	4	6	Why Be Ashamed		Columbia 43558
6/11/66	**22**	7	7	Daydreamer		Columbia 43668
				movie title song		
9/17/66	**15**	6	8	Once I Had A Heart		Columbia 43760
3/25/67	**20**	7	9	World Of Clowns		Columbia 44019
5/13/67	**33**	6	10	One Life, One Dream		Columbia 44100
7/15/67	**29**	4	11	The Sinner		Columbia 44186
3/16/68	**33**	5	12	The Happy Time		Columbia 44466
				from the Broadway musical starring Goulet		
6/8/68	**26**	6	13	What A Wonderful World		Columbia 44548
9/7/68	**17**	10	14	Thirty Days Hath September		Columbia 44618
5/17/69	**33**	3	15	Didn't We		Columbia 44847
				GO WEST		
				British duo of Peter Cox (vocals) and Richard Drummie (guitar, vocals).		
6/30/90	**7**	29	1	**King Of Wishful Thinking**	8	EMI 50307
				from the film *Pretty Woman*		
11/7/92	**3**	33	2	**Faithful**	14	EMI 50411
3/6/93	**3**	20	3	**What You Won't Do For Love**	55	EMI 50443

DEBUT DATE	PEAK POS	WKS CHR	GOLD	ARTIST — Record Title	POP POS	Label & Number
				GRAHAM, Larry		
				Born on 8/14/46 in Beaumont, Texas. To Oakland at the age of two. Bass player with Sly & The Family Stone from 1966-72. Formed Graham Central Station in 1973. Went solo in 1980.		
8/30/80	**37**	6	●	One In A Million You	9	Warner 49221
				GRAMM, Lou		
				Born on 5/2/50 in Rochester, New York. Lead singer of Foreigner. Member of Black Sheep, 1970-75. Left Foreigner in 1991 to form Shadow King; returned in 1992.		
12/2/89	**4**	23		**Just Between You And Me**	6	Atlantic 88781
★★**86**★★				**GRANT, Amy**		
				Born on 11/25/60 in Augusta, Georgia. The first lady of Contemporary Christian music. Married to singer/songwriter Gary Chapman.		
				1)Baby Baby 2)That's What Love Is For 3)The Next Time I Fall		
6/1/85	**7**	16		1 Find A Way	29	A&M 2734
9/7/85	**34**	3		2 Wise Up	66	A&M 2762
11/9/85	**28**	7		3 Everywhere I Go		A&M 2785
9/27/86	**1**²	22		4 The Next Time I Fall..	**1**¹	Full Moon 28597
				PETER CETERA w/AMY GRANT		
11/22/86	**18**	12		5 Stay For Awhile		A&M 2864
10/1/88	**31**	7		6 1974 (We Were Young)		A&M 1243
1/7/89	**32**	7		7 Saved By Love		A&M 1260
3/9/91	**1**³	32		8 Baby Baby	**1**²	A&M 1549
6/15/91	**2**⁶	33		9 Every Heartbeat	**2**¹	A&M 1557
9/28/91	**1**³	32		10 That's What Love Is For...	7	A&M 1566
1/18/92	**4**	29		11 Good For Me	8	A&M 1573
4/18/92	**2**²	33		12 I Will Remember You	20	A&M 1600
				GRANT, Earl		
				Organist/pianist/vocalist born in Oklahoma City in 1931. First recorded for Decca in 1957. In the films *Tender Is The Night, Imitation Of Life* and *Tokyo Night*. Died in an automobile accident on 6/10/70.		
9/29/62	**17**	4		Sweet Sixteen Bars .... [I]	55	Decca 25574
				written by Ray Charles		
				GRANT, Gogi		
				Born Audrey Arinsberg on 9/20/24 in Philadelphia. Moved to Los Angeles at age 12. Performed vocals for the film *The Helen Morgan Story*.		
5/13/67	**23**	17		The Sea..		Monument 1005
				GRASS ROOTS, The		
				Rock group formed in 1964. Lineup from 1971-73: Rob Grill (lead singer, bass), Warren Entner, Reed Kailing, Virgil Webber and Joel Larson.		
7/10/71	**37**	3		1 Sooner Or Later	9	Dunhill 4279
11/6/71	**37**	5		2 Two Divided By Love	16	Dunhill 4289
2/10/73	**31**	6		3 Love Is What You Make It	55	Dunhill 4335
				GRATEFUL DEAD		
				Legendary psychedelic-rock band formed in San Francisco in 1966. By 1987, the group consisted of Jerry Garcia, Bob Weir, Phil Lesh, Brent Mydland, Bill Kreutzmann and Mickey Hart. Mydland died on 7/26/90 (age 37) of a drug overdose; replaced by Tubes keyboardist Vince Welnick.		
8/29/87	**15**	10		Touch Of Grey	9	Arista 9606
				GRAVES, Carl		
				Soul singer from Calgary, Alberta, Canada. With the group Skylark in 1973.		
11/30/74	**23**	8		Baby, Hang Up The Phone	50	A&M 1620
				GRAY, Dobie		
				Born Leonard Victor Ainsworth on 7/26/42 in Brookshire, Texas. Soul vocalist/composer/actor. To Los Angeles in 1960. Worked as an actor on Broadway, and in the L.A. production of *Hair*. Lead singer of Pollution in 1971.		
3/17/73	**12**	10	●	1 Drift Away..	5	Decca 33057
7/28/73	**7**	14		2 Loving Arms...	61	MCA 40100
2/21/76	**22**	9		3 If Love Must Go	78	Capricorn 0249
2/17/79	**44**	3		4 You Can Do It	37	Infinity 50003
				GREAN, Charles Randolph, Sounde		
				Charles (b: 10/1/13 in New York City) is a former artist and repertoire director at RCA and Dot Records. Married singer Betty Johnson.		
6/14/69	**3**	12		1 **Quentin's Theme** .... [I]	13	Ranwood 840
				from the TV series *Dark Shadows*		
2/14/70	**12**	9		2 Peter And The Wolf .... [I]	108	Ranwood 864
				adaptation of Prokofiev's famous symphonic poem		

DEBUT DATE	PEAK POS	WKS CHR	GOLD	ARTIST — Record Title	POP POS	Label & Number
				GREAN, Charles Randolph, Sounde — Cont'd		
5/9/70	**33**	4		3 Come Touch The Sun .... [I]		Ranwood 872
				from the film *Butch Cassidy and the Sundance Kid*		
9/12/70	**32**	4		4 Theme from Borsalino .... [I]		Ranwood 880
				from the film *Borsalino*		
4/29/72	**16**	9		5 The Masterpiece .... [I]		Ranwood 922
				theme from PBS-TV's *Masterpiece Theatre*		
12/13/75	**8**	12		6 Star Trek		Ranwood 1044
				disco version of the theme from the TV series		
				GREAVES, R.B.		
				Born Ronald Bertram Aloysius Greaves on 11/28/44 at the USAF Base in Georgetown, British Guyana. Half American Indian, raised on a Seminole reservation in California. Nephew of Sam Cooke. To England in 1963, as Sonny Childe & The TNT's.		
11/15/69	**21**	5	●	1 Take A Letter Maria	2¹	Atco 6714
1/31/70	**3**	8		**2 Always Something There To Remind Me**	27	Atco 6726
5/9/70	**37**	2		3 Fire & Rain	82	Atco 6745
				GRECCO, Cyndi		
				New York-based songstress.		
5/29/76	**13**	9		Making Our Dreams Come True	25	Private S. 45086
				theme from the TV series *LaVerne & Shirley*		
				GRECO, Buddy		
				Born Armando Greco on 8/14/26 in Philadelphia. Former pianist/vocalist with Benny Goodman.		
8/14/65	**27**	6		1 I Can't Begin To Tell You	132	Epic 9817
				#1 hit for Bing Crosby in 1945		
12/25/65	**36**	4		2 That Darn Cat		Epic 9864
				Walt Disney movie title song		
8/6/66	**24**	8		3 Put Yourself In My Place		Reprise 0495
10/1/66	**21**	7		4 Walking On New Grass		Reprise 0515
				#7 Country hit for Kenny Price in 1966		
3/25/67	**14**	6		5 There She Goes		Reprise 0562
				#26 Pop hit for Jerry Wallace in 1961		
6/24/67	**19**	7		6 Love's Gonna Live Here Again		Reprise 0584
				#1 Country hit for Buck Owens in 1963		
10/4/69	**34**	4		7 From Atlanta To Goodbye		Scepter 12260
				GREEN, Al		
				Born on 4/13/46 in Forest City, Arkansas. Soul singer/songwriter. With gospel group the Greene Brothers. To Grand Rapids, Michigan in 1959. First recorded for Fargo in 1960. In group The Creations from 1964-67. Sang with his brother Robert and Lee Virgins in the group Soul Mates from 1967-68. Went solo in 1969. Wrote most of his songs. Returned to gospel music in 1980.		
1/8/72	**36**	4	●	1 Let's Stay Together	1¹	Hi 2202
7/29/72	**33**	7	●	2 I'm Still In Love With You	3	Hi 2216
11/11/72	**28**	7	●	3 You Ought To Be With Me	3	Hi 2227
12/21/74	**28**	8	●	4 Sha-La-La (Make Me Happy)	7	Hi 2274
11/19/88	**2¹**	19		**5 Put A Little Love In Your Heart**	9	A&M 1255
				ANNIE LENNOX & AL GREEN		
				from the film *Scrooged*		
				GREENE, Lorne		
				Born on 2/12/14 in Ottawa, Canada; died on 9/11/87 of cardiac arrest. Chief newscaster for CBC radio, 1940-43. Acted in films *The Silver Chalice* and *Tight Spot*; starred in TV's *Bonanza* and *Battlestar Galactica*.		
11/14/64	**1⁶**	10		1 Ringo .... [S]	1¹	RCA 8444
2/6/65	**16**	2		2 The Man	72	RCA 8490
3/19/66	**36**	2		3 Five Card Stud	112	RCA 8757
8/20/66	**35**	3		4 Waco .... [S]		RCA 8901
				movie title song		
				GREEN LYTE SUNDAY Featuring Susan Darby ○		
7/25/70	**19**	7		Chelsea Morning		RCA 0365
				#78 Pop hit for Judy Collins in 1969		
				GREENWOOD, Lee		
				Born on 10/27/42 in Los Angeles. Country singer/songwriter/multi-instrumentalist. With Felix Cavaliere (later of the Young Rascals) in the Scotties. Worked as a dealer in Vegas casinos until 1981.		
5/7/83	**4**	22		1 I.O.U.	53	MCA 52199
8/20/83	**15**	12		2 Somebody's Gonna Love You	96	MCA 52257
6/2/84	**26**	9		3 God Bless The USA		MCA 52386
7/14/84	**24**	10		4 To Me *		MCA 52415

DEBUT DATE	PEAK POS	WKS CHR	GOLD	ARTIST — Record Title	POP POS	Label & Number
				GREENWOOD, Lee — Cont'd		
2/23/85	**35**	2		5 It Should Have Been Love By Now *		MCA 52525
				*BARBARA MANDRELL/LEE GREENWOOD		
				GREENWOOD COUNTY SINGERS, The		
8/1/64	**15**	5		1 Frankie And Johnny	75	Kapp 591
4/16/66	**16**	9		2 Please Don't Sell My Daddy No More Wine........................	64	Kapp 742
				THE GREENWOODS		
				GRIFFIN, Clive — see DION, Celine		
				GROCE, Larry		
				Born on 4/22/48 in Dallas. Pop-folk singer/songwriter. Wrote children's songs for Walt Disney Records.		
2/14/76	**33**	8		Junk Food Junkie ....[N]	9	Warner 8165
				recorded live at McCabe's in Santa Monica		
				GROOP, The ☺		
				Australian group.		
10/11/69	**35**	5		The Jet Song (When The Weekend's Over)...........................	112	Bell 822
				GROSS, Henry		
				Rock singer from Brooklyn. Original lead guitarist of Sha-Na-Na.		
3/27/76	**13**	11	●	Shannon	6	Lifesong 45002
				GRUSIN, Dave ☺		
				Jazz pianist. Born on 6/26/34 in Littleton, Colorado. Composer/producer of over 35 film soundtracks, *On Golden Pond* and *Tootsie* among them. Won Academy Award for *Milagro Beanfield War* soundtrack.		
6/2/84	**15**	15		Theme From St. Elsewhere .... [I]		GRP 3005
				from the TV series *St. Elsewhere*		
				GUARALDI, Vince, Trio		
				Born on 7/17/32 in San Francisco; died of a heart attack on 2/6/76. Pianist/leader of own jazz trio. Formerly with Woody Herman and Cal Tjader. Wrote the music for the *Peanuts* TV specials.		
1/12/63	**9**	11		**Cast Your Fate To The Wind** .... [I]	22	Fantasy 563
				GUESS WHO, The		
				Rock group formed in Winnipeg, Canada in 1963. Consisted of Allan "Chad Allan" Kobel (guitar, vocals), Randy Bachman (lead guitar), Garry Peterson (drums), Bob Ashley (piano) and Jim Kale (bass). Recorded as The Reflections, and Chad Allan & The Expressions. Ashley replaced by new lead singer Burton Cummings in 1966. Allan left shortly thereafter.		
11/8/69	**15**	6		Undun...	22	RCA 0195
				flip side "Laughing" made the *Hot 100* (POS 10)		
				GUIDRY, Greg		
				Singer/songwriter/pianist from St. Louis. Born in 1950.		
3/20/82	**11**	15		Goin' Down...	17	Columbia 02691
				GUNHILL ROAD		
				Rock trio: Glen Leopold, Gil Roman and Steven Goldrich.		
6/9/73	**37**	3		Back When My Hair Was Short	40	Kama Sutra 569
				GUTHRIE, Arlo		
				Born on 7/10/47 in Coney Island, New York. Son of legendary folk singer Woody Guthrie. Starred in the 1969 film *Alice's Restaurant* which was based on his 1967 song "Alice's Restaurant Massacree."		
8/12/72	**4**	13		1 The City Of New Orleans	18	Reprise 1103
6/9/73	**23**	8		2 Gypsy Davy..	105	Reprise 1158
				written by Arlo's father, Woody Guthrie		
				GUYS 'N' DOLLS ☺		
				British vocal sextet consisting of three men and three women.		
6/28/75	**15**	10		There's A Whole Lot Of Loving...		Epic 50109

H

HAGGARD, Merle
Born on 4/6/37 in Bakersfield, California. Country singer/songwriter/guitarist. Served nearly three years in San Quentin prison on a burglary charge, 1957-60. Signed to Capitol Records in 1965 and then formed backing band, The Strangers. One of the top male vocalists of the country charts with 38 #1 country singles.

| 1/1/72 | **35** | 3 | | 1 Carolyn .... | 58 | Capitol 3222 |

DEBUT DATE	PEAK POS	WKS CHR	GOLD	ARTIST — Record Title	POP POS	Label & Number
				HAGGARD, Merle — Cont'd		
12/29/73	**16**	8		2 If We Make It Through December	28	Capitol 3746
5/14/83	**21**	12		3 Pancho And Lefty		Epic 03842
				WILLIE NELSON & MERLE HAGGARD		
				HALL, Daryl		
				Born Daryl Franklin Hohl on 10/11/48 in Philadelphia. Half of Hall & Oates duo.		
8/30/86	**24**	7		1 Dreamtime	5	RCA 14387
11/8/86	**21**	7		2 Foolish Pride	33	RCA 5038
2/7/87	**11**	11		3 Someone Like You	57	RCA 5105
★★**51**★★				**HALL, Daryl, & John Oates**		
				Daryl Hall (see previous entry) and John Oates (b: 4/7/49 in New York City) met while students at Temple University in 1967. Hall sang backup for many top soul groups before teaming up with Oates in 1972. In the late 1980s, they passed The Everly Brothers as the #1 charting duo of the rock era.		
				1)*Everything Your Heart Desires* 2)*One On One* 3)*Don't Hold Back Your Love* 4)*So Close* 5)*She's Gone*		
4/17/76	**18**	10	●	1 Sara Smile	4	RCA 10530
8/14/76	**6**	11		2 She's Gone ....[R]	7	Atlantic 3332
				originally made the *Hot 100* on 2/9/74 (POS 60)		
2/10/79	**49**	1		3 I Don't Wanna Lose You	42	RCA 11424
11/24/79	**23**	9		4 Wait For Me	18	RCA 11747
10/11/80	**15**	15		5 You've Lost That Lovin' Feeling	12	RCA 12103
2/14/81	**16**	12	●	6 Kiss On My List	1³	RCA 12142
11/14/81	**33**	5		7 Private Eyes	1²	RCA 12296
11/28/81	**12**	18	●	8 I Can't Go For That (No Can Do)	1¹	RCA 12357
5/1/82	**29**	9		9 Did It In A Minute	9	RCA 13065
11/6/82	**14**	17	●	10 Maneater..	1⁴	RCA 13354
2/5/83	**4**	19		11 **One On One**	7	RCA 13421
6/18/83	**36**	6		12 Family Man	6	RCA 13507
11/5/83	**8**	16		13 **Say It Isn't So**	2⁴	RCA 13654
10/6/84	**8**	19		14 **Out Of Touch**	1²	RCA 13916
1/19/85	**18**	12		15 Method Of Modern Love	5	RCA 13970
3/30/85	**17**	8		16 Some Things Are Better Left Unsaid	18	RCA 14035
6/15/85	**8**	12		17 **Possession Obsession**	30	RCA 14098
9/14/85	**12**	9		18 A Nite At The Apollo Live! The Way You Do The Things You Do/My Girl	20	RCA 14178
				DARYL HALL JOHN OATES with David Ruffin & Eddie Kendrick recorded at the re-opening of New York's Apollo Theatre		
4/16/88	**2**¹	20		19 **Everything Your Heart Desires**	3	Arista 9684
7/16/88	**8**	15		20 **Missed Opportunity**..	29	Arista 9727
10/13/90	**6**	25		21 **So Close**	11	Arista 2085
				produced by Jon Bon Jovi and Danny Kortchmar		
1/19/91	**4**	22		22 **Don't Hold Back Your Love**	41	Arista 2157
5/11/91	**10**	20		23 **Starting All Over Again**		Arista LP Cut
				from the LP *Change Of Season* on Arista 8614; #19 Pop hit for Mel & Tim in 1972		
				HALL, Jimmy		
				Mobile, Alabama native. Leader of the Southern rock band Wet Willie.		
11/8/80	**30**	12		I'm Happy That Love Has Found You	27	Epic 50931
				HALL, Lani		
				Lead vocalist with Sergio Mendes & Brasil '66. Married to Herb Alpert.		
6/6/81	**43**	3		1 Come What May...		A&M 2333
				LANI HALL Featuring Herb Alpert		
10/15/83	**22**	8		2 Never Say Never Again	103	A&M 2596
				title song from the James Bond film		
1/21/84	**18**	10		3 Send In The Clowns		A&M 2616
				#19 Pop hit for Judy Collins in 1977		
4/28/84	**32**	8		4 Come What May..[R]		A&M 2632
				LANI HALL With Herb Alpert		
				HALL, Tom T.		
				Born on 5/25/36 in Olive Hill, Kentucky. Country music storyteller. Wrote "Harper Valley P.T.A." hit for Jeannie C. Riley. Host of *Pop Goes The Country* TV series.		
12/29/73	**2**¹	15		1 I Love	12	Mercury 73436
6/8/74	**24**	8		2 That Song Is Driving Me Crazy	63	Mercury 73488

DEBUT DATE	PEAK POS	WKS CHR	GOLD	ARTIST — Record Title	POP POS	Label & Number
				HAMILTON, George IV		
				Born on 7/19/37 in Winston-Salem, North Carolina. Country-folk-pop singer/songwriter/guitarist. Toured with Buddy Holly, Gene Vincent and The Everly Brothers. Moved to Nashville in 1959 and joined the *Grand Ole Opry*. Own TV series on ABC in 1959, and in Canada in the late 1970s.		
7/27/63	4	8		Abilene	15	RCA 8181
				HAMILTON, JOE FRANK & REYNOLDS		
				Dan Hamilton, Joe Frank Carollo and Tommy Reynolds. Trio were members of The T-Bones. Reynolds left group in 1972 and was replaced by Alan Dennison. Although Reynolds had left, group still recorded as Hamilton, Joe Frank & Reynolds until July 1976.		
6/5/71	4	12	●	1 **Don't Pull Your Love**	4	Dunhill 4276
9/11/71	21	6		2 Annabella	46	Dunhill 4287
6/21/75	1¹	15	●	3 **Fallin' In Love**	1¹	Playboy 6024
11/22/75	5	15		4 **Winners And Losers**	21	Playboy 6054
4/10/76	7	9		5 **Everyday Without You**	62	Playboy 6068
				HAMILTON, JOE FRANK & DENNISON:		
7/10/76	21	7		6 Light Up The World With Sunshine	67	Playboy 6077
10/30/76	50	3		7 Don't Fight The Hands (That Need You)	72	Playboy 6088
				HAMLISCH, Marvin		
				Born on 6/2/44 in New York City. Pianist/composer/conductor for numerous soundtracks. 1973's Best Song Oscar and Grammy winner for "The Way We Were." Won the 1974 Best New Artist Grammy Award.		
2/2/74	1¹	22	●	The Entertainer .... [I]	3	MCA 40174
				written in 1902 by Scott Joplin; featured in the film *The Sting*		
				HAMMER, Jan		
				Jazz-rock keyboard virtuoso born in Prague, Czechoslovakia in 1950. Toured with Sarah Vaughan as conductor/keyboardist. Member of Mahavishnu Orchestra until 1973.		
10/12/85	16	11		1 Miami Vice Theme .... [I]	1¹	MCA 52666
				from TV's *Miami Vice* soundtrack		
3/12/88	42	4		2 Crockett's Theme .... [I]		MCA 53239
				Don Johnson portrayed Det. James "Sonny" Crockett on TV's *Miami Vice*		
				HAMMOND, Albert		
				Born on 5/18/42 in London and raised in Gibraltar, Spain. Member of British group Magic Lanterns, 1971.		
8/19/72	38	3		1 Down By The River	91	Mums 6009
10/28/72	2¹	13	●	2 It Never Rains In Southern California	5	Mums 6011
12/1/73	26	9		3 Half A Million Miles From Home	87	Mums 6024
3/9/74	15	12		4 I'm A Train	31	Mums 6026
3/22/75	1¹	13		5 **99 Miles From L.A.**	91	Mums 6037
				HAMPSHIRE, Keith		
				Singer/songwriter from Canada. Worked as a DJ at CKFH.		
6/16/73	32	4		First Cut Is The Deepest	70	A&M 1432
				written by Cat Stevens		
				HARDY, Hagood		
				Indiana-born vibraphonist based in Toronto. Sideman for Herbie Mann and George Shearing.		
11/8/75	6	15		The Homecoming .... [I]	41	Capitol 4156
				from the made-for-TV pilot film *The Waltons*		
				HARNELL, Joe		
				Born on 8/2/24 in the Bronx. Conductor/arranger for Frank Sinatra, Peggy Lee and others. Musical director for many TV shows, including *The Mike Douglas Show*.		
1/5/63	4	12		1 Fly Me To The Moon-Bossa Nova .... [I]	14	Kapp 497
9/30/67	36	4		2 Serenata .... [I]		Columbia 44244
				HARNEN, Jimmy — see SYNCH		
				HARPERS BIZARRE		
				Santa Cruz, California quintet led by Ted Templeman, who later produced many albums for The Doobie Brothers and Van Halen.		
3/11/67	4	13		1 **The 59th Street Bridge Song (Feelin' Groovy)**	13	Warner 5890
				written by Paul Simon; arranged by Leon Russell		
8/19/67	6	13		2 **Anything Goes**	43	Warner 7063
				written in 1934 by Cole Porter for the musical of the same title		
11/18/67	1²	12		3 **Chattanooga Choo Choo**	45	Warner 7090
				#1 hit for Glenn Miller in 1941		
6/22/68	38	3		4 **Both Sides Now**	123	Warner 7200
				#8 Pop hit for Judy Collins in 1968		
8/17/68	21	7		5 Battle Of New Orleans	95	Warner 7223

DEBUT DATE	PEAK POS	WKS CHR	GOLD	ARTIST — Record Title	POP POS	Label & Number
				HARRIET		
				Harriet Roberts, native of Sheffield, England.		
3/23/91	**24**	10		Temple Of Love..	39	EastWest 98863
				HARRIS, Anita ○		
				British singer.		
10/28/67	**20**	9		Just Loving You	120	Columbia 44236
				HARRIS, Emmylou		
				Born on 4/2/47 in Birmingham, Alabama. Contemporary country vocalist. Sang backup with Gram Parsons until his death in 1973. Own band from 1975. *Grand Ole Opry* in 1992. Also see Southern Pacific.		
3/13/76	**13**	9		1 Here, There And Everywhere	65	Reprise 1346
				written by John Lennon and Paul McCartney; flip side "Together Again" hit #1 on the Country charts		
7/5/80	**10**	14		**2 That Lovin' You Feelin' Again**	55	Warner 49262
				ROY ORBISON & EMMYLOU HARRIS from the film *Roadie*		
2/28/81	**8**	12		**3 Mister Sandman**	37	Warner 49684
7/23/83	**26**	9		4 Wild Montana Skies		RCA 13562
				JOHN DENVER & EMMYLOU HARRIS		
6/20/87	**35**	3		5 Telling Me Lies		Warner 28371
				DOLLY PARTON, LINDA RONSTADT, EMMYLOU HARRIS		
				HARRIS, Johnny, Orchestra ○		
				Harris was a top producer/arranger in England during the late 1960s.		
9/6/69	**31**	7		Footprints On The Moon..[I]		Warner 7319
				HARRIS, Major		
				Born on 2/9/47 in Richmond, Virginia. Soul singer. With The Jarmels, Teenagers and Impacts in the early 1960s. With The Delfonics from 1971-74.		
5/10/75	**33**	10	●	Love Won't Let Me Wait	5	Atlantic 3248
				HARRIS, Phil ○		
				Born on 6/24/04 in Linton, Indiana. Bandleader/drummer/radio-TV-movie personality. Co-hosted a radio program with his wife, actress Alice Faye, from 1947-54.		
3/9/68	**23**	7		But I Loved You		Coliseum 2711
				Gordon Jenkins (orch.)		
				HARRIS, Richard		
				Born on 10/1/30 in Limerick, Ireland. Began prolific acting career in 1958. Portrayed King Arthur in the long-running stage production and film version of *Camelot*.		
6/15/68	**10**	7		**1 MacArthur Park**..	2¹	Dunhill 4134
11/9/68	**23**	4		2 The Yard Went On Forever..	64	Dunhill 4170
6/7/69	**11**	8		3 Didn't We	63	Dunhill 4194
11/13/71	**13**	12		4 My Boy	41	Dunhill 4293
				HARRIS, Rolf		
				Born in Perth, Australia on 3/30/30. Played piano from age nine. Moved to England in the mid-1950s. Developed his unique "wobble board sound" out of a sheet of masonite. Had own BBC-TV series from 1970.		
6/15/63	**1³**	10		**1 Tie Me Kangaroo Down, Sport** ....[N]	3	Epic 9596
3/21/70	**19**	6		2 Two Little Boys	119	MGM 14103
★★153★★				**HARRISON, George**		
				Born on 2/25/43 in Liverpool, England. Formed his first group, the Rebels, at age 13. Joined John Lennon and Paul McCartney in The Quarrymen in 1958; group later evolved into The Beatles, with Harrison as lead guitarist. Organized the Bangladesh benefit concerts at Madison Square Garden in 1971. Member of the 1988 supergroup Traveling Wilburys. In 1992, became the first recipient of The Century Award, *Billboard's* honor for distinguished creative achievement.		
				1)Got My Mind Set On You 2)All Those Years Ago 3)Blow Away		
12/5/70	**10**	11	●	**1 My Sweet Lord**	1⁴	Apple 2995
3/13/71	**31**	4		2 What Is Life..	10	Apple 1828
5/26/73	**4**	11		**3 Give Me Love - (Give Me Peace On Earth)**........................	1¹	Apple 1862
2/19/77	**20**	9		4 Crackerbox Palace	19	Dark Horse 8313
3/17/79	**2¹**	14		**5 Blow Away**	16	Dark Horse 8763
6/23/79	**38**	6		6 Love Comes To Everyone		Dark Horse 8844
5/23/81	**1¹**	15		**7 All Those Years Ago**	2³	Dark Horse 49725
				Paul McCartney (backing vocal); Ringo Starr (drums)		
10/31/87	**1⁴**	20		**8 Got My Mind Set On You**..	1¹	Dark Horse 28178
				originally recorded by James Ray in 1962 (Dynamic Sound 503)		
2/6/88	**10**	13		**9 When We Was Fab**..	23	Dark Horse 28131
5/7/88	**20**	8		10 This Is Love		Dark Horse 27913

DEBUT DATE	PEAK POS	WKS CHR	GOLD	ARTIST — Record Title	POP POS	Label & Number
				HART, Corey		
				Born in Montreal, Canada and raised in Spain and Mexico. Singer/songwriter/keyboardist.		
10/20/84	19	11		1 It Ain't Enough..	17	EMI America 8236
7/6/85	8	18		2 **Never Surrender**	3	EMI America 8268
1/25/86	39	3		3 Everything In My Heart..	30	EMI America 8300
1/10/87	24	8		4 Can't Help Falling In Love	24	EMI America 8368
				HART, Freddie		
				Born Fred Segrest on 12/21/26 in Lochapoka, Alabama. Country singer/songwriter/guitarist.		
10/9/71	28	7	●	Easy Loving	17	Capitol 3115
				HART, Susan		
5/2/81	47	4		Is This A Disco Or A Honky Tonk?......................................	109	Dore 967
				HARTMAN, Dan		
				Multi-instrumentalist/songwriter/producer from Harrisburg, Pennsylvania. Member of the Edgar Winter Group from 1972-76. Own studio called the Schoolhouse in Westport, Connecticut.		
10/17/81	41	5		1 All I Need	110	Blue Sky 02472
6/2/84	7	20		2 I Can Dream About You	6	MCA 52378
				from the film *Streets Of Fire*		
3/2/85	19	7		3 Second Nature..	39	MCA 52519
				HATHAWAY, Donny — see FLACK, Roberta		
				HATHAWAY, Lalah ☉		
				Chicago-born daughter of the late Donny Hathaway. Her mother is classical singer Eulalah Hathaway.		
3/30/91	47	4		It's Somethin'..		Virgin 98834
				HAVENS, Richie		
				Born on 1/21/41 in Brooklyn. Black folk singer/guitarist. Opening act of 1969 Woodstock concert.		
4/24/71	18	8		Here Comes The Sun	16	Stormy F. 656
				written by George Harrison (on Beatles' *Abbey Road* album)		
				HAWKES, Chesney		
				Nineteen-year-old (in 1991) male singer from the U.K. Son of Len "Chip" Hawkes of The Tremeloes. Starred as Roger Daltrey's son in the film *Buddy's Song*.		
11/30/91	46	2		The One And Only..	10	Chrysalis 23730
				written by Nik Kershaw		
				HAWKINS, Edwin, Singers		
				Hawkins (b: August 1943) formed gospel group with Betty Watson in Oakland in 1967 as the Northern California State Youth Choir. Member Dorothy Morrison went on to a solo career.		
5/3/69	22	6	●	Oh Happy Day	4	Pavilion 20001
				featuring Dorothy Combs Morrison		
				HAWKINS, Jennell		
				Keyboardist/vocalist from Los Angeles. Recorded with Richard Berry as Rickey & Jennell for Flair, 1954.		
3/24/62	9	8		**Moments**	50	Amazon 1003
				first released as "Moments To Remember" on the Titanic label		
				HAWKINS, Sophie B.		
				Sophie Ballantine Hawkins, a Manhattan-bred singer. Percussionist in Bryan Ferry's backing band in the early '80s.		
6/20/92	39	7		Damn I Wish I Was Your Lover..	5	Columbia 74164
				HAYES, Isaac		
				Born on 8/20/42 in Covington, Tennessee. Soul singer/songwriter/keyboardist/producer/actor. Session musician for Otis Redding and other artists on the Stax label. Teamed with songwriter David Porter to compose "Soul Man," "Hold On! I'm A Comin'" and many others. Composed film scores for *Shaft*, *Tough Guys* and *Truck Turner*.		
6/5/71	19	6		1 Never Can Say Goodbye...	22	Enterprise 9031
10/23/71	6	11		2 **Theme From Shaft**	1²	Enterprise 9038
				from the Richard Roundtree film *Shaft*		
4/1/72	21	6		3 Let's Stay Together.. [I]	48	Enterprise 9045
10/21/72	12	10		4 Theme From The Men... [I]	38	Enterprise 9058
				from the ABC-TV series *The Men*		
1/19/74	34	6		5 Joy - Pt. I	30	Enterprise 9085
				HAYMAN, Richard		
				Born on 3/27/20 in Cambridge, Massachusetts. Conductor/arranger/harmonica soloist.		
9/18/61	19	1		Night Train .... [I]	80	Mercury 71869

DEBUT DATE	PEAK POS	WKS CHR	G O L D	ARTIST — Record Title	POP POS	Label & Number
				HAYWARD, Justin		
				Lead singer/guitarist of The Moody Blues. Born on 10/14/46 in Swindon, England.		
5/31/75	**29**	7		1 I Dreamed Last Night	47	Threshold 67019
				JUSTIN HAYWARD & JOHN LODGE		
10/14/78	**20**	14		2 Forever Autumn	47	Columbia 10799
				from the musical LP version of H.G. Wells' *War Of The Worlds*		
				HAZLEWOOD, Lee — see SINATRA, Nancy		
				HEAD, Murray		
				British singer/actor. Appeared on the 1970 rock concept LP *Jesus Christ Superstar*. Played juvenile lead in 1971 film *Sunday, Bloody Sunday*.		
5/4/85	**35**	6		One Night In Bangkok..	3	RCA 13988
				from the Tim Rice, Benny Andersson and Bjorn Ulvaeus musical project *Chess*		
				HEALEY, Jeff, Band		
				Toronto-based, blues-rock trio: vocalist/guitarist Healey with drummer Tom Stephen and bassist Joe Rockman. Healey, blind since age one and guitarist since three, appeared in the 1989 film *Road House*.		
8/26/89	**7**	17		1 Angel Eyes	5	Arista 9808
5/8/93	**36**	4		2 Lost In Your Eyes...	91	Arista 12521
				HEART		
				Rock band formed in Seattle in 1973. Originally known as The Army, then White Heart, shortened to Heart in 1974. Group features Ann Wilson (lead singer) and her sister Nancy (guitar, keyboards). Band moved to Vancouver in 1975 when their manager Mike Fisher was drafted, and signed with the new Mushroom label. When amnesty was declared, group returned to Seattle and signed with the CBS Portrait label in 1976. Joining the Wilsons were guitarists Howard Leese and Roger Fisher (brother of Mike), bassist Steve Fossen and drummer Michael DeRosier. The Fishers left the band in 1979; Roger joined Alias in 1990. Fossen and DeRosier left by 1982, replaced by bassist Mark Andes (ex-Spirit, Jo Jo Gunne and Firefall member) and drummer Denny Carmassi (ex-Gamma). Nancy married film director Cameron Crowe.		
				1)These Dreams 2)Alone 3)All I Wanna Do Is Make Love To You		
1/15/77	**17**	9		1 Dreamboat Annie	42	Mushroom 7023
2/17/79	**33**	8		2 Dog & Butterfly	34	Portrait 70025
1/24/81	**43**	4		3 Tell It Like It Is	8	Epic 50950
2/1/86	**1**³	19		**4 These Dreams**	**1**¹	Capitol 5541
6/28/86	**40**	2		**5 Nothin' At All**	10	Capitol 5572
5/30/87	**2**¹	22		**6 Alone**	**1**³	Capitol 44002
3/31/90	**6**	18	●	**7 All I Wanna Do Is Make Love To You**	**2**²	Capitol 44507
9/29/90	**8**	24		**8 Stranded**	13	Capitol 44621
				HEARTSFIELD		
				Six-man Chicago rock band led by vocalist J.C. Heartsfield.		
2/23/74	**40**	7		Music Eyes	95	Mercury 73449
				HEATHERTON, Joey		
				Born on 9/14/44 in Rockville Centre, New York. Movie/TV actress.		
5/20/72	**5**	16		1 Gone	24	MGM 14387
11/25/72	**22**	7		2 I'm Sorry	87	MGM 14434
				HEATWAVE		
				Multi-national, interracial group formed in Germany by brothers Johnnie and Keith Wilder of Dayton, Ohio. Johnnie became a paraplegic due to a car accident in 1979.		
3/11/78	**33**	5	●	Always And Forever..	18	Epic 50490
				HEAVEN BOUND with Tony Scotti		
				Producer/backing vocalist Scotti with Joan Medora (lead vocals), Eddie Medora, Tommy Oliver and Michael Lloyd.		
10/9/71	**40**	2		1 He'd Rather Have The Rain	83	MGM 14284
11/27/71	**12**	9		2 Five Hundred Miles	79	MGM 14314
				HEFTI, Neal		
				Born on 10/29/22 in Hastings, Nebraska. Trumpeter. Gained fame as arranger for Woody Herman (1944-46), Harry James and Count Basie, then as composer of TV themes.		
2/19/66	**12**	8		1 Batman Theme ....[I]	35	RCA 8755
				original theme from the *Batman* TV series		
8/12/67	**38**	3		2 Barefoot In The Park ....[I]		Dot 17020
				movie title song		
				HEIGHTS, The		
				Band made up of cast members from the Fox network prime time TV show of the same name. Show is based on fictional adventures featuring the band. Led by actors/vocalists Shawn Thompson and James Walters.		
10/10/92	**8**	19	●	How Do You Talk To An Angel	**1**²	Capitol 44890

DEBUT DATE	PEAK POS	WKS CHR	GOLD	ARTIST — Record Title	POP POS	Label & Number
				HENDERSON, "Fantastic" Joe ○		
3/29/69	**39**	2		Help Yourself .... [I]		Fontana 1638
				#35 Pop hit for Tom Jones in 1968		
				HENDERSON, Florence ○		
				Born on 2/14/34 in Dale, Indiana. Starred as the mother, Carol Brady, on TV's *The Brady Bunch*.		
1/31/70	**25**	7		Conversations		Decca 732619
				HENDERSON, Joe		
				R&B singer. Born in 1938 in Como, Mississippi and raised in Gary, Indiana. Moved to Nashville in 1958. With the Fairfield Four gospel group. Died in 1966.		
5/26/62	**5**	11		**Snap Your Fingers**	8	Todd 1072
				HENDERSON, Skitch ○		
				Born Lyle Henderson on 1/27/18 in Halstad, Minnesota. Conducted orchestra for *The Steve Allen Show* and Johnny Carson's *Tonight Show*, 1962-66.		
3/12/66	**28**	6		1 Oh, Yeah ....[I-N]		Columbia 43499
				with the *Tonight Show* Orchestra		
2/10/68	**30**	3		2 Green Green Grass Of Home .... [I]	110	Columbia 44333
8/10/68	**40**	2		3 The Girl That I Marry .... [I]		Columbia 44579
				#11 hit for Frank Sinatra in 1946		
				HENHOUSE FIVE PLUS TOO — see STEVENS, Ray		
★★135★★				**HENLEY, Don**		
				Born on 7/22/47 in Gilmer, Texas. Singer/songwriter/drummer. Own band, Shiloh, in the early '70s. Worked with Glenn Frey in Linda Ronstadt's backup band, then the two formed the Eagles with Randy Meisner and Bernie Leadon. Went solo in 1982.		
				1)*Sometimes Love Just Ain't Enough* 2)*The End Of The Innocence* 3)*The Heart Of The Matter*		
11/7/81	**10**	19		1 **Leather And Lace**	6	Modern 7341
				STEVIE NICKS with DON HENLEY		
1/19/85	**33**	4		2 The Boys Of Summer	5	Geffen 29141
6/15/85	**6**	18		3 **Not Enough Love In The World**	34	Geffen 29012
9/28/85	**18**	9		4 Sunset Grill	22	Geffen 28906
7/1/89	**2**[1]	22		5 **The End Of The Innocence**	8	Geffen 22925
				co-written and produced by Bruce Hornsby (also on piano)		
11/11/89	**5**	18		6 **The Last Worthless Evening**	21	Geffen 22771
3/3/90	**3**	29		7 **The Heart Of The Matter**	21	Geffen 19898
11/10/90	**5**	20		8 **New York Minute**	48	Geffen 19660
8/1/92	**1**[4]	34		9 **Sometimes Love Just Ain't Enough**	2[6]	MCA 54403
				PATTY SMYTH with Don Henley		
				HENSON, Jim		
				Creator of The Muppets, that famous crew of puppets starring in TV's *Sesame Street* and *The Muppet Show*, also in the films *The Muppet Movie* and *The Great Muppet Caper*. Jim (b: 9/24/36 in Greenville, Mississippi) was the voice for both Ernie and Kermit. Died of a sudden virus on 5/16/90.		
9/12/70	**36**	1		1 Rubber Duckie .... [N]	16	Columbia 45207
				ERNIE		
9/22/79	**18**	17		2 Rainbow Connection	25	Atlantic 3610
				KERMIT		
				from the original soundtrack of *The Muppet Movie*		
				HESTER, Benny ○		
11/7/81	**41**	8		Nobody Knows Me Like You		Myrrh 228
				HEWETT, Howard		
				Lead vocalist of Shalamar, 1979-85. Born and raised in Akron, Ohio. Married singer/actress Nia Peeples in 1989. Also see Stanley Clarke.		
11/15/86	**31**	4		1 I'm For Real	90	Elektra 69527
				George Duke, Stanley Clarke and Wilton Felder (backing musicians)		
3/19/88	**24**	8		2 Another Chance To Love		Arista 9656
				DIONNE WARWICK & HOWARD HEWETT		
6/9/90	**33**	7		3 Show Me	62	Elektra 64978
2/2/91	**30**	8		4 I Can't Tell You Why		Elektra 64908
3/6/93	**23**	10		5 How Fast Forever Goes		Elektra 64653
				HEYWARD, Nick ○		
				British. Founded and fronted the group Haircut One Hundred in 1981. Group disbanded in 1983.		
12/10/83	**20**	12		Whistle Down The Wind		Arista 9072

HICKMAN, Sara ✪
Dallas-based singer/songwriter. Born on 3/1/63 in Jacksonville, North Carolina and raised in Houston.

3/24/90	38	5		1 Simply		Elektra 64993
9/8/90	47	2		2 Blue Eyes Are Sensitive To The Light		Hollywood 64939
				from the film Arachnophobia		
11/3/90	11	21		3 I Couldn't Help Myself		Elektra 64930

HI-FIVE
R&B teen vocal quintet from Waco, Texas and Oklahoma City: Tony Thompson, Roderick Clark, Russell Neal, Marcus Sanders and Toriano Easley (left after release of first album, replaced by Treston Irby).

6/1/91	42	3	●	1 I Like The Way (The Kissing Game)	1[1]	Jive 1424
				written and produced by Teddy Riley of Guy		
8/24/91	30	10		2 I Can't Wait Another Minute	8	Jive 1445

HIGGINS, Bertie
Singer/songwriter. Born Elbert Higgins on 12/8/44 in Tarpon Springs, Florida. First recorded for ABC in 1964. Worked as a drummer with the Roemans from 1964-66.

12/19/81	1[2]	26		1 Key Largo	8	Kat Family 02524
				inspired by the Humphrey Bogart/Lauren Bacall film		
5/1/82	10	18		2 Just Another Day In Paradise	46	Kat Family 02839
12/17/83	34	8		3 When You Fall In Love		Kat Family 04164

HIGHWAYMEN, The
Folk quintet formed at Wesleyan University in Middletown, Connecticut: Dave Fisher, Bob Burnett, Steve Trott, Steve Butts and Chan Daniels (d: 8/2/75).

8/7/61	1[5]	13		1 Michael	1[2]	United Art. 258
				19th-century folk song ("Michael Row The Boat Ashore")		
11/20/61	12	8		2 The Gypsy Rover/	42	
12/4/61	3	17		3 Cotton Fields	13	United Art. 370
				traditional American ballad, copyrighted in 1850		
7/28/62	19	1		4 The Bird Man	64	United Art. 475
				narration by Burt Lancaster; from film The Bird Man of Alcatraz		

★★151★★ HILL, Dan
Born on 6/3/54 in Toronto. Author/singer/songwriter.
1)Can't We Try 2)Never Thought (That I Could Love) 3)Unborn Heart

12/17/77	10	20	●	1 Sometimes When We Touch	3	20th Century 2355
8/26/78	8	12		2 All I See Is Your Face	41	20th Century 2378
12/23/78	50	3		3 Let The Song Last Forever	91	20th Century 2392
4/25/87	2[3]	29		4 Can't We Try	6	Columbia 07050
				DAN HILL with Vonda Sheppard		
10/31/87	2[3]	23		5 Never Thought (That I Could Love)	43	Columbia 07618
4/16/88	8	13		6 Carmelia		Columbia 07772
5/20/89	3	15		7 Unborn Heart		Columbia 68754
11/23/91	7	27		8 I Fall All Over Again		Quality 15180
6/6/92	30	13		9 Hold Me Now		Quality 19107
				DAN HILL with Rique Franks		

HILL, Warren
Saxophonist from Toronto. Attended Boston's Berklee College of Music. To Los Angeles in 1988.

2/27/93	1[2]	25		1 Tell Me What You Dream	43	RCA 62468
				RESTLESS HEART Featuring Warren Hill		
3/13/93	33	8		2 The Passion Theme ....[I]		Novus LP Cut
				from the soundtrack album Body of Evidence on Novus 66141		

HILLSIDE SINGERS, The
Nine-member vocal group assembled by producer/arranger Al Ham.

11/27/71	5	11		1 I'd Like To Teach The World To Sing (In Perfect Harmony)	13	Metromedia 231
				adapted from a Coca-Cola jingle		
2/19/72	22	4		2 We're Together	100	Metromedia 241
				adapted from a McDonald's jingle		
11/18/72	22	5		3 The Last Happy Song/Look Into Your Brother's Eyes		Metromedia 255

HINES, Gregory — see VANDROSS, Luther

HIROSHIMA ✪
Los Angeles jazz-pop band founded in 1974 by Dan Kuramoto, with varying membership.

| 5/31/86 | 20 | 8 | | 1 One Wish ....[I] | | Epic 05875 |
| 7/1/89 | 41 | 5 | | 2 Come To Me .... | | Epic 68890 |

DEBUT DATE	PEAK POS	WKS CHR	G O L D	ARTIST — Record Title	POP POS	Label & Number
★★113★★				**HIRT, Al** Born Alois Maxwell Hirt on 11/7/22 in New Orleans. Trumpet virtuoso. Toured with Jimmy and Tommy Dorsey, Ray McKinley and Horace Heidt. Formed own Dixieland combo (with Pete Fountain) in the late 1950s.		
				1)Java 2)Cotton Candy 3)Sugar Lips		
2/1/64	**1**⁴	12		1 **Java** .... [I]	4	RCA 8280
4/11/64	**3**	12		2 **Cotton Candy** .... [I]	15	RCA 8346
7/11/64	**3**	7		3 **Sugar Lips** .... [I]	30	RCA 8391
10/10/64	**12**	3		4 Up Above My Head (I Hear Music in the Air)	85	RCA 8439
				#6 R&B hit for Sister Rosetta Tharpe in 1949		
1/23/65	**9**	5		5 **Fancy Pants** .... [I]	47	RCA 8487
				written by Floyd Cramer		
4/17/65	**13**	7		6 Al's Place .... [I]	57	RCA 8542
8/21/65	**19**	7		7 The Silence (Il Silenzio) .... [I]	96	RCA 8653
10/9/65	**30**	4		8 Feelin' Fruggy .... [I]		RCA 8684
2/5/66	**28**	3		9 The Arena * .... [I]	129	RCA 8736
4/2/66	**36**	4		10 Mame *		RCA 8774
				Broadway musical title song		
6/25/66	**27**	8		11 Trumpet Pickin' * .... [I]		RCA 8854
1/21/67	**31**	6		12 Music To Watch Girls By * .... [I]	119	RCA 9060
				AL (He's the King) HIRT, Trumpet		
5/20/67	**18**	8		13 Puppet On A String .... [I]	129	RCA 9198
12/30/67	**23**	4		14 Ludwig .... [I]		RCA 9381
1/27/68	**10**	7		15 **Keep The Ball Rollin'**	100	RCA 9417
4/13/68	**23**	5		16 We Can Fly/Up-Up And Away	129	RCA 9500
2/1/69	**16**	6		17 If	116	RCA 9717
				HITCHCOCK, Russell ⊙ Born on 6/15/49 in Melbourne, Australia. Half of Air Supply duo.		
5/14/88	**39**	4		1 What Becomes Of The Brokenhearted?		Arista 9698
				#7 Pop hit for Jimmy Ruffin in 1966		
1/5/91	**9**	19		2 **Caught In Your Web (Swear To Your Heart)**		Hollywood LP Cut
				from the soundtrack album *Arachnophobia* on Hollywood 60974; Timothy B. Schmit (backing vocal)		
				HO, Don, and the Aliis Don was born on 8/13/30 in Oahu, Hawaii. Nightclub singer/actor.		
12/3/66	**14**	13		Tiny Bubbles	57	Reprise 0507
				HOFFS, Susanna Born on 1/17/57. Former lead singer of The Bangles. Starred in 1987 film *The Allnighter*. Her mother is film director Tamara Hoffs. Married TV producer M. Jay Roach on 4/17/93.		
3/2/91	**27**	9		My Side Of The Bed	30	Columbia 73529
				HOLLAND, Amy Daughter of country singer Esmereldy and opera singer Harry Boersma. Married to Michael McDonald. Also see Chris Christian.		
9/27/80	**34**	8		How Do I Survive	22	Capitol 4884
				produced by Michael McDonald		
				HOLLIES, The Formed in Manchester, England in 1962. Consisted of Allan Clarke (lead vocals), Graham Nash and Tony Hicks (guitars), Eric Haydock (bass) and Don Rathbone (drums). Nash left in December 1968 to join David Crosby and Stephen Stills in new trio, replaced by Terry Sylvester, formerly in the Swinging Blue Jeans. Shuffling personnel since then. Clarke, Nash, Hicks and Elliott regrouped briefly in 1983.		
12/16/72	**31**	4		1 Long Dark Road	26	Epic 10920
5/11/74	**3**	16	●	2 **The Air That I Breathe**	6	Epic 11100
6/11/83	**8**	14		3 Stop In The Name Of Love	29	Atlantic 89819
				HOLM, Michael German singer/songwriter/producer.		
12/7/74	**7**	10		**When A Child Is Born**	53	Mercury 73642
				HOLMAN, Eddie Born on 6/3/46 in Norfolk, Virginia. Soul singer/songwriter. Recorded for Leopard in the early 1960s.		
2/7/70	**36**	3	●	Hey There Lonely Girl	2¹	ABC 11240
				recorded in 1963 by Ruby & The Romantics as "Hey There Lonely Boy"		
				HOLMES, Clint Born on 5/9/46 in Bournemouth, England. Moved to Buffalo, New York as a child.		
3/17/73	**7**	15	●	1 **Playground In My Mind**	2²	Epic 10891
				child's vocal is by producer Paul Vance's son, Philip		

DEBUT DATE	PEAK POS	WKS CHR	G O L D	ARTIST — Record Title	POP POS	Label & Number
				HOLMES, Clint — Cont'd		
9/22/73	**34**	5		2 Shiddle-ee-dee	106	Epic 11033
				HOLMES, Jake		
				Born John Grier Holmes on 12/28/39 in San Francisco. Singer/songwriter.		
10/31/70	**22**	4		So Close	49	Polydor 14041
				HOLMES, Richard "Groove"		
				Born on 5/2/31 in Camden, New Jersey. Died of prostate cancer on 6/29/91. Jazz organist. Discovered by Les McCann. Recorded with Joe Pass, Gene Ammons and Clifford Scott.		
6/25/66	**7**	14		1 Misty ....[I]	44	Prestige 401
9/17/66	**27**	6		2 Secret Love ....[I]	99	Pacific Jazz 88130
				HOLMES, Rupert		
				Born on 2/24/47 in Cheshire, England. Moved to New York at age six. Member of studio group Street People. Wrote and arranged for The Drifters, The Platters and Gene Pitney. Arranged/produced for Barbra Streisand. Wrote The Buoys' hit "Timothy" and the Broadway musical *Drood*.		
11/3/79	**8**	13	●	1 **Escape (The Pina Colada Song)**	1³	Infinity 50035
1/26/80	**4**	16		2 **Him**	6	MCA 41173
5/10/80	**12**	12		3 Answering Machine	32	MCA 41235
11/8/80	**21**	13		4 Morning Man	68	MCA 51019
4/4/81	**21**	9		5 I Don't Need You	56	MCA 51092
11/28/81	**35**	8		6 Loved By The One You Love	103	Elektra 47225
2/20/82	**31**	7		7 The End		Elektra 47409
				HOMI, Amanda, & Brian Jarvis ☺		
5/5/84	**26**	9		Friend Of A Friend		GRP 3004
				HONEYDRIPPERS, The		
				A rock superstar gathering: vocalist Robert Plant (Led Zeppelin), with guitarists Jimmy Page (The Yardbirds, Led Zeppelin, The Firm), Jeff Beck (The Yardbirds) and Nile Rodgers (Chic).		
10/20/84	**1**¹	20		1 **Sea Of Love**	3	Es Paranza 99701
2/2/85	**38**	3		2 Rockin' At Midnight	25	Es Paranza 99686
				recorded by Elvis Presley in 1954 as "Good Rockin' Tonight"		
				HOPKIN, Mary		
				Born on 5/3/50 in Pontardawe, Wales. Discovered by the model Twiggy. Married to producer Tony Visconti (worked with David Bowie) from December 1971 to October 1981.		
10/5/68	**1**⁶	13	●	1 **Those Were The Days**	2³	Apple 1801
				melody based on a traditional Russian folk song		
4/26/69	**6**	10		2 **Goodbye** *	13	Apple 1806
				written by John Lennon and Paul McCartney		
2/21/70	**4**	10		3 **Temma Harbour**	39	Apple 1816
7/4/70	**7**	8		4 **Que Sera, Sera (Whatever Will Be, Will Be)** *	77	Apple 1823
				*produced by Paul McCartney		
12/5/70	**27**	5		5 Think About Your Children	87	Apple 1825
12/2/72	**11**	7		6 Knock Knock Who's There	92	Apple 1855
★★**128**★★				**HORNSBY, Bruce, And The Range**		
				Singer/pianist/songwriter/leader of jazz-influenced pop quintet The Range. Born on 11/23/54 in Williamsburg, Virginia. Moved to Los Angeles in 1980. Backing pianist for Sheena Easton's touring band, 1983. Formed The Range in 1984 with Joe Puerta (bass), John Molo (drums), guitarists George Marinelli and David Mansfield (replaced by Peter Harris who left by 1990). Won the 1986 Best New Artist Grammy Award.		
				1)Mandolin Rain 2)The Way It Is 3)The Valley Road		
8/16/86	**37**	2		1 Every Little Kiss	72	RCA 14361
9/27/86	**1**²	25		2 **The Way It Is**	1¹	RCA 5023
1/24/87	**1**³	19		3 **Mandolin Rain**	4	RCA 5087
5/23/87	**3**	19		4 **Every Little Kiss** ....[R]	14	RCA 5165
4/30/88	**1**¹	23		5 **The Valley Road**	5	RCA 7645
7/30/88	**7**	19		6 **Look Out Any Window**	35	RCA 8678
6/23/90	**8**	20		7 **Across The River**	18	RCA 2621
10/20/90	**16**	14		8 Lost Soul	84	RCA 2704
				Shawn Colvin (female vocal)		
6/8/91	**25**	10	✓	9 Set Me In Motion		RCA 2846
				from the film *Backdraft*		
4/17/93	**13**	15		10 Harbor Lights		RCA 62487
				BRUCE HORNSBY		

DEBUT DATE	PEAK POS	WKS CHR	GOLD	ARTIST — Record Title	POP POS	Label & Number
				HOT		
				Interracial female trio: Gwen Owens, Cathy Carson and Juanita Curiel. First known as Sugar & Spice.		
4/9/77	**8**	15	●	1 **Angel In Your Arms**	6	Big Tree 16085
9/3/77	**37**	4		2 **The Right Feeling At The Wrong Time**....................	65	Big Tree 16099
				HOT BUTTER		
				Hot Butter is Moog synthesizer player Stan Free.		
7/1/72	**4**	16		1 **Popcorn** .... [I]	9	Musicor 1458
4/7/73	**19**	8		2 **Percolator**... [I]	106	Musicor 1473
				#10 Pop hit for Billy Joe & The Checkmates in 1962		
8/25/73	**49**	2		3 **Slag Solution** .... [I]		Musicor 1481
				HOUSTON, David		
				Born on 12/9/38 in Bossier City, Louisiana. Country singer/songwriter/guitarist. Godson of 1920s pop singer Gene Austin and a descendant of Sam Houston and Robert E. Lee.		
3/30/68	**18**	5		1 **Have A Little Faith**	98	Epic 10291
2/22/69	**37**	3		2 **My Woman's Good To Me**		Epic 10430
				HOUSTON, Thelma		
				Soul singer/actress from Leland, Mississippi. In films *Norman...Is That You?*, *Death Scream* and *The Seventh Dwarf*.		
2/26/77	**40**	8		1 **Don't Leave Me This Way**	1[1]	Tamla 54278
6/25/77	**44**	2		2 **If It's The Last Thing I Do**...........................	47	Tamla 54283
6/9/79	**44**	2		3 **Saturday Night, Sunday Morning**	34	Tamla 54297
★★27★★				**HOUSTON, Whitney**		
				Born on 8/9/63 in Newark, New Jersey. Daughter of Cissy Houston and cousin of Dionne Warwick. Began singing career at age 11 with the gospel group New Hope Baptist Junior Choir. As a teen, worked as a backing vocalist for Chaka Khan and Lou Rawls. Pursued modeling career in 1981, appearing in *Glamour* magazine and the cover of *Seventeen*. Married Bobby Brown on 7/18/92.		
				1)I Will Always Love You 2)Greatest Love Of All 3)All The Man That I Need *4)Where Do Broken Hearts Go 5)Saving All My Love For You*		
6/30/84	**6**	17		1 **Hold Me**..	46	Asylum 69720
				TEDDY PENDERGRASS with Whitney Houston		
5/11/85	**4**	21		2 **You Give Good Love**	3	Arista 9274
8/17/85	**1**[3]	19		3 **Saving All My Love For You**	1[1]	Arista 9381
12/14/85	**1**[1]	20		4 **How Will I Know**	1[2]	Arista 9434
3/29/86	**1**[5]	20		5 **Greatest Love Of All**	1[3]	Arista 9466
				originally released as the B-side of "You Give Good Love"		
5/16/87	**1**[3]	22	▲	6 **I Wanna Dance With Somebody (Who Loves Me)**	1[2]	Arista 9598
8/1/87	**1**[3]	18		7 **Didn't We Almost Have It All**..........................	1[2]	Arista 9616
10/31/87	**8**	19		8 **So Emotional**	1[1]	Arista 9642
2/27/88	**1**[3]	21		9 **Where Do Broken Hearts Go**	1[2]	Arista 9674
7/2/88	**10**	14		10 **Love Will Save The Day**	9	Arista 9720
9/10/88	**1**[2]	20		11 **One Moment In Time**	5	Arista 9743
				tune used by NBC-TV for the 1988 Summer Olympics		
10/20/90	**7**	28	●	12 **I'm Your Baby Tonight**...............................	1[1]	Arista 2108
12/22/90	**1**[4]	29	●	13 **All The Man That I Need**	1[2]	Arista 2156
3/2/91	**48**	2	●	14 **The Star Spangled Banner**	20	Arista 2207
				live recording from the National Anthem Ceremony at Super Bowl XXV		
4/13/91	**4**	23		15 **Miracle**	9	Arista 2222
8/10/91	**44**	6		16 **My Name Is Not Susan**	20	Arista 12259
11/14/92	**1**[5]	28	▲[4]	17 **I Will Always Love You**	1[14]	Arista 12490
				2-time #1 Country hit (1974, 1982) and #53 Pop hit (1982) for Dolly Parton; the biggest #1 *Hot 100* hit in history		
1/23/93	**26**	14	●	18 **I'm Every Woman**	4	Arista 12519
2/20/93	**1**[2]	21	●	19 **I Have Nothing**.......................................	4	Arista 12527
6/19/93	**9**	15↑		20 **Run To You**	31	Arista 12570
				above 4 from the film *The Bodyguard* starring Whitney		
				HOWARD, Miki ☺		
				Female session singer/songwriter from Chicago. Former lead singer of Side Effect. Portrayed Billie Holiday in the film *Malcolm X*.		
2/28/87	**38**	3		**Come Share My Love**		Atlantic 89351
				HOWELL, Kurt ☺		
				Former keyboardist/vocalist for Southern Pacific. Native of Tampa.		
7/18/92	**27**	12		1 **We'll Find The Way**		Reprise LP Cut
11/14/92	**18**	21		2 **Does Love Not Open Your Eyes**........................		Reprise LP Cut

DEBUT DATE	PEAK POS	WKS CHR	GOLD	ARTIST — Record Title	POP POS	Label & Number
				HOWELL, Kurt — Cont'd		
5/29/93	**39**	4		3 I'm Over You		Reprise LP Cut
				above 3 from the album *Kurt Howell* on Reprise 26937		
				HUBBARD, Diana ☉		
				Daughter of Scientology founder L. Ron Hubbard.		
3/8/80	**40**	6		Rose Coloured Lights ....[I]		Waterhouse 15003
				HUES CORPORATION, The		
				Black vocal trio formed in Los Angeles in 1969: Bernard Henderson, Fleming Williams and H. Ann Kelley.		
8/18/73	**9**	8		1 **Freedom For The Stallion**	63	RCA 0900
6/15/74	**12**	14	●	2 Rock The Boat	1¹	RCA 0232
				HUGH, Grayson		
				Soul-styled white singer/songwriter/pianist from Connecticut.		
4/1/89	**9**	30		1 **Talk It Over**	19	RCA 8802
10/28/89	**9**	17		2 **Bring It All Back**	87	RCA 9093
2/24/90	**15**	16		3 How 'Bout Us	67	RCA 9163
				GRAYSON HUGH AND BETTY WRIGHT		
				from the film *True Love*		
				HUMAN LEAGUE, The		
				Electro-pop band featuring vocalists Philip Oakey, Joanne Catherall and Susanne Sulley.		
9/27/86	**3**	19		Human	1¹	A&M 2861
★★26★★				**HUMPERDINCK, Engelbert**		
				Born Arnold George Dorsey on 5/2/36 in Madras, India. To Leicester, England in 1947. First recorded for Decca in 1958. Met Tom Jones' manager, Gordon Mills, in 1965, who suggested his name change to Engelbert Humperdinck (a famous German opera composer). Starred in his own musical variety TV series in 1970.		
				1)*After The Lovin'* 2)*This Moment In Time* 3)*Am I That Easy To Forget* 4)*When There's No You* 5)*My Marie*		
5/6/67	**28**	7		1 **Release Me (And Let Me Love Again)**..............................	4	Parrot 40011
9/23/67	**6**	14		2 **The Last Waltz**	25	Parrot 40019
12/30/67	**1¹**	11		3 **Am I That Easy To Forget**	18	Parrot 40023
5/11/68	**3**	15		4 **A Man Without Love**..	19	Parrot 40027
10/19/68	**3**	10		5 **Les Bicyclettes De Belsize**	31	Parrot 40032
3/1/69	**4**	12		6 **The Way It Used To Be**	42	Parrot 40036
8/23/69	**6**	11		7 **I'm A Better Man**	38	Parrot 40040
12/6/69	**3**	14		8 **Winter World Of Love**	16	Parrot 40044
6/27/70	**2³**	11		9 **My Marie**	43	Parrot 40049
10/3/70	**2¹**	11		10 **Sweetheart**	47	Parrot 40054
3/6/71	**1¹**	9		11 **When There's No You**	45	Parrot 40059
8/28/71	**5**	9		12 **Another Time, Another Place**	43	Parrot 40065
3/25/72	**16**	10		13 Too Beautiful To Last	86	Parrot 40069
				theme from the film *Nicholas and Alexandra*		
8/5/72	**12**	8		14 In Time...	69	Parrot 40071
11/4/72	**18**	11		15 I Never Said Goodbye	61	Parrot 40072
5/5/73	**17**	6		16 I'm Leavin' You	99	Parrot 40073
9/15/73	**33**	8		17 Love Is All	91	Parrot 40076
2/16/74	**34**	6	✓	18 Free As The Wind		Parrot 40077
				from the film *Papillon*		
6/8/74	**44**	4		19 Catch Me, I'm Falling		Parrot 40079
6/21/75	**43**	5	✓	20 Forever And Ever..		Parrot 40082
11/1/75	**14**	10		21 This Is What You Mean To Me	102	Parrot 40085
9/11/76	**1²**	26	●	22 After The Lovin'..	8	Epic 50270
4/23/77	**15**	9		23 I Believe In Miracles/		
7/2/77	**37**	6		24 Goodbye My Friend	97	Epic 50365
10/8/77	**33**	10		25 Lover's Holiday..		Epic 50447
4/8/78	**28**	9		26 The Last Of The Romantics		Epic 50526
8/12/78	**44**	4		27 Love's In Need Of Love Today		Epic 50579
				written by Stevie Wonder		
11/11/78	**1²**	18		28 **This Moment In Time**	58	Epic 50632
5/5/79	**44**	4		29 Can't Help Falling In Love...............................		Epic 50692
				#2 Pop hit for Elvis Presley in 1962; #1 Pop hit for UB40 in 1993		
7/7/79	**39**	4		30 A Much, Much Greater Love		Epic 50732
2/23/80	**28**	12		31 Love's Only Love	83	Epic 50844
6/20/81	**41**	5		32 Don't You Love Me Anymore?		Epic 02060

114

DEBUT DATE	PEAK POS	WKS CHR	GOLD	ARTIST — Record Title	POP POS	Label & Number
				HUMPERDINCK, Engelbert — Cont'd		
5/21/83	17	15		33 Til You And Your Lover Are Lovers Again	77	Epic 03817

I

IAN, Janis
Born Janis Eddy Fink on 4/7/51 in New York City. Singer/songwriter/pianist/guitarist.

6/22/74	33	9		1 The Man You Are In Me	104	Columbia 46034
4/5/75	20	8		2 When The Party's Over		Columbia 10119
6/14/75	1²	15		3 **At Seventeen**	3	Columbia 10154
11/15/75	21	9		4 In The Winter		Columbia 10228
3/27/76	43	4		5 Boy I Really Tied One On		Columbia 10297
5/22/76	28	6		6 I Would Like To Dance		Columbia 10331
9/25/76	37	4		7 Roses		Columbia 10391
9/16/78	43	4		8 That Grand Illusion		Columbia 10813
10/18/80	47	4		9 The Other Side Of The Sun		Columbia 11327

ICEHOUSE
Australian rock quartet led by singer/guitarist Iva Davies. First known as Flowers. "Icehouse" is Australian slang for an insane asylum.

4/30/88	36	13		Electric Blue	7	Chrysalis 43201
				co-written by John Oates (of Hall & Oates)		

IFIELD, Frank
Born on 11/30/37 in Coventry, England. Began career as a teenager in Australia with his own radio and TV shows. Signed to Columbia Records in England in 1959.

9/15/62	1¹	10		1 I Remember You	5	Vee-Jay 457
				#9 hit for Jimmy Dorsey in 1942 (from the film *The Fleet's In*)		
10/5/63	16	3		2 I'm Confessin' (That I Love You)	58	Capitol 5032
				Guy Lombardo and Rudy Vallee both had top 5 versions in 1930		

IGLESIAS, Julio
Spanish singer, immensely popular worldwide. Born on 9/23/43 in Madrid. Soccer goalie for the pro Real Madrid team until temporary paralysis from a car crash.

4/23/83	30	8		1 Amor..	105	Columbia 03805
				sung in both Spanish and English by Iglesias; #2 hit for Bing Crosby in 1944		
3/10/84	3	19	▲	2 **To All The Girls I've Loved Before**	5	Columbia 04217
				JULIO IGLESIAS & WILLIE NELSON		
7/7/84	2²	16		3 All Of You	19	Columbia 04507
				JULIO IGLESIAS & DIANA ROSS		
10/6/84	17	10		4 Moonlight Lady	102	Columbia 04645
5/14/88	14	12		5 My Love	80	Columbia 07781
				JULIO IGLESIAS Featuring STEVIE WONDER		

IMPERIALS ✪
Gospel quartet.

5/17/80	43	3		Living Without Your Love		DaySpring 613

INCREDIBLE BONGO BAND, The
Studio band assembled in Canada by producer Michael Viner.

8/18/73	35	4		Bongo Rock.. [I]	57	MGM 14588
				first released on Pride 1015 in 1973		

INDIGO GIRLS
Folk-pop duo of singers/songwriters/guitarists Amy Ray and Emily Saliers from Decatur, Georgia.

8/19/89	48	1		Closer To Fine...	52	Epic 68912

★★71★★ INGRAM, James
R&B vocalist/multi-instrumentalist/composer from Akron, Ohio. To Los Angeles in the late 1970s, with the band Revelation Funk.
1)Baby, Come To Me 2)What About Me 3)I Don't Have The Heart

9/19/81	7	20		1 Just Once *	17	A&M 2357
1/23/82	5	21		2 One Hundred Ways *	14	A&M 2387
				*QUINCY JONES Featuring JAMES INGRAM		
11/20/82	1³	23	●	3 Baby, Come To Me	1²	Qwest 50036
				PATTI AUSTIN with James Ingram		

DEBUT DATE	PEAK POS	WKS CHR	GOLD	ARTIST — Record Title	POP POS	Label & Number
				INGRAM, James — Cont'd		
5/14/83	**5**	20		4 **How Do You Keep The Music Playing**.............................. JAMES INGRAM And PATTI AUSTIN theme from the film *Best Friends*	45	Qwest 29618
1/7/84	**10**	16		5 **Yah Mo B There** .... JAMES INGRAM (with Michael McDonald)	19	Qwest 29394
3/24/84	**7**	18		6 **There's No Easy Way**	58	Qwest 29316
7/28/84	**19**	12		7 **She Loves Me (The Best That I Can Be)**		Qwest 29235
9/15/84	**1**²	19		8 **What About Me?** .... KENNY ROGERS with KIM CARNES and JAMES INGRAM	15	RCA 13899
9/20/86	**13**	11		9 **I Just Can't Let Go** .... DAVID PACK with Michael McDonald and James Ingram		Warner 28605
11/15/86	**4**	28	●	10 **Somewhere Out There** .... LINDA RONSTADT AND JAMES INGRAM from the animated film *An American Tail*	**2**¹	MCA 52973
8/29/87	**40**	1		11 Better Way .... from the film *Beverly Hills Cop II*		MCA 53125
3/31/90	**26**	10	●	12 The Secret Garden (Sweet Seduction Suite) .... QUINCY JONES/Al B. Sure!/James Ingram/El DeBarge/Barry White	31	Qwest 19992
6/2/90	**2**²	38		13 **I Don't Have The Heart**................................	**1**¹	Warner 19911
12/22/90	**29**	11		14 **When Was The Last Time Music Made You Cry**		Warner 19783
11/9/91	**23**	13		15 **Where Did My Heart Go**............................... from the film *City Slickers*		Warner 19197
6/12/93	**34**	5		16 **Someone Like You**		Warner 18531
				INNOCENCE, The Group is actually the singing/songwriting/producing duo of Pete Anders and Vinnie Poncia. Also recorded as The Trade Winds.		
3/4/67	**29**	4		Mairzy Doats.. #1 hit (5 weeks) for The Merry Macs in 1944	75	Kama Sutra 222
				IN PURSUIT ○ Nashville-based pop trio of vocalists: Jay Joyce (guitar), Emma (bass) and Jeff Boggs (drums).		
8/15/87	**33**	6		Thin Line		MTM 72087
				INXS Rock sextet formed in Sydney, Australia as The Farris Brothers. Members since group's formation in 1977: Michael Hutchence (lead singer), Kirk Pengilly (guitar), Garry Beers (bass), and brothers Tim (guitar), Andy (keyboards, guitar) and Jon (drums) Farriss. Hutchence, who starred in the films *Dogs In Space* and *Frankenstein Unbound*, also co-founded the band Max Q. Jon Farriss married actress Leslie Bega.		
10/29/88	**42**	5		1 Never Tear Us Apart	7	Atlantic 89038
3/13/93	**45**	7		2 Beautiful Girl	46	Atlantic 87383
				IRISH ROVERS, The Irish-born folk quintet. Group formed in Alberta, Canada in 1964. Brothers Will (vocals) and George Millar, their cousin Joe Millar, Jimmy Ferguson and Wilcil McDowell.		
3/23/68	**2**¹	13		1 **The Unicorn**...	7	Decca 32254
6/22/68	**9**	8		2 **(The Puppet Song) Whiskey On A Sunday**	75	Decca 32333
9/7/68	**13**	8		3 The Biplane, Ever More...............................	91	Decca 32371
3/8/69	**15**	5		4 Lily The Pink ....[N]	113	Decca 32444
4/4/81	**46**	4		5 Wasn't That A Party .... THE ROVERS	37	Epic 51007
				ISAAK, Chris San Francisco-based singer/songwriter/guitarist. Born in Stockton, California on 6/26/56. Attended college in Japan. Cameo appearances in the films *Married To The Mob*, *Silence Of The Lambs*, others.		
1/5/91	**12**	22	●	1 Wicked Game.. featured in the David Lynch film *Wild at Heart*	6	Reprise 19704
4/17/93	**11**	18		2 Can't Do A Thing (To Stop Me)	105	Reprise 18604
				ISLEY, Ronald — see STEWART, Rod		
				ISLEY, JASPER, ISLEY R&B trio consisting of Ernie Isley, Chris Jasper and Marvin Isley. All were members of The Isley Brothers from 1973-84.		
12/28/85	**16**	13		Caravan Of Love..	51	CBS Assoc. 05611

116

DEBUT DATE	PEAK POS	WKS CHR	GOLD	ARTIST — Record Title	POP POS	Label & Number
				IVES, Burl		
				Born on 6/14/09 in Huntington Township, Illinois. Actor/author/singer. Played semi-pro football. Began Broadway career in the late 1930s. Worked in *This Is The Army* service show during World War II. Own CBS network radio show *The Wayfaring Stranger* in 1944. Appeared in many films, including *Our Man In Havana, East Of Eden, Smokey, Cat On A Hot Tin Roof* and *The Big Country*. Narrated the kids' TV classic *Rudolph The Red-Nosed Reindeer*. Worked on TV series *The Bold Ones* in the early 1970s.		
1/13/62	**1**[1]	11		**1 A Little Bitty Tear**	9	Decca 31330
4/7/62	**3**	11		**2 Funny Way Of Laughin'**	10	Decca 31371
7/28/62	**6**	8		**3 Call Me Mr. In-Between**	19	Decca 31405
11/24/62	**13**	4		**4** Mary Ann Regrets	39	Decca 31433
9/19/64	**12**	5		**5** Pearly Shells	60	Decca 31659
7/13/68	**35**	3		**6** I'll Be Your Baby Tonight	133	Columbia 44508
				written by Bob Dylan		

J

DEBUT DATE	PEAK POS	WKS CHR	GOLD	ARTIST — Record Title	POP POS	Label & Number
				JACKIE & ROY ✪		
				Brother and sister team of Roy and Irene Kral. Irene died of cancer on 8/15/78 (age 46).		
10/14/72	**36**	4		Time & Love		CTI 11
				featuring a sampling of Bach's *Jesu, Joy of Man's Desiring*		
				JACKS, Susan		
				Maiden name: Susan Pesklevits, from Vancouver, Canada. Married Terry Jacks and recorded with him as The Poppy Family; divorced in 1973.		
3/15/75	**18**	8		You're A Part Of Me	90	Mercury 73649
				JACKS, Terry		
				Native of Winnipeg, Canada. Recorded with wife Susan as The Poppy Family.		
1/26/74	**1**[1]	16	●	**1 Seasons In The Sun**	**1**[3]	Bell 45432
				originally recorded by The Kingston Trio in 1964		
6/15/74	**29**	6		**2** If You Go Away	68	Bell 45467
				JACKSON, Freddie		
				Soul singer/songwriter. Born on 10/2/56 and raised in Harlem. Backup singer for Melba Moore, Evelyn King and others. Member of R&B group Mystic Merlin.		
10/5/85	**3**	17		**1 You Are My Lady**	12	Capitol 5495
1/25/86	**28**	6		**2** He'll Never Love You (Like I Do)	25	Capitol 5535
8/19/89	**15**	11		**3** I Do		EMI 50213
				NATALIE COLE with Freddie Jackson		
				JACKSON, Janet		
				Born on 5/16/66 in Gary, Indiana. Sister of The Jacksons (youngest of nine children). Debuted at age seven at the MGM Grand in Las Vegas with her brothers. At age 10, she played Penny Gordon Woods in the TV series *Good Times* (1977-79); in the cast of *Diff'rent Strokes* (1981-82) and later *Fame*. Married James DeBarge of DeBarge in August 1984; marriage annulled in March 1985. Signed a $32 million contract with Virgin Records in 1991. Starred in the 1993 film *Poetic Justice*.		
5/3/86	**38**	4	●	**1** What Have You Done For Me Lately	4	A&M 2812
9/13/86	**10**	13	●	**2 When I Think Of You**	**1**[2]	A&M 2855
1/31/87	**2**[1]	18		**3 Let's Wait Awhile**	**2**[1]	A&M 2906
2/10/90	**16**	14	●	**4** Escapade	**1**[3]	A&M 1490
7/7/90	**1**[3]	23		**5 Come Back To Me**	**2**[2]	A&M 1475
1/12/91	**33**	14	●	**6** Love Will Never Do (Without You)	**1**[1]	A&M 1538
5/8/93	**16**	21↑	▲	**7** That's The Way Love Goes	**1**[8]	Virgin 12650
				JACKSON, Jermaine		
				Born on 12/11/54 in Gary, Indiana. Fourth oldest of the Jackson family. Vocalist/bassist of The Jackson 5 until group left Motown in 1976. Married Hazel Joy Gordy, daughter of Berry Gordy, Jr., on 12/15/73; later divorced. Rejoined The Jacksons in 1984 for their *Victory* album and tour.		
10/27/84	**1**[3]	21		**1** Do What You Do	13	Arista 9279
3/8/86	**5**	14		**2** I Think It's Love	16	Arista 9444
				JACKSON, Joe		
				Born on 8/11/55 in Burton-on-Trent, England. Singer/songwriter/pianist, featuring an ever-changing music style. Moved to New York City in 1982.		
10/9/82	**4**	19		**1** Steppin' Out	6	A&M 2428
2/5/83	**8**	15		**2** Breaking Us In Two	18	A&M 2510

117

DEBUT DATE	PEAK POS	WKS CHR	G O L D	ARTIST — Record Title	POP POS	Label & Number
				JACKSON, Joe — Cont'd		
5/12/84	**13**	15		3 You Can't Get What You Want (Till You Know What You Want)..	15	A&M 2628
★★45★★				**JACKSON, Michael**		

Born on 8/29/58 in Gary, Indiana. The seventh of nine children. Became lead singer of his brothers' group, The Jackson 5 (later known as The Jacksons), at age five. Played the Scarecrow in the 1978 movie musical *The Wiz*. His 1982 *Thriller* album, with sales of over 40 million copies, is the best-selling album in history. Starred in the 15-minute film *Captain Eo*, which was shown exclusively at Disneyland and Disneyworld. His 1988 autobiography, *Moonwalker*, became a film the same year. Winner of 12 Grammy Awards; awarded Grammy's Living Legends Award in 1993. Michael signed a $1 billion multimedia contract with Sony Software on 3/20/91.

1)The Girl Is Mine 2)I Just Can't Stop Loving You 3)Human Nature 4)Man In The Mirror 5)Ben

DEBUT DATE	PEAK POS	WKS CHR	G O L D	ARTIST — Record Title	POP POS	Label & Number
11/20/71	**14**	7		1 Got To Be There...	4	Motown 1191
9/2/72	**3**	12		2 **Ben**	1¹	Motown 1207
				title song from the film about a trained rat		
5/19/73	**23**	5		3 With A Child's Heart.......................................	50	Motown 1218
9/30/78	**40**	3		4 Ease On Down The Road..................................	41	MCA 40947
				DIANA ROSS MICHAEL JACKSON		
				from the film *The Wiz*		
11/17/79	**21**	14	▲	5 Rock With You..	1⁴	Epic 50797
4/26/80	**4**	19	●	6 She's Out Of My Life.....................................	10	Epic 50871
5/9/81	**37**	5		7 One Day In Your Life.....................................	55	Motown 1512
				recorded in 1975		
11/6/82	**1**⁴	18	●	8 The Girl Is Mine	2³	Epic 03288
				MICHAEL JACKSON/PAUL McCARTNEY		
2/12/83	**9**	18	▲	9 Billie Jean..	1⁷	Epic 03509
7/23/83	**2**⁴	17		10 Human Nature..	7	Epic 04026
10/15/83	**3**	21	▲	11 Say Say Say	1⁶	Columbia 04168
				PAUL McCARTNEY AND MICHAEL JACKSON		
11/12/83	**37**	4		12 P.Y.T. (Pretty Young Thing)............................	10	Epic 04165
2/11/84	**24**	11	▲	13 Thriller...	4	Epic 04364
6/9/84	**20**	11		14 Farewell My Summer Love	38	Motown 1739
				re-mix of a recording from 8/13/73		
8/8/87	**1**³	17	●	15 I Just Can't Stop Loving You	1¹	Epic 07253
				Siedah Garrett (backing vocal)		
10/3/87	**33**	8		16 Bad...	1²	Epic 07418
				Jimmy Smith (organ solo)		
12/5/87	**9**	17		17 The Way You Make Me Feel..............................	1¹	Epic 07645
2/13/88	**2**¹	19		18 Man In The Mirror......................................	1²	Epic 07668
				Siedah Garrett, The Winans and the Andrea Crouch Choir (backing vocals)		
8/20/88	**44**	6		19 Another Part Of Me.....................................	11	Epic 07962
11/30/91	**23**	12	▲	20 Black Or White	1⁷	Epic 74100
				rap by Bill Bottrell; features Slash (Guns N' Roses) on guitar		
2/1/92	**15**	14	●	21 Remember The Time	3	Epic 74200
12/5/92	**9**	30		22 Heal The World..	27	Epic 74708
7/17/93	**5**	11↑		23 Will You Be There......................................	7	MJJ 77060
				from the film *Free Willy*		
				JACKSON, Wanda		

Born on 10/20/37 in Maud, Oklahoma. Country-rockabilly singer/songwriter/guitarist. First recorded for Decca in 1954. Toured with Elvis Presley from 1955-56.

DEBUT DATE	PEAK POS	WKS CHR	G O L D	ARTIST — Record Title	POP POS	Label & Number
8/21/61	**9**	3		1 Right Or Wrong..	29	Capitol 4553
4/28/62	**16**	6		2 If I Cried Every Time You Hurt Me	58	Capitol 4723
				JACKSON 5, The		

Quintet of brothers formed and managed by their father beginning in 1966 in Gary, Indiana. Consisted of Sigmund "Jackie" (b: 5/4/51), Toriano "Tito" (b: 10/15/53), Jermaine (b: 12/11/54), Marlon (b: 3/12/57) and lead singer Michael (b: 8/29/58).

DEBUT DATE	PEAK POS	WKS CHR	G O L D	ARTIST — Record Title	POP POS	Label & Number
10/17/70	**24**	6		I'll Be There	1⁵	Motown 1171
				JACOBY, Don "Jake" ۞		
7/13/68	**23**	4		Theme From Elvira Madigan............................[I]		Pompeii 6670
				tune is based upon a Mozart Piano Concerto; from the film *Elvira Madigan*		
				JAKATA ۞		
4/27/85	**39**	2		Golden Girl		Motown 1778

DEBUT DATE	PEAK POS	WKS CHR	G O L D	ARTIST — Record Title	POP POS	Label & Number
				JAMAL, Ahmad ○		
				Born Fritz Jones on 7/2/30 in Pittsburgh. Jazz pianist/leader. Formed own trio, the Three Strings, with Ray Crawford (guitar) and Eddie Calhoun (bass). Recorded for Okeh in 1951.		
12/30/67	**37**	3		A Beautiful Friendship		Cadet 5581
				#74 Pop hit for Ella Fitzgerald in 1956		
				JAMES, Etta		
				R&B pioneer. Born Jamesetta Hawkins on 1/25/38 in Los Angeles. Nicknamed "Miss Peaches." Inducted into the Rock and Roll Hall of Fame in 1993.		
10/12/63	**16**	3		Two Sides (To Every Story)	63	Argo 5452
				JAMES, Rick		
				Punk-funk singer/songwriter/guitarist. Born James Johnson on 2/1/52 in Buffalo. In Mynah Birds band with Neil Young in the late '60s. To London; formed the band Main Line. Returned to the U.S. and formed Stone City Band; produced Teena Marie, Mary Jane Girls, Eddie Murphy and others.		
1/21/84	**35**	5		Ebony Eyes	43	Gordy 1714
				RICK JAMES Featuring SMOKEY ROBINSON		
				JAMES, Sonny		
				Born James Loden on 5/1/29 in Hackleburg, Alabama. Country singer/songwriter/guitarist. Nicknamed "The Southern Gentleman." Brought to Capitol Records in Nashville by Chet Atkins. In the films *Second Fiddle To A Steel Guitar*, *Nashville Rebel*, *Las Vegas Hillbillies* and *Hillbillys In A Haunted House*.		
1/23/65	**22**	1		1 You're The Only World I Know	91	Capitol 5280
2/15/69	**32**	4		2 Only The Lonely..	92	Capitol 2370
10/11/69	**26**	5		3 Since I Met You, Baby	65	Capitol 2595
2/7/70	**31**	3		4 It's Just A Matter Of Time	87	Capitol 2700
				JAMES, Tommy		
				Born Thomas Jackson on 4/29/47 in Dayton, Ohio. To Niles, Michigan at age 11. Formed pop group The Shondells at age 12. Began recording as a solo artist in 1970.		
8/2/69	**27**	4		1 Crystal Blue Persuasion...................................	2³	Roulette 7050
				TOMMY JAMES AND THE SHONDELLS		
6/19/71	**6**	12		2 Draggin' The Line	4	Roulette 7103
9/9/72	**40**	2		3 Love Song	67	Roulette 7130
2/2/80	**1¹**	15		4 Three Times In Love	19	Millennium 11785
				JAMESON, Cody		
				Songstress from New York City.		
4/16/77	**35**	5		Brooklyn	74	Atco 7073
				JAMESTOWN MASSACRE		
8/19/72	**30**	4		Summer Sun	90	Warner 7603
				JANKOWSKI, Horst		
				Born on 1/30/36 in Berlin. Jazz pianist.		
5/8/65	**1²**	14		1 A Walk In The Black Forest .... [I]	12	Mercury 72425
8/14/65	**15**	9		2 Simpel Gimpel .... [I]	91	Mercury 72465
11/13/65	**39**	1		3 Heide .... [I]		Mercury 72492
1/8/66	**19**	7		4 Play A Simple Melody .... [I]		Mercury 72520
				#2 hit for Bing Crosby & Gary Crosby in 1950		
5/14/66	**21**	10		5 Black Forest Holiday .... [I]		Mercury 72567
10/8/66	**19**	7		6 So What's New? .... [I]		Mercury 72615
				also recorded by Herb Alpert & The Tijuana Brass on the album *What Now My Love*		
5/25/68	**27**	6		7 Zabadak.. [I]		Mercury 72809
				#52 Pop hit for Dave Dee, Dozy, Beaky, Mick & Tich		
				JANZ, Paul ○		
				Singer/songwriter/keyboardist/producer born in Three Hills, Alberta, Canada.		
10/24/87	**25**	11		Believe In Me		A&M 2978
★★141★★				**JARREAU, Al**		
				Born on 3/12/40 in Milwaukee. Soul-jazz vocalist. Has masters degree in psychology from the University of Iowa. Worked clubs in San Francisco with George Duke.		
				1)Moonlighting 2)Mornin' 3)We're In This Love Together		
8/15/81	**6**	23		1 We're In This Love Together	15	Warner 49746
1/9/82	**30**	6		2 Breakin' Away	43	Warner 49842
3/13/82	**19**	14		3 Teach Me Tonight	70	Warner 50032
3/12/83	**2³**	21		4 Mornin' *	21	Warner 29720
9/17/83	**10**	16		5 Trouble In Paradise *	63	Warner 29501
				*JARREAU		
10/20/84	**6**	17		6 After All	69	Warner 29262

DEBUT DATE	PEAK POS	WKS CHR	GOLD	ARTIST — Record Title	POP POS	Label & Number
				JARREAU, Al — Cont'd		
3/8/86	**16**	12		7 The Music Of Goodbye		MCA 52784
				MELISSA MANCHESTER AND AL JARREAU		
				love theme from the film *Out Of Africa*		
6/6/87	**1**¹	18		8 Moonlighting	23	MCA 53124
9/19/87	**10**	12		9 Since I Fell For You		MCA 53187
				#4 Pop hit for Lenny Welch in 1963; above 2 from the TV series *Moonlighting*		
12/10/88	**27**	12		10 So Good		Reprise 27664
6/24/89	**40**	5		11 All Or Nothing At All		Reprise 27550
				JAY & THE AMERICANS		
				Group formed in late 1959 by New York University students as the Harbor-Lites: John "Jay" Traynor (formerly with the Mystics), Sandy Yaguda, Kenny Vance (later a Hollywood musical director) and Howie Kane. Guitarist Marty Sanders joined during production of their first album in 1961. Traynor left after their first hit and was replaced by lead singer Jay Black (real name: David Blatt; b: 11/2/38) in 1962.		
2/8/69	**11**	8	●	1 This Magic Moment	6	United Art. 50475
6/7/69	**31**	6		2 Hushabye	62	United Art. 50535
11/22/69	**8**	15		3 Walkin' In The Rain	19	United Art. 50605
4/11/70	**32**	4		4 Capture The Moment	57	United Art. 50654
				JEFFERSON		
				English vocalist.		
1/24/70	**19**	7		Baby Take Me In Your Arms	23	Janus 106
★★172★★				**JEFFERSON STARSHIP**		
				Formed as Jefferson Airplane in San Francisco, 1965. Consisted of Marty Balin and Signe Anderson (vocals), Paul Kantner (vocals, guitar), Jorma Kaukonen (guitar), Jack Casady (bass) and Alexander "Skip" Spence (drums). Grace Slick and Spencer Dryden joined in 1966, replacing Anderson and Spence. Balin left in 1971, rejoined in 1975, by which time group was renamed Jefferson Starship and consisted of Slick, Kantner, Papa John Creach (Hot Tuna; violin), David Freiberg (bass), Craig Chaquico (pronounced: chuck-ee-so; guitar), Pete Sears (bass) and John Barbata (drums). In 1979, singer Mickey Thomas joined (replaced Balin), along with Aynsley Dunbar. Kantner left in 1984, and, due to legal difficulties, band's name was shortened to Starship, whose lineup included Slick, Thomas, Sears, Chaquico and Don Baldwin. Slick left in early 1988. In 1989, the original 1966 lineup — Balin, Slick, Kantner, Kaukonen and Casady — reunited as Jefferson Airplane. Continuing as Starship were Thomas, Chaquico, Baldwin, Brett Bloomfield (bass) and Mark Morgan (keyboards). Starship disbanded in 1990.		
				1)Sara 2)Nothing's Gonna Stop Us Now 3)With Your Love		
10/4/75	**17**	10		1 Miracles	3	Grunt 10367
8/14/76	**6**	11		2 With Your Love	12	Grunt 10746
4/8/78	**15**	11		3 Count On Me	8	Grunt 11196
7/1/78	**37**	8		4 Runaway	12	Grunt 11274
				STARSHIP:		
11/30/85	**37**	2	●	5 We Built This City	1²	Grunt 14170
1/18/86	**1**³	19		6 Sara	1¹	Grunt 14253
2/14/87	**1**²	18	●	7 Nothing's Gonna Stop Us Now	1²	Grunt 5109
				from the film *Mannequin*		
3/5/88	**9**	16		8 Set The Night To Music		RCA/Grunt 6964
9/9/89	**30**	12		9 It's Not Enough	12	RCA 9032
9/23/89	**15**	10		10 Summer Of Love....................................		Epic LP Cut
				JEFFERSON AIRPLANE		
				from the album *Jefferson Airplane* on Epic 45271		
				JENNINGS, Waylon		
				Born on 6/15/37 in Littlefield, Texas. While working as a DJ in Lubbock, Texas, Waylon befriended Buddy Holly. Holly produced Waylon's first record "Jole Blon" in 1958. Waylon then joined with Buddy's backing band as bass guitarist on the fateful "Winter Dance Party" tour in 1959. Established himself in the mid-1970s as a leader of the "outlaw" movement in country music. Married to Jessi Colter since 1969. In the films *Nashville Rebel* and *MacKintosh And T.J.* Narrator for TV's *The Dukes Of Hazzard*. Hazzard.		
3/13/76	**16**	8		1 Good Hearted Woman *	25	RCA 10529
6/4/77	**16**	11		2 Luckenbach, Texas (Back to the Basics of Love)	25	RCA 10924
				Willie Nelson (ending vocal)		
3/4/78	**33**	5		3 Mammas Don't Let Your Babies Grow Up To Be Cowboys *	42	RCA 11198
				*WAYLON & WILLIE		
6/9/79	**40**	6		4 Amanda..	54	RCA 11596
10/15/83	**31**	5		5 Take It To The Limit	102	Columbia 04131
				WILLIE NELSON & WAYLON JENNINGS		
				JERICHO HARP ✪		
				Jim Thomas and Tom Schmidt.		
2/18/78	**46**	3		Is It Really Love At All..............................		United Art. 1121

DEBUT DATE	PEAK POS	WKS CHR	G O L D	ARTIST — Record Title	POP POS	Label & Number
				JEROME, Henry, his Chorus & Orch. ✪		
				Bandleader/composer popular in the late '40s and '50s. Born on 11/12/17 in New York City.		
6/10/67	**39**	2		Illya Darling...		United Art. 50146
				Broadway musical title song		
				JETS, The		
				Minneapolis-based family band consisting of eight brothers and sisters: Leroy, Eddie, Eugene, Haini, Rudy, Kathi, Elizabeth and Moana Wolfgramm. Their parents are from the South Pacific country of Tonga. All members play at least two instruments. Eugene left group and formed duo Boys Club in 1988.		
12/27/86	**1**[2]	23		1 **You Got It All**..	3	MCA 52968
4/30/88	**1**[3]	20		2 **Make It Real**...	4	MCA 53311
11/19/88	**35**	5	✓	3 Anytime...		MCA 53446
				written and produced by Rupert Holmes		
10/21/89	**15**	16		4 The Same Love..	87	MCA 53734
				JIGSAW		
				Pop-rock quartet from England: Des Deyer (lead vocals), Clive Scott, Tony Campbell and Barrie Bernard.		
10/18/75	**4**	13		1 Sky High...	3	Chelsea 3022
				from the film *The Dragon Flies*		
2/14/76	**20**	10		2 Love Fire...	30	Chelsea 3037
				JIMENEZ, Jose		
				Real name: Bill Dana. Born William Szarthmary on 10/5/24 in Quincy, Massachusetts. Head writer for TV's *Steve Allen Show*. Star of own TV series from 1963-65. Created the Latin American comic character Jose Jimenez for Steve Allen's TV series.		
9/25/61	**4**	6		**The Astronaut (Parts 1 & 2)**.........................[C]	19	Kapp 409
				interviewed by Don Hinckley		
				JIVE BUNNY And The Mastermixers		
				British dance outfit: DJ Les Hemstock and mixers John Pickles, Andy Pickles and Ian Morgan.		
12/2/89	**38**	8	●	Swing The Mood...	11	Music Fac. 99140
				includes samplings of these tunes: Let's Twist Again (Chubby Checker)/ In The Mood (Glenn Miller)/Rock Around The Clock (Bill Haley)/ Rock-A-Beatin' Boogie (Bill Haley)/Tutti-Frutti (Little Richard)/ Wake Up Little Susie (Everly Brothers)/C'mon Everybody (Eddie Cochran)/ Hound Dog (Elvis)/Shake, Rattle And Roll (Bill Haley)/All Shook Up (Elvis)/ Jailhouse Rock (Elvis)/At The Hop (Danny & The Juniors); Elvis samplings are by a sound-a-like		
				JO, Damita		
				Born Damita Jo DuBlanc in Austin, Texas. Featured singer with Steve Gibson & The Red Caps (married to Gibson), 1951-53 and 1959-60. Regular on Red Foxx's TV variety series in 1977.		
8/14/65	**30**	4		1 Nobody Knows You When You're Down And Out................		Epic 9821
				#15 hit for Bessie Smith in 1929		
12/3/66	**10**	13		2 If You Go Away	68	Epic 10061
7/29/67	**34**	2		3 Yellow Days		Epic 10176
12/9/67	**28**	4		4 Walk Away..		Epic 10235
				from the Broadway musical *How Now, Dow Jones*		
				JO, Sami		
				Alabama-bred, country-pop songstress.		
2/23/74	**14**	14		1 Tell Me A Lie	21	MGM South 7029
6/29/74	**31**	8		2 It Could Have Been Me.................................	46	MGM South 7034
★★18★★				**JOEL, Billy**		
				Born William Martin Joel on 5/9/49 in Hicksville, Long Island, New York. Formed his first band, The Echoes, in 1964, which later became The Lost Souls. Member of Long Island group The Hassles in the late 1960s. Later formed rock duo, Attila, with The Hassles' drummer, Jon Small. Signed solo to Columbia Records in 1973. Involved in a serious motorcycle accident in Long Island in 1982. Married supermodel Christie Brinkley on 3/23/85. Toured and recorded in Russia in 1987. Won Grammy's Living Legends Award in 1990.		
				1)*Just The Way You Are* 2)*This Is The Time* 3)*The Longest Time* 4)*Leave A Tender Moment Alone* 5)*Tell Her About It*		
3/2/74	**4**	14		1 Piano Man	25	Columbia 45963
8/24/74	**31**	7		2 Travelin' Prayer.......................................	77	Columbia 10015
12/21/74	**30**	9		3 The Entertainer.......................................	34	Columbia 10064
12/3/77	**1**[4]	23	●	4 Just The Way You Are..................................	3	Columbia 10646
4/29/78	**40**	4		5 Movin' Out (Anthony's Song)..........................	17	Columbia 10708
8/12/78	**2**[2]	23		6 She's Always A Woman	17	Columbia 10788
11/11/78	**2**[5]	18	●	7 My Life...	3	Columbia 10853
4/28/79	**9**	13		8 Honesty...	24	Columbia 10959
4/26/80	**48**	1		9 You May Be Right......................................	7	Columbia 11231

DEBUT DATE	PEAK POS	WKS CHR	G O L D	ARTIST — Record Title	POP POS	Label & Number
				JOEL, Billy — Cont'd		
6/7/80	45	5	●	10 It's Still Rock And Roll To Me	1[2]	Columbia 11276
8/9/80	1[2]	18		11 **Don't Ask Me Why**	19	Columbia 11331
10/24/81	35	5		12 Say Goodbye To Hollywood	17	Columbia 02518
11/28/81	4	19		13 **She's Got A Way**	23	Columbia 02628
				originally released on Family 0900 in 1973		
1/22/83	19	10		14 Allentown	17	Columbia 03413
7/30/83	1[2]	19		15 **Tell Her About It**	1[1]	Columbia 04012
10/1/83	2[4]	19	●	16 **Uptown Girl**	3	Columbia 04149
12/24/83	1[1]	21		17 **An Innocent Man**	10	Columbia 04259
3/24/84	1[2]	21		18 **The Longest Time**	14	Columbia 04400
7/7/84	1[2]	18		19 **Leave A Tender Moment Alone**	27	Columbia 04514
1/19/85	3	19		20 **Keeping The Faith**	18	Columbia 04681
7/13/85	2[3]	19		21 **You're Only Human (Second Wind)**	9	Columbia 05417
10/19/85	13	8		22 The Night Is Still Young	34	Columbia 05657
6/14/86	7	12		23 **Modern Woman**	10	Epic 06118
				from the film *Ruthless People*		
8/30/86	17	13		24 A Matter Of Trust	10	Columbia 06108
11/22/86	1[3]	20		25 **This Is The Time**	18	Columbia 06526
3/21/87	3	15		26 **Baby Grand**	75	Columbia 06994
				BILLY JOEL Featuring Ray Charles		
10/14/89	5	18	●	27 **We Didn't Start The Fire**	1[2]	Columbia 73021
1/20/90	4	17		28 **I Go To Extremes**	6	Columbia 73091
4/28/90	18	11		29 The Downeaster "Alexa"	57	Columbia 73333
7/21/90	5	25		30 **And So It Goes**	37	Columbia 73602
1/4/92	40	6		31 Shameless		Columbia 74188
				#1 Country hit for Garth Brooks in 1991; above 5 from Joel's 1989 album *Storm Front*		
8/8/92	15	14		32 All Shook Up	92	Epic Snd. 74422
				#1 Pop hit for Elvis Presley in 1957; from the film *Honeymoon In Vegas*		

★★3★★ **JOHN, Elton**

Born Reginald Kenneth Dwight on 3/25/47 in Pinner, Middlesex, England. Formed his first group Bluesology in 1966. Group backed visiting U.S. soul artists and later became Long John Baldry's backing band. Took the name of Elton John from the first names of Bluesology members Elton Dean and John Baldry. Teamed up with lyricist Bernie Taupin beginning in 1969. Formed Rocket Records in 1973. Played the Pinball Wizard in the film version of *Tommy*.

1)The One 2)You Gotta Love Someone 3)Simple Life 4)That's What Friends Are For 5)Blue Eyes

DEBUT DATE	PEAK POS	WKS CHR	G O L D	ARTIST — Record Title	POP POS	Label & Number
12/26/70	9	11		1 **Your Song**	8	Uni 55265
3/27/71	17	7		2 Friends	34	Uni 55277
				British movie title song		
4/8/72	35	3		3 Tiny Dancer	41	Uni 55318
5/13/72	39	2		4 Rocket Man	6	Uni 55328
8/26/72	6	8		5 Honky Cat	8	Uni 55343
12/23/72	11	8	●	6 Crocodile Rock	1[3]	MCA 40000
4/14/73	1[2]	13		7 **Daniel**	2[1]	MCA 40046
11/3/73	7	18	●	8 **Goodbye Yellow Brick Road**	2[3]	MCA 40148
7/6/74	3	13	●	9 **Don't Let The Sun Go Down On Me**	2[2]	MCA 40259
				also see new version with George Michael (#42 below)		
7/26/75	36	6	●	10 Someone Saved My Life Tonight	4	MCA 40421
11/8/75	27	8	●	11 Island Girl	1[3]	MCA 40461
2/7/76	21	8		12 I Feel Like A Bullet (In The Gun Of Robert Ford)	flip	MCA 40505
				made the *Hot 100* as the B-side of "Grow Some Funk Of Your Own" (POS 14)		
5/22/76	18	7		13 Love Song		MCA 1938
				Lesley Duncan (female vocal); available only as a promo single		
7/10/76	1[1]	13	●	14 **Don't Go Breaking My Heart**	1[4]	Rocket 40585
				ELTON JOHN and KIKI DEE		
11/13/76	1[1]	15	●	15 **Sorry Seems To Be The Hardest Word**	6	MCA/Rocket 40645
11/25/78	40	7		16 Part-Time Love	22	MCA 40973
3/10/79	37	4		17 Song For Guy	[I] 110	MCA 40993
6/16/79	1[1]	18	●	18 **Mama Can't Buy You Love**	9	MCA 41042
5/10/80	1[2]	20	●	19 **Little Jeannie**	3	MCA 41236
8/30/80	45	6		20 (Sartorial Eloquence) Don't Ya Wanna Play This Game No More?	39	MCA 41293
5/16/81	23	11		21 Nobody Wins	21	Geffen 49722
8/1/81	16	12		22 Chloe	34	Geffen 49788

DEBUT DATE	PEAK POS	WKS CHR	GOLD	ARTIST — Record Title	POP POS	Label & Number
				JOHN, Elton — Cont'd		
3/27/82	**18**	18		23 Empty Garden (Hey Hey Johnny)..	13	Geffen 50049
7/17/82	**1**²	22		**24 Blue Eyes**..	12	Geffen 29954
6/4/83	**28**	13		**25 I'm Still Standing**...	12	Geffen 29639
11/5/83	**2**³	24		**26 I Guess That's Why They Call It The Blues**.................	4	Geffen 29460
				Stevie Wonder (harmonica solo)		
6/9/84	**2**⁶	19		**27 Sad Songs (Say So Much)**..	5	Geffen 29292
9/22/84	**11**	12		28 Who Wears These Shoes?	16	Geffen 29189
12/8/84	**11**	16		29 In Neon	38	Geffen 29111
11/9/85	**1**²	22	●	30 That's What Friends Are For..	1⁴	Arista 9422
				DIONNE AND FRIENDS: Elton John, Gladys Knight and Stevie Wonder		
1/25/86	**3**	18		**31 Nikita**...	7	Geffen 28800
				George Michael (backing vocal)		
7/4/87	**32**	4		32 Flames Of Paradise..	36	Epic 07119
				JENNIFER RUSH with Elton John		
10/3/87	**2**²	24		**33 Candle In The Wind**	6	MCA 53196
				tribute to Marilyn Monroe; first recorded for his 1973 *Goodbye Yellow Brick Road* LP		
3/5/88	**37**	5		34 Take Me To The Pilot..		MCA 53260
				above 2 are live recordings with the Melbourne Symphony Orchestra; first recorded for his 1974 LP *Elton John*		
6/18/88	**1**¹	23		**35 I Don't Wanna Go On With You Like That**	2¹	MCA 53345
9/24/88	**4**	19		**36 A Word In Spanish**...	19	MCA 53408
4/15/89	**3**	18		37 Through The Storm..	16	Arista 9809
				ARETHA FRANKLIN AND ELTON JOHN		
9/2/89	**1**¹	19		**38 Healing Hands**	13	MCA 53692
11/18/89	**3**	28		**39 Sacrifice**	18	MCA 53750
4/21/90	**2**⁴	25		**40 Club At The End Of The Street**..	28	MCA 79026
11/3/90	**1**⁵	23		**41 You Gotta Love Someone**	43	MCA 53953
12/7/91	**1**²	23	●	**42 Don't Let The Sun Go Down On Me**...........................[R]	1¹	Columbia 74086
				GEORGE MICHAEL/ELTON JOHN recorded live in London, March 1991		
6/27/92	**1**⁶	30		**43 The One**	9	MCA 54423
10/17/92	**2**²	30		**44 The Last Song**	23	MCA 54510
2/6/93	**1**³	27		**45 Simple Life**	30	MCA 54581
				JOHN, Robert		
				Born Robert John Pedrick, Jr. in Brooklyn in 1946. First recorded at age 12 for Big Top Records. In 1963, recorded as lead singer with Bobby & The Consoles.		
1/8/72	**6**	13	●	**1 The Lion Sleeps Tonight**	3	Atlantic 2846
				adaptation of a South African song (adapted in 1952 as "Wimoweh")		
5/19/79	**10**	25	●	**2 Sad Eyes**	1¹	EMI America 8015
11/10/79	**42**	2		3 Only Time	102	EMI America 8023
1/19/80	**49**	2		4 Lonely Eyes	41	EMI America 8030
8/2/80	**10**	16		**5 Hey There Lonely Girl**	31	EMI America 8049
				JOHNNY HATES JAZZ		
				Englishmen Clark Datchler (vocals) and Calvin Hayes (son of producer Mickie Most) with American Mike Nocito. Datchler left in late 1988, replaced by producer/ex-Cure member Phil Thornalley.		
4/9/88	**1**¹	19		**1 Shattered Dreams**	2³	Virgin 99383
7/16/88	**15**	13		2 I Don't Want To Be A Hero	31	Virgin 99304
10/22/88	**5**	20		**3 Turn Back The Clock**...		Virgin 99308
				JOHNS, Sammy		
				Born on 2/7/46 in Charlotte, North Carolina. Own band, the Devilles, from 1963-73.		
9/28/74	**19**	11		1 Early Morning Love..	68	GRC 2021
7/5/75	**34**	7		2 Rag Doll	52	GRC 2062
7/10/76	**11**	11		3 Peas In A Pod		Warner 8224
				JOHNSON, Don — see STREISAND, Barbra		
				JOHNSON, Kevin		
				Singer/songwriter/guitarist from Australia.		
11/10/73	**43**	7		Rock 'N Roll (I Gave You The Best Years of My Life)	73	Mainstream 5548
				JOHNSON, Michael		
				Born on 8/8/44 in Alamosa, Colorado and raised in Denver. Studied classical guitar in 1966 in Spain. In the Chad Mitchell Trio with John Denver in 1968.		
4/29/78	**1**³	21		**1 Bluer Than Blue**	12	EMI America 8001

123

DEBUT DATE	PEAK POS	WKS CHR	G O L D	ARTIST — Record Title	POP POS	Label & Number
				JOHNSON, Michael — Cont'd		
8/19/78	**4**	15		2 Almost Like Being In Love	32	EMI America 8004
1/20/79	**44**	4		3 Sailing Without A Sail		EMI America 8008
8/4/79	**5**	19		4 This Night Won't Last Forever	19	EMI America 8019
1/26/80	**29**	10		5 The Very First Time	101	EMI America 8031
9/20/80	**34**	6		6 You Can Call Me Blue	86	EMI America 8054
9/5/81	**32**	10	✔	7 You're Not Easy To Forget		EMI America 8086
				JOLI, France French Canadian singer born in 1963 in Montreal.		
11/17/79	**47**	1		Come To Me	15	Prelude 8001
				JON & VANGELIS Jon Anderson (lead singer of Yes) and Greek keyboardist Evangelos Papathanassiou.		
6/19/82	**41**	5		I'll Find My Way Home	51	Polydor 2205
				JONES, Davy Born on 12/30/45 in Manchester, England. Member of The Monkees.		
7/3/71	**26**	6		Rainy Jane .... *written by Neil Sedaka*	52	Bell 45111
				JONES, Glenn Vocalist from Jacksonville, Florida. Sang with the gospel group, Bivens Special, from age eight. Had own gospel group, the Modulations, from age 14. In the Broadway musical *Sing Mahalia, Sing*.		
2/2/85	**12**	10		1 Finder Of Lost Loves .... **DIONNE WARWICK & GLENN JONES** TV series title song		Arista 9281
10/24/87	**36**	4		2 We've Only Just Begun (The Romance Is Not Over)	66	Jive 1049
				JONES, Howard Born on 2/23/55 in Southampton, England. Pop singer/songwriter/synth wizard.		
6/8/85	**38**	5		1 Things Can Only Get Better	5	Elektra 69651
8/17/85	**16**	10		2 Life In One Day	19	Elektra 69631
4/26/86	**1**¹	21		3 No One Is To Blame	4	Elektra 69549
4/8/89	**1**²	25		4 Everlasting Love	12	Elektra 69308
4/18/92	**10**	17		5 Lift Me Up	32	Elektra 64779
★★31★★				**JONES, Jack** Born on 1/14/38 in Los Angeles. Son of actress Irene Hervey and actor/singer Allan Jones, who had the #8 pop hit "The Donkey Serenade" the year Jack was born. *1)Lady 2)The Impossible Dream (The Quest) 3)The Race Is On 4)Now I Know 5)A Day In The Life Of A Fool*		
3/10/62	**12**	6		1 Lollipops And Roses	66	Kapp 435
11/23/63	**9**	10		2 Wives And Lovers .... *inspired by the film of the same title*	14	Kapp 551
3/28/64	**19**	1		3 Love With The Proper Stranger .... *movie title song*	62	Kapp 571
7/4/64	**12**	4		4 The First Night Of The Full Moon	59	Kapp 589
8/22/64	**12**	4		5 Where Love Has Gone	62	Kapp 608
11/28/64	**6**	11		6 Dear Heart .... *above 2 are movie title songs*	30	Kapp 635
3/27/65	**1**¹	7		7 The Race Is On	15	Kapp 651
6/5/65	**9**	10		8 Seein' The Right Love Go Wrong	46	Kapp 672
9/25/65	**5**	10		9 Just Yesterday/	73	
10/23/65	**27**	3		10 The True Picture	134	Kapp 699
11/27/65	**5**	11		11 Love Bug	71	Kapp 722
2/5/66	**20**	8		12 The Weekend	123	Kapp 736
5/7/66	**1**¹	22		13 The Impossible Dream (The Quest) .... *from the musical Man Of La Mancha*	35	Kapp 755
10/22/66	**4**	13		14 A Day In The Life Of A Fool	62	11 781
1/14/67	**1**⁴	18		15 Lady	39	Kapp 800
5/6/67	**19**	7		16 Afterthoughts .... *flip side "I'm Indestructible" made the Hot 100 (POS 81)*		Kapp 818
6/3/67	**3**	12		17 Now I Know	73	Kapp 833
8/26/67	**13**	8		18 Our Song.......................................	92	Kapp 847
10/28/67	**26**	6		19 Open For Business As Usual	130	Kapp 860
11/18/67	**9**	10		20 Live For Life .... *movie title song*	99	RCA 9365

DEBUT DATE	PEAK POS	WKS CHR	GOLD	ARTIST — Record Title	POP POS	Label & Number
				JONES, Jack — Cont'd		
2/17/68	**5**	7		21 **If You Ever Leave Me**	92	RCA 9441
5/11/68	**20**	6		22 **Follow Me**	117	RCA 9510
7/13/68	**15**	9		23 **I Really Want To Know You**		RCA 9564
10/12/68	**33**	5		24 **The Way That I Live**		RCA 9639
				from the film *The Bliss of Mrs. Blossom*		
12/21/68	**21**	8		25 **L.A. Break Down (And Take Me In)**	106	RCA 9687
				featuring Doug Talbert on piano		
6/20/70	**24**	4		26 **Sweet Changes**		RCA 0350
12/19/70	**38**	2		27 **I Didn't Count On Love**		RCA 9934
5/22/71	**18**	7		28 **Let Me Be The One**		RCA 0475
12/28/74	**45**	4		29 **She Doesn't Live Here Anymore**		RCA 10025
6/28/75	**25**	9		30 **What I Did For Love**		RCA 10317
				from the Broadway musical *A Chorus Line*		
4/30/77	**21**	13	✓	31 **With One More Look At You**		RCA 10955
				from the film *A Star Is Born*		
1/26/80	**37**	5		32 **Love Boat Theme**		MGM 14851
				from the TV series *Love Boat*		

JONES, Quincy

Born Quincy Delight Jones, Jr. on 3/14/33 in Chicago and raised in Seattle. Composer/producer/conductor/arranger. Wrote scores for many films, 1965-73. Scored TV series *Roots* in 1977. Produced Michael Jackson's mega-albums *Off The Wall*, *Thriller* and *Bad*. Established own Qwest label in 1981. Most nominated artist in Grammy history with 76 nominations and 25 wins. Won the Grammy's Trustees Award in 1989. Won Grammy's Living Legends Award in 1990. His biographical film *Listen Up: The Lives Of Quincy Jones* was released in 1990.

5/23/70	**29**	4		1 **Killer Joe** .... [I]	74	A&M 1163
8/4/73	**30**	8		2 **Summer In The City** .... [I]	102	A&M 1455
				Valerie Simpson has a 30-second vocal; #1 Pop hit for The Lovin' Spoonful in 1966		
3/12/77	**21**	6		3 **"Roots" Medley** .... [I]	57	A&M 1909
				Motherland/Theme From *Roots* (Roots Mural Theme); Bill Summers (bata drums)		
9/19/81	**7**	20		4 **Just Once** *	17	A&M 2357
1/23/82	**5**	21		5 **One Hundred Ways** *	14	A&M 2387
				*QUINCY JONES Featuring JAMES INGRAM		
1/6/90	**30**	9		6 **I'll Be Good To You**	18	Qwest 22697
				QUINCY JONES Featuring Ray Charles and Chaka Khan		
3/31/90	**26**	10	●	7 **The Secret Garden (Sweet Seduction Suite)**	31	Qwest 19992
				QUINCY JONES/Al B. Sure!/James Ingram/El DeBarge/Barry White		

JONES, Rickie Lee

Born on 11/8/54 in Chicago. Pop-jazz-styled singer/songwriter. Moved to Los Angeles in 1977. Won the 1979 Best New Artist Grammy Award.

5/19/79	**20**	11		1 **Chuck E.'s In Love**	4	Warner 8825
10/6/84	**37**	3		2 **The Real End**	83	Warner 29191

JONES, Tamiko

Born Barbara Tamiko Ferguson in 1945 in Kyle, West Virginia and raised in Detroit. First recorded for Atlantic in 1966. Moved to London; married to John Abbey (publisher of *Blues & Soul* magazine). Smokey Robinson's manager in 1991.

10/29/66	**9**	14		**A Man And A Woman**	88	Atlantic 2362
				TAMIKO JONES with HERBIE MANN		
				movie title song		

★★35★★				**JONES, Tom**		

Born Thomas Jones Woodward on 6/7/40 in Pontypridd, South Wales. Worked local clubs as Tommy Scott; formed own trio The Senators in 1963. Began solo career in London in 1964. Won the 1965 Best New Artist Grammy Award. Host of own TV musical variety series from 1969-71.

1)I'll Never Fall In Love Again 2)Without Love (There Is Nothing) 3)Daughter Of Darkness 4)Love Me Tonight 5)I (Who Have Nothing)

6/5/65	**3**	5		1 **It's Not Unusual**	10	Parrot 9737
8/28/65	**3**	10		2 **With These Hands**	27	Parrot 9787
12/4/65	**5**	12		3 **Thunderball**	25	Parrot 9801
				from the James Bond film *Thunderball*		
2/12/66	**11**	9		4 **Promise Her Anything**	74	Parrot 9809
				movie title song		
1/28/67	**12**	7		5 **Green, Green Grass Of Home**	11	Parrot 40009
9/16/67	**28**	4		6 **I'll Never Fall In Love Again**	49	Parrot 40018
1/20/68	**30**	3		7 **I'm Coming Home**	57	Parrot 40024
3/30/68	**8**	12		8 **Delilah**	15	Parrot 40025
8/24/68	**3**	13		9 **Help Yourself**	35	Parrot 40029
12/14/68	**4**	14		10 **A Minute Of Your Time**	48	Parrot 40035

DEBUT DATE	PEAK POS	WKS CHR	GOLD	ARTIST — Record Title	POP POS	Label & Number
				JONES, Tom — Cont'd		
5/24/69	**2**⁴	12		11 Love Me Tonight	13	Parrot 40038
8/2/69	**1**¹	14	●	12 **I'll Never Fall In Love Again** ....[R]	6	Parrot 40018
1/3/70	**1**¹	11	●	13 **Without Love (There Is Nothing)**	5	Parrot 40045
5/2/70	**1**¹	11		14 **Daughter Of Darkness**	13	Parrot 40048
8/22/70	**2**³	9		15 I (Who Have Nothing)	14	Parrot 40051
11/28/70	**3**	8		16 Can't Stop Loving You	25	Parrot 40056
2/6/71	**4**	12	●	17 **She's A Lady**	2¹	Parrot 40058
				written by Paul Anka		
10/30/71	**4**	8		18 **Till**	41	Parrot 40067
4/22/72	**14**	9		19 The Young New Mexican Puppeteer	80	Parrot 40070
5/12/73	**11**	10		20 Letter To Lucille	60	Parrot 40074
10/5/74	**23**	10		21 Somethin' 'Bout You Baby I Like		Parrot 40080
1/4/75	**19**	10		22 Pledging My Love		Parrot 40081
				#17 Pop hit for Johnny Ace in 1955		
1/8/77	**3**	18		23 **Say You'll Stay Until Tomorrow**	15	Epic 50308
5/28/77	**32**	6		24 Take Me Tonight	101	Epic 50382
				adapted from Tchaikovsky's *Pathetique Symphony*		
11/19/77	**47**	5		25 What A Night		Epic 50468
5/16/81	**45**	6		26 Darlin'	103	Mercury 76100
				JONES, Universal — see McDANIELS, Gene		

JONES GIRLS, The
Detroit soul sister trio: Shirley, Brenda and Valorie Jones. Backup singers for Lou Rawls, Teddy Pendergrass and Aretha Franklin. With Diana Ross from 1975-78. Sang with Le Pamplemousse.

| 12/15/79 | **50** | 1 | | We're A Melody .... | | Phil. Int. 3722 |

JORDAN, Marc ☉
Canadian-American singer.

| 9/29/90 | **44** | 3 | | Edge Of The World .... | | RCA 2547 |

JOSH ☉

| 7/21/73 | **13** | 12 | | Was A Sunny Day .... | | Bell 45,369 |
| | | | | written by Paul Simon | | |

JOURNEY
Rock group formed in San Francisco in 1973. Core lineup: Steve Perry (lead vocals), Neal Schon (guitar) and Jonathan Cain (keyboards). Schon and Cain joined Bad English in 1989.

8/15/81	**14**	17		1 Who's Crying Now	4	Columbia 02241
1/30/82	**7**	19		2 Open Arms	2⁶	Columbia 02687
7/31/82	**37**	4		3 Still They Ride	19	Columbia 02883
5/14/83	**24**	13		4 Faithfully	12	Columbia 03840
11/5/83	**27**	12		5 Send Her My Love	23	Columbia 04151
12/27/86	**7**	19		6 **I'll Be Alright Without You**	14	Columbia 06301
5/9/87	**24**	6		7 Why Can't This Night Go On Forever	60	Columbia 07043
1/9/93	**30**	10		8 Lights ....[R]	74	Columbia 74842
				live version of #68 Pop hit for Journey in 1978		

JOY ☉

| 5/15/71 | **33** | 3 | | Next Year (Bashana Habana) ....[F] | | Kama Sutra 523 |

JOY OF COOKING
Berkeley, California country-rock quintet led by female vocalists Terry Garthwaite and Toni Brown.

| 5/22/71 | **27** | 3 | | Brownsville .... | 66 | Capitol 3075 |

JUDD, Wynonna
Country singer. Born Christina Ciminella on 5/30/64 in Ashland, Kentucky. Half of The Judds duo with her mother, Naomi, from 1983-91. Moved to Hollywood in 1968. Appeared in *More American Graffiti*. To Nashville in 1979.

4/25/92	**25**	12		1 She Is His Only Need		Curb/MCA 54320
1/16/93	**35**	13		2 No One Else On Earth	83	Curb/MCA 54449
6/26/93	**24**	7		3 Tell Me Why	77	Curb/MCA 54606

JULIE
Actress/singer Julie Budd.

| 1/3/76 | **34** | 8 | | One Fine Day .... | 93 | Tom Cat 10454 |

DEBUT DATE	PEAK POS	WKS CHR	GOLD	ARTIST — Record Title	POP POS	Label & Number
				JUMP 'N THE SADDLE		
				Chicago-based band — Peter Quinn, lead singer.		
12/17/83	29	8		The Curly Shuffle ....[N]	15	Atlantic 89718
				a Three Stooges parody; first released on Acme 416 in 1983		
				JUST US		
				Consists of New York City producers Chip Taylor and Al Gorgoni.		
3/26/66	3	11		I Can't Grow Peaches On A Cherry Tree...........................	34	Colpix 803
				first released on Minuteman 203 in 1966		

K

DEBUT DATE	PEAK POS	WKS CHR	GOLD	ARTIST — Record Title	POP POS	Label & Number
				KADISON, Joshua ○		
				Songwriter/pianist/singer. Born on 2/8/65 in Los Angeles.		
5/29/93	25	15↑		Jessie	106↑	SBK 50429
★★104★★				**KAEMPFERT, Bert, And His Orchestra**		
				Born on 10/16/23 in Hamburg, Germany. Multi-instrumentalist/bandleader/producer/composer/arranger for Polydor Records in Germany. Produced first Beatles recording session. Died on 6/21/80 in Switzerland.		
				1)Red Roses For A Blue Lady 2)Bye Bye Blues 3)I Can't Give You Anything But Love		
8/7/61	14	6		1 Now And Forever ....[I]	48	Decca 31279
1/27/62	10	9		2 **Afrikaan Beat** ....[I]	42	Decca 31350
1/23/65	3	13		3 **Red Roses For A Blue Lady** ....[I]	11	Decca 31722
				#3 hit for Vaughn Monroe in 1949		
5/1/65	10	8		4 **Three O'Clock In The Morning**........................[I]	33	Decca 31778
				there were 6 top 10 versions of this tune from 1921-30		
7/3/65	6	13		5 **Moon Over Naples** ....[I]	59	Decca 31812
				tune later known as "Spanish Eyes"		
1/15/66	5	13		6 **Bye Bye Blues** ....[I]	54	Decca 31882
				#5 hit in 1930 for Bert Lown's orchestra (their theme song)		
5/7/66	8	15		7 **Strangers In The Night** ....[I]	124	Decca 31945
				theme from the film *A Man Could Get Killed*; #1 Pop hit for Frank Sinatra in 1966		
9/10/66	6	11		8 **I Can't Give You Anything But Love** ....[I]	100	Decca 32008
				there were 6 top 20 versions of this tune from 1928-29		
4/1/67	37	2	✓	9 Hold Me ....[I]		Decca 32094
				#3 hit for the Hotel Commodore Orchestra in 1933		
8/26/67	39	3		10 Talk ....[I]		Decca 32159
1/13/68	10	8		11 **Caravan**...[I]		Decca 32241
				#4 hit for Duke Ellington in 1937		
3/30/68	30	3		12 The First Waltz...[I]		Decca 32283
6/15/68	12	10	✓	13 Mister Sandman ....[I]		Decca 32329
				#1 hit for The Chordettes in 1954		
10/5/68	17	5		14 (You Are) My Way Of Life ....[I]		Decca 32379
8/9/69	30	7		15 Games People Play ....[I]		Decca 732518
				#12 Pop hit for Joe South in 1969		
3/21/70	27	5		16 Someday We'll Be Together.....................................		Decca 732647
				#1 Pop hit for The Supremes in 1969		
12/19/70	24	8		17 Sweet Caroline (Good Times Never Seemed So Good) ....[I]		Decca 32772
				#4 Pop hit for Neil Diamond in 1969		
				KALLEN, Kitty		
				Born on 5/25/22 in Philadelphia. Big band singer with Jack Teagarden, Jimmy Dorsey and Harry James.		
12/29/62	7	9		**My Coloring Book**	18	RCA 8124
				KALLMANN, Gunter, Chorus		
				German chorus.		
11/26/66	2²	18		1 **Wish Me A Rainbow**	63	4 Corners 138
				from the film *This Property Is Condemned*		
3/11/67	28	6		2 Chanson D'Amour		4 Corners 139
				#6 Pop hit for Art & Dotty Todd in 1958		
				KANE GANG, The		
				English soul-styled pop trio: vocalists Martin Brammer and Paul Woods with guitarist David Brewis. Band's name derived from the film *Citizen Kane*.		
11/7/87	12	16		Motortown	36	Capitol 44062

DEBUT DATE	PEAK POS	WKS CHR	GOLD	ARTIST — Record Title	POP POS	Label & Number
				KANSAS Progressive rock group formed in Topeka in 1970. Consisted of Steve Walsh (lead vocals, keyboards), Kerry Livgren (guitar, keyboards), Phil Ehart (drums), Robby Steinhardt (violin), Rich Williams (guitar) and Dave Hope (bass). Walsh left in 1981 and was replaced by John Elefante (later a prolific Christian rock producer). Livgren became a popular Contemporary Christian artist in the '80s. Revised lineup in 1986: Walsh, Ehart, Williams, Steve Morse (guitarist from Dixie Dregs) and Billy Greer (bass).		
2/4/78	**6**	17	●	1 Dust In The Wind	6	Kirshner 4274
12/20/86	**14**	15		2 All I Wanted .... featuring new guitarist Steve Morse (Dixie Dregs)	19	MCA 52958
				KAPU, Sam ○ Pop singer from Hawaii. Discovered by Don Ho.		
9/11/71	**39**	2		Chotto Matte Kudasai (Never Say Goodbye)......................		Anthem 51000
				KARAZOV, Alexandrow ○		
4/12/69	**24**	8		Castschok..[I] Russian title means "Life's A Dance"	120	Jamie 1372
				KAREN, Kenny Singer/songwriter from Toronto.		
9/15/73	**29**	3		That's Why You Remember...................................	82	Big Tree 16007
				KASHIF — see WARWICK, Dionne		
				KATRINA And The WAVES British-based, pop-rock quartet fronted by Kansas-born Katrina Leskanich, with American Vince de la Cruz (bass) and Britons Alex Cooper (drums) and Kimberley Rew (guitar; Soft Boys).		
6/8/85	**21**	11		Walking On Sunshine	9	Capitol 5466
				KAYE, Sammy Born on 3/13/10 in Rocky River, Ohio; died on 6/2/87 of cancer. Durable leader of popular "sweet" dance band with the slogan "Swing and Sway with Sammy Kaye." Also played clarinet and alto sax.		
4/11/64	**10**	6		Charade ....[I] movie title song	36	Decca 31589
				KAZAN, Lainie ○ Born Lainie Levine on 5/16/40 in New York City. Film actress. Appeared in such films as *One From the Heart* and *My Favorite Year*.		
12/31/66	**29**	10		Kiss Tomorrow Goodbye....................................	123	MGM 13657
				KC And The SUNSHINE BAND Disco-R&B band formed in Florida in 1973 by lead singer/keyboardist Harry "KC" Casey (b: 1/31/51, Hialeah, Florida) and bassist Richard Finch (b: 1/25/54, Indianapolis). Interracial band contained from seven to 11 members.		
9/3/77	**36**	11		1 Keep It Comin' Love	2³	T.K. 1023
10/20/79	**27**	9		2 Please Don't Go	1¹	T.K. 1035
11/24/79	**1²**	20	●	3 Yes, I'm Ready .... TERI DeSARIO with K.C.	2²	Casablanca 2227
2/19/83	**12**	14		4 Don't Run (Come Back To Me) .... with Teri DeSario	103	Epic 03556
				KEEP IT DARK ○		
8/16/86	**36**	3		Dreamer		Elektra 69529
				KELLAWAY, Roger ○ Born on 11/1/39 in Waban, Massachusetts. Composer/pianist. Wrote for numerous TV shows and films.		
1/29/72	**31**	4		Remembering You ....[I] closing theme from the TV series *All In The Family*		A&M 1321
				KENDALL, Leslie ○		
10/5/74	**28**	7		This Is Your Song... written by Paul Anka; #86 Pop hit for Don Goodwin in 1973		Warner 8022
				KENDRICK, Eddie Born on 12/17/39 in Union Springs, Alabama and raised in Birmingham. Joined R&B group the Primes in Detroit in the late '50s. Group later evolved into The Temptations; Eddie sang lead from 1960-71. Died of lung cancer on 10/5/92.		
9/14/85	**12**	9		1 A Nite At The Apollo Live! The Way You Do The Things You Do/My Girl .... DARYL HALL JOHN OATES with David Ruffin & Eddie Kendrick recorded at the re-opening of New York's Apollo Theatre	20	RCA 14178
12/26/87	**48**	3		2 I Couldn't Believe It.. DAVID RUFFIN & EDDIE KENDRICK		RCA 5313

DEBUT DATE	PEAK POS	WKS CHR	GOLD	ARTIST — Record Title	POP POS	Label & Number
				KENNEDY, Joyce Vocalist from Chicago. Formed Mother's Finest with husband Glen Murdoch in 1968.		
9/15/84	**37**	6		The Last Time I Made Love.................. JOYCE KENNEDY & JEFFREY OSBORNE	40	A&M 2656
				KENNY, Michael ○ Los Angeles-based singer.		
8/30/75	**30**	10		Morning		Tom Cat 10327
★★99★★				**KENNY G** Born Kenny Gorelick on 7/6/56 in Seattle. Fusion saxophonist. Joined Barry White's Love Unlimited Orchestra at age 17. Graduated Phi Beta Kappa and Magna Cum Laude from the University of Washington with an accounting degree. *1)Missing You Now 2)Forever In Love 3)By The Time This Night Is Over*		
4/4/87	**3**	29		**1 Songbird**.................... [I]	4	Arista 9588
9/5/87	**2**³	22		**2 Don't Make Me Wait For Love** .... Lenny Williams (original lead singer for Tower Of Power), vocal; originally hit the R&B charts on 12/13/86 on Arista 9544 (POS 77)	15	Arista 9625
10/15/88	**2**¹	29		**3 Silhouette**.................... [I]	13	Arista 9751
2/4/89	**4**	20		**4 We've Saved The Best For Last**.......... KENNY G with Smokey Robinson	47	Arista 9785
12/23/89	**5**	20		**5 Going Home**.................... [I]	56	Arista 9913
7/27/91	**32**	9		**6** Theme From Dying Young .... [I] from the film *Dying Young*		Arista 2267
1/25/92	**1**³	30		**7 Missing You Now** .... MICHAEL BOLTON Featuring Kenny G	12	Columbia 74184
11/21/92	**1**²	34		**8 Forever In Love** .... [I]	18	Arista 12482
5/15/93	**1**²	20↑		**9 By The Time This Night Is Over**.......... [I] KENNY G & PEABO BRYSON	25	Arista 12565
				KENTON, Stan Progressive jazz bandleader/pianist/composer. Born on 2/19/12 in Wichita, Kansas; died in Los Angeles on 8/25/79. Organized his first jazz band in 1941. Third person named to the Jazz Hall of Fame.		
10/27/62	**12**	7		**1** Mama Sang A Song .... [S]	32	Capitol 4847
2/4/67	**40**	1		**2** Dragnet.................... [I] theme from the TV series; #2 hit for Ray Anthony in 1953		Capitol 5828
				KERMIT — see HENSON, Jim		
				KERR, Anita, Singers ○ Anita was born Anita Jean Grob on 10/13/27 in Memphis.		
4/1/67	**19**	8		**1** One In A Row .... #19 Country hit for Willie Nelson in 1966		Warner 7010
9/9/67	**15**	8		**2** I Can't Help Remembering You .... written by Bert Kaempfert		Warner 7065
12/2/67	**30**	4		**3** In The Morning		Warner 7085
				KHAN, Chaka Born Yvette Marie Stevens on 3/23/53 in Great Lakes, Illinois. Became lead singer of Rufus in 1972. Recorded solo and with Rufus since 1978. Sister of vocalists Taka Boom and Mark Stevens (Jamaica Boys). Chaka's daughter Milini is a member of Pretty In Pink.		
5/4/85	**16**	11		**1** Through The Fire	60	Warner 29025
1/6/90	**30**	9		**2** I'll Be Good To You .... QUINCY JONES Featuring Ray Charles and Chaka Khan	18	Qwest 22697
10/17/92	**5**	29		**3** Feels Like Heaven .... PETER CETERA with CHAKA KHAN	71	Warner 18651
				KHAN, Sajid ○ Indian youth who starred in the TV series *Maya* as Raji.		
2/8/69	**29**	4		Dream......................... #1 hit for the Pied Pipers in 1945	119	Colgems 1034
				KIDS NEXT DOOR, The Vocal group featuring Mary Sinclair.		
10/23/65	**23**	6		Inky Dinky Spider (The Spider Song) .... [N]	84	4 Corners 129
				KIM, Andy Born Andrew Joachim on 12/5/46 in Montreal. His parents were from Lebanon. Pop singer/songwriter. Teamed with Jeff Barry to write "Sugar, Sugar."		
8/2/69	**31**	2	●	**1** Baby, I Love You	9	Steed 716
11/21/70	**24**	6		**2** Be My Baby	17	Steed 729
4/10/71	**40**	2		**3** I Wish I Were	62	Steed 731

DEBUT DATE	PEAK POS	WKS CHR	G O L D	ARTIST — Record Title	POP POS	Label & Number
				KIM, Andy — Cont'd		
7/13/74	**40**	7	●	4 Rock Me Gently	1¹	Capitol 3895
				KING, Ben E.		
				Born Benjamin Earl Nelson on 9/23/38 in Henderson, North Carolina. To New York in 1947. Worked with The Moonglows for six months while still in high school. Joined the Five Crowns in 1957, who became the new Drifters in 1959. Wrote lyrics to "There Goes My Baby," his first lead performance with The Drifters. Went solo in May 1960.		
8/3/63	**10**	7		1 **I (Who Have Nothing)**	29	Atco 6267
11/1/86	**10**	16		2 **Stand By Me** ....[R]	9	Atlantic 89361
				featured song in the film of the same title; originally made the *Hot 100* on 5/8/61 on Atco 6194 (POS 4)		
★★**68**★★				**KING, Carole**		
				Born Carole Klein on 2/9/42 in Brooklyn. Singer/songwriter/pianist. Neil Sedaka wrote his 1959 hit "Oh! Carol" about her. Married lyricist Gerry Goffin in 1958; team wrote four #1 hits: "Will You Love Me Tomorrow," "Go Away Little Girl," "Take Good Care Of My Baby" and "The Loco-Motion." Divorced Goffin in 1968. First solo album in 1970. In 1971, won four Grammys. King and Goffin's daughter, Louise, began a solo career in 1979. One of the most successful female songwriters of the rock era. She and Goffin were inducted as a songwriting team into the Rock and Roll Hall of Fame in 1990.		
				1)It's Too Late 2)Nightingale 3)Only Love Is Real		
5/22/71	**1**⁵	14	●	1 **It's Too Late**..	1⁵	Ode 66015
9/4/71	**3**	10		2 **So Far Away**/	14	
		10		3 Smackwater Jack	flip	Ode 66019
2/5/72	**2**¹	10		4 **Sweet Seasons**	9	Ode 66022
12/9/72	**1**¹	8		5 **Been To Canaan**...	24	Ode 66031
7/21/73	**6**	9		6 **You Light Up My Life**/	67	
		6		7 Believe In Humanity	28	Ode 66035
10/20/73	**5**	14		8 **Corazon**..[I]	37	Ode 66039
9/14/74	**4**	12		9 **Jazzman**..	2¹	Ode 66101
1/11/75	**1**¹	12		10 **Nightingale**	9	Ode 66106
2/21/76	**1**¹	12		11 **Only Love Is Real**	28	Ode 66119
6/5/76	**40**	5		12 High Out Of Time	76	Ode 66123
7/30/77	**8**	14		13 **Hard Rock Cafe**	30	Capitol 4455
11/19/77	**37**	3		14 Simple Things		Capitol 4497
12/2/78	**43**	7		15 Morning Sun		Capitol 4649
5/24/80	**11**	20		16 **One Fine Day**	12	Capitol 4864
4/17/82	**20**	13		17 One To One...	45	Atlantic 4026
4/8/89	**14**	15		18 City Streets..		Capitol 44336
8/1/92	**18**	18		19 Now And Forever		Columbia LP Cut
				from the soundtrack album *A League Of Their Own* on Columbia 52919		
				KING, Claude		
				Born on 2/5/33 in Shreveport, Louisiana. Country singer/songwriter/guitarist. Acted in the TV miniseries *The Blue And The Gray* in 1982.		
6/9/62	**3**	14	●	1 **Wolverton Mountain**	6	Columbia 42352
				title is an actual place in Arkansas where Clifton Clowers lived		
10/13/62	**20**	1		2 The Burning Of Atlanta	53	Columbia 42581
				KING, Evelyn "Champagne"		
				Born on 6/29/60 in the Bronx. To Philadelphia in 1970. Employed as a cleaning woman at Sigma Studios when discovered.		
6/1/85	**35**	4		Till Midnight		RCA 14048
				KING, Jonathan		
				Born Kenneth King on 12/6/44 in London. Successful singer/songwriter/producer. Formed U.K. Records in 1972. Produced Hedgehoppers Anonymous.		
7/3/71	**34**	6		Lazybones		Parrot 3027
				#1 hit for Ted Lewis in 1933		
				KING, Morgana ○		
				Jazz-pop singer/film actress. Born on 6/4/30 in Pleasantville, New York. Played Mama Corleone in *The Godfather* and *The Godfather, Part II*.		
9/9/67	**34**	4		I Have Loved Me A Man		Reprise 0604
				KING CURTIS		
				Born Curtis Ousley on 2/7/34 in Fort Worth, Texas. Stabbed to death on 8/13/71 in New York City. R&B saxophonist.		
12/11/65	**13**	10		1 Spanish Harlem ....[I]	89	Atco 6387
3/23/68	**32**	4		2 (Sittin' On) The Dock Of The Bay ....[I]	84	Atco 6562
				KING CURTIS & THE KINGPINS		

DEBUT DATE	PEAK POS	WKS CHR	GOLD	ARTIST — Record Title	POP POS	Label & Number
				KING HARVEST Six-man, pop-rock group based in Olcott, New York. Formed by Ron Altback (piano), Rod Novak (sax), Eddie Tulya (guitar) and Doc Robinson (bass).		
1/27/73	22	5		Dancing In The Moonlight..	13	Perception 515
				KING RICHARD'S FLUEGEL KNIGHTS ○ Instrumental troupe led by Dick (King Richard) Behrke.		
8/6/66	19	7		1 A Sign Of The Times .... [I]		MTA 107
				#11 Pop hit for Petula Clark in 1966		
4/22/67	11	11		2 Everybody Loves My Baby .... [I]	126	MTA 120
				#5 hit for Aileen Stanley in 1925		
9/2/67	19	9		3 Horn Duey .... [I]		MTA 131
1/6/68	12	6		4 Camelot .... [I]	107	MTA 138
				Broadway musical title song		
5/18/68	36	4		5 Feelin' Good .... [I]		MTA 151
3/8/69	31	6		6 One Of Those Songs .... [I]		MTA 166
				THE FLUEGEL KNIGHTS		
				KINGSTON TRIO, The Folk trio formed in San Francisco in 1957: Dave Guard (banjo), Bob Shane and Nick Reynolds (guitars). Big break came at San Francisco's Purple Onion, where they stayed for eight months. Guard left in 1961 to form the Whiskeyhill Singers; John Stewart replaced him. Disbanded in 1968, Shane formed New Kingston Trio. Guard died on 3/22/91 (age 56) of lymphoma. Current trio consists of Shane, Reynolds and George Grove (joined group in 1972). The originators of the folk music craze of the 1960s.		
1/27/62	4	12		1 Where Have All The Flowers Gone	21	Capitol 4671
2/23/63	6	6		2 Greenback Dollar	21	Capitol 4898
8/24/63	12	5		3 Desert Pete..	33	Capitol 5005
12/4/65	30	6		4 Parchment Farm (Blues)...		Decca 31860
				KINKS, The Rock group formed in London in 1963 by Ray Davies (lead singer, guitar) and his brother Dave Davies (lead guitar, vocals). Ray appeared in the 1986 film *Absolute Beginners*. 1987 lineup consisted of Ray & Dave Davies, Ian Gibbons (keyboards, left by 1989), Bob Henrit (drums) and Jim Rodford (bass). Henrit and Rodford were members of Argent. Group inducted into the Rock and Roll Hall of Fame in 1990.		
6/4/83	16	14		1 Come Dancing..	6	Arista 1054
8/20/83	23	10		2 Don't Forget To Dance..	29	Arista 9075
				KIRBY, Kathy British songstress.		
8/28/65	22	7		The Way Of Love	88	Parrot 9775
				KIRK, Jim, And The TM Singers Jim was vice president of TM Communications, a radio syndicator organization.		
2/23/80	40	4		Voice Of Freedom...	71	Capitol 4834
				KISS Hard-rock band formed in New York City in 1973. Consisted of Gene Simmons (bass), Paul Stanley (guitar), Ace Frehley (lead guitar) and Peter Criss (drums). Noted for elaborate makeup and highly theatrical stage shows.		
10/2/76	14	13	●	Beth	7	Casablanca 863
				KISSIN' COUSINS, The ○		
5/13/67	34	4		Listen To Your Heart		Project 3 1312
				KISSOON, Mac And Katie Brother and sister from Port-of-Spain, Trinidad. Moved to England in the late '50s.		
7/31/71	10	11		Chirpy Chirpy Cheep Cheep	20	ABC 11306
				KLUGH, Earl ○ Born on 9/16/53 in Detroit. Jazz acoustic guitarist/pianist.		
7/12/80	36	11		Doc .... [I]	105	United Art. 1355
				KLYMAXX Black female band founded by drummer/producer Bernadette Cooper in Los Angeles in 1979. Lead vocals by Lorena Porter Shelby and Joyce "Fenderella" Irby.		
11/16/85	3	17		1 I Miss You	5	Constellation 52606
5/16/87	8	21		2 I'd Still Say Yes	18	Constellation 53028

DEBUT DATE	PEAK POS	WKS CHR	GOLD	ARTIST — Record Title	POP POS	Label & Number
	★★108★★			**KNIGHT, Gladys, & The Pips**		
				R&B family group from Atlanta, formed in 1952 when lead singer Gladys was eight years old. Consisted of Gladys (b: 5/28/44, Atlanta), her brother Merald "Bubba" Knight and sister Brenda, and cousins William and Eleanor Guest. Named "Pips" for their manager, cousin James "Pip" Woods. First recorded for Brunswick in 1958. Brenda and Eleanor replaced by cousins Edward Patten and Langston George in 1959. Langston left group in 1962 and group has remained a quartet with the same members ever since. Due to legal problems, Gladys could not record with the Pips from 1977-80. Gladys was a cast member of the 1985 TV series *Charlie & Co.*		
				1)That's What Friends Are For 2)The Way We Were/Try To Remember 3)So Sad The Song		
4/8/72	25	6		1 Help Me Make It Through The Night	33	Soul 35094
3/24/73	15	5		2 Neither One Of Us (Wants To Be The First To Say Goodbye)	2²	Soul 35098
6/30/73	18	7		3 Where Peaceful Waters Flow...................................	28	Buddah 363
9/15/73	19	11	●	4 Midnight Train To Georgia...................................	1²	Buddah 383
3/2/74	10	13	●	**5 Best Thing That Ever Happened To Me**........................	3	Buddah 403
3/1/75	40	4		6 Love Finds It's Own Way	47	Buddah 453
5/3/75	2¹	16		**7 The Way We Were/Try To Remember**	11	Buddah 463
11/22/75	17	11		8 Part Time Love	22	Buddah 513
10/9/76	3	16		**9 So Sad The Song**	47	Buddah 544
				from the film *Pipe Dreams* starring Gladys Knight		
12/3/83	23	11		10 Hero	104	Columbia 04219
				#1 Pop hit in 1989 for Bette Midler as "Wind Beneath My Wings"		
11/9/85	1²	22	●	**11 That's What Friends Are For**	1⁴	Arista 9422
				DIONNE AND FRIENDS: Elton John, Gladys Knight and Stevie Wonder		
9/20/86	16	10		12 Loving On Borrowed Time		Scotti Br. 06267
				GLADYS KNIGHT and BILL MEDLEY		
				love theme from the film *Cobra*		
3/19/88	45	1		13 Love Overboard...................................	13	MCA 53210
7/15/89	18	9		14 Licence To Kill		MCA 53676
				GLADYS KNIGHT		
				from the James Bond film *Licence To Kill*		
3/17/90	10	22		15 If I Knew Then What I Know Now		Reprise 19972
				KENNY ROGERS (with Gladys Knight)		
				flip side "Maybe" (Kenny Rogers with Holly Dunn) made the Country charts (POS 25)		
				KNOBLOCK, Fred		
				Born in Jackson, Mississippi. With the rock band Let's Eat in the late 1970s. Member of the country trios Schuyler, Knobloch & Overstreet (SKO) and Schuyler, Knobloch & Bickhardt (SKB).		
7/19/80	1²	16		1 Why Not Me	18	Scotti Br. 600
				released earlier on Scotti Br. 518		
11/22/80	5	19		2 Killin' Time...................................	28	Scotti Br. 609
				FRED KNOBLOCK AND SUSAN ANTON		
9/12/81	28	10		3 Memphis	102	Scotti Br. 02434
				#2 Pop hit for Johnny Rivers in 1964		
				KOLOC, Bonnie ○		
9/21/74	12	11		You're Gonna Love Yourself In The Morning......................		Ovation 1049
	★★182★★			**KOOL & THE GANG**		
				R&B group formed in Jersey City, New Jersey in 1964 by bass player Robert "Kool" Bell as the Jazziacs. Session work in New York City, 1964-68. First recorded for De-Lite in 1969. Added lead singer James "J.T." Taylor in 1979. Current lineup consists of brothers Robert and Ronald Bell (sax, keyboards), George Brown (drums), Curtis "Fitz" Williams (keyboards) and Charles Smith (guitar). Taylor left in 1988; replaced by lead singers Gary Brown, Odeen Mays and former Dazz Band lead vocalist Skip Martin. Brown left by 1990.		
				1)Cherish 2)Joanna 3)Fresh		
2/2/80	11	15	●	1 Too Hot	5	De-Lite 802
2/14/81	34	4	▲	2 Celebration	1²	De-Lite 807
11/19/83	2²	24	●	3 Joanna...................................	2¹	De-Lite 829
3/30/85	5	18		4 Fresh	9	De-Lite 880623
7/6/85	1⁶	22	●	**5 Cherish**	2³	De-Lite 880869
12/6/86	35	9		6 Victory	10	Mercury 888074
2/21/87	11	15		7 Stone Love	10	Mercury 888292
10/10/87	6	17		8 Special Way	72	Mercury 888867
				KORGIS, The		
				British pop duo: James Warren and Andy Davis (both formerly with Stackridge).		
11/15/80	22	11		Everybody's Got To Learn Sometime	18	Asylum 47055

DEBUT DATE	PEAK POS	WKS CHR	GOLD	ARTIST — Record Title	POP POS	Label & Number
				KORONA		
				Korona is Bruce Blackman from Greenville, Mississippi, leader of Eternity's Children and Starbuck.		
4/26/80	**49**	2		Let Me Be	43	United Art. 1341
				KOZ, Dave ✪		
				Saxophonist born in San Fernando Valley, California. Touring member of Jeff Lorber's band. Member of *The Pat Sajak Show* band.		
12/15/90	**13**	18		1 Castle Of Dreams .... [I]		Capitol 44641
4/13/91	**20**	13		2 Nothing But The Radio On		Capitol 44674
				DAVE KOZ (Featuring Joey Diggs)		
				KRAFTWERK		
				Synthesizer band formed in 1970 in Dusseldorf, Germany by Ralf Hutter and Florian Schneider. Kraftwerk is German for power station.		
4/26/75	**43**	4		Autobahn .... [I]	25	Vertigo 203
				KRAL — see JACKIE & ROY		
				KRAMER, Billy J., With The Dakotas		
				Billy was born William Ashton on 8/19/43 near Liverpool, England. Discovered by The Beatles' manager, Brian Epstein, who teamed him with the group The Dakotas.		
5/9/64	**6**	2		1 Little Children	7	Imperial 66027
7/10/65	**10**	6		2 Trains And Boats And Planes	47	Imperial 66115
				KRAVITZ, Lenny		
				Singer/songwriter/multi-instrumentalist raised in New York City and later Los Angeles. Three-year member of the California Boys Choir. Married for a time to actress Lisa Bonet. Son of actress Roxie Roker (played Helen Willis on TV's *The Jeffersons*).		
6/29/91	**5**	22		It Ain't Over Til It's Over..	2[1]	Virgin 98795
				KRISTOFFERSON, Kris		
				Born on 6/22/36 in Brownsville, Texas. Singer/songwriter/actor. Attended England's Oxford University on a Rhodes scholarship. Married to Rita Coolidge from 1973-80. Wrote "Me And Bobby McGee," "For The Good Times" and "Help Me Make It Through The Night." Has starred in many films since 1972.		
8/28/71	**4**	12		1 Loving Her Was Easier (Than Anything I'll Ever Do Again)..	26	Monument 8525
7/21/73	**28**	5	●	2 Why Me..	16	Monument 8571
				KRIS KRISTOFFERSON & RITA COOLIDGE:		
11/10/73	**12**	13		3 A Song I'd Like To Sing	49	A&M 1475
3/2/74	**25**	11		4 Loving Arms	86	A&M 1498
12/21/74	**44**	5		5 Rain		Monument 8630
2/15/75	**42**	4		6 Lover Please		Monument 8636
				#7 Pop hit for Clyde McPhatter in 1962		
				KULIS, Charlie		
				Twenty-four-year-old (in 1975) singer/guitarist, based in New York.		
3/1/75	**40**	7		Runaway	46	Playboy 6023
				KUNKEL, Leah — see TAYLOR, Livingston		

L

DEBUT DATE	PEAK POS	WKS CHR	GOLD	ARTIST — Record Title	POP POS	Label & Number
				LaBELLE, Patti		
				Born Patricia Holt on 5/24/44 in Philadelphia. Lead singer of The Blue Belles and LaBelle.		
4/12/86	**2[2]**	21	●	1 On My Own..	1[3]	MCA 52770
				PATTI LaBELLE AND MICHAEL McDONALD		
4/25/87	**15**	11		2 The Last Unbroken Heart		MCA 53064
				PATTI LaBELLE AND BILL CHAMPLIN from the TV series *Miami Vice*		
7/29/89	**11**	17		3 If You Asked Me To	79	MCA 53358
				from the James Bond film *Licence To Kill*		
				LaBOUNTY, Bill		
				Singer/songwriter/pianist from Los Angeles.		
6/17/78	**46**	3		1 This Night Won't Last Forever	65	Warner 8529
9/2/78	**36**	7		2 In 25 Words Or Less		Warner 8642
5/29/82	**22**	11		3 Never Gonna Look Back	110	Warner 50065

DEBUT DATE	PEAK POS	WKS CHR	G O L D	ARTIST — Record Title	POP POS	Label & Number
				LACEY, Flo ○		
2/4/78	**34**	10		1 What's Expected Of Me Now/		
		10		2 Bluebird		Krugerrand 101
				LADD, Cheryl		
				Born Cheryl Stoppelmoor on 7/2/51 in Huron, South Dakota. Played Kris Monroe on the TV series *Charlie's Angels*. Voice on the cartoon series *Josie & The Pussycats*. Married to David Ladd (son of actor Alan Ladd) from 1973-79. Married producer/songwriter Brian Russell (Brian & Brenda) in 1981.		
8/26/78	**44**	4		Think It Over	34	Capitol 4599
				LaFORGE, Jack		
				Born on 8/8/24 in New York City. Pianist/composer/conductor.		
2/6/65	**22**	2		Goldfinger ....[I]	96	Regina 1323
				a James Bond movie title song		
				LAI, Francis		
				French composer/conductor.		
2/6/71	**21**	5		Theme From Love Story ....[I]	31	Paramount 0064
				from the film *Love Story*; Georges Pludermacher (piano solo)		
★★133★★				**LAINE, Frankie**		
				Born Frank Paul LoVecchio on 3/30/13 in Chicago. To Los Angeles in the early 1940s. First recorded for Exclusive in 1945. With Johnny Moore's Three Blazers. Signed to Mercury label in 1947. Dynamic style found favor with black and white audiences.		
				1)You Gave Me A Mountain 2)To Each His Own 3)I'll Take Care Of Your Cares		
5/18/63	**17**	5		1 Don't Make My Baby Blue	51	Columbia 42767
1/14/67	**2**²	17		2 I'll Take Care Of Your Cares	39	ABC 10891
4/15/67	**2**¹	12		3 Making Memories	35	ABC 10924
7/1/67	**5**	11		4 You Wanted Someone To Play With (I Wanted		
				Someone To Love)	48	ABC 10946
8/19/67	**23**	6		5 Laura, What's He Got That I Ain't Got...............	66	ABC 10967
				#1 Country hit for Leon Ashley in 1967		
10/7/67	**6**	10		6 You, No One But You	83	ABC 10983
1/27/68	**2**⁴	9		7 To Each His Own	82	ABC 11032
				there were 3 #1 versions of this tune in 1946		
3/30/68	**26**	2		8 I Don't Want To Set The World On Fire/		
				Horace Heidt, The Ink Spots, and Tommy Tucker all had top 5 versions of this tune in 1941		
4/6/68	**19**	6		9 I Found You	118	ABC/TRC 11057
7/6/68	**18**	6		10 Take Me Back	115	ABC 11097
9/28/68	**30**	4	✓	11 Please Forgive Me...		ABC 11129
1/25/69	**1**²	16		**12 You Gave Me A Mountain**	24	ABC 11174
				written by Marty Robbins; produced by Jimmy Bowen		
				LAKE, Greg		
				Born on 11/10/48 in Bournemouth, England. Guitarist/bassist with King Crimson and Emerson, Lake & Palmer.		
8/20/77	**46**	4		C'est La Vie..	91	Atlantic 3405
				from the Emerson, Lake & Palmer album *Works, Volume 1*		
				LANDIS, Richard ○		
				Singer/songwriter. Produced several hits for Juice Newton.		
3/18/72	**35**	2		1 A Man Who Sings	102	Dunhill 4300
4/29/72	**40**	1		2 Natural Causes		Dunhill 4307
				LANG, k.d.		
				Kathryn Dawn Lang from Consort, Alberta, Canada. Born on 11/2/61. Named her group The Reclines, in honor of Patsy Cline. Left country music in 1992.		
12/12/87	**28**	9		1 Crying		Virgin 99388
				ROY ORBISON/K.D. LANG		
				from the film *Hiding Out*; remake of Roy's 1961 Pop hit (POS 2)		
6/20/92	**2**¹	27		**2 Constant Craving**	38	Sire 18942
1/23/93	**40**	2		3 Crying ....[R]		Virgin LP Cut
				ROY ORBISON & K.D. LANG		
				from the Roy Orbison album *King Of Hearts* on Virgin 86520		
2/27/93	**32**	8		4 Miss Chatelaine...		Sire 18608
				LaROSA, Julius		
				Born on 1/2/30 in Brooklyn. Regular singer on *Arthur Godfrey And His Friends* TV show until he was fired on-the-air on 10/19/53.		
5/14/66	**21**	7		1 You're Gonna Hear From Me		MGM 13497
				from the film *Inside Daisy Clover*		

DEBUT DATE	PEAK POS	WKS CHR	GOLD	ARTIST — Record Title	POP POS	Label & Number
				LaROSA, Julius — Cont'd		
10/18/69	**24**	6		2 Where Do I Go?		Crewe 335
				JULIUS LA ROSA with The Bob Crewe Generation		
				from the Broadway musical *Hair*; #86 Pop hit for Carla Thomas in 1968		
				LARSEN-FEITEN BAND		
				Top session musicians Neil Larsen (keyboards) and Buzz Feiten (guitar). Feiten, a former member of the Paul Butterfield Blues Band and Stevie Wonder's band, joined Mr. Mister in 1989.		
9/27/80	**22**	11		Who'll Be The Fool Tonight	29	Warner 49282
				LARSON, Nicolette		
				Born on 7/17/52 in Helena, Montana and raised in Kansas City. To San Francisco in 1974. Session vocalist with Neil Young, Linda Ronstadt, Van Halen and many others.		
12/9/78	**1**[1]	23		1 **Lotta Love**	8	Warner 22
				written by Neil Young		
4/28/79	**38**	6		2 Rhumba Girl	47	Warner 8795
6/23/79	**19**	14		3 Give A Little	104	Warner 8851
				Linda Ronstadt and Ted Templeman (backing vocals)		
1/19/80	**9**	10		4 **Let Me Go, Love**	35	Warner 49130
				duet with Michael McDonald		
8/7/82	**15**	13		5 I Only Want To Be With You.....................................	53	Warner 29948
				LAST, James		
				Born on 4/17/29 in Bremen, Germany. Producer/arranger/conductor of big cabaret band.		
2/6/71	**22**	6		1 Washington Square/		
				#2 Pop hit for The Village Stompers in 1963		
		5		2 Proud Mary		Polydor 15017
				#2 Pop hit for Creedence Clearwater Revival in 1969		
12/4/71	**18**	11		3 Music From Across The Way	84	Polydor 15028
4/12/80	**22**	12		4 The Seduction (Love Theme)........................... [I]	28	Polydor 2071
				JAMES LAST BAND		
				from the film *American Gigolo*		
				LATTISAW, Stacy		
				Born on 11/25/66 in Washington, D.C. Soul singer. Recorded her first album at age 12. Childhood friend of Johnny Gill. Her younger brother Jerry is a member of Me-2-U.		
10/18/80	**34**	10		1 Let Me Be Your Angel	21	Cotillion 46001
7/18/81	**19**	10		2 Love On A Two Way Street	26	Cotillion 46015
				LAUPER, Cyndi		
				Born on 6/20/53 in Queens, New York. Recorded an album for Polydor Records in 1980 with the group Blue Angel. Supported by The Hooters, 1983-84. Won the 1984 Best New Artist Grammy Award. In the 1988 film *Vibes*. Married actor David Thornton on 11/24/91.		
4/21/84	**1**[3]	20	●	1 Time After Time	**1**[2]	Portrait 04432
10/13/84	**4**	18		2 All Through The Night	5	Portrait 04639
9/6/86	**5**	15		3 True Colors	**1**[2]	Portrait 06247
4/11/87	**29**	5		4 What's Going On	12	Portrait 06970
7/1/89	**43**	5		5 I Drove All Night..	6	Epic 68759
★★**56**★★				**LAWRENCE, Steve**		
				Born Sidney Leibowitz on 7/8/35 in Brooklyn. Regular performer on Steve Allen's *Tonight Show* for five years. First recorded for King in 1953. Married singer Eydie Gorme on 12/29/57; they recorded as Parker & Penny in 1979. Steve and Eydie remain a durable nightclub act.		
				1)Go Away Little Girl 2)I've Gotta Be Me 3)We Can Make It Together 4)I Want To Stay Here 5)Poor Little Rich Girl		
7/17/61	**13**	4		1 My Claire De Lune/	68	
				adapted from Debussy's *Suite Bergamesque*		
8/14/61	**19**	1		2 In Time..	94	United Art. 335
				adapted from Tchaikovsky's *Pathetique Symphony*		
11/6/61	**16**	3		3 Somewhere Along The Way	67	United Art. 364
				#8 hit for Nat King Cole in 1952		
12/8/62	**1**[6]	13	●	4 Go Away Little Girl	**1**[2]	Columbia 42601
3/9/63	**12**	9		5 Don't Be Afraid, Little Darlin'...................................	26	Columbia 42699
6/1/63	**11**	6		6 Poor Little Rich Girl	27	Columbia 42795
6/20/64	**18**	1		7 Everybody Knows	72	Columbia 43047
9/5/64	**15**	4		8 Yet...I Know	77	Columbia 43095
8/21/65	**11**	10		9 Millions Of Roses	106	Columbia 43362
2/5/66	**24**	7		10 The Week-End	131	Columbia 43487
8/27/66	**36**	3		11 The Ballad Of The Sad Young Men............................		Columbia 43758

135

DEBUT DATE	PEAK POS	WKS CHR	G O L D	ARTIST — Record Title	POP POS	Label & Number
				LAWRENCE, Steve — Cont'd		
4/15/67	**23**	6		12 Sweet Maria		Columbia 44084
				written by Bert Kaempfert		
12/16/67	**6**	12	✓	13 **I've Gotta Be Me**		Calendar 1001
				from the Broadway musical *Golden Rainbow*; #11 Pop hit for Sammy Davis, Jr. in 1969		
9/14/68	**27**	7		14 Runaround...		Calendar 1005
				written, produced and arranged by Teddy Randazzo		
9/27/69	**14**	7		15 The Drifter		RCA 0237
2/28/70	**38**	2		16 Mama, A Rainbow		RCA 0303
				from the musical *Minnie's Boys*		
7/18/70	**25**	3		17 Groovin'		RCA 0357
				#1 Pop hit for The Young Rascals in 1967		
4/1/72	**24**	6		18 Ain't No Sunshine/You Are My Sunshine		MGM 14368
				#3 Pop hit for Bill Withers in 1971/#7 Pop hit for Ray Charles in 1962		
10/13/73	**46**	3		19 The End (At The End Of A Rainbow)		MGM 14631
				#7 Pop hit for Earl Grant in 1958		
11/29/75	**16**	11		20 Now That We're In Love		20th Century 2246
				from the film *Whiffs*		
				STEVE LAWRENCE & EYDIE GORME:		
8/17/63	**8**	7		21 **I Want To Stay Here**..................................	28	Columbia 42815
1/25/64	**14**	3		22 I Can't Stop Talking About You	35	Columbia 42932
2/4/67	**14**	8	✓	23 The Honeymoon Is Over...............................		Columbia 43930
				from the Broadway musical *I Do, I Do*		
6/15/68	**33**	6		24 The Two Of Us		Calendar 1003
4/5/69	**20**	7		25 Real True Lovin'	119	RCA 0123
4/25/70	**21**	5		26 (You're My) Soul And Inspiration		RCA 0334
2/13/71	**37**	3		27 Love Is Blue/Autumn Leaves		RCA 0420
				#1 Pop hit for Paul Mauriat in 1968/#1 Pop hit for Roger Williams in 1955		
8/26/72	**7**	14		28 **We Can Make It Together**	68	MGM 14383
				STEVE & EYDIE featuring The Osmonds		
2/24/73	**31**	5		29 Feelin'		MGM 14493
8/4/79	**46**	5		30 Hallelujah		Warner/Curb 8877
				PARKER & PENNY		
				LAWRENCE, Vicki		
				Born on 5/26/49 in Inglewood, California. Regular on Carol Burnett's CBS-TV series from 1967-78. Also starred in TV's *Mama's Family*, 1982-83.		
3/3/73	**6**	9	●	1 **The Night The Lights Went Out In Georgia**	1²	Bell 45303
				written by Vicki's husband, Bobby Russell (also #3 below)		
6/16/73	**14**	9		2 He Did With Me..	75	Bell 45362
11/17/73	**49**	3		3 Ships In The Night		Bell 45409
				LAWS, Hubert ✪		
				Born in 1939 in Houston. Oldest brother of Ronnie, Eloise and Debra Laws. Jazz flutist. With the Swingsters (later the Jazz Crusaders), in 1954. With Mongo Santamaria from 1958.		
9/20/75	**43**	5		The Chicago Theme (Love Loop)		CTI 27
				LAWSON, Janet ✪		
7/18/70	**35**	2		Two Little Rooms	124	United Art. 50671
				LEAHY, Joe ✪		
9/18/65	**33**	3		Life ....[I]		Tower 150
				LEAPY LEE		
				Born Lee Graham on 7/2/42 in Eastbourne, England. Acted on stage and TV in England. Nicknamed "Leapy" in school because "I was always a leaper!"		
11/2/68	**38**	4		Little Arrows	16	Decca 32380
				LeBLANC & CARR		
				Lenny LeBlanc (b: 6/17/51, Leominster, Massachusetts) and Pete Carr (b: 4/22/50, Daytona Beach). Lenny (bass) and Pete (lead guitar) were both session musicians at Muscle Shoals, Alabama. Lenny later recorded Christian Contemporary music.		
11/5/77	**11**	17		1 Falling	13	Big Tree 16100
5/20/78	**40**	4		2 Midnight Light..	91	Big Tree 16114
4/18/81	**47**	4		3 Somebody Send My Baby Home	55	Capitol 4979
				LENNY LeBLANC		

DEBUT DATE	PEAK POS	WKS CHR	GOLD	ARTIST — Record Title	POP POS	Label & Number
	★★61★★			**LEE, Brenda** Born Brenda Mae Tarpley on 12/11/44 in Lithonia, Georgia. Professional singer since age six. Signed to Decca Records in 1956. Became known as "Little Miss Dynamite." Successful country singer from 1971-85. *1)All Alone Am I 2)Losing You 3)Too Many Rivers 4)Everybody Loves Me But You* *5)Johnny One Time*		
4/14/62	**2**¹	11		1 Everybody Loves Me But You	6	Decca 31379
7/7/62	**4**	10		2 Heart In Hand........................	15	Decca 31407
9/29/62	**1**⁵	15		3 All Alone Am I	3	Decca 31424
1/26/63	**12**	7		4 Your Used To Be/	32	
1/26/63	**15**	6		5 She'll Never Know	47	Decca 31454
4/20/63	**2**³	11		6 Losing You	6	Decca 31478
7/27/63	**8**	6		7 My Whole World Is Falling Down/	24	
7/27/63	**9**	5		8 I Wonder	25	Decca 31510
10/5/63	**7**	7		9 The Grass Is Greener........................	17	Decca 31539
12/21/63	**5**	10		10 As Usual	12	Decca 31570
3/14/64	**4**	8		11 Think........................	25	Decca 31599
6/20/64	**8**	5		12 Alone With You	48	Decca 31628
8/15/64	**8**	4		13 When You Loved Me	47	Decca 31654
4/10/65	**9**	5		14 Truly, Truly, True	54	Decca 31762
6/5/65	**2**²	14		15 Too Many Rivers/	13	
5/29/65	**25**	1		16 No One........................	98	Decca 31792
10/2/65	**3**	12		17 Rusty Bells	33	Decca 31849
1/11/69	**3**	16		18 Johnny One Time........................	41	Decca 32428
5/17/69	**32**	6		19 You Don't Need Me For Anything Anymore	84	Decca 32491
7/4/70	**37**	1		20 I Think I Love You Again	97	Decca 32675
				LEE, Dickey Born Dickey Lipscomb on 9/21/36 in Memphis. Pop-country singer/songwriter. First recorded for Sun Records in 1957.		
9/4/65	**12**	7		The Girl From Peyton Place........................	73	TCF Hall 111
				LEE, Johnny Born John Lee Ham on 7/3/46 in Texas City and raised in Alta Loma, Texas. Country singer/songwriter. Married to actress Charlene Tilton from 1982-84.		
7/26/80	**10**	15	●	Lookin' For Love .... from the film *Urban Cowboy*	5	Full Moon 47004
				LEE, Larry Original member of the Ozark Mountain Daredevils.		
5/22/82	**19**	13		Don't Talk	81	Columbia 02740
				LEE, Michele Born Michele Dusiak on 6/24/42. TV-film actress. Plays Karen McKenzie on TV's *Knots Landing*.		
2/10/68	**9**	13		1 L. David Sloane	52	Columbia 44413
7/27/68	**37**	4	✓	2 I Didn't Come To New York To Meet A Guy From My Home Town........................		Columbia 44554
12/14/68	**32**	5	✓	3 Knowing When To Leave .... from the musical *Promises, Promises*		Columbia 44698
	★★136★★			**LEE, Peggy** Born Norma Jean Egstrom on 5/26/20 in Jamestown, North Dakota. Jazz singer with Jack Wardlow band (1936-40), Will Osborne (1940-41) and Benny Goodman (1941-43). Went solo in March 1943. In films *Mister Music* (1950), *The Jazz Singer* (1953) and *Pete Kelly's Blues* (1955). Co-wrote many songs with husband Dave Barbour (married, 1943-52). Awarded nearly $4 million in court for her singing in the animated film *Lady and The Tramp*. *1)Is That All There Is 2)I Feel It 3)Big Spender*		
3/13/65	**20**	1		1 Pass Me By........................ main theme from the film *Father Goose* starring Cary Grant	93	Capitol 5346
10/23/65	**29**	7		2 Free Spirits		Capitol 5521
1/29/66	**9**	12		3 Big Spender .... from the Broadway show *Sweet Charity*		Capitol 5557
4/9/66	**31**	5		4 That Man		Capitol 5605
6/18/66	**36**	4		5 You've Got Possibilities .... from Broadway's *It's A Bird, It's A Plane, It's Superman*		Capitol 5653
10/15/66	**20**	7		6 So What's New/ also recorded by Herb Alpert & The Tijuana Brass on the album *What Now My Love*		
10/22/66	**14**	11		7 Walking Happy .... from the musical of the same title		Capitol 5758
9/30/67	**8**	10		8 I Feel It		Capitol 5988

DEBUT DATE	PEAK POS	WKS CHR	GOLD	ARTIST — Record Title	POP POS	Label & Number
				LEE, Peggy — Cont'd		
5/3/69	**24**	6		9 Spinning Wheel		Capitol 2477
				#2 Pop hit for Blood, Sweat & Tears in 1969		
9/13/69	**1²**	12		10 Is That All There Is	11	Capitol 2602
12/20/69	**13**	6	✓	11 Whistle For Happiness		Capitol 2696
2/7/70	**26**	5		12 Love Story	105	Capitol 2721
				written by Randy Newman		
5/9/70	**16**	6		13 You'll Remember Me...		Capitol 2817
10/3/70	**21**	5		14 One More Ride On The Merry-Go-Round		Capitol 2910
				written by Neil Sedaka and Howard Greenfield		
10/7/72	**34**	4		15 Love Song..		Capitol 3439
11/2/74	**22**	8		16 Let's Love..		Atlantic 3215
				written and produced by Paul McCartney		
				LEFEVRE, Raymond		
				Conductor/pianist/flutist from Paris.		
2/10/68	**4**	16		1 Ame Caline (Soul Coaxing).. [I]	37	Four Corners 147
5/25/68	**23**	5		2 La La La (He Gives Me Love) .... [I]	110	Four Corners 149
				LeGRAND, Michel		
				Pianist/composer/conductor/arranger. Born on 2/24/32 in Paris. Scored over 50 motion pictures including *Summer Of '42* and *Thomas Crown Affair*.		
1/29/72	**17**	8		Brian's Song .... [I]	56	Bell 45171
				from the TV film *Brian's Song* (Chicago Bears' Brian Piccolo)		
				LENNON, John		
				Born on 10/9/40 in Liverpool, England. Founding member of The Beatles. Married Cynthia Powell on 8/23/62, had son Julian. Divorced Cynthia on 11/8/68. Met Yoko Ono in 1966 and married her on 3/20/69. Formed Plastic Ono Band in 1969. To New York City in 1971. Fought deportation from the U.S., 1972-76, until he was granted a permanent visa. Lennon was shot to death on 12/8/80 in New York City. Won Grammy's Lifetime Achievement Award in 1991.		
10/23/71	**7**	9		1 Imagine	3	Apple 1840
				JOHN LENNON PLASTIC ONO BAND		
12/1/73	**33**	6		2 Mind Games	18	Apple 1868
11/29/80	**17**	15	●	3 (Just Like) Starting Over..	1⁵	Geffen 49604
1/24/81	**4**	13	●	4 Woman..	2³	Geffen 49644
4/4/81	**6**	14		5 Watching The Wheels	10	Geffen 49695
1/28/84	**11**	12		6 Nobody Told Me	5	Polydor 817254
				recorded in 1980		
10/22/88	**22**	7		7 Jealous Guy	80	Capitol 44230
				JOHN LENNON AND THE PLASTIC ONO BAND (with The Flux Fiddlers) from the film documentary *Imagine: John Lennon*; originally released on John's *Imagine* album in 1971		
				LENNON, Julian		
				Born John Charles Julian Lennon on 4/8/63. Son of John and Cynthia Lennon. First child to be born to any of The Beatles.		
11/3/84	**4**	17		1 Valotte	9	Atlantic 89609
1/26/85	**1²**	18		2 Too Late For Goodbyes	5	Atlantic 89589
5/4/85	**6**	13		3 Say You're Wrong...	21	Atlantic 89567
				LENNON SISTERS, The		
				Four sisters from Venice, California: Dianne, Peggy, Kathy and Janet Lennon. TV debut on Lawrence Welk's Christmas Eve show in 1955. Left Welk in 1967.		
9/25/61	**13**	5		Sad Movies (Make Me Cry)...	56	Dot 16255
				Billy Vaughn (orch.)		
				LENNOX, Annie		
				Born on 12/25/54 in Aberdeen, Scotland. Lead singer of the Eurythmics.		
11/19/88	**2¹**	19		1 Put A Little Love In Your Heart..................................	9	A&M 1255
				ANNIE LENNOX & AL GREEN from the film *Scrooged*		
5/30/92	**6**	21		2 Why..	34	Arista 12419
9/12/92	**6**	27		3 Walking On Broken Glass...	14	Arista 12452
				LEONETTI, Tommy		
				Born on 9/10/29 in Bergen, New Jersey; died on 9/15/79. Vocalist with Charlie Spivak and other bands. Featured singer on TV's *Your Hit Parade*.		
12/16/67	**40**	2		1 You Knew About Her All The Time		Columbia 44267
7/27/68	**34**	6		2 All The Brave Young Faces Of The Night		Columbia 44568

DEBUT DATE	PEAK POS	WKS CHR	G O L D	ARTIST — Record Title	POP POS	Label & Number
				LEONETTI, Tommy — Cont'd		
12/28/68	4	14		3 **Kum Ba Yah**	54	Decca 32421
				based on a traditional Afro-American slave song		
4/21/73	38	4		4 Wasn't It Nice In New York City		Columbia 45807
				LESTER, Ketty		
				Born Revoyda Frierson on 8/16/34 in Hope, Arkansas. To Los Angeles in 1955. Acted in several films and TV shows (formerly a cast member of *Days Of Our Lives*, *Rituals* and *Little House On The Prairie*).		
6/23/62	10	7		**But Not For Me**	41	Era 3080
				the George & Ira Gershwin classic, written in 1930		
★★33★★				**LETTERMEN, The**		
				Harmonic vocal group formed in Los Angeles in 1960. Consisted of Tony Butala (b: 11/20/40), Jim Pike (b: 11/6/38) and Bob Engemann (b: 2/19/36). First recorded for Warner Bros. Engemann replaced by Gary Pike (Jim's brother) in 1968.		
				1)*When I Fall In Love* 2)*Hurt So Bad* 3)*Goin' Out Of My Head/Can't Take My Eyes Off You* 4)*Theme From "A Summer Place"* 5)*The Way You Look Tonight*		
10/2/61	3	9		1 **The Way You Look Tonight**	13	Capitol 4586
				#1 hit for Fred Astaire in 1936		
11/27/61	1¹	13		2 **When I Fall In Love**	7	Capitol 4658
				#20 hit for Doris Day in 1952		
2/17/62	3	11		3 **Come Back Silly Girl**	17	Capitol 4699
5/19/62	16	6		4 How Is Julie?	42	Capitol 4746
6/19/65	2¹	12		5 **Theme From "A Summer Place"**	16	Capitol 5437
				from the film *A Summer Place* starring Sandra Dee/Troy Donahue		
9/18/65	8	10		6 **Secretly**	64	Capitol 5499
12/11/65	24	8		7 Sweet September	114	Capitol 5544
6/4/66	4	10		8 **I Only Have Eyes For You**	72	Capitol 5649
				#2 hit for Ben Selvin in 1934		
10/29/66	8	9		9 **Chanson D'Amour**	112	Capitol 5749
				#6 Pop hit for Art & Dotty Todd in 1958		
1/14/67	16	8		10 Our Winter Love	72	Capitol 5813
5/27/67	17	9		11 Volare		Capitol 5913
				#1 Pop hit for Domenico Modugno in 1958		
12/23/67	2²	14		12 **Goin' Out Of My Head/Can't Take My Eyes Off You**.......	7	Capitol 2054
3/30/68	9	8		13 **Sherry Don't Go**	52	Capitol 2132
11/9/68	8	13		14 **Put Your Head On My Shoulder**	44	Capitol 2324
3/1/69	16	8		15 I Have Dreamed	129	Capitol 2414
				from the musical *The King And I*; #91 Pop hit for Chad & Jeremy in 1965		
5/10/69	2³	24		16 **Hurt So Bad**	12	Capitol 2482
10/11/69	8	8		17 **Shangri-La**	64	Capitol 2643
12/20/69	3	12		18 **Traces/Memories Medley**	47	Capitol 2697
3/28/70	18	6		19 Hang On Sloopy	93	Capitol 2774
6/6/70	6	9		20 **She Cried**	73	Capitol 2820
10/24/70	17	4		21 Hey, Girl	104	Capitol 2938
				#10 Pop hit for Freddie Scott in 1963		
1/2/71	34	5		22 Morning Girl..		Capitol 3006
				The Lettermen Present JIM PIKE		
				#17 Pop hit for Neon Philharmonic in 1969		
1/23/71	6	8		23 **Everything Is Good About You**........................	74	Capitol 3020
6/5/71	33	4		24 Feelings		Capitol 3098
10/9/71	8	10		25 **Love**..	42	Capitol 3192
				written by John Lennon		
6/9/73	25	6		26 Summer Song		Capitol 3619
				#7 Pop hit for Chad & Jeremy in 1964		
7/27/74	31	9		27 Touch Me In The Morning/The Way We Were		Capitol 3912
				#1 Pop hits for Diana Ross in 1973 and for Barbra Streisand in 1974		
2/1/75	16	11		28 Eastward		Capitol 4005
6/28/75	28	7		29 You Are My Sunshine Girl		Capitol 4096
				LEVEL 42		
				Band from Manchester, England: Mark King (lead vocals), Mike Lindup, and brothers Phil and Boon Gould.		
4/12/86	10	17		1 **Something About You**.................................	7	Polydor 883362
9/27/86	32	7		2 Leaving Me Now		Polydor 885284
				LEWIS, Barbara		
				Born on 2/9/43 in South Lyon, Michigan. R&B singer/multi-instrumentalist/songwriter (since age nine). First recorded in Chicago in 1961. Inactive since the early 1970s.		
8/31/63	15	5		Straighten Up Your Heart	43	Atlantic 2200

DEBUT DATE	PEAK POS	WKS CHR	GOLD	ARTIST — Record Title	POP POS	Label & Number
				LEWIS, Ephraim		
				Pop-soul singer. Born of Jamaican parentage in Birmingham, England.		
8/22/92	**12**	17		Drowning In Your Eyes	72	Elektra 64710
				LEWIS, Gary, And The Playboys		
				Pop group formed in Los Angeles in 1964. Consisted of Gary (vocals, drums), Al Ramsey, John West (guitars), David Walker (keyboards) and David Costell (bass). Lewis (b: Cary Levitch on 7/31/45, name changed at age two) is the son of comedian Jerry Lewis. Group worked regularly at Disneyland in 1964. Lewis inducted into the Army on New Year's Day in 1967, resumed career after discharge in 1968.		
7/31/65	**1**³	8		**1 Save Your Heart For Me**	2¹	Liberty 55809
8/10/68	**32**	5		**2** Sealed With A Kiss	19	Liberty 56037
★★111★★				**LEWIS, Huey, and the News**		
				Born Hugh Cregg, III on 7/5/50 in New York City. Joined the country-rock band Clover in the late '70s. Formed his six-man, pop-rock band, the News, in San Francisco in 1980: Huey (lead singer), Chris Hayes (lead guitar), Mario Cipollina (bass; brother of Quicksilver Messenger Service guitarist John Cipollina), Bill Gibson (drums), Sean Hopper (keyboards) and Johnny Colla (sax, guitar).		
				1)Stuck With You 2)Doing It All For My Baby 3)Perfect World		
7/28/84	**5**	17		**1 If This Is It**...	6	Chrysalis 42803
7/20/85	**6**	20	●	**2 The Power Of Love**	1²	Chrysalis 42876
				from the film *Back To The Future*		
8/2/86	**1**³	19		**3 Stuck With You**	1³	Chrysalis 43019
11/8/86	**20**	12		**4** Hip To Be Square	3	Chrysalis 43065
1/31/87	**17**	12		**5** Jacob's Ladder	1¹	Chrysalis 43097
				written by Bruce Hornsby		
5/16/87	**30**	5		**6** I Know What I Like	9	Chrysalis 43108
7/25/87	**2**¹	19		**7 Doing It All For My Baby**	6	Chrysalis 43143
7/23/88	**2**¹	19		**8 Perfect World**	3	Chrysalis 43265
10/22/88	**19**	11		**9** Small World	25	Chrysalis 43306
1/28/89	**42**	4		**10** Give Me The Keys (And I'll Drive You Crazy)	47	Chrysalis 43335
7/27/91	**10**	17		**11 It Hit Me Like A Hammer**	21	EMI 50364
12/14/91	**40**	6		**12** He Don't Know		EMI LP Cut
				from the album *Hard At Play* on EMI 93355		
5/22/93	**7**	17↑		**13** It's Alright		Shanachie LP Cut
				from the album *People Get Ready: A Tribute To Curtis Mayfield* on Shanachie 9004; #4 Pop hit for The Impressions in 1963		
				LEWIS, Jerry Lee		
				Born on 9/29/35 in Ferriday, Louisiana. Played piano since age nine, professionally since age 15. Cousin to country singer Mickey Gilley and TV evangelist Jimmy Swaggart. Inducted into the Rock and Roll Hall of Fame in 1986. Jerry's early career is documented in the 1989 film *Great Balls Of Fire* starring Dennis Quaid.		
12/11/71	**39**	3		**1** Me And Bobby McGee	40	Mercury 73248
				made the Country charts as the B-side of "Would You Take Another Chance On Me"		
3/25/72	**23**	6		**2** Chantilly Lace	43	Mercury 73273
				LEWIS, Ramsey		
				Ramsey (b: 5/27/35, Chicago; piano) formed the Gentlemen Of Swing, a jazz-oriented trio, in 1956 in Chicago. Consisted of Ramsey, Eldee Young (bass) and Isaac "Red" Holt (drums). All had been in The Clefs in the early '50s. First recorded for Chess/Argo in 1956. Disbanded in 1965; Young and Holt then formed the Young-Holt Trio. Lewis re-formed his trio with Cleveland Eaton (bass) and Maurice White (later with Earth, Wind & Fire; drums). Reunited with Young and Holt in 1983.		
				1)A Hard Day's Night 2)Wade In The Water 3)Hang On Sloopy		
12/4/65	**18**	6		**1** Hang On Sloopy * ....[I]	11	Cadet 5522
1/22/66	**10**	8		**2 A Hard Day's Night** * ....[I]	29	Cadet 5525
3/26/66	**27**	4		**3** Hi Heel Sneakers - Pt. 1 * ....[I]	70	Cadet 5531
7/9/66	**11**	14		**4** Wade In The Water ....[I]	19	Cadet 5541
11/5/66	**37**	3		**5** Up Tight ....[I]	49	Cadet 5547
12/24/66	**27**	5		**6** Day Tripper ....[I]	74	Cadet 5553
9/16/67	**36**	4		**7** Dancing In The Street ....[I]	84	Cadet 5573
10/25/69	**21**	5		**8** Julia ....[I]	76	Cadet 5640
				written by John Lennon		
1/10/70	**32**	4		**9** My Cherie Amour * ....[I]		Cadet 5662
				#4 Pop hit for Stevie Wonder in 1969		
5/25/74	**46**	2		**10** The Everywhere Calypso.................................[I]		Columbia 46037
				*****RAMSEY LEWIS TRIO**		
				LIA, Orsa		
				Country-pop singer born and raised in Virginia. Sang several TV jingles in the mid-1970s.		
2/24/79	**1**¹	17		**I Never Said I Love You**	84	Infinity 50004

DEBUT DATE	PEAK POS	WKS CHR	GOLD	ARTIST — Record Title	POP POS	Label & Number
				LIGHT, Enoch, and the Light Brigade		
				Enoch was born on 8/18/07 in Canton, Ohio. Died in New York City on 7/31/78. Conductor of own orchestra, The Light Brigade, since 1935. President of Grand Award label and managing director for Command Records, for whom he produced a long string of hit stereo percussion albums in the '60s.		
5/20/67	**38**	3		I Love, I Live, I Love .... [I]		Project 3 1310
★★97★★				**LIGHTFOOT, Gordon**		
				Born on 11/17/38 in Orillia, Ontario, Canada. Folk-pop-country singer/songwriter/guitarist. Worked on *Country Hoedown*, CBC-TV series. Teamed with Jim Whalen as the Two Tones in the mid-1960s. Wrote hit "Early Mornin' Rain" for Peter, Paul and Mary. First recorded for Chateau in 1965.		
				1)Sundown 2)Carefree Highway 3)Rainy Day People		
1/2/71	**1**¹	13		1 **If You Could Read My Mind**	5	Reprise 0974
6/26/71	**11**	7		2 Talking In Your Sleep	64	Reprise 1020
6/3/72	**30**	4		3 Beautiful	58	Reprise 1088
2/3/73	**32**	4		4 You Are What I Am	101	Reprise 1128
4/6/74	**1**²	18	●	5 **Sundown**	**1**¹	Reprise 1194
8/31/74	**1**¹	16		6 **Carefree Highway**	10	Reprise 1309
4/5/75	**1**¹	12		7 **Rainy Day People**	26	Reprise 1328
9/18/76	**9**	14		8 **The Wreck Of The Edmund Fitzgerald**	2²	Reprise 1369
				true story of an ore vessel that sank in Lake Superior on 11/10/75		
3/5/77	**13**	9		9 Race Among The Ruins	65	Reprise 1380
2/11/78	**3**	15		10 **The Circle Is Small (I Can See It In Your Eyes)**	33	Warner 8518
6/3/78	**16**	10		11 Daylight Katy		Warner 8579
5/17/80	**25**	11		12 Dream Street Rose		Warner 49230
3/27/82	**17**	15		13 Baby Step Back	50	Warner 50012
7/12/86	**13**	13		14 Anything For Love		Warner 28655
				LIGHTHOUSE		
				Rock band from Toronto — Bob McBride, lead singer.		
10/16/71	**30**	4		1 One Fine Morning	24	Evolution 1048
12/8/73	**38**	6		2 Pretty Lady	53	Polydor 14198
				LIGHTNING SEEDS, The		
				Band with fluctuating lineup spearheaded by U.K. producer/vocalist Ian Broudie (former member of Big In Japan who produced Echo & The Bunnymen and others).		
7/28/90	**31**	6		Pure	31	MCA 53816
				LIMAHL		
				Real name: Chris Hamill (Limahl is an anagram of his last name). Ex-lead singer of Kajagoogoo.		
5/11/85	**6**	15		**Never Ending Story**	17	EMI America 8230
				from the film *The Never Ending Story*		
				LINDISFARNE		
				Folk-rock quintet from England — Alan Hull, lead singer. Group's name is an island off of Northumberland, U.K.		
11/4/78	**43**	10		Run For Home	33	Atco 7093
				LINDSAY, Mark		
				Born on 3/9/42 in Cambridge, Idaho. Lead singer/saxophonist of Paul Revere & The Raiders. Also recorded with Raider, Keith Allison, and Steve Alaimo as The Unknowns.		
7/19/69	**24**	6		1 First Hymn From Grand Terrace	81	Columbia 44875
12/27/69	**16**	10	●	2 Arizona	10	Columbia 45037
4/18/70	**20**	5		3 Miss America	44	Columbia 45125
6/27/70	**7**	9		4 Silver Bird	25	Columbia 45180
10/3/70	**5**	12		5 And The Grass Won't Pay No Mind	44	Columbia 45229
				written by Neil Diamond		
1/16/71	**35**	3		6 Problem Child	80	Columbia 45286
12/18/71	**36**	4		7 Something Big		Columbia 45506
				movie title song		
10/16/76	**22**	10		8 Sing Your Own Song		Greedy 106
				LISA LISA AND CULT JAM		
				Harlem trio: Lisa Velez (b: 1/15/67; lead vocals), Mike Hughes and Alex "Spanador" Moseley. Assembled and produced by Full Force.		
9/26/87	**27**	9	●	Lost In Emotion	**1**¹	Columbia 07267
				LITTLE RICHARD — see BEACH BOYS		

DEBUT DATE	PEAK POS	WKS CHR	GOLD	ARTIST — Record Title	POP POS	Label & Number
				★★146★★ LITTLE RIVER BAND		
				Pop-rock group formed in Australia in 1975. Consisted of Glenn Shorrock (lead singer), Rick Formosa, Beeb Birtles and Graham Goble (guitars), Roger McLachlan (bass) and Derek Pellicci (drums). McLachlan replaced by George McArdle in 1977 and Formosa replaced by David Briggs in 1978. American bassist Wayne Nelson replaced McLachlan in 1980. In 1983, Shorrock replaced by John Farnham and Briggs replaced by Steve Housden. By 1985, Pellicci replaced by Steven Prestwich, and Birtles had left and keyboardist David Hirschfelder joined. Pellicci and Shorrock returned in 1987. By 1992, Goble had left and Peter Beckett, ex-leader of Player, had joined. Band named after a resort town near Melbourne.		
				1)The Other Guy 2)Lady 3)Cool Change		
8/5/78	**10**	18		1 **Reminiscing**	3	Harvest 4605
1/20/79	**7**	18		2 **Lady**	10	Harvest 4667
8/4/79	**15**	13		3 Lonesome Loser	6	Capitol 4748
11/3/79	**8**	16		4 **Cool Change**	10	Capitol 4789
9/26/81	**33**	10		5 The Night Owls	6	Capitol 5033
1/9/82	**14**	15		6 Take It Easy On Me	10	Capitol 5057
5/15/82	**26**	12		7 Man On Your Mind	14	Capitol 5061
11/20/82	**6**	20		8 **The Other Guy**	11	Capitol 5185
5/28/83	**17**	15		9 We Two	22	Capitol 5231
7/2/88	**18**	13		10 Love Is A Bridge		MCA 53291
3/17/90	**22**	10		11 If I Get Lucky		MCA 53767
6/23/90	**27**	9		12 Every Time I Turn Around		MCA LP Cut
				from the album *Get Lucky* on MCA 6369		
				★★87★★ LOBO		
				Pop singer/songwriter/guitarist. Born Roland Kent Lavoie on 7/31/43 in Tallahassee, Florida. Played with the Legends in Tampa in 1961. The Legends included Jim Stafford, Gerald Chambers, Gram Parsons and Jon Corneal. Lobo is Spanish for wolf. Lavoie formed own publishing company, Boo Publishing, in 1974.		
				1)Where Were You When I Was Falling In Love 2)Me And You And A Dog Named Boo 3)Don't Expect Me To Be Your Friend		
4/10/71	**1**²	12		1 **Me And You And A Dog Named Boo**	5	Big Tree 112
7/10/71	**14**	7		2 I'm The Only One/	flip	
		7		3 She Didn't Do Magic	46	Big Tree 116
9/11/71	**19**	5		4 California Kid And Reemo	72	Big Tree 119
7/8/72	**17**	7		5 A Simple Man	56	Big Tree 141
9/30/72	**1**¹	13	●	6 **I'd Love You To Want Me**	2²	Big Tree 147
1/13/73	**1**²	10		7 **Don't Expect Me To Be Your Friend**	8	Big Tree 158
4/14/73	**3**	9		8 **It Sure Took A Long, Long Time**	27	Big Tree 16001
6/23/73	**4**	12		9 How Can I Tell Her	22	Big Tree 16004
11/3/73	**29**	7		10 There Ain't No Way	68	Big Tree 16012
4/27/74	**25**	7		11 Standing At The End Of The Line...........	37	Big Tree 15001
7/20/74	**8**	11		12 Rings	43	Big Tree 15008
3/22/75	**2**¹	11		13 **Don't Tell Me Goodnight**	27	Big Tree 16033
7/19/75	**44**	4		14 Would I Still Have You		Big Tree 16040
7/21/79	**1**²	20		15 **Where Were You When I Was Falling In Love**	23	MCA 41065
12/1/79	**13**	11		16 Holdin' On For Dear Love	75	MCA 41152
				LODGE, John — see HAYWARD, Justin		
				LOGGINS, Dave		
				Born on 11/10/47 in Mountain City, Tennessee. Pop-country singer/songwriter. Cousin of Kenny Loggins.		
5/18/74	**1**¹	18		1 **Please Come To Boston**	5	Epic 11115
6/9/79	**22**	13		2 Pieces Of April.......................................		Epic 50711
				DAVID LOGGINS #19 Pop hit for Three Dog Night in 1972		
9/8/84	**10**	17		3 **Nobody Loves Me Like You Do**		Capitol 5401
				ANNE MURRAY with Dave Loggins		
				★★101★★ LOGGINS, Kenny		
				Born on 1/7/47 in Everett, Washington. Raised in Alhambra, California. Pop-rock singer/songwriter/guitarist. Cousin of Dave Loggins. In band Gator Creek (later with producer Michael Omartian, later in Second Helping. Worked as a songwriter for Wingate Music; wrote Nitty Gritty Dirt Band's "House At Pooh Corner." Signed as a solo artist with Columbia in 1971 where he met and recorded with Jim Messina from 1972-76.		
				1)Meet Me Half Way 2)Heart To Heart 3)The Real Thing		
7/30/77	**37**	6		1 I Believe In Love	66	Columbia 10569
8/19/78	**9**	23		2 **Whenever I Call You "Friend"**	5	Columbia 10794
				Stevie Nicks (harmony vocal)		

DEBUT DATE	PEAK POS	WKS CHR	G O L D	ARTIST — Record Title	POP POS	Label & Number
				LOGGINS, Kenny — Cont'd		
11/10/79	**17**	15		3 This Is It..	11	Columbia 11109
3/22/80	**40**	7		4 Keep The Fire..	36	Columbia 11215
12/4/82	**3**	20		**5 Heart To Heart**....................................	15	Columbia 03377
3/19/83	**17**	13		6 Welcome To Heartlight........................	24	Columbia 03555
				inspired by the writings of children from Heartlight School		
6/1/85	**5**	24		**7 Forever**..	40	Columbia 04931
11/2/85	**33**	3		8 I'll Be There..	88	Columbia 05625
4/18/87	**2**[1]	21		**9 Meet Me Half Way**............................	11	Columbia 06690
				from the film *Over The Top* starring Sylvester Stallone		
9/10/88	**42**	7		10 Nobody's Fool.......................................	8	Columbia 07971
				theme from the film *Caddyshack II*		
10/26/91	**9**	26		**11 Conviction Of The Heart**	65	Columbia 74029
2/1/92	**5**	29		**12 The Real Thing**..............................		Columbia 74186
5/30/92	**9**	28		**13 If You Believe**................................		Columbia LP Cut
12/5/92	**34**	12		14 Now Or Never.......................................		Columbia LP Cut
				above 4 from the album *Leap Of Faith* on Columbia 46140		

LOGGINS & MESSINA

Duo of Kenneth Clarke Loggins (see previous entry) and James Messina (b: 12/5/47, Maywood, California). Messina was raised in Harlingen, Texas and played in bands from age 13. Worked as a recording engineer and producer from 1965. Member of Buffalo Springfield and Poco. Duo formed in 1970.

12/23/72	**19**	8	●	1 Your Mama Don't Dance...................	4	Columbia 45719
				KENNY LOGGINS AND JIM MESSINA		
3/31/73	**7**	11		**2 Thinking Of You**..............................	18	Columbia 45815
11/10/73	**10**	15		**3 My Music**..	16	Columbia 45952
3/9/74	**36**	5		4 Watching The River Run...................	71	Columbia 46010
4/12/75	**18**	8		5 Growin'...	52	Columbia 10118

LONDONBEAT

Britain-based soul outfit. Vocal trio of Americans Jimmy Helms and George Chandler, with Trinidad native Jimmy Chambers. Backed by British producer/multi-instrumentalist Willy M.

3/16/91	**7**	20	●	1 I've Been Thinking About You	1[1]	Radioactive 54005
6/22/91	**37**	7		2 A Better Love	18	Radioactive 54101

LONDON SYMPHONY ORCHESTRA — see WILLIAMS, John

LONGET, Claudine

Born on 1/29/42 in France. Singer/actress. Formerly married to Andy Williams. Jailed, for a time, for fatally shooting skier Spider Savich.

3/11/67	**19**	8		1 Here, There And Everywhere...............................	126	A&M 832
				written by Lennon and McCartney; #65 Pop hit for Emmylou Harris in 1976		
5/6/67	**8**	11		**2 Hello, Hello**...	91	A&M 846
8/26/67	**36**	3		3 Good Day Sunshine	100	A&M 864
				written by John Lennon and Paul McCartney		
9/30/67	**12**	7		4 Small Talk		A&M 877
3/9/68	**28**	8		5 Love Is Blue (L'Amour Est Bleu).................[F]	71	A&M 909
5/25/68	**30**	4		6 White Horses		A&M 936
8/24/68	**23**	9		7 Walk In The Park		A&M 967
12/28/68	**28**	7		8 A Flea In Her Ear..		A&M 1002
				movie title song		
2/15/69	**30**	4		9 Hurry On Down		A&M 1024

LOOKING GLASS

Rock quartet formed by singer/guitarist Elliot Lurie while at Rutgers University in New Jersey.

7/1/72	**7**	11	●	**1 Brandy (You're A Fine Girl)**	1[1]	Epic 10874
11/25/72	**37**	3	✓	2 Golden Rainbow		Epic 10900
6/30/73	**16**	18		3 Jimmy Loves Mary-Anne	33	Epic 11001

★★129★★ LOPEZ, Trini

Born Trinidad Lopez, III on 5/15/37 in Dallas. Pop-folk singer/guitarist. Discovered by Don Costa while performing at PJs nightclub in Los Angeles. Portrayed Pedro Jiminez in the film *The Dirty Dozen*.

1)Lemon Tree 2)I'm Comin' Home, Cindy 3)The Bramble Bush

11/30/63	**13**	7		1 Kansas City	23	Reprise 20236
8/29/64	**7**	7		**2 Michael**	42	Reprise 0300
1/23/65	**2**[4]	7		**3 Lemon Tree**	20	Reprise 0336
5/1/65	**22**	1		4 Sad Tomorrows	94	Reprise 0328
6/5/65	**25**	4		5 Are You Sincere	85	Reprise 0376

DEBUT DATE	PEAK POS	WKS CHR	GOLD	ARTIST — Record Title	POP POS	Label & Number
				LOPEZ, Trini — Cont'd		
10/9/65	**12**	11		6 Sinner Man	54	Reprise 0405
				from the film *Marriage On The Rocks*		
2/26/66	**36**	2		7 Made In Paris	113	Reprise 0435
				movie title song		
4/2/66	**2**¹	13		8 I'm Comin' Home, Cindy	39	Reprise 0455
6/25/66	**9**	6		9 La Bamba - Part I ....[F]	86	Reprise 0480
1/28/67	**6**	12		10 Gonna Get Along Without Ya' Now..............	93	Reprise 0547
7/8/67	**4**	11		11 The Bramble Bush....................................		Reprise 0596
				from the film *The Dirty Dozen*		
9/16/67	**30**	4		12 Together		Reprise 0618
3/2/68	**30**	3		13 Sally Was A Good Old Girl	99	Reprise 0659
5/18/68	**18**	7		14 Mental Journey		Reprise 0687
10/12/68	**24**	5		15 Malaguena Salerosa		Reprise 0770
				LORENZ, Trey		
				Born on 1/19/69 in Florence, South Carolina. Attended New York's Fairleigh Dickinson University; earned advertising degree. Sang backup on Mariah Carey's first two albums; male vocal on her hit "I'll Be There."		
10/3/92	**18**	12		Someone To Hold	19	Epic 74482
				co-written and co-produced by Mariah Carey		
				LORING, Gloria		
				Born on 12/10/46. Played Liz Curtis on the TV soap *Days Of Our Lives*. Married to actor Alan Thicke for 14 years.		
7/19/86	**1**²	19		Friends And Lovers....................................	2²	USA Carrere 06122
				GLORIA LORING & CARL ANDERSON		
				LOS DIABLOS ✪		
				Spanish quintet.		
9/19/70	**35**	4		Un Rayo De Sol....................................[F]		Crazy Horse 5097
				LOS INDIOS TABAJARAS		
				Brazilian Indian brothers: Natalicio and Antenor Lima.		
10/5/63	**3**	12		Maria Elena ....[I]	6	RCA 8216
				#1 hit in 1941 for Jimmy Dorsey & His Orchestra		
				LOS LOBOS		
				Hispanic-American rock quintet formed in East Los Angeles in 1973 by David Hidalgo (lead vocals), Cesar Rosas, Conrad Lozano and Louie Perez. Former Blasters' saxophonist, Steve Berlin, joined in 1983.		
8/1/87	**4**	14		1 La Bamba...[F]	1³	Slash 28336
10/31/87	**35**	5		2 Come On, Let's Go	21	Slash 28186
				above 2 from the film *La Bamba*		
				LOS POP TOPS — see POP-TOPS		
				LOVE, Marian ✪		
				Songstress from New York City.		
3/6/71	**27**	3		I Believe In Music	111	A&R 7100/505
				written by Mac Davis; #22 Pop hit for Gallery in 1972		
				LOVE AND MONEY		
				Scottish pop trio: James Grant (guitar, vocals), Bobby Paterson (bass) and Paul McGeechan (keyboards). Drummer Stuart Kerr of the group Texas was an early member.		
4/1/89	**44**	2		Halleluiah Man	75	Mercury 870596
				LOVE GENERATION, The		
				Pop group consisting of four men and two women.		
7/27/68	**19**	9		Montage From How Sweet It Is (I Know That You Know)	86	Imperial 66310
				from the film *How Sweet It Is* starring James Garner/Debbie Reynolds		
				LOVERBOY		
				Rock quintet formed in Vancouver, Canada in 1978: Mike Reno (lead singer), Paul Dean (lead guitar), Scott Smith (bass), Matt Frenette (drums) and Doug Johnson (keyboards, left by 1989).		
3/15/86	**30**	8		This Could Be The Night................................	10	Columbia 05765
				LOVE SOUNDS ✪		
12/13/75	**26**	8		Ebb Tide...[I]		Pye 71039
				#2 hit for Frank Chacksfield in 1953		
				LOVE UNLIMITED ORCHESTRA		
				Studio orchestra conducted and arranged by Barry White.		
12/15/73	**1**²	17	●	1 Love's Theme....................................[I]	1¹	20th Century 2069
5/4/74	**34**	7		2 Rhapsody In White ....[I]	63	20th Century 2090

144

DEBUT DATE	PEAK POS	WKS CHR	GOLD	ARTIST — Record Title	POP POS	Label & Number
				LOVE UNLIMITED ORCHESTRA — Cont'd		
3/1/75	39	7		3 Satin Soul......................[I]	22	20th Century 2162
9/25/76	30	11		4 My Sweet Summer Suite......................[I]	48	20th Century 2301
1/29/77	27	7		5 Theme From King Kong (Pt. I)......................[I]	68	20th Century 2325
				from the Dino DeLaurentis film *King Kong*		
				LOWE, Nick		
				Born on 3/25/49 in Woodbridge, Suffolk, England. With Brinsley Schwarz (1970-75) and Rockpile. Married Carlene Carter on 8/18/79; later divorced. Produced albums for Elvis Costello, Graham Parker & The Rumour and others. Co-founder of Little Village.		
9/22/79	36	5		Cruel To Be Kind......................	12	Columbia 11018
				LULU		
				Born Marie Lawrie on 11/3/48 near Glasgow, Scotland. Married to Maurice Gibb (Bee Gees) from 1969-73. Starred in the 1967 film *To Sir With Love*. Hosted own U.K. TV show in 1968.		
11/15/69	36	3		1 Oh Me Oh My (I'm A Fool For You Baby)......................	22	Atco 6722
5/9/70	26	5		2 Hum A Song (From Your Heart) *......................	54	Atco 6749
7/18/70	20	5		3 After The Feeling Is Gone *......................	117	Atco 6761
				*LULU with The Dixie Flyers		
8/15/81	2³	18		4 I Could Never Miss You (More Than I Do)......................	18	Alfa 7006
11/14/81	27	13		5 If I Were You......................	44	Alfa 7011
				LUNDBERG, Victor		
				Ex-DJ/newsman born in 1923 in Grand Rapids, Michigan.		
11/18/67	40	2		An Open Letter To My Teenage Son......................[S]	10	Liberty 55996
				LURIE, Elliot ☉		
				Lead singer/guitarist of Looking Glass.		
8/3/74	39	7		Your Love Song......................		Epic 11153
				LYMAN, Arthur, Group		
				Born on the island of Kauai, Hawaii in 1934. Plays vibraphone, guitar, piano and drums. Formerly with the Martin Denny Trio.		
7/17/61	2²	5		1 Yellow Bird......................[I]	4	Hi Fi 5024
3/2/63	13	5		2 Love For Sale......................[I]	43	Hi Fi 5066
				Libby Holman's version of the Cole Porter tune hit #5 in 1931		
				LYNN, Cheryl		
				Born on 3/11/57 in Los Angeles. Soul singer. Discovered on TV's *Gong Show*. Cousin of soul singer D'La Vance. Also see Toto.		
3/9/85	39	2		At Last You're Mine......................		Private I 04736
				from the film *Heavenly Bodies*		
				LYNN, Judy ☉		
				Born Judy Lynn Voiten on 4/12/36 in Boise, Idaho. For 21 years a featured artist in Nevada casinos. Retired in 1980 to become an ordained minister.		
5/1/71	18	4		Married To A Memory......................	104	Amaret 131
				LYNN, Vera		
				Born Vera Margaret Welsh on 3/20/19 in London. England's most popular female singer during World War II.		
2/11/67	7	13		It Hurts To Say Goodbye......................		United Art. 50119
				LYNNE, Gloria		
				Born on 11/23/31 in New York City. Jazz-styled vocalist.		
9/11/61	19	1		1 Impossible......................	95	Everest 19418
2/15/64	10	5		2 I Wish You Love......................	28	Everest 2036
4/11/64	16	4		3 I Should Care......................	64	Everest 2042
				there were 4 top 20 versions of this song in 1945		
7/18/64	16	1		4 Don't Take Your Love From Me......................	76	Everest 2044
				#26 hit for Glen Gray in 1944		
6/5/65	36	1		5 Watermelon Man......................	62	Fontana 1511

M

MacDONALD, Ralph

Session percussionist/bandleader. Formerly with Roberta Flack, and the jazz sextet, The Writers.

8/25/84	6	14		**In The Name Of Love**......................	58	Polydor 881221
				RALPH MacDONALD with Bill Withers		

DEBUT DATE	PEAK POS	WKS CHR	GOLD	ARTIST — Record Title	POP POS	Label & Number
				MacGREGOR, Byron		
				Twenty-five-year-old news director at CKLW-Detroit when he did the narration for "Americans." Narration was originally written and delivered as an editorial by Gordon Sinclair for CFRB-Toronto on 6/5/73.		
1/19/74	**26**	6	●	Americans ....[S]	4	Westbound 222
				backed by instrumental version of "America The Beautiful"		
				MacGREGOR, Mary		
				Born on 5/6/48 in St. Paul, Minnesota. Pop singer.		
11/6/76	**1**²	21	●	1 Torn Between Two Lovers	1²	Ariola Am. 7638
4/23/77	**27**	9		2 This Girl (Has Turned Into A Woman)............................	46	Ariola Am. 7662
8/6/77	**38**	5		3 For A While	90	Ariola Am. 7667
				above 3 written and produced by Peter Yarrow (Peter, Paul & Mary)		
4/1/78	**29**	8		4 I've Never Been To Me		Ariola 7677
				#3 Pop hit for Charlene in 1982		
11/18/78	**23**	11		5 The Wedding Song (There Is Love)	81	Ariola 7726
8/11/79	**11**	14		6 Good Friend	39	RSO 938
				from the film Meatballs		
4/26/80	**31**	8		7 Dancin' Like Lovers	72	RSO 1025
				MADISON STREET ✪		
				Pop group from Queens, New York. Consisted of brothers Dominick and Frank Safuto, Mike Zero and Vinny Corella. The Safuto brothers and Zero are former members of Randy & The Rainbows.		
2/4/78	**41**	9		1 Minstrel Man		Millennium 605
10/28/78	**50**	1		2 A Simple Love Song		Millennium 621
★★**57**★★				**MADONNA**		
				Born Madonna Louise Ciccone on 8/16/58 in Bay City, Michigan. To New York in the late '70s; performed with the Alvin Ailey dance troupe. Short-lived member of the Breakfast Club, early '80s. Married to actor Sean Penn from 1985-89. Acted in the films Desperately Seeking Susan, Dick Tracy, A League Of Their Own and Body Of Evidence among others. Appeared in Broadway's Speed-The-Plow. Released concert tour documentary film Truth Or Dare in 1991. Released adults-only picture book Sex in 1992. The top female pop artist since 1984.		
				1)Live To Tell 2)Cherish 3)La Isla Bonita 4)Crazy For You 5)Like A Prayer		
6/2/84	**23**	16		1 Borderline..	10	Sire 29354
9/8/84	**19**	11		2 Lucky Star	4	Sire 29177
12/8/84	**29**	8	●	3 Like A Virgin...	1⁶	Sire 29210
3/16/85	**2**¹	17	●	4 Crazy For You	1¹	Geffen 29051
				from the film Vision Quest		
4/20/85	**38**	2		5 Material Girl...	2²	Sire 29083
5/11/85	**5**	17	●	6 Angel	5	Sire 29008
				gold certification is for the 12" single		
9/21/85	**32**	7		7 Dress You Up	5	Sire 28919
4/19/86	**1**³	18		8 Live To Tell...	1¹	Sire 28717
				from the film At Close Range		
7/5/86	**16**	13		9 Papa Don't Preach	1²	Sire 28660
10/11/86	**5**	16		10 True Blue	3	Sire 28591
12/27/86	**12**	14		11 Open Your Heart	1¹	Sire 28508
4/4/87	**1**¹	17		12 La Isla Bonita	4	Sire 28425
7/18/87	**5**	14		13 Who's That Girl...	1¹	Sire 28341
10/10/87	**37**	5		14 Causing A Commotion	2³	Sire 28224
				above 2 from the film Who's That Girl		
3/18/89	**3**	18	▲	15 Like A Prayer...	1³	Sire 27539
6/10/89	**12**	15	●	16 Express Yourself..	2²	Sire 22948
8/26/89	**1**²	19		17 Cherish..	2²	Sire 22883
2/17/90	**32**	11	●	18 Keep It Together	8	Sire 19986
5/5/90	**23**	13	▲²	19 Vogue..	1³	Sire 19863
				from the Dick Tracy soundtrack		
7/4/92	**4**	20	●	20 This Used To Be My Playground	1¹	Sire 18822
				from the film A League Of Their Own (not on soundtrack album)		
				MAGNA CARTA ✪		
				British group.		
12/19/70	**39**	2		Airport Song	111	Dunhill 4257
				MAHARIS, George		
				Born on 9/1/28 in New York City. Film/TV actor. Played Buz Murdock on TV's Route 66.		
5/5/62	**8**	9		1 Teach Me Tonight...	25	Epic 9504
				there were 5 top 30 versions of this song in 1954		
8/18/62	**17**	4		2 Love Me As I Love You...	54	Epic 9522

146

DEBUT DATE	PEAK POS	WKS CHR	GOLD	ARTIST — Record Title	POP POS	Label & Number
				MAIN INGREDIENT, The		
				New York soul trio formed as the Poets in 1964. Consisted of Donald McPherson (d: 7/4/71), Luther Simmons, Jr. and Tony Sylvester. First recorded as the Poets for Red Bird in 1965. McPherson replaced by Cuba Gooding in 1971; Gooding's son, Cuba Jr., acted in films *Boyz N The Hood*, *Gladiator* and *A Few Good Men*.		
9/16/72	25	7	●	1 Everybody Plays The Fool	3	RCA 0731
4/27/74	42	5	●	2 Just Don't Want To Be Lonely	10	RCA 0205
				MAKEBA, Miriam		
				Born Zensi Miriam Makeba on 3/4/32 in Johannesburg, South Africa. Folk singer. Her five husbands included Hugh Masekela (1964-66) and black-power activist Stokeley Carmichael (married in 1968).		
10/21/67	36	6		Pata Pata [F]	12	Reprise 0606
				MALMKVIST, Siw - Umberto Marcato		
				Siw is a female ballad singer; born on 12/31/36 in Umea, Sweden. Umberta is a male vocalist from Italy.		
7/18/64	11	5		Sole Sole Sole [F]	58	Jubilee 5479
				MALO		
				Latin-rock band formed by Jorge Santana (brother of Carlos). Malo is Spanish for Bad.		
3/18/72	8	11		Suavecito	18	Warner 7559
				MAMA CASS		
				Born Ellen Naomi Cohen on 9/19/41 in Baltimore. Died of a heart attack on 7/29/74 in London. Cass Elliot of The Mamas & The Papas.		
				1)Dream A Little Dream Of Me 2)New World Coming 3)Make Your Own Kind Of Music		
7/13/68	2³	14		1 **Dream A Little Dream Of Me**	12	Dunhill 4145
				with The Mamas & The Papas		
4/5/69	32	3		2 Move In A Little Closer, Baby	58	Dunhill 4184
6/28/69	13	15		3 It's Getting Better	30	Dunhill 4195
10/25/69	6	9		4 **Make Your Own Kind Of Music** *	36	Dunhill 4214
1/31/70	4	9		5 **New World Coming** *	42	Dunhill 4225
8/1/70	25	4		6 A Song That Never Comes *	99	Dunhill 4244
				*MAMA CASS ELLIOT		
10/31/70	19	5		7 The Good Times Are Coming	104	Dunhill 4253
				from the film *Monte Walsh*		
12/19/70	34	4		8 Don't Let The Good Life Pass You By	110	Dunhill 4264
				MAMAS & THE PAPAS, The		
				Quartet formed in New York City in 1963. Consisted of John Phillips (b: 8/30/35, Paris Island, South Carolina); Holly Michelle Gilliam Phillips (b: 6/4/45, Long Beach, California); Dennis Doherty (b: 11/29/41, Halifax, Nova Scotia, Canada) and Cass Elliot (see Mama Cass above). Michelle and John's daughter, Chynna, is a member of the trio Wilson Phillips.		
3/4/72	25	8		Step Out	81	Dunhill 4301
★★75★★				**MANCHESTER, Melissa**		
				Born on 2/15/51 in the Bronx. Vocalist/pianist/composer. Father is a bassoon player with the New York Metropolitan Opera Orchestra. She studied songwriting under Paul Simon at the University School of the Arts in the early '70s. Former backup singer for Bette Midler.		
				1)Midnight Blue 2)Just Too Many People 3)Just You And I		
4/19/75	1²	18		1 **Midnight Blue**	6	Arista 0116
10/4/75	2¹	12		2 **Just Too Many People**	30	Arista 0146
2/14/76	3	11		3 **Just You And I**	27	Arista 0168
5/1/76	9	10		4 **Better Days**	71	Arista 0183
7/31/76	33	6		5 Happy Endings		Arista 0196
				flip side "Rescue Me" made the *Hot 100* (POS 78)		
11/18/78	9	18		6 **Don't Cry Out Loud**	10	Arista 0373
3/24/79	13	14		7 Theme From Ice Castles (Through The Eyes Of Love)	76	Arista 0405
				theme song from the film *Ice Castles*		
11/10/79	26	7		8 Pretty Girls	39	Arista 0456
2/9/80	8	14		9 **Fire In The Morning**	32	Arista 0485
9/20/80	19	13		10 If This Is Love	102	Arista 0551
3/7/81	25	8		11 Lovers After All	54	Arista 0587
				MELISSA MANCHESTER AND PEABO BRYSON		
5/15/82	10	26		12 **You Should Hear How She Talks About You**	5	Arista 0676
3/5/83	22	9		13 Nice Girls	42	Arista 1045
5/7/83	33	4		14 My Boyfriend's Back		Arista 1057
				#1 Pop hit for The Angels in 1963		
11/5/83	34	6		15 No One Can Love You More Than Me	78	Arista 9087
11/10/84	18	12		16 Thief Of Hearts	86	Casablanca 880308
				movie title song		

DEBUT DATE	PEAK POS	WKS CHR	GOLD	ARTIST — Record Title	POP POS	Label & Number
				MANCHESTER, Melissa — Cont'd		
3/8/86	16	12		17 The Music Of Goodbye		MCA 52784
				MELISSA MANCHESTER AND AL JARREAU love theme from the film *Out Of Africa*		
11/4/89	6	19		18 **Walk On By**		Mika 873012
				#6 Pop hit for Dionne Warwick in 1964		
★★55★★				**MANCINI, Henry**		
				Born on 4/16/24 in Cleveland and raised in Aliquippa, Pennsylvania. Leading film and TV composer/arranger/conductor. Staff composer for Universal Pictures, 1952-58. Won more Oscars (four) and Grammys (20) than any other pop artist. Married to Ginny O'Connor, an original member of Mel Torme's Mel-Tones.		
				1)Love Theme From Romeo & Juliet 2)Theme From Love Story 3)Moon River 4)Wait Until Dark 5)Hawaii (Main Title)		
10/23/61	3	18		1 **Moon River**	11	RCA 7916
				from the film *Breakfast At Tiffany's*		
2/9/63	10	15		2 **Days Of Wine And Roses** *	33	RCA 8120
1/18/64	15	5		3 Charade *	36	RCA 8256
4/11/64	10	7		4 **The Pink Panther Theme** * ....[I]	31	RCA 8286
12/12/64	14	6		5 Dear Heart *	77	RCA 8458
7/17/65	23	11		6 The Sweetheart Tree..	117	RCA 8624
				from the film *The Great Race*		
12/25/65	27	6	✓	7 Moment To Moment *		RCA 8718
10/15/66	6	17		8 **Hawaii (Main Title)** * ....[I]		RCA 8951
6/10/67	17	8	✓	9 Two For The Road *		RCA 9200
10/28/67	4	11		10 **Wait Until Dark** * ....[I]		RCA 9340
5/18/68	21	5		11 Norma La De Guadalajara..............................[I]		RCA 9521
				written by Perez Prado		
11/9/68	36	3		12 A Man, A Horse, And A Gun ....[I]		RCA 9654
				from the film *The Stranger Returns*		
5/10/69	1⁸	17	●	13 Love Theme From Romeo & Juliet * ....[I]	1²	RCA 0131
8/16/69	15	8		14 Moonlight Sonata ....[I]	87	RCA 0212
				written by Beethoven in 1802		
12/27/69	39	3		15 There's Enough To Go Around		RCA 0297
				from the film *Gaily, Gaily*		
3/7/70	17	7		16 Theme From "Z" (Life Goes On)...................[I]	115	RCA 0315
				from the film *"Z"*		
6/13/70	26	6		17 Darling Lili *		RCA 9857
12/19/70	2²	16		18 **Theme From Love Story** * ....[I]	13	RCA 9927
11/20/71	14	8		19 Theme from "Cade's County" ** ....[I]		RCA 0575
10/7/72	38	3		20 Theme from The Mancini Generation ** ....[I]		RCA 0756
				from the Henry Mancini syndicated musical variety TV series		
6/30/73	38	3		21 Oklahoma Crude * ....[I]		RCA 0974
7/27/74	21	8		22 Hangin' Out...[I]		RCA 0323
				HANK MANCINI AND THE MOULDY SEVEN from the film *99 and 44/100% Dead!*		
10/4/75	45	5		23 Once Is Not Enough *		RCA 10355
2/21/76	40	7		24 African Symphony.......................................[I]		RCA 10463
8/14/76	38	4		25 Slow Hot Wind (Lujon) ....[I]		RCA 10731
				HENRY MANCINI AND HIS CONCERT ORCHESTRA (above 2)		
4/2/77	22	12		26 Theme from Charlie's Angels ** ....[I]	45	RCA 10888
				*movie title songs; **TV series title songs		
				MANDRELL, Barbara		
				Born on 12/25/48 in Houston and raised in Oceanside, California. Country singer. Moved to Nashville in 1971. Host of own TV variety series *Barbara Mandrell & The Mandrell Sisters*, 1980-82. Suffered severe injuries in an auto accident in 1984, from which she fully recovered.		
2/11/78	49	2		1 Woman To Woman	92	ABC/Dot 17736
3/31/79	6	16		2 **(If Loving You Is Wrong) I Don't Want To Be Right**..	31	ABC 12451
9/1/79	26	11		3 Fooled By A Feeling...	89	MCA 41077
2/2/80	38	6		4 Years	102	MCA 41162
2/21/81	26	13		5 Sometime, Somewhere, Somehow		MCA 51062
				charted as the B-side of the Country hit "Love Is Fair" (POS 13)		
11/21/81	40	10		6 Wish You Were Here		MCA 51171
5/15/82	25	14		7 'Till You're Gone		MCA 52038
7/14/84	24	10		8 To Me *		MCA 52415

DEBUT DATE	PEAK POS	WKS CHR	GOLD	ARTIST — Record Title	POP POS	Label & Number
				MANDRELL, Barbara — Cont'd		
2/23/85	**35**	2		**9** It Should Have Been Love By Now *		MCA 52525
				*BARBARA MANDRELL/LEE GREENWOOD		
				MANGIONE, Chuck		
				Born on 11/29/40 in Rochester, New York. Flugelhorn/bandleader/composer. Recorded with older brother Gaspare ("Gap") as The Jazz Brothers for Riverside in 1960. To New York City in 1965; played with Maynard Ferguson, Kai Winding, and Art Blakey's Jazz Messengers.		
7/3/71	**32**	5		**1** Hill Where The Lord Hides .... [I]	76	Mercury 73208
				featuring Gerry Niewood on flute		
2/28/76	**49**	2		**2** Bellavia (Bella Veeya) .... [I]		A&M 1773
2/4/78	**1**¹	27		**3** Feels So Good .... [I]	4	A&M 2001
10/28/78	**44**	5		**4** Children Of Sanchez .... [I]	104	A&M 2088
				movie title song		
3/17/79	**41**	4		**5** Bellavia (Bella Veeya) ....[I-R]		A&M 2118
				new version of #2 above		
9/29/79	**44**	3		**6** Land Of Make Believe ....[I-R]		A&M 2167
				live version of Mangione's 1977 *Hot 100* hit (POS 86)		
1/26/80	**1**³	16		**7** Give It All You Got.............................. [I]	18	A&M 2211
				featured song by ABC Sports for the 1980 Winter Olympics		
5/17/80	**49**	2		**8** Fun And Games .... [I]		A&M 2236
				MANHATTANS, The		
				Soul vocal group from Jersey City, New Jersey. Consisted of George "Smitty" Smith (d: 1970, spinal meningitis; lead vocals), Winfred "Blue" Lovett (bass), Edward "Sonny" Bivins and Kenneth "Wally" Kelly (tenors) and Richard Taylor (baritone). Smith replaced by Gerald Alston in 1971. First recorded for Piney in 1962. Taylor (aka Abdul Rashid Talhah) left in 1976; died on 12/7/87 (age 47) following lengthy illness. Featured female vocalist Regina Belle began solo career in 1987. Alston went solo in 1988.		
6/19/76	**12**	11	▲	**1** Kiss And Say Goodbye	1²	Columbia 10310
5/24/80	**21**	17	●	**2** Shining Star	5	Columbia 11222
3/2/85	**8**	13		**3** You Send Me	81	Columbia 04754
				MANHATTAN TRANSFER, The		
				Versatile vocal harmony quartet formed in New York City in 1972: Tim Hauser, Alan Paul, Janis Siegel and Cheryl Bentyne (replaced Laurel Masse in 1979).		
				1)*Boy From New York City* 2)*Spice Of Life* 3)*Mystery*		
10/25/75	**34**	8		**1** Operator	22	Atlantic 3292
1/15/77	**16**	9		**2** Chanson D'Amour		Atlantic 3374
				#6 Pop hit for Art & Dotty Todd in 1958		
5/30/81	**4**	16		**3** Boy From New York City	7	Atlantic 3816
10/31/81	**41**	6		**4** Smile Again (Dedicated To Angela From Alan)................		Atlantic 3855
5/8/82	**22**	13		**5** Route 66	78	Atlantic 4034
				from the film *Sharky's Machine* starring Burt Reynolds		
9/10/83	**5**	17		**6** Spice Of Life	40	Atlantic 89786
3/24/84	**6**	17		**7** Mystery	102	Atlantic 89695
12/15/84	**14**	13		**8** Baby Come Back To Me (The Morse Code Of Love).............	83	Atlantic 89594
12/26/87	**25**	11		**9** Soul Food To Go (Sina)...........................		Atlantic 89156
				guest vocalist: Djavan		
★★**7**★★				**MANILOW, Barry**		
				Born Barry Alan Pincus on 6/17/46 in Brooklyn. Vocalist/pianist/composer. Studied at New York's Juilliard School. Music director for the WCBS-TV series *Callback*. Worked at New York's Continental Baths bathhouse/nightclub in New York as Bette Midler's accompanist in 1972; later produced her first two albums. First recorded solo as Featherbed. Wrote and sang jingles for Dr. Pepper, Pepsi and McDonald's ("You Deserve A Break Today").		
				1)*Read 'Em And Weep* 2)*Looks Like We Made It* 3)*Even Now* 4)*The Old Songs* 5)*Can't Smile Without You*		
11/9/74	**1**²	15	●	**1** Mandy	1¹	Bell 45613
				originally made the *Hot 100* in 1972 as "Brandy" by Scott English		
3/15/75	**1**¹	11		**2** It's A Miracle	12	Arista 0108
7/5/75	**4**	11		**3** Could It Be Magic..................................	6	Arista 0126
				first released on Bell 45-133 in 1971 as by Featherbed Featuring Barry Manilow; inspired by Chopin's prelude in C minor		
11/15/75	**1**²	13	●	**4** I Write The Songs	1¹	Arista 0157
				written by the Beach Boys' Bruce Johnston		
3/20/76	**1**¹	11		**5** Tryin' To Get The Feeling Again	10	Arista 0172
9/18/76	**1**¹	13		**6** This One's For You	29	Arista 0206
11/27/76	**1**¹	17		**7** Weekend In New England	10	Arista 0212
5/7/77	**1**³	20	●	**8** Looks Like We Made It	1¹	Arista 0244
10/1/77	**7**	16		**9** Daybreak	23	Arista 0273

DEBUT DATE	PEAK POS	WKS CHR	G O L D	ARTIST — Record Title	POP POS	Label & Number
				MANILOW, Barry — Cont'd		
12/17/77	33	5		10 It's Just Another New Year's Eve ....[X]		Arista 11
				available only as a promotional single; live recording		
2/4/78	1²	18	●	11 **Can't Smile Without You**	3	Arista 0305
5/6/78	1³	16		12 **Even Now**	19	Arista 0330
6/17/78	6	15	●	13 **Copacabana (At The Copa)**	8	Arista 0339
9/2/78	5	19		14 **Ready To Take A Chance Again**	11	Arista 0357
				above 2 from the film Foul Play		
12/16/78	4	16		15 **Somewhere In The Night**	9	Arista 0382
10/13/79	4	14		16 **Ships**	9	Arista 0464
12/15/79	1¹	19		17 **When I Wanted You**	20	Arista 0481
4/12/80	2²	19		18 **I Don't Want To Walk Without You**	36	Arista 0501
11/22/80	4	18		19 **I Made It Through The Rain**	10	Arista 0566
				all of above produced by Manilow and Ron Dante		
3/21/81	7	12		20 **Lonely Together**	45	Arista 0596
10/10/81	1³	18		21 **The Old Songs**	15	Arista 0633
12/19/81	1²	20		22 **Somewhere Down The Road**	21	Arista 0658
3/20/82	6	15		23 **Let's Hang On**	32	Arista 0675
8/14/82	24	8		24 **Oh Julie**	38	Arista 0698
11/20/82	8	18		25 **Memory**	39	Arista 1025
				theme from the musical Cats		
2/26/83	4	17		26 **Some Kind Of Friend**	26	Arista 9003
				also released on Arista 1046 in 1983		
11/19/83	1⁶	18		27 **Read 'Em And Weep**	18	Arista 9101
3/17/84	25	7		28 You're Lookin' Hot Tonight		Arista 9185
11/17/84	6	12		29 **When October Goes**		Arista 9295
				available only as a 12" single		
1/26/85	24	5		30 Paradise Cafe		Arista 9318
4/13/85	12	9		31 Run To Me		Arista 9341
				DIONNE WARWICK with Barry Manilow #16 Pop hit for the Bee Gees in 1972		
11/16/85	11	10		32 In Search Of Love		RCA 14223
3/29/86	22	8		33 He Doesn't Care (But I Do)		RCA 14302
11/14/87	13	14		34 Brooklyn Blues		Arista LP Cut
				featuring saxophonist Tom Scott; from the album Swing Street on Arista 8527		
5/6/89	7	15		35 **Keep Each Other Warm**		Arista 9838
9/9/89	25	7		36 The One That Got Away		Arista 9883
5/5/90	41	7		37 If You Remember Me		Arista 9948
				written by Marvin Hamlisch and Carole Bayer Sager; live recording		
12/22/90	38	5		38 Because It's Christmas (For All The Children) ....[X]		Arista 2094
10/31/92	33	7		39 Another Life		Arista LP Cut
				from the album The Complete Collection And Then Some... on Arista 18714		
				MANN, Barry		
				Born Barry Iberman on 2/9/39 in Brooklyn. One of pop music's most prolific songwriters. Wrote with wife, Cynthia Weil, "You've Lost That Lovin' Feelin'," "(You're My) Soul & Inspiration," "Kicks," "Hungry," "We Gotta Get Out Of This Place," and many others. Established own publishing company, Dyad Music.		
2/12/72	40	1		1 When You Get Right Down To It	105	New Design 1005
3/3/79	30	8		2 Almost Gone		Warner 8752
				MANN, Herbie		
				Born Herbert Jay Solomon on 4/16/30 in Brooklyn. Renowned jazz flutist. First recorded with Mat Mathews Quintet for Brunswick in 1953. First recorded as a solo for Bethlehem in 1954.		
10/29/66	9	14		1 A Man And A Woman	88	Atlantic 2362
				TAMIKO JONES with HERBIE MANN movie title song		
10/14/67	11	9		2 To Sir, With Love ....[I]	93	Atlantic 2444
12/9/67	33	4		3 Live For Life	101	Atlantic 2451
				CARMEN McRAE & HERBIE MANN movie title song		
7/12/69	37	4		4 Memphis Underground ....[I]	44	Atlantic 2621
3/2/74	48	3		5 Spin Ball ....[I]		Atlantic 3009
2/10/79	47	5		6 Superman	26	Atlantic 3547
				MANN, Johnny, Singers		
				Born on 8/30/28 in Baltimore. Johnny was musical director for Joey Bishop's TV talk show.		
2/18/67	35	3		1 A Joyful Noise		Liberty 55938
				Broadway show title song		

DEBUT DATE	PEAK POS	WKS CHR	GOLD	ARTIST — Record Title	POP POS	Label & Number
				MANN, Johnny, Singers — Cont'd		
6/10/67	**24**	5		2 Up-Up And Away...	91	Liberty 55972
1/13/68	**21**	6		3 Instant Happy/		
1/27/68	**33**	2		4 Don't Look Back		Liberty 56010
				#83 Pop hit for The Temptations in 1966		
1/4/69	**31**	5		5 If I Only Had Time		Liberty 56083
				#95 Pop hit for Nick DeCaro in 1969		
				MANTOVANI AND HIS ORCHESTRA		
				Born Annunzio Paolo Mantovani on 11/15/05 in Venice, Italy; died on 3/29/80. Played classical violin in England before forming his own orchestra in the early 1930s.		
8/17/68	**36**	3		Theme From Villa Rides .... [I]		London 20040
				from the film *Villa Rides*		
				MARDONES, Benny		
				Savage, Maryland native.		
6/3/89	**20**	19		Into The Night .... [R]	20	Polydor 889368
				originally hit the *Hot 100* in 1980 (POS 11) on Polydor 2091; newly recorded version released on Curb 10549 in 1989		
				MARIACHI BRASS — see BAKER, Chet		
				MARK-ALMOND		
				British sessionmen Jon Mark and Johnny Almond (b: 7/20/46, Enfield, Middlesex, England). Former musicians with John Mayall.		
7/3/71	**37**	3		1 The City..		Blue Thumb 201
3/4/72	**39**	2		2 One Way Sunday	94	Blue Thumb 206
				MARKETTS, The		
				Hollywood instrumental surf quintet led by Tommy Tedesco.		
12/13/69	**27**	5		1 They Call The Wind Maria .... [I]		Uni 55173
				from the film *Paint Your Wagon*		
7/4/76	**36**	7		2 Song From M*A*S*H.. [I]		Farr 007
				THE NEW MARKETTS		
				disco version of the theme from the movie and TV series *M*A*S*H*		
				MARKS, Guy		
				Born Mario Scarpa, from South Philadelphia. Comedian-impressionist/TV actor. Died on 11/28/87 (age 64).		
4/6/68	**17**	6		Loving You Has Made Me Bananas .... [N]	51	ABC 11055
				MARMALADE, The		
				Scottish pop quintet led by vocalist Dean Ford (real name: Thomas McAleese).		
4/25/70	**21**	9		1 Reflections Of My Life	10	London 20058
8/8/70	**7**	10		2 Rainbow	51	London 20059
4/17/71	**31**	4		3 My Little One	123	London 20066
5/1/76	**34**	5		4 Falling Apart At The Seams...............................	49	Ariola Am. 7619
				MARSHALL HAIN		
				British duo: Julian Marshall and Kit Hain. Marshall later formed duo Eye To Eye.		
1/20/79	**33**	8		Dancing In The City	43	Harvest 4648
				MARSHALL TUCKER BAND, The		
				Southern-rock band formed in South Carolina in 1971: Doug Gray (lead singer), brothers Toy (lead guitarist; d: 2/25/93 of respiratory failure [age 45]) and Tommy (bass; d: 4/28/80 in auto accident [age 30]; replaced by Franklin Wilkie) Caldwell, George McCorkle (rhythm guitar), Paul Riddle (drums) and Jerry Eubanks (sax, flute). Caldwell left band in 1984. Marshall Tucker was the owner of the band's rehearsal hall.		
5/28/77	**25**	8		Heard It In A Love Song	14	Capricorn 0270
				MARTIKA		
				Born Marta Marrera on 5/18/69. Los Angeles-based, Cuban-American singer/writer/actress/dancer. Starred in TV program *Kids, Incorporated*. Appeared in the 1982 film musical *Annie*.		
7/1/89	**37**	10	●	1 Toy Soldiers	1[2]	Columbia 68747
9/28/91	**40**	5		2 Love...Thy Will Be Done	10	Columbia 73853
				written by Prince and Martika		
				MARTIN, Bobbi		
				Born Barbara Anne Martin on 11/29/43 in Brooklyn; raised in Baltimore. Toured the Far East with Bob Hope's Christmas shows.		
				1)For The Love Of Him 2)Don't Forget I Still Love You 3)I Can't Stop Thinking Of You		
2/6/65	**2**[1]	2		1 Don't Forget I Still Love You	19	Coral 62426
3/13/65	**9**	7		2 I Can't Stop Thinking Of You...........................	46	Coral 62447
5/29/65	**16**	9		3 I Love You So	70	Coral 62452
7/31/65	**21**	8		4 I Don't Want To Live (Without Your Love)	115	Coral 62457

151

DEBUT DATE	PEAK POS	WKS CHR	GOLD	ARTIST — Record Title	POP POS	Label & Number
				MARTIN, Bobbi — Cont'd		
9/25/65	**29**	3		5 There Are No Rules	13	Coral 62466
12/6/69	**1**[2]	16		6 For The Love Of Him	13	United Art. 50602
7/11/70	**17**	4		7 Give A Woman Love..	97	United Art. 50687
10/16/71	**32**	3		8 Tomorrow		Buddah 253
2/26/72	**16**	7		9 Something Tells Me (Something's Gonna Happen Tonight)..		Buddah 286

★★28★★ **MARTIN, Dean**

Born Dino Crocetti on 6/7/17 in Steubenville, Ohio. Vocalist/actor. To California in 1937, worked local clubs. Teamed with comedian Jerry Lewis in Atlantic City in 1946. First film, *My Friend Irma* in 1949. Team broke up after 16th film *Hollywood Or Bust* in 1956. Appeared in many films since then; own TV series from 1965-74.

1)Everybody Loves Somebody 2)In The Chapel In The Moonlight 3)In The Misty Moonlight
4)The Door Is Still Open To My Heart 5)You're Nobody Till Somebody Loves You

DEBUT DATE	PEAK POS	WKS CHR	GOLD	ARTIST — Record Title	POP POS	Label & Number
7/4/64	**1**[8]	14	●	1 Everybody Loves Somebody	**1**[1]	Reprise 0281
9/26/64	**1**[1]	11		2 The Door Is Still Open To My Heart........................	6	Reprise 0307
12/12/64	**1**[1]	9		3 You're Nobody Till Somebody Loves You/	25	
12/26/64	**13**	4		4 You'll Always Be The One I Love	64	Reprise 0333
2/20/65	**5**	9		5 Send Me The Pillow You Dream On	22	Reprise 0344
5/22/65	**7**	8		6 (Remember Me) I'm The One Who Loves You	32	Reprise 0369
8/7/65	**2**[1]	9		7 Houston...	21	Reprise 0393
10/30/65	**3**	12		8 I Will...	10	Reprise 0415
2/12/66	**2**[2]	13		9 Somewhere There's A Someone	32	Reprise 0443
5/7/66	**4**	11		10 Come Running Back	35	Reprise 0466
7/23/66	**4**	11		11 A Million And One	41	Reprise 0500
10/8/66	**6**	10		12 Nobody's Baby Again	60	Reprise 0516
12/10/66	**7**	9		13 (Open Up The Door) Let The Good Times In............	55	Reprise 0538
4/29/67	**6**	10		14 Lay Some Happiness On Me	55	Reprise 0571
7/15/67	**1**[3]	11		15 In The Chapel In The Moonlight	25	Reprise 0601
8/26/67	**5**	9		16 Little Ole Wine Drinker, Me	38	Reprise 0608
12/9/67	**1**[2]	11		17 In The Misty Moonlight	46	Reprise 0640
3/23/68	**7**	12		18 You've Still Got A Place In My Heart	60	Reprise 0672
8/17/68	**9**	10		19 April Again/	105	
8/24/68	**19**	6		20 That Old Time Feelin'....................................	104	Reprise 0761
11/2/68	**4**	10		21 Not Enough Indians	43	Reprise 0780
2/22/69	**9**	8		22 Gentle On My Mind..	103	Reprise 0812
8/9/69	**15**	10		23 I Take A Lot Of Pride In What I Am	75	Reprise 0841
10/11/69	**15**	7		24 One Cup Of Happiness (And One Peace Of Mind)............	107	Reprise 0857
10/31/70	**36**	2		25 Detroit City	101	Reprise 0955
5/8/71	**36**	2		26 She's A Little Bit Country.................................		Reprise 1004
8/18/73	**50**	2		27 Get On With Your Livin'		Reprise 1166

MARTIN, George

Born on 1/3/26 in London. The Beatles' producer from 1962-70. Also produced Billy J. Kramer, Gerry And The Pacemakers, America, Jeff Beck and others.

DEBUT DATE	PEAK POS	WKS CHR	GOLD	ARTIST — Record Title	POP POS	Label & Number
8/8/64	**7**	7		Ringo's Theme (This Boy)................................[I] from The Beatles' *A Hard Days Night* soundtrack	53	United Art. 745

MARTIN, Marilyn

Raised in Louisville. Background vocalist for Stevie Nicks, Tom Petty, Kenny Loggins and Joe Walsh.

DEBUT DATE	PEAK POS	WKS CHR	GOLD	ARTIST — Record Title	POP POS	Label & Number
10/12/85	**1**[3]	19		1 Separate Lives .... PHIL COLLINS and MARILYN MARTIN love theme from the film *White Nights*	**1**[1]	Atlantic 89498
5/10/86	**34**	5		2 Move Closer		Atlantic 89424

MARTIN, Moon

Real name: John Martin. Pop-rock singer/songwriter/guitarist from Oklahoma. Wrote Robert Palmer's hit "Bad Case Of Loving You." Moved to Los Angeles in 1968. Lead guitarist of group Southwind.

DEBUT DATE	PEAK POS	WKS CHR	GOLD	ARTIST — Record Title	POP POS	Label & Number
12/8/79	**36**	6		No Chance	50	Capitol 4794

MARTIN, Tony

Born Alvin Morris, Jr. on 12/25/12 in Oakland. Vocalist/actor. In many films from 1936-57, including *Casbah* in 1948. Married to actress/dancer Cyd Charisse.

DEBUT DATE	PEAK POS	WKS CHR	GOLD	ARTIST — Record Title	POP POS	Label & Number
2/11/67	**22**	6		Theme From "The Sand Pebbles" (And We Were Lovers) .... from the film *The Sand Pebbles*		Dunhill 4073

DEBUT DATE	PEAK POS	WKS CHR	G O L D	ARTIST — Record Title	POP POS	Label & Number
				MARTINE, Layng		
				Singer/songwriter from Greenwich, Connecticut. Wrote Elvis Presley's "Way Down."		
10/9/71	**36**	4		Rub It In	65	Barnaby 2041
★★**17**★★				**MARTINO, Al**		
				Born Alfred Cini on 10/7/27 in Philadelphia. Encouraged by success of boyhood friend, Mario Lanza. Winner on *Arthur Godfrey's Talent Scouts* in 1952. Portrayed singer Johnny Fontane in the 1972 film *The Godfather*.		
				1)Spanish Eyes 2)Mary In The Morning 3)More Than The Eye Can See 4)I Love You Because 5)Daddy's Little Girl		
8/7/61	**17**	2		1 Here In My Heart...[R]	86	Capitol 4593
				Al's original version charted in 1952 (POS 1)		
4/27/63	**1**²	12		**2 I Love You Because**	3	Capitol 4930
8/10/63	**3**	10		**3 Painted, Tainted Rose**	15	Capitol 5000
11/2/63	**8**	9		**4 Living A Lie**	22	Capitol 5060
2/8/64	**3**	9		**5 I Love You More And More Every Day**	9	Capitol 5108
5/23/64	**7**	7		**6 Tears And Roses**	20	Capitol 5183
8/22/64	**4**	7		**7 Always Together**	33	Capitol 5239
11/14/64	**6**	5		**8 We Could**	41	Capitol 5293
1/23/65	**11**	4		9 My Heart Would Know	52	Capitol 5341
				written by Hank Williams		
3/27/65	**11**	6		10 Somebody Else Is Taking My Place	53	Capitol 5384
6/5/65	**26**	4		11 My Cherie	88	Capitol 5434
9/25/65	**7**	10		12 Forgive Me..	61	Capitol 5506
11/27/65	**1**⁴	17		13 **Spanish Eyes**	15	Capitol 5542
2/26/66	**2**¹	11		14 Think I'll Go Somewhere And Cry Myself To Sleep........	30	Capitol 5598
5/14/66	**3**	11		15 Wiederseh'n	57	Capitol 5652
7/23/66	**12**	12		16 Just Yesterday	77	Capitol 5702
10/22/66	**12**	9		17 The Wheel Of Hurt	59	Capitol 5741
1/28/67	**2**²	14		18 Daddy's Little Girl	42	Capitol 5825
				#5 hit for The Mills Brothers in 1950		
5/27/67	**1**²	15		19 Mary In The Morning	27	Capitol 5904
9/16/67	**1**²	16		20 More Than The Eye Can See...........................	54	Capitol 5989
12/9/67	**5**	10		21 A Voice In The Choir	80	Capitol 2053
2/10/68	**3**	9		22 Love Is Blue	57	Capitol 2102
4/20/68	**7**	11		23 Lili Marlene	87	Capitol 2158
10/26/68	**21**	5		24 Wake Up To Me Gentle	120	Capitol 2285
				from the rock musical *Alison*		
11/30/68	**10**	10		25 I Can't Help It (If I'm Still In Love With You)	97	Capitol 2355
4/19/69	**13**	9		26 Sausalito	99	Capitol 2468
11/8/69	**19**	11		27 I Started Loving You Again................................	86	Capitol 2674
				written by Merle Haggard		
2/14/70	**5**	8		28 Can't Help Falling In Love	51	Capitol 2746
6/6/70	**9**	6		29 Walking In The Sand....................................	123	Capitol 2830
11/14/70	**33**	2		30 True Love Is Greater Than Friendship...................		Capitol 2956
				written by Carl Perkins; from the film *Little Fauss & Big Halsy*		
3/13/71	**30**	7		31 Come Into My Life (Lass Das Weinen Sein)...........		Capitol 3056
7/3/71	**39**	3		32 Losing My Mind		Capitol 3120
				from the Stephen Sondheim musical *Follies*		
4/29/72	**24**	4		33 Speak Softly Love	80	Capitol 3313
				love theme from the film *The Godfather*		
10/7/72	**37**	4		34 Canta Libre (Sing Free).................................		Capitol 3444
				written by Neil Diamond		
12/14/74	**7**	13		**35 To The Door Of The Sun (Alle Porte Del Sole)**	17	Capitol 3987
9/20/75	**9**	14		**36 Volare**...	33	Capitol 4134
4/10/76	**43**	4		37 My Thrill		Capitol 4241
9/11/76	**24**	7		38 Sing My Love Song......................................		Capitol 4322
				Mike Curb Congregation (backing vocals)		
7/30/77	**26**	7		39 Kentucky Mornin'		Capitol 4444
11/12/77	**6**	16		**40 The Next Hundred Years**...............................	49	Capitol 4508
3/18/78	**44**	6		41 One Last Time...		Capitol 4551
				#78 Pop hit for Glen Campbell in 1973		

DEBUT DATE	PEAK POS	WKS CHR	GOLD	ARTIST — Record Title	POP POS	Label & Number

★★78★★ MARX, Richard
Born on 9/16/63 in Chicago. Pop-rock singer/songwriter. Professional jingle singer since age five. Backing singer for Lionel Richie. Co-wrote Kenny Rogers' hit "What About Me." On 1/8/89, married Cynthia Rhodes, lead singer of Animotion.

1)Right Here Waiting 2)Keep Coming Back 3)Hazard

DEBUT DATE	PEAK POS	WKS CHR	GOLD	ARTIST — Record Title	POP POS	Label & Number
11/7/87	20	15		1 Should've Known Better	3	Manhattan 50083
				Fee Waybill (Tubes) and Timothy B. Schmit (backing vocals)		
2/6/88	2²	24		2 Endless Summer Nights	2²	EMI-Man. 50113
5/28/88	3	27		3 Hold On To The Nights	1¹	EMI-Man. 50106
7/8/89	1⁶	23	▲	4 Right Here Waiting	1³	EMI 50219
10/14/89	2²	20		5 Angelia	4	EMI 50218
3/10/90	47	2		6 Too Late To Say Goodbye	12	EMI 50234
5/5/90	6	20		7 Children Of The Night	13	EMI 50288
				tribute to the Los Angeles organization helping child prostitutes		
11/2/91	1⁴	22		8 Keep Coming Back	12	Capitol 44753
2/8/92	1¹	32		9 Hazard	9	Capitol 44796
6/13/92	4	37		10 Take This Heart	20	Capitol 44782
10/17/92	9	24		11 Chains Around My Heart	44	Capitol 44848

MASEKELA, Hugh
Born Hugh Ramapolo Masekela on 4/4/39 in Wilbank, South Africa. Trumpeter/bandleader/arranger. Played trumpet since age 14. To England in 1959; New York City in 1960. Formed own band in 1964. Married to Miriam Makeba from 1964-66.

DEBUT DATE	PEAK POS	WKS CHR	GOLD	ARTIST — Record Title	POP POS	Label & Number
7/13/68	15	9	●	Grazing In The Grass .... [I]	1²	Uni 55066

MASON, Dave
Born on 5/10/46 in Worcester, England. Vocalist/composer/guitarist. Original member of Traffic from March through December 1967 and from June 1968 on. Joined Delaney & Bonnie for a short time in 1970.

DEBUT DATE	PEAK POS	WKS CHR	GOLD	ARTIST — Record Title	POP POS	Label & Number
10/8/77	19	12		1 We Just Disagree	12	Columbia 10575
1/30/88	11	12	✓	2 Dreams I Dream		MCA 53205
				DAVE MASON with Phoebe Snow		

★★20★★ MATHIS, Johnny
Born on 9/30/35 in San Francisco. Studied opera from age 13. Track scholarship at the San Francisco State College. Invited to Olympic try-outs, chose singing career instead. Discovered by George Avakian of Columbia Records. To New York City in 1956. Initially recorded as jazz-styled singer. Columbia A&R executive Mitch Miller switched him to singing pop ballads. One of the top album artists of the rock era, Mathis has charted over 60 entries on *Billboard*'s Top Pop Albums chart.

1)Too Much, Too Little, Too Late 2)I'm Coming Home 3)Gina 4)What Will Mary Say 5)Stardust

DEBUT DATE	PEAK POS	WKS CHR	GOLD	ARTIST — Record Title	POP POS	Label & Number
9/29/62	2³	11		1 Gina...............................	6	Columbia 42582
2/2/63	3	11		2 What Will Mary Say	9	Columbia 42666
6/1/63	10	6		3 Every Step Of The Way	30	Columbia 42799
10/19/63	19	2		4 Your Teenage Dreams...............................	68	Mercury 72184
				flip side "Come Back" made the *Hot 100* in 1963 (POS 61)		
2/29/64	17	2		5 Bye Bye Barbara	53	Mercury 72229
10/24/64	11	5		6 Listen Lonely Girl	62	Mercury 72339
6/12/65	32	4		7 Take The Time...............................	104	Mercury 72432
7/24/65	21	10		8 Sweetheart Tree	108	Mercury 72464
				from the film *The Great Race*; also released on Mercury 72568		
11/6/65	6	15		9 On A Clear Day You Can See Forever	98	Mercury 72493
9/10/66	17	7		10 So Nice (Samba de Verao)		Mercury 72610
3/4/67	38	2		11 Two Tickets And A Candy Heart...............................		Mercury 72653
9/9/67	21	5	✓	12 Don't Talk To Me/		
				written by Bert Kaempfert		
9/16/67	40	2		13 Misty Roses...............................		Columbia 44266
6/22/68	23	3		14 Venus...............................	111	Columbia 44517
				#1 Pop hit for Frankie Avalon in 1959		
10/12/68	35	4		15 You Make Me Think About You		Columbia 44637
				from the film *With Six, You Get Egg Roll*		
3/1/69	39	2	✓	16 The 59th Street Bridge Song (Feelin' Groovy)...............................		Columbia 44728
				written by Paul Simon; #13 Pop hit for Harpers Bizarre in 1967		
5/17/69	35	3		17 I'll Never Fall In Love Again		Columbia 44837
				from the musical *Promises, Promises*; #6 Pop hit for Dionne Warwick in 1970		
7/5/69	8	13		18 Love Theme From "Romeo And Juliet" (A Time For Us) .	96	Columbia 44915
				from the film *Romeo And Juliet*		
11/15/69	20	5		19 Midnight Cowboy...............................		Columbia 45022
				movie title song; #10 Pop hit for Ferrante & Teicher in 1970		

DEBUT DATE	PEAK POS	WKS CHR	G O L D	ARTIST — Record Title	POP POS	Label & Number
				MATHIS, Johnny — Cont'd		
3/21/70	**30**	3	✓	20 Odds And Ends		Columbia 45104
				#43 Pop hit for Dionne Warwick in 1969		
6/27/70	**17**	4		21 Wherefore And Why		Columbia 45183
				written by Gordon Lightfoot		
9/12/70	**9**	8		**22 Pieces Of Dreams**		Columbia 45223
				movie title song		
11/14/70	**30**	4		23 Evil Ways		Columbia 45263
				#9 Pop hit for Santana in 1970		
3/6/71	**32**	2		24 Ten Times Forever More		Columbia 45323
7/15/72	**16**	9		25 Make It Easy On Yourself	103	Columbia 45635
				#20 Pop hit for Jerry Butler in 1962		
12/2/72	**37**	5		26 Soul And Inspiration/Just Once In My Life		Columbia 45729
				Pop hits for The Righteous Brothers in 1966 (POS 1) & 1965 (POS 9)		
3/3/73	**40**	2		27 Take Good Care Of Her		Columbia 45777
				#7 Pop hit for Adam Wade in 1961		
5/12/73	**36**	3	✓	28 Show And Tell		Columbia 45835
				#1 Pop hit for Al Wilson in 1974		
8/25/73	**1**[1]	18		**29 I'm Coming Home**	75	Columbia 45908
12/22/73	**8**	15		**30 Life Is A Song Worth Singing**	54	Columbia 45975
6/1/74	**35**	5	✓	31 Sweet Child		Columbia 46048
2/15/75	**39**	5		32 Sail On White Moon		Columbia 10080
				written and produced by Johnny Bristol		
3/29/75	**16**	9		33 I'm Stone In Love With You		Columbia 10112
				#10 Pop hit for The Stylistics in 1972		
11/29/75	**4**	12		**34 Stardust**..		Columbia 10250
				there have been 17 charted versions of this Hoagy Carmichael classic		
3/13/76	**36**	5	✓	35 One Day In Your Life		Columbia 10291
				#55 Pop hit for Michael Jackson in 1981		
7/24/76	**44**	3		36 Yellow Roses On Her Gown		Columbia 10350
10/2/76	**25**	9	✓	37 Do Me Wrong, But Do Me		Columbia 10404
4/2/77	**29**	5	✓	38 Loving You-Losing You		Columbia 10496
7/23/77	**24**	9		39 Arianne..		Columbia 10574
3/11/78	**1**[1]	19	●	**40 Too Much, Too Little, Too Late ***	**1**[1]	Columbia 10693
7/8/78	**16**	11		41 You're All I Need To Get By *	47	Columbia 10772
				*JOHNNY MATHIS & DENIECE WILLIAMS		
2/24/79	**15**	12	✓	42 The Last Time I Felt Like This		Columbia 10902
				JOHNNY MATHIS/JANE OLIVOR		
				from the film *Same Time Next Year*		
7/21/79	**37**	5	✓	43 Begin The Beguine.......................................		Columbia 11001
				#1 hit for Artie Shaw (of the Cole Porter classic) in 1938		
4/24/82	**5**	17		**44 Friends In Love**	38	Arista 0673
				DIONNE WARWICK AND JOHNNY MATHIS		
3/24/84	**14**	13		45 Love Won't Let Me Wait	106	Columbia 04379
				JOHNNY MATHIS with Deniece Williams		
				#5 Pop hit for Major Harris in 1975		
5/26/84	**6**	16		**46 Simple**	81	Columbia 04468
5/18/85	**38**	2		47 Right From The Heart		Columbia 04856
				from the TV series *Ryan's Hope*		
7/2/88	**27**	12		48 I'm On The Outside Looking In		Columbia 07797
				#15 Pop hit for Little Anthony & The Imperials in 1964		
				MATTEA, Kathy ☉		
				Born on 6/21/59 in Cross Lane, West Virginia. Country singer/guitarist.		
3/31/84	**23**	9		1 Someone Is Falling In Love		Mercury 818289
2/3/90	**25**	10		2 Where've You Been		Mercury 876262
				MATTHEWS, Ian		
				Born Ian Matthew MacDonald in Lincolnshire, England in June 1946. Founder of Fairport Convention and Matthews' Southern Comfort. From 1984-87, in A&R for Island and Windham Hill record labels.		
4/10/71	**17**	7		1 Woodstock	23	Decca 32774
				MATTHEWS' SOUTHERN COMFORT		
1/13/79	**21**	10		2 Shake It	13	Mushroom 7039
3/24/79	**43**	6		3 Give Me An Inch	67	Mushroom 7040
				written by Robert Palmer		
6/2/79	**42**	5		4 Don't Hang Up Your Dancing Shoes		Mushroom 7041

DEBUT DATE	PEAK POS	WKS CHR	GOLD	ARTIST — Record Title	POP POS	Label & Number
				MAURIAT, Paul		
				French conductor/arranger; born in 1925. Moved to Paris at age 10. Formed own touring orchestra at 17.		
12/16/67	1[11]	24	●	1 Love Is Blue ....[I]	1[5]	Philips 40495
				the #1 hit in Adult Contemporary chart history		
5/4/68	7	12		2 Love In Every Room ....[I]	60	Philips 40530
8/17/68	16	9		3 San Francisco (Wear Some Flowers In Your Hair) ....[I]	103	Philips 40550
				#4 Pop hit for Scott McKenzie in 1967		
11/23/68	24	10		4 Chitty Chitty Bang Bang ....[I]	76	Philips 40574
				movie title song		
3/15/69	24	2		5 Hey Jude ....[I]	119	Philips 40594
				#1 Pop hit for The Beatles in 1968		
1/10/70	35	2		6 Je T'aime Moi Non Plus ....[F]		Philips 40647
				#58 Pop hit for Jane Birkin & Serge Gainsbourg in 1970		
9/5/70	32	3		7 Gone Is Love ....[I]		Philips 40683
9/16/72	21	7		8 Apres Toi (Come What May) ....[I]		MGM/Verve 10682
				MAXWELL, Robert		
				Born on 4/19/21 in New York City. Jazz harpist/composer. With NBC Symphony under Toscanini at age 17. Also recorded as Mickey Mozart.		
4/11/64	4	9		1 Shangri-La ....[I]	15	Decca 25622
7/11/64	13	3		2 Peg O' My Heart ....[I]	64	Decca 25637
				there were 4 #1 versions of this tune from 1913-47		
				MAY, Billy, And His Orchestra		
				Born on 1/10/16 in Pittsburgh. Arranger/conductor/sideman for many of the big bands. After leading his own band in early '50s, Billy went on to arrange/conduct for Frank Sinatra and compose movie scores.		
1/25/75	20	11		Front Page Rag ....[I]		MCA 40352
				from the film The Front Page		
				MAYA, Johnnie ○		
5/24/75	41	5		If I Could Love You		Ranwood 1021
				MAYE, Marilyn ○		
				1)Step To The Rear 2)Sherry! 3)Cabaret		
10/1/66	9	13	✓	1 Cabaret		RCA 8936
				from the Broadway musical; #72 Pop hit for Herb Alpert in 1968		
2/4/67	8	13		2 Sherry!		RCA 9076
				from the Broadway musical		
7/15/67	25	7		3 When We All Get Together		RCA 9234
11/11/67	2[1]	13		4 Step To The Rear		RCA 9347
				from the musical How Now, Dow Jones		
4/13/68	35	4		5 Till You Come Back		RCA 9487
12/21/68	14	14	✓	6 Feelin'		RCA 9689
7/19/69	17	8		7 Think Summer		RCA 9751
				ED & MARILYN		
5/30/70	38	3		8 Think Summer ....[R]		RCA 9843
				ED AMES and MARILYN MAYE		
				McANALLY, Mac		
				Born Lyman McAnally, Jr. in 1957 in Red Bay, Alabama. Session singer/guitarist/songwriter.		
7/9/77	10	11		1 It's A Crazy World	37	Ariola Am. 7665
5/13/78	47	3		2 Opinion On Love		Ariola 7688
3/12/83	7	19		3 Minimum Love	41	Geffen 29736
				McCAFFREY, Mary ○		
				Session singer. Sang background vocals for Melanie in the late-1970s.		
11/9/74	38	7		(I Believe In) Happy Endings		Playboy 6006
				McCALL, C.W.		
				Born William Fries on 11/15/28 in Audubon, Iowa. The character "C.W. McCall" was created for the Mertz Bread Company. Fries was their advertising man. Elected mayor of Ouray, Colorado in the early '80s.		
12/20/75	19	8	●	1 Convoy ....[N]	1[1]	MGM 14839
5/8/76	50	1		2 There Won't Be No Country Music (There Won't Be No Rock 'N' Roll) ....[S]	73	Polydor 14310
				McCANN, Peter		
				Connecticut native; staffwriter with ABC Music. Wrote Jennifer Warnes' hit "Right Time Of The Night."		
5/28/77	22	14	●	Do You Wanna Make Love	5	20th Century 2335

DEBUT DATE	PEAK POS	WKS CHR	GOLD	ARTIST — Record Title	POP POS	Label & Number

★★24★★   McCARTNEY, Paul/Wings

Born James Paul McCartney on 6/18/42 in Liverpool, England. Writer of over 50 top 10 singles. Founding member/ bass guitarist of The Beatles. Married Linda Eastman on 3/12/69. First solo album in 1970. Formed group Wings in 1971 with wife Linda (keyboards, backing vocals), Denny Laine (ex-Moody Blues; guitar) and Denny Seiwell (drums). Henry McCullough (guitar) joined in 1972. Seiwell and McCullough left in 1973. In 1975, Joe English (drums) and ex-Thunderclap Newman guitarist Jimmy McCulloch (d: 9/27/79 [age 26] of heart failure) joined; both left in 1977. Wings officially disbanded in April 1981. McCartney starred in own film *Give My Regards To Broad Street* (1984). Won Lifetime Achievement Grammy in 1990.

1)Ebony And Ivory 2)The Girl Is Mine 3)My Love 4)Let 'Em In 5)Silly Love Songs

3/13/71	4	11		1 **Another Day**	5	Apple 1829
				PAUL McCARTNEY		
8/21/71	9	10	●	2 **Uncle Albert/Admiral Halsey**	1¹	Apple 1837
				PAUL & LINDA McCARTNEY		
				WINGS:		
7/1/72	29	4		3 Mary Had A Little Lamb	28	Apple 1851
4/28/73	1³	13	●	4 **My Love** *	1⁴	Apple 1861
7/7/73	8	10	●	5 **Live And Let Die**	2³	Apple 1863
				a James Bond movie title song		
5/11/74	22	9	●	6 **Band On The Run** *	1¹	Apple 1873
12/7/74	7	12		7 **Sally G** *	17	Apple 1875
				flip side "Junior's Farm" made the *Hot 100* (POS 3)		
6/14/75	8	12	●	8 **Listen To What The Man Said**	1¹	Capitol 4091
4/24/76	1¹	11	●	9 **Silly Love Songs**	1⁵	Capitol 4256
7/10/76	1¹	12	●	10 **Let 'Em In**	3	Capitol 4293
1/28/78	45	2		11 Mull Of Kintyre		Capitol 4504
				flip side "Girls' School" made the *Hot 100* (POS 33)		
4/8/78	5	16		12 **With A Little Luck**	1²	Capitol 4559
9/16/78	17	9		13 London Town	39	Capitol 4625
4/14/79	30	11	●	14 Goodnight Tonight	5	Columbia 10939
9/22/79	29	5		15 Arrow Through Me	29	Columbia 11070
5/31/80	48	4	●	16 Coming Up (Live at Glasgow) *	1³	Columbia 11263
				*PAUL McCARTNEY & WINGS		
4/10/82	1⁵	22	●	17 **Ebony And Ivory**	17	Columbia 02860
				PAUL McCARTNEY with Stevie Wonder		
				PAUL McCARTNEY:		
7/10/82	6	19		18 **Take It Away**	10	Columbia 03018
10/16/82	31	5		19 Tug Of War	53	Columbia 03235
11/6/82	1⁴	18	●	20 **The Girl Is Mine**	2³	Epic 03288
				MICHAEL JACKSON/PAUL McCARTNEY		
10/15/83	3	21	▲	21 **Say Say Say**	1⁶	Columbia 04168
				PAUL McCARTNEY AND MICHAEL JACKSON		
1/7/84	3	19		22 **So Bad**	23	Columbia 04296
10/13/84	2⁴	19		23 **No More Lonely Nights**	6	Columbia 04581
				from the film *Give My Regards To Broad Street*		
2/7/87	9	13		24 **Only Love Remains**		Capitol 5672
5/27/89	4	14		25 **My Brave Face**	25	Capitol 44367
				written by Elvis Costello and McCartney		
9/16/89	28	8		26 This One	94	Capitol 44438
12/23/89	47	5		27 Figure Of Eight	92	Capitol 44489
4/14/90	11	13		28 Put It There		Capitol 44570
				a tribute to McCartney's Dad		
1/30/93	9	15		29 Hope Of Deliverance	83	Capitol 44904
5/15/93	27	8		30 Off The Ground		Capitol 44924

McCLINTON, Delbert

Born on 11/4/40 in Lubbock, Texas. Played harmonica on Bruce Channel's hit "Hey Baby." Leader of the Ron-Dels.

2/21/81	35	4		Giving It Up For Your Love	8	Capitol 4948

McCOO, Marilyn, & Billy Davis, Jr.

Marilyn (b: 9/30/43, Jersey City, New Jersey) and husband Billy (b: 6/26/39, St. Louis) were members of The 5th Dimension. Marilyn co-hosted TV's *Solid Gold* from 1981-84.

3/27/76	9	9		1 I Hope We Get To Love In Time	91	ABC 12170
9/11/76	6	24	●	2 **You Don't Have To Be A Star (To Be In My Show)**	1¹	ABC 12208
4/9/77	21	8		3 Your Love	15	ABC 12262
9/3/77	29	6		4 Look What You've Done To My Heart	51	ABC 12298
1/21/78	38	6		5 My Reason To Be Is You		ABC 12324

157

DEBUT DATE	PEAK POS	WKS CHR	G O L D	ARTIST — Record Title	POP POS	Label & Number
				McCORMICK, Gayle		
				Born in St. Louis. Former lead singer of the group Smith.		
7/24/71	**20**	5		1 Gonna Be Alright Now..	84	Dunhill 4281
10/2/71	**9**	9		2 It's A Cryin' Shame	44	Dunhill 4288
10/11/75	**46**	6		3 Coming In, Out Of The Rain...		Shady Brook 017
				McCOY, Van, & The Soul City Symphony		
				Pianist/producer/songwriter/singer. Born on 1/6/44 in Washington, D.C.; died on 7/6/79 of a heart attack. Formed own Rock'N label in 1960. A&R man at Scepter/Wand from 1961-64. Own MAXX label, mid-1960s. Produced The Shirelles, Gladys Knight, The Stylistics and Brenda & The Tabulations.		
6/29/74	**22**	12		1 Love Is The Answer ....[I]		Avco 4639
5/17/75	**2**²	14	●	2 The Hustle ....[I]	1¹	Avco 4653
				McCRAE, George		
				Born on 10/19/44 in West Palm Beach, Florida. Duets with wife Gwen McCrae; became her manager.		
6/29/74	**19**	9		Rock Your Baby..	1²	T.K. 1004
				McDANIELS, Gene		
				Born Eugene B. McDaniels on 2/12/35 in Kansas City. To Omaha, early 1940s, sang in choirs, attended Omaha Conservatory of Music. Own band, early '50s. Appeared in the film It's Trad, Dad in 1962.		
9/7/63	**20**	1		1 It's A Lonely Town (Lonely Without You)	64	Liberty 55597
9/16/72	**37**	2		2 River	115	MGM/Verve 10677
				UNIVERSAL JONES		
				McDONALD, Duncan ۝		
				Los Angeles-based singer/songwriter. Worked in the charts department of Billboard magazine.		
7/20/74	**17**	15		You Can Take My Love...		United Art. 436
★★★144★★★				**McDONALD, Michael**		
				Born on 12/2/52 in St. Louis, Missouri. Vocalist/keyboardist. First recorded for RCA in 1972. Formerly with Steely Dan and The Doobie Brothers. Married to singer Amy Holland. Also see Nicolette Larson.		
				1)On My Own 2)Sweet Freedom 3)Take It To Heart		
8/21/82	**8**	18		1 I Keep Forgettin' (Every Time You're Near).....................	4	Warner 29933
11/27/82	**28**	11		2 I Gotta Try...	44	Warner 29862
1/7/84	**10**	16		3 Yah Mo B There	19	Qwest 29394
				JAMES INGRAM (with Michael McDonald)		
8/17/85	**18**	9		4 No Lookin' Back	34	Warner 28960
11/30/85	**40**	2		5 Lost In The Parade		Warner 28847
4/12/86	**2**²	21	●	6 On My Own	1³	MCA 52770
				PATTI LaBELLE AND MICHAEL McDONALD		
6/28/86	**4**	17		7 Sweet Freedom	7	MCA 52857
				theme from the film Running Scared		
9/20/86	**13**	11		8 I Just Can't Let Go		Warner 28605
				DAVID PACK with Michael McDonald and James Ingram		
5/19/90	**4**	24		9 Take It To Heart..	98	Reprise 19828
10/6/90	**27**	9		10 Tear It Up		Reprise 19710
2/15/92	**11**	22		11 Ever Changing Times		Arista 12394
				ARETHA FRANKLIN Featuring Michael McDonald		
				McDOWELL, Carrie ۝		
				Vocalist from Des Moines, Iowa. At the age of 10, made three appearances on the Tonight Show and was the opening act for George Burns, Liberace, and Danny Thomas.		
11/7/87	**45**	5		When A Woman Loves A Man		Motown 1910
				McDOWELL, Ronnie		
				Country singer/songwriter. Born on 3/26/50 in Portland, Tennessee. Sang on soundtrack for the film Elvis.		
9/24/77	**42**	6	●	1 The King Is Gone..	13	Scorpion 135
				a tribute to Elvis Presley		
3/4/78	**50**	2		2 I Love You, I Love You, I Love You	81	Scorpion 149
				McELROY, Taffy ۝		
				Thirteen-year-old vocalist (in 1981).		
6/13/81	**48**	5		Who's That Look In Your Eye..		MCA 51090
				McFERRIN, Bobby		
				Born on 3/11/50 in New York City. Unaccompanied, jazz-styled improvisation vocalist. Sang the 1987 Cosby Show theme and the Levi's 501 Blues jingle. Father was a baritone with the New York Metropolitan Opera.		
8/13/88	**7**	17	●	Don't Worry Be Happy	1²	EMI-Man. 50146
				featured in the film Cocktail		

DEBUT DATE	PEAK POS	WKS CHR	GOLD	ARTIST — Record Title	POP POS	Label & Number
				McGEE, Parker		
				Pop singer/songwriter from Mississippi. Wrote "I'd Really Love To See You Tonight" and "Nights Are Forever Without You" for England Dan & John Ford Coley.		
2/5/77	**7**	12		**I Just Can't Say No To You**	42	Big Tree 16082
★★162★★				**McGOVERN, Maureen**		
				Born on 7/27/49 in Youngstown, Ohio. Pop singer. Sang theme of TV show *Angie*. Cameo roles in *The Towering Inferno* and *Airplane* (as Sister Angelina). Starred in Broadway's *Pirates Of Penzance* for 14 months.		
				1)Different Worlds 2)Can You Read My Mind 3)The Morning After		
6/16/73	**6**	12	●	**1 The Morning After**	1²	20th Century 2010
				love theme from the film *The Poseidon Adventure*		
10/6/73	**14**	10		2 I Won't Last A Day Without You	89	20th Century 2051
3/2/74	**28**	7		3 Nice To Be Around	101	20th Century 2072
				from the film *Cinderella Liberty*		
8/3/74	**12**	10		4 Give Me A Reason To Be Gone	71	20th Century 2109
1/18/75	**20**	10		5 We May Never Love Like This Again	83	20th Century 2158
				from the film *The Towering Inferno*		
11/8/75	**24**	8		6 Love Songs Are Getting Harder To Sing		20th Century 2234
2/17/79	**5**	19		**7 Can You Read My Mind**	52	Warner 8750
				love theme from the film *Superman*		
6/30/79	**1²**	21		**8 Different Worlds**	18	Warner 8835
				theme from the TV series *Angie*		
12/1/79	**27**	9		9 Can't Take My Eyes Off You		Warner 49129
				#2 Pop hit for Frankie Valli in 1967		
2/23/80	**16**	10		10 We Could Have It All		Warner 49177
				love theme from *The Last Married Couple In America*		
4/11/81	**24**	14		11 Halfway Home		Maiden Voyage 120
				theme from the film *The Earthling*		
				McGUINN, CLARK & HILLMAN		
				Roger McGuinn (b: 7/13/42; vocals, guitar), Gene Clark (b: 11/17/44; d: 5/24/91; guitar) and Chris Hillman (b: 6/4/42; bass). All are former members of The Byrds.		
4/7/79	**17**	12		1 Don't You Write Her Off	33	Capitol 4693
7/28/79	**45**	5		2 Surrender To Me	104	Capitol 4739
				McGUIRE, Phyllis		
				The youngest of The McGuire Sisters (see below).		
12/12/64	**13**	2		I Don't Want To Walk Without You	79	Reprise 0310
				#1 hit for Harry James in 1942		
				McGUIRE SISTERS, The		
				Sisters Christine (b: 7/30/29), Dorothy (b: 2/13/30) and Phyllis (b: 2/14/31) from Middletown, Ohio. Replaced the Chordettes on *Arthur Godfrey And His Friends* show in 1953. Phyllis went solo in 1964. Reunited in 1986.		
7/24/61	**12**	5		1 Tears On My Pillow	59	Coral 62276
				written by Gene Autry and Fred Rose		
3/5/66	**30**	6		2 Truer Than You Were		ABC-Para. 10776
				M.C. HAMMER		
				Born Stanley Kirk Burrell on 3/30/63 in Oakland. Rapper/producer/founder/leader of The Posse, an eight-member group of dancers, DJs and singers.		
9/1/90	**42**	4	●	Have You Seen Her	4	Capitol 44573
				McKEE, Maria ○		
				Born in 1964. Former lead singer of Lone Justice from Los Angeles.		
10/6/90	**28**	11		Show Me Heaven		Geffen 19674
				from the film *Days Of Thunder*		
				McKNIGHT, Brian		
				R&B singer/composer. Born on 6/5/69 in Buffalo, New York. His older brother is Claude McKnight of Take 6.		
2/6/93	**1³**	34↑		1 Love Is	3	Giant 18630
				VANESSA WILLIAMS & BRIAN McKNIGHT		
6/26/93	**16↑**	14↑		2 One Last Cry	13	Mercury 862404
★★130★★				**McLEAN, Don**		
				Born on 10/2/45 in New Rochelle, New York. Singer/songwriter/poet. The hit "Killing Me Softly With His Song" was inspired by Don.		
				1)American Pie - Parts I & II 2)Wonderful Baby 3)Crying		
2/27/71	**40**	1		1 Castles In The Air		Mediarts 108
				made the *Hot 100* in 1972 as the B-side of "Vincent" and again in 1981 (POS 36)		
12/11/71	**1³**	14	●	2 American Pie - Parts I & II	1⁴	United Art. 50856
				inspired by the death of Buddy Holly		

DEBUT DATE	PEAK POS	WKS CHR	G O L D	ARTIST — Record Title	POP POS	Label & Number
				McLEAN, Don — Cont'd		
3/25/72	**2**[3]	11		**3 Vincent**	12	United Art. 50887
				a tribute to artist Vincent Van Gogh		
1/6/73	**7**	9		**4 Dreidel**	21	United Art. 51100
3/31/73	**12**	7		**5 If We Try**	58	United Art. 206
2/9/74	**25**	7		**6 Fool's Paradise**	107	United Art. 363
4/19/75	**1**[1]	12		**7 Wonderful Baby**	93	United Art. 614
				written as a tribute to Fred Astaire		
1/24/81	**2**[4]	17		**8 Crying**	5	Millennium 11799
4/18/81	**6**	15		**9 Since I Don't Have You**	23	Millennium 11804
8/1/81	**20**	13		**10 It's Just The Sun**	83	Millennium 11809
10/24/81	**7**	18		**11 Castles In The Air** ....[R]	36	Millennium 11819
				new version of Don's 1971 hit		
				McLEAN, Phil		
				Veteran DJ; born in Detroit.		
12/4/61	**6**	10		**Small Sad Sam** .... [S-N]	21	Versatile 107
				parody of Jimmy Dean's "Big Bad John"		
				McRAE, Carmen		
				Born on 4/8/20 in New York City. Jazz singer/pianist. Active into the 1990s.		
8/20/66	**29**	8		**1 Alfie**		Mainstream 650
				from the film *Alfie*; #15 Pop hit for Dionne Warwick in 1967		
12/9/67	**33**	4		**2 Live For Life**	101	Atlantic 2451
				CARMEN McRAE & HERBIE MANN		
				movie title song		
3/2/68	**35**	6		**3 Elusive Butterfly**		Atlantic 2485
				#5 Pop hit for Bob Lind in 1966		
				McVIE, Christine		
				Born Christine Perfect on 7/12/43 in Birmingham, England. Vocalist with Fleetwood Mac since 1970. Married to Fleetwood Mac bassist John McVie, 1968-77. Quit touring with group after 1990.		
2/4/84	**1**[4]	20		**1 Got A Hold On Me**	10	Warner 29372
5/19/84	**32**	8		**2 Love Will Show Us How**	30	Warner 29313
				MEAD, Sister Janet		
				Australian nun; born in 1938. Gained prominence through her weekly cathedral rock masses and weekly radio programs.		
2/23/74	**2**[1]	12	●	**The Lord's Prayer**	4	A&M 1491
				Biblical text with new music by Arnold Strals		
				MEAT LOAF		
				Born Marvin Lee Aday on 9/27/47 in Dallas. Rock singer. Sang lead vocals on Ted Nugent's 1976 *Free-For-All* LP. Played Eddie in the Los Angeles production and film of *The Rocky Horror Picture Show*. Appeared in films *Americathon*, *Roadie*, *Out Of Bounds*, *The Squeeze* and *Leap Of Faith*.		
5/27/78	**31**	12	●	**Two Out Of Three Ain't Bad**	11	Epic 50513
				MECO		
				Disco producer Meco Monardo; born on 11/29/39 in Johnsonburg, Pennsylvania. Played trombone in Cadet Band at West Point. Later moved to New York and became a session musician and arranger. Co-produced Gloria Gaynor's hit "Never Can Say Goodbye."		
8/27/77	**18**	13	▲	**1 Star Wars Theme/Cantina Band** ....[I]	1[2]	Millennium 604
1/14/78	**30**	9		**2 Theme From Close Encounters** ....[I]	25	Millennium 608
9/30/78	**30**	6		**3 Themes From The Wizard Of Oz** ....[N]	35	Millennium 620
				all of above inspired by movie themes		
2/13/82	**17**	13		**4 Pop Goes The Movies Part I** ....[I]	35	Arista 0660
				20th Century Fox Trademark/Tara's Theme/The Magnificent Seven/ The James Bond Theme/Goldfinger/The Good, The Bad And The Ugly/ Theme From The Apartment/Theme From The High & The Mighty		
5/29/82	**18**	9		**5 Big Band Medley** ....[I]	101	Arista 0686
				Pennsylvania 6-5000/String Of Pearls/In The Mood/Don't Be That Way/ I've Got A Girl In Kalamazoo/Moonlight Serenade/Opus No. 1/Two O'Clock Jump		
				MEDEIROS, Glenn		
				Born on 6/24/70 and raised in Hawaii. Discovered through a local radio station talent search.		
4/4/87	**4**	19		**1 Nothing's Change My Love For You**	12	Amherst 311
11/24/90	**35**	8		**2 Me-U=Blue**	78	MCA 53945
				GLENN MEDEIROS Featuring The Stylistics		
				MEDICAL MISSIONARIES OF MARY CHORAL GROUP ☺		
2/5/66	**31**	6		**Angels (Watching Over Me)**	117	Kapp 731

DEBUT DATE	PEAK POS	WKS CHR	GOLD	ARTIST — Record Title	POP POS	Label & Number
				MEDLEY, Bill		
				Born on 9/19/40 in Santa Ana, California. Baritone of The Righteous Brothers duo. Co-owner of a Las Vegas nightclub named Kicks with Paul Revere of The Raiders.		
3/28/81	29	8		1 Don't Know Much	88	Liberty 1402
11/6/82	31	7		2 Right Here And Now	58	Planet 13317
6/30/84	25	9		3 I Still Do		RCA 13753
9/20/86	16	10		4 Loving On Borrowed Time		Scotti Br. 06267
				GLADYS KNIGHT and BILL MEDLEY love theme from the film *Cobra*		
8/8/87	1⁴	26	●	5 (I've Had) The Time Of My Life	1¹	RCA 5224
				BILL MEDLEY AND JENNIFER WARNES love theme from the film *Dirty Dancing*		
7/16/88	49	2		6 He Ain't Heavy, He's My Brother		Scotti Br. 07938
				from the film *Rambo III*; #7 Pop hit for The Hollies in 1970		
				MELANIE		
				Born Melanie Safka on 2/3/47 in Queens, New York. Neighborhood Records formed by Melanie and her husband/producer Peter Schekeryk.		
11/20/71	5	12	●	1 Brand New Key	1³	Neighborhood 4201
2/5/72	18	8		2 Ring The Living Bell	31	Neighborhood 4202
2/5/72	30	5		3 The Nickel Song	35	Buddah 268
3/3/73	12	7		4 Bitter Bad	36	Neighborhood 4210
1/5/74	42	5		5 Will You Love Me Tomorrow?	82	Neighborhood 4213
				MELLENCAMP, John Cougar		
				Born on 10/7/51 in Seymour, Indiana. Rock singer/songwriter/producer. Worked outside of music until 1975. Given name Johnny Cougar by David Bowie's manager, Tony DeFries. First recorded for MCA in 1976. Directed and starred in the 1992 film *Falling from Grace*; leader of the Buzzin' Cousins group that appeared in the film. Married model Elaine Irwin on 9/5/92.		
10/26/85	37	3		1 Lonely Ol' Night	6	Riva 880984
11/23/85	13	13		2 Small Town	6	Riva 884202
3/15/86	36	2		3 R.O.C.K. In The U.S.A.	2¹	Riva 884455
				a salute to 60's rock		
11/14/87	12	18		4 Cherry Bomb	8	Mercury 888934
7/29/89	31	6		5 Jackie Brown	48	Mercury 874644
3/28/92	46	3		6 Again Tonight..................................	36	Mercury 866414
				JOHN MELLENCAMP		
				MELVIN, Harold, And The Blue Notes		
				Philadelphia soul group, The Blue Notes, formed in 1954: Harold Melvin, Bernard Williams, Jesse Gillis, Jr., Franklin Peaker and Roosevelt Brodie. First recorded for Josie in 1956. Numerous personnel changes until 1970, when Teddy Pendergrass joined as drummer and lead singer. Pendergrass went solo in 1976, replaced by David Ebo.		
12/29/73	48	2	●	1 The Love I Lost (Part 1)	7	Phil. Int. 3533
1/24/76	34	8		2 Wake Up Everybody (Part 1)	12	Phil. Int. 3579
				MEN AT WORK		
				Melbourne, Australia rock quintet formed in 1979. Colin Hay (lead singer, guitar), Ron Strykert (lead guitar), Greg Ham (sax, keyboards), Jerry Speiser (drums) and John Rees (bass). Won the 1982 Best New Artist Grammy Award. Speiser and Rees left in 1984. Hay went solo as Colin James Hay in 1987.		
12/11/82	13	18	●	1 Down Under	1⁴	Columbia 03303
4/9/83	6	16		2 Overkill	3	Columbia 03795
7/9/83	10	15		3 It's A Mistake	6	Columbia 03959
7/6/85	34	2		4 Everything I Need..............................	47	Columbia 04929
★★39★★				**MENDES, Sergio, & Brasil '66**		
				Sergio was born on 2/11/41 in Niteroi, Brazil. Pianist/leader of Latin-styled group originating from Brazil. Member Lani Hall (vocals) married Herb Alpert.		
				1)The Fool On The Hill 2)Never Gonna Let You Go 3)The Look Of Love 4)Scarborough Fair 5)Pretty World		
8/6/66	4	17		1 Mas Que Nada................................. [F]	47	A&M 807
12/24/66	11	9		2 Constant Rain (Chove Chuva)	71	A&M 825
3/11/67	16	8		3 For Me	98	A&M 836
5/27/67	8	12		4 Night And Day	82	A&M 853
				there's been 7 top 25 hits since 1932 of this Cole Porter classic		
9/23/67	21	5		5 The Frog	126	A&M 872
2/10/68	21	4		6 Say A Little Prayer .... [I]	106	Atlantic 2472
				SERGIO MENDES #4 Pop hit for Dionne Warwick in 1967		
3/2/68	31	4		7 With A Little Help From My Friends *		A&M 910

DEBUT DATE	PEAK POS	WKS CHR	G O L D	ARTIST — Record Title	POP POS	Label & Number
				MENDES, Sergio, & Brasil '66 — Cont'd		
5/4/68	2⁵	18		8 **The Look Of Love**	4	A&M 924
				from the film *Casino Royale*		
8/10/68	1⁶	15		9 **The Fool On The Hill** *	6	A&M 961
11/16/68	2¹	13		10 Scarborough Fair	16	A&M 986
5/3/69	4	9		11 **Pretty World**	62	A&M 1049
6/21/69	12	8		12 (Sittin' On) The Dock Of The Bay	66	A&M 1073
11/29/69	34	2		13 Wichita Lineman	95	A&M 1132
2/28/70	32	4		14 Norwegian Wood *	107	A&M 1164
				*written by John Lennon and Paul McCartney		
8/22/70	10	8		15 **For What It's Worth**	101	A&M 1209
				#7 Pop hit for Buffalo Springfield in 1967		
11/7/70	21	6		16 Chelsea Morning		A&M 1226
				#78 Pop hit for Judy Collins in 1969; written by Joni Mitchell		
				SERGIO MENDES & BRASIL '77:		
3/31/73	24	6		17 Love Music	113	Bell 45,335
7/28/73	36	3	✓	18 Where Is The Love		Bell 45,372
				#5 Pop hit for Roberta Flack & Donny Hathaway		
				SERGIO MENDES:		
2/5/77	50	2		19 The Real Thing		Elektra 45360
				written by Stevie Wonder		
4/16/83	1⁴	27		20 **Never Gonna Let You Go**	4	A&M 2540
				Joe Pizzulo and Leza Miller (vocals)		
8/6/83	6	16		21 **Rainbow's End**	52	A&M 2563
				Dan Sembello (vocal)		
4/7/84	18	8		22 Olympia	58	A&M 2623
5/26/84	5	21		23 **Alibis**	29	A&M 2639
9/29/84	17	9		24 Real Life		A&M 2672
3/16/85	33	3		25 Let's Give A Little More This Time		A&M 2706
11/1/86	14	16		26 **Take This Love**		A&M 2875
				SERGIO MENDES BRASIL '66		
3/14/87	19	9		27 What Do We Mean To Each Other		A&M 2917
				Joe Pizzulo (vocal, above 6)		

MERCY
Florida group led by Jack Sigler, Jr.

DEBUT DATE	PEAK POS	WKS CHR	G O L D	ARTIST — Record Title	POP POS	Label & Number
4/12/69	2³	13	●	1 **Love (Can Make You Happy)**	2²	Sundi 6811
6/28/69	24	6		2 Forever	79	Warner 7297

MESSINA, Jimmy
Born on 12/5/47 in Maywood, California; raised in Harlingen, Texas. Member of Buffalo Springfield, 1967-68, then Poco 1968-70. Formed duo with Kenny Loggins from 1971-76. Joined the re-formed Poco in 1989.

DEBUT DATE	PEAK POS	WKS CHR	G O L D	ARTIST — Record Title	POP POS	Label & Number
11/17/79	43	4		New And Different Way		Columbia 11094

MFSB
Large interracial studio band formed by producers Kenny Gamble and Leon Huff. Also recorded as The James Boys, and Family. Name means "Mother, Father, Sister, Brother."

DEBUT DATE	PEAK POS	WKS CHR	G O L D	ARTIST — Record Title	POP POS	Label & Number
3/9/74	1²	16	●	TSOP (The Sound Of Philadelphia) .... [I]	1²	Phil. Int. 3540
				MFSB featuring The Three Degrees theme from the TV show *Soul Train*		

MGM SINGING STRINGS ✪

DEBUT DATE	PEAK POS	WKS CHR	G O L D	ARTIST — Record Title	POP POS	Label & Number
5/7/66	28	5		Lara's Theme from "Dr. Zhivago" .... [I]		MGM 13448
				arranged, conducted and produced by Teddy Randazzo		

MIAMI SOUND MACHINE — see ESTEFAN, Gloria

★★46★★ MICHAEL, George/Wham!
Born Georgios Kyriacos Panayiotou on 6/26/63 in Bushey, England. Wham!, formed in early '80s, centered around George's vocals and songwriting, and included Andrew Ridgeley (b: 1/26/63, Bushey, England) on guitar. Their association ended in 1986. Ridgeley pursued race car driving, then solo career in 1990.

1)*Careless Whisper* 2)*One More Try* 3)*Don't Let The Sun Go Down On Me* 4)*Kissing A Fool* 5)*I Knew You Were Waiting (For Me)*

WHAM!:

DEBUT DATE	PEAK POS	WKS CHR	G O L D	ARTIST — Record Title	POP POS	Label & Number
10/6/84	4	16	▲	1 **Wake Me Up Before You Go-Go**	1³	Columbia 04552
12/15/84	1⁵	22	▲	2 **Careless Whisper**	1³	Columbia 04691
				WHAM! Featuring George Michael originally released as a solo single by George Michael		
4/6/85	4	18	●	3 **Everything She Wants**	1²	Columbia 04840

DEBUT DATE	PEAK POS	WKS CHR	GOLD	ARTIST — Record Title	POP POS	Label & Number
				MICHAEL, George/Wham! — Cont'd		
8/3/85	**4**	17		4 **Freedom**....................	3	Columbia 05409
12/14/85	**13**	14		5 I'm Your Man....................	3	Columbia 05721
5/3/86	**6**	14		6 A Different Corner	7	Columbia 05888
				GEORGE MICHAEL		
7/26/86	**22**	9		7 The Edge Of Heaven....................	10	Columbia 06182
10/25/86	**33**	6		8 Where Did Your Heart Go?....................	50	Columbia 06294
3/7/87	**2**³	16		9 **I Knew You Were Waiting (For Me)**....................	1²	Arista 9559
				ARETHA FRANKLIN AND GEORGE MICHAEL		
				GEORGE MICHAEL:		
11/7/87	**5**	17	●	10 **Faith**	1⁴	Columbia 07623
1/23/88	**3**	19		11 **Father Figure**....................	1²	Columbia 07682
4/16/88	**1**³	20	●	12 **One More Try**....................	1³	Columbia 07773
10/8/88	**1**¹	18		13 **Kissing A Fool**....................	5	Columbia 08050
3/11/89	**3**	18		14 **Heaven Help Me**....................	5	Mika 871538
				DEON ESTUS with George Michael		
9/1/90	**4**	16		15 **Praying For Time**....................	1¹	Columbia 73512
11/10/90	**27**	14		16 Freedom	8	Columbia 73559
				different tune than Michael's 1985 Wham! hit		
1/19/91	**22**	15		17 Waiting For That Day/	27	
				samples The Rolling Stones' "You Can't Always Get What You Want"		
3/2/91	**41**	4		18 Mother's Pride	46	Columbia 73663
12/7/91	**1**²	23	●	19 **Don't Let The Sun Go Down On Me**....................	1¹	Columbia 74086
				GEORGE MICHAEL/ELTON JOHN		
				recorded live in London, March 1991		
5/8/93	**42**	7		20 Somebody To Love....................	30	Hollywood 64647
				GEORGE MICHAEL and QUEEN		
				#13 Pop hit for Queen in 1977		
				MICHAELANGELO ✪		
4/17/71	**18**	5		300 Watt Music Box........................ [I]		Columbia 45328
				MICHAELS, Marilyn ✪		
				Comedienne.		
12/9/67	**29**	3		I Wonder Who's Kissing Him Now....................		ABC 10979
				female version of Henry Burr's #1 hit in 1909		
				MICKY ✪		
1/8/77	**37**	7		Bye, Bye Fraulein.................... [F]		Ariola Am. 7655
★★69★★				**MIDLER, Bette**		
				Born on 12/1/45 in Paterson, New Jersey. Vocalist/actress. Raised in Hawaii. In the Broadway show *Fiddler On The Roof* for three years. Won the 1973 Best New Artist Grammy Award. Barry Manilow was her arranger/accompanist in early years. Nominated for an Oscar for performance in *The Rose* (1979). Also in films *Down And Out In Beverly Hills, Ruthless People, Beaches, For The Boys* and others.		
				1)From A Distance 2)The Rose 3)Boogie Woogie Bugle Boy		
1/13/73	**8**	11		1 **Do You Want To Dance?**	17	Atlantic 2928
5/19/73	**1**²	14		2 **Boogie Woogie Bugle Boy**....................	8	Atlantic 2964
9/29/73	**9**	10		3 **Friends**	40	Atlantic 2980
2/2/74	**18**	7		4 In The Mood....................	51	Atlantic 3004
				above 3 produced by Barry Manilow		
3/27/76	**45**	5		5 Strangers In The Night		Atlantic 3319
				disco version of Frank Sinatra's #1 Pop hit in 1966		
5/1/76	**36**	6		6 Old Cape Cod		Atlantic 3325
				#3 Pop hit for Patti Page in 1957		
2/26/77	**11**	19		7 You're Movin' Out Today	42	Atlantic 3379
12/24/77	**37**	11		8 Storybook Children (Daybreak)	57	Atlantic 3431
3/29/80	**1**⁵	21	●	9 **The Rose**	3	Atlantic 3656
				movie title song		
12/13/80	**8**	16		10 **My Mother's Eyes**	39	Atlantic 3771
				from the film *Divine Madness*		
9/10/83	**39**	5		11 **All I Need To Know**	77	Atlantic 89789
2/18/89	**2**²	27	▲	12 **Wind Beneath My Wings**	1¹	Atlantic 88972
				from the film *Beaches* starring Bette; won Grammys for 1989's Best Song and Best Record; #65 Pop hit for Lou Rawls in 1983		
10/6/90	**1**⁶	28	▲	13 **From A Distance**	2¹	Atlantic 87820
1/26/91	**15**	15		14 Night And Day	62	Atlantic 87825
8/17/91	**19**	15		15 The Gift Of Love		Atlantic 87633

DEBUT DATE	PEAK POS	WKS CHR	G O L D	ARTIST — Record Title	POP POS	Label & Number
				MIDLER, Bette — Cont'd		
11/30/91	**15**	14		16 Every Road Leads Back To You	78	Atlantic 87572
2/29/92	**20**	14		17 In My Life		Atlantic 87525
				written by John Lennon and Paul McCartney; above 2 from the film *For The Boys*		
				MIKE + THE MECHANICS		
				Rock quintet consisting of bassist Mike Rutherford (Genesis), vocalists Paul Carrack (Ace, Squeeze) and Paul Young (Sad Cafe), drummer Peter Van Hooke (Van Morrison) and keyboardist Adrian Lee.		
2/1/86	**7**	13		1 Silent Running (On Dangerous Ground)	6	Atlantic 89488
				title track from the film *On Dangerous Ground*		
4/19/86	**7**	18		2 All I Need Is A Miracle	5	Atlantic 89450
7/12/86	**7**	17		3 Taken In	32	Atlantic 89404
1/21/89	**1**⁴	23		4 **The Living Years**	1¹	Atlantic 88964
7/22/89	**41**	4		5 Nobody Knows..		Atlantic 88990
6/15/91	**24**	10		6 Everybody Gets A Second Chance...................		Atlantic 87679
				MILLER, Glenn, Orchestra ✪		
				Born on 3/1/04 in Clarinda, Iowa. Leader of the most popular big band of all time. Glenn disappeared in a plane flight from England to France on 12/15/44.		
9/17/66	**12**	9		1 I'm Gettin' Sentimental Over You ....[I]		Epic 10057
				orchestra directed by Buddy DeFranco; Tommy Dorsey's famous theme song		
3/12/77	**36**	2		2 In The Mood... [I-R]		Buddah 548
				new version of Glenn's #1 hit from 1940		
				MILLER, Jody		
				Born in Phoenix on 11/29/41 and raised in Blanchard, Oklahoma. Pop-country singer.		
5/15/65	**4**	6		1 **Queen Of The House**	12	Capitol 5402
				answer song to Roger Miller's "King Of The Road"		
6/12/71	**2**²	13		2 He's So Fine	53	Epic 10734
10/2/71	**21**	7		3 Baby, I'm Yours	91	Epic 10785
3/25/72	**35**	4		4 Be My Baby		Epic 10835
				#2 Pop hit for The Ronettes in 1963		
7/1/72	**23**	7		5 There's A Party Goin' On	115	Epic 10878
12/1/73	**41**	3		6 The House Of The Rising Sun		Epic 11056
				#1 Pop hit for The Animals in 1964		
				MILLER, Joe ✪		
11/13/76	**45**	6		Lonely People		Polydor 14350
				MILLER, Mrs.		
				Mrs. Elva Miller. Tone-deaf singer from Claremont, California.		
4/23/66	**13**	8		1 A Lover's Concerto/	[N] 95	
4/30/66	**9**	7		2 **Downtown** ....[N]	82	Capitol 5640
				MILLER, Ned		
				Born Henry Ned Miller on 4/12/25 in Rains, Utah. Country singer/songwriter. To California in 1956. Signed with Fabor in 1956. Wrote the Gale Storm and Bonnie Guitar hit "Dark Moon."		
2/9/63	**3**	7		From A Jack To A King	6	Fabor 114
				originally released on Dot 15601 in 1957		
★★106★★				**MILLER, Roger**		
				Country vocalist/humorist/guitarist/composer. Born on 1/2/36 in Fort Worth, Texas and raised in Erick, Oklahoma. To Nashville in the mid-1950s, began songwriting career. With Faron Young as writer/drummer in 1962. Won six Grammys in 1965. Own TV show in 1966. Songwriter of 1985's Tony Award-winning Broadway musical *Big River.* Died of cancer on 10/25/92.		
				1)*King Of The Road* 2)*England Swings* 3)*Engine Engine #9*		
1/30/65	**1**¹⁰	13	●	1 King Of The Road	4	Smash 1965
5/8/65	**2**³	9		2 Engine Engine #9....................................	7	Smash 1983
7/10/65	**8**	7		3 One Dyin' And A Buryin'/	34	
7/17/65	**26**	5		4 It Happened Just That Way	105	Smash 1994
9/18/65	**3**	7		5 Kansas City Star.................................[N]	31	Smash 1998
10/30/65	**1**¹	14		6 England Swings	8	Smash 2010
2/12/66	**2**¹	12		7 Husbands And Wives	26	Smash 2024
6/25/66	**17**	7		8 You Can't Roller Skate In A Buffalo Herd ....[N]	40	Smash 2043
4/1/67	**6**	8		9 Walkin' In The Sunshine	37	Smash 2081
3/2/68	**5**	10		10 Little Green Apples	39	Smash 2148
11/30/68	**15**	8		11 Vance	80	Smash 2197
7/28/73	**20**	9		12 Open Up Your Heart	105	Columbia 45873

DEBUT DATE	PEAK POS	WKS CHR	GOLD	ARTIST — Record Title	POP POS	Label & Number
				MILLER, Steve, Band		
				Born on 10/5/43 in Milwaukee; moved to Dallas at age six. Blues-rock singer/songwriter/guitarist. To San Francisco in 1966; formed the Steve Miller Band, which featured a fluctuating lineup.		
2/12/77	**38**	7	●	1 Fly Like An Eagle	2²	Capitol 4372
				STEVE MILLER		
8/28/82	**28**	9	●	2 Abracadabra	1²	Capitol 5126
7/3/93	**27**	9		3 Wide River	64	Sailor 859194
				MILLIONS LIKE US		
				British duo: John O'Kane and Jeep. Jeep toured with Talk Talk.		
10/10/87	**28**	6		Guaranteed For Life	69	Virgin 99412
				MILLI VANILLI		
				Europop act formed in Germany by producer Frank Farian (creator of Boney M and Far Corporation). Milli Vanilli is Turkish for Positive Energy. Originally thought to be Rob Pilatus (from Germany) and Fabrice Morvan (from France). Stripped of their 1989 Best New Artist Grammy Award when it was revealed that they did not sing on their debut album. Actual vocalists are Charles Shaw, John Davis and Brad Howe.		
9/23/89	**21**	11	●	1 Girl I'm Gonna Miss You	1²	Arista 9870
11/18/89	**27**	13	▲	2 Blame It On The Rain	1²	Arista 9904
				MILLS, Frank		
				Born in Toronto in 1943. Pianist/composer/producer/arranger.		
2/19/72	**8**	9		1 Love Me, Love Me Love	46	Sunflower 118
2/3/79	**4**	18	●	2 Music Box Dancer .... [I]	3	Polydor 14517
11/3/79	**6**	14		3 Peter Piper .... [I]	48	Polydor 2002
12/20/80	**41**	7		4 Happy Song .... [I]		Polydor 2148
				MILLS, Stephanie		
				Born in 1957 in Brooklyn. R&B singer/actress.		
8/23/80	**5**	24	●	Never Knew Love Like This Before	6	20th Century 2460
				MILLS BROTHERS, The		
				Smooth family vocal group from Piqua, Ohio. Consisted of John, Jr. (b: 1911; d: 1936), Herbert (b: 1912; d: 4/12/89 [age 77]), Harry (b: 1913; d: 6/28/82 [age 68]) and Donald (b: 1915). Originally featured unusual vocal style of imitating instruments. Achieved national fame via radio broadcasts and appearances in films. Father, John, Sr., joined group in 1936, replacing John, Jr.; remained in group until 1956 (d: 12/8/67). Group continued as a trio until 1982. Donald and his son John, III continued singing as a duo.		
2/17/68	**3**	13		1 Cab Driver	23	Dot 17041
5/11/68	**4**	12		2 My Shy Violet	73	Dot 17096
10/19/68	**16**	8		3 The Ol' Race Track	83	Dot 17162
2/1/69	**13**	8		4 The Jimtown Road		Dot 17198
				Tommy Morgan (harmonica solo)		
★★66★★				**MILSAP, Ronnie**		
				Born on 1/16/46 in Robbinsville, North Carolina. Country singer/pianist/guitarist. Blind since birth; multi-instrumentalist by age 12. With J.J. Cale band; own band from 1965.		
				1)Any Day Now 2)Smoky Mountain Rain 3)(There's) No Gettin' Over Me		
6/25/77	**7**	23		1 It Was Almost Like A Song	16	RCA 10976
1/7/78	**19**	11		2 What A Difference You've Made In My Life	80	RCA 11146
6/17/78	**24**	10		3 Only One Love In My Life	63	RCA 11270
10/7/78	**33**	6		4 Let's Take The Long Way Around The World		RCA 11369
11/29/80	**1**¹	21		5 Smoky Mountain Rain	24	RCA 12084
7/4/81	**2**⁴	21		6 (There's) No Gettin' Over Me	5	RCA 12264
11/7/81	**3**	21		7 I Wouldn't Have Missed It For The World	20	RCA 12342
5/8/82	**1**⁵	21		8 Any Day Now	14	RCA 13216
8/21/82	**15**	14		9 He Got You	59	RCA 13286
12/4/82	**27**	16		10 Inside/		RCA 13362
			16	11 Carolina Dreams		RCA 13362
4/2/83	**8**	16		12 Stranger In My House	23	RCA 13470
8/13/83	**12**	14		13 Don't You Know How Much I Love You	58	RCA 13564
12/10/83	**17**	14		14 Show Her	103	RCA 13658
6/2/84	**29**	9		15 Still Losing You		RCA 13805
7/20/85	**8**	15		16 Lost In The Fifties Tonight (In The Still of the Night) ...		RCA 14135
5/24/86	**35**	6		17 Happy, Happy Birthday Baby		RCA 14286
9/19/87	**42**	3		18 Make No Mistake, She's Mine		RCA 5209
				RONNIE MILSAP & KENNY ROGERS		
				all of above (except #11 and 12) were #1 Country hits		

DEBUT DATE	PEAK POS	WKS CHR	GOLD	ARTIST — Record Title	POP POS	Label & Number
				MILSAP, Ronnie — Cont'd		
8/3/91	**25**	12		19 Since I Don't Have You..		RCA 2848
				MINOGUE, Kylie		
				Singer/actress. Born on 5/28/68 in Melbourne, Australia. Began TV acting career at age 11. Was a longtime cast member of the popular Australian soap *Neighbours*.		
10/29/88	**39**	8	●	The Loco-Motion	3	Geffen 27752
				MISSION ☉		
10/20/73	**36**	7		Together (Body And Soulin')....................................	108	Paramount 0213
				Dorothy Lerner (lead vocal)		
				MR. BIG		
				Rock quartet: Eric Martin (vocals), Pat Torpey (former drummer of Ted Nugent's band and Impellitteri), Billy Sheehan (bass) and Paul Gilbert (guitar). Group took their name from the title of a song by Free.		
1/25/92	**11**	21	●	To Be With You..	1³	Atlantic 87580
				MR. MISTER		
				Los Angeles-based, pop-rock quartet: Richard Page (vocals), Steve George, Pat Mastelotto and Steve Farris (left in 1989; replaced by Buzz Feiten, ex-guitarist of Paul Butterfield Blues Band, Stevie Wonder's band, and the Larsen-Feiten Band).		
11/2/85	**3**	17		1 Broken Wings	1²	RCA 14136
1/25/86	**11**	13		2 Kyrie	1²	RCA 14258
				MITCHELL, Barbara — see ROBINSON, Smokey		
				MITCHELL, Chad, Trio		
				Leader of folk-pop trio which included Mike Kobluk and Joe Frazier. Formed while sophomores at Gonzaga University in Spokane, Washington.		
1/11/64	**20**	1		The Marvelous Toy ....[N]	43	Mercury 72197
				MITCHELL, Joni		
				Born Roberta Joan Anderson on 11/7/43 in Fort McLeod, Alberta, Canada and raised in Saskatoon, Saskatchewan. Singer/songwriter/guitarist/pianist. Moved to New York in 1966. Wrote the hits "Both Sides Now" and "Woodstock." Married her producer/bassist, Larry Klein, in 1982.		
6/6/70	**33**	4		1 Big Yellow Taxi	67	Reprise 0906
12/9/72	**13**	10		2 You Turn Me On, I'm A Radio	25	Asylum 11010
2/9/74	**40**	4		3 Raised On Robbery	65	Asylum 11029
3/16/74	**1¹**	18		4 Help Me	7	Asylum 11034
7/20/74	**2¹**	15		5 Free Man In Paris..	22	Asylum 11041
1/18/75	**27**	7		6 Big Yellow Taxi ....[R]	24	Asylum 45221
				live version of Joni's 1970 studio hit		
2/21/76	**32**	8		7 In France They Kiss On Main Street	66	Asylum 45296
				MITCHELL, Willie		
				Born in Ashland, Mississippi in 1928. Trumpeter/keyboardist/composer/arranger/producer. Eventually became president of Hi Records.		
4/27/68	**32**	5		Soul Serenade ....[I]	23	Hi 2140
				MIXTURES, The		
				Pop group from Melbourne, Australia.		
3/6/71	**19**	9		Pushbike Song	44	Sire 350
				MOCEDADES		
				Sextet from Bilbao, Spain, featuring the Amezaga sisters, Amaya and Izaskum.		
11/17/73	**8**	24		1 Eres Tu (Touch The Wind) ....[F]	9	Tara 100
				B-side is sung in English		
6/8/74	**48**	3		2 Dime Senor...		Tara 105
				MODERN ROMANCE ☉		
				British pop quintet led by vocalists Michael J. Mullins and David Jaymes.		
3/3/84	**40**	4		Just My Imagination (Running Away With Me)....................		Atlantic 89711
				#1 Pop hit for The Temptations in 1971		
				MONEY, Eddie		
				Born Edward Mahoney on 3/2/49 in Brooklyn, New York. Rock singer discovered and subsequently managed by the late West Coast promoter Bill Graham. Formerly an officer with the New York Police Department.		
3/7/87	**33**	4		1 I Wanna Go Back	14	Columbia 06569
1/20/90	**34**	7		2 Peace In Our Time..	11	Columbia 73047
12/21/91	**7**	27		3 I'll Get By..	21	Columbia 74109
5/16/92	**16**	12		4 Fall In Love Again..	54	Columbia 74262

DEBUT DATE	PEAK POS	WKS CHR	G O L D	ARTIST — Record Title	POP POS	Label & Number

MONKEES, The

Formed in Los Angeles in 1965. Chosen from over 400 applicants for new Columbia TV series. Consisted of Davy Jones (b: 12/30/45, Manchester, England; vocals), Michael Nesmith (b: 12/30/42, Houston; guitar, vocals), Peter Tork (b: 2/13/44, Washington, D.C.; bass, vocals) and Micky Dolenz (b: 3/8/45, Tarzana, California; drums, vocals). TV show dropped after 58 episodes, 1966-68. Tork left in 1968. Group disbanded in 1969; re-formed (minus Nesmith) in 1986.

9/20/69	29	6		1 Good Clean Fun	82	Colgems 5005
7/26/86	24	8		2 That Was Then, This Is Now............................	20	Arista 9505
				MICKEY DOLENZ AND PETER TORK OF THE MONKEES		

MONRO, Matt

Born Terrence Parsons on 12/1/32 in London; died of liver cancer on 2/7/85. Sang with Cyril Stapleton's Orchestra before going solo.

7/17/61	6	7		1 My Kind Of Girl..	18	Warwick 636
11/28/64	5	9		2 Walk Away	23	Liberty 55745
10/1/66	35	2		3 Born Free	126	Capitol 5623
				movie title song		
2/11/67	11	10		4 The Lady Smiles		Capitol 5823
				written by Bert Kaempfert		
8/5/67	22	6		5 What To Do?		Capitol 5947
				from the film Woman Times Seven		
7/20/68	15	10		6 The Music Played..		Capitol 2207
				written, arranged and conducted by George Martin		

MONTAN, Chris ✪

New Jersey native. Keyboardist/guitarist with Karla Bonoff from 1977-79.

11/8/80	37	11		1 Is This The Way Of Love		20th Century 2470
				CHRIS MONTAN with Lauren Wood		
2/14/81	17	12		2 Let's Pick It Up (Where We Left Off).....................	106	20th Century 2480

MONTENEGRO, Hugo

Born in 1925 and raised in New York City; died on 2/6/81. Conductor/composer. Composed and conducted the film soundtrack of Hurry Sundown.

1/27/68	1³	26		1 The Good, The Bad And The Ugly .... [I]	2¹	RCA 9423
6/22/68	6	15		2 Hang 'Em High .... [I]	82	RCA 9554
				above 2 are movie title songs		
6/21/69	29	4		3 Happy Together..	112	RCA 0160
				#1 Pop hit for The Turtles in 1967		

MONTEZ, Chris

Born Ezekiel Christopher Montanez on 1/17/43 in Los Angeles. Protege of Ritchie Valens.

12/18/65	2¹	19		1 Call Me	22	A&M 780
4/16/66	2⁴	16		2 The More I See You......................................	16	A&M 796
8/13/66	4	10		3 There Will Never Be Another You	33	A&M 810
11/26/66	12	6		4 Time After Time	36	A&M 822
3/18/67	25	5		5 Because Of You..	71	A&M 839
2/24/68	15	7		6 The Face I Love		A&M 906
9/14/68	38	2		7 Love Is Here To Stay		A&M 958
				#15 hit for Larry Clinton & His Orchestra in 1938		

MONTGOMERY, Wes

Born John Leslie Montgomery on 3/6/25 in Indianapolis; died on 6/15/68. Jazz guitarist. His brother Monk plays bass and brother Buddy plays piano.

11/25/67	10	13		1 Windy .... [I]	44	A&M 883
4/6/68	36	5		2 Wind Song .... [I]	103	A&M 916
7/6/68	34	4		3 Georgia On My Mind .... [I]	91	A&M 940
1/25/69	39	2		4 Where Have All The Flowers Gone?.............. [I]	119	A&M 1008

MOODY BLUES, The

Formed in Birmingham, England in 1964. Consisted of Denny Laine (guitar, vocals), Ray Thomas (flute, vocals), Mike Pinder (keyboards, vocals), Clint Warwick (bass) and Graeme Edge (drums). Laine and Warwick left in the summer of 1966, replaced by Justin Hayward (lead vocals, lead guitar) and John Lodge (vocals, bass). Laine joined Wings in 1971. Switzerland-born Patrick Moraz (former keyboardist of Yes) replaced Pinder in 1978; left group in early 1992.

11/4/72	37	3	●	1 Nights In White Satin...............................	2²	Deram 85023
				released from their 1968 album Days of Future Passed		
11/4/78	38	7		2 Driftwood...	59	London 273
8/22/81	16	14		3 The Voice...	15	Threshold 602
4/26/86	1²	22		4 Your Wildest Dreams	9	Threshold 883906
8/23/86	18	11		5 The Other Side Of Life	58	Polydor 885201
				also released on Polydor 885212 in 1986		

DEBUT DATE	PEAK POS	WKS CHR	GOLD	ARTIST — Record Title	POP POS	Label & Number
				MOODY BLUES, The — Cont'd		
6/11/88	**9**	19		6 I Know You're Out There Somewhere	30	Polydor 887600
10/29/88	**15**	14		7 No More Lies		Polydor 870990
7/20/91	**31**	8		8 Say It With Love		Polydor 867136
				MOORE, Bob		
				Born on 11/30/32 in Nashville. Top session bass player. Led the band on Roy Orbison's sessions for Monument Records. Also worked as sideman for Elvis Presley, Brenda Lee, Pat Boone and others.		
8/14/61	**1**[1]	15		Mexico ....[I]	7	Monument 446
				MOORE, Dorothy		
				Born in Jackson, Mississippi in 1946. Lead singer of The Poppies. Also a popular gospel artist.		
5/15/76	**14**	11		1 Misty Blue..	3	Malaco 1029
7/31/76	**46**	3		2 Funny How Time Slips Away	58	Malaco 1033
9/3/77	**24**	11		3 I Believe You	27	Malaco 1042
				MOORE, Gary		
				Guitarist from Belfast, Ireland. Brief member of Thin Lizzy.		
2/23/91	**43**	4		Still Got The Blues	97	Charisma 98854
				MOORE, Sally ○		
				Native of Rowlett, Texas.		
8/11/90	**42**	3		My Heart Has A Mind Of Its Own		Curb 76833
				MOORE, Tim		
				Pop singer/songwriter/guitraist/keyboardist from New York City.		
7/6/74	**41**	9		Second Avenue	58	Asylum 45208
				MORGAN, Jane		
				Born Jane Currier in Boston and raised in Florida. Popular singer in France before achieving U.S. fame via TV and nightclub entertaining.		
10/2/65	**25**	8		1 Side By Side..		Epic 9847
				#3 hit for Nick Lucas and Paul Whiteman in 1927 and for Kay Starr in 1953		
6/4/66	**16**	9		2 1-2-3	135	Epic 10032
				#2 Pop hit for Len Barry in 1965		
9/24/66	**9**	11		**3 Elusive Butterfly**		Epic 10058
				#5 Pop hit for Bob Lind in 1966		
12/31/66	**30**	9		4 Kiss Tomorrow Goodbye..	121	Epic 10113
10/14/67	**24**	5		5 Somebody Someplace		ABC 10969
				from the musical *Henry Sweet Henry*		
12/23/67	**27**	6		6 I Promise You		ABC 11002
3/30/68	**39**	2		7 A Child		ABC 11054
				MORGAN, Jaye P.		
				Born Mary Margaret Morgan in Mancos, Colorado on 12/3/31. Sang with Frank DeVol's band from 1950-53. Featured on many TV game shows from the 1950s-'70s. Sister of recording group The Morgan Brothers.		
1/3/70	**37**	2		1 Love Of A Gentle Man...		Beverly Hills 9337
3/21/70	**40**	1		2 What Are You Doing The Rest Of Your Life		Beverly Hills 9344
				from the film *The Happy Ending*		
				MORNING MIST		
				Singing/songwriting/production team of Terry Cashman and Tommy West. Also recorded as Cashman & West.		
7/31/71	**30**	5		California On My Mind	96	Event 206
				MORODER, Giorgio		
				Born on 4/26/40 in Ortisei, Italy. Electronic composer/conductor/producer for numerous soundtracks. Produced seven of Donna Summer's albums.		
2/24/79	**42**	4		Chase ....[I]	33	Casablanca 956
				from the film *Midnight Express*		
				MORRIS, Gary — see GAYLE, Crystal		
				MORRIS, Marlowe, Quintet		
3/31/62	**20**	1		Play The Thing ....[I]	95	Columbia 42218
				MORRISON, Van		
				Born George Ivan on 8/31/45 in Belfast, Ireland. Blue-eyed soul singer/songwriter. Leader of Them. Wrote the classic hit "Gloria." Inducted into the Rock and Roll Hall of Fame in 1993.		
4/9/88	**28**	9		1 Someone Like You		Mercury LP Cut
				from the album *Poetic Champions Compose* on Mercury 832585		
9/9/89	**12**	14		2 Have I Told You Lately		Mercury LP Cut
				from the album *Avalon Sunset* on Mercury 839262		
12/15/90	**34**	8		3 Real Real Gone		Mercury 879202

DEBUT DATE	PEAK POS	WKS CHR	GOLD	ARTIST — Record Title	POP POS	Label & Number
				MOTELS, The		
				Los Angeles-based quintet led by vocalist Martha Davis. Formed in Berkeley. To Los Angeles in the early '70s. Re-formed in 1978, signed to Capitol in 1979. Disbanded in 1987.		
7/24/82	**27**	10		1 Only The Lonely..	9	Capitol 5114
10/8/83	**18**	15		2 Suddenly Last Summer	9	Capitol 5271
8/31/85	**22**	7		3 Shame..	21	Capitol 5497
				MOTEN, Wendy		
				Memphis native. R&B singer. Starred in the off-Broadway play *Mama I Want To Sing*.		
1/16/93	**5**	26		**Come In Out Of The Rain**...................................	55	EMI 50417
				MOTTOLA, Tony ☉		
				Born on 4/18/18 in Kearney, New Jersey. Latin-style guitarist. Produced by Enoch Light.		
8/3/68	**22**	7		This Guy's In Love With You .... [I]		Project 3 1337
				#1 Pop hit for Herb Alpert in 1968		
				MOUTH & MACNEAL		
				Dutch duo: Willem Duyn and Maggie Macneal (real name: Sjoukje Van't Spijker).		
7/29/72	**37**	4	●	How Do You Do?	8	Philips 40715
				MOVING PICTURES		
				Australian six-man pop group led by Alex Smith (vocals). Member Garry Frost later formed the group 1927.		
9/30/89	**43**	8		What About Me......................................[R]	46	Geffen 22859
				originally hit the *Hot 100* on 9/18/82 (POS 29) on Network 69952		
				MULDAUR, Maria		
				Born Maria D'Amato on 9/12/43 in New York City. Member of Jim Kweskin's Jug Band with former husband Geoff Muldaur (divorced in 1972). Maria later became an Inspirational recording artist.		
2/16/74	**7**	18		1 Midnight At The Oasis	6	Reprise 1183
1/4/75	**4**	13		2 I'm A Woman..	12	Reprise 1319
5/10/75	**42**	4		3 Gringo En Mexico		Reprise 1331
5/8/76	**14**	10		4 Sad Eyes		Reprise 1352
				written by Neil Sedaka		
				MUNGO JERRY		
				British skiffle quartet: Ray Dorset (lead vocals), Colin Earl, Paul King and Mike Cole.		
8/15/70	**30**	5	●	In The Summertime	3	Janus 125
				MURDOCK, Shirley		
				Former gospel singer from Toledo. Discovered by Roger Troutman (aka Roger) who hired her as backup singer for his family funk group, Zapp.		
3/7/87	**21**	9		As We Lay..	23	Elektra 69518
				MURMAIDS, The		
				Los Angeles teenage trio: sisters Carol and Terry Fischer, with Sally Gordon.		
11/30/63	**2**[3]	13		**Popsicles And Icicles**..	3	Chattahoochee 628
				written by David Gates of Bread		
				MURPHEY, Michael Martin		
				Born Michael Martin Murphey in Dallas. Progressive country singer/songwriter. Toured as Travis Lewis of The Lewis & Clarke Expedition in 1967. Worked as a staff writer for Screen Gems. Lived in Austin from 1971-74; Colorado from 1974-79. Based in Taos, New Mexico since 1979.		
4/19/75	**1**[1]	15	●	1 Wildfire *	3	Epic 50084
8/30/75	**4**	12		2 Carolina In The Pines *	21	Epic 50131
				made the Country charts in 1985 (POS 9) on EMI America 8265		
7/17/82	**4**	22		3 What's Forever For	19	Liberty 1466
12/11/82	**28**	11		4 Still Taking Chances *	76	Liberty 1486
9/24/83	**16**	13		5 Don't Count The Rainy Days *	106	Liberty 1505
				*MICHAEL MURPHEY		
5/12/84	**12**	14		6 Disenchanted..		Liberty 1517
1/19/85	**39**	2		7 What She Wants		EMI America 8243
				MURPHY, Walter		
				Born in 1952 in New York City. Studied classical and jazz piano at Manhattan School of Music. Former arranger for Doc Severinsen and *The Tonight Show* orchestra.		
5/29/76	**13**	11	●	1 A Fifth Of Beethoven............................. [I]	**1**[1]	Private S. 45073
				WALTER MURPHY & THE BIG APPLE BAND		
				based on Beethoven's *Fifth Symphony*		
11/20/76	**12**	11		2 Flight '76 .... [I]	44	Private S. 45123
				based on Rymsky-Korsakov's *Flight Of The Bumble Bee*		
4/23/77	**36**	6		3 Rhapsody In Blue .... [I]	102	Private S. 45146
				#3 hit for Paul Whiteman with George Gershwin in 1924		

DEBUT DATE	PEAK POS	WKS CHR	GOLD	ARTIST — Record Title	POP POS	Label & Number
				MURPHY, Walter — Cont'd		
8/21/82	**26**	11		**4** Themes From E.T. (The Extra-Terrestrial) ....[I]	47	MCA 52099
				from the all-time #1 box-office hit *E.T.*		
★★**10**★★				**MURRAY, Anne**		
				Born Morna Anne Murray on 6/20/45 in Springhill, Nova Scotia. High school teacher for one year after college. With CBC-TV show *Sing Along Jubilee*. First recorded for ARC in 1969. Regular on Glen Campbell's *Goodtime Hour* TV series. Currently resides in Toronto.		
				1)*Snowbird* 2)*Broken Hearted Me* 3)*I Just Fall In Love Again* 4)*Shadows In The Moonlight* 5)*You Won't See Me*		
7/4/70	**1**⁶	17	●	**1 Snowbird**..	8	Capitol 2738
12/12/70	**21**	6		**2** Sing High - Sing Low	83	Capitol 2988
9/4/71	**7**	9		**3 Talk It Over In The Morning**	57	Capitol 3159
10/23/71	**13**	5		**4** I Say A Little Prayer/By The Time I Get To		
				Phoenix	81	Capitol 3200
				GLEN CAMPBELL/ANNE MURRAY		
1/29/72	**32**	5		**5** Cotton Jenny	71	Capitol 3260
				written by Gordon Lightfoot		
1/6/73	**1**²	15		**6 Danny's Song**	7	Capitol 3481
				written by Kenny Loggins for his nephew (also wrote #9)		
5/19/73	**2**²	10		**7 What About Me**	64	Capitol 3600
7/21/73	**10**	10		**8 Send A Little Love My Way**	72	Capitol 3648
				from the film *Oklahoma Crude*		
12/15/73	**1**¹	17		**9 Love Song**	12	Capitol 3776
4/20/74	**1**²	15		**10 You Won't See Me**	8	Capitol 3867
				written by John Lennon & Paul McCartney (also #12 & 25); flip side "He Thinks I Still Care" made the Country charts (POS 1²)		
11/30/74	**50**	2		**11** Just One Look	86	Capitol 3955
				flip side "Son Of A Rotten Gambler" made the Country charts (POS 5)		
1/11/75	**40**	6		**12** Day Tripper	59	Capitol 4000
10/18/75	**13**	12		**13** Sunday Sunrise	98	Capitol 4142
2/7/76	**6**	12		**14 The Call**	91	Capitol 4207
6/5/76	**44**	3		**15** Golden Oldie		Capitol 4265
9/11/76	**12**	14		**16** Things	89	Capitol 4329
3/5/77	**42**	2		**17** Sunday School To Broadway		Capitol 4375
1/21/78	**15**	14		**18** Walk Right Back	103	Capitol 4527
				#7 Pop hit for The Everly Brothers in 1961		
5/13/78	**3**	36	●	**19 You Needed Me**	1¹	Capitol 4574
1/27/79	**1**⁴	16		**20 I Just Fall In Love Again**	12	Capitol 4675
5/19/79	**1**³	24		**21 Shadows In The Moonlight**	25	Capitol 4716
9/22/79	**1**⁵	18		**22 Broken Hearted Me**	12	Capitol 4773
1/5/80	**1**¹	14		**23 Daydream Believer**	12	Capitol 4813
4/5/80	**8**	13		**24 Lucky Me**	42	Capitol 4848
6/21/80	**13**	14		**25** I'm Happy Just To Dance With You	64	Capitol 4878
9/13/80	**3**	19		**26 Could I Have This Dance**	33	Capitol 4920
				from the film *Urban Cowboy*		
4/11/81	**10**	14		**27 Blessed Are The Believers**	34	Capitol 4987
6/27/81	**33**	12		**28** We Don't Have To Hold Out		Capitol 5013
9/12/81	**14**	19		**29 It's All I Can Do**	53	Capitol 5023
1/23/82	**11**	15		**30** Another Sleepless Night	44	Capitol 5083
8/7/82	**26**	11		**31** Hey! Baby!		Capitol 5145
				#1 Pop hit for Bruce Channel in 1962		
12/18/82	**36**	10		**32** Somebody's Always Saying Goodbye		Capitol 5183
9/24/83	**11**	17		**33 A Little Good News**	74	Capitol 5264
2/4/84	**12**	17		**34** That's Not The Way (It's S'posed To Be)	106	Capitol 5305
4/28/84	**7**	19		**35 Just Another Woman In Love**		Capitol 5344
9/8/84	**10**	17		**36 Nobody Loves Me Like You Do**	103	Capitol 5401
				ANNE MURRAY with Dave Loggins		
1/26/85	**11**	13		**37** Time Don't Run Out On Me		Capitol 5436
5/18/85	**30**	5		**38** I Don't Think I'm Ready For You		Capitol 5472
				from the film *Stick*		
2/1/86	**7**	17		**39 Now And Forever (You And Me)**	92	Capitol 5547
5/24/86	**26**	8		**40** Who's Leaving Who		Capitol 5576
6/6/87	**33**	6		**41** Are You Still In Love With Me		Capitol 44005
				MUSICAL CAST OF TOYS — see WENDY & LISA		

DEBUT DATE	PEAK POS	WKS CHR	GOLD	ARTIST — Record Title	POP POS	Label & Number
				MYLES, Alannah		
				Rock singer born in Toronto and raised in Buckhorn, Canada.		
2/3/90	**7**	22	●	**Black Velvet**	**1**²	Atlantic 88742
				MYSTIC MOODS, The		
				Hollywood studio orchestra produced by Brad Miller.		
11/27/71	**21**	7		**1** Sensuous Woman .... [I]	106	Warner 7534
				melody is from Sergio Mendes' "The Look Of Love"		
4/21/73	**25**	6		**2** Cosmic Sea... [I]	83	Warner 7686
8/23/75	**35**	7		**3** Honey Trippin' .... [I]	98	Sound Bird 5002

N

DEBUT DATE	PEAK POS	WKS CHR	GOLD	ARTIST — Record Title	POP POS	Label & Number
				NAJEE		
				Jazz saxophonist. Born in Manhattan and raised in Queens, New York. Session work for George Benson, Kashif and Lillo Thomas.		
9/5/92	**48**	2		I Adore Mi Amor... [I]		EMI 50395
				NAKED EYES		
				English duo: Pete Byrne (vocals) and Rob Fisher (keyboards, synthesizer). Split in 1984. Fisher later in duo Climie Fisher.		
5/28/83	**31**	11		**1** Always Something There To Remind Me	8	EMI America 8155
8/13/83	**19**	16		**2** Promises, Promises	11	EMI America 8170
				NASH, Johnny		
				Born on 8/19/40 in Houston. Vocalist/guitarist/actor. Appeared on local TV from age 13. With Arthur Godfrey's TV and radio shows from 1956-63. In the film *Take A Giant Step* in 1959. Own JoDa label in 1965. Began recording in Jamaica in the late '60s.		
10/19/68	**20**	6		**1** Hold Me Tight...	5	JAD 207
12/13/69	**38**	3		**2** Cupid	39	JAD 220
				originally released as the B-side of "Hold Me Tight"		
9/9/72	**1**⁴	15	●	**3 I Can See Clearly Now**...	**1**⁴	Epic 10902
2/17/73	**6**	12		**4** Stir It Up	12	Epic 10949
				written by Bob Marley		
6/23/73	**34**	5		**5** My Merry-Go-Round	77	Epic 11003
9/29/73	**38**	6		**6** Ooh What A Feeling	103	Epic 11034
5/22/76	**34**	5		**7** (What A) Wonderful World	103	Epic 50219
				#12 Pop hit for Sam Cooke in 1960		
				NATASHA'S BROTHER AND RACHELE CAPPELLI ○		
				Robert Matarazzo from Pequannock, New Jersey. Brooklyn, New York-born Rachele Cappelli was a jingle singer and a session singer (worked with Lenny White, Carly Simon, Fatback and others).		
12/22/90	**12**	18		Always Come Back To You		Atlantic 87776
				NAUGHTON, David		
				Singer/dancer/actor. Born on 2/13/52. Starred in the 1981 film *An American Werewolf In London* and TV shows *Makin' It* and *My Sister Sam.*		
7/7/79	**48**	4	●	Makin' It	5	RSO 916
				from the film *Meatballs*		
				NAYLOR, Jerry		
				Born on 3/6/39 in Stephenville, Texas. Replaced Joe B. Mauldin in The Crickets in 1961.		
3/28/70	**5**	8		**But For Love**	69	Columbia 45106
				NEELY, Sam		
				Born on 8/22/48 in Cuero, Texas. Performing since age 11. Worked with local rock groups. Played clubs in Corpus Christi, especially at The Rogue, in the late '60s. Long residency at the Electric Eel in Corpus Christi in the late '70s.		
9/23/72	**24**	10		**1** Loving You Just Crossed My Mind	29	Capitol 3381
2/3/73	**9**	7		**2 Rosalie**	43	Capitol 3510
9/21/74	**15**	12		**3** You Can Have Her	34	A&M 1612
				NEIGHBORHOOD, The		
				Seven-man, two-woman vocal group.		
7/25/70	**30**	7		Big Yellow Taxi	29	Big Tree 102

DEBUT DATE	PEAK POS	WKS CHR	GOLD	ARTIST — Record Title	POP POS	Label & Number
				★★174★★ NELSON, Rick		
				Born Eric Hilliard Nelson on 5/8/40 in Teaneck, New Jersey. Died on 12/31/85 in a plane crash in DeKalb, Texas. Son of bandleader Ozzie Nelson and vocalist Harriet Hilliard. Rick and brother David appeared on Nelson's radio show from March 1949, later on TV, 1952-66. Formed own Stone Canyon Band in 1969. In films *Rio Bravo*, *Wackiest Ship In The Army* and *Love And Kisses*. Married Kristin Harmon (sister of actor Mark Harmon) in 1963; divorced in 1982. Their daughter Tracy is a film/TV actress. Their twin sons began recording as Nelson in 1990. Ricky was one of the first teen idols of the rock era. Inducted into the Rock and Roll Hall of Fame in 1987.		
				1)Garden Party 2)For You 3)Teen Age Idol		
8/18/62	2¹	10		1 **Teen Age Idol**	5	Imperial 5864
12/15/62	4	12		2 It's Up To You	6	Imperial 5901
1/11/64	1²	9		3 **For You**	6	Decca 31574
4/25/64	11	4		4 The Very Thought Of You	26	Decca 31612
				#1 hit for Ray Noble in 1934		
8/22/64	18	1		5 There's Nothing I Can Say	47	Decca 31656
10/25/69	27	3		6 She Belongs To Me *	33	Decca 32550
				written by Bob Dylan		
3/14/70	21	5		7 Easy To Be Free	48	Decca 32635
2/13/71	15	6		8 Life *	109	Decca 32779
8/12/72	1²	15	●	9 Garden Party *	6	Decca 32980
3/23/74	46	2		10 Windfall *		MCA 40187
				*RICK NELSON & The Stone Canyon Band		
4/14/79	29	8		11 Dream Lover		Epic 50674
				re-entered the Country charts in 1986 (POS 88) on Epic 06066		
				★★117★★ NELSON, Willie		
				Born on 4/30/33 in Ft. Worth, Texas; raised in Abbott, Texas. Prolific country singer/songwriter (writer of Patsy Cline's "Crazy" and Faron Young's "Hello Walls"). Played bass for Ray Price. Moved to Nashville in 1960. Moved back to Texas in 1970. Pioneered the "outlaw" country movement. Appeared in several films including *The Electric Horseman* (1979), *Honeysuckle Rose* (1980) and *Barbarosa* (1982). Won Grammy's Living Legends Award in 1989. Elected to the Country Music Hall Of Fame in 1993.		
				1)Always On My Mind 2)To All The Girls I've Loved Before 3)On The Road Again		
10/18/75	12	10		1 Blue Eyes Crying In The Rain	21	Columbia 10176
3/13/76	16	8		2 Good Hearted Woman *	25	RCA 10529
3/4/78	33	5		3 Mammas Don't Let Your Babies Grow Up To Be Cowboys * .	42	RCA 11198
				*WAYLON & WILLIE		
4/8/78	24	10		4 Georgia On My Mind	84	Columbia 10704
				written in 1930 by Hoagy Carmichael		
7/22/78	32	11		5 Blue Skies		Columbia 10784
				written in 1927 by Irving Berlin		
2/23/80	29	9		6 My Heroes Have Always Been Cowboys	44	Columbia 11186
				from the film *The Electric Horseman*		
9/27/80	7	18		7 **On The Road Again**	20	Columbia 11351
				from the film *Honeysuckle Rose*		
4/25/81	36	4		8 Mona Lisa		Columbia 02000
				#1 hit for Nat King Cole in 1950		
3/20/82	2⁷	26	▲	9 **Always On My Mind**	5	Columbia 02741
8/14/82	11	18		10 Let It Be Me	40	Columbia 03073
12/25/82	19	12		11 Everything's Beautiful (In It's Own Way)	102	Monument 03408
				DOLLY PARTON WILLIE NELSON		
5/14/83	21	12		12 Pancho And Lefty		Epic 03842
				WILLIE NELSON & MERLE HAGGARD		
10/15/83	31	5		13 Take It To The Limit	102	Columbia 04131
				WILLIE NELSON & WAYLON JENNINGS		
				#4 Pop hit for the Eagles in 1976		
3/10/84	3	19	▲	14 **To All The Girls I've Loved Before**	5	Columbia 04217
				JULIO IGLESIAS & WILLIE NELSON		
8/18/84	30	9		15 City Of New Orleans		Columbia 04568
				#18 Pop hit for Arlo Guthrie in 1972		
				NENA		
				Gabriele "Nena" Kerner (b: 3/26/60) with four-member backup group from Hagen, Germany.		
3/17/84	42	5	●	99 Luftballons .... [F]	2¹	Epic 04108
				NEON PHILHARMONIC, The		
				Chamber-sized orchestra of Nashville Symphony Orchestra musicians. Project headed by Tupper Saussy (composer) and Don Gant (vocals). Gant died on 3/6/87 (age 44).		
5/3/69	39	2		1 Morning Girl	17	Warner 7261
9/19/70	37	3		2 Flowers For Your Pillow		Warner 7419

DEBUT DATE	PEAK POS	WKS CHR	GOLD	ARTIST — Record Title	POP POS	Label & Number
				NERO, Peter		
				Born on 5/22/34 in Brooklyn. Pop-jazz-classical pianist. Won the 1961 Best New Artist Grammy Award.		
10/30/71	**6**	13		1 **Theme From "Summer Of '42"** .... [I]	21	Columbia 45399
				from the film *Summer Of '42*		
2/12/72	**30**	4		2 Brian's Song .... [I]	105	Columbia 45544
				TV film theme song; #56 Pop hit for Michel LeGrand in 1972		
4/5/75	**37**	6		3 Emmanuelle .... [I]		Arista 0112
				movie title song		
				NESMITH, Michael, & The First National Band		
				Born on 12/30/43 in Houston. Michael was a professional musician before joining The Monkees. Wrote Linda Ronstadt's hit "Different Drum." Formed own video production company, Pacific Arts, in 1977; produced films *Elephant Parts*, *Repo Man* and others.		
8/22/70	**6**	11		1 Joanne	21	RCA 0368
11/28/70	**7**	9		2 Silver Moon	42	RCA 0399
				NEVIL, Robbie		
				Pop singer/songwriter/guitarist from Los Angeles.		
1/24/87	**37**	4		C'est La Vie	2²	Manhattan 50047
★★145★★				**NEVILLE, Aaron**		
				Born on 1/24/41 in New Orleans. Member of the New Orleans family group The Neville Brothers. Brother Art was keyboardist of The Meters. Bassist/singer Ivan Neville is his son.		
				1)Don't Know Much 2)All My Life 3)Everybody Plays The Fool		
9/30/89	**1**⁵	26		1 **Don't Know Much** *	2²	Elektra 69261
1/20/90	**1**³	24		2 **All My Life** *	11	Elektra 64987
5/5/90	**5**	17		3 **When Something Is Wrong With My Baby** *	78	Elektra 64968
				*LINDA RONSTADT featuring Aaron Neville		
6/9/90	**31**	9		4 Bird On A Wire		A&M 1499
				THE NEVILLE BROTHERS (Aaron Neville, vocal); movie title song		
7/13/91	**1**¹	31		5 **Everybody Plays The Fool**	8	A&M 1563
11/23/91	**6**	19		6 Somewhere, Somebody		A&M 1577
3/28/92	**38**	7		7 Close Your Eyes		A&M LP Cut
				AARON NEVILLE with LINDA RONSTADT		
				above 3 from the Aaron Neville album *Warm Your Heart* on A&M 5354;		
				above 3 co-produced by Linda Ronstadt		
5/1/93	**4**	22↑		8 Don't Take Away My Heaven	56	A&M 0240
				NEWBURY, Mickey		
				Born Milton S. Newbury, Jr. on 5/19/40 in Houston. Moved to Nashville in 1963, worked as staff writer for Acuff-Rose. Wrote "Just Dropped In (To See What Condition My Condition Was In)."		
11/6/71	**9**	12		1 **An American Trilogy**	26	Elektra 45750
				Dixie/Battle Hymn Of The Republic/All My Trials;		
				re-entered the Country charts in 1988 on Airborne 10005		
7/7/73	**16**	7		2 Sunshine	87	Elektra 45853
				NEW CHRISTY MINSTRELS, The		
				Folk/balladeer troupe named after the Christy Minstrels (formed in 1842 by Edwin "Pop" Christy). Group founded and led by Randy Sparks — Barry McGuire, lead singer. Kenny Rogers was briefly a member in 1966.		
7/20/63	**3**	9		1 **Green, Green**	14	Columbia 42805
4/25/64	**4**	12		2 Today	17	Columbia 43000
				from the film *Advance To The Rear*		
4/24/65	**20**	4		3 Chim, Chim, Cheree	81	Columbia 43215
				from the film *Mary Poppins*		
4/17/71	**36**	3		4 Brother		Gregar 0106
				NEW COLONY SIX, The		
				Soft-rock group from Chicago: Patrick McBride, Ronnie Rice, Gerry Van Kollenburg, Les Kummel, Chuck Jobes and William Herman. Ray Graffia joined in 1969. Kummel died on 12/18/78 (age 33).		
2/22/69	**17**	8		1 Things I'd Like To Say	16	Mercury 72858
6/7/69	**36**	4		2 I Could Never Lie To You	50	Mercury 72920
9/20/69	**32**	4		3 I Want You To Know	65	Mercury 72961
1/31/70	**37**	2		4 Barbara, I Love You	78	Mercury 73004
9/25/71	**31**	4		5 Roll On	56	Sunlight 1001
				NEW ESTABLISHMENT, The		
				Four-man, one-woman vocal group.		
10/11/69	**16**	6		1 (One Of These Days) Sunday's Gonna' Come On Tuesday	92	Colgems 5006
3/7/70	**26**	5		2 I'll Build A Bridge		Colgems 5009

DEBUT DATE	PEAK POS	WKS CHR	G O L D	ARTIST — Record Title	POP POS	Label & Number
				NEW ESTABLISHMENT, The — Cont'd		
2/6/71	**40**	2		3 Love Will Keep Us Going...........................		RCA 0394
				NEW KIDS ON THE BLOCK		
				Boston teen vocal quintet: Joe McIntyre (b: 12/31/72), Donny Wahlberg (b: 8/17/69), Danny Wood (b: 5/14/69), and brothers Jordan (b: 5/17/70) and Jon Knight (b: 11/29/68). Formed in the summer of 1984 by New Edition's founder/producer, Maurice Starr. Also see Tommy Page.		
5/6/89	**3**	21	●	1 I'll Be Loving You (Forever).......................	1[1]	Columbia 68671
10/21/89	**12**	15		2 Didn't I (Blow Your Mind).......................	8	Columbia 68960
				flip side "Hangin' Tough" made the *Hot 100* (POS 1[1])		
12/16/89	**27**	7	●	3 This One's For The Children ....[X]	7	Columbia 73064
				NEWLEY, Anthony		
				Born on 9/24/31 in London. Actor/singer/composer/comedian. In films *Oliver Twist, Doctor Doolittle, Fire Down Below, The Garbage Pail Kids Movie* and others.		
7/24/76	**12**	9		Teach The Children.................................		United Art. 825
				NEWMAN, Randy		
				Born on 11/28/43 in New Orleans. Singer/composer/pianist. Nephew of composers Alfred, Emil and Lionel Newman. Scored the films *Ragtime, The Natural* and *Avalon*.		
11/26/77	**25**	13	●	1 Short People ....[N]	2[3]	Warner 8492
2/19/83	**36**	4		2 The Blues..	51	Warner 29803
				RANDY NEWMAN AND PAUL SIMON		
				NEW MARKETTS — see MARKETTS		
★★195★★				**NEW SEEKERS, The**		
				British-Australian group formed by former Seekers' member Keith Potger after disbandment of The Seekers in 1969. Consisted of Eve Graham, Lyn Paul, Peter Doyle, Marty Kristian and Paul Layton.		
				1)Look What They've Done To My Song Ma 2)Beautiful People 3)Nickel Song		
9/5/70	**4**	11		1 Look What They've Done To My Song Ma	14	Elektra 45699
1/2/71	**11**	10		2 Beautiful People/	67	
1/2/71	**33**	3		3 When There's No Love Left		Elektra 45710
3/6/71	**13**	6		4 Nickel Song	81	Elektra 45719
				all of above (except #3) written by Melanie		
12/4/71	**27**	10	●	5 I'd Like To Teach The World To Sing (In Perfect Harmony)	7	Elektra 45762
4/15/72	**15**	7		6 Beg, Steal Or Borrow.........................	81	Elektra 45780
7/1/72	**27**	8		7 Circles..	87	Elektra 45787
9/30/72	**24**	6		8 Dance, Dance, Dance	84	Elektra 45805
				written by Neil Young		
12/23/72	**21**	6		9 Come Softly To Me	95	Verve 10698
4/7/73	**34**	4		10 Pinball Wizard/See Me, Feel Me	29	Verve 10709
				from the rock opera *Tommy*		
7/28/73	**16**	8		11 The Greatest Song I've Ever Heard		MGM 14586
1/12/74	**18**	9	✓	12 You Won't Find Another Fool Like Me		MGM 14691
★★140★★				**NEWTON, Juice**		
				Born Judy Kay Newton on 2/18/52 in New Jersey; raised in Virginia Beach. Pop/country singer. Performed folk music from age 13. Moved to Los Angeles with own Silver Spur band in 1974; recorded for RCA in 1975. Group disbanded in 1978. Juice is an accomplished equestrian.		
				1)Angel Of The Morning 2)Break It To Me Gently 3)The Sweetest Thing (I've Ever Known)		
2/28/81	**1**[3]	16	●	1 Angel Of The Morning........................	4	Capitol 4976
6/13/81	**2**[3]	22	●	2 Queen Of Hearts	2[2]	Capitol 4997
10/24/81	**1**[1]	24		3 The Sweetest Thing (I've Ever Known)	7	Capitol 5046
5/15/82	**4**	20		4 Love's Been A Little Bit Hard On Me	7	Capitol 5120
8/21/82	**1**[2]	23		5 Break It To Me Gently	11	Capitol 5148
12/4/82	**4**	19		6 Heart Of The Night.........................	25	Capitol 5192
8/27/83	**14**	10		7 Tell Her No.................................	27	Capitol 5265
				flip side "Stranger At My Door" made the Country charts (POS 45)		
6/9/84	**7**	13		8 A Little Love................................	44	RCA 13823
★★73★★				**NEWTON, Wayne**		
				Born on 4/3/42 in Roanoke, Virginia. Singer/multi-instrumentalist. Top Las Vegas entertainer. Began singing career with regular appearances on Jackie Gleason's TV variety show in 1962. Appeared in the 1990 film *The Adventures Of Ford Fairlane*.		
				1)Daddy Don't You Walk So Fast 2)Danke Schoen 3)Can't You Hear The Song?		
				4)Red Roses For A Blue Lady 5)Summer Wind		
8/3/63	**3**	9		1 Danke Schoen	13	Capitol 4989

DEBUT DATE	PEAK POS	WKS CHR	G O L D	ARTIST — Record Title	POP POS	Label & Number
				NEWTON, Wayne — Cont'd		
11/23/63	**18**	3		2 Shirl Girl	58	Capitol 5058
				above 2 with Wayne's brother, Jerry		
3/13/65	**4**	7		**3 Red Roses For A Blue Lady**	23	Capitol 5366
5/29/65	**17**	5		4 I'll Be With You In Apple Blossom Time	52	Capitol 5419
				#2 hit for Charles Harrison in 1920		
7/31/65	**9**	8		**5 Summer Wind**	78	Capitol 5470
10/9/65	**15**	7		6 Remember When	69	Capitol 5514
12/25/65	**23**	6		7 Some Sunday Morning	123	Capitol 5553
5/28/66	**23**	7		8 Stagecoach To Cheyenne	113	Capitol 5643
				from the film Stagecoach		
10/15/66	**22**	8		9 Games That Lovers Play	86	Capitol 5754
3/25/67	**23**	5		10 Sunny Day Girl.......................................		Capitol 5842
7/29/67	**20**	6		11 Summer Colors		Capitol 5954
10/7/67	**26**	7		12 Through The Eyes Of Love		Capitol 5993
11/4/67	**33**	5		13 Love Of The Common People	106	Capitol 2016
				above 2 arranged by Leon Russell		
2/17/68	**26**	6	✓	14 All The Time...		MGM 13891
				#1 Country hit for Jack Greene in 1967		
6/29/68	**14**	8		15 Dreams Of The Everyday Housewife	60	MGM 13955
12/14/68	**28**	7	✓	16 Husbands And Wives		MGM 14014
				#26 Pop hit for Roger Miller in 1966		
10/18/69	**28**	2		17 (I Guess) The Lord Must Be In New York City		MGM 14083
				#34 Pop hit for Nilsson in 1969		
5/6/72	**3**	15	●	18 Daddy Don't You Walk So Fast	4	Chelsea 0100
9/23/72	**3**	10		19 Can't You Hear The Song?.......................	48	Chelsea 0105
9/29/73	**26**	7		20 Pour Me A Little More Wine		Chelsea 0091
11/16/74	**47**	3		21 Lady Lay	101	Chelsea 3003
4/24/76	**11**	13		22 The Hungry Years	82	Chelsea 3041
				written by Neil Sedaka		
11/24/79	**45**	3		23 I Apologize		Aries II 107
2/16/80	**40**	5		24 Years	35	Aries II 108
★★14★★				**NEWTON-JOHN, Olivia**		

Born on 9/26/48 in Cambridge, England. To Australia in 1953. At age 16, won talent contest trip to England; sang with Pat Carroll as Pat & Olivia. With the group Toomorrow, in a British film of the same name. Granddaughter of Nobel Prize-winning German physicist Max Born. In films *Grease, Xanadu* and *Two Of A Kind.* Married actor Matt Lattanzi in 1984. Opened own chain of clothing boutiques (Koala Blue) in 1984. Battled breast cancer in 1992.

1)Magic 2)I Honestly Love You 3)Something Better To Do 4)If Not For You 5)Please Mr. Please

DEBUT DATE	PEAK POS	WKS CHR	G O L D	ARTIST — Record Title	POP POS	Label & Number
6/19/71	**1**³	15		**1 If Not For You**...................................	25	Uni 55281
				written by Bob Dylan		
10/23/71	**34**	5		2 Banks Of The Ohio	94	Uni 55304
3/4/72	**34**	3		3 What Is Life		Uni 55317
				#10 Pop hit for George Harrison in 1971		
9/8/73	**3**	25	●	**4 Let Me Be There**	6	MCA 40101
4/13/74	**2**²	17	●	**5 If You Love Me (Let Me Know)**	5	MCA 40209
8/3/74	**1**³	17	●	**6 I Honestly Love You**	1²	MCA 40280
2/1/75	**1**¹	13	●	**7 Have You Never Been Mellow**	1¹	MCA 40349
6/7/75	**1**³	13	●	**8 Please Mr. Please**	3	MCA 40418
9/27/75	**1**³	11		**9 Something Better To Do**	13	MCA 40459
12/6/75	**1**²	14		10 Let It Shine/	30	
		14		11 He Ain't Heavy...He's My Brother	flip	MCA 40495
3/13/76	**1**¹	10		**12 Come On Over**....................................	23	MCA 40525
				written by Barry and Robin Gibb		
8/7/76	**1**¹	12		**13 Don't Stop Believin'**	33	MCA 40600
10/30/76	**6**	13		**14 Every Face Tells A Story**	55	MCA 40642
1/29/77	**1**²	17		**15 Sam**	20	MCA 40670
6/18/77	**20**	9		16 Making A Good Thing Better....................	87	MCA 40737
12/3/77	**49**	1	●	17 I Honestly Love You ....[R]	48	MCA 40811
4/22/78	**23**	13	▲	18 You're The One That I Want	1¹	RSO 891
				JOHN TRAVOLTA AND OLIVIA NEWTON-JOHN		
7/15/78	**7**	16	●	**19 Hopelessly Devoted To You**	3	RSO 903
8/12/78	**21**	11	●	20 Summer Nights	5	RSO 906
				JOHN TRAVOLTA, OLIVIA NEWTON-JOHN & CAST		
				above 3 from the film Grease		
12/2/78	**4**	21	●	**21 A Little More Love**	3	MCA 40975

DEBUT DATE	PEAK POS	WKS CHR	GOLD	ARTIST — Record Title	POP POS	Label & Number
				NEWTON-JOHN, Olivia — Cont'd		
4/28/79	**4**	14		**22 Deeper Than The Night**	11	MCA 41009
8/4/79	**25**	12		**23 Dancin' 'Round And 'Round**	82	MCA 41074
				flip side "Totally Hot" made the *Hot 100* (POS 52)		
4/5/80	**8**	13		**24 I Can't Help It**	12	RSO 1026
				ANDY GIBB AND OLIVIA NEWTON-JOHN		
5/31/80	**1**5	20	●	**25 Magic**	**1**4	MCA 41247
8/23/80	**2**2	22		**26 Xanadu**	8	MCA 41285
				OLIVIA NEWTON-JOHN/ELECTRIC LIGHT ORCHESTRA		
10/25/80	**4**	20		**27 Suddenly**	20	MCA 51007
				OLIVIA NEWTON-JOHN AND CLIFF RICHARD		
				above 3 from the film *Xanadu*		
10/31/81	**29**	13	▲	**28 Physical**	**1**10	MCA 51182
2/20/82	**6**	17	●	**29 Make A Move On Me**	5	MCA 52000
11/26/83	**3**	17		**30 Take A Chance**		MCA 52284
				OLIVIA NEWTON-JOHN AND JOHN TRAVOLTA		
				from the film *Two Of A Kind*; flip side "Twist Of Fate" made the *Hot 100* (POS 5)		
10/19/85	**20**	9		**31 Soul Kiss**	20	MCA 52686
5/31/86	**6**	16		**32 The Best Of Me**	80	Atlantic 89420
				DAVID FOSTER AND OLIVIA NEWTON-JOHN		
8/20/88	**33**	6		**33 The Rumour**	62	MCA 53294
				written and produced by Elton John		
1/6/90	**32**	10		**34 Reach Out For Me**		Geffen 22736
				#20 Pop hit for Dionne Warwick in 1964		
8/22/92	**20**	12		**35 Deeper Than A River**		Geffen LP Cut
				from the album *Back To Basics - The Essential Collection* on Geffen 24470		
				NEW VAUDEVILLE BAND, The		
				Creation of British composer/record producer Geoff Stephens (b: 10/1/34, London).		
11/12/66	**1**4	13	●	**1 Winchester Cathedral**	**1**3	Fontana 1562
2/18/67	**16**	8		**2 Peek-A-Boo**	72	Fontana 1573
6/3/67	**24**	9		**3 Finchley Central**	102	Fontana 1589
				NEW YORK CITY		
				New York City R&B quartet: Tim McQueen, John Brown, Ed Shell and Claude Johnston. First recorded for Buddah as Triboro Exchange. Name changed in 1972.		
4/14/73	**8**	10		**I'm Doin' Fine Now**	17	Chelsea 0113
				NICHOLAS, Paul		
				Born Paul Beuselinck on 12/3/45 in Peterborough, England. British theater/film actor. Played Billy Shears' brother in the 1978 film *Sgt. Pepper's Lonely Hearts Club Band*.		
9/10/77	**23**	12	●	**Heaven On The 7th Floor**	6	RSO 878
				NICKS, Stevie		
				Born Stephanie Nicks on 5/26/48 in Phoenix; raised in California. Became vocalist of Bay-area group Fritz and subsequently met guitarist Lindsey Buckingham. Teamed up and recorded album *Buckingham-Nicks* in 1973. Vocalist with Fleetwood Mac since January 1975. Quit touring with band after 1990.		
11/7/81	**10**	19		**1 Leather And Lace**	6	Modern 7341
				STEVIE NICKS with DON HENLEY		
7/3/82	**36**	5		**2 After The Glitter Fades**	32	Modern 7405
2/11/84	**39**	3		**3 Nightbird**	33	Modern 99799
				STEVIE NICKS with Sandy Stewart		
12/7/85	**14**	13		**4 Talk To Me**	4	Modern 99582
5/31/86	**31**	6		**5 Has Anyone Ever Written Anything For You**	60	Modern 99532
5/27/89	**16**	15		**6 Rooms On Fire**	16	Modern 99216
				NIELSEN/PEARSON		
				Sacramento pop quartet fronted by lead vocalists/guitarists Reed Nielsen and Mark Pearson.		
11/15/80	**35**	4		**1 If You Should Sail**	38	Capitol 4910
8/29/81	**31**	5		**2 The Sun Ain't Gonna Shine Anymore**	56	Capitol 5032
				NIGHT — see THOMPSON, Chris		
				NIGHTINGALE, Maxine		
				Born on 11/2/52 in Wembly, England. First recorded in 1968. In productions of *Hair*, *Jesus Christ Superstar*, *Godspell* and *Savages* in the early '70s.		
3/6/76	**5**	13	●	**1 Right Back Where We Started From**	**2**2	United Art. 752
7/17/76	**22**	8		**2 Gotta Be The One**	53	United Art. 820
5/12/79	**1**7	26	●	**3 Lead Me On**	5	Windsong 11530

DEBUT DATE	PEAK POS	WKS CHR	GOLD	ARTIST — Record Title	POP POS	Label & Number
				NIKKI		
				Twenty-one-year-old American male singer/multi-instrumentalist born in Okinawa, Japan and raised in Dayton, Ohio. Backing member of the soul-funk group Sun. Jingle writer of TV commercials.		
6/16/90	**11**	16		Notice Me	21	Geffen 19946
				NILSSON		
				Born Harry Edward Nelson, III on 6/15/41 in Brooklyn. Wrote Three Dog Night's hit "One"; scored the film *Skidoo* and TV's *The Courtship Of Eddie's Father*. Close friend of John Lennon and Ringo Starr.		
				1)Without You 2)Everybody's Talkin' 3)Me And My Arrow		
8/30/69	**2**²	12		**1 Everybody's Talkin'**..	6	RCA 0161
				theme song from the film *Midnight Cowboy*		
11/1/69	**7**	7		**2 I Guess The Lord Must Be In New York City**	34	RCA 0261
3/14/70	**40**	1		3 Waiting		RCA 0310
				from the film *Jenny*		
3/13/71	**3**	15		**4 Me And My Arrow**..	34	RCA 0443
12/25/71	**1**⁵	16	●	**5 Without You**	1⁴	RCA 0604
				written by Badfinger's Pete Ham and Tom Evans		
12/30/72	**21**	6		6 Remember (Christmas)..	53	RCA 0855
8/18/73	**35**	6		7 As Time Goes By	86	RCA 0039
5/25/74	**37**	4		8 Daybreak	39	RCA 0246
				from the film *Son of Dracula*		
				NITE-LITERS, The		
				R&B band formed in Louisville in 1963 by Harvey Fuqua and Tony Churchill. Expanded to 17 members with two vocal groups and band. Renamed New Birth, Inc., with The Nite-Liters making up the instrumental section.		
8/21/71	**15**	9		K-Jee .... [I]	39	RCA 0461
				NITTY GRITTY DIRT BAND		
				Country-folk-rock group from Long Beach, California. Led by Jeff Hanna (b: 7/11/47; vocals, guitar) and John McEuen (b: 12/19/45; banjo, mandolin). Changed name to Dirt Band in 1976 when Hanna left the group.		
11/7/70	**10**	18		**1 Mr. Bojangles**..	9	Liberty 56197
				prologue: Uncle Charlie And His Dog Teddy		
7/12/75	**30**	7		2 (All I Have To Do Is) Dream	66	United Art. 655
				THE DIRT BAND:		
12/15/79	**16**	12		**3 An American Dream**	13	United Art. 1330
				Linda Ronstadt (harmony vocal)		
7/5/80	**12**	12		4 Make A Little Magic	25	United Art. 1356
				Nicolette Larson (backing vocal)		
				NOBLE, Nick		
				Born Nicholas Valkan on 6/21/36 in Chicago. Attended Loyola University.		
1/6/68	**38**	3		1 You're The Right One For Me		Date 1582
9/16/78	**43**	5		2 Stay With Me		Churchill 7713
				NOLAN, Kenny		
				Los Angeles-based singer/songwriter. Wrote "My Eyes Adored You," "Lady Marmalade" and "Get Dancin'." Fronted studio group The Eleventh Hour.		
12/4/76	**4**	18	●	**1 I Like Dreamin'**...	3	20th Century 2287
4/9/77	**3**	18		**2 Love's Grown Deep**...	20	20th Century 2331
9/24/77	**42**	10		3 My Eyes Get Blurry	97	20th Century 2352
2/16/80	**36**	7		4 Us And Love (We Go Together)...................................	44	Casablanca 2234
				NOONE, Peter ○		
				Born on 11/5/47 in Manchester, England. Lead singer of Herman's Hermits.		
8/17/74	**22**	9		1 Meet Me On The Corner Down At Joe's Cafe......................	101	Casablanca 0106
3/18/89	**19**	9		2 I'm Into Something Good..		Cypress 0019
				from the film *The Naked Gun*; #13 Pop hit in 1964 for Noone's group, Herman's Hermits		
				NORMAN, Chris — see QUATRO, Suzi		
				NUNN, Terri — see CARRACK, Paul		
				NU SHOOZ		
				Portland, Oregon group centered around husband-and-wife team of guitarist/songwriter John Smith and lead singer Valerie Day.		
6/21/86	**38**	2	●	I Can't Wait...	3	Atlantic 89446

DEBUT DATE	PEAK POS	WKS CHR	GOLD	ARTIST — Record Title	POP POS	Label & Number
				NYLONS, The		
				Canadian a cappella quartet formed in 1979: Marc Connors, Paul Cooper, Claude Morrison and Arnold Robinson. Connors died on 3/25/91 (age 41).		
5/16/87	**10**	16		1 **Kiss Him Goodbye**	12	Open Air 0022
8/22/87	**16**	11		2 Happy Together	75	Open Air 0024
				NYRO, Laura		
				Born Laura Nigro on 10/18/47 in the Bronx, New York. White soul-gospel singer/songwriter. Wrote "Stoned Soul Picnic," "Wedding Bell Blues," "And When I Die" and "Stoney End."		
10/3/70	**30**	4		Up On The Roof	92	Columbia 45230

O

DEBUT DATE	PEAK POS	WKS CHR	GOLD	ARTIST — Record Title	POP POS	Label & Number
				OAK RIDGE BOYS		
				Country-pop vocal group formed as a gospel quartet in 1940 in Oak Ridge, Tennessee. Disbanded after World War II; re-formed in 1957. Many personnel changes. Lineup since early 1970s: Duane Allen (lead), Joe Bonsall (tenor), Richard Sterban (bass) and Bill Golden (baritone; left for a solo career in 1987, replaced by the group's guitarist, Steve Sanders).		
5/19/79	**29**	9		1 Sail Away		ABC 12463
9/29/79	**45**	5		2 Dream On		MCA 41078
				#32 Pop hit for The Righteous Brothers in 1974		
9/6/80	**49**	4		3 Heart Of Mine	105	MCA 41280
5/30/81	**8**	16	▲	4 **Elvira**	5	MCA 51084
9/19/81	**17**	17		5 Fancy Free	104	MCA 51169
1/30/82	**19**	13		6 Bobbie Sue	12	MCA 51231
				OCASEK, Ric		
				Born Richard Otcasek on 3/23/49 in Baltimore. Lead singer/guitarist/songwriter of The Cars. Appeared in the 1987 film *Made In Heaven*. Married supermodel/actress Paulina Porizkova in 1989. His son Christopher Otcasek is leader of Glamour Camp.		
10/18/86	**8**	17		**Emotion In Motion**	15	Geffen 28617
				OCEAN		
				Canadian pop quintet: Janice Morgan (vocals), David Tamblyn, Greg Brown, Jeff Jones and Charles Slater.		
3/20/71	**4**	12	●	1 **Put Your Hand In The Hand**	2¹	Kama Sutra 519
8/21/71	**37**	3		2 We Got A Dream	82	Kama Sutra 529
9/9/72	**30**	5		3 One More Chance	76	Kama Sutra 556
★★**100**★★				**OCEAN, Billy**		
				Born Leslie Sebastian Charles on 1/21/50 in Trinidad. Raised in England, worked as a tailor. Did session work in London. Moved to the U.S. in the late '70s.		
				1)Love Is Forever 2)Suddenly 3)There'll Be Sad Songs (To Make You Cry)		
9/8/84	**7**	20	●	1 **Caribbean Queen (No More Love On The Run)**	1²	Jive 9199
3/30/85	**1²**	23		2 **Suddenly**	4	Jive 9323
7/13/85	**5**	15		3 **Mystery Lady**	24	Jive 9374
11/2/85	**24**	5		4 The Long And Winding Road		Jive 9421
				#1 Pop hit for The Beatles in 1970		
12/14/85	**2²**	19		5 **When The Going Gets Tough, The Tough Get Going**	2¹	Jive 9432
				from the film *The Jewel of the Nile*		
4/19/86	**1¹**	20		6 **There'll Be Sad Songs (To Make You Cry)**	1¹	Jive 9465
8/2/86	**5**	16		7 **Love Zone**	10	Jive 9510
11/1/86	**1³**	22		8 **Love Is Forever**	16	Jive 9540
2/20/88	**5**	21		9 **Get Outta My Dreams, Get Into My Car**	1²	Jive 9678
6/4/88	**2¹**	22		10 **The Colour Of Love**	17	Jive 9707
6/26/93	**43**	3		11 **Everything's So Different Without You**		Jive 42135
				O'CONNOR, Carroll, And Jean Stapleton		
				Archie and Edith Bunker of TV's *All In The Family*. Veteran actors, both born in New York City — Carroll on 8/2/24 and Jean (real name: Jeanne Murray) on 1/19/23.		
12/25/71	**30**	7		Those Were The Days [N]	43	Atlantic 2847
				All In The Family TV theme		

DEBUT DATE	PEAK POS	WKS CHR	G O L D	ARTIST — Record Title	POP POS	Label & Number
				O'CONNOR, Sinead		
				Pronounced: shin-NAYD. Born on 12/8/67 in Dublin, Ireland. Female singer/songwriter.		
3/31/90	2³	19	▲	**Nothing Compares 2 U**	1⁴	Ensign 23488
				written by Prince		
				O'DAY, Alan		
				Born on 10/3/40 in Hollywood. Singer/songwriter/pianist. Wrote Helen Reddy's #1 hit "Angie Baby" and the Righteous Brothers' "Rock And Roll Heaven."		
5/28/77	**31**	12	●	Undercover Angel..	1¹	Pacific 001
				ODYSSEY		
				New York soul-disco trio: Manila-born Tony Reynolds, and sisters Lillian and Louise Lopez, originally from the Virgin Islands.		
1/14/78	**28**	7		Native New Yorker..	21	RCA 11129
				O'HARA, Ronnie & Natalie ☉		
				Brother-and-sister Ronnie (b: 12/17/43) and Natalie (b: 6/23/46) Pollock from Winnipeg, Canada. Discovered by Dionne Warwick in 1968. First single released on Capitol 2391 (produced by Dionne Warwick) in 1969. Own TV show in Winnipeg, *Pollock & Pollock Gossip Show*, 1985-89.		
10/26/74	**23**	12		1 You Foxy Thing, I Love You		Legacy 103
5/3/75	**28**	10		2 Smile On Me...		Legacy 104
9/6/75	**35**	8		3 Dance Music..		Legacy 105
				OHTA-SAN ☉		
				Ukelele player Herb Ohta.		
5/4/74	**26**	10		1 Song For Anna (Chanson D'Anna) .... [I]	104	A&M 1505
1/25/75	**43**	6		2 One Day Of Love (Un Jour L'Amour)............................... [I]		A&M 1647
				O'JAYS, The		
				R&B group from Canton, Ohio. 1978 lineup: Eddie Levert, Walter Williams and Sammy Strain.		
6/17/78	**21**	13	●	Use Ta Be My Girl	4	Phil. Int. 3642
				O'KEEFE, Danny		
				Singer/songwriter born in Spokane, Washington.		
9/2/72	**5**	14		**Good Time Charlie's Got The Blues**	9	Signpost 70006
				OLDFIELD, Mike		
				Born on 5/15/53 in Reading, England. Classical-rock, multi-instrumentalist/composer.		
3/23/74	**15**	11		Tubular Bells .... [I]	7	Virgin 55100
				theme from the film *The Exorcist*		
				OLIVER		
				Born William Oliver Swofford on 2/22/45 in North Wilkesboro, North Carolina.		
5/24/69	**3**	13		1 **Good Morning Starshine**	3	Jubilee 5659
				from the Broadway musical *Hair*		
8/16/69	**1⁴**	14	●	2 **Jean**...	2²	Crewe 334
				from the film *The Prime Of Miss Jean Brodie*		
12/6/69	**14**	9		3 Sunday Mornin'...	35	Crewe 337
4/18/70	**26**	5		4 Angelica	97	Crewe 341
7/25/70	**24**	4	✓	5 I Can Remember...		Crewe 346
4/3/71	**38**	2		6 Early Mornin' Rain...	124	United Art. 50762
				written by Gordon Lightfoot; #91 Pop hit for Peter, Paul & Mary in 1965		
				OLIVOR, Jane		
				Lyrical stylist from New York City.		
5/13/78	**21**	9		1 He's So Fine	77	Columbia 10724
2/24/79	**15**	12		2 The Last Time I Felt Like This		Columbia 10902
				JOHNNY MATHIS/JANE OLIVOR		
				from the film *Same Time Next Year*		
				OLSSON, Nigel		
				Born on 2/10/49 in Merseyside, England. Drummer for Elton John's band from 1971-76.		
1/13/79	**8**	15		1 **Dancin' Shoes**	18	Bang 740
4/28/79	**9**	10		2 **Little Bit Of Soap**	34	Bang 4800
				ONE G PLUS THREE ☉		
				Pop quartet based in Los Angeles.		
11/7/70	**38**	2		Poquito Soul .... [I]	122	Paramount 0054
				originally released on Gordo 705 in 1970		

DEBUT DATE	PEAK POS	WKS CHR	G O L D	ARTIST — Record Title	POP POS	Label & Number
				ONE 2 MANY		
				Norwegian trio: keyboardist Dag Kolsrud, guitarist Jan Gisle Ytterdal and female vocalist Camilla Griehsel. Kolsrud was a-ha's world tour musical director.		
4/15/89	**18**	12		1 Downtown..	37	A&M 1272
8/12/89	**49**	2		2 Writing On The Wall..		A&M LP Cut
				from the album *Mirror* on A&M 5237		
				ORBISON, Roy		
				Born on 4/23/36 in Vernon, Texas. Had own band, the Wink Westerners, in 1952. Attended North Texas University with Pat Boone. First recorded for Je-Wel in early 1956 as leader of The Teen Kings. Toured with Sun Records shows to 1958. Toured with The Beatles in 1963. Wife Claudette killed in a motorcycle accident on 6/7/66; two sons died in a fire in 1968. Resurgence in career beginning in 1985. Inducted into the Rock and Roll Hall of Fame in 1987. Member of the supergroup Traveling Wilburys in 1988. Died of a heart attack on 12/6/88 in Madison, Tennessee.		
				1)*You Got It* 2)*In Dreams* 3)*Falling*		
3/30/63	**3**	6		1 In Dreams	7	Monument 806
6/15/63	**7**	6		2 Falling	22	Monument 815
12/14/63	**10**	6		3 Pretty Paper...[X]	15	Monument 830
				written by Willie Nelson		
7/5/80	**10**	14		4 That Lovin' You Feelin' Again	55	Warner 49262
				ROY ORBISON & EMMYLOU HARRIS		
				from the film *Roadie*		
12/12/87	**28**	9		5 Crying ....[R]		Virgin 99388
				ROY ORBISON/K.D. LANG (also see #10 below)		
				from the film *Hiding Out*; remake of Roy's 1961 Pop hit (POS 2)		
1/28/89	**1**²	22		6 You Got It	9	Virgin 99245
				written by Roy Orbison, Jeff Lynne and Tom Petty (also see #8 below)		
4/22/89	**23**	10		7 She's A Mystery To Me		Virgin 99227
				written by David Evans (The Edge) & Paul Hewson (Bono) of U2		
7/22/89	**44**	4		8 California Blue		Virgin 99202
12/9/89	**48**	2		9 Oh Pretty Woman ....[R]		Virgin 99159
				recorded live in September 1987 at the Coconut Grove In Los Angeles; backing vocals by Bruce Springsteen, among others; revival of Roy's #1 Pop hit in 1964		
1/23/93	**40**	2	✓	10 Crying ....[R]		Virgin LP Cut
				ROY ORBISON & K.D. LANG		
				from the album *King Of Hearts* on Virgin 86520 (also see #5 above)		
				ORCHESTRAL MANOEUVRES IN THE DARK		
				English electro-pop quartet: keyboardists/vocalists Paul Humphreys and Andrew McCluskey, with drummer Malcolm Holmes and multi-instrumentalist Martin Cooper. Humphreys left band in 1991.		
2/1/86	**37**	2		1 Secret...	63	A&M 2794
4/12/86	**24**	11		2 If You Leave	4	A&M 2811
				from the film *Pretty In Pink*		
11/22/86	**25**	7		3 (Forever) Live And Die	19	A&M 2872
				ORIGINAL CASTE, The		
				Canadian quintet — Dixie Lee Innes, lead singer.		
1/10/70	**25**	7		One Tin Soldier	34	T-A 186
				from the film *Billy Jack*		
				ORLANDO, Tony		
				Born Michael Anthony Orlando Cassavitis on 4/3/44 in New York City of Greek/Puerto Rican parents. Discovered by producer Don Kirshner. Lead singer of Dawn, 1970-77. Hosted weekly TV variety show *Tony Orlando & Dawn*, 1974-76.		
7/29/78	**48**	1		1 Don't Let Go		Elektra 45501
				#13 Pop hit for Roy Hamilton in 1958		
7/7/79	**20**	12		2 Sweets For My Sweet	54	Casablanca 991
				ORLEANS		
				Rock group founded in New York City by John Hall with the Hoppen brothers (Lawrence and Lance), Wells Kelly and Jerry Marotta. Hall and Marotta left in 1977, replaced by Bob Leinbach and R.A. Martin.		
8/2/75	**6**	12		1 Dance With Me	6	Asylum 45261
8/28/76	**33**	10		2 Still The One	5	Asylum 45336
3/19/77	**47**	2		3 Reach	51	Asylum 45375
4/28/79	**13**	10		4 Love Takes Time	11	Infinity 50006
10/6/79	**24**	10		5 Forever..		Infinity 50036
				ORR, Benjamin		
				Born Benjamin Orzechowski in Cleveland. Bassist/vocalist of The Cars.		
11/8/86	**2**¹	21		Stay The Night...	24	Elektra 69506

DEBUT DATE	PEAK POS	WKS CHR	GOLD	ARTIST — Record Title	POP POS	Label & Number
				★★184★★ OSBORNE, Jeffrey		
				Born on 3/9/48 in Providence, Rhode Island. Soul singer/songwriter/drummer. Lead singer of L.T.D. until 1980.		
				1)Love Power 2)You Should Be Mine (The Woo Woo Song) 3)We're Going All The Way		
10/2/82	7	20		1 On The Wings Of Love	29	A&M 2434
2/26/83	18	13		2 Eenie Meenie	76	A&M 2530
9/10/83	29	6		3 Don't You Get So Mad	25	A&M 2561
3/3/84	6	20		**4 We're Going All The Way**	48	A&M 2618
9/15/84	37	6		5 The Last Time I Made Love	40	A&M 2656
				JOYCE KENNEDY & JEFFREY OSBORNE		
6/7/86	2²	18		**6 You Should Be Mine (The Woo Woo Song)**	13	A&M 2814
12/13/86	15	14		7 In Your Eyes		A&M 2894
7/4/87	1¹	19		**8 Love Power ***	12	Arista 9567
11/4/89	25	8		9 Take Good Care Of You And Me *		Arista 9901
				***DIONNE WARWICK and JEFFREY OSBORNE**		
				★★157★★ OSMOND, Donny		
				Born on 12/9/57 in Ogden, Utah. Seventh son of George and Olive Osmond, Donny became a member of The Osmonds in 1963. Owner of production company Night Star. Burst back on to pop charts in March 1989.		
				1)Sacred Emotion 2)The Twelfth Of Never 3)I'll Be Good To You		
8/14/71	14	10	●	1 Go Away Little Girl	1³	MGM 14285
12/4/71	21	7	●	2 Hey Girl	9	MGM 14322
6/24/72	23	6		3 Too Young	13	MGM 14407
9/23/72	19	8		4 Why	13	MGM 14424
3/17/73	7	9	●	**5 The Twelfth Of Never**	8	MGM 14503
7/21/73	26	8		6 Young Love/	25	
		5		7 A Million To One	23	MGM 14583
12/8/73	31	9		8 When I Fall In Love/	55	
		9		9 Are You Lonesome Tonight	14	MGM 14677
3/1/75	45	4		10 I Have A Dream	50	MGM 14781
6/26/76	25	7		11 C'mon Marianne	38	Polydor 14320
4/29/89	20	15		12 Soldier Of Love	2¹	Capitol 44369
7/8/89	4	20		13 Sacred Emotion	13	Capitol 44379
1/6/90	10	15		14 I'll Be Good To You		Capitol 44508
4/20/91	24	9		15 Love Will Survive		Capitol 44707
				OSMOND, Donny And Marie		
				Brother and sister co-hosts of own musical/variety TV series from 1976-78. Starred in the film *Goin' Coconuts* (1978).		
7/20/74	1¹	14	●	**1 I'm Leaving It (All) Up To You**	4	MGM 14735
11/30/74	1¹	13		**2 Morning Side Of The Mountain**	8	MGM 14765
6/21/75	31	8		3 Make The World Go Away	44	MGM 14807
12/20/75	8	14		**4 Deep Purple**	14	MGM 14840
12/25/76	17	11		5 Ain't Nothing Like The Real Thing	21	Polydor 14363
11/26/77	18	12		6 (You're My) Soul And Inspiration	38	Polydor 14439
10/21/78	25	13		7 On The Shelf	38	Polydor 14510
				OSMOND, Marie		
				Born Olive Marie Osmond on 10/13/59 in Ogden, Utah. Began performing in concert with her brothers at age 14. Co-hosted the TV series *Ripley's Believe It Or Not* from 1985-86. Emerged as a top country artist in the '80s.		
9/15/73	1¹	16	●	**1 Paper Roses**	5	MGM 14609
3/8/75	21	6		2 Who's Sorry Now	40	MGM 14786
				above 2 produced by Sonny James		
				OSMONDS, The		
				Family group from Ogden, Utah. Alan (b: 6/22/49), Wayne (b: 8/28/51), Merrill (b: 4/30/53), Jay (b: 3/2/55) and Donny (b: 12/9/57). Began as a quartet in 1959, singing religious and barbershop-quartet songs. Regulars on Andy Williams' TV show from 1962-67. Alan, Wayne, Merrill and Jay turned to country music as The Osmond Brothers in the early '80s.		
1/30/71	37	2	●	1 One Bad Apple	1⁵	MGM 14193
8/26/72	7	14		**2 We Can Make It Together**	68	MGM 14383
				STEVE & EYDIE featuring The Osmonds		
9/15/73	4	10		3 Let Me In	36	MGM 14617
9/7/74	2¹	14		4 Love Me For A Reason	10	MGM 14746
8/9/75	1¹	10		5 The Proud One	22	MGM 14791
11/1/75	38	6		6 I'm Still Gonna Need You		MGM 14831
10/9/76	38	5		7 I Can't Live A Dream	46	Polydor 14348

★★175★★ O'SULLIVAN, Gilbert
Born Raymond O'Sullivan on 12/1/46 in Waterford, Ireland.

1)Alone Again (Naturally) 2)Clair 3)Out Of The Question

DEBUT DATE	PEAK POS	WKS CHR	GOLD	ARTIST — Record Title	POP POS	Label & Number
6/10/72	1⁶	16	●	1 Alone Again (Naturally)	1⁶	MAM 3619
10/28/72	1³	15	●	2 Clair	2²	MAM 3626
3/10/73	2¹	13		3 Out Of The Question	17	MAM 3628
6/23/73	3	13	●	4 Get Down	7	MAM 3629
10/13/73	29	10		5 Ooh Baby	25	MAM 3633
3/23/74	23	9		6 Happiness Is Me And You	62	MAM 3636
1/25/75	17	8		7 You Are You		MAM 3642
2/21/81	13	13		8 What's In A Kiss		Epic 50967

OUTFIELD, The
British pop-rock trio: Tony Lewis (lead singer; bass), John Spinks (guitar, keyboards, vocals) and Alan Jackman (drums). Jackman left by 1990; Lewis and Spinks continued as a duo.

12/1/90	21	14		For You	21	MCA 53935

OWENS, Buck
Country singer/guitarist/songwriter. Has charted 21 #1 country hits. Born Alvis Edgar Owens on 8/12/29 in Sherman, Texas; raised in Mesa, Arizona. Moved to Bakersfield, California in 1951. Co-host of TV's *Hee Haw*, 1969-86. Backing group: The Buckaroos.

9/5/64	18	1		1 I Don't Care (Just as Long as You Love Me)	92	Capitol 5240
5/15/65	20	2		2 Before You Go	83	Capitol 5410

OZARK MOUNTAIN DAREDEVILS
Country-rock group from Springfield, Missouri. Nucleus: Larry Lee (keyboards, guitar), Steve Cash (harp), John Dillon (guitar) and Michael Granda (bass).

2/12/77	18	10		You Know Like I Know	74	A&M 1888

P

PABLO CRUISE
San Francisco pop-rock quartet formed in 1973: Dave Jenkins (vocals, guitar), Bud Cockrell (member of It's A Beautiful Day; vocals, bass), Cory Lerios (keyboards) and Stephen Price (drums). Cockrell replaced by Bruce Day in 1977. John Pierce replaced Day, and guitarist Angelo Rossi joined in 1980.

7/15/78	28	11		1 Love Will Find A Way	6	A&M 2048
1/20/79	29	9		2 I Go To Rio	46	A&M 2112
7/11/81	14	16		3 Cool Love	13	A&M 2349

PACK, David
Born on 7/15/53. Lead singer of Ambrosia. Also see David Benoit.

5/10/86	16	12		1 That Girl Is Gone		Warner 28892
9/20/86	13	11		2 I Just Can't Let Go		Warner 28605

DAVID PACK with Michael McDonald and James Ingram

PAGANO, John ✪
Native of Providence, Rhode Island. Friendship with boxer Mike Tyson led to a meeting with MCA.

4/17/93	24	10		The Best I Ever Was		MCA 54576

written and produced by Barry Mann

PAGE, Gene ✪
Keyboardist/arranger/conductor from Los Angeles. Staff arranger with Reprise and Motown Records.

2/22/75	37	5		All Our Dreams Are Coming True	104	Atlantic 3247

produced by Barry White

PAGE, Larry, Orchestra ✪
British producer/arranger. Founded the Page One record label.

11/30/68	37	3		1 Those Were The Days	[I]	Page One 21,010

#2 Pop hit for Mary Hopkin in 1968

2/1/69	33	4		2 Wichita Lineman	[I]	Page One 21,018

#3 Pop hit for Glen Campbell in 1969

DEBUT DATE	PEAK POS	WKS CHR	GOLD	ARTIST — Record Title	POP POS	Label & Number
★★**98**★★				**PAGE, Patti**		

Born Clara Ann Fowler on 11/8/27 in Muskogee, Oklahoma. One of 11 children. Raised in Tulsa. On radio KTUL with Al Klauser & His Oklahomans, as "Ann Fowler," late 1940s. Another singer was billed as "Patti Page" for the Page Milk Company show on KTUL. When she left, Fowler took her place and name. With the Jimmy Joy band in 1947. On *Breakfast Club*, Chicago radio in 1947; signed by Mercury Records. Used multi-voice effect on records from 1947. Own TV series *The Patti Page Show*, 1955-58 and *The Big Record*, 1957-58. In the 1960 film *Elmer Gantry*.

1)*Hush, Hush, Sweet Charlotte* 2)*Gentle On My Mind* 3)*Most People Get Married*

DEBUT DATE	PEAK POS	WKS CHR	GOLD	ARTIST — Record Title	POP POS	Label & Number
7/17/61	11	3		1 You'll Answer To Me/	46	
7/17/61	14	1		2 Mom And Dad's Waltz	58	Mercury 71823
1/13/62	9	6		3 Go On Home	42	Mercury 71906
4/21/62	8	8		4 **Most People Get Married**	27	Mercury 71950
4/24/65	2¹	14		5 **Hush, Hush, Sweet Charlotte**	8	Columbia 43251
				movie title song		
8/14/65	11	8		6 You Can't Be True, Dear	94	Columbia 43345
				there were 8 top 20 versions of this tune in 1948		
11/13/65	35	4	✓	7 Ribbons And Roses		Columbia 43429
2/26/66	26	7		8 Custody	126	Columbia 43517
6/11/66	15	7		9 In This Day And Age		Columbia 43647
9/10/66	20	8		10 Almost Persuaded	113	Columbia 43794
				#24 Pop hit for David Houston in 1966		
12/10/66	37	3		11 Music And Memories		Columbia 43909
6/10/67	16	14	✓	12 Same Old You/		
6/10/67	16	6		13 Walkin' - Just Walkin'		Columbia 44115
9/30/67	23	6		14 All The Time		Columbia 44257
				#1 Country hit for Jack Greene in 1967		
12/30/67	7	12		15 **Gentle On My Mind**	66	Columbia 44353
6/22/68	12	12		16 Little Green Apples	96	Columbia 44556
10/26/68	20	7		17 Stand By Your Man	121	Columbia 44666
				#19 Pop hit for Tammy Wynette in 1969		
3/15/69	25	7	✓	18 The Love Song		Columbia 44778
1/16/71	26	8		19 Give Him Love		Mercury 73162

PAGE, Tommy

Born on 5/24/69 in West Caldwell, New Jersey.

DEBUT DATE	PEAK POS	WKS CHR	GOLD	ARTIST — Record Title	POP POS	Label & Number
3/17/90	31	7	●	I'll Be Your Everything	1¹	Sire 19959
				backing vocals by 3 members of New Kids On The Block		

PALM BEACH BAND BOYS, The ☉

Vocal trio led by Roger Rigney and arranged by Billy Mure.

DEBUT DATE	PEAK POS	WKS CHR	GOLD	ARTIST — Record Title	POP POS	Label & Number
12/31/66	25	5		I'm Gonna Sit Right Down And Write Myself A Letter	117	RCA 9026
				#3 Pop hit for Billy Williams in 1957		

PALMER, Robert

Born Alan Palmer on 1/19/49 in Batley, England and raised on the Mediterranean island of Malta. Formed first band, Mandrake Paddle Steamer, in 1969. Lead singer of short-lived supergroup The Power Station.

DEBUT DATE	PEAK POS	WKS CHR	GOLD	ARTIST — Record Title	POP POS	Label & Number
5/27/78	22	9		1 Every Kinda People	16	Island 100
2/23/91	4	24		2 **Mercy Mercy Me (The Ecology)/I Want You**	16	EMI 50344
				medley of Marvin Gaye's #2 Pop hit (1971) and #15 Pop hit (1976)		
5/9/92	8	16		3 **Every Kinda People**	[R]	Island LP Cut
				from the album *Addictions* Volume 2 on Island 510345; new version of #1 above		

PAPA JOE'S MUSIC BOX ☉

Featuring session pianist, Jerry Smith.

DEBUT DATE	PEAK POS	WKS CHR	GOLD	ARTIST — Record Title	POP POS	Label & Number
11/15/69	32	4		Papa Joe's Thing	[I]	ABC 11246

PAPER LACE

English quintet formed in 1969: Phil Wright (b: 4/9/48; lead singer, drums), Cliff Fish (bass), Michael Vaughan (lead guitar) and Chris Morris (guitar). Morris later replaced by Carlo Santanna.

DEBUT DATE	PEAK POS	WKS CHR	GOLD	ARTIST — Record Title	POP POS	Label & Number
8/17/74	27	6	●	The Night Chicago Died	1¹	Mercury 73492

PARIS, Mica

Mica (pronounced: MEE-sha) was born on 4/27/69 in London. Real name: Michelle Wallen.

DEBUT DATE	PEAK POS	WKS CHR	GOLD	ARTIST — Record Title	POP POS	Label & Number
5/20/89	8	19		**My One Temptation**	97	Island 99252

PARIS SISTERS, The

Albeth, Priscilla and Sherrell Paris from San Francisco.

DEBUT DATE	PEAK POS	WKS CHR	GOLD	ARTIST — Record Title	POP POS	Label & Number
2/17/62	7	7		**He Knows I Love Him Too Much**	34	Gregmark 10

DEBUT DATE	PEAK POS	WKS CHR	G O L D	ARTIST — Record Title	POP POS	Label & Number
				PARK, Simon, Orchestra ✪		
				Simon was born in 1946 in England.		
12/22/73	**29**	9		Eye Level .... [I]		Vanguard 35175
				PARKER, Graham, And The Shot		
				Born on 11/18/50 in East London. Pub-rock vocalist/guitarist/songwriter.		
6/8/85	**26**	7		Wake Up (Next To You)	39	Elektra 69654
				PARKER, Ray Jr./Raydio		
				Born on 5/1/54 in Detroit. Prominent session guitarist in California; worked with Stevie Wonder, Barry White and others. Formed band Raydio in 1977 with Arnell Carmichael, Jerry Knight, Larry Tolbert, Darren Carmichael and Charles Fearing. Parker went solo in 1982. Knight later recorded in duo Ollie & Jerry.		
				1)Jamie 2)That Old Song 3)Ghostbusters		
				RAYDIO:		
5/19/79	**25**	12		1 You Can't Change That	9	Arista 0399
				RAY PARKER JR. & RAYDIO:		
6/7/80	**34**	6		2 Two Places At The Same Time	30	Arista 0494
4/4/81	**11**	18		3 A Woman Needs Love (Just Like You Do)............	4	Arista 0592
7/25/81	**7**	15		4 **That Old Song**...	21	Arista 0616
				RAY PARKER JR.:		
6/5/82	**33**	8		5 The Other Woman	4	Arista 0669
11/26/83	**10**	19		6 **I Still Can't Get Over Loving You**....................	12	Arista 9116
7/21/84	**9**	13	●	7 **Ghostbusters**	1[3]	Arista 9212
				from 1984's #1 box-office film		
11/24/84	**6**	16		8 Jamie	14	Arista 9293
10/3/87	**42**	3		9 I Don't Think That Man Should Sleep Alone	68	Geffen 28417
2/20/88	**38**	6		10 Over You		Geffen 28152
				RAY PARKER JR. with NATALIE COLE		
				PARKER & PENNY — see LAWRENCE, Steve, and/or GORME, Eydie		
				PARKS, Michael		
				Born on 4/4/38 in Corona, California. Film and TV actor/singer. In films *The Man Who Came To Dinner*, *Night Must Fall*, *Wild Seed* and *Back In Town*. Starred in the 1963 TV series *Channing*; portrayed Jim Bronson in the 1969 TV series *Then Came Bronson*.		
2/21/70	**5**	13		Long Lonesome Highway	20	MGM 14104
				from the TV series *Then Came Bronson*		
				PARR, John		
				Singer/songwriter, born in Nottingham, England.		
8/24/85	**16**	12		St. Elmo's Fire (Man In Motion)............................	1[2]	Atlantic 89541
				from the film of the same title		
				PARRIS, Fred — see FIVE SATINS, The		
				PARSONS, Alan, Project		
				Duo formed in London in 1975. Consisted of producer Alan Parsons (guitar, keyboards) and lyricist Eric Woolfson (vocals, keyboards). Both had worked at the Abbey Road Studios; Parsons was an engineer, Woolfson a songwriter. Parsons engineered Pink Floyd's *Dark Side Of The Moon* and The Beatles' *Abbey Road* albums. Project features varying musicians and vocalists.		
6/6/81	**10**	16		1 **Time**	15	Arista 0598
7/10/82	**3**	24		2 **Eye In The Sky**...	3	Arista 0696
3/5/83	**21**	12		3 Old And Wise		Arista 1048
3/10/84	**4**	19		4 **Don't Answer Me**	15	Arista 9160
5/26/84	**10**	16		5 **Prime Time**..	34	Arista 9208
4/27/85	**11**	16		6 Days Are Numbers (The Traveller)	71	Arista 9349
	★★**59**★★			**PARTON, Dolly**		
				Born on 1/19/46 in Sevier County, Tennessee. Leading female artist of the Country charts. Worked on Knoxville radio show at age 11. First recorded for Gold Band in 1957. To Nashville in 1964. Replaced Norma Jean on the Porter Wagoner TV show, 1967-74. Joined the *Grand Ole Opry* in 1969. Starred in the films *9 To 5*, *The Best Little Whorehouse In Texas*, *Steel Magnolias* and *Straight Talk*. Hosted own TV variety show in 1987.		
				1)Islands In The Stream 2)9 To 5 3)Here You Come Again 4)Baby I'm Burnin'		
				5)Save The Last Dance For Me		
2/9/74	**44**	4		1 Jolene	60	RCA 0145
11/2/74	**38**	5		2 Love Is Like A Butterfly	105	RCA 10031
2/22/75	**35**	4		3 The Bargain Store		RCA 10164
10/22/77	**2**[2]	20	●	4 **Here You Come Again**	3	RCA 11123

DEBUT DATE	PEAK POS	WKS CHR	GOLD	ARTIST — Record Title	POP POS	Label & Number
				PARTON, Dolly — Cont'd		
3/25/78	**12**	13		**5** Two Doors Down..	19	RCA 11240
				flip side "It's All Wrong, But It's All Right" made the Country charts (POS 1²)		
8/26/78	**12**	13		**6** Heartbreaker..	37	RCA 11296
12/16/78	**11**	14		**7** Baby I'm Burnin'/	25	
		14		**8** I Really Got The Feeling....................................		RCA 11420
6/9/79	**14**	12		**9** You're The Only One....................................	59	RCA 11577
10/13/79	**41**	5		**10** Sweet Summer Lovin'....................................	77	RCA 11705
4/5/80	**35**	7		**11** Starting Over Again....................................	36	RCA 11926
				written by Donna Summer and her husband Bruce Sudano		
12/13/80	**1²**	22	●	**12** 9 To 5..	**1²**	RCA 12133
				movie title song		
4/18/81	**14**	10		**13** But You Know I Love You....................................	41	RCA 12200
9/12/81	**30**	6		**14** The House Of The Rising Sun....................................	77	RCA 12282
8/14/82	**17**	12		**15** I Will Always Love You.................................... [R]	53	RCA 13260
				Dolly's original version hit #1 on the Country charts on 6/8/74; from the film *The Best Little Whorehouse In Texas*		
12/25/82	**19**	12		**16** Everything's Beautiful (In It's Own Way)....................	102	Monument 03408
				DOLLY PARTON WILLIE NELSON		
8/27/83	**1⁴**	24	▲	**17** Islands In The Stream....................................	**1²**	RCA 13615
				KENNY ROGERS with Dolly Parton		
				written by the Bee Gees		
12/24/83	**12**	14		**18** Save The Last Dance For Me....................................	45	RCA 13703
				The Jordanaires (backing vocals)		
4/14/84	**20**	8		**19** Downtown	80	RCA 13756
1/5/85	**40**	2		**20** The Greatest Gift Of All.................................... [X]	81	RCA 13945
				KENNY ROGERS & DOLLY PARTON		
				from their Christmas TV special		
2/23/85	**12**	13		**21** Don't Call It Love....................................		RCA 13987
5/25/85	**13**	14		**22** Real Love..	91	RCA 14058
				DOLLY PARTON (with Kenny Rogers)		
6/20/87	**35**	3		**23** Telling Me Lies....................................		Warner 28371
				DOLLY PARTON, LINDA RONSTADT, EMMYLOU HARRIS		
1/16/88	**43**	3		**24** The River Unbroken....................................		Columbia 07665
3/5/88	**22**	8		**25** I Know You By Heart....................................		Columbia 07727
				DOLLY PARTON with Smokey Robinson		

PARTRIDGE FAMILY, The

Popularized through *The Partridge Family* TV series, broadcast from 1970-74. Recordings by series stars David Cassidy (lead singer) and real-life stepmother Shirley Jones (backing vocals). David, son of actor Jack Cassidy, was born on 4/12/50 in New York City; raised in California. Shirley, born on 3/31/34 in Smithton, Pennsylvania, starred in the film musicals *Oklahoma* and *The Music Man*; married David's father in 1956.

1)*It's One Of Those Nights (Yes Love)* 2)*I'll Meet You Halfway*
3)*Doesn't Somebody Want To Be Wanted*

DEBUT DATE	PEAK POS	WKS CHR	GOLD	ARTIST — Record Title	POP POS	Label & Number
				THE PARTRIDGE FAMILY Starring Shirley Jones Featuring David Cassidy:		
10/17/70	**8**	11	●	**1** I Think I Love You....................................	**1³**	Bell 910
2/13/71	**6**	11	●	**2 Doesn't Somebody Want To Be Wanted**	6	Bell 963
5/15/71	**4**	10		**3 I'll Meet You Halfway**	9	Bell 996
8/28/71	**14**	6		**4** I Woke Up In Love This Morning....................................	13	Bell 45130
1/1/72	**2¹**	7		**5 It's One Of Those Nights (Yes Love)**	20	Bell 45160
4/22/72	**36**	3		**6** Am I Losing You....................................	59	Bell 45200
7/22/72	**30**	4		**7** Breaking Up Is Hard To Do....................................	28	Bell 45235
12/23/72	**9**	7		**8 Looking Through The Eyes Of Love**	39	Bell 45301

PASTOR, Tony, Jr. ✪

Son of tenor saxophonist, Tony Pastor. Member of The Pastors.

DEBUT DATE	PEAK POS	WKS CHR	GOLD	ARTIST — Record Title	POP POS	Label & Number
2/26/66	**29**	6		I'll Forgive You (But I Won't Forget)....................................		Tower 204

PASTORS, The ✪

Brothers Guy, John and Tony Pastor, Jr.

DEBUT DATE	PEAK POS	WKS CHR	GOLD	ARTIST — Record Title	POP POS	Label & Number
7/28/73	**41**	10		I Need You/Isn't Life Strange/Without You....................		Alithia 6051
				medley: #9/'72 America; #29/'72 Moody Blues; #1/'72 Nilsson		

PATSY ✪

Patsy Maharam.

DEBUT DATE	PEAK POS	WKS CHR	GOLD	ARTIST — Record Title	POP POS	Label & Number
2/5/83	**44**	6		Just A Little Imagination		Roperry 817

DEBUT DATE	PEAK POS	WKS CHR	GOLD	ARTIST — Record Title	POP POS	Label & Number
				PATTON, Robbie		
				English singer/songwriter. Toured with Fleetwood Mac as a guest in 1979.		
8/15/81	**41**	5		1 Don't Give It Up	26	Liberty 1420
3/19/83	**16**	18		2 Smiling Islands..	52	Atlantic 89955
				Stevie Nicks (backing vocal)		
				PAUL, Billy		
				Born Paul Williams on 12/1/34 in Philadelphia. Soul singer; sang on Philadelphia radio broadcasts at age 11. First recorded for Jubilee in 1952.		
12/16/72	**10**	7	●	Me And Mrs. Jones..	1³	Phil. Int. 3521
				PAUL, Christopher		
				Made the *Hot 100* charts in 1975 as a duo: Christopher Paul & Shawn.		
10/13/73	**28**	7		Venus		MGM South 7026
				#1 Pop hit for Frankie Avalon in 1959		
				PAUL & PAULA		
				Real names: Ray Hildebrand (b: 12/21/40, Joshua, Texas) and Jill Jackson (b: 5/20/42, McCaney, Texas). Formed duo at Howard Payne College, Brownwood, Texas.		
3/16/63	**3**	10		Young Lovers..	6	Philips 40096
				PEACHES & HERB		
				Soul duo from Washington, D.C.: Herb Fame (born Herbert Feemster, 1942) and Francine Barker (born Francine Hurd, 1947). Fame had been recording solo, Francine sang in vocal group Sweet Things. Marlene Mack filled in for Francine from 1968-69. Re-formed with Fame and Linda Green in 1977.		
3/31/79	**4**	17	▲	1 Reunited	1⁴	Polydor 14547
8/4/79	**43**	4		2 We've Got Love	44	Polydor 14577
2/9/80	**33**	7		3 I Pledge My Love	19	Polydor 2053
				PEARL, Leslie		
				Pop singer/songwriter/producer from Pennsylvania. Wrote jingles for Pepsi, Ford, Gillette and others.		
6/12/82	**7**	17		If The Love Fits Wear It	28	RCA 13235
				PEARSON, Johnny, & His Orch. ✪		
2/19/72	**23**	6		Sleepy Shores ....[I]		Mercury 73270
				PEBBLES		
				Born Perri Alette McKissack. Native of Oakland. Nicknamed "Pebbles" by her family for her resemblance to cartoon character Pebbles Flintstone. R&B-dance singer.		
1/19/91	**24**	11		Love Makes Things Happen	13	MCA 53973
				Babyface (backing vocal)		
				PEEK, Dan		
				Born on 11/1/50 in Panama City, Florida. Member of America. Popular Contemporary Christian artist.		
6/30/79	**6**	33		All Things Are Possible	78	Lamb & Lion 814
				PEEPLES, Nia		
				Born on 12/10/61. Singer/actress. Played Nicole Chapman for three seasons on the TV series *Fame*. Hosted *Top Of The Pops* TV show and own syndicated music video dance TV program, *Party Machine*. Married Howard Hewett in 1989.		
7/11/92	**33**	6		Faces Of Love	88	Charisma 98568
				Howard Hewett (guest vocal)		
				PENDERGRASS, Teddy		
				Born on 3/26/50 in Philadelphia. Worked local clubs, became drummer for Harold Melvin's Blue Notes in 1969; lead singer with same group in 1970. Went solo in 1976. In the 1982 film *Soup For One*. Auto accident on 3/18/82 left him partially paralyzed.		
6/30/84	**6**	17		1 Hold Me	46	Asylum 69720
				TEDDY PENDERGRASS with Whitney Houston		
4/5/86	**31**	4		2 Love 4/2...		Asylum 69568
10/6/90	**37**	5		3 Glad To Be Alive		Elektra 64960
				TEDDY PENDERGRASS & LISA FISHER		
				from the film *The Adventures of Ford Fairlane*		
12/15/90	**37**	5		4 Make It With You		Elektra 64916
				PENN, Michael		
				Los Angeles-based singer/songwriter. Older brother of actors Sean and Christopher Penn. Son of actor/director Leo Penn and actress Eileen Ryan.		
12/16/89	**22**	17		1 No Myth	13	RCA 9111
5/19/90	**39**	5		2 This & That..	53	RCA 2512

DEBUT DATE	PEAK POS	WKS CHR	GOLD	ARTIST — Record Title	POP POS	Label & Number
				PEPPERMINT RAINBOW, The		
				Baltimore group: Doug Lewis (guitar), Skip Harris (bass), Tony Corey (drums), and sisters/vocalists Bonnie and Pat Lamdin. Discovered by producer Paul Leka (Steam).		
4/12/69	**22**	6		1 Will You Be Staying After Sunday	32	Decca 32410
6/21/69	**21**	8		2 Don't Wake Me Up In The Morning, Michael	54	Decca 32498
				PERICOLI, Emilio		
				Singer/actor, born in 1928 in Cesenatico, Italy.		
6/2/62	**3**	12		Al Di La' .... [F]	6	Warner 5259
				from the film *Rome Adventure*		
				PERREY, Jean Jacques ○		
				French synthesizer player.		
5/23/70	**20**	7		Passport To The Future .... [I]	106	Vanguard 35105
				PERRY, Steve		
				Born on 1/22/49 in Hanford, California. Lead singer of Journey since 1978.		
6/2/84	**33**	9		1 Oh Sherrie	3	Columbia 04391
12/1/84	**2**³	22		2 Foolish Heart	18	Columbia 04693
				PETER AND GORDON		
				Pop duo formed in London in 1963: Peter Asher (b: 6/22/44, London) and Gordon Waller (b: 6/4/45, Braemar, Scotland). Peter's sister Jane was Paul McCartney's girlfriend, and Paul wrote their first three chart hits. Toured the U.S. in 1964, appeared on *Shindig*, *Hullabaloo* and Ed Sullivan TV shows. Disbanded in 1967. Asher went into production and management, including work with Linda Ronstadt, James Taylor and 10,000 Maniacs.		
10/17/64	**9**	1		1 I Don't Want To See You Again	16	Capitol 5272
				written by John Lennon & Paul McCartney		
4/8/67	**34**	3		2 Sunday For Tea	31	Capitol 5864
★★96★★				**PETER, PAUL & MARY**		
				Folk group formed in New York City in 1961. Consisted of Mary Travers (b: 11/7/37, Louisville); Peter Yarrow (b: 5/31/38, New York City); and Paul Stookey (b: 11/30/37, Baltimore). Yarrow had worked the Newport Folk Festival in 1960. Stookey had done TV work, and Travers had been in the Broadway musical *The Next President*. Disbanded in 1971, reunited in 1978.		
				1)*Blowin' In The Wind* 2)*Leaving On A Jet Plane* 3)*Puff The Magic Dragon*		
5/12/62	**12**	7		1 Lemon Tree	35	Warner 5274
1/19/63	**14**	6		2 Settle Down (Goin' Down That Highway)	56	Warner 5334
3/16/63	**1**²	14		3 Puff The Magic Dragon	2¹	Warner 5348
7/13/63	**1**⁵	13		4 Blowin' In The Wind *	2¹	Warner 5368
9/21/63	**2**¹	9		5 Don't Think Twice, It's All Right *	9	Warner 5385
12/7/63	**17**	4		6 Stewball	35	Warner 5399
3/21/64	**7**	4		7 Tell It On The Mountain	33	Warner 5418
1/23/65	**5**	7		8 For Lovin' Me **	30	Warner 5496
5/29/65	**23**	1		9 When The Ship Comes In *	91	Warner 5625
				*written by Bob Dylan		
9/25/65	**13**	10		10 Early Morning Rain **	91	Warner 5659
				**written by Gordon Lightfoot		
4/16/66	**4**	10		11 The Cruel War	52	Warner 5809
10/1/66	**33**	3		12 The Other Side Of This Life	100	Warner 5849
1/14/67	**37**	3		13 Hurry Sundown	123	Warner 5883
5/10/69	**7**	10		14 Day Is Done	21	Warner 7279
10/25/69	**1**³	16	●	15 Leaving On A Jet Plane	1¹	Warner 7340
				written by John Denver		
				PETERS, Bernadette		
				Born Bernadette Lazzara on 2/28/44 in Queens, New York. Broadway/TV/film star. Appeared in the films *The Jerk* and *Annie* among others, and the TV series *All's Fair* (1976-77).		
3/29/80	**3**	21		Gee Whiz	31	MCA 41210
				PETERS & LEE ○		
				British duo: Lennie Peters (who is blind) and Dianne Lee. Duo split in 1980. Peters died on 10/10/92 (age 59) of cancer.		
8/18/73	**26**	16		Welcome Home	119	Philips 40729
				PETERSEN, Paul		
				Born on 9/23/45 in Glendale, California. Member of Disney's "Mouseketeers" and played Jeff Stone on TV's *Donna Reed Show* (1958-66). Became a paperback novelist in the '70s.		
12/1/62	**2**¹	14		My Dad	6	Colpix 663

DEBUT DATE	PEAK POS	WKS CHR	G O L D	ARTIST — Record Title	POP POS	Label & Number
				PETERSON, Ray		
				Born on 4/23/39 in Denton, Texas. Started singing in his early teens, while being treated for polio at a Texas hospital. Formed own Dunes label in 1961.		
9/25/61	**7**	7		**Missing You**	29	Dunes 2006
				PET SHOP BOYS		
				British duo: Neil Tennant (vocals) and Chris Lowe (keyboards). Tennant was a writer for the British fan magazine *Smash Hits*. In 1989, Tennant also recorded with the group Electronic.		
4/26/86	**26**	8		1 West End Girls	1[1]	EMI America 8307
1/23/88	**14**	12		2 What Have I Done To Deserve This?	2[2]	EMI-Man. 50107
				PET SHOP BOYS and Dusty Springfield		
				PETTY, Tom		
				Born on 10/20/53 in Gainesville, Florida. Appeared in the 1987 film *Made In Heaven*. Member of the supergroup Traveling Wilburys. The Heartbreakers consist of Mike Campbell, Benmont Tench, Howard Epstein and Stan Lynch.		
12/9/89	**17**	14		1 Free Fallin'	7	MCA 53748
8/10/91	**36**	8		2 Learning To Fly	28	MCA 54124
				TOM PETTY AND THE HEARTBREAKERS written by Tom Petty and Jeff Lynne		
				PHILADELPHIA LUV ENSEMBLE, The ○		
				Studio group assembled by producer Jerry Ross.		
5/24/80	**20**	19		Love Fantasy..[I]		Pavillion 6404
				PHILHARMONIC 2000 ○		
11/13/76	**43**	4		Disconcerto		Mercury 73854
				disco version of Tchaikovsky's *Piano Concerto in B Flat*		
				PHILLIPS, Esther		
				Born Esther Mae Jones on 12/23/35 in Galveston, Texas. One of the first female superstars of R&B. Vocalist/ multi-instrumentalist. Moved to Los Angeles in 1940. Recorded and toured with The Johnny Otis Orchestra as "Little Esther," 1948-54; scored seven top 10 hits on the R&B charts in 1950. Bouts with drug addiction interrupted her career and led to her death on 8/7/84 (liver, kidney failure).		
6/5/65	**14**	5		1 And I Love Him	54	Atlantic 2281
				female version of The Beatles' "And I Love Her"		
7/24/65	**28**	5		2 Moonglow & Theme From Picnic	115	Atlantic 2294
				#1 Pop hit for Morris Stoloff in 1956		
10/4/75	**29**	9		3 What A Diff'rence A Day Makes	20	Kudu 925
				PHILLIPS, John		
				Born on 8/30/35 in Paris Island, South Carolina. Co-founder of The Mamas & The Papas. Father of actress MacKenzie Phillips and singer Chynna Phillips. Co-wrote The Beach Boys' 1988 #1 hit "Kokomo."		
5/23/70	**13**	9		Mississippi	32	Dunhill 4236
				PHILLIPS, Shawn		
				Born on 2/3/43 in Fort Worth, Texas. Soft-rock vocalist.		
2/24/73	**20**	5		Lost Horizon..	63	A&M 1405
				movie title song		
				PHOTOGLO, Jim		
				Pop vocalist from the South Bay area of Los Angeles.		
3/22/80	**14**	19		1 We Were Meant To Be Lovers *	31	20th Century 2446
8/23/80	**44**	3		2 When Love Is Gone *..	106	20th Century 2458
				***PHOTOGLO**		
4/4/81	**12**	20		3 Fool In Love With You	25	20th Century 2487
10/3/81	**36**	5		4 More To Love		20th Century 2498
				PICKETTYWITCH		
				English sextet — Polly Brown, lead singer.		
6/20/70	**34**	4		That Same Old Feeling	67	Janus 118
				PIKE, Jim — see LETTERMEN		
				PIPKINS, The		
				British vocal duo: Roger Greenaway and Tony Burrows (low voice). Worked together in studio group White Plains.		
5/30/70	**20**	5		Gimme Dat Ding ....[N]	9	Capitol 2819
				background tune used on TV's *Benny Hill Show*		

DEBUT DATE	PEAK POS	WKS CHR	G O L D	ARTIST — Record Title	POP POS	Label & Number
				PITNEY, Gene		
				Born on 2/17/41 in Hartford, Connecticut and raised in Rockville, Connecticut. Own band at Rockville High School. Recorded for Decca in 1959, with Ginny Arnell as Jamie & Jane. Recorded for Blaze in 1960 as Billy Bryan. First recorded under own name for Festival in 1960. Wrote "Hello Mary Lou," "He's A Rebel" and "Rubber Ball." Recorded with George Jones as George & Gene.		
9/15/62	1²	14		1 Only Love Can Break A Heart	2¹	Musicor 1022
12/22/62	5	7		2 Half Heaven - Half Heartache	12	Musicor 1026
4/6/63	4	9		3 Mecca	12	Musicor 1028
8/10/63	5	6		4 True Love Never Runs Smooth............................	21	Musicor 1032
10/26/63	6	9		5 Twenty Four Hours From Tulsa...........................	17	Musicor 1034
				PLATTERS, The		
				R&B group formed in Los Angeles in 1953. Consisted of Tony Williams (lead), David Lynch (tenor), Paul Robi (baritone), Herb Reed (bass) and Zola Taylor. Williams left to go solo, replaced by Sonny Turner in 1961. Taylor replaced by Sandra Dawn; Robi replaced by Nate Nelson (formerly in The Flamingos) in 1966. Lynch died of cancer on 1/2/81 (age 61). Robi died of cancer on 2/1/89. Williams died on 8/14/92 of diabetes and emphysema. Group inducted into the Rock and Roll Hall of Fame in 1990. Several unrelated groups use The Platters' famous name today.		
7/31/61	7	8		I'll Never Smile Again	25	Mercury 71847
				#1 hit for Tommy Dorsey in 1940		
				PLAYER		
				Pop-rock group formed in Los Angeles: Peter Beckett (vocals, guitar), John Crowley (vocals, guitar), Ronn Moss (bass), John Friesen (drums) and Wayne Cooke (keyboards). Moss plays Ridge Forrester on the TV soap *The Bold & The Beautiful*. Crowley began solo country career in 1988. Beckett joined Little River Band by 1992.		
10/29/77	20	19	●	1 Baby Come Back	1³	RSO 879
4/1/78	20	13		2 This Time I'm In It For Love	10	RSO 890
				PM ○		
				St. Louis trio originally known as the Peter Mayer Group: brothers Jim (bass) and Peter (vocals, guitar) Mayer with Roger Guth (drums). Jim and Peter were raised in Tamilnadu, India where their parents worked as missionaries.		
10/8/88	11	18		Piece Of Paradise		Warner 27779
				PM DAWN		
				Jersey City, New Jersey rap duo of brothers Attrell (b: 5/15/70) and Jarrett (b: 7/17/71) Cordes — nicknamed Prince Be and DJ Minutemix. PM Dawn means "from the darkest hour comes the light."		
7/17/93	31	10		Looking Through Patient Eyes	6	Gee Street 862024
★★156★★				**POCO**		
				Country-rock band formed in Los Angeles by Rusty Young (pedal steel guitar) and Buffalo Springfield members Richie Furay (rhythm guitar) and Jim Messina (lead guitar). Randy Meisner (later of the Eagles) left in 1969, replaced by bassist Timothy B. Schmit. Messina left in 1970, replaced by Paul Cotton, and Furay left in 1973. Grantham and Schmit (joined Eagles) left in 1977; replacements: Charlie Harrison, Kim Bullard and Steve Chapman. Disbanded in 1984. In 1989, Young, Furay, Messina, Grantham and Meisner reunited.		
				1)*Crazy Love* 2)*Call It Love* 3)*Heart Of The Night*		
10/4/75	23	8		1 Keep On Tryin'	50	ABC 12126
9/10/77	39	5		2 Indian Summer	50	ABC 12295
1/20/79	1⁷	21		3 Crazy Love..	17	ABC 12439
5/26/79	5	23		4 Heart Of The Night	20	MCA 41023
10/11/80	42	9		5 Midnight Rain	74	MCA 41326
2/13/82	35	9		6 Sea Of Heartbreak	109	MCA 52001
				#21 Pop hit for Don Gibson in 1961		
12/18/82	10	21		7 Shoot For The Moon	50	Atlantic 89919
9/16/89	2¹	18		8 Call It Love	18	RCA 9038
12/9/89	10	15		9 Nothin' To Hide	39	RCA 9131
				written and produced by Richard Marx		
6/23/90	24	10		10 What Do People Know		RCA 2623
				POINDEXTER, Buster, and his Banshees of Blue		
				Buster is David Johansen. Born on 1/9/50 in Staten Island. Founder and lead singer of the pre-punk group the New York Dolls, 1971-75. Assumed the Buster Poindexter persona in 1987. Appeared in the films *Married To The Mob*, *Let It Ride*, *Tales From The Darkside: The Movie* and *Freejack*.		
4/15/89	40	5		Hit The Road Jack		RCA 8914
				from the film *The Dream Team*; #1 Pop hit for Ray Charles in 1961		
				POINTER, Bonnie		
				Born on 7/11/51 in East Oakland, California. Member of the Pointer Sisters, 1971-78.		
9/1/79	43	4		Heaven Must Have Sent You................................	11	Motown 1459

DEBUT DATE	PEAK POS	WKS CHR	GOLD	ARTIST — Record Title	POP POS	Label & Number
				★★115★★ **POINTER SISTERS**		
				Soul group formed in Oakland in 1971, consisting of sisters Ruth, Anita, Bonnie and June Pointer. Parents were ministers. Group was originally a trio, joined by youngest sister June in the early '70s. First recorded for Atlantic in 1971. Backup work for Cold Blood, Elvin Bishop, Boz Scaggs, Grace Slick and many others. Sang in nostalgic 1940s style, 1973-77. In the 1976 film *Car Wash*. Bonnie went solo in 1978, group continued as trio in new musical style.		
				1)Slow Hand 2)American Music 3)Jump (For My Love)		
11/9/74	13	11		1 Fairytale	13	ABC/Blue Thumb 254
3/15/75	31	6		2 Live Your Life Before You Die	89	ABC/Blue Thumb 262
1/20/79	21	14	●	3 Fire	2²	Planet 45901
				written by Bruce Springsteen		
8/30/80	13	16	●	4 He's So Shy	3	Planet 47916
6/20/81	6	21	●	5 Slow Hand	2³	Planet 47929
2/13/82	19	13		6 Should I Do It	13	Planet 47960
7/3/82	9	15		7 American Music	16	Planet 13254
10/29/83	15	13		8 I Need You	48	Planet 13639
3/17/84	36	10		9 Automatic	5	Planet 13730
6/9/84	11	18		10 Jump (For My Love)	3	Planet 13780
9/1/84	25	13		11 I'm So Excited [R]	9	Planet 13857
				originally made the *Hot 100* in 1982 (POS 30) on Planet 13327		
2/2/85	23	11		12 Neutron Dance	6	Planet 13951
				from the film *Beverly Hills Cop*		
8/24/85	32	7		13 Dare Me	11	RCA 14126
11/23/85	16	9		14 Freedom	59	RCA 14224
12/6/86	27	7		15 Goldmine	33	RCA 5062
2/28/87	36	4		16 All I Know Is The Way I Feel	93	RCA 5112
6/4/88	36	5		17 I'm In Love		RCA 8378
				POLICE, The		
				Rock trio formed in England in 1977: Gordon "Sting" Sumner (b: 10/2/51; vocals, bass), Andy Summers (b: 12/31/42; guitar) and Stewart Copeland (b: 7/16/52; drums). First guitarist was Henri Padovani, replaced by Summers in 1977. Copeland had been with Curved Air. Inactive as a group since appearance at "Amnesty '86." Sting began recording solo in 1985. Copeland formed group Animal Logic in 1989.		
6/18/83	5	20	●	1 Every Breath You Take	1⁸	A&M 2542
10/1/83	33	8		2 King Of Pain	3	A&M 2569
1/28/84	13	16		3 Wrapped Around Your Finger	8	A&M 2614
				POLNAREFF, Michel		
				Pop vocalist/keyboardist/guitarist.		
3/20/76	41	3		If You Only Believe (Jesus For Tonite)	48	Atlantic 3314
				POPPY FAMILY, The		
				Canadian pop quartet: Susan (vocals) and husband Terry Jacks (guitar, composer), Craig MacCaw (guitar) and Satwan Singh (percussion). Group and marriage broke up in 1973; Susan and Terry began solo careers.		
4/25/70	6	12	●	1 Which Way You Goin' Billy? *	2²	London 129
8/22/70	7	10		2 That's Where I Went Wrong *	29	London 139
				*THE POPPY FAMILY Featuring Susan Jacks		
8/7/71	16	9		3 Where Evil Grows	45	London 148
3/4/72	34	3		4 Good Friends?	105	London 172
				THE POPPY FAMILY Vocal: Susan Jacks		
				POP-TOPS		
				Vocal septet based in Spain. Lead singer Phil Tris is from the West Indies.		
10/9/71	28	7		Mammy Blue	57	ABC 11311
				PORTNOY, Gary		
				Pop singer/songwriter from Valley Stream, New York.		
4/2/83	28	12		Where Everybody Knows Your Name	83	Applause 106
				theme from the TV show *Cheers*		
				POST, Mike		
				Born on 9/29/44 in Los Angeles. Record producer/composer of numerous TV and film scores. Orchestra leader for two TV variety shows: *The Andy Williams Show* (1969-71) and *The Mac Davis Show* (1974-76).		
6/14/75	16	10		1 The Rockford Files * [I]	10	MGM 14772
10/18/75	28	8		2 Manhattan Spiritual [I]	56	MGM 14829
9/19/81	4	21		3 The Theme From Hill Street Blues * [I]	10	Elektra 47186
				featuring guitarist Larry Carlton		
4/10/82	40	6		4 Theme From Magnum P.I. * [I]	25	Elektra 47400

DEBUT DATE	PEAK POS	WKS CHR	GOLD	ARTIST — Record Title	POP POS	Label & Number
				POST, Mike — Cont'd		
2/6/88	**13**	16		5 Theme From L.A. Law * .... [I] *theme songs from TV series		Polydor 887145
				POTTER, Don ☉ Folk singer/guitarist based in Rochester, New York. Wrote several country hits for The Judds.		
12/7/74	**33**	5		Just Leave Me Alone..		Columbia 10059
				POURCEL, Franck Frank was born on 1/1/15 in Marseilles, France. String orchestra leader/composer/arranger/violinist.		
4/26/69	**38**	3		1 The Lonely Season .... [I] FRANK POURCEL And His Orchestra		Blue 1002
4/1/72	**22**	5		2 I Only Want To Say (Gethsemane)................................. [I] from the rock opera *Jesus Christ Superstar*		Paramount 0151
				POWERS, Joey Born in 1939 in Canonsburg, Pennsylvania. Produced *The John Hills Exercise Show* for NBC-TV. Wrestling instructor at Ohio State University.		
11/23/63	**7**	11		Midnight Mary	10	Amy 892
				POZO-SECO SINGERS Native Texan trio: Susan Taylor, Lofton Kline and country star Don Williams (lead singer).		
3/26/66	**3**	6		1 Time .... first released on Edmark 10017 in 1965	47	Columbia 43437
6/18/66	**34**	4		2 I'll Be Gone	92	Columbia 43646
3/18/67	**8**	14		3 I Believed It All	96	Columbia 44041
				PRATT & McCLAIN Truett Pratt and Jerry McClain, with backing group Brother Love.		
4/24/76	**7**	11		Happy Days .... TV series title song	5	Reprise 1351
				PRELUDE English folk-based trio: Ian Vardy with Brian and Irene Hume (husband-and-wife).		
10/12/74	**11**	10		1 After The Goldrush.. written by Neil Young	22	Island 002
3/27/76	**42**	2		2 Best Of A Bad Time		Pye 71045
★★5★★				**PRESLEY, Elvis** "The King of Rock & Roll." Born on 1/8/35 in Tupelo, Mississippi. Died at Graceland mansion in Memphis on 8/16/77 (age 42) of heart failure caused by prescription drug abuse. Won talent contest at age eight, singing "Old Shep." Moved to Memphis in 1948. First recorded for Sun in 1954. Signed to RCA Records on 11/22/55. In U.S. Army from 3/24/58 to 3/5/60. Starred in 33 films (beginning with *Love Me Tender* in 1956). Married Priscilla Beaulieu on 5/1/67; divorced on 10/11/73. Priscilla pursued acting in the 1980s beginning with a role on TV's *Dallas*. Their only child Lisa Marie was born on 2/1/68. Elvis' last live performance was in Indianapolis on 6/26/77. Won the Lifetime Achievement Grammy in 1971. Inducted into the Rock and Roll Hall of Fame in 1986. The first rock 'n' roll artist to be honored by the U.S. Postal Service with an Elvis commemorative stamp on 1/8/93. *1)Crying In The Chapel 2)Can't Help Falling In Love 3)I'm Yours 4)(Such An) Easy Question 5)My Boy*		
8/28/61	**2**²	11	●	1 (Marie's the Name) His Latest Flame .... flip side "Little Sister" made the *Hot 100* (POS 5)	4	RCA 47-7908
1/13/62	**1**⁶	9	▲	2 Can't Help Falling In Love .... from the film *Blue Hawaii*; flip side "Rock-A-Hula Baby" made the *Hot 100* (POS 23)	**2**¹	RCA 47-7968
3/17/62	**6**	8		3 Anything That's Part Of You .... flip side "Good Luck Charm" made the *Hot 100* (POS 1²)	31	RCA 47-7992
5/12/62	**5**	6		4 Follow That Dream .... from the film and the E.P. of the same title	15	RCA EPA-4368
8/4/62	**2**²	10	●	5 She's Not You/	5	
9/8/62	**14**	1		6 Just Tell Her Jim Said Hello...................................	55	RCA 47-8041
5/1/65	**1**⁷	13	▲	7 Crying In The Chapel... recorded on 10/31/60	3	RCA 447-0643
7/3/65	**1**²	7		8 (Such An) Easy Question.. flip side "It Feels So Right" made the *Hot 100* (POS 55)	11	RCA 47-8585
8/28/65	**1**³	14	●	9 I'm Yours .... above 2 from th 1962 album *Pot Luck; flip side "(It's A) Long Lonely Highway" Bubbled Under (POS 112)	11	RCA 47-8657
11/13/65	**3**	12	●	10 Puppet On A String .... from the film *Girl Happy*; flip side "Wooden Heart" Bubbled Under (POS 110); made the Country charts on 8/12/78 on RCA 11320 (POS 78)	14	RCA 447-0650
3/26/66	**3**	8	●	11 Frankie And Johnny .... version of the classic song written around 1850; movie title song; flip side "Please Don't Stop Loving Me" made the *Hot 100* (POS 45)	25	RCA 47-8780

DEBUT DATE	PEAK POS	WKS CHR	GOLD	ARTIST — Record Title	POP POS	Label & Number
				PRESLEY, Elvis — Cont'd		
7/30/66	**38**	3		12 Love Letters	19	RCA 47-8870
				#11 hit for Dick Haymes in 1945; flip side "Come What May" Bubbled Under (POS 109)		
10/8/66	**9**	11		13 **All That I Am**	41	RCA 47-8941
				from the film *Spinout*; flip side "Spinout" made the *Hot 100* (POS 41)		
11/18/67	**34**	2		14 **You Don't Know Me**	44	RCA 47-9341
				#14 Pop hit for Jerry Vale in 1956; flip side "Big Boss Man" made the *Hot 100* (POS 38)		
3/22/69	**7**	7		15 **Memories**	35	RCA 47-9731
				from the NBC-TV special *Elvis*		
5/17/69	**8**	11	▲	16 **In The Ghetto**	3	RCA 47-9741
8/2/69	**37**	2	●	17 Clean Up Your Own Back Yard	35	RCA 47-9747
				from the film *The Trouble With Girls (and how to get into it)*		
10/4/69	**4**	8	▲	18 **Suspicious Minds**	1¹	RCA 47-9764
12/6/69	**3**	11	▲	19 **Don't Cry Daddy**	6	RCA 47-9768
2/21/70	**3**	9	●	20 **Kentucky Rain**	16	RCA 47-9791
				written by Eddie Rabbitt		
5/23/70	**1¹**	9	●	21 **The Wonder Of You**	9	RCA 47-9835
				recorded live in Las Vegas		
8/1/70	**5**	10	●	22 **I've Lost You/**	32	
		10		23 The Next Step Is Love	flip	RCA 47-9873
10/24/70	**1¹**	11	●	24 **You Don't Have To Say You Love Me**	11	RCA 47-9916
1/2/71	**2²**	9	●	25 **I Really Don't Want To Know/**	21	
				#11 hit for Les Paul & Mary Ford in 1954		
		9		26 There Goes My Everything	flip	RCA 47-9960
3/20/71	**18**	5		27 Where Did They Go, Lord	33	RCA 47-9980
5/15/71	**8**	7		28 **Life**	53	RCA 47-9985
7/17/71	**2¹**	8		29 **I'm Leavin'**	36	RCA 47-9998
10/30/71	**19**	5		30 It's Only Love/	51	
		4		31 The Sound Of Your Cry		RCA 48-1017
2/12/72	**9**	7		32 **Until It's Time For You To Go/**	40	
		7		33 We Can Make The Morning		RCA 74-0619
5/13/72	**31**	4		34 An American Trilogy	66	RCA 74-0672
				Dixie/Battle Hymn Of The Republic/All My Trials; recorded live at Las Vegas		
8/26/72	**9**	14		35 **It's A Matter Of Time/**		
		12	▲	36 Burning Love	2¹	RCA 74-0769
12/2/72	**3**	12	●	37 **Separate Ways**	20	RCA 74-0815
				featured in the film *Elvis On Tour*; flip side "Always On My Mind" made the Country charts (POS 16)		
4/28/73	**12**	8		38 Fool	flip	RCA 74-0910
				flip side "Steamroller Blues" made the *Hot 100* (POS 17)		
9/29/73	**27**	7		39 Raised On Rock	41	RCA APBO-0088
				flip side "For Ol' Times Sake" made the Country charts (POS 42)		
2/9/74	**27**	10		40 Take Good Care Of Her/	flip	
		10		41 I've Got A Thing About You Baby	39	RCA APBO-0196
6/8/74	**6**	14		42 **If You Talk In Your Sleep**	17	RCA APBO-0280
				flip side "Help Me" made the Country charts (POS 6)		
10/26/74	**8**	11		43 **It's Midnight/**		
		11		44 Promised Land	14	RCA PB-10074
2/8/75	**1¹**	12		45 **My Boy**	20	RCA PB-10191
6/14/75	**42**	4		46 T-R-O-U-B-L-E	35	RCA PB-10278
4/10/76	**7**	10		47 **Hurt**	28	RCA PB-10601
1/8/77	**2²**	14		48 **Moody Blue**	31	RCA PB-10857
7/2/77	**14**	19	●	49 Way Down	18	RCA PB-10998
11/12/77	**6**	13	●	50 **My Way**	22	RCA PB-11165
				recorded live from Elvis' tour; written in 1969 by Paul Anka		
2/14/81	**16**	9		51 Guitar Man ....[R]	28	RCA PB-12158
				original version made the *Hot 100* on 1/27/68 (POS 43) on RCA 47-9425		
11/27/82	**31**	8		52 The Elvis Medley	71	RCA PB-13351
				Jailhouse Rock/(Let Me Be Your) Teddy Bear/Hound Dog/Don't Be Cruel (To A Heart That's True)/Burning Love/Suspicious Minds		

PRESTON, Billy

Born on 9/9/46 in Houston. R&B vocalist/keyboardist. To Los Angeles at an early age. With Mahalia Jackson in 1956. Played piano in film *St. Louis Blues*, 1958. Regular on *Shindig* TV show. Recorded with The Beatles on "Get Back" and "Let It Be"; worked Concert For Bangladesh in 1969. Prominent session man, played on Sly & The Family Stone hits. With The Rolling Stones U.S. tour in 1975.

5/27/72	23	6	●	1 Outa-Space .... [I]	2¹	A&M 1320
				flip side "I Wrote A Simple Song" made the *Hot 100* (POS 77)		
10/6/73	34	8	●	2 Space Race .... [I]	4	A&M 1463
7/27/74	15	13	●	3 Nothing From Nothing	1¹	A&M 1544
12/15/79	2¹	25		4 With You I'm Born Again *	4	Motown 1477
7/12/80	42	5		5 One More Time For Love *	52	Tamla 54312
				*BILLY PRESTON & SYREETA		
9/4/82	38	9		6 I'm Never Gonna Say Goodbye	88	Motown 1625

PRETENDERS, The

Rock quartet featuring lead singer/songwriter/guitarist Chrissie Hynde (b: 9/7/51, Akron, Ohio). Hynde was married to Jim Kerr of Simple Minds. With the exception of Hynde, numerous personnel changes since 1985.

11/29/86	28	8		Don't Get Me Wrong..	10	Sire 28630

PRICE, Ray

Country singer. Born on 1/12/26 in Perryville, Texas and raised in Dallas. Ray charted over 80 top 40 singles on *Billboard*'s country charts. Known as "The Cherokee Cowboy."

8/15/70	9	25		1 For The Good Times..	11	Columbia 45178
3/20/71	4	14		2 I Won't Mention It Again.......................................	42	Columbia 45329
8/7/71	26	8		3 I'd Rather Be Sorry	70	Columbia 45425
8/4/73	21	10		4 You're The Best Thing That Ever Happened To Me............	82	Columbia 45889

PRIDE, Charley

Born on 3/18/38 in Sledge, Mississippi. The most successful black country performer. Discovered by Red Sovine in 1963. Charley has charted 29 #1 singles on the country charts.

1/1/72	7	9	●	Kiss An Angel Good Mornin'	21	RCA 0550

PRIEST, Maxi

Born Max Elliott in London to Jamaican parents. Dancehall reggae singer.

12/10/88	10	14		1 Wild World..	25	Virgin 99269
9/8/90	15	20	●	2 Close To You..	1¹	Charisma 98951
9/28/91	2¹	28		3 Set The Night To Music	6	Atlantic 87607
				ROBERTA FLACK with MAXI PRIEST		

PRINCE

Born Prince Roger Nelson on 6/7/58 in Minneapolis. Vocalist/multi-instrumentalist/composer/producer/actor. Prince formed new band, New Power Generation (named for the oldest Prince fan club in Britain), in 1990, featuring Levi Seacer, Jr. (guitar), Sonny T. (bass), Tommy Barbarella (keyboard), dancer/percussionists Kirk Johnson and Damon Dickson, Michael Bland (drums), rapper Tony M. and Rosie Gaines (keyboards, vocals; replaced by Mayte [pronounced: my-tie] by 1992). Prince announced that he would no longer record on 4/27/93. Changed his name on 6/7/93 to a combination male/female symbol and announced his separation from New Power Generation.

10/28/89	21	13		1 The Arms Of Orion..	36	Warner 22757
				PRINCE with Sheena Easton		
				from the film *Batman*		
2/15/92	40	5		2 Diamonds And Pearls	3	Paisley P. 19083
				PRINCE AND THE N.P.G.		

PRINCIPAL, Victoria — see GIBB, Andy

PROPAGANDA ✪

Electronic dance quartet formed in Dusseldorf, Germany: Michael Mertens, ex-Simple Minds members Derek Forbes and Brian McGee, and American-born vocalist Betsi Miller.

7/21/90	22	10		Heaven Give Me Words		Charisma 98952

PRYSOCK, Arthur

Born on 1/2/29 in Spartanburg, South Carolina. R&B Singer. First recorded with Buddy Johnson, 1944. Solo, 1952. Popular nightclub act, often appearing with brother, saxophonist Wilbert "Red" Prysock.

8/7/65	8	6		1 It's Too Late, Baby Too Late	56	Old Town 1183
7/2/66	28	7		2 Let It Be Me	124	Old Town 1196
				#7 Pop hit for The Everly Brothers in 1960		
1/13/68	24	5		3 A Working Man's Prayer	74	Verve 10574

DEBUT DATE	PEAK POS	WKS CHR	G O L D	ARTIST — Record Title	POP POS	Label & Number
				PUCKETT, Gary, And The Union Gap		
				Singer/guitarist Puckett (b: 10/17/42, Hibbing, Minnesota) formed The Union Gap in San Diego in 1967; named after the town of Union Gap, Washington. Included Kerry Chater (bass), Paul Whitebread (drums), Dwight Bement (sax) and Gary Withem (keyboards).		
3/16/68	34	5	●	1 Young Girl	2³	Columbia 44450
				THE UNION GAP Featuring Gary Puckett		
7/13/68	26	4	●	2 Lady Willpower	2²	Columbia 44547
9/21/68	3	12	●	3 Over You	7	Columbia 44644
3/22/69	13	7		4 Don't Give In To Him..	15	Columbia 44788
8/30/69	2¹	11		5 This Girl Is A Woman Now	9	Columbia 44967
3/14/70	16	4		6 Let's Give Adam And Eve Another Chance	41	Columbia 45097
				GARY PUCKETT:		
10/31/70	14	8		7 I Just Don't Know What To Do With Myself........................	61	Columbia 45249
2/6/71	28	5		8 Keep The Customer Satisfied	71	Columbia 45303
5/1/71	24	3		9 Life Has Its Little Ups And Downs		Columbia 45358
				PURE PRAIRIE LEAGUE		
				Country-rock group formed in Cincinnati in 1971. Numerous personnel changes. Craig Fuller, guitarist/vocalist from 1971-75, joined Little Feat by 1988. Country singer Vince Gill was lead singer from late 1979-83.		
3/22/75	20	8		1 Amie	27	RCA 10184
5/17/80	1³	26		2 Let Me Love You Tonight	10	Casablanca 2266
5/2/81	4	16		3 Still Right Here In My Heart...	28	Casablanca 2332
				PURSELL, Bill		
				Pianist from Tulare, California. Appeared with the Nashville Symphony Orchestra. Taught musical composition at Vanderbilt University.		
2/16/63	4	12		Our Winter Love ....[I]	9	Columbia 42619

Q

DEBUT DATE	PEAK POS	WKS CHR	G O L D	ARTIST — Record Title	POP POS	Label & Number
				QUARTERFLASH		
				Rock group from Portland, Oregon led by the husband-and-wife team of Marv (guitar) and Rindy (vocals, saxophone) Ross. Originally known as Seafood Mama.		
1/23/82	41	3	●	1 Harden My Heart	3	Geffen 49824
				originally released as by Seafood Mama on Whitefire in 1980		
7/2/83	28	13		2 Take Me To Heart	14	Geffen 29603
				QUATRO, Suzi		
				Rock singer born on 6/3/50 in Detroit. Moved to England in 1970, signed with Mickie Most's RAK label. Played Leather Tuscadero on TV's *Happy Days* in 1977. Her older sister Patti was a bassist with Fanny.		
2/24/79	4	19	●	Stumblin' In	4	RSO 917
				SUZI QUATRO AND CHRIS NORMAN (lead singer of Smokie)		
				QUEEN		
				Rock group formed in England in 1972: Freddie Mercury (born Fred Bulsara on 9/5/46 in Zanzibar; d: 11/24/91 of AIDS; vocals), Brian May (guitar), John Deacon (bass) and Roger Taylor (drums). May and Taylor had been in the group Smile. Mercury had recorded as Larry Lurex. Wrote soundtrack for the film *Flash Gordon* in 1980.		
1/19/80	17	10	●	1 Crazy Little Thing Called Love	1⁴	Elektra 46579
5/8/93	42	7		2 Somebody To Love	30	Hollywood 64647
				GEORGE MICHAEL and QUEEN		
				#13 Pop hit for Queen in 1977		
				QUINN, Anthony ✪		
				Born on 4/21/15 in Chihuahua, Mexico. Popular film actor. Oscar winner for *Viva Zapata!* (1952) and *Lust For Life* (1956). Best known for the leading role in *Zorba The Greek*.		
7/1/67	28	6		Sometimes ....[S]		Capitol 5930
				with the Harold Spina Singers; same melody as "I Love You (And You Love Me)" by The Billy Vaughn Singers		

194

R

★★72★★ **RABBITT, Eddie**

Born Edward Thomas Rabbitt on 11/27/44 in Brooklyn; raised in East Orange, New Jersey. Country singer/songwriter/guitarist. First recorded for 20th Century in 1964. Moved to Nashville in 1968. Became established after Elvis Presley recorded his song "Kentucky Rain."

1)I Love A Rainy Night 2)You And I 3)You Can't Run From Love

8/14/76	48	1		1 Rocky Mountain Music	76	Elektra 45315
6/24/78	18	12		2 You Don't Love Me Anymore	53	Elektra 45488
10/21/78	47	2		3 I Just Want To Love You		Elektra 45531
2/10/79	26	11		4 Every Which Way But Loose	30	Elektra 45554
				movie title song		
6/16/79	9	19		5 **Suspicions**	13	Elektra 46053
3/29/80	35	14		6 Gone Too Far	82	Elektra 46613
7/12/80	3	18	●	7 **Drivin' My Life Away**	5	Elektra 46656
				from the film Roadie		
11/15/80	1³	21	●	8 **I Love A Rainy Night**	1²	Elektra 47066
8/1/81	3	20		9 **Step By Step**	5	Elektra 47174
11/28/81	10	16		10 **Someone Could Lose A Heart Tonight**	15	Elektra 47239
4/17/82	9	20		11 **I Don't Know Where To Start**	35	Elektra 47435
10/16/82	2⁵	28		12 **You And I**	7	Elektra 69936
				EDDIE RABBITT with CRYSTAL GAYLE		
4/2/83	2²	19		13 **You Can't Run From Love**	55	Warner 29712
				above 12 (except #11) were #1 Country hits		
9/3/83	15	11		14 **You Put The Beat In My Heart**	81	Warner 29512
1/14/84	38	5		15 Nothing Like Falling In Love		Warner 29431
5/26/84	36	6		16 B-B-B-Burnin' Up With Love		Warner 29279
11/16/85	35	3		17 A World Without Love		RCA 14192

RAFFERTY, Gerry

Born on 4/16/47 in Paisley, Scotland. Singer/songwriter/guitarist. Co-leader of Stealers Wheel.

5/6/78	4	18	●	1 **Baker Street**	2⁶	United Art. 1192
				Raphael Ravenscroft (sax solo)		
8/26/78	1⁴	22		2 **Right Down The Line**	12	United Art. 1233
1/20/79	26	6		3 Home And Dry	28	United Art. 1266
6/16/79	17	9		4 Days Gone Down (Still Got The Light In Your Eyes)	17	United Art. 1298
8/25/79	15	11		5 Get It Right Next Time	21	United Art. 1316

RAIDERS — see REVERE, Paul

★★166★★ **RAITT, Bonnie**

Born on 11/8/49 in Burbank, California. Veteran blues-rock singer/guitarist. Daughter of Broadway actor/singer John Raitt. Winner of four Grammys for her 1989 album *Nick Of Time*. Married actor Michael O'Keefe (*Caddyshack* film and TV's *Against The Law*) on 4/28/91.

1)Not The Only One 2)Have A Heart 3)Something To Talk About

9/16/89	10	15		1 Nick Of Time	92	Capitol 44364
2/3/90	3	20		2 **Have A Heart**	49	Capitol 44501
				theme from the film Heart Condition		
6/23/90	35	6		3 Love Letter		Capitol LP Cut
				from the album Nick Of Time on Capitol 91268		
7/6/91	5	34		4 **Something To Talk About**	5	Capitol 44724
10/12/91	6	36		5 **I Can't Make You Love Me**	18	Capitol 44729
3/21/92	2¹	29		6 **Not The Only One**	34	Capitol 44764
7/25/92	10	20		7 **Come To Me**		Capitol LP Cut
				from the album Luck Of The Draw on Capitol 96111; also on the B-side of #8 below		
12/19/92	17	16		8 All At Once		Capitol 5679

RAMBEAU, Eddie

Born Edward Flurie on 6/30/43 in Hazleton, Pennsylvania. Pop singer/songwriter.

6/12/65	13	4		1 Concrete And Clay	35	DynoVoice 204
7/17/65	30	4		2 My Name Is Mud	112	DynoVoice 207

DEBUT DATE	PEAK POS	WKS CHR	GOLD	ARTIST — Record Title	POP POS	Label & Number
				RANDALL, Frankie ✪		
				Los Angeles-based singer/songwriter.		
4/1/67	**38**	2		**1** Nice 'N Easy		RCA 9126
				#60 Pop hit for Frank Sinatra in 1960		
12/2/67	**40**	2		**2** The Happy Time		RCA 9346
				Broadway musical title song		
				RANDAZZO, Teddy — see MGM SINGING STRINGS		
				RANDOLPH, Boots		
				Born Homer Louis Randolph, III on 6/3/27 in Paducah, Kentucky. Premier Nashville session saxophonist.		
12/24/66	**28**	6		**1** The Shadow Of Your Smile	93	Monument 976
6/24/67	**30**	6		**2** Temptation ....[I]	93	Monument 1009
3/16/68	**39**	2	✔	**3** Fred ....[I]		Monument 1056
7/27/68	**19**	6	✔	**4** Gentle On My Mind ....[I]		Monument 1081
				#30 Pop hit for Glen Campbell in 1967		
5/16/70	**40**	1		**5** Anna	111	Monument 1199
				#54 Pop hit for Jorgen Ingmann in 1961		
				RANEY, Sue ✪		
				Singer from New York City. Founder of Rayel Records production company.		
1/7/67	**33**	3		**1** There Goes My Everything		Imperial 66222
				#20 Pop hit for Engelbert Humperdinck in 1967		
12/9/67	**22**	6		**2** Parade (A Banda)		Imperial 66265
				#35 Pop hit for Herb Alpert & The Tijuana Brass in 1967		
12/28/68	**16**	8		**3** Early Morning Blues And Greens		Imperial 66340
				RANKIN, Kenny ✪		
				Singer/songwriter/acoustic guitarist.		
3/20/76	**28**	6		**1** Sunday Kind Of Love		Little David 732
				#15 hit for Jo Stafford in 1947		
7/19/80	**33**	7		**2** Regrets		Atlantic 3663
★★**188**★★				**RAWLS, Lou**		
				Born on 12/1/35 in Chicago. With the Pilgrim Travelers gospel group, 1957-59. Summer replacement TV show *Lou Rawls & The Golddiggers* in 1969. In films *Angel Angel, Down We Go* and *Believe In Me*. Voice of many Budweiser beer ads and featured singer in the *Garfield* TV specials.		
				1)You'll Never Find Another Love Like Mine 2)Lady Love 3)Wind Beneath My Wings		
6/5/65	**27**	4		**1** Three O'Clock In The Morning	83	Capitol 5424
9/13/69	**35**	3		**2** Your Good Thing (Is About To End)	18	Capitol 2550
3/21/70	**31**	2		**3** You've Made Me So Very Happy	95	Capitol 2734
10/2/71	**14**	9		**4** A Natural Man	17	MGM 14262
11/18/72	**34**	5		**5** Walk On In	106	MGM 14428
				written by Carole King		
6/12/76	**1**[1]	14	●	**6** You'll Never Find Another Love Like Mine	2[2]	Phil. Int. 3592
10/23/76	**19**	10		**7** Groovy People	64	Phil. Int. 3604
12/10/77	**5**	22		**8** Lady Love	24	Phil. Int. 3634
5/13/78	**10**	13		**9** One Life To Live		Phil. Int. 3643
9/9/78	**33**	7		**10** There Will Be Love		Phil. Int. 3653
3/19/83	**10**	15		**11** Wind Beneath My Wings	65	Epic 03758
				RAYDIO — see PARKER, Ray Jr.		
				RAYE, Collin ✪		
				Country singer. Born on 8/22/59 in DeQueen, Arkansas.		
12/5/92	**21**	14		In This Life		Epic 74791
				RAY, GOODMAN & BROWN		
				Soul group consisting of Harry Ray (tenor), Al Goodman (bass) and Billy Brown (falsetto). Formerly known as The Moments. Ray died of a stroke on 10/1/92 (age 45).		
2/16/80	**17**	12	●	**1** Special Lady	5	Polydor 2033
9/6/80	**19**	10		**2** My Prayer	47	Polydor 2116
				REA, Chris		
				Born on 3/4/51 in Middlesborough, England. Pop singer/songwriter.		
7/22/78	**1**[3]	18		**1** Fool (If You Think It's Over)	12	United Art. 1198
6/17/89	**9**	18		**2** On The Beach		Geffen 22938

DEBUT DATE	PEAK POS	WKS CHR	G O L D	ARTIST — Record Title	POP POS	Label & Number
				READ, John Dawson British singer/songwriter/guitarist.		
8/9/75	**18**	9		A Friend Of Mine Is Going Blind	72	Chrysalis 2105
				READY FOR THE WORLD Black sextet from Flint, Michigan, formed in 1982: Melvin Riley, Jr. (lead singer), Gordon Strozier, Gregory Potts, Willie Triplett, John Eaton and Gerald Valentine.		
2/14/87	**24**	6		Love You Down	9	MCA 52947
				REDDINGS, The Consisted of Otis Redding's sons Dexter (vocals, bass) and Otis III (guitar), and cousin Mark Locket (vocals, drums, keyboards).		
6/12/82	**15**	16		(Sittin' On) The Dock Of The Bay	55	Believe 02836
★★**34**★★				**REDDY, Helen** Born on 10/25/41 in Melbourne, Australia. Family was in show business; Helen made stage debut at age four. Own TV series in the early '60s. Migrated to New York in 1966. To Los Angeles in 1968. Acted in the films *Airport 1975* (1974), *Pete's Dragon* (1977) and *Sgt. Pepper's Lonely Hearts Club Band* (1978). *1)Leave Me Alone (Ruby Red Dress) 2)Delta Dawn 3)Keep On Singing 4)You And Me Against The World 5)Angie Baby*		
5/22/71	**12**	7		1 I Don't Know How To Love Him .... from the rock opera *Jesus Christ Superstar*	13	Capitol 3027
7/31/71	**8**	12		2 Crazy Love.. written by Van Morrison	51	Capitol 3138
12/25/71	**32**	4		3 No Sad Song	62	Capitol 3231
6/24/72	**2**²	22	●	4 I Am Woman.. from the film *Stand Up And Be Counted*	**1**¹	Capitol 3350
2/17/73	**2**²	13		5 Peaceful	12	Capitol 3527
6/23/73	**1**²	16	●	6 Delta Dawn	**1**¹	Capitol 3645
11/10/73	**1**⁴	16	●	7 Leave Me Alone (Ruby Red Dress)	3	Capitol 3768
3/16/74	**1**²	13		8 Keep On Singing	15	Capitol 3845
6/15/74	**1**¹	18		9 You And Me Against The World	9	Capitol 3897
11/2/74	**1**¹	13	●	10 Angie Baby	**1**¹	Capitol 3972
2/8/75	**1**¹	12		11 Emotion	22	Capitol 4021
7/5/75	**5**	8		12 Bluebird.. written by Leon Russell	35	Capitol 4108
8/23/75	**1**¹	11		13 Ain't No Way To Treat A Lady	8	Capitol 4128
11/29/75	**2**¹	14		14 Somewhere In The Night	19	Capitol 4192
8/14/76	**1**¹	11		15 I Can't Hear You No More	29	Capitol 4312
11/13/76	**10**	12		16 Gladiola		Capitol 4350
4/16/77	**5**	21		17 You're My World	18	Capitol 4418
10/8/77	**14**	11		18 The Happy Girls .... flip side "Laissez Les Bontemps Rouler" made the Country charts (POS 98)	57	Capitol 4487
12/24/77	**27**	10		19 Candle On The Water .... from the film *Pete's Dragon*		Capitol 4521
4/22/78	**12**	9	✓	20 We'll Sing In The Sunshine.. #4 Pop hit for Gale Garnett in 1964		Capitol 4555
7/1/78	**28**	8		21 Ready Or Not	73	Capitol 4582
6/9/79	**41**	5		22 Make Love To Me	60	Capitol 4712
11/10/79	**43**	5		23 Let Me Be Your Woman		Capitol 4786
5/23/81	**42**	4		24 I Can't Say Goodbye To You	88	MCA 51106
				REDNOW, Eivets — see WONDER, Stevie		
				REED, Jerry Born Jerry Reed Hubbard on 3/20/37 in Atlanta. Country singer/guitarist/songwriter/actor. Among his many films, co-starred in *Gator* and *Smokey & The Bandit I* and *II*. Own TV series *Concrete Cowboys*. Elvis Presley recorded two of Reed's songs: "U.S. Male" and "Guitar Man."		
5/22/71	**6**	10		1 When You're Hot, You're Hot ....[N]	9	RCA 9976
9/11/71	**29**	4		2 Ko-Ko Joe	51	RCA 1011
6/23/73	**32**	7		3 Lord, Mr. Ford ....[N]	68	RCA 0960
				REESE, Della Born Delloreese Patricia Early on 7/6/31 in Detroit. With Mahalia Jackson gospel troupe from 1945-49, and Erskine Hawkins in the early '50s. Solo since 1957. Actress/singer on many TV shows. Appeared in the 1958 film *Let's Rock* and the 1989 film *Harlem Nights*. Own series *Della* in 1970. Played "Della Rogers" on the TV series *Chico & The Man* from 1976-78. On TV's *The Royal Family*.		
7/10/65	**21**	7		After Loving You	95	ABC-Para. 10691

DEBUT DATE	PEAK POS	WKS CHR	GOLD	ARTIST — Record Title	POP POS	Label & Number
				REEVES, Dianne ○		
				Jazz singer. Born in Detroit in 1956; raised in Denver. Niece of jazz bassist Charles Burrell.		
4/14/90	45	4		Never Too Far..		EMI 50242
				REEVES, Jim		
				Born James Travis Reeves on 8/20/24 in Panola County, Texas. Killed in a plane crash on 7/31/64 in Nashville. Joined the *Grand Ole Opry* in 1955. Own ABC-TV series in 1957. In the 1963 film *Kimberley Jim*. Posthumously, he continued to have many country hits into the 1980s.		
12/4/61	20	1		1 Losing Your Love......................................	89	RCA 7950
8/29/64	17	4		2 I Guess I'm Crazy......................................	82	RCA 8383
11/21/64	15	2		3 I Won't Forget You	93	RCA 8461
3/13/65	18	1		4 This Is It..	88	RCA 8508
8/14/65	10	7		5 Is It Really Over?....................................	79	RCA 8625
8/20/66	15	8		6 Blue Side Of Lonesome	59	RCA 8902
				REILLY, Mike		
				New York City-based singer/songwriter discovered by Tom Smothers.		
2/27/71	38	3		1927 Kansas City	88	Paramount 0053
				REISMAN, Joe		
				Born on 9/16/24 in Dallas. Conductor/composer/arranger for TV, Broadway and films. Musical conductor at RCA during 1950s. Headed RCA's A&R section in Los Angeles from 1962-77. Died of a heart attack on 9/25/87 (age 63).		
7/24/61	14	4		The Guns Of Navarone.................................... [I]	74	Landa 674
				movie title song		
				REJOICE!		
				Husband-wife duo of Tom and Nancy Brown from Sausalito, California.		
3/8/69	31	4		November Snow	126	Dunhill 4176
				R.E.M.		
				Athens, Georgia rock quartet formed in 1980: Michael Stipe (vocals), Peter Buck (guitar), Mike Mills (bass) and Bill Berry (drums). R.E.M. is abbreviation for Rapid Eye Movement, the dream stage of sleep. Developed huge following with college audiences in the early 1980s as one of the first "alternative rock" bands. Buck, Mills and Berry recorded with Warren Zevon as the Hindu Love Gods in 1990.		
6/1/91	28	9	●	1 Losing My Religion	4	Warner 19392
9/21/91	48	1		2 Shiny Happy People....................................	10	Warner 19242
3/27/93	46	4		3 Man On The Moon	30	Warner 18642
				REMBRANDTS, The		
				Duo of Danny Wilde and Phil Solem. Both were members of the L.A. pop band Great Buildings.		
3/30/91	12	16		Just The Way It Is, Baby................................	14	Atco 98874
				RENAY, Diane		
				Philadelphian Renee Diane Kushner.		
2/8/64	1¹	10		Navy Blue	6	20th Century 456
				RENE & RENE		
				Mexican-American duo from Laredo, Texas: Rene Ornelas (b: 8/26/36) and Rene Herrera (b: 10/2/35).		
11/23/68	2¹	14		Lo Mucho Que Te Quiero (The More I Love You)...........	14	White Whale 287
				RENO, Mike, and Ann Wilson		
				Lead singers of Loverboy and Heart, respectively.		
5/19/84	1¹	22		Almost Paradise...Love Theme From Footloose	7	Columbia 04418
				from the film *Footloose*		
				REO SPEEDWAGON		
				Rock quintet from Champaign, Illinois: Kevin Cronin (lead vocals, rhythm guitar), Gary Richrath (lead guitar), Neal Doughty (keyboards), Bruce Hall (bass) and Alan Gratzer (drums). Group named after a 1911 fire truck.		
9/5/81	26	7		1 In Your Letter	20	Epic 02457
1/26/85	3	19	●	2 Can't Fight This Feeling..............................	1³	Epic 04713
4/20/85	10	16		3 One Lonely Night	19	Epic 04848
8/15/87	6	23		4 In My Dreams..	19	Epic 07255
7/9/88	9	19		5 Here With Me	20	Epic 07901
				RESTLESS HEART		
				Nashville country-rock quintet consisting of former session musicians Larry Stewart (vocals), David Innis, Greg Jennings, Paul Gregg and John Dittrich. Stewart went solo in early 1992. Keyboardist Innis left in early 1993. Remaining three continued on with two backing musicians.		
2/21/87	3	24		1 I'll Still Be Loving You	33	RCA 5065
8/22/87	11	18		2 Why Does It Have To Be (Wrong or Right)		RCA 5132
11/7/87	23	13		3 New York (Hold Her Tight)		RCA 5280
				flip side "Wheels" made the Country charts (POS 1¹)		

DEBUT DATE	PEAK POS	WKS CHR	G O L D	ARTIST — Record Title	POP POS	Label & Number
				RESTLESS HEART — Cont'd		
3/14/92	**33**	7		4 'Til I Loved You ....[R]		RCA LP Cut
				originally made the Country charts in 1986 (POS 10) on RCA 14292; from the album *The Best Of Restless Heart* on RCA 61041		
10/31/92	**2**[7]	33		**5 When She Cries**	11	RCA 62412
2/27/93	**1**[2]	25		**6 Tell Me What You Dream**	43	RCA 62468
				RESTLESS HEART Featuring Warren Hill		
				REUNION		
				RCA studio group — Joey Levine (Ohio Express), lead singer.		
6/3/72	**38**	3		Smile (Theme From Modern Times)		Bell 45,222
				music written by Charlie Chaplin		
				REVERE, Paul, And The Raiders		
				Pop-rock group formed in Portland, Oregon in 1960. Group featured Paul Revere (b: 1/7/42, Boise, Idaho; keyboards) and Mark Lindsay (lead singer). To Los Angeles in 1965. On daily ABC-TV show *Where The Action Is* in 1965. Own TV show *Happening* in 1968. Lindsay and Raider member, Keith Allison, recorded with Steve Alaimo as The Unknowns. Group had many personnel changes.		
				RAIDERS:		
5/29/71	**11**	10	●	1 Indian Reservation (The Lament Of The Cherokee Reservation Indian)	**1**[1]	Columbia 45332
9/18/71	**11**	8		2 Birds Of A Feather	23	Columbia 45453
2/12/72	**28**	4		3 Country Wine	51	Columbia 45535
				RHODES, Cynthia — see STALLONE, Frank		
				RHYTHM HERITAGE		
				Los Angeles studio group assembled by prolific producers Steve Barri and Michael Omartian (keyboards). Vocals by Oren and Luther Waters. Omartian was in band Gator Creek with Kenny Loggins.		
11/29/75	**6**	17	●	1 Theme From S.W.A.T. ....[I]	**1**[1]	ABC 12135
				from the ABC-TV series *S.W.A.T.*		
5/1/76	**14**	11		2 Baretta's Theme ("Keep Your Eye On The Sparrow")	20	ABC 12177
				from the Robert Blake TV series *Baretta*		
2/26/77	**49**	2		3 Theme From Rocky (Gonna Fly Now) ....[I]	94	ABC 12243
				from the Sylvester Stallone film *Rocky*		
10/15/77	**48**	4		4 Theme From Starsky & Hutch ....[I]		ABC 12273
				from the TV series *Starsky & Hutch*		
★★91★★				**RICH, Charlie**		
				Born on 12/14/32 in Colt, Arkansas. Rockabilly-country singer/pianist/songwriter. First played jazz and blues. Own jazz group, the Velvetones, mid-1950s, while in U.S. Air Force. Session work with Sun Records in 1958. Known as the "Silver Fox."		
				1)The Most Beautiful Girl 2)A Very Special Love Song 3)Every Time You Touch Me (I Get High)		
4/11/70	**39**	2		1 July 12, 1939	85	Epic 10585
10/31/70	**34**	5		2 Nice 'N' Easy ....[R]		Epic 10662
				originally Bubbled Under (POS 131) in 1964 on Groove 0041		
5/12/73	**8**	15	●	3 Behind Closed Doors...............................	15	Epic 10950
9/29/73	**1**[3]	23	●	4 The Most Beautiful Girl	**1**[2]	Epic 11040
2/16/74	**15**	10		5 There Won't Be Anymore.............................	18	RCA 0195
2/23/74	**1**[2]	15		**6 A Very Special Love Song**	11	Epic 11091
5/11/74	**9**	11		**7 I Don't See Me In Your Eyes Anymore**	47	RCA 0260
8/10/74	**1**[1]	13		**8 I Love My Friend**.................................	24	Epic 20006
10/26/74	**41**	5		9 She Called Me Baby.................................	47	RCA 10062
				above 7 were #1 Country hits		
2/8/75	**16**	9		10 My Elusive Dreams	49	Epic 50064
5/31/75	**1**[1]	13		**11 Every Time You Touch Me (I Get High)**..........	19	Epic 50103
9/27/75	**33**	8		12 All Over Me.......................................		Epic 50142
1/17/76	**11**	11		13 Since I Fell For You	71	Epic 50182
5/29/76	**42**	3		14 America, The Beautiful (1976).....................		Epic 50222
9/25/76	**31**	4		15 Road Song		Epic 50268
7/16/77	**32**	10		16 Rollin' With The Flow	101	Epic 50392
8/11/79	**13**	13		17 Life Goes On		United Art. 1307

DEBUT DATE	PEAK POS	WKS CHR	GOLD	ARTIST — Record Title	POP POS	Label & Number
★★171★★				**RICHARD, Cliff**		
				Born Harry Rodger Webb on 10/14/40 in Lucknow, India, of British parentage. Vocalist/actor/guitarist. To England in 1948. Worked in skiffle groups, mid-1950s. Backing band: The Drifters (later: The Shadows). Cliff also recorded Inspirational music since 1967. The Shadows disbanded in 1969. Superstar in England, with over 80 charted hits, including 10 #1 singles. British films *Expresso Bongo*, *The Young Ones*, *Summer Holiday* and *Wonderful Life*.		
				1)Daddy's Home 2)Suddenly 3)We Don't Talk Anymore		
1/18/64	**10**	7		1 It's All In The Game	25	Epic 9633
7/24/76	**30**	8	●	2 Devil Woman	6	Rocket 40574
9/17/77	**48**	2		3 Try A Smile		Rocket 40771
11/10/79	**5**	17		4 We Don't Talk Anymore	7	EMI America 8025
10/4/80	**21**	16		5 Dreaming	10	EMI America 8057
10/25/80	**4**	20		6 Suddenly	20	MCA 51007
				OLIVIA NEWTON-JOHN AND CLIFF RICHARD from the film *Xanadu*		
1/17/81	**6**	15		7 A Little In Love	17	EMI America 8068
1/30/82	**3**	16		8 Daddy's Home	23	EMI America 8103
10/23/82	**26**	12		9 The Only Way Out	64	EMI America 8135
10/22/83	**23**	7		10 Never Say Die (Give A Little Bit More)	73	EMI America 8180
2/18/84	**17**	11		11 Donna		EMI America 8193
				#2 Pop hit for Ritchie Valens in 1959		
				RICHARDS, Barry ✪		
9/28/74	**33**	10		Come Fill Your Cup Again		A&M 1543
★★25★★				**RICHIE, Lionel**		
				Born on 6/20/49 in Tuskegee, Alabama. Grew up on the campus of Tuskegee Institute where his grandfather worked. Former lead singer of the Commodores. Appeared in the film *Thank God It's Friday* (1978).		
				1)Hello 2)You Are 3)Stuck On You		
7/11/81	**1**[3]	27	▲	1 Endless Love	**1**[9]	Motown 1519
				DIANA ROSS & LIONEL RICHIE movie title song		
10/16/82	**1**[4]	21	●	2 Truly	**1**[2]	Motown 1644
1/15/83	**1**[6]	20		3 You Are	4	Motown 1657
4/16/83	**1**[4]	18		4 My Love	5	Motown 1677
9/24/83	**1**[4]	23	●	5 All Night Long (All Night)	**1**[4]	Motown 1698
12/3/83	**6**	21		6 Running With The Night	7	Motown 1710
3/3/84	**1**[6]	24	●	7 Hello	**1**[2]	Motown 1722
6/23/84	**1**[5]	20		8 Stuck On You	3	Motown 1746
10/6/84	**1**[4]	19		9 Penny Lover	8	Motown 1762
11/9/85	**1**[5]	20	●	10 Say You, Say Me	**1**[4]	Motown 1819
				featured in the film (not album) *White Nights*		
7/19/86	**3**	17		11 Dancing On The Ceiling	**2**[2]	Motown 1843
10/4/86	**1**[2]	21		12 Love Will Conquer All	9	Motown 1866
12/13/86	**1**[4]	20		13 Ballerina Girl/	7	
12/27/86	**28**	11		14 Deep River Woman	71	Motown 1873
				LIONEL RICHIE with Alabama		
4/4/87	**5**	15		15 Se La	20	Motown 1883
5/2/92	**3**	26		16 Do It To Me	21	Motown 2160
8/15/92	**7**	22		17 My Destiny		Motown 2176
				RIDDLE, Nelson		
				Born on 6/1/21 in Oradell, New Jersey; died on 10/6/85. Trombonist/arranger with Charlie Spivak and Tommy Dorsey in the '40s. One of the most in-demand of all arranger/conductors for many top artists, including Frank Sinatra (several classic '50s albums), Nat King Cole, Ella Mae Morse, and more recently, Linda Ronstadt; also arranger/musical director for many films.		
7/7/62	**9**	7		1 Route 66 Theme .... [I]	30	Capitol 4741
				from the CBS-TV series *Route 66*		
4/1/67	**33**	2		2 Thoroughly Modern Millie		Liberty 55952
				movie title song		
10/29/83	**5**	17		3 What's New *	53	Asylum 69780
				#2 hit for Bing Crosby in 1939		
2/18/84	**7**	13		4 I've Got A Crush On You *		Asylum 69752
				#21 hit for Frank Sinatra in 1948 ***LINDA RONSTADT & THE NELSON RIDDLE ORCHESTRA**		

DEBUT DATE	PEAK POS	WKS CHR	G O L D	ARTIST — Record Title	POP POS	Label & Number
				RIFF		
				Male vocal quintet from Paterson, New Jersey formed at Eastside High School: Kenny Kelly, Steven Capers, Jr., Anthony Fuller, Dwayne Jones and Michael Best. Appeared as themselves (singing the alma mater) in the 1989 film *Lean On Me*, which was based on their school.		
3/30/91	29	11		My Heart Is Failing Me	25	SBK 07342
				RIGHTEOUS BROTHERS, The		
				Blue-eyed soul duo: Bill Medley (b: 9/19/40, Santa Ana, California; baritone) and Bobby Hatfield (b: 8/10/40, Beaver Dam, Wisconsin; tenor). Formed duo in 1962. First recorded as the Paramours for Smash in 1962. On *Hullabaloo* and *Shindig* TV shows. Split up from 1968-74. Medley went solo, replaced by Jimmy Walker (The Knickerbockers); rejoined Hatfield in 1974.		
5/28/66	37	4		1 Rat Race .... [I]		Verve 10403
				THE RIGHTEOUS BROTHERS BAND Orchestra conducted by Michael Patterson		
6/8/74	38	6		2 Rock And Roll Heaven	3	Haven 7002
11/16/74	6	11		3 Dream On	32	Haven 7006
8/25/90	1²	22		4 Unchained Melody .... [R]	13	Verve F. 871882
				featured in the film *Ghost*; originally made the *Hot 100* on 7/17/65 (POS 4) on Philles 129; a newly recorded version also made the *Hot 100* in 1990 on Curb 76842 (POS 19)		
				RILEY, Jeannie C.		
				Born Jeanne Carolyn Stephenson on 10/19/45 in Anson, Texas. Country singer.		
8/31/68	4	10	●	Harper Valley P.T.A.	1¹	Plantation 3
				RIOS, Miguel		
				Born in Granada, Spain in 1944.		
6/13/70	1²	9		A Song Of Joy	14	A&M 1193
				based on the last movement of Beethoven's 9th Symphony; Waldo de los Rios, conductor		
				RIOS, Waldo de los		
				Spanish conductor/composer; died on 3/28/77.		
6/12/71	25	6		Mozart Symphony No. 40 in G Minor K.550, 1st Movement .... [I]	67	United Art. 50772
				RIPERTON, Minnie		
				Born on 11/8/47 in Chicago; died of cancer on 7/12/79 in Los Angeles. Recorded as "Andrea Davis" on Chess in 1966. Lead singer of the rock-R&B sextet Rotary Connection from 1967-70. In Stevie Wonder's backup group Wonderlove in 1973.		
1/25/75	4	14	●	1 Lovin' You	1¹	Epic 50057
11/22/75	45	3		2 Simple Things		Epic 50166
				RITCHIE FAMILY, The		
				Philadelphia disco group named for arranger/producer Ritchie Rome. Group featured various session singers and musicians.		
8/16/75	5	11		Brazil .... [I]	11	20th Century 2218
				RITENOUR, Lee		
				Born on 1/11/52 in Los Angeles. Guitarist/composer/arranger. Top session guitarist, has appeared on more than 200 albums. Nicknamed "Captain Fingers." Member of jazz outfits Brass Fever and Fourplay.		
5/23/81	15	13		Is It You	15	Elektra 47124
				RIVERS, Johnny		
				Born John Ramistella on 11/7/42 in New York City; raised in Baton Rouge. Rock and roll singer/guitarist/songwriter/producer. Recorded with the Spades for Suede in 1956. Named Johnny Rivers by DJ Alan Freed in 1958. To Los Angeles in 1961. Began own Soul City label in 1966. Recorded Christian music in the early 1980s.		
5/22/71	38	2		1 Sea Cruise	84	United Art. 50778
8/2/75	38	6		2 Help Me Rhonda	22	Epic 50121
7/23/77	8	18	●	3 Swayin' To The Music (Slow Dancin')	10	Big Tree 16094
12/24/77	4	15		4 Curious Mind (Um, Um, Um, Um, Um, Um)	41	Big Tree 16106
				ROBBINS, Marty		
				Born Martin David Robinson on 9/26/25 in Glendale, Arizona; died of a heart attack on 12/8/82. Country singer/guitarist/songwriter. Own radio show with K-Bar Cowboys, late 1940s. Own TV show, *Western Caravan*, KPHO-Phoenix, 1951. First recorded for Columbia in 1952. Regular on the *Grand Ole Opry* since 1953. Own Robbins label in 1958. Raced stock cars. Films: *Road To Nashville* and *Guns Of A Stranger*.		
9/25/61	12	5		1 It's Your World	51	Columbia 42065
1/20/62	19	2		2 I Told The Brook	81	Columbia 42246
				flip side "Sometimes I'm Tempted" made the Country charts (POS 12)		
4/28/62	18	5		3 Love Can't Wait	69	Columbia 42375
12/1/62	4	8		4 Ruby Ann	18	Columbia 42614
3/21/70	23	7		5 My Woman My Woman, My Wife	42	Columbia 45091

DEBUT DATE	PEAK POS	WKS CHR	G O L D	ARTIST — Record Title	POP POS	Label & Number
				ROBERTS, Austin		
				Born on 9/19/45 in Newport News, Virginia. Writer of several country songs. Collaborator on cartoon series *Scooby Doo* and *Josie & The Pussycats*. Replaced Gene Pistilli in Buchanan Brothers/Cashman, Pistilli & West trio in 1972.		
11/4/72	16	10		1 Something's Wrong With Me	12	Chelsea 0101
2/10/73	22	7		2 Keep On Singing...	50	Chelsea 0110
9/20/75	22	8		3 Rocky...	9	Private S. 45020
				ROBERTS, Malcolm ○		
2/14/70	40	2		Love Is All		Columbia 45074
				ROBERTSON, Robbie ○		
				Born Jaime Robbie Robertson on 7/5/44 in Toronto, Canada. Guitarist of The Band.		
4/23/88	47	2		Somewhere Down The Crazy River...................................		Geffen 28111
				ROBINSON, Freddy		
				Born on 2/24/39 in Memphis. Jazz-rock guitarist. With Little Walter's Band, Howling Wolf and John Mayall.		
8/1/70	32	7		Black Fox .... [I]	56	World Pac. 88155
★★80★★				**ROBINSON, Smokey**		
				Born William Robinson on 2/19/40 in Detroit. Formed The Miracles (then called the Matadors) at Northern High School in 1955. First recorded for End in 1958. Married Miracles' member Claudette Rogers in 1963. Left The Miracles on 1/29/72. Wrote dozens of hit songs for Motown artists. Vice President of Motown Records, 1985-1988. Inducted into the Rock and Roll Hall of Fame in 1987. Won Grammy's Living Legends Award in 1989.		
				1)Just To See Her 2)Everything You Touch 3)One Heartbeat		
12/1/79	34	8		1 Cruisin'	4	Tamla 54306
3/14/81	4	20	●	2 **Being With You**	2³	Tamla 54321
2/6/82	31	7		3 Tell Me Tomorrow - Part I	33	Tamla 1601
5/15/82	32	7		4 Old Fashioned Love	60	Tamla 1615
7/2/83	5	15		5 **Blame It On Love**	48	Tamla 1684
				SMOKEY ROBINSON And BARBARA MITCHELL (member of High Inergy)		
11/19/83	36	8		6 Don't Play Another Love Song	103	Tamla 1700
1/21/84	35	5		7 Ebony Eyes	43	Gordy 1714
				RICK JAMES Featuring SMOKEY ROBINSON		
2/22/86	18	8		8 Hold On To Your Love		Tamla 1828
3/14/87	1¹	24		9 **Just To See Her**	8	Motown 1877
7/25/87	2¹	22		10 **One Heartbeat**	10	Motown 1897
11/14/87	15	13		11 What's Too Much	79	Motown 1911
3/5/88	22	8		12 I Know You By Heart		Columbia 07727
				DOLLY PARTON with Smokey Robinson		
4/9/88	24	11		13 Love Don't Give No Reason		Motown 1925
2/4/89	4	20		14 **We've Saved The Best For Last**	47	Arista 9785
				KENNY G with Smokey Robinson		
2/24/90	2³	23		15 **Everything You Touch**		Motown 2031
5/26/90	32	8		16 (It's The) Same Old Love..		Motown 2046
8/25/90	34	6		17 Take Me Through The Night...		Motown 2056
10/19/91	12	13		18 Double Good Everything	91	SBK 07370
				ROBINSON, Vicki Sue		
				Born in Philadelphia in 1955. Disco vocalist. Appeared in the original Broadway productions of *Hair* and *Jesus Christ Superstar*.		
8/14/76	43	4		Turn The Beat Around...	10	RCA 10562
				RODGERS, Jimmie		
				Born James Frederick Rodgers on 9/18/33 in Camas, Washington. Vocalist/guitarist/pianist. Formed first group while in the Air Force. Own NBC-TV variety series in 1959. Career hampered following mysterious assault on the San Diego Freeway on 12/1/67, which left him with a fractured skull. Returned to performing a year later. Starred in films *The Little Shepherd From Kingdom Come* and *Back Door To Hell*.		
				1)It's Over 2)The World I Used To Know 3)No One Will Ever Know		
9/4/61	16	4		1 A Little Dog Cried .... [S]	71	Roulette 4384
9/15/62	14	8		2 No One Will Ever Know	43	Dot 16378
12/15/62	16	4		3 Rainbow At Midnight	62	Dot 16407
6/20/64	9	6		4 **The World I Used To Know**..	51	Dot 16595
				written by Rod McKuen (also #6 below)		
5/21/66	5	10		5 **It's Over**	37	Dot 16861
4/22/67	20	6		6 I'll Say Goodbye		A&M 842
10/7/67	21	7		7 Child Of Clay	31	A&M 871
2/24/68	25	4		8 I Believed It All..		A&M 902

DEBUT DATE	PEAK POS	WKS CHR	GOLD	ARTIST — Record Title	POP POS	Label & Number
				RODGERS, Jimmie — Cont'd		
10/12/68	**19**	9		9 Today.................................... #17 Pop hit for the New Christy Minstrels in 1964	104	A&M 976
12/20/69	**39**	2		10 Tomorrow Is My Friend....................... from the film *Gaily, Gaily*; written by Henry Mancini		A&M 1152
3/4/72	**30**	5		11 Froggy's Fable............................. #32 Pop hit for The Brothers Four in 1961		Epic 10828
10/7/78	**46**	4		12 Secretly ....[R] original version made the *Hot 100* in 1958 (POS 3) on Roulette 4070		Scrimshaw 1318
				ROE, Tommy Born on 5/9/42 in Atlanta. Pop-rock singer/guitarist/composer.		
9/11/71	**34**	4		Stagger Lee	25	ABC 11307
				ROGER Born Roger Troutman from Hamilton, Ohio. Leader of the family group Zapp. Worked with Sly Stone and George Clinton. Father of male singer Lynch.		
1/9/88	**22**	9		I Want To Be Your Man	3	Reprise 28229
				ROGERS, Dann Kenny Rogers' nephew, Danny Wayne Rogers.		
10/27/79	**6**	17		1 Looks Like Love Again	41	ia 500
4/5/80	**34**	7		2 China...................................		ia 503
				ROGERS, Julie Born Julie Rolls on 4/6/43 in London.		
11/21/64	**1**[3]	11		1 The Wedding	10	Mercury 72332
2/13/65	**12**	3		2 Like A Child	67	Mercury 72380
★★★4★★				**ROGERS, Kenny/First Edition** Born Kenneth Donald Rogers on 8/21/38 in Houston. With high school band the Scholars in 1958. Bass player of jazz group the Bobby Doyle Trio, recorded for Columbia. In Kirby Stone Four and The New Christy Minstrels, mid-1960s. Formed and fronted The First Edition in 1967. Original lineup included Thelma Camacho, Mike Settle, Terry Williams and Mickey Jones. All but Jones were members of The New Christy Minstrels. Group hosted own syndicated TV variety show *Rollin* in 1972. Rogers split from group in 1973. Starred in films *The Gambler, The Gambler II, Gambler III, Coward Of The County* and *Six Pack*.		
				1)I Don't Need You 2)Islands In The Stream 3)Lady 4)Love Will Turn You Around 5)She Believes In Me		
				THE FIRST EDITION:		
2/8/69	**18**	8		1 But You Know I Love You.....................	19	Reprise 0799
				KENNY ROGERS AND THE FIRST EDITION:		
6/28/69	**6**	12		2 **Ruby, Don't Take Your Love To Town** .... written by Mel Tillis	6	Reprise 0829
10/18/69	**29**	4		3 Ruben James .... title also shown as "Reuben James"	26	Reprise 0854
8/1/70	**8**	7		4 **Tell It All Brother**	17	Reprise 0923
10/31/70	**20**	5		5 Heed The Call.............................	33	Reprise 0953
3/20/71	**4**	9		6 **Someone Who Cares** .... love theme from the film *Fools*	51	Reprise 0999
				KENNY ROGERS:		
4/23/77	**10**	15	●	7 Lucille	5	United Art. 929
8/6/77	**13**	15		8 Daytime Friends...........................	28	United Art. 1027
11/19/77	**29**	13		9 Sweet Music Man	44	United Art. 1095
4/8/78	**44**	6		10 Every Time Two Fools Collide	101	United Art. 1137
				KENNY ROGERS & DOTTIE WEST		
6/10/78	**12**	14		11 Love Or Something Like It	32	United Art. 1210
10/28/78	**3**	26		12 The Gambler	16	United Art. 1250
4/14/79	**38**	8		13 All I Ever Need Is You .... **KENNY ROGERS** with DOTTIE WEST #7 Pop hit for Sonny & Cher in 1971	102	United Art. 1276
4/28/79	**1**[2]	16	●	14 **She Believes In Me**	5	United Art. 1273
9/22/79	**2**[1]	15		15 **You Decorated My Life**	7	United Art. 1315
11/17/79	**5**	15	●	16 **Coward Of The County**	3	United Art. 1327
3/29/80	**2**[4]	19		17 **Don't Fall In Love With A Dreamer** .... **KENNY ROGERS** with Kim Carnes	4	United Art. 1345
6/21/80	**8**	12		18 **Love The World Away**.................... from the film *Urban Cowboy*	14	United Art. 1359
10/4/80	**1**[4]	20	●	19 **Lady** .... written by Lionel Richie	**1**[6]	Liberty 1380

DEBUT DATE	PEAK POS	WKS CHR	G O L D	ARTIST — Record Title	POP POS	Label & Number
				ROGERS, Kenny/First Edition — Cont'd		
4/11/81	**7**	20		20 **What Are We Doin' In Love**........................	14	Liberty 1404
				DOTTIE WEST with Kenny Rogers		
6/13/81	**1**⁶	19		21 **I Don't Need You**...................................	3	Liberty 1415
9/5/81	**1**²	19		22 **Share Your Love With Me**......................	14	Liberty 1430
12/5/81	**25**	7		23 **Blaze Of Glory**....................................	66	Liberty 1441
1/16/82	**1**²	18		24 **Through The Years**..............................	13	Liberty 1444
				above 6 (except #20) produced by Lionel Richie		
7/3/82	**1**²	20		25 **Love Will Turn You Around**.................	13	Liberty 1471
				from the film *Six Pack* starring Kenny Rogers		
10/23/82	**10**	18		26 **A Love Song**......................................	47	Liberty 1485
1/29/83	**2**⁵	18		27 **We've Got Tonight**.............................	6	Liberty 1492
				KENNY ROGERS and SHEENA EASTON		
4/30/83	**2**²	19		28 **All My Life**..	37	Liberty 1495
8/27/83	**1**⁴	24	▲	29 **Islands In The Stream**........................	**1**²	RCA 13615
				KENNY ROGERS with Dolly Parton		
1/21/84	**2**³	19		30 **This Woman**......................................	23	RCA 13710
				flip side "Buried Treasure" made the Country charts (POS 3)		
4/21/84	**4**	16		31 **Eyes That See In The Dark**..................	79	RCA 13774
				above 3 feature writing and production work by the Bee Gees		
9/15/84	**1**²	19		32 **What About Me?**................................	15	RCA 13899
				KENNY ROGERS with KIM CARNES and JAMES INGRAM		
1/5/85	**40**	2		33 The Greatest Gift Of All......................[X]	81	RCA 13945
				KENNY ROGERS & DOLLY PARTON		
				from their Christmas TV special		
1/19/85	**5**	18		34 **Crazy**...	79	RCA 13975
4/13/85	**35**	4		35 Love Is What We Make It.......................		Liberty 1524
5/25/85	**13**	14		36 Real Love..	91	RCA 14058
				DOLLY PARTON (with Kenny Rogers)		
10/19/85	**8**	16		37 **Morning Desire**..................................	72	RCA 14194
6/14/86	**30**	6		38 The Pride Is Back..................................		RCA 14384
				KENNY ROGERS with NICKIE RYDER		
				tune used for a Chrysler Corporation jingle		
10/11/86	**10**	14		39 **They Don't Make Them Like They Used To**..................		RCA 5016
				theme from the film *Tough Guys*		
1/31/87	**15**	12		40 Twenty Years Ago.................................		RCA 5078
9/19/87	**42**	3		41 Make No Mistake, She's Mine.................		RCA 5209
				RONNIE MILSAP & KENNY ROGERS		
8/6/88	**17**	15		42 When You Put Your Heart In It...............		Reprise 27812
8/5/89	**26**	9		43 (Something Inside) So Strong.................		Reprise 22853
3/17/90	**10**	22		44 If I Knew Then What I Know Now............		Reprise 19972
				KENNY ROGERS (with Gladys Knight)		
				flip side "Maybe" (Kenny Rogers with Holly Dunn) made the Country charts (POS 25)		
11/17/90	**9**	21		45 Crazy In Love......................................		Reprise 19504
				flip side "Lay My Body Down" made the Country charts (POS 69)		
6/1/91	**43**	4		46 Walk Away..		Reprise 19324
8/29/92	**42**	5		47 I'll Be There For You............................		Reprise LP Cut
				from the album *Back Home Again* on Reprise 26740		

ROGERS, Roy

"King Of The Cowboys." Born Leonard Slye on 11/5/11 in Cincinnati. Original member of the famous western group, the Sons Of The Pioneers. Roy starred in close to 100 movie Westerns, then in a popular radio and TV series with his wife Dale Evans.

12/21/74	**33**	9		Hoppy, Gene And Me.........................[N]	65	20th Century 2154
				tribute to Hopalong Cassidy, Gene Autry and Roy Rogers		

ROLLING STONES, The

British R&B-influenced rock group formed in London in January 1963. Consisted of Mick Jagger (b: 7/26/43; vocals), Keith Richards (b: 12/18/43; lead guitar), Brian Jones (b: 2/28/42; guitar), Bill Wyman (b: 10/24/36; bass) and Charlie Watts (b: 6/2/41; drums). Jones left group shortly before drowning on 7/3/69. Replaced by Mick Taylor (b: 1/17/48). In 1975, Ron Wood (ex-Jeff Beck Group, ex-Faces) replaced Taylor.

1/1/66	**10**	8		1 **As Tears Go By**..................................	6	London 9808
10/6/73	**38**	7	●	2 **Angie**...	**1**¹	Rolling S. 19105

ROMAN, Dick

Pop singer from Brooklyn. Real name: Ricardo De Giacomo. Regular on TV's *The Liberace Show*, 1958-59. Died from a heart attack on 10/21/76 (age 39).

8/25/62	**16**	4		Theme from A Summer Place.....................	64	Harmon 1004
				from the film *A Summer Place*		

DEBUT DATE	PEAK POS	WKS CHR	GOLD	ARTIST — Record Title	POP POS	Label & Number
				ROMEOS, The		
				Philadelphia soul quintet featuring producers Kenny Gamble and Thom Bell.		
5/6/67	**39**	2		Precious Memories .... [I]	67	Mark II 101
	★★**21**★★			**RONSTADT, Linda**		
				Born on 7/15/46 in Tucson, Arizona. While in high school formed folk trio The Three Ronstadts (with sister and brother). To Los Angeles in 1964. Formed the Stone Poneys with Bobby Kimmel (guitar) and Ken Edwards (keyboards); recorded for Sidewalk in 1965. Went solo in 1968. In 1971 formed backing band with Glenn Frey, Don Henley, Randy Meisner and Bernie Leadon (later became the Eagles). In *Pirates Of Penzance* operetta in New York City in 1980, also in film of same name in 1983.		
				1)Don't Know Much 2)All My Life 3)Ooh Baby Baby 4)Blue Bayou 5)When Will I Be Loved		
9/12/70	**20**	7		1 Long Long Time	25	Capitol 2846
1/23/71	**17**	6		2 (She's A) Very Lovely Woman/	70	
		3		3 The Long Way Around	flip	Capitol 3021
12/22/73	**23**	10		4 Love Has No Pride	51	Asylum 11026
1/4/75	**10**	11		**5 You're No Good**..	1¹	Capitol 3990
				flip side "I Can't Help It (If I'm Still In Love With You)" made the Country charts (POS 2)		
4/26/75	**3**	14		**6 When Will I Be Loved/**	2²	
8/9/75	**20**	8		7 It Doesn't Matter Anymore	47	Capitol 4050
10/25/75	**19**	8		**8 Heat Wave**	5	Asylum 45282
				flip side "Love Is A Rose" made the *Hot 100* (POS 63)		
12/27/75	**4**	13		**9 Tracks Of My Tears**	25	Asylum 45295
				flip side "The Sweetest Gift" (with Emmylou Harris) made the Country charts (POS 12)		
8/21/76	**16**	12		10 That'll Be The Day	11	Asylum 45340
12/25/76	**38**	7		11 Someone To Lay Down Beside Me	42	Asylum 45361
				flip side "Crazy" made the Country charts (POS 6)		
6/18/77	**43**	3		12 Lose Again	76	Asylum 45402
9/10/77	**3**	22	▲	**13 Blue Bayou**	3	Asylum 45431
11/19/77	**37**	9		14 It's So Easy	5	Asylum 45438
2/11/78	**27**	8		15 Poor Poor Pitiful Me	31	Asylum 45462
5/13/78	**30**	6		16 I Never Will Marry/	32	Asylum 45479
		6		17 Tumbling Dice		
9/9/78	**30**	7		18 Back In The U.S.A.	16	Asylum 45519
11/18/78	**2²**	15		**19 Ooh Baby Baby**	7	Asylum 45546
2/24/79	**5**	10		**20 Just One Look**	44	Asylum 46011
				flip side "Love Me Tender" made the Country charts (POS 59)		
5/5/79	**30**	6		21 Alison		Asylum 46034
				written by Elvis Costello		
4/19/80	**25**	8		**22 Hurt So Bad**...	8	Asylum 46624
7/26/80	**48**	3		23 I Can't Let Go	31	Asylum 46654
1/15/83	**29**	10		24 I Knew You When	37	Asylum 69853
3/26/83	**7**	19		**25 Easy For You To Say**	54	Asylum 69838
10/29/83	**5**	17		**26 What's New**	53	Asylum 69780
				#2 hit for Bing Crosby in 1939		
2/18/84	**7**	13		**27 I've Got A Crush On You**		Asylum 69752
				#21 hit for Frank Sinatra in 1948		
				LINDA RONSTADT & THE NELSON RIDDLE ORCHESTRA (above 2)		
12/1/84	**12**	12		28 Skylark	101	Asylum 69671
				#5 hit for Dinah Shore in 1942		
3/16/85	**24**	7		29 When I Fall In Love		Asylum 69653
				#20 hit for Doris Day in 1952		
11/15/86	**4**	28	●	**30 Somewhere Out There**	2¹	MCA 52973
				LINDA RONSTADT AND JAMES INGRAM		
				from the animated film *An American Tail*		
12/6/86	**32**	6		31 When You Wish Upon A Star......................................		Asylum 69507
				#1 hit for Glenn Miller in 1940		
6/20/87	**35**	3		32 Telling Me Lies...		Warner 28371
				DOLLY PARTON, LINDA RONSTADT, EMMYLOU HARRIS		
9/30/89	**1⁵**	26	●	**33 Don't Know Much**	2²	Elektra 69261
				tune also known as "All I Need To Know"		
1/20/90	**1³**	24		**34 All My Life**	11	Elektra 64987
5/5/90	**5**	17		**35 When Something Is Wrong With My Baby**...............	78	Elektra 64968
				LINDA RONSTADT featuring Aaron Neville (above 3)		
8/4/90	**9**	14		**36 Adios**		Elektra 64943
11/16/91	**13**	17		37 Dreams To Dream		MCA 54203
				from the film *An American Tail-Fievel Goes West*		

DEBUT DATE	PEAK POS	WKS CHR	GOLD	ARTIST — Record Title	POP POS	Label & Number
				RONSTADT, Linda — Cont'd		
3/28/92	**38**	7		38 Close Your Eyes		A&M LP Cut
				AARON NEVILLE with LINDA RONSTADT from the Aaron Neville album *Warm Your Heart* on A&M 5354		
				ROOFTOP SINGERS, The Folk trio from New York City: Erik Darling, Willard Svanoe and Lynne Taylor (d: 1982). Disbanded in 1967. Darling was a member of The Tarriers in 1956 and The Weavers, 1958-62. Taylor was a vocalist with Benny Goodman and Buddy Rich.		
1/12/63	**1**⁵	12	●	1 **Walk Right In**	1²	Vanguard 35017
8/31/63	**20**	1		2 Mama Don't Allow	55	Vanguard 35020
				ROSE, David Born on 6/15/10 in London; died on 8/23/90 of heart disease. Moved to Chicago at an early age. Conductor/ composer/arranger for numerous films. Scored many TV series, such as *The Red Skelton Show, Bonanza* and *Little House On The Prairie*. Married to Martha Raye (1938-41) and Judy Garland (1941-43).		
6/23/62	**1**²	11	●	**The Stripper** ....[I]	1¹	MGM 13064
				ROSE COLORED GLASS Mary Owens with Larry Meletio, Bob Caldwell and Bill Tillman.		
5/15/71	**30**	7		Can't Find The Time	54	Bang 584
				ROSELLI, Jimmy Italian singer.		
4/30/66	**29**	7		1 I'm Gonna Change Everything		United Art. 996
				#95 Pop hit for Jim Reeves in 1962		
7/8/67	**13**	13		2 There Must Be A Way	93	United Art. 50179
				#1 Country hit for Jack Greene in 1967		
10/14/67	**19**	9	✓	3 All The Time		United Art. 50217
1/13/68	**31**	4	✓	4 Please Believe Me		United Art. 50234
5/25/68	**35**	3		5 Oh What It Seemed To Be		United Art. 50287
				#1 hit for both Frank Sinatra and Frankie Carle in 1946		
3/1/69	**38**	4		6 Buona Sera, Mrs. Campbell		United Art. 50490
				movie title song		
				ROSE ROYCE Eight-member backing band formed in Los Angeles in early '70s. Backed Edwin Starr as Total Concept Unlimited in 1973. Backed The Temptations, became regular band for Undisputed Truth. Lead vocalist Gwen Dickey added, name changed to Rose Royce in 1976. Did soundtrack for the film *Car Wash*.		
4/9/77	**9**	12		I Wanna Get Next To You	10	MCA 40662
				ROSS, Charlie Born in Greenville, Mississippi. DJ on WDDT radio. Moved to California in the late 1960s, worked with Eternity's Children. DJ at KFJZ-Ft. Worth in the mid-1970s.		
2/1/75	**23**	8		Thanks For The Smiles	61	Big Tree 16025
★★**29**★★				**ROSS, Diana** Born Diane Earle on 3/26/44 in Detroit. In vocal group The Primettes, first recorded for LuPine in 1960. Lead singer of The Supremes from 1961-69. Went solo in late 1969. Oscar nominee for the 1972 film *Lady Sings The Blues*. Appeared in the films *Mahogany* and *The Wiz*. Own Broadway show *An Evening With Diana Ross*, 1976. Married Norwegian shipping magnate Arne Naess in 1986.		
				1)*Endless Love* 2)*Last Time I Saw Him* 3)*Touch Me In The Morning* 4)*Theme From Mahogany (Do You Know Where You're Going To)* 5)*Why Do Fools Fall In Love*		
5/16/70	**18**	6		1 Reach Out And Touch (Somebody's Hand)	20	Motown 1165
8/15/70	**6**	11		2 **Ain't No Mountain High Enough**	1³	Motown 1169
1/2/71	**20**	7		3 Remember Me	16	Motown 1176
5/8/71	**16**	7		4 Reach Out I'll Be There	29	Motown 1184
1/27/73	**8**	6		5 **Good Morning Heartache**	34	Motown 1211
				from the film *Lady Sings The Blues* starring Diana Ross		
6/2/73	**1**¹	15		6 **Touch Me In The Morning**	1¹	Motown 1239
10/20/73	**43**	4		7 You're A Special Part Of Me	12	Motown 1280
				DIANA ROSS & MARVIN GAYE		
12/29/73	**1**³	17		8 **Last Time I Saw Him**	14	Motown 1278
3/8/75	**17**	9		9 Sorry Doesn't Always Make It Right....................		Motown 1335
10/25/75	**1**¹	14		10 **Theme From Mahogany (Do You Know Where You're Going To)**	1¹	Motown 1377
				from the film *Mahogany* starring Diana Ross		
3/20/76	**4**	8		11 **I Thought It Took A Little Time (But Today I Fell In Love)**	47	Motown 1387
5/1/76	**19**	10		12 Love Hangover	1²	Motown 1392
8/14/76	**31**	7		13 One Love In My Lifetime	25	Motown 1398

DEBUT DATE	PEAK POS	WKS CHR	GOLD	ARTIST — Record Title	POP POS	Label & Number
				ROSS, Diana — Cont'd		
11/5/77	**8**	14		14 **Gettin' Ready For Love**	27	Motown 1427
5/6/78	**9**	13		15 **You Got It**	49	Motown 1442
9/30/78	**40**	3		16 Ease On Down The Road	41	MCA 40947
				DIANA ROSS MICHAEL JACKSON		
				from the film *The Wiz* (starring Ross and Jackson)		
8/18/79	**41**	7		17 The Boss	19	Motown 1462
8/16/80	**18**	17	●	18 Upside Down	1⁴	Motown 1494
11/8/80	**9**	21		19 It's My Turn	9	Motown 1496
				movie title song		
7/11/81	**1³**	27	▲	20 **Endless Love**	1⁹	Motown 1519
				DIANA ROSS & LIONEL RICHIE		
				movie title song		
10/24/81	**2³**	17		21 **Why Do Fools Fall In Love**	7	RCA 12349
11/13/82	**36**	9		22 Muscles	10	RCA 13348
				written and produced by Michael Jackson		
2/19/83	**13**	12		23 So Close	40	RCA 13424
7/7/84	**2²**	16		24 **All Of You**	19	Columbia 04507
				JULIO IGLESIAS & DIANA ROSS		
12/1/84	**4**	26		25 **Missing You**	10	RCA 13966
				dedicated to Marvin Gaye; produced and written by Lionel Richie		
12/7/85	**25**	13		26 Chain Reaction	95	RCA 14244
11/26/88	**23**	13		27 If We Hold On Together		MCA 53448
				from the film *The Land Before Time*		
9/14/91	**26**	13		28 When You Tell Me That You Love Me		Motown 2139
				ROSS, Jack		
				West Coast nightclub entertainer/trumpet player. Died on 12/16/82 (age 66).		
1/20/62	**15**	5		Happy Jose (Ching, Ching) ....[I-N]	57	Dot 16302
				ROSS, Jerry, Symposium ○		
				Studio group assembled by producer Jerry Ross (executive with the Colossus record label).		
5/30/70	**37**	3		Ma Belle Amie .... [I]		Colossus 113
				#5 Pop hit for The Tee Set in 1970		
				ROSSO, Nini ○		
				Born Celeste Rosso on 9/19/26 in Turin, Italy. Jazz Trumpeter.		
10/16/65	**32**	5		Il Silenzio .... [I]	101	Columbia 43363
				ROTA, Nino		
				Composer; died on 4/10/79 (age 68).		
5/20/72	**24**	3		Love Theme From "The Godfather" .... [I]	66	Paramount 0152
				conducted by Carlo Savina; from the film *The Godfather*		
				ROTH, David Lee		
				Born on 10/10/55 in Bloomington, Indiana. Former lead singer of Van Halen.		
2/16/85	**29**	6		California Girls	3	Warner 29102
				#3 Pop hit for The Beach Boys in 1965		
				ROUSSOS, Demis		
				Greek singer; born on 6/15/47 in Alexandria, Egypt. Formed rock band, Aphrodites Child, in France with Vangelis, 1968 to early '70s.		
6/3/78	**50**	4		That Once In A Lifetime	47	Mercury 73992
				ROVERS — see IRISH ROVERS		
				ROWLES, John		
				Native of New Zealand.		
11/21/70	**19**	12		Cheryl Moana Marie	64	Kapp 2102
★★200★★				**ROXETTE**		
				Male/female Swedish pop-rock duo: Marie Fredriksson (b: 5/30/58; vocals) and Per Gessle (b: 6/12/59; songwriter).		
				1)Listen To Your Heart 2)It Must Have Been Love 3)Fading Like A Flower (Every Time You Leave)		
9/30/89	**2²**	24		1 **Listen To Your Heart**	1¹	EMI 50223
2/10/90	**21**	10		2 Dangerous	2²	EMI 50233
4/21/90	**2¹**	28	●	3 **It Must Have Been Love**	1²	EMI 50283
				from the film *Pretty Woman*		
4/6/91	**21**	16		4 Joyride	1¹	EMI 50342
6/29/91	**5**	23		5 **Fading Like A Flower (Every Time You Leave)**	2¹	EMI 50355
11/16/91	**20**	16		6 Spending My Time	32	EMI 50366
3/21/92	**24**	9		7 Church Of Your Heart	36	EMI 50380

DEBUT DATE	PEAK POS	WKS CHR	GOLD	ARTIST — Record Title	POP POS	Label & Number
				ROXETTE — Cont'd		
6/19/93	**45**	3		**8** Almost Unreal...	94	Capitol 44942
				from the film *Super Mario Bros.*		
				ROXY MUSIC		
				English art-rock band. Nucleus consisted of Bryan Ferry (vocals, keyboards), Phil Manzanera (guitar) and Andy Mackay (horns).		
5/26/79	**38**	8		Dance Away	44	Atco 7100
				ROYAL PHILHARMONIC ORCHESTRA, The		
				British — Louis Clark, conductor (born in Birmingham, England; arranger for ELO).		
10/24/81	**8**	21		Hooked On Classics...[I]	10	RCA 12304
				Tchaikovsky Piano Concerto No. 1/Flight of the Bumble Bee/ Mozart Symphony No. 40 in G Minor/Rhapsody In Blue/Karelia Suite/ The Marriage of Figaro/Romeo & Juliet/Trumpet Voluntary/Hallelujah Chorus/ Grieg Piano Concerto in A Minor/March of the Toreadors		
				ROYAL SCOTS DRAGOON GUARDS, The		
				The Pipes and Drums and The Military Band of Scotland's armored regiment. Led by Pipe Major Tony Crease.		
5/20/72	**9**	8		Amazing Grace...[I]	11	RCA 0709
				THE PIPES AND DRUMS AND THE MILITARY BAND OF THE ROYAL SCOTS DRAGOON GUARDS Pipe Major Tony Crease (bagpipes solo)		
				RTZ		
				Boston-based rock quintet spearheaded by Brad Delp (vocals) and Barry Goudreau (guitar), former members of the group Boston. Goudreau was also a member of Orion The Hunter. RTZ stands for Return To Zero.		
2/15/92	**36**	11		Until Your Love Comes Back Around...................................	26	Giant 19051
				RUBICON		
				Bay area septet led by horn player Jerry Martini (member of Sly & The Family Stone, 1966-76). Group included Jack Blades and Brad Gillis of Night Ranger.		
4/8/78	**45**	5		I'm Gonna Take Care Of Everything	28	20th Century 2362
				RUBY AND THE ROMANTICS		
				Akron, Ohio R&B quintet: Ruby Nash Curtis (b: 11/12/39, New York City; lead), Ed Roberts (d: 8/10/93 [age 57] of cancer) and George Lee (tenors), Ronald Mosley (baritone) and Leroy Fann (bass; d: 1973).		
6/1/63	**6**	9		**1** My Summer Love	16	Kapp 525
8/24/63	**5**	7		**2** Hey There Lonely Boy	27	Kapp 544
11/16/63	**15**	4		**3** Young Wings Can Fly (Higher Than You Know)...................	47	Kapp 557
4/11/64	**14**	3		**4** Our Everlasting Love...	64	Kapp 578
10/3/64	**15**	2		**5** When You're Young And In Love	48	Kapp 615
				RUFFELLE, Frances — see CROSS, Christopher		
				RUFFIN, David		
				Born Davis Eli Ruffin on 1/18/41 in Meridian, Mississippi. Brother of Jimmy Ruffin. With the Dixie Nightingales gospel group. Recorded for Anna in 1960. Co-lead singer of The Temptations from 1963-68. Died of a drug overdose on 6/1/91.		
9/14/85	**12**	9		**1** A Nite At The Apollo Live! The Way You Do The Things You Do/My Girl	20	RCA 14178
				DARYL HALL JOHN OATES with David Ruffin & Eddie Kendrick recorded at the re-opening of New York's Apollo Theatre		
12/26/87	**48**	3		**2** I Couldn't Believe It...		RCA 5313
				DAVID RUFFIN & EDDIE KENDRICK		
				RUFFIN, Jimmy		
				Born on 5/7/39 in Collinsville, Mississippi. Brother of David Ruffin. Backup work at Motown in the early '60s. First recorded for Miracle in 1961.		
3/22/80	**32**	8		Hold On To My Love	10	RSO 1021
				written and produced by Robin Gibb		
				RUNDGREN, Todd		
				Born on 6/22/48 in Upper Darby, Pennsylvania. Virtuoso musician/songwriter/producer/engineer. Leader of groups Nazz and Utopia. Produced Meat Loaf's *Bat Out Of Hell* album and produced albums for Badfinger, Grand Funk Railroad, The Tubes, XTC, Patti Smith and many others.		
5/6/72	**12**	8		**1** I Saw The Light...	16	Bearsville 0003
11/3/73	**17**	14		**2** Hello It's Me...	5	Bearsville 0009
				original version by Rundgren's group, Nazz, made the *Hot 100* in 1969		
6/19/76	**32**	7		**3** Good Vibrations	34	Bearsville 0309
7/29/78	**45**	2		**4** Can We Still Be Friends	29	Bearsville 0324

DEBUT DATE	PEAK POS	WKS CHR	G O L D	ARTIST — Record Title	POP POS	Label & Number
				RUSH, Jennifer		
				Native of Queens, New York.		
7/4/87	**32**	4		Flames Of Paradise	36	Epic 07119
				JENNIFER RUSH with Elton John		
				RUSH, Merrilee, & The Turnabouts		
				From Seattle, Washington. Discovered by fellow Northwesterners, Paul Revere & The Raiders.		
6/29/68	**37**	3		1 Angel Of The Morning	7	Bell 705
7/2/77	**49**	2		2 Save Me	54	United Art. 993
				MERRILEE RUSH		
				RUSSELL, Andy ○		
6/10/67	**1**[1]	13		1 It's Such A Pretty World Today	119	Capitol 5917
				#1 Country hit for Wynn Stewart in 1967		
9/9/67	**10**	9		2 I'm Still Not Through Missin' You		Capitol 5971
12/2/67	**32**	2	✓	3 Your Love Is Everywhere		Capitol 2009
2/3/68	**29**	4		4 If My Heart Had Windows		Capitol 2072
				RUSSELL, Bobby		
				Born on 4/19/41 in Nashville. Died of a heart attack on 11/19/92. Wrote "The Night The Lights Went Out In Georgia," "Honey," "Little Green Apples" and "The Joker Went Wild." First husband of Vicki Lawrence.		
10/26/68	**9**	8		1 1432 Franklin Pike Circle Hero	36	Elf 90020
8/16/69	**31**	5		2 Better Homes And Gardens		Elf 90031
7/4/70	**33**	2		3 As Far As I'm Concerned		National G. 005
6/12/71	**13**	13		4 Saturday Morning Confusion .... [N]	28	United Art. 50788
				RUSSELL, Brenda		
				Soul singer/keyboardist/composer. Born Brenda Gordon in Brooklyn. To Toronto at age 12. Recorded as duo, Brian & Brenda, with former husband Brian Russell in 1978; co-hosted the Canadian TV series *Music Machine*. Session work for Barbra Streisand, Elton John, Bette Midler and many others. Also see Michael Franks.		
8/25/79	**8**	16		1 So Good, So Right	30	Horizon 123
12/28/85	**15**	12		2 When I Give My Love To You		Warner 28819
				MICHAEL FRANKS Featuring Brenda Russell		
3/19/88	**3**	25		3 Piano In The Dark	6	A&M 3003
				featuring vocalist Joe Esposito (Brooklyn Dreams)		
8/4/90	**13**	20		4 Stop Running Away		A&M 1514
7/13/91	**40**	7		5 If You're Not The One For Me		GRP LP Cut
				TOM SCOTT with Brenda Russell & Bill Champlin from the Tom Scott album *Keep This Love Alive* on GRP 9646		
7/3/93	**46**	2		6 No Time For Time		EMI 50435
				RUSSELL, Leon		
				Born on 4/2/41 in Lawton, Oklahoma. Rock singer/songwriter/multi-instrumentalist sessionman. Wrote "Superstar" and "This Masquerade."		
9/6/75	**13**	12		1 Lady Blue	14	Shelter 40378
1/24/76	**45**	4		2 Back To The Island	53	Shelter 40483
				RYDELL, Bobby		
				Born Robert Ridarelli on 4/26/42 in Philadelphia. Regular on Paul Whiteman's amateur TV show, 1951-54. Drummer with Rocco & His Saints, which included Frankie Avalon on trumpet in 1956. First recorded for Veko in 1957. In films *Bye Bye Birdie* and *That Lady From Peking*.		
12/28/63	**3**	9		1 Forget Him	4	Cameo 280
2/13/65	**23**	1		2 Diana	98	Capitol 5352
2/28/76	**27**	9		3 Sway .... [R]		PIP 6515
				disco version of Rydell's #14 Pop hit from 1960 on Cameo 182		
				RYDER, John & Anne		
				Husband-wife duo from Sheffield, England.		
10/4/69	**17**	10		1 I Still Believe In Tomorrow	70	Decca 32506
1/24/70	**34**	2		2 A Sign For Love		Decca 32596
				RYDER, Nickie — see ROGERS, Kenny		
				RYSER, Jimmy		
				Guitarist/violinist/vocalist born on 1/31/65 in Cleveland. Raised in Columbus, Indiana.		
8/11/90	**33**	7		Same Old Look	78	Arista 2039

S

★★164★★ **SADE**

Born Helen Folasade Adu on 1/16/59 in Ibadan, Nigeria; moved to London at age four. Name pronounced: SHAH-day. Appeared in the 1986 film *Absolute Beginners*. Former designer of menswear. Won the 1985 Best New Artist Grammy Award.

1)Smooth Operator 2)The Sweetest Taboo 3)Paradise

3/16/85	1²	21		1 Smooth Operator	5	Portrait 04807
6/29/85	8	13		2 Your Love Is King	54	Portrait 05408
11/30/85	1¹	22		3 The Sweetest Taboo	5	Portrait 05713
3/29/86	6	14		4 Never As Good As The First Time	20	Portrait 05846
7/5/86	32	7		5 Is It A Crime		Portrait 06121
5/21/88	3	18		6 Paradise	16	Epic 07904
9/3/88	21	10		7 Nothing Can Come Between Us		Epic 07977
11/14/92	14	20		8 No Ordinary Love	28	Epic 74734
3/27/93	20	13		9 Kiss Of Life	78	Epic 74848

SADLER, SSgt Barry

Born on 11/1/40 in Carlsbad, New Mexico. Staff Sergeant of U.S. Army Special Forces (aka Green Berets). Served in Vietnam until injuring leg in booby trap. Shot in the head during a 1988 robbery attempt at his Guatemala home; suffered brain damage. Died of heart failure on 11/5/89 in Tennessee.

2/12/66	1⁵	12	●	1 The Ballad Of The Green Berets	1⁵	RCA 8739
4/23/66	6	9		2 The "A" Team	28	RCA 8804

SA-FIRE

Latin American dance singer from New York City.

4/15/89	4	19		Thinking Of You	12	Cutting 872502

SAGER, Carole Bayer

Born on 3/8/46 in New York City. Prolific pop lyricist. Married Burt Bacharach in 1982. Collaborated in writing "A Groovy Kind Of Love," "Midnight Blue," "Nobody Does It Better," "When I Need You" and many others. Wrote lyrics for many film scores.

5/23/81	14	14		Stronger Than Before	30	Boardwalk 02054

SAILCAT

Country-rock duo: Court Pickett and John Wyker.

7/8/72	12	10		Motorcycle Mama	12	Elektra 45782

SAINTE-MARIE, Buffy

Folk singer/songwriter. Born on 2/20/41 of Cree Indian parents on Piapot Reserve, Saskatchewan, Canada. Raised in Maine. Co-writer of "Up Where We Belong." Semi-regular of TV's *Sesame Street* cast from 1976-1991.

4/29/72	29	3		Mister Can't You See	38	Vanguard 35151

SAKAMOTO, Kyu

Native of Kawasaki, Japan. Kyu (pronounced: cue) was one of 520 people killed in the crash of the Japan Airlines 747 near Tokyo on 8/12/85 (age 43).

5/25/63	1⁵	12	●	1 Sukiyaki	[F]	1³	Capitol 4945
				released in Japan as "Ue O Muite Aruko" (I Look Up When I Walk)			
9/7/63	19	1		2 China Nights (Shina No Yoru)	[F]	58	Capitol 5016

SALSOUL ORCHESTRA

Disco orchestra conducted by Philadelphia producer/arranger Vincent Montana, Jr. Vocalists included Phyllis Rhodes, Ronni Tyson, Carl Helm and Philip Hurt.

1/31/76	11	12		Tangerine	[I]	18	Salsoul 2004
				#1 hit for Jimmy Dorsey in 1942			

SANBORN, David

Born on 7/30/45 in Tampa, Florida; raised in St. Louis. Saxophonist/flutist. Stricken with polio as a child. Played with Paul Butterfield from 1967-71; Stevie Wonder from 1972-73. Formed own group in 1975.

6/13/87	25	7		1 Chicago Song	[I]		Warner 28392
				written and produced by Marcus Miller			
8/15/92	23	12		2 Bang Bang		53	Elektra 64735
				#63 pop hit for the Joe Cuba Sextet in 1966			

SANDALWOOD ☺

6/2/73	19	7		Lovin' Naturally	111	Bell 45,348

DEBUT DATE	PEAK POS	WKS CHR	GOLD	ARTIST — Record Title	POP POS	Label & Number
				SANDLER, Tony, And Ralph Young ○		
				Vocal duo — Tony (Belgian-born) and Ralph (New York-born).		
12/17/66	**18**	8	✓	**1** Dominique		Capitol 5795
				Tony sings "Dominique" while Ralph sings "Deep River," "Nobody Knows The Trouble I've Seen," "Swing Low, Sweet Chariot" and "When The Saints Go Marching In"; #1 Pop hit for The Singing Nun in 1963		
7/8/67	**16**	7		**2** More And More		Capitol 5928
				#10 hit for the Tommy Dorsey Orchestra in 1945		
1/27/68	**11**	8		**3** In The Sunshine Days (Hilo de Seda)......................		Capitol 2083
				SANDLER & YOUNG:		
12/28/68	**40**	2		**4** Life Is		Capitol 2362
				from the musical *Zorba*		
10/11/69	**36**	2		**5** On Days Like These...		Capitol 2636
				from the movie *The Italian Job*		
★★189★★				**SANDPIPERS, The**		
				Los Angeles-based trio: Jim Brady (b: 8/24/44), Michael Piano (b: 10/26/44) and Richard Shoff (b: 4/30/44); met while in the Mitchell Boys Choir.		
				1)Guantanamera 2)Cuando Sali De Cuba 3)Come Saturday Morning		
8/6/66	**3**	14		**1** Guantanamera......................................[F]	9	A&M 806
10/29/66	**24**	7		**2** Louie, Louie.......................................[F]	30	A&M 819
2/18/67	**31**	3	✓	**3** For Baby		A&M 835
				written by John Denver		
8/19/67	**20**	6		**4** Bon Soir Dame		A&M 861
				written by Bud Dashiel (of Bud & Travis)		
10/21/67	**3**	12		**5** Cuando Sali De Cuba ....[F]		A&M 880
6/1/68	**16**	6		**6** Quando M'Innamoro ....[F]	124	A&M 939
				Italian version of Engelbert Humperdinck's 1968 hit "A Man Without Love"		
9/7/68	**39**	2		**7** Softly		A&M 968
				written by Gordon Lightfoot		
11/16/68	**36**	5		**8** Let Go!		A&M 997
11/15/69	**8**	24		**9** Come Saturday Morning	17	A&M 1134
				from the film *The Sterile Cuckoo*; originally charted for 13 weeks (POS 9); re-entered on 4/18/70 (A&M 1185)		
8/29/70	**17**	7		**10** Santo Domingo		A&M 1208
				recitation by Michael Piano		
11/28/70	**11**	10		**11** Free To Carry On.......................................	94	A&M 1227
				SANDS, Evie		
				Born in New York City. Hit the New York charts as a teenage rocker, 1965-68.		
3/14/70	**30**	5		**1** But You Know I Love You	110	A&M 1175
				#19 Pop hit for The First Edition in 1969		
12/13/75	**36**	9		**2** Yesterday Can't Hurt Me		Haven 7020
				SANFORD/TOWNSEND BAND, The		
				Los Angeles-based rock band led by Ed Sanford and John Townsend.		
8/20/77	**34**	7		Smoke From A Distant Fire	9	Warner 8370
				SANG, Samantha		
				Born Cheryl Gray on 8/5/53 in Melbourne, Australia. Began career on Melbourne radio at age eight.		
12/3/77	**5**	23	▲	**1** Emotion	3	Private S. 45178
				backing vocal by Barry Gibb; written by Barry and Robin Gibb		
5/13/78	**34**	7		**2** You Keep Me Dancing......................................	56	Private S. 45188
				SAN REMO GOLDEN STRINGS		
				Group of master violinists.		
9/11/65	**3**	10		Hungry For Love ....[I]	27	Ric-Tic 104
				SANTA FE ○		
7/17/76	**24**	9		Adios		Chelsea 3042
				disco version of Glenn Miller's Pop hit in 1941 (POS 13)		
				SANTAMARIA, Mongo		
				Born Ramon Santamaria on 4/7/22 in Havana, Cuba. Bandleader/conga, bongo and percussion player. Member of bands led by Perez Prado, Tito Puente and Cal Tjader. Own group from 1961. In the film *Made In Paris* in 1966.		
4/6/63	**3**	8		**1** Watermelon Man ....[I]	10	Battle 45909
				written by Herbie Hancock		
3/15/69	**30**	3		**2** Cloud Nine ....[I]	32	Columbia 44740

DEBUT DATE	PEAK POS	WKS CHR	GOLD	ARTIST — Record Title	POP POS	Label & Number

SANTANA
Latin-rock group formed in San Francisco in 1966. Consisted of Carlos Santana (b: 7/20/47, Autlan de Navarro, Mexico; vocals, guitar), Gregg Rolie (keyboards) and David Brown (bass). Added percussionists Michael Carabello, Jose Chepitos Areas and Michael Shrieve in 1969. Worked Fillmore West and Woodstock in 1969. Neal Schon (guitar) added in 1971. Santana began solo work in 1972. Schon and Rolie formed Journey in 1973. Shrieve left in 1975 to form Automatic Man.

2/7/70	19	7		1 Evil Ways	9	Columbia 45069
12/5/70	29	4		2 Black Magic Woman	4	Columbia 45270
2/20/71	11	7		3 Oye Como Va ....[F]	13	Columbia 45330
1/20/79	19	9		4 Stormy	32	Columbia 10873
10/30/82	34	4		5 Hold On...	15	Columbia 03160
8/18/90	31	7		6 Gypsy Woman..................................		Columbia LP Cut

from the album *Spirits Dancing In The Flesh* on Columbia 46065; #3 Pop hit for Brian Hyland in 1970

SANTO & JOHNNY
Brooklyn-born guitar duo: Santo Farina (b: 10/24/37; steel guitar) and his brother Johnny (b: 4/30/41; rhythm guitar). Sister Ann Farina helped with songwriting.

2/22/64	20	2		I'll Remember (In The Still Of The Night)..................[I]	58	Canadian A. 164

SANTOS, Larry
Born on 6/2/41 in Oneonto, New York. Wrote "Candy Girl" by the 4 Seasons. Worked as a jingle singer.

4/10/76	26	7		1 We Can't Hide It Anymore	36	Casablanca 844
11/20/76	38	5		2 Long, Long Time	109	Casablanca 869

#25 Pop hit for Linda Ronstadt in 1970

SARIDIS, Saverio
Born on 6/16/33 in Brooklyn. Worked as a New York City policeman.

3/3/62	20	1		Love Is The Sweetest Thing	86	Warner 5243

#1 hit (5 weeks) in 1933 for Ray Noble

SARSTEDT, Peter
British singer. Brother of Eden Kane (Richard Sarstedt).

4/19/69	29	4		Where Do You Go To (My Lovely)	70	World Pac. 77911

SAVALAS, Telly ○
Born Aristotle Savalas on 1/21/24 in Garden City, New York. Popular TV/film actor. Gained fame as the star of TV's *Kojak*.

11/2/74	12	10		If ....[S]		MCA 40301

#4 Pop hit for Bread in 1971

SAWYER BROWN ○
Five-member country band from Nashville — Mark Miller, lead singer.

4/24/93	42	5		All These Years		Curb LP Cut

from the album *Cafe On The Corner* on Curb 77574

SAYER, Leo
Born Gerard Sayer on 5/21/48 in Shoreham, England. With Patches in the early '70s. Songwriting team with David Courtney, 1972-75. Own British TV show in 1978 and again in 1983.

11/20/76	19	13	●	1 You Make Me Feel Like Dancing	1¹	Warner 8283
3/19/77	1¹	17	●	2 When I Need You................................	1¹	Warner 8332
7/30/77	27	8		3 How Much Love	17	Warner 8319
10/7/78	9	15		4 Raining In My Heart..........................	47	Warner 8682
10/11/80	1³	20	●	5 More Than I Can Say	2⁵	Warner 49565
2/21/81	12	8		6 Living In A Fantasy	23	Warner 49657

SCAGGS, Boz
Born William Royce Scaggs on 6/8/44 in Ohio; raised in Texas. Joined Steve Miller's band, The Marksmen, in 1959 in Dallas. Hooked up with Miller at UW-Madison in The Ardells, later known as The Fabulous Night Trains. Joined R&B band The Wigs in 1963. To Europe in 1964, toured as a folk singer. Re-joined Miller in 1967, solo since 1969. Retired from music and opened a restaurant in San Francisco, 1983-87. Made comeback in 1988.

7/31/76	11	11	●	1 Lowdown.......................................	3	Columbia 10367
12/18/76	35	8		2 What Can I Say	42	Columbia 10440
7/5/80	29	9		3 JoJo	17	Columbia 11281
8/30/80	3	16		4 Look What You've Done To Me	14	Columbia 11349
12/20/80	13	12		5 Miss Sun	14	Columbia 11406
				Lisa Dal Bello (backing vocal)		
5/7/88	3	21		6 Heart Of Mine................................	35	Columbia 07780
9/3/88	39	5		7 Cool Running		Columbia 07981

DEBUT DATE	PEAK POS	WKS CHR	G O L D	ARTIST — Record Title	POP POS	Label & Number
				SCARBURY, Joey		
				Born on 6/7/55 in Ontario, California. Session singer for producer Mike Post.		
9/1/73	**36**	5		1 I'm Gonna Sit Right Down And Write Myself A Letter		Big Tree 16008
				#3 Pop hit for Billy Williams in 1957		
5/30/81	**3**	19	●	**2 Theme From "Greatest American Hero" (Believe It or Not)**	2²	Elektra 47147
				from the TV series *Greatest American Hero*		
				SCARLETT & BLACK		
				Keyboardist/singer/songwriter Robin Hild and songwriter Sue West (former backing vocalist for Doctor And The Medics).		
3/19/88	**13**	12		You Don't Know	20	Virgin 99405
				SCHIFRIN, Lalo		
				Born Boris Schifrin on 6/21/32 in Buenos Aires, Argentina. Pianist/conductor/composer. To the U.S. in 1958. Scored films *Bullitt*, *Dirty Harry*, *Brubaker* and many others.		
2/10/68	**7**	9		**Mission-Impossible** .... [I]	41	Dot 17059
				from the TV series of the same title		
				SCHMIT, Timothy B.		
				Born on 10/30/47 in Sacramento. Member of Poco, 1970-77, and the Eagles, 1977-82.		
10/23/82	**27**	12		1 So Much In Love	59	Full Moon 69939
				from the film *Fast Times At Ridgemont High*		
1/16/88	**30**	6		2 Don't Give Up		MCA 53233
				SCHNEIDER, John		
				Born on 4/8/59 in Mount Kisco, New York. Moved to Atlanta at age 14. Country singer/actor. Played "Bo Duke" on TV's *The Dukes Of Hazzard*. Appeared in many TV films. Scriptwriter/director.		
6/6/81	**5**	18		1 It's Now Or Never	14	Scotti Br. 02105
10/10/81	**32**	6		2 Still	69	Scotti Br. 02489
				flip side "Them Good Ol' Boys Are Bad" made the Country charts (POS 13)		
5/22/82	**21**	13		3 Dreamin'	45	Scotti Br. 02889
				SCHWARTZ, David ✪		
				David composed, produced and plays the fretless bass for his hit.		
11/7/92	**15**	12		Theme From Northern Exposure .... [I]		MCA 54552
				from the TV series *Northern Exposure*		
				SCHWARTZ, Eddie		
				Canadian singer/songwriter. Wrote Pat Benatar's "Hit Me With Your Best Shot."		
1/30/82	**40**	6		All Our Tomorrows	28	Atco 7342
				SCORPIONS		
				German heavy-metal rock quintet: Rudolf Schenker (Michael Schenker's brother; lead guitar), Klaus Meine (lead singer), Matthias Jabs (guitar), Francis Buchholz (bass) and Herman Rarebell (drums). Buchholz left band in 1992.		
10/5/91	**43**	3	●	Wind Of Change	4	Mercury 868180
				SCOTT, Linda		
				Born Linda Joy Sampson on 6/1/45 in Queens, New York. Moved to Teaneck, New Jersey at age 11. Vocalist on Arthur Godfrey's CBS radio show, late 1950s. Co-host of TV's *Where The Action Is*. Joined Army, 1970-72. Later earned a degree in Theology and is currently a music teacher/director at the Christian Academy in New York.		
7/17/61	**3**	10		**1 Don't Bet Money Honey**	9	Canadian A. 127
12/11/61	**4**	8		**2 I Don't Know Why**	12	Canadian A. 129
				#2 hit for Wayne King in 1931		
2/24/62	**16**	4		3 Bermuda	70	Canadian A. 134
4/21/62	**10**	7		**4 Count Every Star**	41	Canadian A. 133
				3 versions of this tune made the top 10 in 1950		
7/14/62	**15**	5		5 Never In A Million Years	56	Congress 103
				#2 hit for Bing Crosby in 1937		
				SCOTT, Tom		
				Born on 5/19/48 in Los Angeles. Pop-jazz-fusion saxophonist. Session work for Joni Mitchell, Steely Dan, Carole King and others. Composer of films and TV scores. Led the house band for TV's *Pat Sajak Show*. Son of Nathan Scott, a composer of TV scores for *Dragnet*, *Wagon Train*, *My Three Sons* and others.		
2/28/76	**46**	3		1 Uptown & Country .... [I]	80	Ode 66118
7/13/91	**40**	7		2 If You're Not The One For Me		GRP LP Cut
				TOM SCOTT with Brenda Russell & Bill Champlin		
				from the album *Keep This Love Alive* on GRP 9646		

DEBUT DATE	PEAK POS	WKS CHR	GOLD	ARTIST — Record Title	POP POS	Label & Number
				SEALS, Dan		
				Born on 2/8/48 in McCamey Texas and raised in Dallas. Half of the duo England Dan & John Ford Coley (both formerly with Southwest F.O.B.). Brother of Jim Seals of Seals & Crofts. A hot country artist since 1983, Dan's charted 11 #1 country hits through 1992.		
8/9/80	**28**	11		1 Late At Night	57	Atlantic 3674
				ENGLAND DAN SEALS		
2/8/86	**10**	15		2 Bop	42	EMI America 8289
★★**114**★★				**SEALS & CROFTS**		
				Pop duo: Jim Seals (b: 10/17/41, Sidney, Texas; guitar, fiddle, saxophone) and Dash Crofts (b: 8/14/40, Cisco, Texas; drums, mandolin, keyboards, guitar). With Dean Beard, recorded for Edmoral and Atlantic in 1957. To Los Angeles in 1958. With the Champs from 1958-65. Own group, the Dawnbreakers, in the late 1960s; entire band converted to Baha'i faith in 1969. Jim is the brother of "England" Dan Seals.		
				1)You're The Love 2)Get Closer 3)We May Never Pass This Way (Again)		
10/21/72	**4**	10		1 **Summer Breeze**	6	Warner 7606
2/3/73	**12**	9		2 **Hummingbird**	20	Warner 7671
6/2/73	**4**	13		3 **Diamond Girl**	6	Warner 7708
9/29/73	**2**[1]	13		4 **We May Never Pass This Way (Again)**	21	Warner 7740
6/1/74	**26**	9		5 King Of Nothing..	60	Warner 7810
3/29/75	**4**	14		6 **I'll Play For You**	18	Warner 8075
9/20/75	**21**	9	✓	7 Castles In The Sand		Warner 8130
4/10/76	**2**[2]	15		8 **Get Closer**	6	Warner 8190
				featuring Carolyn Willis (Honey Cone/Bob B. Soxx & The Blue Jeans)		
11/27/76	**14**	11		9 Baby, I'll Give It To You............................	58	Warner 8277
3/12/77	**10**	10	✓	10 **Goodbye Old Buddies**............................		Warner 8330
9/3/77	**11**	17		11 My Fair Share	28	Warner 8405
				love theme from the film *One On One*		
4/15/78	**2**[3]	19		12 **You're The Love**	18	Warner 8551
9/27/80	**37**	6		13 First Love..		Warner 49522
				SEBASTIAN, John		
				Born on 3/17/44 in New York City. Played with the Even Dozen Jug Band as "John Benson" in 1964. Did session work for Elektra Records and toured with Mississippi John Hurt. Formed The Lovin' Spoonful in 1965. Went solo in 1968. Continues to write and perform into the '90s.		
4/17/76	**1**[2]	9	●	**Welcome Back**	**1**[1]	Reprise 1349
				from the ABC-TV series *Welcome Back Kotter*		
				SECADA, Jon		
				Cuban-born, Miami-raised singer/songwriter. Left Cuba at age eight. Earned a master's degree in jazz at the University of Miami. Co-wrote six songs on Gloria Estefan's album *Into The Light* and a backing vocalist for that tour.		
5/2/92	**2**[2]	38	●	1 **Just Another Day**	5	SBK 07383
				Gloria Estefan (backing vocal)		
9/26/92	**3**	37		2 Do You Believe In Us...............................	13	SBK 50408
1/23/93	**3**	28		3 Angel	18	SBK 50406
6/19/93	**4**	15↑		4 I'm Free	27	SBK 50434
★★**110**★★				**SEDAKA, Neil**		
				Born on 3/13/39 in Brooklyn. Pop singer/songwriter/pianist. Studied piano since elementary school. Formed songwriting team with lyricist Howard Greenfield while attending Lincoln High School (partnership lasted over 20 years). Recorded with The Tokens on Melba in 1956. Attended Juilliard School for classical piano. Prolific hit songwriter. Career revived in 1974 after signing with Elton John's new Rocket label.		
				1)Laughter In The Rain 2)Breaking Up Is Hard To Do 3)The Immigrant		
10/12/74	**1**[2]	14		1 **Laughter In The Rain**	**1**[1]	Rocket 40313
3/22/75	**1**[1]	10		2 **The Immigrant**	22	Rocket 40370
7/12/75	**7**	10		3 **That's When The Music Takes Me**	27	Rocket 40426
9/27/75	**25**	8	●	4 Bad Blood	**1**[3]	Rocket 40460
				Elton John (backing vocal)		
12/13/75	**1**[1]	13		5 **Breaking Up Is Hard To Do** ....[R]	8	Rocket 40500
				slow version of Sedaka's 1962 *Hot 100* hit (POS 1[2])		
4/17/76	**4**	9		6 **Love In The Shadows**	16	Rocket 40543
7/24/76	**45**	2		7 Steppin' Out...	36	Rocket 40582
9/11/76	**7**	13		8 **You Gotta Make Your Own Sunshine**........	53	Rocket 40614
6/4/77	**4**	9		9 **Amarillo**	44	Elektra 45406
8/6/77	**17**	11		10 Alone At Last	104	Elektra 45421
4/12/80	**3**	17		11 **Should've Never Let You Go**	19	Elektra 46615
				NEIL SEDAKA and DARA SEDAKA (Neil's daughter)		
8/29/81	**36**	4		12 My World Keeps Slipping Away		Elektra 47184

DEBUT DATE	PEAK POS	WKS CHR	GOLD	ARTIST — Record Title	POP POS	Label & Number
				SEDAKA, Neil — Cont'd		
12/3/83	**15**	16		13 Your Precious Love..		MCA/Curb 52307
				NEIL SEDAKA with DARA SEDAKA		
				#5 Pop hit for Marvin Gaye & Tammi Terrell in 1967		
7/28/84	**37**	3		14 Rhythm Of The Rain		MCA/Curb 52400
				#3 Pop hit for The Cascades in 1963		
				SEDUCTION		
				Female vocal trio from New York: Idalis Leon (b: 6/15/66), April Harris (b: 3/25/67) and Michelle Visage (b: 9/20/68). Leon left in 1990, replaced by Sinoa Loren (b: 12/6/66). Visage a member of The S.O.U.L. S.Y.S.T.E.M. by 1992.		
7/14/90	**21**	14		Could This Be Love..	11	A&M 1509
				SEEKERS, The		
				Pop-folk, Australian-born quartet: Judith Durham (b: 7/3/43; lead singer), Keith Potger (guitar), Bruce Woodley (Spanish guitar) and Athol Guy (standup bass). Potger formed the New Seekers in 1970.		
5/29/65	**2**[1]	4		**1 I'll Never Find Another You**	4	Capitol 5383
5/29/65	**2**[1]	11		**2 A World Of Our Own**	19	Capitol 5430
11/27/65	**27**	4		3 The Carnival Is Over	105	Capitol 5531
1/28/67	**7**	7	●	4 Georgy Girl..	2[2]	Capitol 5756
				movie title song		
2/25/67	**13**	10		5 Morningtown Ride...	44	Capitol 5787
10/21/67	**14**	8		6 When The Good Apples Fall		Capitol 2013
3/16/68	**21**	7		7 Love Is Kind, Love Is Wine	135	Capitol 2122
				SEELY, Jeannie		
				Born Marilyn Jeanne Seely on 7/6/40 in Titusville, Pennsylvania. Country singer/songwriter. Married briefly to country star Hank Cochran, who wrote many of her country hits.		
5/28/66	**29**	6		Don't Touch Me..	85	Monument 933
★★**168**★★				**SEGER, Bob, & The Silver Bullet Band**		
				Born on 5/6/45 in Dearborn, Michigan and raised in Detroit. Rock singer/songwriter/guitarist. Formed own backing group, The Silver Bullet Band, in 1976: Alto Reed (horns), Robyn Robbins (keyboards), Drew Abbott (guitar), Chris Campbell (bass) and Charlie Allen Martin (drums). Various personnel changes since then; Campbell is the only remaining original member.		
				1)Shame On The Moon 2)The Real Love 3)Understanding		
6/10/78	**27**	10		1 Still The Same..	4	Capitol 4581
11/25/78	**29**	11		2 We've Got Tonite	13	Capitol 4653
3/8/80	**31**	10		3 Fire Lake *	6	Capitol 4836
5/17/80	**8**	13		4 Against The Wind *	5	Capitol 4863
8/16/80	**17**	15		5 You'll Accomp'ny Me *	14	Capitol 4904
				*BOB SEGER		
12/25/82	**1**[2]	20		6 Shame On The Moon....................................	2[4]	Capitol 5187
11/10/84	**7**	17		7 Understanding	17	Capitol 5413
				from the film *Teachers*		
5/31/86	**21**	11		8 Like A Rock	12	Capitol 5592
9/6/86	**22**	9		9 It's You	52	Capitol 5623
8/24/91	**4**	21		10 The Real Love	24	Capitol 44743
12/7/91	**45**	5		11 The Fire Inside		Capitol 44793
				SEMBELLO, Michael		
				Born on 4/17/54 in Philadelphia. Session guitarist/producer/composer/arranger/vocalist. Guitarist on Stevie Wonder's albums from 1974-79.		
9/3/83	**34**	9		1 Maniac	1[2]	Casablanca 812516
				from the film *Flashdance*		
2/4/84	**25**	10		2 Talk		Warner 29381
				vocal duet with Cruz Baca Sembello		
				SERENDIPITY SINGERS, The		
				Nine member pop-folk group organized at the University of Colorado.		
3/28/64	**2**[6]	10		**1 Don't Let The Rain Come Down (Crooked Little Man)**..	6	Philips 40175
6/6/64	**5**	6		**2 Beans In My Ears** ....[N]	30	Philips 40198
				SEVELLE, Taja		
				Soulful songstress from Minneapolis. Discovered by Prince. Volunteer DJ at KMOJ-Minneapolis.		
9/26/87	**48**	2		Love Is Contagious	62	Reprise 28257

DEBUT DATE	PEAK POS	WKS CHR	G O L D	ARTIST — Record Title	POP POS	Label & Number
				SEVERINSEN, Doc ⊙		
				Born Carl H. Severinsen on 7/7/27 in Arlington, Oregon. Trumpet virtuoso — leader of the *Tonight Show* band (1967-92). With Charlie Barnet (1947-49), Tommy Dorsey (1949-50), and Sauter-Finegan (1952-53).		
6/11/66	**34**	3		1 Mothers And Daughters ....[I]		Command 4084
				DOC SEVERINSEN and His SEXTET		
3/24/73	**33**	3		2 The Last Tango In Paris ....[I]	106	RCA 0904
				movie title song		
1/22/77	**34**	7		3 Melody (Aria) ....[I]		Epic 50318
				SEVILLE, David — see CHIPMUNKS, The		
				SEYMOUR, Phil		
				Born on 5/15/52 in Tulsa, Oklahoma. Died of lymphoma on 8/17/93. Vocalist/drummer/bassist. Formerly with the Dwight Twilley Band.		
3/7/81	**34**	6		Precious To Me...	22	Boardwalk 5703
				SHAKESPEAR'S SISTER		
				Female duo of British native Siobhan Fahey and Detroit native Marcella Detroit. Fahey, wife of Dave Stewart (Eurythmics), was a member of Bananarama. Detroit is Marcy Levy who recorded with Robin Gibb, sang backup for Eric Clapton and co-wrote "Lay Down Sally."		
8/29/92	**39**	7	●	Stay	4	London 869730
				SHALAMAR		
				Black vocal trio formed in 1978 by Don Cornelius, the producer/host of TV's *Soul Train*. Consisted of vocalists/dancers Jody Watley and Jeffrey Daniels with Gerald Brown. Howard Hewett replaced Brown in early 1979.		
3/1/80	**47**	3	●	The Second Time Around	8	Solar 11709
				SHA NA NA		
				Fifties rock & roll specialists led by John "Bowzer" Baumann (b: 9/14/47, Queens, New York). Formed at Columbia University in 1969. Own syndicated variety TV show, 1977-81. Henry Gross was a member, left in 1970. Many personnel changes.		
5/31/75	**47**	4		(Just Like) Romeo And Juliet.............................	55	Kama Sutra 602
				SHANGO		
				Quartet member Tommy Reynolds was later part of Hamilton, Joe Frank & Reynolds.		
3/15/69	**17**	7		Day After Day (It's Slippin' Away)........................	57	A&M 1014
				SHANICE — see WILSON, Shanice		
				SHANK, Bud		
				Born Clifford E. Shank on 5/27/26 in Dayton, Ohio. Jazz-oriented saxophonist. Played with Charlie Barnet, Art Mooney and Stan Kenton from 1947-51. TV and movie studio musician.		
1/8/66	**12**	11		Michelle ....[I]	65	World Pac. 77814
				SHANNON		
				Shannon is actually British rock singer Marty Wilde.		
7/26/69	**22**	7		Abergavenny	47	Heritage 814
				SHANNON, Del		
				Born Charles Westover on 12/30/34 in Coopersville, Michigan. With U.S. Army *Get Up And Go* radio show in Germany. Discovered by Ann Arbor D.J./producer Ollie McLaughlin. Formed own Berlee label in 1963. Wrote "I Go To Pieces" for Peter & Gordon. To Los Angeles in 1966; production work. Died on 2/8/90 of a self-inflicted gunshot wound.		
9/22/62	**19**	1		1 The Swiss Maid	64	Big Top 3117
				written by Roger Miller		
1/23/82	**36**	6		2 Sea Of Love	33	Network 47951
				produced by Tom Petty		
				SHEILA E.		
				Born Sheila Escovedo on 12/12/59 in San Francisco. Singer/percussionist.		
3/21/87	**36**	3		Hold Me..	68	Paisley P. 28580
				SHELLEY, Peter		
				British songwriter/producer. Worked as an executive at Magnet Records in Britain.		
12/7/74	**13**	10		Gee Baby	81	Bell 45614
				SHEPARD, Vonda		
				Born in New York and raised in Los Angeles. Former backing vocalist/keyboardist for Rickie Lee Jones and Al Jarreau.		
4/25/87	**2**[3]	29		1 Can't We Try..	6	Columbia 07050
				DAN HILL with Vonda Sheppard		
1/6/90	**17**	12		2 Don't Cry Ilene		Reprise 22777
9/15/90	**37**	7		3 I Shy Away		Reprise 19703

DEBUT DATE	PEAK POS	WKS CHR	GOLD	ARTIST — Record Title	POP POS	Label & Number
				SHEPPARD, T.G.		
				Born William Browder on 7/20/42 in Alamo, Tennessee. Country singer. Moved to Memphis in 1960. Worked as backup singer with Travis Wammack's band.		
7/10/76	29	7		1 Solitary Man	100	Hitsville 6032
3/21/81	3	18		2 I Loved 'Em Every One	37	Warner 49690
2/6/82	20	10		3 Only One You	68	Warner 49858
4/24/82	17	12		4 Finally..	58	Warner 50041
2/25/84	36	4		5 Make My Day .... [N]	62	Warner 29343
				T.G. SHEPPARD WITH CLINT EASTWOOD inspired by the film *Sudden Impact*		
10/13/84	42	1		6 Home Again		Elektra 69697
				JUDY COLLINS with T.G. SHEPPARD		
				SHERIFF		
				Canadian rock quintet — Freddy Curci, lead singer. Disbanded in 1983. Members Wolf Hassell and Arnold Lanni are now the duo Frozen Ghost. Bandmates Curci and Steve DeMarchi formed Alias in 1990.		
12/24/88	1¹	20	●	When I'm With You .... [R]	1¹	Capitol 44302
				originally made the *Hot 100* on 5/14/83 (POS 61) on Capitol 5199		
				SHERMAN, Allan		
				Born Allan Copelon on 11/30/24 in Chicago; died on 11/21/73. Began as a professional comedy writer for Jackie Gleason, Joe E. Lewis and others. Creator/producer of TV's *I've Got A Secret*.		
8/1/64	9	5		1 Hello Mudduh, Hello Fadduh! (A Letter From Camp - New 1964 Version) .... [C]	59	Warner 5449
				original version made the *Hot 100* on 8/3/63 (POS 2) on Warner 5378		
3/27/65	6	8		2 Crazy Downtown .... [C]	40	Warner 5614
				parody of Petula Clark's "Downtown"		
12/4/65	21	5		3 The Drinking Man's Diet .... [C]	98	Warner 5672
★★193★★				**SHERMAN, Bobby**		
				Born on 7/18/43 in Santa Monica, California. Regular on TV's *Shindig*; played Jeremy Bolt on TV's *Here Come The Brides*. Currently involved in TV production. 1)*Easy Come, Easy Go* 2)*Julie, Do Ya Love Me* 3)*The Drum*		
11/29/69	14	10	●	1 La La La (If I Had You)	9	Metromedia 150
2/14/70	2⁴	12	●	2 Easy Come, Easy Go	9	Metromedia 177
5/23/70	3	8		3 Hey, Mister Sun	24	Metromedia 188
8/1/70	2²	12	●	4 Julie, Do Ya Love Me	5	Metromedia 194
2/13/71	9	8		5 Cried Like A Baby	16	Metromedia 206
5/8/71	2²	9		6 The Drum	29	Metromedia 217
10/16/71	9	8		7 Jennifer	60	Metromedia 227
7/12/75	34	6		8 Our Last Song Together		Janus 254
				written by Neil Sedaka & Howard Greenfield		
				SHERMAN, Joe, and The Arena Brass		
				Sherman was a prolific record producer in the 1960s.		
1/8/66	19	12		1 Feeling Good .... [I]		Epic 9877
				from the musical *The Roar Of The Greasepaint*		
4/23/66	32	6		2 Happiness Is .... [I]		Epic 10008
				SHERWOOD, Holly ☺		
3/24/73	30	5		Yesterday And You...................................	117	Rocky Road 30068
				SHIFRIN, Su ☺		
				Singer/songwriter from Miami. Currently married to David Cassidy.		
5/3/75	40	5		All I Wanna Do		Motown 1343
				SHIRLEY, Don, Trio		
				Born on 1/27/27 in Kingston, Jamaica. Pianist/organist.		
7/17/61	10	14		Water Boy .... [I]	40	Cadence 1392
				SHOCKED, Michelle		
				Folk singer Karen Michelle Johnson. An American expatriate of Mormon upbringing.		
1/21/89	42	2		Anchorage	66	Mercury 870611
				SIEGEL, Dan ☺		
				Jazz pianist. Scored the film *Reform School Girls*.		
3/12/88	28	7		Feelin' Happy .... [I]		CBS Assoc. 07667

DEBUT DATE	PEAK POS	WKS CHR	GOLD	ARTIST — Record Title	POP POS	Label & Number
				SILVER		
				Country-rock quintet led by John Batdorf (of Batdorf & Rodney). Included organist Brent Mydland, who later joined the Grateful Dead (died on 7/26/90 of a drug overdose at the age of 37).		
8/7/76	**22**	9		Wham Bam..	16	Arista 0189
				title also shown as "Wham Bam Shang-A-Lang"		
				SILVER CONVENTION		
				German studio disco act assembled by producer Michael Kunze and writer/arranger Silvester Levay. Female vocal trio formed in 1976 consisting of Penny McLean, Ramona Wolf and Linda Thompson.		
11/8/75	**6**	12	●	1 Fly, Robin, Fly .... [I]	1³	Midland I. 10339
5/1/76	**25**	10	●	2 Get Up And Boogie (That's Right)	2³	Midland I. 10571
				SILVETTI		
				Argentinian Bebu Silvetti.		
2/19/77	**13**	11		Spring Rain .... [I]	39	Salsoul 2014
				SIMEONE, Harry, Chorale		
				Harry was born on 5/9/11 in Newark, New Jersey. Arranger/conductor for film and TV shows. Began career in 1939 as an arranger for Fred Waring.		
12/18/61	**6**	3		1 **The Little Drummer Boy**.. [X-R]	22	20th Fox 121
				originally made the *Hot 100* on 12/22/58 (POS 13)		
12/15/62	**6**	3		2 **The Little Drummer Boy**.. [X-R]	28	20th Fox 121
8/14/65	**20**	6		3 Summer Wind	109	Kapp 55
				ROGER WILLIAMS & The HARRY SIMEONE CHORALE		
				#25 Pop hit for Frank Sinatra in 1966		
12/17/66	**15**	10		4 Anyone Can Move A Mountain		Columbia 43926
				from the TV musical *Ballad Of Smokey The Bear*		
★★32★★				**SIMON, Carly**		
				Born on 6/25/45 in New York City. Pop vocalist/songwriter. Father is co-founder of Simon & Schuster publishing. Folk duo with sister Lucy (The Simon Sisters), mid-1960s. Won the 1971 Best New Artist Grammy Award. Married James Taylor on 11/3/72, divorced in 1983.		
				1)*Nobody Does It Better* 2)*You're So Vain* 3)*Haven't Got Time For The Pain* 4)*Devoted To You* 5)*Anticipation*		
5/1/71	**6**	16		1 That's The Way I've Always Heard It Should Be............	10	Elektra 45724
12/18/71	**3**	13		2 **Anticipation**	13	Elektra 45759
4/1/72	**11**	8		3 Legend In Your Own Time	50	Elektra 45774
12/16/72	**1²**	11	●	4 **You're So Vain**	1³	Elektra 45824
				Mick Jagger (backing vocal)		
3/31/73	**4**	12		5 **The Right Thing To Do**	17	Elektra 45843
2/16/74	**10**	12	●	6 **Mockingbird**	5	Elektra 45880
				CARLY SIMON & JAMES TAYLOR		
5/18/74	**2¹**	14		7 **Haven't Got Time For The Pain**	14	Elektra 45887
6/7/75	**18**	7		8 Attitude Dancing	21	Elektra 45246
7/26/75	**21**	8		9 Waterfall	78	Elektra 45263
7/4/76	**27**	5		10 It Keeps You Runnin'	46	Elektra 45323
10/2/76	**39**	3		11 Half A Chance		Elektra 45341
7/16/77	**1⁷**	25	●	12 **Nobody Does It Better**	2³	Elektra 45413
				from the film *The Spy Who Loved Me*		
4/29/78	**4**	19		13 **You Belong To Me**...	6	Elektra 45477
8/19/78	**2¹**	14		14 **Devoted To You**..	36	Elektra 45506
				CARLY SIMON and JAMES TAYLOR		
9/1/79	**34**	7		15 Spy		Elektra 46514
8/16/80	**8**	18	●	16 **Jesse**	11	Warner 49518
10/15/83	**36**	5		17 You Know What To Do	83	Warner 29484
7/20/85	**34**	4		18 Tired Of Being Blonde	70	Epic 05419
9/6/86	**5**	25		19 **Coming Around Again**	18	Arista 9525
				from the film *Heartburn*		
5/16/87	**5**	17		20 **Give Me All Night**..	61	Arista 9587
8/22/87	**8**	17		21 **The Stuff That Dreams Are Made Of**		Arista 9619
11/28/87	**7**	20		22 **All I Want Is You**	54	Arista 9653
2/11/89	**11**	15		23 Let The River Run	49	Arista 9793
				theme from the film *Working Girl*		
10/6/90	**4**	21		24 **Better Not Tell Her**		Arista 2083
3/23/91	**36**	5		25 Holding Me Tonight		Arista LP Cut
				from the album *Have You Seen Me Lately?* on Arista 8650		
4/18/92	**16**	15		26 Love Of My Life		Qwest LP Cut
				from the soundtrack album *This Is My Life* on Qwest 26901		

DEBUT DATE	PEAK POS	WKS CHR	GOLD	ARTIST — Record Title	POP POS	Label & Number
	★★62★★			**SIMON, Paul**		
				Born on 11/5/41 in Newark, New Jersey; raised in Queens, New York. Vocalist/composer/guitarist. Met Art Garfunkel in high school, recorded together as Tom & Jerry in 1957. Worked as Jerry Landis, Paul Kane, Harrison Gregory and True Taylor in the early '60s. To England from 1963-64. Returned to the U.S. and recorded first album with Garfunkel in 1965. Went solo in 1971. Married to actress Carrie Fisher from 1983-85. Married Edie Brickell on 5/30/92. In the films *Annie Hall* and *One-Trick Pony*. Winner of 12 Grammy Awards.		
				1)(What A) Wonderful World 2)Loves Me Like A Rock 3)50 Ways to Leave Your Lover 4)Kodachrome 5)Slip Slidin' Away		
2/12/72	4	12		1 **Mother And Child Reunion**	4	Columbia 45547
4/15/72	6	10		2 **Me And Julio Down By The Schoolyard**	22	Columbia 45585
7/22/72	30	5		3 **Duncan**..	52	Columbia 45638
5/26/73	2²	11		4 **Kodachrome**	2²	Columbia 45859
8/4/73	1²	16	●	5 **Loves Me Like A Rock**	2¹	Columbia 45907
				The Dixie Hummingbirds (backing vocals)		
12/15/73	8	11		6 **American Tune**..	35	Columbia 45900
5/25/74	50	1	✓	7 **The Sound Of Silence**		Columbia 46038
				live version of Simon & Garfunkel's #1 *Hot 100* hit in 1965 on Columbia 43396		
8/30/75	9	10		8 **Gone At Last**	23	Columbia 10197
				PAUL SIMON/PHOEBE SNOW and The Jessy Dixon Singers		
12/27/75	1²	14	●	9 **50 Ways To Leave Your Lover**..	1³	Columbia 10270
5/8/76	5	11		10 **Still Crazy After All These Years**	40	Columbia 10332
10/15/77	4	20		11 **Slip Slidin' Away**	5	Columbia 10630
1/28/78	1⁵	14		12 **(What A) Wonderful World**...	17	Columbia 10676
				ART GARFUNKEL with JAMES TAYLOR & PAUL SIMON		
4/8/78	45	6		13 **Stranded In A Limousine**...		Columbia 10711
8/9/80	7	16		14 **Late In The Evening**	6	Warner 49511
11/1/80	17	13		15 **One-Trick Pony**	40	Warner 49601
				above 2 from the film *One-Trick Pony*		
2/19/83	36	4		16 **The Blues**...	51	Warner 29803
				RANDY NEWMAN AND PAUL SIMON		
11/12/83	26	10		17 **Allergies**	44	Warner 29453
4/21/84	26	9		18 **Think Too Much**		Warner 29333
8/23/86	15	22		19 **You Can Call Me Al**	23	Warner 28667
				originally charted for 13 weeks; re-entered on 5/2/87 (POS 22)		
12/6/86	34	3		20 **Graceland**	81	Warner 28522
	★★163★★			**SIMON & GARFUNKEL**		
				Folk-rock duo from New York City: Paul Simon and Art Garfunkel. Recorded as Tom & Jerry in 1957. Duo split in 1964; Simon was working solo in England, Garfunkel was in graduate school. They re-formed in 1965 and stayed together until 1971. Reunited briefly in 1981 for national tour. Inducted into the Rock and Roll Hall of Fame in 1990.		
				1)Bridge Over Troubled Water 2)My Little Town 3)The Boxer		
3/9/68	5	11		1 **Scarborough Fair (/Canticle)**..	11	Columbia 44465
				song also known as "Parsley, Sage, Rosemary And Thyme"		
5/4/68	4	13	●	2 **Mrs. Robinson**..	1³	Columbia 44511
				above 2 from the film *The Graduate*		
4/19/69	3	9		3 **The Boxer**..	7	Columbia 44785
2/14/70	1⁶	10	●	4 **Bridge Over Troubled Water**	1⁶	Columbia 45079
5/16/70	31	4	●	5 **Cecilia**	4	Columbia 45133
9/19/70	6	10		6 **El Condor Pasa**	18	Columbia 45237
9/16/72	27	4		7 **For Emily, Whenever I May Find Her**	53	Columbia 45663
11/1/75	1²	12		8 **My Little Town**	9	Columbia 10230
4/10/82	5	13		9 **Wake Up Little Susie**	27	Warner 50053
				recorded live in New York's Central Park on 9/19/81		
				SIMPLE MINDS		
				Scottish rock group. Nucleus of band: Jim Kerr (lead singer; formerly married to Chrissie Hynde of The Pretenders, later married Patsy Kensit of Eighth Wonder), Michael MacNeil (keyboards), Charles Burchill (guitar), Mel Gaynor (drums) and John Giblin (bass). MacNeil left in 1989.		
5/25/85	36	4		**Don't You (Forget About Me)**..	1¹	A&M 2703
				from the film *The Breakfast Club*		
	★★181★★			**SIMPLY RED**		
				Manchester, England group: vocalist Mick "Red" Hucknall (b: 6/8/60), keyboardists Fritz McIntyre & Tim Kellett, Tony Bowers (bass), Chris Joyce (drums) and Sylvan Richardson (guitar). 1991 lineup: Hucknall, McIntyre, Kellett, saxophonist Ian Kirkham, Brazilian guitarist Heitor T.P. and Japanese drummer Gota.		
				1)If You Don't Know Me By Now 2)Holding Back The Years 3)You've Got It		
3/29/86	4	23		1 **Holding Back The Years**...	1¹	Elektra 69564

DEBUT DATE	PEAK POS	WKS CHR	G O L D	ARTIST — Record Title	POP POS	Label & Number
				SIMPLY RED — Cont'd		
9/12/87	**28**	7		2 Maybe Someday..		Elektra 69448
2/25/89	**19**	9		3 It's Only Love	57	Elektra 69317
5/20/89	**1**[6]	24	●	4 If You Don't Know Me By Now	**1**[1]	Elektra 69297
9/23/89	**7**	18		5 You've Got It		Elektra 69269
9/28/91	**21**	14		6 Something Got Me Started	23	EastWest 98711
1/4/92	**8**	34		7 Stars	44	EastWest 98636
5/16/92	**24**	13		8 For Your Babies		EastWest 98570

★★**8**★★ **SINATRA, Frank**

Born Francis Albert Sinatra on 12/12/15 in Hoboken, New Jersey. With Harry James from 1939-40, first recorded for Brunswick in 1939; with Tommy Dorsey, 1940-42. Went solo in late 1942 and charted 40 top 10 hits through 1954. Appeared in many films from 1941 on. Won an Oscar for the film *From Here To Eternity* in 1953. Own TV show in 1957. Own Reprise record company in 1961, sold to Warner Bros. in 1963. Won the Lifetime Achievement Grammy in 1965. Married to actress Ava Gardner from 1951-57. Married to actress Mia Farrow from 1966 to 1968. Announced his retirement in 1970, but made comeback in 1973. Regarded by many as the greatest popular singer of the 20th century.

1)*Somethin' Stupid* 2)*Strangers In The Night* 3)*The World We Knew (Over And Over)* 4)*That's Life* 5)*Summer Wind*

DEBUT DATE	PEAK POS	WKS CHR	G O L D	ARTIST — Record Title	POP POS	Label & Number
7/17/61	**15**	2		1 Granada	64	Reprise 20010
10/23/61	**12**	6		2 I'll Be Seeing You	58	Reprise 20023
				#1 hit in 1944 for Bing Crosby		
1/6/62	**9**	6		3 Pocketful Of Miracles....................................	34	Reprise 20040
				movie title song		
3/24/62	**20**	1		4 Stardust	98	Reprise 20059
				one of the most recorded, charted and popular tunes of all time		
12/29/62	**18**	2		5 Me And My Shadow ....[N]	64	Reprise 20128
				FRANK SINATRA and SAMMY DAVIS JR.		
				#1 hit for "Whispering" Jack Smith in 1927		
5/4/63	**20**	2		6 Call Me Irresponsible	78	Reprise 20151
				from the film *Papa's Delicate Condition*		
9/5/64	**4**	11		7 Softly, As I Leave You..	27	Reprise 0301
12/19/64	**4**	12		8 Somewhere In Your Heart	32	Reprise 0332
3/13/65	**11**	5		9 Anytime At All	46	Reprise 0350
5/22/65	**16**	7		10 Tell Her (You Love Her Every Day)	57	Reprise 0373
6/26/65	**13**	7		11 Forget Domani	78	Reprise 0380
				from the film *The Yellow Rolls Royce*		
9/4/65	**10**	7		12 When Somebody Loves You	102	Reprise 0398
10/23/65	**18**	9		13 I'll Only Miss Her When I Think Of Her/		
11/6/65	**25**	7		14 Everybody Has The Right To Be Wrong! (At Least Once)	131	Reprise 0410
				from the Broadway musical *Skyscraper*		
12/25/65	**1**[1]	17		15 It Was A Very Good Year/	28	
12/25/65	**18**	7		16 Moment To Moment	115	Reprise 0429
				movie title song		
4/30/66	**1**[7]	20		17 Strangers In The Night..	**1**[1]	Reprise 0470
				from the film *A Man Could Get Killed*		
9/3/66	**1**[1]	13		18 Summer Wind	25	Reprise 0509
11/19/66	**1**[3]	13		19 That's Life	4	Reprise 0531
3/18/67	**1**[9]	17	●	20 Somethin' Stupid..	**1**[4]	Reprise 0561
				NANCY SINATRA & FRANK SINATRA		
8/12/67	**1**[5]	14		21 The World We Knew (Over And Over)	30	Reprise 0610
11/4/67	**17**	5		22 This Town...	53	Reprise 0631
				from the film *The Cool Ones*		
4/13/68	**4**	11		23 I Can't Believe I'm Losing You	60	Reprise 0677
8/24/68	**3**	11		24 My Way Of Life/	64	
10/19/68	**2**[3]	15		25 Cycles	23	Reprise 0764
12/28/68	**3**	11		26 Rain In My Heart	62	Reprise 0798
3/29/69	**2**[3]	13		27 My Way	27	Reprise 0817
				written by Paul Anka		
9/13/69	**8**	8		28 Loves Been Good To Me	75	Reprise 0852
11/22/69	**14**	7		29 Goin' Out Of My Head/	79	
11/22/69	**16**	2		30 Forget To Remember	flip	Reprise 0865
3/21/70	**4**	8		31 I Would Be In Love (Anyway)	88	Reprise 0895
6/20/70	**31**	1		32 What's Now Is Now	123	Reprise 0920
1/9/71	**30**	4		33 Feelin' Kinda Sunday		Reprise 0980
				NANCY SINATRA AND FRANK SINATRA		

DEBUT DATE	PEAK POS	WKS CHR	GOLD	ARTIST — Record Title	POP POS	Label & Number
				SINATRA, Frank — Cont'd		
1/16/71	**22**	6		34 Bein' Green		Reprise 0981
11/24/73	**23**	10		35 Let Me Try Again	63	Reprise 1181
2/9/74	**39**	5		36 You Will Be My Music		Reprise 1190
3/30/74	**31**	8		37 Bad, Bad Leroy Brown	83	Reprise 1196
7/6/74	**11**	12		38 You Turned My World Around.................	83	Reprise 1208
4/12/75	**10**	10		39 **Anytime (I'll Be There)**.....................	75	Reprise 1327
8/2/75	**2**¹	12		40 **I Believe I'm Gonna Love You**	47	Reprise 1335
2/21/76	**43**	6		41 Empty Tables		Reprise 1343
7/31/76	**21**	9		42 Stargazer		Reprise 1364
				written by Neil Diamond; Sam Butera (sax solo)		
11/27/76	**31**	5		43 Like A Sad Song....................................		Reprise 1377
				#36 Pop hit for John Denver in 1976		
1/8/77	**43**	7		44 I Love My Wife		Reprise 1382
				Broadway musical title song		
4/16/77	**29**	7	✓	45 Everybody Ought To Be In Love		Reprise 1386
				#75 Pop hit for Paul Anka in 1977		
5/3/80	**10**	12		46 **Theme From New York, New York**	32	Reprise 49233
				from the film New York, New York		
8/16/80	**42**	5		47 You And Me (We Wanted It All)		Reprise 49517
8/11/84	**34**	8		48 L.A. Is My Lady		Qwest 29223
★★159★★				**SINATRA, Nancy**		

SINATRA, Nancy
Born on 6/8/40 in Jersey City, New Jersey. First child of Frank and Nancy Sinatra. Moved to Los Angeles while a child. Made national TV debut with father and Elvis Presley in 1959. Married to Tommy Sands, 1960-65. Appeared on *Hullabaloo*, *American Bandstand*, and own specials, mid-'60s. In films *For Those Who Think Young*, *Get Yourself A College Girl*, *The Oscar* and *Speedway*.

1)Somethin' Stupid 2)Sugar Town 3)You Only Live Twice

DEBUT DATE	PEAK POS	WKS CHR	GOLD	ARTIST — Record Title	POP POS	Label & Number
12/3/66	**1**²	13	●	1 Sugar Town	5	Reprise 0527
				flip side "Summer Wine" (with Lee Hazlewood) made the *Hot 100* (POS 49)		
3/18/67	**1**⁹	17	●	2 Somethin' Stupid	**1**⁴	Reprise 0561
				NANCY SINATRA & FRANK SINATRA		
4/22/67	**30**	7		3 Love Eyes	15	Reprise 0559
6/24/67	**3**	15		4 **You Only Live Twice/**	44	
				a James Bond movie title song		
7/22/67	**39**	3		5 Jackson	14	Reprise 0595
				NANCY SINATRA & LEE HAZLEWOOD		
4/6/68	**29**	5		6 100 Years	69	Reprise 0670
7/20/68	**18**	7		7 Happy	74	Reprise 0756
4/5/69	**40**	1		8 God Knows I Love You	97	Reprise 0813
5/17/69	**19**	5		9 Here We Go Again	98	Reprise 0821
12/5/70	**17**	6		10 How Are Things In California?		Reprise 0968
				The Baylor Bros. (backing vocals)		
1/9/71	**30**	4		11 Feelin' Kinda Sunday.............................		Reprise 0980
				NANCY SINATRA AND FRANK SINATRA		

SINGING NUN, The
Sister Luc-Gabrielle (real name: Jeanine Deckers) from the Fichermont, Belgium convent. Recorded under the name Soeur Sourire ("Sister Smile"). Committed suicide on 3/31/85 (age 52).

DEBUT DATE	PEAK POS	WKS CHR	GOLD	ARTIST — Record Title	POP POS	Label & Number
11/9/63	**1**⁴	13		Dominique .... [F]	**1**⁴	Philips 40152

SISTER SLEDGE
Sisters Debra, Joan, Kim and Kathie Sledge from North Philadelphia. First recorded as Sisters Sledge for Money Back label in 1971. Worked as backup vocalists. Began producing their own albums in 1981.

DEBUT DATE	PEAK POS	WKS CHR	GOLD	ARTIST — Record Title	POP POS	Label & Number
6/2/79	**30**	12	●	1 We Are Family	**2**²	Cotillion 44251
1/30/82	**2**²	19		2 **My Guy**	23	Cotillion 47000
6/22/85	**15**	10		3 Frankie	75	Atlantic 89547

SKELLERN, Peter
British singer/pianist. Had a bit part in the film *Lassiter*.

DEBUT DATE	PEAK POS	WKS CHR	GOLD	ARTIST — Record Title	POP POS	Label & Number
11/25/72	**11**	9		You're A Lady	50	London 20075

SKELTON, Red
Born Richard Skelton on 7/18/13 in Vincennes, Indiana. Popular comedian/actor. Own TV variety show from 1951-72. Still active into the '90s.

DEBUT DATE	PEAK POS	WKS CHR	GOLD	ARTIST — Record Title	POP POS	Label & Number
3/22/69	**25**	5		The Pledge Of Allegiance .... [S]	44	Columbia 44798
				as reviewed on TV's *Red Skelton Hour* on 1/14/69; musical background: "Red's White and Blue March"		

DEBUT DATE	PEAK POS	WKS CHR	GOLD	ARTIST — Record Title	POP POS	Label & Number
				SKYLARK Group from Vancouver. Lead singers Donny Gerrard and B.J. (Bonnie Jean) Cook with keyboardist David Foster and drummer Duris Maxwell. Foster was later with Attitudes, then a hit songwriter/solo artist.		
3/24/73	**5**	11		1 **Wildflower**	9	Capitol 3511
8/25/73	**39**	5		2 I'll Have To Go Away	106	Capitol 3661
				SLY & THE FAMILY STONE San Francisco interracial "psychedelic soul" group formed by Sylvester "Sly Stone" Stewart (b: 3/15/44, Dallas; lead singer, keyboards). Group inducted into the Rock and Roll Hall of Fame in 1993.		
3/4/72	**26**	4		Runnin' Away	23	Epic 10829
				SMITH, Hurricane Born Norman Smith in northern England in 1923. Vocalist/producer/engineer/session musician. Produced early Pink Floyd albums and did some engineering for The Beatles.		
11/18/72	**2²**	14		1 **Oh, Babe, What Would You Say?**	3	Capitol 3383
3/31/73	**12**	6		2 Who Was It?	49	Capitol 3455
				SMITH, Jerry, and his Pianos Session pianist. Wrote and performed on The Dixiebelles' "(Down At) Papa Joe's."		
5/24/69	**13**	8		1 Truck Stop [I]	71	ABC 11162
9/6/69	**38**	2		2 Sweet 'N' Sassy [I]		ABC 11230
				SMITH, Kate ○ Born on 5/1/07 in Greenville, Alabama; died on 6/17/86. Tremendously popular soprano who was for years one of the most-listened-to of all radio singers. Later hosted own TV variety series, 1951-52, 1960. Kate introduced the classic Irving Berlin hit "God Bless America."		
7/1/67	**30**	7		1 Anyone Can Move A Mountain		RCA 9217
				from the TV musical *Ballad of Smokey the Bear*		
5/18/74	**42**	5		2 Smile, Smile, Smile		Atlantic 3022
				Dr. John (guest artist)		
				SMITH, Margo ○ Born Bette Lou Miller on 4/9/42 in Dayton, Ohio. Sang with the Apple Sisters vocal group while in high school. Writes almost all of her hits.		
3/4/78	**40**	5		1 Don't Break The Heart That Loves You	104	Warner 8508
				#1 Pop hit for Connie Francis in 1962		
9/16/78	**37**	8		2 Little Things Mean A Lot		Warner 8653
				#1 Pop hit for Kitty Kallen in 1954		
				SMITH, Michael W. Contemporary Christian singer/keyboardist/songwriter from Kenova, West Virginia. To Nashville in 1978. Touring keyboardist for Amy Grant in 1982. Wrote Amy Grant's hits "Find A Way" and "Stay For Awhile."		
3/30/91	**5**	32		1 **Place In This World**	6	Reunion 19019
				co-written by Amy Grant		
9/7/91	**20**	14		2 For You	60	Reunion 19103
9/12/92	**1²**	27		3 **I Will Be Here For You**	27	Reunion 19139
2/6/93	**10**	19		4 Somebody Love Me	71	Reunion 62465
				SMITH, O.C. Born Ocie Lee Smith on 6/21/36 in Mansfield, Louisiana. To Los Angeles in 1939. Sang while in U.S. Air Force from 1953-57. First recorded for Cadence in 1956. With Count Basie from 1961-63.		
				1)Little Green Apples 2)Primrose Lane 3)Daddy's Little Man		
8/24/68	**4**	15	●	1 Little Green Apples	2¹	Columbia 44616
2/22/69	**19**	6		2 Honey (I Miss You)	44	Columbia 44751
5/31/69	**17**	6		3 Friend, Lover, Woman, Wife	47	Columbia 44859
8/30/69	**6**	9		4 **Daddy's Little Man**	34	Columbia 44948
3/14/70	**38**	1		5 Moody	114	Columbia 45098
5/23/70	**4**	10		6 **Primrose Lane**	86	Columbia 45160
8/29/70	**21**	7		7 Baby, I Need Your Loving	52	Columbia 45206
10/5/74	**36**	6		8 La La Peace Song	62	Columbia 10031
11/27/76	**14**	13		9 Together		Caribou 9017
10/14/78	**29**	14		10 Love To Burn		Shady Brook 1045
				SMITH, Rex Born on 9/19/56 in Jacksonville, Florida. Vocalist/actor. Starred in several Broadway musicals and in the TV film *Sooner Or Later*. Appeared in films *The Pirates Of Penzance* and *Streethawk*. Younger brother of Starz's lead singer, Michael Lee Smith.		
5/12/79	**11**	11	●	1 You Take My Breath Away	10	Columbia 10908
7/21/79	**31**	9	✓	2 Simply Jessie	✓	Columbia 11032
				above 2 from the TV movie *Sooner Or Later*		

DEBUT DATE	PEAK POS	WKS CHR	GOLD	ARTIST — Record Title	POP POS	Label & Number
				SMITH, Rex — Cont'd		
7/18/81	**31**	9		**3** Everlasting Love	32	Columbia 02169
				REX SMITH/RACHEL SWEET		
				SMITH, Sammi		
				Born on 8/5/43 in Orange, California and raised in Oklahoma. Country singer. Moved to Nashville in 1967.		
1/23/71	**3**	15	●	**1** Help Me Make It Through The Night	8	Mega 0015
5/29/71	**30**	3		**2** Then You Walk In	118	Mega 0026
8/26/72	**35**	5		**3** I've Got To Have You	77	Mega 0079
				SMITH, Whistling Jack		
				Studio session production featuring the Mike Sammes Singers. Billy Moeller (b: 2/2/46, Liverpool, England) was later hired to tour as Whistling Jack Smith.		
4/29/67	**8**	11		I Was Kaiser Bill's Batman.............................. [I]	20	Deram 85005
				SMITHEREENS, The		
				New Jersey pop quartet formed in 1980: Pat DiNizio (vocals), Jim Babjak, Dennis Diken and Mike Mesaros.		
4/11/92	**32**	9		Too Much Passion	37	Capitol 44784
				SMOKE RING, The		
2/15/69	**24**	5		No Not Much	85	Buddah 77
				SMOKIE		
				British pop-rock quartet: Chris Norman (lead singer), Alan Silson (guitar), Terry Utley (bass) and Pete Spencer (drums).		
1/8/77	**24**	9		Living Next Door To Alice.......................................	25	RSO 860
				SMOTHERMAN, Michael ☉		
				Singer/songwriter/keyboardist. Former member of Buckwheat.		
3/6/82	**35**	5		Do I Ever Cross Your Mind		Epic 02711
				SMYTH, Patty		
				Born on 6/26/57 in New York City. Lead singer of Scandal. In the 1980s was married to punk rocker Richard Hell.		
8/1/92	**1**⁴	34	●	**1** Sometimes Love Just Ain't Enough.............................	2⁶	MCA 54403
				PATTY SMYTH with Don Henley		
12/26/92	**4**	23		**2** No Mistakes	33	MCA 54554
				SNEAKER		
				Los Angeles-based, pop-rock sextet — Mitch Crane, lead singer.		
11/21/81	**17**	15		More Than Just The Two Of Us..................................	34	Handshake 02557
				SNOW, Phoebe		
				Born Phoebe Laub on 7/17/52 in New York City; raised in New Jersey. Vocalist/guitarist/songwriter. Began performing in Greenwich Village in the early '70s.		
1/18/75	**1**¹	15		**1** Poetry Man	5	Shelter 40353
5/24/75	**20**	8		**2** Harpo's Blues		Shelter 40400
8/30/75	**9**	10		**3** Gone At Last..	23	Columbia 10197
				PAUL SIMON/PHOEBE SNOW and The Jessy Dixon Singers		
1/30/88	**11**	12		**4** Dreams I Dream		MCA 53205
				DAVE MASON with Phoebe Snow		
4/1/89	**13**	13		**5** If I Can Just Get Through The Night.........................		Elektra 69305
7/22/89	**29**	9		**6** Something Real...		Elektra 69290
				SOBULE, Jill ☉		
				Singer/guitarist/songwriter from Denver. Moved to Nashville in 1988.		
9/22/90	**17**	12		Too Cool To Fall In Love.......................................		MCA 53938
				produced by Todd Rundgren		
				SOMMERS, Joanie		
				Born on 2/24/41 in Buffalo; moved to California in 1954. Sang Pepsi-Cola jingles in the early and mid-1960s.		
8/6/66	**9**	10		**1** Alfie..		Columbia 43731
				from the film Alfie; #15 Pop hit for Dionne Warwick in 1967		
1/18/69	**29**	5		**2** Talk Until Daylight..		Warner 7251
				SONIA ☉		
				Dance singer from Liverpool, England.		
5/9/92	**13**	12		Be Young, Be Foolish, Be Happy		I.Q./RCA 62246
				#61 Pop hit for The Tams in 1968		

DEBUT DATE	PEAK POS	WKS CHR	GOLD	ARTIST — Record Title	POP POS	Label & Number
				SONNY & CHER		
				Husband-and-wife duo: Sonny and Cher Bono. Session singers for Phil Spector. First recorded as Caesar & Cleo for Vault in 1963. Married in 1963; divorced in 1974. In the films *Good Times* (1966) and *Chastity* (1968). Own CBS-TV variety series from 1971-74. Brief TV reunion in 1975. Each recorded solo.		
10/23/71	**1**5	14		1 **All I Ever Need Is You**...............	7	Kapp 2151
3/11/72	**4**	10		2 **A Cowboys Work Is Never Done**........	8	Kapp 2163
7/15/72	**2**3	10		3 **When You Say Love**...............	32	Kapp 2176
				adapted from a Budweiser jingle		
				SONOMA ○		
11/10/73	**33**	8		Love For You...............	112	Dunhill 4365
				SOUL, David		
				Born David Solberg on 8/28/43 in Chicago. Played Ken Hutchinson on TV's *Starsky & Hutch* (1975-79). Began career as a folk singer and appeared several times on *The Merv Griffin Show* as "The Covered Man" (wore a ski mask).		
2/12/77	**1**1	14	●	1 **Don't Give Up On Us**...............	**1**1	Private S. 45129
5/14/77	**14**	11		2 **Going In With My Eyes Open**...............	54	Private S. 45150
9/17/77	**23**	11		3 **Silver Lady**...............	52	Private S. 45163
				SOULSISTER		
				Belgian male duo: Jan Leyers and Paul Michiels.		
10/14/89	**5**	20		**The Way To Your Heart**...............	41	EMI 50217
				SOUL II SOUL		
				South London soul outfit led by the duo of Beresford "Jazzie B." Romeo and Nellee Hooper. Features female vocalists Caron Wheeler, Do'Reen and Rose Windross and musical backing by the Reggae Philharmonic Orchestra. Wheeler left in 1990.		
9/16/89	**37**	5	▲	Keep On Movin'...............	11	Virgin 99205
				SOUNDS OF SUNSHINE		
				Studio group assembled by producer Randy Wood (d: 10/6/80).		
4/10/71	**5**	19		1 **Love Means (You Never Have To Say You're Sorry)**........	39	Ranwood 896
11/13/76	**46**	2		2 **Nadia's Theme**...............		PIP 6527
				vocal theme from the TV series *The Young And The Restless*; #8 Pop hit for Barry DeVorzon & Perry Botkin, Jr. in 1976		
				SOUNDS ORCHESTRAL		
				British studio project produced by John Schroeder. Included arranger/producer Johnny Pearson on piano.		
3/27/65	**1**3	13		1 **Cast Your Fate To The Wind**............... [I]	10	Parkway 942
7/17/65	**14**	7		2 **Canadian Sunset**............... [I]	76	Parkway 958
12/4/65	**30**	3		3 **A Boy And A Girl**............... [I]	104	Parkway 968
				featuring Johnny Pearson on piano		
7/18/70	**39**	2		4 **Louie Louie**............... [I]		Janus 124
				#2 Pop hit for The Kingsmen in 1963		
				SOUTH, Joe		
				Born Joe Souter on 2/28/40 in Atlanta. Successful Nashville session guitarist/songwriter in the mid-1960s. Wrote "Down In The Boondocks," "Hush" and "Rose Garden."		
9/20/69	**16**	7		1 **Don't It Make You Want To Go Home** *...............	41	Capitol 2592
1/10/70	**3**	9		2 **Walk A Mile In My Shoes** *...............	12	Capitol 2704
				*JOE SOUTH and The Believers		
4/11/70	**32**	4		3 **Children**...............	51	Capitol 2755
				SOUTHER, J.D.		
				John David Souther, born in Detroit and raised in Amarillo, Texas. Formed Longbranch Pennywhistle with Glenn Frey. Teamed with Chris Hillman and Richie Furay as the Souther, Hillman, Furay Band in 1974.		
9/29/79	**1**5	21		1 **You're Only Lonely**...............	7	Columbia 11079
3/1/80	**46**	5		2 **White Rhythm And Blues**...............	105	Columbia 11196
3/14/81	**5**	13		3 **Her Town Too**...............	11	Columbia 60514
				JAMES TAYLOR AND J.D. SOUTHER		
				SOUTHERN PACIFIC ○		
				Band formed in Los Angeles in 1985. Consisted of John McFee (formerly with The Doobie Brothers; guitar, fiddle), Stu Cook (formerly with Creedence Clearwater Revival; bass), Keith Knudsen (formerly with The Doobie Brothers; drums), Kurt Howell (keyboards), and lead vocalist Tim Goodman. Goodman replaced by David Jenkins (formerly with Pablo Cruise) in 1986. Jenkins left in early 1989. Group disbanded in 1991.		
4/22/89	**19**	11		All Is Lost...............		Warner 27530
				SOVEREIGN COLLECTION ○		
4/17/71	**33**	2		Mozart 40............... [I]		Capitol 3094
				#67 Pop hit for Waldo de los Rios in 1971 as "Mozart Symphony No. 40"		

SPANDAU BALLET

English quintet: Tony Hadley (lead singer), Steve Norman, John Keeble, and brothers Gary and Martin Kemp. The Kemps starred in the 1990 film *The Krays*. Gary Kemp, later in *The Bodyguard*, married actress Sadie Frost (of the 1992 film *Dracula*).

DEBUT DATE	PEAK POS	WKS CHR	GOLD	ARTIST — Record Title	POP POS	Label & Number
8/20/83	1¹	22		1 **True**..	4	Chrysalis 42720
				PM Dawn's "Set Adrift On Memory Bliss" is based on this tune		
11/19/83	17	14		2 Gold..	29	Chrysalis 42743
8/18/84	35	8		3 Only When You Leave...................	34	Chrysalis 42792

SPANKY AND OUR GANG

Folk-pop group formed in Chicago in 1966 featuring lead singer Elaine "Spanky" McFarlane (b: 6/19/42, Peoria, Illinois). Included Malcolm Hale, Kenny Hodges, Lefty Baker, Nigel Pickering and John Seiter. Spanky became lead singer of the new Mamas & The Papas, early '80s.

11/4/67	24	5		1 Lazy Day....................................	14	Mercury 72732
2/24/68	39	2		2 Sunday Mornin'...........................	30	Mercury 72765
5/18/68	24	7		3 Like To Get To Know You..............	17	Mercury 72795

SPENCER, Jeremy, Band ✪

Jeremy was born on 7/4/48 in Lancashire, England. Guitarist of Fleetwood Mac, 1967-70.

8/4/79	21	11		1 Cool Breeze..............................		Atlantic 3601
12/15/79	41	6		2 Travellin'.................................		Atlantic 3624

SPIN DOCTORS

Rock quartet formed at New York's New School of Jazz: Christopher Barron (vocals), Eric Schenkman, Mark White and Aaron Comess.

7/17/93	24	11↑		Two Princes	7	Epic 74804

★★190★★ SPINNERS

R&B vocal group from Ferndale High School near Detroit, originally known as the Domingoes. Discovered by producer/lead singer of The Moonglows, Harvey Fuqua, and became the Spinners in 1961. First recorded on Fuqua's Tri-Phi label. Many personnel changes. G.C. Cameron was lead singer from 1968-72. 1972 hit lineup included Phillippe Wynne (tenor; d: 7/14/84), Bobbie Smith (tenor), Billy Henderson (tenor), Henry Fambrough (baritone) and Pervis Jackson (bass). Wynne left group in 1977 and toured with Parliament/Funkadelic; replaced by John Edwards.

1)*They Just Can't Stop It the (Games People Play)* 2)*Cupid/I've Loved You For A Long Time* 3)*Then Came You*

11/11/72	31	5	●	1 I'll Be Around............................	3	Atlantic 2904
1/20/73	14	8	●	2 Could It Be I'm Falling In Love.......	4	Atlantic 2927
5/26/73	19	7	●	3 One Of A Kind (Love Affair)...........	11	Atlantic 2962
8/25/73	20	6		4 Ghetto Child..............................	29	Atlantic 2973
8/3/74	3	16	●	5 Then Came You..........................	1¹	Atlantic 3202
				DIONNE WARWICKE AND SPINNERS		
				originally released on Atlantic 3029 earlier in 1974		
8/16/75	2¹	15	●	6 They Just Can't Stop It the (Games People Play)...........	5	Atlantic 3284
10/1/77	43	4		7 Heaven On Earth (So Fine)............	89	Atlantic 3425
1/19/80	5	17	●	8 Working My Way Back To You/Forgive Me, Girl............	2²	Atlantic 3637
5/17/80	3	17		9 Cupid/I've Loved You For A Long Time............	4	Atlantic 3664
3/28/81	45	3		10 Yesterday Once More/Nothing Remains The Same..............	52	Atlantic 3798

★★150★★ SPRINGFIELD, Dusty

Born Mary O'Brien on 4/16/39 in London. Vocalist/guitarist. In The Lana Sisters vocal group. With brother Tom Springfield and Tim Feild in folk trio, The Springfields, 1960-63.

1)*A Brand New Me* 2)*The Windmills Of Your Mind* 3)*Wishin' And Hopin'*

9/5/64	4	2		1 **Wishin' And Hopin'**....................	6	Philips 40207
6/25/66	8	9		2 **You Don't Have To Say You Love Me**..........	4	Philips 40371
9/24/66	33	5		3 All I See Is You...........................	20	Philips 40396
10/7/67	31	2		4 The Look Of Love.........................	22	Philips 40465
				from the film *Casino Royale*		
5/17/69	3	9		5 **The Windmills Of Your Mind**..........	31	Atlantic 2623
10/4/69	27	4		6 In The Land Of Make Believe..........	113	Atlantic 2673
11/8/69	3	14		7 A Brand New Me.........................	24	Atlantic 2685
3/14/70	25	4		8 Silly, Silly, Fool..........................	76	Atlantic 2705
5/23/70	25	4		9 I Wanna Be A Free Girl.................	105	Atlantic 2729
4/28/73	33	6		10 Mama's Little Girl......................	118	Dunhill 4344
				also released as the B-side of #11 below		
7/14/73	33	5		11 Learn To Say Goodbye................		Dunhill 4357
				from the TV movie *Say Goodbye, Maggie Cole*		
10/3/87	12	14		12 Something In Your Eyes...............		A&M 2940
				RICHARD CARPENTER with Dusty Springfield		

DEBUT DATE	PEAK POS	WKS CHR	GOLD	ARTIST — Record Title	POP POS	Label & Number
				SPRINGFIELD, Dusty — Cont'd		
1/23/88	**14**	12		13 What Have I Done To Deserve This?	2²	EMI-Man. 50107
				PET SHOP BOYS and Dusty Springfield		
12/24/88	**7**	15		14 **As Long As We Got Each Other**..		Reprise 27878
				STEVE DORFF & FRIENDS		
				B.J. Thomas and Dusty Springfield (vocals; Dorff is the producer); theme from the TV show *Growing Pains*		
				SPRINGFIELD, Rick		
				Born on 8/23/49 in Sydney, Australia. Singer/actor/songwriter. With top Australian teen-idol band Zoot before going solo in 1972. Turned to acting in the late '70s, played Noah Drake on the TV soap opera *General Hospital* in the early '80s. Starred in the film *Hard To Hold* in 1984.		
9/2/72	**16**	9		1 Speak To The Sky	14	Capitol 3340
5/1/82	**30**	8		2 Don't Talk To Strangers	2⁴	RCA 13070
12/1/84	**16**	11		3 Taxi Dancing...	59	RCA 13861
				RICK SPRINGFIELD & RANDY CRAWFORD		
				from the film *Hard To Hold*		
				SPRINGSTEEN, Bruce		
				Born on 9/23/49 in Freehold, New Jersey. Rock singer/songwriter/guitarist. Married to model/actress Julianne Phillips from 1985-89. Appeared in the 1987 film *Hail! Hail! Rock 'N' Roll*. Split from the E-Street Band in November 1989. Married Patti Scialfa, former singer with the E-Street Band, on 6/8/91.		
3/9/85	**6**	19		1 **I'm On Fire**	6	Columbia 04772
12/14/85	**1¹**	15		2 **My Hometown**	6	Columbia 05728
10/3/87	**5**	17		3 **Brilliant Disguise**	5	Columbia 07595
12/26/87	**13**	13		4 **Tunnel Of Love**	9	Columbia 07663
3/12/88	**3**	16		5 **One Step Up**	13	Columbia 07726
3/21/92	**8**	18		6 **Human Touch**	16	Columbia 74273
				SPYRO GYRA		
				Jazz-pop band formed in 1975 in Buffalo, New York. Led by saxophonist Jay Beckenstein (b: 5/14/51).		
6/24/78	**16**	14		1 Shaker Song ....[I]	90	Amherst 730
4/28/79	**1¹**	27		2 **Morning Dance** ....[I]	24	Infinity 50011
3/1/80	**15**	13		3 Catching The Sun ....[I]	68	MCA 41180
8/2/80	**48**	4		4 Percolator ....[I]	105	MCA 41275
1/31/81	**14**	10		5 Cafe Amore ....[I]	77	MCA 51035
				SQUEEZE		
				English pop-rock group led by Chris Difford and Glenn Tilbrook. Originally known as UK Squeeze due to confusion with American band Tight Squeeze. Paul Carrack (Ace, Mike + The Mechanics) was lead singer of fluctuating lineup in 1981; re-joined in 1993.		
12/5/87	**45**	3		Hourglass	15	A&M 2967
				STAFFORD, Jim		
				Born on 1/16/44 in Eloise, Florida. Singer/songwriter/guitarist. Moved to Nashville after high school graduation. Own summer variety TV show in 1975, and co-host of *Those Amazing Animals* from 1980-81. Married Bobbie Gentry in 1978.		
7/7/73	**31**	3		1 Swamp Witch..	39	MGM 14496
12/8/73	**28**	11	●	2 Spiders & Snakes	3	MGM 14648
4/13/74	**9**	13		3 My Girl Bill ....[N]	12	MGM 14718
7/27/74	**29**	6		4 Wildwood Weed ....[N]	7	MGM 14737
				STAFFORD, Terry		
				Born in Hollis, Oklahoma and raised in Amarillo, Texas. Elvis Presley sound-alike. Moved to California in 1960. Appeared in the film *Wild Wheels*.		
5/30/64	**4**	7		**I'll Touch A Star**	25	Crusader 105
				STALLONE, Frank/Cynthia Rhodes		
1/21/84	**16**	9		I'm Never Gonna Give You Up		RSO 815882
				from the film *Staying Alive*		
				STAMPEDERS		
				Pop-rock trio from Calgary: Rick Dodson, Ronnie King and Kim Berly.		
8/14/71	**5**	13		**Sweet City Woman**	8	Bell 45120
				STAMPLEY, Joe		
				Born on 6/6/43 in Springhill, Louisiana. Country singer. Leader of The Uniques.		
1/27/73	**17**	8		Soul Song	37	Dot 17442

DEBUT DATE	PEAK POS	WKS CHR	G O L D	ARTIST — Record Title	POP POS	Label & Number
				STANSFIELD, Lisa		
				Born on 4/11/66. Lead singer of Blue Zone from Roachdale, England. Vocalist on Coldcut's 1989 club hit "People Hold On."		
3/17/90	7	20	▲	1 All Around The World..	3	Arista 9928
7/14/90	26	8		2 You Can't Deny It..	14	Arista 2024
9/29/90	35	5		3 This Is The Right Time	21	Arista 2049
11/30/91	13	16		4 Change	27	Arista 12362
3/21/92	21	13		5 All Woman	56	Arista 12398
				STAPLE SINGERS, The		
				Family soul group consisting of Roebuck "Pop" Staples (b: 12/28/15, Winoma, Mississippi), with his son Pervis (who left in 1971) and daughters Cleotha, Yvonne and lead singer Mavis Staples.		
3/16/74	27	9		Touch A Hand, Make A Friend	23	Stax 0196
				STARBABIES ○		
4/28/79	47	2		Oh Boy..		20th Century 2400
				#10 Pop hit for The Crickets in 1958		
				STARBUCK		
				Atlanta pop-rock septet — Bruce Blackman, lead singer.		
5/15/76	2¹	16		1 Moonlight Feels Right	3	Private S. 45039
9/4/76	11	12		2 I Got To Know	43	Private S. 45104
12/18/76	42	6		3 Lucky Man	73	Private S. 45125
5/21/77	41	5		4 Everybody Be Dancin'..	38	Private S. 45144
				STARK & McBRIEN		
				Pop duo: Fred Stark and Rod McBrien. Best known for their music and voices on jingles for McDonald's, Miller Beer, Wrangler and Coca-Cola.		
11/30/74	18	10		1 Isn't It Lonely Together	85	RCA 10109
7/19/75	27	9	✓	2 Big Star..		RCA 10314
6/26/76	17	9		3 If You Like The Music (Suicide And Vine)		RCA 10697
				STARLAND VOCAL BAND		
				Washington, D.C.-based pop quartet: Bill and wife Taffy Danoff, John Carroll and future wife Margot Chapman. Bill and Taffy had fronted the folk quintet Fat City. Bill co-wrote "Take Me Home, Country Roads" with friend John Denver. Denver owned Windsong record label. Won the 1976 Best New Artist Grammy.		
4/24/76	5	16	●	1 Afternoon Delight...	1²	Windsong 10588
10/9/76	20	9		2 California Day	66	Windsong 10785
8/27/77	17	14		3 The Light Of My Life		Windsong 11067
1/26/80	13	13		4 Loving You With My Eyes	71	Windsong 11899
				STARR, Brenda K.		
				Born Brenda Kaplan on 10/15/66 in Manhattan. Singer/film actress from New York City of Puerto Rican heritage. Daughter of Harvey Kaplan (Spiral Starecase).		
4/16/88	14	18		I Still Believe	13	MCA 53288
				STARR, Kay		
				Born Katherine Starks on 7/21/22 in Dougherty, Oklahoma and raised in Dallas and Memphis. With Joe Venuti's orchestra at age 15, and sang briefly with Glenn Miller, Charlie Barnet and Bob Crosby before launching solo career in 1945. In the films *Make Believe Ballroom* and *When You're Smiling*.		
11/6/65	23	7	✓	1 Never Dreamed I Could Love Someone New		Capitol 5492
3/19/66	26	5		2 Old Records/		
4/2/66	19	5		3 Tears And Heartaches..		Capitol 5601
12/16/67	24	6		4 When The Lights Go On Again (All Over The World)		ABC 11013
				California Dreamers (backing vocals)		
				STARR, Lucille		
				Singer born in St. Boniface, Manitoba, Canada.		
6/13/64	15	4		The French Song.. [F]	54	Almo 204
				arranged by Herb Alpert		
				STARR, Ringo		
				Born Richard Starkey on 7/7/40 in Liverpool, England. Played with Rory Storm and the Hurricanes before joining The Beatles following ousting of drummer Pete Best in 1962. First solo album in 1970. Acted in films *Candy* (made in 1967, released in 1969), *The Magic Christian*, *200 Motels*, *Born To Boogie*, *Blindman*, *That'll Be The Day*, *Cave Man* and Paul McCartney's *Give My Regards To Broad Street*. Played Mr. Conductor on PBS-TV's *Shining Time Station* from 1989-91. Married actress Barbara Bach in 1981.		
6/5/71	24	4	●	1 It Don't Come Easy	4	Apple 1831
10/13/73	3	16	●	2 Photograph..	1¹	Apple 1865
12/22/73	2¹	15	●	3 You're Sixteen	1¹	Apple 1870
3/16/74	24	10		4 Oh My My	5	Apple 1872

DEBUT DATE	PEAK POS	WKS CHR	GOLD	ARTIST — Record Title	POP POS	Label & Number
				STARR, Ringo — Cont'd		
11/23/74	**1**¹	13		5 Only You	6	Apple 1876
10/30/76	**44**	2		6 A Dose Of Rock 'N' Roll	26	Atlantic 3361
				STARSHIP — see JEFFERSON STARSHIP		
				STARS on 45		
				Dutch session vocalists and musicians assembled by producer Jaap Eggermont. The John Lennon vocals by Bas Muys.		
4/18/81	**11**	16	●	1 Medley: Intro "Venus"	**1**¹	Radio 3810
				Sugar Sugar/No Reply/I'll Be Back/Drive My Car/Do You Want To Know A Secret/ We Can Work It Out/I Should Have Known Better/Nowhere Man/ You're Going To Lose That Girl/Stars on 45		
4/17/82	**31**	6		2 Stars on 45 III	28	Radio 4019
				STARS ON (A Tribute To Stevie Wonder) Uptight Everything's All Right/My Cherie Amour/Yester Me, Yester You/ Master Blaster/You Are The Sunshine Of My Life/Isn't She Lovely/Stars On Jingle/ Sir Duke/I Wish/I Was Made To Love Her/Superstition/Fingertips		
				STATLER BROTHERS, The		
				Country vocal quartet from Staunton, Virginia. Consisted of brothers Harold and Don Reid, Phil Balsley and Lew DeWitt. In 1983, Jimmy Fortune replaced DeWitt who died from Crohn's disease on 8/15/90 (age 52).		
4/15/72	**18**	7		Do You Remember These	105	Mercury 73275
				STATON, Candi		
				Born in Hanceville, Alabama. Sang with the Jewel Gospel Trio from age 10. Went solo in 1968. Married for a time to Clarence Carter.		
8/21/76	**50**	1		Young Hearts Run Free	20	Warner 8181
				STEALERS WHEEL		
				Scottish group led by Gerry Rafferty (vocals, guitar) and Joe Egan (vocals, keyboards).		
4/21/73	**13**	6		1 Stuck In The Middle With You	6	A&M 1416
7/7/73	**23**	9		2 Everyone's Agreed That Everything Will Turn Out Fine	49	A&M 1450
1/26/74	**6**	14		3 Star	29	A&M 1483
				STEELE, Jevetta — see WHALUM, Kirk		
				STEELY DAN		
				Los Angeles-based, pop/jazz-styled group formed by Donald Fagen (b: 1/10/48, Passaic, New Jersey; keyboards, vocals) and Walter Becker (b: 2/20/50, New York City; bass, vocals). Group, primarily known as a studio unit, featured Fagen and Becker with various studio musicians. Actor/comedian Chevy Chase was their drummer in band's formative years. Duo went their separate ways in 1981. Drummer Jimmy Hodder drowned on 6/5/90 (age 42). Fagen and Becker reunited for a concert tour in 1993.		
1/27/73	**34**	5		1 Do It Again	6	ABC 11338
6/1/74	**15**	10		2 Rikki Don't Lose That Number	4	ABC 11439
1/28/78	**30**	9		3 Peg	11	ABC 12320
5/13/78	**40**	5		4 Deacon Blues	19	ABC 12355
9/30/78	**44**	3		5 Josie	26	ABC 12404
12/20/80	**11**	16		6 Hey Nineteen	10	MCA 51036
3/28/81	**13**	9		7 Time Out Of Mind	22	MCA 51082
				STEVENS, April — see TEMPO, Nino		
★★180★★				**STEVENS, Cat**		
				Born Steven Georgiou on 7/21/47 in London. Began career playing folk music at Hammersmith College in 1966. Contracted tuberculosis in 1968 and spent over a year recuperating. Adopted new style when he re-emerged. Lived in Brazil in the mid-'70s. Converted to Muslim religion in 1979, took name Yusef Islam.		
				1)Peace Train 2)Morning Has Broken 3)Oh Very Young		
3/27/71	**21**	7		1 Wild World	11	A&M 1231
7/10/71	**10**	8		2 Moon Shadow	30	A&M 1265
10/2/71	**1**³	13		3 Peace Train	7	A&M 1291
4/8/72	**1**¹	12		4 Morning Has Broken	6	A&M 1335
12/9/72	**17**	7		5 Sitting	16	A&M 1396
7/14/73	**38**	6		6 The Hurt	31	A&M 1418
3/23/74	**2**¹	18		7 Oh Very Young	10	A&M 1503
8/10/74	**13**	12		8 Another Saturday Night	6	A&M 1602
8/9/75	**39**	6		9 Two Fine People	33	A&M 1700
7/16/77	**28**	6		10 (Remember The Days Of The) Old Schoolyard	33	A&M 1948

★★152★★ STEVENS, Ray

Born Ray Ragsdale on 1/24/39 in Clarkdale, Georgia. Attended Georgia State University, studied music theory and composition. Production work in the mid-'60s. Numerous appearances on Andy Williams' TV show in the late '60s. Own TV show in summer of 1970. Featured on *Music Country* TV show, 1973-74. The #1 novelty recording artist of the past 30 years.

1)Everything Is Beautiful 2)A Mama And A Papa 3)All My Trials

DEBUT DATE	PEAK POS	WKS CHR	GOLD	ARTIST — Record Title	POP POS	Label & Number
4/18/70	1³	12	●	1 Everything Is Beautiful	1²	Barnaby 2011
7/25/70	12	7		2 America, Communicate With Me....................................	45	Barnaby 2016
11/7/70	17	6		3 Sunset Strip	81	Barnaby 2021
5/1/71	4	7		4 A Mama And A Papa	82	Barnaby 2029
8/28/71	6	8		5 All My Trials	70	Barnaby 2039
11/13/71	24	7		6 Turn Your Radio On..	63	Barnaby 2048
7/14/73	44	5		7 Nashville...		Barnaby 5020
4/27/74	12	9	●	8 The Streak ....[N]	1³	Barnaby 600
11/23/74	18	10		9 Everybody Needs A Rainbow		Barnaby 610
3/29/75	8	12		10 Misty	14	Barnaby 614
1/17/76	44	2		11 Young Love..	93	Barnaby 618
1/15/77	38	4		12 In The Mood ....[N]	40	Warner 8301
				HENHOUSE FIVE PLUS TOO		
9/9/78	50	1		13 Be Your Own Best Friend		Warner 8603
3/31/79	11	13		14 I Need Your Help Barry Manilow ....[N]	49	Warner 8785

STEVENS, Shakin'

Born Michael Barratt on 3/4/48 in Ely, Wales. Rockabilly singer/songwriter.

DEBUT DATE	PEAK POS	WKS CHR	GOLD	ARTIST — Record Title	POP POS	Label & Number
4/14/84	13	16		I Cry Just A Little Bit...	67	Epic 04338

STEVENSON, B.W.

Born Louis Stevenson on 10/5/49 in Dallas; died on 4/28/88 after heart surgery.

DEBUT DATE	PEAK POS	WKS CHR	GOLD	ARTIST — Record Title	POP POS	Label & Number
7/8/72	38	4		1 Say What I Feel	114	RCA 0728
6/2/73	31	6		2 Shambala..	66	RCA 0952
8/4/73	1¹	14		3 My Maria	9	RCA 0030
12/1/73	32	9		4 The River Of Love..	53	RCA 0171
8/10/74	40	5		5 Little Bit Of Understanding		RCA 10012

STEVIE B

Miami-born Steven B. Hill. R&B singer/self-taught musician. In high school band with Howard Johnson.

DEBUT DATE	PEAK POS	WKS CHR	GOLD	ARTIST — Record Title	POP POS	Label & Number
11/3/90	1²	24	●	1 Because I Love You (The Postman Song).....................	1⁴	LMR 2724
3/9/91	16	13		2 I'll Be By Your Side	12	LMR 52758

STEWART, Al

Born on 9/5/45 in Glasgow, Scotland. Pop-rock singer/composer/guitarist.

DEBUT DATE	PEAK POS	WKS CHR	GOLD	ARTIST — Record Title	POP POS	Label & Number
1/8/77	8	16		1 Year Of The Cat	8	Janus 266
				written about British comedian Tony Hancock		
4/30/77	23	9		2 On The Border...	42	Janus 267
10/14/78	1¹⁰	19		3 Time Passages	7	Arista 0362
2/10/79	10	11		4 Song On The Radio	29	Arista 0389
				all of above produced by Alan Parsons		
9/13/80	13	18		5 Midnight Rocks...	24	Arista 0552

STEWART, Andy

Born in Glasgow, Scotland in 1933. Singer/composer/actor/comedian/impressionist.

DEBUT DATE	PEAK POS	WKS CHR	GOLD	ARTIST — Record Title	POP POS	Label & Number
8/21/61	17	4		Donald Where's Your Troosers? ....[N]	77	Warwick 665
				backed by The White Heather Group		

STEWART, David A., Introducing Candy Dulfer

David was born on 9/9/52 in England. Half of the Eurythmics duo. Multi-instrumentalist/composer/producer. Married Siobhan Fahey (Bananarama, Shakespear's Sister) on 8/1/87. Dulfer is a saxophonist from Holland.

DEBUT DATE	PEAK POS	WKS CHR	GOLD	ARTIST — Record Title	POP POS	Label & Number
6/8/91	6	21		Lily Was Here...[I]	11	Arista 2187
				Dutch film title song		

STEWART, James ✪

Born on 5/20/08 in Indiana, Pennsylvania. One of America's all-time leading actors. Oscar winner for *The Philadelphia Story* (1940).

DEBUT DATE	PEAK POS	WKS CHR	GOLD	ARTIST — Record Title	POP POS	Label & Number
7/10/65	33	2		The Legend Of Shenandoah ....[S]	133	Decca 31795
				inspired by the film *Shenandoah* (starring Stewart); orchestra directed by Charles "Bud" Dant		

STEWART, John

Born on 9/5/39 in San Diego. Member of The Kingston Trio from 1961-67. Wrote "Daydream Believer."

DEBUT DATE	PEAK POS	WKS CHR	GOLD	ARTIST — Record Title	POP POS	Label & Number
7/7/79	42	7		1 Gold	5	RSO 931

DEBUT DATE	PEAK POS	WKS CHR	GOLD	ARTIST — Record Title	POP POS	Label & Number
				STEWART, John — Cont'd		
9/29/79	**49**	1		**2** Midnight Wind	28	RSO 1000
				backing vocals on above 2 by Stevie Nicks and Lindsey Buckingham		
12/22/79	**18**	10		**3** Lost Her In The Sun	34	RSO 1016
★★**48**★★				**STEWART, Rod**		
				Born Roderick Stewart on 1/10/45 in London. Worked as a folksinger in Europe in the early '60s. Recorded for English Decca in 1964. With the Hoochie Coochie Men, Steampacket and Shotgun Express. Joined Jeff Beck Group, 1967-69. With Faces from 1969-75, also recorded solo during this time. Left Faces in December 1975. Won Grammy's Living Legends Award in 1989. Married to actress Alana Hamilton from 1979-84. Married supermodel Rachel Hunter on 12/15/90.		
				1)Have I Told You Lately 2)This Old Heart Of Mine 3)Downtown Train		
10/30/76	**42**	5	●	**1** Tonight's The Night (Gonna Be Alright)................	1[8]	Warner 8262
3/5/77	**43**	5		**2** The First Cut Is The Deepest...........................	21	Warner 8321
				written by Cat Stevens		
11/26/77	**17**	14	●	**3** You're In My Heart (The Final Acclaim)	4	Warner 8475
5/13/78	**31**	10		**4** I Was Only Joking	22	Warner 8568
2/2/80	**44**	2		**5** I Don't Want To Talk About It	46	Warner 49138
10/27/84	**32**	7		**6** Some Guys Have All The Luck	10	Warner 29215
6/14/86	**5**	16		**7** Love Touch	6	Warner 28668
				theme from the film *Legal Eagles*		
9/3/88	**3**	24		**8** Forever Young	12	Warner 27796
12/17/88	**3**	26		**9** My Heart Can't Tell You No............................	4	Warner 27729
12/2/89	**1**[1]	21		**10** Downtown Train	3	Warner 22685
3/24/90	**1**[5]	24		**11** This Old Heart Of Mine ....[R]	10	Warner 19983
				ROD STEWART (with Ronald Isley)		
				Rod's original version made the *Hot 100* in 1976 (POS 83) on Warner 8170		
9/1/90	**2**[1]	24		**12** I Don't Want To Talk About It ....[R]		Warner LP Cut
				from the album *Storyteller/The Complete Anthology: 1964-1990* on Warner 25987; new version of Rod's 1980 hit		
3/16/91	**2**[2]	29		**13** Rhythm Of My Heart	5	Warner 19366
7/6/91	**3**	29		**14** The Motown Song	10	Warner 19322
				The Temptations (backing vocals)		
10/19/91	**3**	27		**15** Broken Arrow	20	Warner 19274
				written by Robbie Robertson (The Band)		
1/25/92	**6**	14		**16** Your Song	48	Polydor 865944
				all artist royalties donated to worldwide AIDS charities		
11/28/92	**33**	16		**17** Have I Told You Lately		Warner LP Cut
				from the album *Vagabond Heart* on Warner 26300		
4/24/93	**1**[5]	23↑	●	**18 Have I Told You Lately** ....[R]	5	Warner 18511
				live version from the album *Unplugged...And Seated*		
				STEWART, Sandy		
				Born Sandra Galitz on 7/10/37 in Philadelphia. Regular on the Eddie Fisher and Perry Como TV shows.		
1/5/63	**8**	9		**My Coloring Book**	20	Colpix 669
				STIGERS, Curtis		
				Vocalist/saxophonist from Boise, Idaho. Twenty-five years old in 1991.		
10/5/91	**5**	32		**1** I Wonder Why...	9	Arista 12331
				Angel Rogers, Alfie Silas and Tata Vega (backing vocals)		
2/8/92	**17**	16		**2** You're All That Matters To Me........................	98	Arista 12391
9/5/92	**5**	20		**3** Never Saw A Miracle	107	Arista 12459
				STILLS, Stephen		
				Born on 1/3/45 in Dallas. Member of Buffalo Springfield and Crosby, Stills & Nash. Group Manassas included Chris Hillman (The Byrds), Dallas Taylor, Fuzzy Samuels, Paul Harris, Al Perkins and Joe Lala.		
1/2/71	**32**	5		**1** Love The One You're With	14	Atlantic 2778
10/27/84	**17**	12		**2** Can't Let Go..	67	Atlantic 89611
				STEPHEN STILLS FEATURING MICHAEL FINNIGAN		
				STING		
				Born Gordon Sumner on 10/2/51 in Wallsend, England. Lead singer/bass guitarist of The Police. In the films *Quadrophenia, Dune, The Bride, Plenty* and others. Married actress/producer Trudie Styler in early 1992. Nicknamed "Sting" because of a yellow and black jersey he liked to wear.		
				1)Fields Of Gold 2)If I Ever Lose My Faith In You 3)All This Time		
7/13/85	**39**	2		**1** If You Love Somebody Set Them Free................	3	A&M 2738
10/5/85	**32**	8		**2** Fortress Around Your Heart	8	A&M 2767
12/7/85	**20**	8		**3** Love Is The Seventh Wave	17	A&M 2787
1/30/88	**37**	7		**4** Be Still My Beating Heart	15	A&M 2992
5/7/88	**48**	3		**5** Englishman In New York	84	A&M 1200

DEBUT DATE	PEAK POS	WKS CHR	GOLD	ARTIST — Record Title	POP POS	Label & Number
				STING — Cont'd		
1/26/91	9	20		6 All This Time	5	A&M 1541
7/4/92	47	3		7 It's Probably Me		A&M 2407
				STING with Eric Clapton		
				from the film *Lethal Weapon 3*; available only as a CD single		
2/20/93	8	25		8 If I Ever Lose My Faith In You	17	A&M 0111
6/5/93	2⁵	17↑		9 Fields Of Gold...	23	A&M 0259
				STONE, Kirby, Four — see TOKENS		
				STONEBOLT		
				Pop-rock quintet from Vancouver, Canada — David Wills, lead singer.		
8/19/78	20	13		I Will Still Love You	29	Parachute 512
				STOOKEY, Paul		
				Born on 11/30/37 in Baltimore. Paul of Peter, Paul & Mary.		
7/31/71	3	14		**Wedding Song (There Is Love)**.....................	24	Warner 7511
				STORM ○		
5/6/72	26	5		This I Find Is Beautiful...........................		Sunflower 120
				STRAIGHT A'S, The ○		
8/16/69	39	2		Blue Moon		Kapp 2017
				#1 Pop hit for The Marcels in 1961		
				STRANGE, Billy		
				Top Hollywood session guitarist. Born in Long Beach, California in 1930.		
8/29/64	10	8		1 The James Bond Theme .... [I]	58	GNP Cresc. 320
				from the film *From Russia With Love*		
1/23/65	10	5		2 Goldfinger .... [I]	55	GNP Cresc. 334
				movie title song		
				STRAWBERRY ALARM CLOCK		
				West Coast psychedelic rock sextet: Ed King (lead guitar), Mark Weitz (keyboards), Lee Freeman (guitar), Gary Lovetro (bass), George Bunnel (bass) and Randy Seol (drums). King joined Lynyrd Skynyrd, 1973-75. Originally known as the Sixpence.		
9/21/68	39	2		Barefoot In Baltimore	67	Uni 55076
				STREAMLINERS WITH JOANNE, The ○		
7/3/65	40	1		Frankfurter Sandwiches .... [N]	117	United Art. 880
				1930's-styled novelty tune		
				STREET, Janey		
				Pop-rock singer originally from New York City.		
2/23/85	18	9		Under The Clock		Arista 9304
★★1★★				**STREISAND, Barbra**		
				Born Barbara Joan Streisand on 4/24/42 in Brooklyn. Made Broadway debut in *I Can Get It For You Wholesale*, 1962. Lead role in Broadway's *Funny Girl*, 1964. Film debut in *Funny Girl* in 1968 (tied with Katharine Hepburn for Best Actress Oscar); also starred in *A Star Is Born*, *Hello Dolly*, *Funny Lady*, *The Way We Were* and many others. Produced/directed/starred in the films *Yentl* and *Prince Of Tides*. Married to actor Elliott Gould from 1963-71.		
				1)*Love Theme From "A Star Is Born" (Evergreen)* 2)*Woman In Love* 3)*My Heart Belongs To Me* 4)*What Kind Of Fool* 5)*People*		
5/2/64	1³	15		1 People	5	Columbia 42965
9/19/64	6	8		2 Funny Girl...	44	Columbia 43127
				above 2 from the Broadway musical *Funny Girl*		
4/3/65	15	5		3 Why Did I Choose You	77	Columbia 43248
				from the Broadway musical *The Yearling*		
6/26/65	17	8		4 My Man	79	Columbia 43323
9/25/65	2¹	14		5 He Touched Me	53	Columbia 43403
				from the Broadway musical *Drat! The Cat!*		
12/18/65	5	11		6 Second Hand Rose	32	Columbia 43469
2/5/66	4	12		7 Where Am I Going?/	94	
3/12/66	18	6		8 You Wanna Bet...		Columbia 43518
				above 2 from the Broadway musical *Sweet Charity*		
4/30/66	23	8		9 The Minute Waltz/		
5/14/66	9	8		10 Sam, You Made The Pants Too Long............................	98	Columbia 43612
				parody, written by Milton Berle in 1940, of "Lawd, You Made The Night Too Long"		
8/6/66	15	5		11 Non...C'est Rien .... [F]		Columbia 43739
9/24/66	8	10		12 Free Again..	83	Columbia 43808

DEBUT DATE	PEAK POS	WKS CHR	GOLD	ARTIST — Record Title	POP POS	Label & Number
				STREISAND, Barbra — Cont'd		
8/5/67	**2**[2]	12		13 **Stout-Hearted Men**	92	Columbia 44225
				from the Broadway musical *The New Moon*		
11/11/67	**29**	4		14 Lover Man (Oh, Where Can You Be?)		Columbia 44331
3/30/68	**19**	5		15 Our Corner Of The Night	107	Columbia 44474
9/7/68	**25**	2		16 Funny Girl/	[R]	
9/14/68	**19**	10		17 I'd Rather Be Blue Over You (Than Happy With Somebody Else)		Columbia 44622
				above 2 from the movie *Funny Girl*		
8/16/69	**35**	4		18 Honey Pie		Columbia 44921
				recorded by The Beatles on their *White* album		
1/31/70	**23**	4		19 Before The Parade Passes By		Columbia 45072
				from the film *Hello Dolly!*		
5/9/70	**19**	9		20 The Best Thing You've Ever Done		Columbia 45147
10/24/70	**2**[1]	16		21 **Stoney End**	6	Columbia 45236
3/20/71	**3**	8		22 **Time And Love**	51	Columbia 45341
5/22/71	**7**	5		23 **Flim Flam Man**	82	Columbia 45384
				above 3 written by Laura Nyro		
7/24/71	**3**	9		24 **Where You Lead**	40	Columbia 45414
10/30/71	**24**	4		25 Mother	79	Columbia 45471
				written by John Lennon		
7/8/72	**15**	10		26 Sweet Inspiration/Where You Lead	37	Columbia 45626
8/5/72	**28**	4		27 Sing A Song/Make Your Own Kind Of Music	94	Columbia 45686
12/16/72	**22**	5		28 Didn't We	82	Columbia 45739
10/20/73	**1**[2]	26	●	29 **The Way We Were**	1[3]	Columbia 45944
				movie title song		
3/30/74	**10**	9		30 **All In Love Is Fair**	63	Columbia 46024
				written by Stevie Wonder		
5/17/75	**27**	7		31 How Lucky Can You Get		Arista 0123
				from the film *Funny Lady*		
9/6/75	**11**	11		32 My Father's Song		Columbia 10198
12/11/76	**1**[6]	22	●	33 **Love Theme From "A Star Is Born" (Evergreen)**	1[3]	Columbia 10450
				love theme from the film *A Star Is Born*		
6/4/77	**1**[4]	18		34 **My Heart Belongs To Me**	4	Columbia 10555
6/17/78	**1**[2]	15		35 **Songbird**	25	Columbia 10756
9/23/78	**48**	2		36 Love Theme From "Eyes Of Laura Mars" (Prisoner)	21	Columbia 10777
				from the film *Eyes Of Laura Mars*		
10/28/78	**3**	18	●	37 **You Don't Bring Me Flowers**	1[2]	Columbia 10840
				BARBRA & NEIL		
3/24/79	**29**	7		38 Superman		Columbia 10931
6/23/79	**2**[1]	19	●	39 **The Main Event/Fight**	3	Columbia 11008
				from the film *The Main Event*		
10/27/79	**7**	12	●	40 **No More Tears (Enough Is Enough)**	1[2]	Columbia 11125
				BARBRA STREISAND/DONNA SUMMER		
				12" single available on Casablanca 20199		
1/5/80	**9**	11		41 Kiss Me In The Rain	37	Columbia 11179
9/6/80	**1**[5]	23	●	42 **Woman In Love**	1[3]	Columbia 11364
11/1/80	**5**	18	●	43 **Guilty ***	3	Columbia 11390
2/7/81	**1**[4]	17		44 **What Kind Of Fool ***	10	Columbia 11430
				***BARBRA STREISAND & BARRY GIBB**		
5/16/81	**8**	17		45 **Promises**	48	Columbia 02065
				above 4 written and produced by Barry Gibb (Bee Gees)		
11/14/81	**2**[6]	20		46 **Comin' In And Out Of Your Life**	11	Columbia 02621
2/27/82	**9**	13		47 Memory	52	Columbia 02717
				theme from the musical *Cats*		
10/22/83	**1**[2]	19		48 **The Way He Makes Me Feel**	40	Columbia 04177
2/25/84	**26**	8		49 Papa, Can You Hear Me?		Columbia 04357
				above 2 from the film *Yentl*		
9/15/84	**4**	12		50 **Left In The Dark**	50	Columbia 04605
12/15/84	**8**	17		51 **Make No Mistake, He's Mine**	51	Columbia 04695
				BARBRA STREISAND (With KIM CARNES)		
3/9/85	**14**	9		52 Emotion	79	Columbia 04707
11/30/85	**5**	17		53 **Somewhere**	43	Columbia 05680
				from the musical *West Side Story*		
3/8/86	**25**	10		54 Send In The Clowns		Columbia 05837
				from the musical *A Little Night Music*		

DEBUT DATE	PEAK POS	WKS CHR	GOLD	ARTIST — Record Title	POP POS	Label & Number
				STREISAND, Barbra — Cont'd		
0/22/88	3	15		55 Till I Loved You..	25	Columbia 08062
				BARBRA STREISAND AND DON JOHNSON love theme from the Broadway musical *Goya*		
2/24/88	15	14		56 All I Ask Of You..		Columbia 08026
				from the Broadway musical *The Phantom Of The Opera*		
4/8/89	32	7		57 What Were We Thinking Of		Columbia 68691
9/30/89	10	13		58 **We're Not Makin' Love Anymore**		Columbia 73016
				written by Michael Bolton and Diane Warren		
2/16/89	25	9		59 Someone That I Used To Love..................................		Columbia LP Cut
				from the album *A Collection Greatest Hits...And More* on Columbia 45369		
1/4/92	43	5		60 Places That Belong To You		Columbia LP Cut
				from the soundtrack album *The Prince Of Tides* on Columbia 48627		
				STRING-A-LONGS, The		
				Instrumental quintet: Keith McCormack, Aubrey Lee de Cordova, Richard Stephens and Jimmy Torres (guitars) and Don Allen (drums).		
7/17/61	10	4		**Should I** .... [I]	42	Warwick 654
				STRUNK, Jud		
				Born Justin Strunk, Jr. on 6/11/36 in Jamestown, New York and raised in Farmington, Maine. Killed in a plane crash on 10/15/81. Regular on TV's *Laugh In*.		
1/6/73	4	20		1 **Daisy A Day**	14	MGM 14463
7/7/73	22	8		2 Next Door Neighbor's Kid......................................		MGM 14572
				STYLE COUNCIL, The		
				English duo: Paul Weller (ex-vocalist of The Jam) and Mick Talbot (keyboards). Expanded to a trio in 1988 with the addition of female vocalist Dee C. Lee.		
5/5/84	34	8		1 My Ever Changing Moods	29	Geffen 29359
7/21/84	31	7		2 You're The Best Thing	76	Geffen 29248
★★186★★				**STYLISTICS, The**		
				Soul group from Philadelphia formed in 1968. Consisted of Russell Thompkins, Jr. (b: 3/21/51; lead), Airron Love, James Smith, James Dunn and Herbie Murrell. Thompkins, Love and Smith sang with the Percussions; Murrell and Dunn with the Monarchs from 1965-68. First recorded for Sebring in 1969.		
				1)You'll Never Get To Heaven 2)You Make Me Feel Brand New 3)Betcha By Golly, Wow		
2/11/71	24	8	●	1 You Are Everything..	9	Avco 4581
3/18/72	7	11	●	2 **Betcha By Golly, Wow**	3	Avco 4591
6/10/72	25	5		3 People Make The World Go Round	25	Avco 4595
11/4/72	27	7	●	4 I'm Stone In Love With You	10	Avco 4603
2/24/73	21	7	●	5 Break Up To Make Up	5	Avco 4611
5/19/73	4	9		6 **You'll Never Get To Heaven (If You Break My Heart)**......	23	Avco 4618
12/1/73	44	5		7 Rockin' Roll Baby	14	Avco 4625
4/27/74	6	14	●	8 **You Make Me Feel Brand New**	2²	Avco 4634
8/17/74	26	9		9 Let's Put It All Together	18	Avco 4640
1/25/75	27	8		10 Star On A TV Show	47	Avco 4649
7/19/75	34	7		11 Can't Give You Anything (But My Love)............................	51	Avco 4656
3/6/76	26	8		12 You Are Beautiful..	79	Avco 4664
1/24/90	35	8		13 Me-U=Blue	78	MCA 53945
				GLENN MEDEIROS Featuring The Stylistics		
				STYX		
				Chicago-based rock quintet: Dennis DeYoung (vocals, keyboards), Tommy Shaw (lead guitar), James Young (guitar), and twin brothers John (drums) and Chuck Panozzo (bass). Band earlier known as TW4. Shaw replaced John Curulewski in 1976. Most songs written by Dennis DeYoung and/or Tommy Shaw. Band broke up when DeYoung and Shaw went solo in 1984. Reunited in 1990 with guitarist Glen Burtnick replacing Shaw, who joined the Damn Yankees. In Greek mythology, Styx is a river of Hades.		
0/20/79	9	16	●	1 **Babe**	1²	A&M 2188
2/7/81	26	8		2 The Best Of Times	3	A&M 2300
5/14/83	13	15		3 Don't Let It End	6	A&M 2543
12/8/90	3	31		4 **Show Me The Way**	3	A&M 1536
4/13/91	13	19		5 Love At First Sight	25	A&M 1548
				SUGAR SHOPPE, The ○		
				Two-man, two-woman pop group from Canada.		
1/30/68	31	12		Poor Papa		Capitol 2326
				#10 hit for "Whispering" Jack Smith in 1926		

DEBUT DATE	PEAK POS	WKS CHR	GOLD	ARTIST — Record Title	POP POS	Label & Number
				SULLIVAN, Tom ○		
				Born on 3/27/47 in West Roxbury, Massachusetts. Singer/songwriter/actor; blind since birth.		
5/15/76	44	5		Yes, I'm Ready	103	ABC 12174
				#5 Pop hit for Barbara Mason in 1965		
★★142★★				**SUMMER, Donna**		
				Born Adrian Donna Gaines on 12/31/48 in Boston. With group Crow, played local clubs. In German production of *Hair*, European productions of *Godspell*, *The Me Nobody Knows* and *Porgy And Bess*. Settled in Germany, where she recorded "Love To Love You Baby." In the film *Thank God It's Friday* in 1979. Married Bruce Sudano (Alive & Kicking and Brooklyn Dreams) in 1980. Dubbed "The Queen of Disco."		
				1)This Time I Know It's For Real 2)No More Tears (Enough Is Enough) 3)Winter Melody		
5/15/76	47	3		1 Could It Be Magic	52	Oasis 405
2/26/77	8	9		2 **Winter Melody**	43	Casablanca 874
9/17/77	45	4	●	3 I Feel Love..	6	Casablanca 884
8/5/78	42	4	●	4 Last Dance	3	Casablanca 926
				from the film *Thank God It's Friday*		
9/23/78	24	11	●	5 MacArthur Park	1³	Casablanca 939
1/27/79	17	13	●	6 Heaven Knows	4	Casablanca 959
				DONNA SUMMER with Brooklyn Dreams		
10/27/79	44	3	●	7 Dim All The Lights	2²	Casablanca 2201
10/27/79	7	12	●	8 **No More Tears (Enough Is Enough)**	1²	Columbia 11125
				BARBRA STREISAND/DONNA SUMMER		
				12" single available on Casablanca 20199		
2/2/80	26	7	●	9 On The Radio..	5	Casablanca 2236
1/15/83	17	16		10 The Woman In Me	33	Geffen 29805
1/28/84	19	12		11 Love Has A Mind Of Its Own	70	Mercury 814922
				with Matthew Ward of the gospel group "2nd Chapter of Acts"		
8/25/84	17	10		12 There Goes My Baby	21	Geffen 29291
9/19/87	38	4		13 Dinner With Gershwin	48	Geffen 28418
12/19/87	14	14		14 Only The Fool Survives		Geffen 28165
				DONNA SUMMER with MICKEY THOMAS		
5/13/89	2⁴	24	●	15 This Time I Know It's For Real	7	Atlantic 88899
				SUNNY & THE SUNGLOWS		
				Group from San Antonio, Texas, formed in 1959. Group led by Sunny Ozuna, with Jesse, Oscar and Ray Villanueva, Tony Tostado, Gilbert Fernandez and Alfred Luna.		
10/5/63	4	8		Talk To Me	11	Tear Drop 3014
				SUNSHINE COMPANY, The		
				Southern California pop quintet featuring lead singer Mary Nance.		
8/3/68	31	6		On A Beautiful Day...	106	Imperial 66308
				SUPERTRAMP		
				British rock quintet: Roger Hodgson (vocals, guitar), Rick Davies (vocals, keyboards), John Helliwell (sax), Dougie Thomson (bass) and Bob Siebenberg (drums). Hodgson went solo in 1983.		
8/18/79	32	6		1 Goodbye Stranger..	15	A&M 2162
11/3/79	28	8		2 Take The Long Way Home	10	A&M 2193
11/6/82	5	17		3 **It's Raining Again**	11	A&M 2502
2/12/83	16	12		4 My Kind Of Lady	31	A&M 2517
12/19/87	42	5		5 I'm Beggin' You		A&M 2985
				SUPREMES, The		
				R&B vocal group from Detroit, formed as the Primettes in 1959. Consisted of lead singer Diana Ross (b: 3/26/44), Mary Wilson (b: 3/6/44), Florence Ballard (b: 6/30/43; d: 2/22/76 of cardiac arrest) and Barbara Martin. Recorded for LuPine in 1960. Signed to Motown's Tamla label in 1960. Changed name's to The Supremes in 1961; Martin left shortly thereafter. Worked as backing vocalists for Motown until 1964. Backed Marvin Gaye on "Can I Get A Witness." Ballard discharged from group in 1967, replaced by Cindy Birdsong, formerly with Patti LaBelle's Blue Belles. Ross left in 1969 for solo career, replaced by Jean Terrell. Birdsong left in 1972, replaced by Lynda Lawrence. Inducted into the Rock and Roll Hall of Fame in 1988.		
11/29/69	12	9		1 Someday We'll Be Together	1¹	Motown 1156
				DIANA ROSS & THE SUPREMES		
4/11/70	28	5		2 Up The Ladder To The Roof	10	Motown 1162
8/8/70	29	5		3 Everybody's Got The Right To Love	21	Motown 1167
11/21/70	24	6		4 Stoned Love	7	Motown 1172
5/15/71	29	6		5 Nathan Jones	16	Motown 1182
2/5/72	33	7		6 Floy Joy	16	Motown 1195
5/13/72	17	7		7 Automatically Sunshine	37	Motown 1200
10/28/72	17	7		8 I Guess I'll Miss The Man...............................	85	Motown 1213
				from the Broadway musical *Pippin*		

DEBUT DATE	PEAK POS	WKS CHR	GOLD	ARTIST — Record Title	POP POS	Label & Number
				SURFACE		
				Soul trio from New Jersey: Bernard Jackson (lead singer), David Townsend (son of producer/songwriter Ed Townsend) and Dave Conley (former horn player with Mandrill).		
6/20/87	**24**	8		1 Happy	20	Columbia 06611
8/12/89	**3**	18	●	2 Shower Me With Your Love	5	Columbia 68746
11/10/90	**1²**	28	●	3 The First Time	1²	Columbia 73502
5/4/91	**17**	18		4 Never Gonna Let You Down...........................	17	Columbia 73643
				SURVIVOR		
				Midwest rock group: Dave Bickler (lead singer), Jim Peterik (keyboards; former lead singer of Ides Of March), Frankie Sullivan (guitar), Gary Smith (drums) and Dennis Johnson (bass). Smith and Johnson replaced by Marc Droubay and Stephan Ellis in 1981. Bickler replaced by Jimi Jamison in 1984. Droubay and Ellis left in 1988.		
7/31/82	**27**	12	▲	1 Eye Of The Tiger	1⁶	Scotti Br. 02912
				from the film *Rocky III*		
5/4/85	**1⁴**	22		2 The Search Is Over	4	Scotti Br. 04871
1/25/86	**35**	4		3 Burning Heart	2²	Scotti Br. 05663
				from the film *Rocky IV*		
12/20/86	**25**	10		4 Is This Love	9	Scotti Br. 06381
2/4/89	**16**	12		5 Across The Miles	74	Scotti Br. 68526
				SWAN, Billy		
				Born on 5/12/42 in Cape Girardeau, Missouri. Singer/songwriter/keyboardist/guitarist. Wrote "Lover Please" for Clyde McPhatter. Produced Tony Joe White's first three albums. Toured with Kris Kristofferson from the early '70s. Formed band Black Tie with Randy Meisner in 1986.		
10/19/74	**6**	13	●	I Can Help	1²	Monument 8621
				SWAYZE, Patrick (featuring Wendy Fraser)		
				Film actor Swayze was born on 8/18/52 in Houston, Texas. Starred in *Red Dawn*, *Dirty Dancing*, *Road House*, *Ghost* and others.		
1/9/88	**1²**	21		She's Like The Wind	3	RCA 5363
				from the film *Dirty Dancing*		
				SWEDEN HEAVEN AND HELL Soundtrack		
9/6/69	**12**	7		Mah-Na-Mah-Na ....[I-N]	55	Ariel 500
				from the film *Sweden Heaven And Hell*; tune used on TV's *Benny Hill Show*		
				SWEET, Rachel — see SMITH, Rex		
				SWEET SENSATION		
				Eight-member soul group from Manchester, England led by Marcel King (vocals), with additional vocals by St. Clair Palmer, Vincent James and Junior Daye.		
12/14/74	**18**	13		Sad Sweet Dreamer...................................	14	Pye 71002
				SWEET SENSATION		
				Female trio from New York City: Betty LeBron, and sisters Margie and Mari Fernandez. Mari replaced in 1989 by Sheila Bega.		
7/7/90	**8**	19		If Wishes Came True.................................	1¹	Atco 98953
				SWING OUT SISTER		
				British jazz-pop trio: Corinne Drewery (vocals), Andy Connell and Martin Jackson. Drewery was a fashion designer. Reduced to a duo in 1989 with departure of Jackson.		
9/12/87	**1²**	20		1 Breakout...	6	Mercury 888016
12/26/87	**7**	17		2 Twilight World	31	Mercury 888484
6/25/88	**37**	4		3 Surrender...		Mercury 888243
5/20/89	**6**	17		4 Waiting Game	86	Fontana 874190
9/16/89	**23**	8		5 You On My Mind....................................		Fontana 874904
8/15/92	**1¹**	19		6 Am I The Same Girl	45	Fontana 864170
12/12/92	**22**	13		7 Notgonnachange		Fontana 866855
				only available as a maxi-single		
				SYLVESTER, Terry ☺		
				Born on 1/8/47 in England. Member of The Swinging Blue Jeans (1966-68) and The Hollies (1969-81).		
10/19/74	**48**	3		For The Peace Of All Mankind.........................		Epic 20002
				SYLVIA		
				Born Sylvia Vanderpool on 5/6/36 in New York City. Singer/songwriter/producer. First recorded with Hot Lips Page for Columbia in 1950, as Little Sylvia. Half of Mickey & Sylvia duo. Married Joe Robinson, owner of All-Platinum/Vibration Records (later known as Sugar Hill). Their son Joey was leader of West Street Mob.		
5/26/73	**27**	5	●	Pillow Talk	3	Vibration 521

DEBUT DATE	PEAK POS	WKS CHR	GOLD	ARTIST — Record Title	POP POS	Label & Number
				SYLVIA Country singer Sylvia Kirby. Born on 12/9/56 in Kokomo, Indiana. Moved to Nashville in 1975. Worked as a secretary for producer Tom Collins. Solo debut in 1979.		
9/11/82	5	21	●	1 Nobody	15	RCA 13223
6/23/84	44	5		2 Victims Of Goodbye..		RCA 13755
				SYMS, Sylvia Dubbed the "world's greatest saloon singer" by Frank Sinatra. Born on 12/2/17 in Brooklyn. Discovered by actress Mae West in 1948. Star of several musical comedies. Collapsed onstage during a Manhattan performance on 5/10/92 and died of a heart attack.		
1/29/66	28	10		There's Gotta Be Something Better Than This....................		Columbia 43475
				from the musical *Sweet Charity*		
				SYNCH Pop-rock sextet from Wilkes-Barre, Pennsylvania — Jimmy Harnen, lead singer.		
5/6/89	3	21		Where Are You Now?..	10	WTG 68625
				JIMMY HARNEN w/SYNCH originally made the *Hot 100* (as SYNCH) on 3/1/86 (POS 77) on Columbia 05788		
				SYREETA — see PRESTON, Billy		
				SYSTEM, The New York City-based, techno-funk duo: Mic Murphy (b: Raleigh, North Carolina; vocals, guitar) and David Frank (b: Dayton, Ohio; synthesizer).		
7/11/87	35	6		Don't Disturb This Groove....................................	4	Atlantic 89320
				SZABO, Gabor ⊙ Born on 3/8/36 in Budapest, Hungary; died on 2/26/82. Jazz guitarist/composer.		
12/19/70	40	2		(They Long To Be) Close To You ....[I]		Blue Thumb 7118
				#1 Pop hit for the Carpenters in 1970		

T

DEBUT DATE	PEAK POS	WKS CHR	GOLD	ARTIST — Record Title	POP POS	Label & Number
				TACO Born Taco Ockerse in 1955 to Dutch parents in Jaharta, Indonesia. German-based singer.		
7/2/83	12	14	●	Puttin' On The Ritz	4	RCA 13574
				written in 1929 by Irving Berlin; #1 hit for Harry Richman in 1930		
				TANNER, Gary		
6/3/78	30	6		Over The Rainbow	69	20th Century 2373
				#1 hit for Glenn Miller in 1939		
				TASTE OF HONEY, A Soul-disco quartet, formed in Los Angeles in 1972. Consisted of Janice Marie Johnson (vocals, guitar), Hazel Payne (vocals, bass), Perry Kimble (keyboards) and Donald Johnson (drums). Re-formed in 1980 with Janice Johnson and Hazel Payne. Won the 1978 Best New Artist Grammy Award.		
3/7/81	1²	21	●	1 Sukiyaki...	3	Capitol 4953
4/17/82	29	7		2 I'll Try Something New.......................................	41	Capitol 5099
				TAUPIN, Bernie ⊙ Born on 5/22/50 in Lincolnshire, England. Known as "The Brown Dirt Cowboy." Began highly successful songwriting collaboration with Elton John in 1969. Married Stephanie Haymes (daughter of big band singer Dick Haymes and singer Fran Jeffries) on 8/21/93.		
8/1/87	35	1		Citizen Jane		RCA 5216
				TAVARES Family R&B group from New Bedford, Massachusetts. Consisted of brothers Ralph, Antone "Chubby," Feliciano "Butch," Arthur "Pooch" and Perry Lee "Tiny" Tavares. Worked as Chubby & The Turnpikes from 1964-69. Butch was married to Lola Falana.		
7/31/76	18	10	●	1 Heaven Must Be Missing An Angel (Part 1).................	15	Capitol 4270
5/7/77	31	8		2 Whodunit..	22	Capitol 4398
11/27/82	15	16		3 A Penny For Your Thoughts	33	RCA 13292
				TAYLOR, Faron ⊙		
8/6/66	33	4		I Can't Believe That You're In Love With Me		Columbia 43630

DEBUT DATE	PEAK POS	WKS CHR	G O L D	ARTIST — Record Title	POP POS	Label & Number
	★★23★★			**TAYLOR, James**		
				Born on 3/12/48 in Boston. Singer/songwriter/guitarist. With older brother Alex in the Fabulous Corsairs in 1964. In New York group The Flying Machine in 1967, with friend Danny Kortchmar. Moved to England in 1968, recorded for Peter Asher. Married Carly Simon on 11/3/72, divorced in 1983. In film *Two Lane Blacktop* with Dennis Wilson in 1973. Sister Kate and brothers Alex and Livingston also recorded. Their father, Isaac, was the dean of the University of North Carolina medical school until 1971.		
				1)(What A) Wonderful World 2)Handy Man 3)Shower The People *4)How Sweet It Is (To Be Loved By You) 5)You've Got A Friend*		
9/26/70	**7**	12		1 **Fire And Rain**	3	Warner 7423
2/13/71	**9**	8		2 **Country Road**...	37	Warner 7460
6/26/71	**1**[1]	11	●	3 **You've Got A Friend**..	**1**[1]	Warner 7498
10/9/71	**4**	8		4 **Long Ago And Far Away**	31	Warner 7521
				Joni Mitchell (backing vocal, above 2)		
12/16/72	**3**	10		5 **Don't Let Me Be Lonely Tonight**	14	Warner 7655
2/16/74	**10**	12	●	6 **Mockingbird**..	5	Elektra 45880
				CARLY SIMON & JAMES TAYLOR		
10/5/74	**26**	6		7 **Walking Man**		Warner 8028
7/5/75	**1**[1]	13		8 **How Sweet It Is (To Be Loved By You)**...............	5	Warner 8109
10/11/75	**5**	10		9 **Mexico**	49	Warner 8137
6/26/76	**1**[1]	14		10 **Shower The People**	22	Warner 8222
12/4/76	**20**	9	✓	11 **Woman's Gotta Have It**		Warner 8278
				#60 Pop hit for Bobby Womack in 1972		
6/18/77	**1**[1]	20		12 **Handy Man**	4	Columbia 10557
				flip side "Bartender's Blues" made the Country charts (POS 88)		
10/8/77	**6**	17		13 **Your Smiling Face**	20	Columbia 10602
1/28/78	**1**[5]	14		14 **(What A) Wonderful World**	17	Columbia 10676
				ART GARFUNKEL with JAMES TAYLOR & PAUL SIMON		
8/19/78	**2**[1]	14		15 **Devoted To You**	36	Elektra 45506
				CARLY SIMON and JAMES TAYLOR		
5/26/79	**7**	21		16 **Up On The Roof**...	28	Columbia 11005
3/14/81	**5**	13		17 **Her Town Too**	11	Columbia 60514
				JAMES TAYLOR AND J.D. SOUTHER		
6/13/81	**23**	9		18 Hard Times/	72	
8/1/81	**25**	8		19 Summer's Here		Columbia 02093
10/26/85	**3**	21		20 **Everyday**	61	Columbia 05681
				written by Buddy Holly		
2/1/86	**6**	15		21 **Only One**		Columbia 05785
5/17/86	**8**	14		22 **That's Why I'm Here**		Columbia 05884
2/6/88	**3**	18		23 **Never Die Young**	80	Columbia 07616
7/9/88	**16**	15		24 Baby Boom Baby		Columbia 07948
12/24/88	**37**	6		25 Sweet Potato Pie		Columbia 08493
2/18/89	**23**	11		26 City Lights...		Critique 99255
				LIVINGSTON TAYLOR with James Taylor		
10/5/91	**13**	18		27 Copperline		Columbia LP Cut
2/8/92	**28**	10		28 (I've Got To) Stop Thinkin' 'Bout That...............		Columbia 74214
6/13/92	**19**	13		29 Everybody Loves To Cha Cha Cha		Columbia LP Cut
				#31 Pop hit for Sam Cooke in 1959 as "Everybody Likes To Cha Cha Cha"		
10/10/92	**31**	8		30 Like Everyone She Knows		Columbia LP Cut
				above 4 from the album *New Moon Shine* on Columbia 46038		

TAYLOR, James "J.T." — see BELLE, Regina

TAYLOR, Kate
Born on 8/15/49 in Boston. James Taylor's younger sister.

9/10/77	**13**	11		It's In His Kiss (The Shoop Shoop Song)..........................	49	Columbia 10596
				produced and arranged by James Taylor		

TAYLOR, Livingston
Born on 11/21/50 in Boston. James Taylor's younger brother. Hosted TV's *This Week's Music* in 1984.

11/4/78	**15**	17		1 I Will Be In Love With You	30	Epic 50604
3/3/79	**8**	12		2 I'll Come Running..	82	Epic 50667
7/5/80	**13**	20		3 First Time Love	38	Epic 50894
8/20/88	**14**	16		4 Loving Arms		Critique 99275
				LIVINGSTON TAYLOR with LEAH KUNKEL		
2/18/89	**23**	11		5 City Lights...		Critique 99255
				LIVINGSTON TAYLOR with James Taylor		

DEBUT DATE	PEAK POS	WKS CHR	GOLD	ARTIST — Record Title	POP POS	Label & Number
				TAYLOR, R. Dean		
				Born in Toronto in 1939. First recorded for Parry in 1960. Co-wrote The Supremes' hit "Love Child."		
4/22/72	**28**	4		Taos New Mexico	83	Rare Earth 5041
				TEACH-IN ✪		
5/17/75	**22**	8		Ding-A-Dong		Philips 40800
				TEARS FOR FEARS		
				British duo: Roland Orzabal (b: 8/22/61; vocals, guitar, keyboards) and Curt Smith (b: 6/24/61; vocals, bass). Adopted name from Arthur Janev's book *Prisoners Of Pain*. Assisted by Manny Elias (drums) and Ian Stanley (keyboards). Smith left duo by 1992.		
4/20/85	**2**¹	22		1 **Everybody Wants To Rule The World**	1²	Mercury 880659
9/28/85	**5**	17		2 **Head Over Heels**	3	Mercury 880899
10/7/89	**29**	9		3 Sowing The Seeds Of Love	2¹	Fontana 874710
12/23/89	**37**	7		4 Woman In Chains	36	Fontana 876248
				Oletta Adams (female vocal)		
3/17/90	**24**	9		5 Advice For The Young At Heart	89	Fontana 876894
				TEMPO, Nino, & April Stevens		
				Nino (born Antonio Lo Tempio on 1/6/35) and sister April (born Carol Lo Tempio on 4/29/36) from Niagara Falls, New York. Prior to teaming up, Nino was a session saxophonist and April had recorded solo.		
12/28/63	**4**	8		1 Whispering	11	Atco 6281
				#1 hit for Paul Whiteman & His Orchestra in 1920		
2/29/64	**13**	2		2 Stardust	32	Atco 6286
				#1 hit for Isham Jones & His Orchestra in 1931		
9/22/73	**18**	9		3 Sister James .... [I]	53	A&M 1461
				NINO TEMPO AND 5th AVE. SAX		
4/12/75	**38**	5		4 You Turn Me On		A&M 1674
				NINO & APRIL		
				TEMPTATIONS, The		
				Detroit soul group formed in 1960. Consisted of Eddie Kendricks (d: 10/5/92 of lung cancer at age 52), Paul Williams (d: 8/17/73), Melvin Franklin, Otis Williams and Elbridge Bryant, who was replaced by David Ruffin in 1964. Originally called the Primes and Elgins, first recorded for Miracle in 1961. Ruffin (d: 6/1/91 of drug overdose at age 50; cousin of Billy Stewart) replaced by Dennis Edwards (ex-Contours) in 1968. Kendricks and Paul Williams left in 1971, replaced by Ricky Owens (ex-Vibrations) and Richard Street. Owens was replaced by Damon Harris. Harris left in 1975, replaced by Glenn Leonard. Edwards left group, 1977-79, replaced by Louis Price. Ali Ollie Woodson replaced Edwards from 1984-87. 1988 lineup: Williams, Franklin, Street, Edwards and Ron Tyson. Recognized as America's all-time favorite soul group. Inducted into the Rock and Roll Hall of Fame in 1989. Also see Rod Stewart.		
3/13/71	**33**	5		1 Just My Imagination (Running Away With Me)	1²	Gordy 7105
3/31/84	**17**	11		2 Sail Away	54	Gordy 1720
5/17/86	**28**	5		3 A Fine Mess		Motown 1837
				movie title song		
11/21/87	**36**	9		4 I Wonder Who She's Seeing Now		Motown 1908
12/14/91	**27**	9		5 My Girl .... [R]		Epic Soundtrax 74108
				movie title song; original #1 Pop and R&B hit from 1965 on Gordy 7038		
				10cc		
				English art-rock group which evolved from Hotlegs. Consisted of Eric Stewart (guitar), Graham Gouldman (bass), Lol Creme (guitar, keyboards) and Kevin Godley (drums). Stewart and Gouldman were members of The Mindbenders. Godley and Creme left in 1976, replaced by drummer Paul Burgess. Added members Rick Fenn, Stuart Tosh and Duncan MacKay in 1978. Gouldman later in duo Wax.		
5/31/75	**10**	14		1 I'm Not In Love	2³	Mercury 73678
1/22/77	**12**	11	●	2 The Things We Do For Love	5	Mercury 73875
6/4/77	**23**	8		3 People In Love	40	Mercury 73917
				10,000 MANIACS		
				Jamestown, New York group formed in 1981: Natalie Merchant (vocals), Robert Buck (guitar), Dennis Drew (keyboards), Steven Gustafson (bass), Jerome Augustyniak (drums) and John Lombardo (guitar). Lombardo left in July 1986. Merchant left the band in August of 1993.		
6/10/89	**7**	17		1 Trouble Me	44	Elektra 69298
11/28/92	**34**	9		2 These Are Days	66	Elektra 64700
				TERRELL, Tammi — see GAYE, Marvin		
				TERRY, Tony		
				Born 3/12/64 in Pinehurst, North Carolina and raised in Washington, D.C. Soul-funk singer. Former backing vocalist for Sweet Sensation and Boogie Boys.		
11/30/91	**45**	3		With You	14	Epic 73713

TESH, John ○
New Age multi-instrumentalist. Born on 7/9/52 in Long Island, New York. Co-host of TV's *Entertainment Tonight* since 1986. Appeared in the film *Shocker*. Married actress Connie Sellecca on 4/4/92.

| 2/24/90 | **46** | 3 | | You Break It .... | | Cypress LP Cut |

Diana DeWitt (vocal); from the album *Garden City* on Cypress 0133

TEXTOR, Keith, Singers ○
Keith was born on 7/21/21 in Coon Rapids, Iowa. Singer/songwriter. Composed many commercials.

| 9/19/70 | **26** | 6 | | Measure The Valleys.. | 112 | A&R 500 |

THIRTY EIGHT SPECIAL
Florida Southern-rock group led by Donnie Van Zant (younger brother of Lynyrd Skynyrd's Ronnie Van Zant).

| 2/18/89 | **1**² | 31 | | **Second Chance**... | 6 | A&M 1273 |

★★41★★   THOMAS, B.J.
Born Billy Joe Thomas on 8/7/42 in Hugo, Oklahoma; raised in Rosenberg, Texas. Sang in church choir as a teenager. Joined band, the Triumphs, while in high school. B.J. has featured gospel music since 1976.

1)Raindrops Keep Fallin' On My Head 2)I Just Can't Help Believing 3)(Hey Won't You Play) Another Somebody Done Somebody Wrong Song 4)Rock And Roll Lullaby 5)Don't Worry Baby

| 5/3/69 | **37** | 2 | | 1 It's Only Love .... | 45 | Scepter 12244 |
| 11/1/69 | **1**⁷ | 18 | ● | 2 Raindrops Keep Fallin' On My Head .... | **1**⁴ | Scepter 12265 |

from the film *Butch Cassidy And The Sundance Kid*

4/11/70	**3**	8		3 Everybody's Out Of Town...............................	26	Scepter 12277
6/27/70	**1**¹	14		4 I Just Can't Help Believing...........................	9	Scepter 12283
12/5/70	**2**¹	11		5 Most Of All	38	Scepter 12299
2/27/71	**4**	12		6 No Love At All...	16	Scepter 12307
6/26/71	**8**	11		7 Mighty Clouds Of Joy	34	Scepter 12320
11/6/71	**13**	7		8 Long Ago Tomorrow	61	Scepter 12335
2/12/72	**1**¹	13		9 Rock And Roll Lullaby.................................	15	Scepter 12344

featuring Duane Eddy (guitar) and The Blossoms (backing vocals)

| 7/29/72 | **38** | 4 | | 10 That's What Friends Are For .... | 74 | Scepter 12354 |

Paul Williams (backing vocal)

| 9/30/72 | **31** | 5 | | 11 Happier Than The Morning Sun...................... | 100 | Scepter 12364 |

written by Stevie Wonder (Stevie also plays harmonica)

7/7/73	**41**	4		12 Songs		Paramount 0218
2/8/75	**1**¹	15	●	13 (Hey Won't You Play) Another Somebody Done Somebody Wrong Song	**1**¹	ABC 12054
9/20/75	**5**	12		14 Help Me Make It (To My Rockin' Chair)............	64	ABC 12121
6/25/77	**2**²	20		15 Don't Worry Baby	17	MCA 40735
11/5/77	**8**	12		16 Still The Lovin' Is Fun	77	MCA 40812
1/21/78	**2**²	14		17 Everybody Loves A Rain Song......................	43	MCA 40854
12/15/78	**38**	6		18 God Bless The Children...........................[X]		MCA/Songbird 41134
4/12/80	**30**	10		19 Walkin' On A Cloud		MCA/Songbird 41207

above 2 written and produced by Chris Christian

| 4/11/81 | **34** | 7 | | 20 Some Love Songs Never Die .... | | MCA 51087 |
| 6/19/82 | **27** | 9 | | 21 But Love Me .... | | MCA 52053 |

written by Kenny Nolan

3/5/83	**13**	17		22 Whatever Happened To Old Fashioned Love	93	Cleve. Int. 03492
2/25/84	**44**	3		23 Two Car Garage......................................		Cleve. Int. 04237
12/24/88	**7**	15		24 As Long As We Got Each Other		Reprise 27878

STEVE DORFF & FRIENDS
B.J. Thomas and Dusty Springfield (vocals; Dorff is the producer); theme from the TV show *Growing Pains*

| 9/30/89 | **39** | 7 | | 25 Don't Leave Love (Out There All Alone)................ | | Reprise 22837 |

THOMAS, Ian
Canadian singer/songwriter. Brother of SCTV comedian Dave Thomas, aka Doug McKenzie.

| 11/24/73 | **28** | 9 | | Painted Ladies .... | 34 | Janus 224 |

THOMAS, Mickey — see SUMMER, Donna

THOMPSON, Chris
Lead singer, guitarist of Manfred Mann, 1976-79 (continues as guest vocalist with group).

| 6/30/79 | **7** | 24 | | 1 If You Remember Me.................................... | 17 | Planet 45909 |

CHRIS THOMPSON & NIGHT
first released on Planet 45904 in 1979 as by Chris Thompson; from the film *The Champ*

DEBUT DATE	PEAK POS	WKS CHR	GOLD	ARTIST — Record Title	POP POS	Label & Number
				THOMPSON, Chris — Cont'd		
11/19/83	19	13		2 All The Right Moves	85	Casablanca 814603
				JENNIFER WARNES/CHRIS THOMPSON		
				movie title song		
				THOMPSON, Sue		
				Born Eva Sue McKee on 7/19/26 in Nevada, Missouri and raised in San Jose, California. Became a popular country singer in the '70s.		
9/4/61	1¹	14		**1 Sad Movies (Make Me Cry)**..	5	Hickory 1153
3/31/62	8	7		**2 Two Of A Kind**	42	Hickory 1166
6/30/62	9	9		**3 Have A Good Time**	31	Hickory 1174
9/27/75	40	7		4 Big Mable Murphy		Hickory 354
				THOMPSON TWINS		
				British trio: Tom Bailey (b: 1/18/56, England; lead singer, synthesizer), Alannah Currie (b: 9/28/57, New Zealand; xylophone, percussion) and Joe Leeway (b: 11/15/57, London; conga, synthesizer). Leeway left in 1986.		
2/25/84	8	20		**1 Hold Me Now**..	3	Arista 9164
6/16/84	35	9		2 Doctor! Doctor!	11	Arista 9209
10/5/85	14	15		3 Lay Your Hands On Me	6	Arista 9396
2/1/86	13	14		**4 King For A Day**	8	Arista 9450
				THOMSON, Ali		
				Singer/songwriter from Glasgow, Scotland. Younger brother of Supertramp's Dougie Thomson.		
7/5/80	4	16		**1 Take A Little Rhythm**	15	A&M 2243
10/25/80	39	4		2 Live Every Minute...	42	A&M 2260
				THREE DEGREES, The		
				Philadelphia R&B trio discovered by Richard Barrett. Originally consisted of Fayette Pinkney, Linda Turner and Shirley Porter. Turner and Porter replaced by Sheila Ferguson and Valerie Holiday in 1966.		
3/9/74	1²	16	●	**1 TSOP (The Sound Of Philadelphia)** ....[I]	1²	Phil. Int. 3540
				MFSB featuring The Three Degrees		
				theme from the TV show *Soul Train*		
10/12/74	1¹	14	●	**2 When Will I See You Again**	2¹	Phil. Int. 3550
6/28/75	24	7		3 Take Good Care Of Yourself		Phil. Int. 3568
3/24/79	50	1		4 Woman In Love		Ariola 7742
★★196★★				**THREE DOG NIGHT**		
				Los Angeles pop-rock group formed in 1968 featuring lead singers Danny Hutton (b: 9/10/42), Cory Wells (b: 2/5/42) and Chuck Negron (b: 6/8/42). Disbanded in the mid-1970s. Re-formed in the mid-1980s.		
				1)Black & White 2)An Old Fashioned Love Song 3)Shambala		
9/19/70	11	8		1 Out In The Country	15	Dunhill 4250
11/20/71	1¹	11	●	**2 An Old Fashioned Love Song**....................................	4	Dunhill 4294
1/22/72	18	6		3 Never Been To Spain	5	Dunhill 4299
4/15/72	27	5		4 The Family Of Man	12	Dunhill 4306
8/19/72	1¹	13	●	**5 Black & White**	1¹	Dunhill 4317
12/2/72	6	10		**6 Pieces Of April**	19	Dunhill 4331
5/26/73	3	11	●	**7 Shambala**	3	Dunhill 4352
7/19/75	11	11		8 Til The World Ends	32	ABC 12114
7/10/76	44	3		9 Everybody Is A Masterpiece.......................................		ABC 12192
				THUNDERKLOUD, Billy, & The Chieftones		
				Group of Indian musicians from Northwest British Columbia.		
5/24/75	32	5		What Time Of Day	92	20th Century 2181
				TIERRA		
				East Los Angeles group formed in 1972. Band led by the Salas brothers: Steve (trombone, timbales) and Rudy (guitar); both formerly with El Chicano.		
1/24/81	30	6		Together	18	Boardwalk 5702
				TIFFANY		
				Tiffany Darwisch, born on 10/2/71. California pop singer, originally from Oklahoma.		
10/24/87	38	8		1 I Think We're Alone Now	1²	MCA 53167
12/12/87	1¹	18		**2 Could've Been**..	1²	MCA 53231
7/9/88	43	4		3 Feelings Of Forever	50	MCA 53325
12/10/88	10	19		**4 All This Time**	6	MCA 53371
5/20/89	37	6		5 Hold An Old Friend's Hand		MCA 53612
				TILLIS, Mel ○		
				Born Lonnie Melvin Tillis on 8/8/32 in Tampa, Florida; raised in Pahokee, Florida. Country singer.		
6/3/78	44	6		I Believe In You		MCA 40900

DEBUT DATE	PEAK POS	WKS CHR	GOLD	ARTIST — Record Title	POP POS	Label & Number
★★**197**★★				**TILLOTSON, Johnny**		
				Born on 4/20/39 in Jacksonville, Florida; raised in Palatka, Florida. On local radio *Young Folks Revue* from age nine. DJ on WWPF. Appeared on the *Toby Dowdy* TV show in Jacksonville, then own show. Signed by Cadence Records in 1958. In the film *Just For Fun*.		
				1)You Can Never Stop Me Loving You 2)She Understands Me 3)Heartaches By The Number		
8/18/62	**5**	8		1 **Send Me The Pillow You Dream On**.............................	17	Cadence 1424
11/3/62	**8**	8		2 **I Can't Help It (If I'm Still In Love With You)**.............	24	Cadence 1432
3/30/63	**11**	6		3 Out Of My Mind..	24	Cadence 1434
8/24/63	**4**	8		4 **You Can Never Stop Me Loving You**.......................	18	Cadence 1437
10/26/63	**16**	5		5 Funny How Time Slips Away................................	50	Cadence 1441
				written by Willie Nelson		
12/14/63	**6**	8		6 **Talk Back Trembling Lips**...............................	7	MGM 13181
7/25/64	**5**	7		7 **Worry**..	45	MGM 13255
11/14/64	**4**	10		8 **She Understands Me**.....................................	31	MGM 13284
8/28/65	**4**	10		9 **Heartaches By The Number**..............................	35	MGM 13376
				'TIL TUESDAY		
				Boston pop quartet: Aimee Mann (lead singer, bass), Michael Hausmann (drums), Robert Holmes (guitar) and Joey Pesce (keyboards; replaced by Michael Montes in 1988).		
12/3/88	**32**	10		(Believed You Were) Lucky................................	95	Epic 08059
				TIMMY -T-		
				Born Timmy Torres on 9/23/67 in Fresno, California.		
2/16/91	**4**	20	▲	One More Try...	1[1]	Quality 15114
				TIN TIN		
				Australian duo: Steve Kipner (keyboards) and Steve Groves (guitar). Disbanded in 1973. Kipner later co-wrote Chicago's "Hard Habit To Break" and Olivia Newton-John's "Physical" and "Twist Of Fate."		
5/1/71	**10**	6		1 **Toast And Marmalade For Tea**............................	20	Atco 6794
9/25/71	**36**	3		2 Is That The Way...	59	Atco 6821
				above 2 produced by Maurice Gibb of the Bee Gees		
				TJADER, Cal		
				Born on 7/16/25 in St. Louis; died on 5/5/82. Latin jazz vibraphonist.		
6/5/65	**21**	6		Soul Sauce (Guacha Guaro) ....[I]	88	Verve 10345
				written by Dizzy Gillespie		
				TOAD THE WET SPROCKET		
				Pop quartet from Santa Barbara, California: Glen Phillips (vocals), Todd Nichols (guitar), Dean Dinning (bass) and Randy Guss (drums). Name taken from a Monty Python skit.		
8/8/92	**14**	23		1 All I Want..	15	Columbia 74355
1/23/93	**31**	12		2 Walk On The Ocean.......................................	18	Columbia 74706
				TOBY BEAU		
				Texas pop quintet: Balde Silva (vocals), Danny McKenna, Rob Young, Steve Zipper and Ron Rose.		
6/17/78	**1**[1]	17		1 **My Angel Baby**..	13	RCA 11250
8/11/79	**7**	13		2 **Then You Can Tell Me Goodbye**..........................	57	RCA 11670
				TODAY'S PEOPLE		
8/18/73	**37**	4		He	90	20th Century 2032
				TOKENS, The		
				Vocal group formed in Brooklyn: Hank Medress and Jay Siegel, with brothers Phil and Mitch Margo. Medress left to produce Tony Orlando & Dawn while the others recorded as Cross Country in 1973.		
8/8/64	**20**	1		1 He's In Town...	43	B.T. Puppy 502
1/21/67	**23**	5		2 Life Is Groovy..	110	B.T. Puppy 524
				UNITED STATES DOUBLE QUARTET: THE TOKENS THE KIRBY STONE FOUR		
1/3/70	**34**	3		3 She Lets Her Hair Down (Early In The Morning).................	61	Buddah 151
				TOMLINSON, Michael ☉		
				Seattle-based singer/songwriter born in Amarillo, Texas.		
10/31/87	**12**	15		1 Dawning On A New Day		Cypress 661122
3/26/88	**24**	7		2 Highway Rain		Cypress 661128
				TOOKES, Darryl ☉		
				Born in the Bronx, New York and raised in Tallahassee, Florida. Graduated magna cum laude in physics from Florida A&M. Prolific backing and jingle singer. Sang backup for Roberta Flack, Leonard Bernstein and Diana Ross among others.		
9/23/89	**43**	3		Lifeguard		SBK 07301

DEBUT DATE	PEAK POS	WKS CHR	G O L D	ARTIST — Record Title	POP POS	Label & Number

TORME, Mel
Born Melvin Howard on 9/13/25 in Chicago. Jazz singer/songwriter/pianist/drummer/actor. Wrote Nat King Cole's "The Christmas Song." Frequently appeared as himself on TV's *Night Court*.

| 7/29/67 | 6 | 11 | | Lover's Roulette .... | | Columbia 44180 |

★★160★★ TOTO
Pop-rock group formed in Los Angeles in 1978. Consisted of Bobby Kimball (b: Robert Toteaux; vocals), Steve Lukather (guitar), David Paich and Steve Porcaro (keyboards), David Hungate (bass) and Jeff Porcaro (drums; d: 8/5/92 [age 38] from hardening of arteries due to prolonged cocaine use). Prominent session musicians, most notably behind Boz Scaggs in the late '70s. Hungate was replaced by Mike Porcaro in 1983. (The Porcaros are brothers.) Kimball replaced by Fergie Frederiksen in 1984; Frederiksen replaced by Joseph Williams (conductor John's son) in 1986. Steve Porcaro left in 1988. South African native Jean-Michel Byron replaced Frederiksen in 1990. Paich and his father, Marty, won an Emmy for writing the theme to the TV series *Ironside*.

1)I Won't Hold You Back 2)I'll Be Over You 3)Africa

6/9/79	49	2		1 Georgy Porgy	48	Columbia 10944
				Cheryl Lynn (backing vocal)		
1/26/80	19	8		2 99	26	Columbia 11173
5/22/82	17	18	●	3 Rosanna	2⁵	Columbia 02811
11/6/82	5	22	●	4 Africa	1¹	Columbia 03335
3/19/83	1³	18		5 I Won't Hold You Back	10	Columbia 03597
7/23/83	27	7		6 Waiting For Your Love	73	Columbia 03981
9/6/86	1²	22		7 I'll Be Over You	11	Columbia 06280
1/17/87	7	14		8 Without Your Love	38	Columbia 06570
3/26/88	9	16		9 Pamela	22	Columbia 07715
9/24/88	47	5		10 Anna		Columbia 08010

TOWER OF POWER
Interracial Oakland-based, R&B-funk band formed by sax player Emilio "Mimi" Castillo in the late '60s. Lenny Williams sang lead from 1972-75. Originally known as the Motowns. Also see Kenny G.

| 7/7/73 | 36 | 4 | | 1 So Very Hard To Go .... | 17 | Warner 7687 |
| 9/15/73 | 46 | 3 | | 2 This Time It's Real .... | 65 | Warner 7733 |

TRAVELING WILBURYS
Supergroup masquerading as a band of brothers. Spearheaded by Nelson (George Harrison), with Lucky (Bob Dylan), Otis (Jeff Lynne of ELO), Lefty (Roy Orbison) and Charlie T. Junior (Tom Petty) Wilbury. Orbison died on 12/6/88 (age 52).

| 11/5/88 | 30 | 10 | | 1 Handle With Care .... | 45 | Wilbury 27732 |
| 2/25/89 | 28 | 10 | | 2 End Of The Line .... | 63 | Wilbury 27637 |

TRAVERS, Mary
Born on 11/7/37 in Louisville. Member of the folk trio Peter, Paul & Mary. Chorus singer in the short-lived Broadway show *The Next President*, 1957.

5/8/71	3	13		1 Follow Me	56	Warner 7481
				written by John Denver		
9/11/71	29	5		2 The Song Is Love		Warner 7517
10/13/73	50	1		3 Oh, What A Feeling		Warner 7731
5/4/74	42	5		4 Circles		Warner 7790
				written by Harry Chapin		
3/4/78	42	5		5 The Air That I Breathe		Chrysalis 2202
				#6 Pop hit for The Hollies in 1974		

TRAVOLTA, John
Born on 2/18/54 in Englewood, New Jersey. Actor/singer. Played Vinnie Barbarino on the TV series *Welcome Back Kotter*. Starred in the films *Saturday Night Fever*, *Grease*, *Urban Cowboy*, *Look Who's Talking* and others. Married actress Kelly Preston on 9/5/91.

6/19/76	16	11		1 Let Her In	10	Midland I. 10623
10/30/76	26	8		2 Whenever I'm Away From You	38	Midland I. 10780
3/19/77	35	5		3 All Strung Out On You	34	Midland I. 10907
4/22/78	23	13	▲	4 You're The One That I Want	1¹	RSO 891
				JOHN TRAVOLTA AND OLIVIA NEWTON-JOHN		
8/12/78	21	11	●	5 Summer Nights	5	RSO 906
				JOHN TRAVOLTA, OLIVIA NEWTON-JOHN & CAST		
				above 2 from the film *Grease*		
11/26/83	3	17		6 Take A Chance		MCA 52284
				OLIVIA NEWTON-JOHN AND JOHN TRAVOLTA		
				from the film *Two Of A Kind*; flip side "Twist Of Fate" made the *Hot 100* (POS 5)		

DEBUT DATE	PEAK POS	WKS CHR	GOLD	ARTIST — Record Title	POP POS	Label & Number
				TRIPLETS, The		
				Triplet sisters Diana, Sylvia and Vicky Villegas. Born on 4/18/65, seven minutes apart. Raised in Mexico by their American mother and Mexican father. Gained recognition after winning an *MTV Basement Tapes* competition in 1986.		
5/4/91	25	9		1 You Don't Have To Go Home Tonight	14	Mercury 878864
8/3/91	16	15		2 Sunrise		Mercury 868414
12/21/91	35	8		3 Light A Candle		Mercury 866098
				TROCCOLI, Kathy		
				New York City native. Grammy-nominated Contemporary Christian artist. Backing singer with Taylor Dayne.		
2/22/92	6	24		**1 Everything Changes**	14	Reunion 19118
6/20/92	7	18		**2 You've Got A Way**		Reunion 19126
				TROYER, Eric		
				Pop session vocalist from New York City.		
8/23/80	43	4		Mirage	92	Chrysalis 2445
				TRUE, Andrea, Connection		
				Disco act led by white Nashville-born vocalist Andrea True. Andrea moved to New York in 1968 and wrote commercials for radio and TV. Her break came while singing at the Riverboat in the Empire State Building in 1974.		
5/1/76	23	10	●	More, More, More Pt. 1	4	Buddah 515
				TUCKER, Louise		
				English classical-styled vocalist. Male vocal on only hit: Charlie Skarbek.		
6/4/83	10	19		**Midnight Blue**	46	Arista 9022
				based on Beethoven's *Pathetique Piano Sonata No. 8*; Charlie Skarbek (male vocal)		
				TUCKER, Tanya		
				Born on 10/10/58 in Seminole, Texas and raised in Wilcox, Arizona. Prominent country singer. Bit part in the film *Jeremiah Johnson* in 1972.		
5/3/75	7	11		**1 Lizzie And The Rainman**	37	MCA 40402
9/25/76	25	9		2 Here's Some Love	82	MCA 40598
★★187★★				**TURNER, Tina**		
				Born Anna Mae Bullock on 11/26/38 in Brownsville, Tennessee. R&B-rock vocalist/actress. Half of Ike & Tina Turner duo, when married to Ike from 1958-76. In films *Tommy* (1975; cast as the Acid Queen) and *Mad Max-Beyond Thunderdome* (1985). With Ike, inducted into the Rock And Roll Hall of Fame in 1991.		
				1)*I Don't Wanna Fight* 2)*We Don't Need Another Hero (Thunderdome)* 3)*What's Love Got To Do With It*		
6/23/84	8	20	●	**1 What's Love Got To Do With It**	1[3]	Capitol 5354
2/2/85	30	13		2 Private Dancer	7	Capitol 5433
7/13/85	3	19		**3 We Don't Need Another Hero (Thunderdome)**	2[1]	Capitol 5491
				from the film *Mad Max-Beyond Thunderdome*		
10/4/86	23	9		4 Typical Male	2[3]	Capitol 5615
11/29/86	12	14		5 Two People	30	Capitol 5644
10/21/89	43	4		6 The Best	15	Capitol 44442
				Edgar Winter (sax solo)		
2/10/90	8	18		**7 Look Me In The Heart**		Capitol 44510
5/15/93	1[7]	20↑		**8 I Don't Wanna Fight**	9	Virgin 12652
				from Tina's autobiographical film *What's Love Got To Do With It*		
				TUXEDO JUNCTION		
				Female disco studio group assembled by producers W. Michael Lewis and Lauren Rinder.		
4/8/78	18	15		1 Chattanooga Choo Choo..	32	Butterfly 1205
				#1 hit for Glenn Miller in 1941		
9/2/78	42	6		2 Moonlight Serenade	103	Butterfly 1210
				#3 hit for Glenn Miller in 1939		
				TWITTY, Conway		
				Superstar country singer who charted over 30 #1 solo country hits. Born Harold Lloyd Jenkins on 9/1/33 in Friars Point, Mississippi and raised in Helena, Arkansas. Died of an abdominal aneurysm on 6/5/93.		
9/29/73	37	3		You've Never Been This Far Before	22	MCA 40094
				TYLER, Bonnie		
				Born Gaynor Hopkins on 6/8/53 in Swansea, Wales. Worked local clubs until the mid-1970s. Distinctive raspy vocals caused by operation to remove throat nodules in 1976.		
4/22/78	10	16	●	**1 It's A Heartache**	3	RCA 11249
9/3/83	7	18	●	**2 Total Eclipse Of The Heart**.................................	1[4]	Columbia 03906

DEBUT DATE	PEAK POS	WKS CHR	GOLD	ARTIST — Record Title	POP POS	Label & Number
				TYMES, The		
				Soul group formed in Philadelphia in 1956. Consisted of George Williams (lead), George Hilliard, Donald Banks, Albert Berry and Norman Burnett. First called the Latineers. Berry and Hilliard were replaced by female singers Terri Gonzalez and Melanie Moore in the early '70s.		
9/14/63	**2**⁴	7		**1** Wonderful! Wonderful!	7	Parkway 884
12/28/63	**8**	7		**2** Somewhere..	19	Parkway 891
9/14/74	**31**	8		**3** You Little Trustmaker	12	RCA 10022
				TZUKE, Judie ☺		
				Pronounced: ZOOK. British singer/songwriter.		
1/5/80	**47**	6		Stay With Me Till Dawn......................................	101	Rocket 41133

U

DEBUT DATE	PEAK POS	WKS CHR	GOLD	ARTIST — Record Title	POP POS	Label & Number
				UB40		
				British interracial reggae octet formed in 1978 — Ali Campbell (b: 2/15/59, Birmingham, England), lead singer. Took name from a British unemployment benefit form. Members include Ali's brother Robin Campbell, Earl Falconer, Michael Virtue, Astro, Norman Hassan, Brian Travers and James Brown.		
10/1/88	**13**	12	●	**1** Red Red Wine ....[R]	1¹	A&M 1244
				originally made the *Hot 100* on 1/28/84 (POS 34) on A&M 2600		
12/1/90	**21**	11	●	**2** The Way You Do The Things You Do	6	Virgin 98978
				#11 Pop hit for The Temptations in 1964		
6/22/91	**44**	6		**3** Here I Am (Come And Take Me)......................	7	Virgin 99141
				#10 Pop hit for Al Green in 1973		
7/10/93	**11**	12↑ ▲		**4** Can't Help Falling In Love..............................	1⁷	Virgin 12653
				from the film *Sliver*; #2 Pop and #1 Adult hit for Elvis Presley in 1962		
				UGGAMS, Leslie		
				Born on 5/25/43 in New York City. Actress/singer. Played Kizzy in the TV mini-series *Roots*. Regular on TV's *Sing Along With Mitch*.		
1/27/68	**36**	4		A House Built On Sand		Atlantic 2469
				ULLMAN, Tracey		
				Born on 12/30/59 in Buckinghamshire, England. Actress/singer/comedienne. Own variety-style TV show on Fox network, 1987-90. In films *I Love You To Death*, *Plenty* and *Give My Regards To Broad Street*.		
3/17/84	**11**	15		They Don't Know..	8	MCA 52347
				UNDISPUTED TRUTH, The		
				Soul group consisting of Joe Harris, Billie Calvin and Brenda Evans.		
9/11/71	**34**	2		Smiling Faces Sometimes	3	Gordy 7108
				UNION GAP, The — see PUCKETT, Gary		
				UNITED STATES DOUBLE QUARTET — see TOKENS		
				UNIT FOUR plus TWO		
				English pop-rock sextet — Tommy Moeller, lead singer.		
6/5/65	**9**	5		Concrete And Clay	28	London 9751
				USA for AFRICA		
				USA: United Support of Artists — a collection of 46 major artists formed to help the suffering people of Africa and the U.S.		
3/23/85	**1**²	15	▲⁴	We Are The World..	1⁴	Columbia 04839
				soloists (in order): Lionel Richie, Stevie Wonder, Paul Simon, Kenny Rogers, James Ingram, Tina Turner, Billy Joel, Michael Jackson, Diana Ross, Dionne Warwick, Willie Nelson, Al Jarreau, Bruce Springsteen, Kenny Loggins, Steve Perry, Daryl Hall, Huey Lewis, Cyndi Lauper, Kim Carnes, Bob Dylan, and Ray Charles; written by Michael Jackson and Lionel Richie		
				U2		
				Rock band formed in Dublin, Ireland in 1976. Consists of Paul "Bono" Hewson (vocals), Dave "The Edge" Evans (guitar), Adam Clayton (bass) and Larry Mullen, Jr. (drums). Emerged in 1987 as a leading rock act. Released concert tour documentary film *Rattle And Hum* in 1988.		
5/9/87	**23**	9		**1** With Or Without You.......................................	1³	Island 99469
7/25/87	**16**	14		**2** I Still Haven't Found What I'm Looking For........	1²	Island 99430
2/4/89	**38**	5		**3** Angel Of Harlem	14	Island 99254
				a tribute to Billie Holiday		
4/4/92	**24**	13		**4** One..	10	Island 866533
				U2's royalties to benefit AIDS research		

DEBUT DATE	PEAK POS	WKS CHR	GOLD	ARTIST — Record Title	POP POS	Label & Number

V

★★**70**★★ **VALE, Jerry**
Born Genero Vitaliano on 7/8/32 in the Bronx. Pop ballad singer.
1)Have You Looked Into Your Heart 2)Dommage, Dommage (Too Bad, Too Bad)
3)In The Back Of My Heart 4)Don't Tell My Heart To Stop Loving You
5)Time Alone Will Tell (Non Pensare A Me)

DEBUT DATE	PEAK POS	WKS CHR	GOLD	ARTIST — Record Title	POP POS	Label & Number
12/19/64	1¹	12		1 **Have You Looked Into Your Heart**	24	Columbia 43181
3/13/65	13	4		2 For Mama	54	Columbia 43232
6/5/65	30	4		3 Tears Keep On Falling	96	Columbia 43252
7/31/65	19	10		4 Where Were You When I Needed You.............	99	Columbia 43337
10/9/65	16	8		5 Deep In Your Heart	118	Columbia 43413
				from the musical *Drat! The Cat!*		
1/8/66	28	6	✓	6 Ashamed		Columbia 43473
4/23/66	14	12	✓	7 Less Than Tomorrow.............................		Columbia 43605
7/16/66	14	8		8 It'll Take A Little Time	120	Columbia 43696
9/10/66	5	12		9 **Dommage, Dommage (Too Bad, Too Bad)**	93	Columbia 43774
1/7/67	32	3		10 I've Lost My Heart Again	132	Columbia 43895
3/4/67	36	3		11 Signs/		
3/18/67	30	5		12 Have You Seen The One I Love Go By		Columbia 44027
4/15/67	6	11		13 **Time Alone Will Tell (Non Pensare A Me)**	126	Columbia 44087
7/15/67	5	12	✓	14 **In The Back Of My Heart**		Columbia 44185
9/23/67	26	4	✓	15 Blame It On Me		Columbia 44274
2/10/68	6	8		16 **Don't Tell My Heart To Stop Loving You**.......		Columbia 44432
5/11/68	25	5		17 My Love, Forgive Me (Amore, Scusami)		Columbia 44512
				#16 Pop hit for Robert Goulet in 1965		
7/6/68	30	6		18 With Pen In Hand		Columbia 44572
				#35 Pop hit for Vikki Carr in 1969		
9/28/68	39	2	✓	19 Till Now/		
10/19/68	37	2		20 That Girl Would Be So Pretty		Columbia 44615
3/1/69	28	4		21 Life		Columbia 44753
7/19/69	34	4	✓	22 He Who Loves		Columbia 44914
9/20/69	26	5	✓	23 This Is My Life (La Vita)		Columbia 44969
2/14/70	27	4	✓	24 Stay Awhile		Columbia 45043
4/25/70	40	1	✓	25 Hello And Goodbye		Columbia 45118
9/19/70	27	5		26 I Climbed The Mountain		Columbia 45216
5/8/71	36	2	✓	27 My Little Girl (Angel All A-glow)...............		Columbia 45361

VALENTI, John
Blue-eyed soul singer from Chicago.

DEBUT DATE	PEAK POS	WKS CHR	GOLD	ARTIST — Record Title	POP POS	Label & Number
10/23/76	49	3		Anything You Want...........................	37	Ariola Am. 7625

VALERY, Dana
Session singer. Sang backup for Leslie West in the mid-1970s.

DEBUT DATE	PEAK POS	WKS CHR	GOLD	ARTIST — Record Title	POP POS	Label & Number
12/15/79	23	13		I Don't Want To Be Lonely...................	87	Scotti Br. 509

VALJEAN
Born Valjean Johns on 11/19/34 in Shattuck, Oklahoma. Pianist.

DEBUT DATE	PEAK POS	WKS CHR	GOLD	ARTIST — Record Title	POP POS	Label & Number
6/2/62	10	7		**Theme From Ben Casey**...................... [I]	28	Carlton 573
				from the TV series *Ben Casey*		

★★**161**★★ **VALLI, Frankie**
Born Francis Castellucio on 5/3/37 in Newark, New Jersey. Recorded his first solo single in 1953 as Frank Valley on the Corona label. Formed own group, the Variatones, in 1955 and changed their name to the Four Lovers in 1956, which evolved into The 4 Seasons by 1961. Began solo work in 1965. Suffered from a disease which caused hearing loss in the late 1970s, corrected by surgery.
1)Our Day Will Come 2)My Eyes Adored You 3)Where Did We Go Wrong

DEBUT DATE	PEAK POS	WKS CHR	GOLD	ARTIST — Record Title	POP POS	Label & Number
1/27/68	17	4		1 To Give (The Reason I Live)	29	Philips 40510
7/5/69	32	4		2 The Girl I'll Never Know (Angels Never Fly This Low)	52	Philips 40622
11/9/74	2¹	15	●	3 **My Eyes Adored You**	1¹	Private S. 45003
5/17/75	9	12		4 **Swearin' To God**	6	Private S. 45021
11/1/75	2²	11		5 **Our Day Will Come**	11	Private S. 45043
4/3/76	9	10		6 **Fallen Angel**	36	Private S. 45074

DEBUT DATE	PEAK POS	WKS CHR	G O L D	ARTIST — Record Title	POP POS	Label & Number
				VALLI, Frankie — Cont'd		
7/31/76	**27**	9		7 We're All Alone..	78	Private S. 45098
				written by Boz Scaggs		
4/23/77	**26**	5		8 Easily..	108	Private S. 45140
6/24/78	**13**	18	▲	9 Grease...	1²	RSO 897
				movie title song		
11/11/78	**48**	3		10 Save Me, Save Me...		Warner 8670
				written by Barry Gibb		
2/3/79	**36**	5		11 Fancy Dancer..	77	Warner 8734
6/21/80	**4**	17		12 **Where Did We Go Wrong**............................	90	MCA 41253
				FRANKIE VALLI Introducing Chris Forde		
★★138★★				**VANDROSS, Luther**		
				Born on 4/20/51 in New York City. Soul singer/producer/songwriter. Commercial jingle singer, then a top session vocalists/arranger. Sang lead on a few of Change's early albums. Appeared in the film *The Meteor Man*.		
				1)Power Of Love/Love Power 2)Here And Now 3)How Many Times Can We Say Goodbye		
10/8/83	**4**	17		1 **How Many Times Can We Say Goodbye**........................	27	Arista 9073
				DIONNE WARWICK AND LUTHER VANDROSS		
1/17/87	**7**	15		2 **Stop To Love**...	15	Epic 06523
4/25/87	**20**	7		3 There's Nothing Better Than Love........................	50	Epic 06978
				LUTHER VANDROSS (With GREGORY HINES)		
10/15/88	**12**	15		4 Any Love..	44	Epic 08047
2/11/89	**17**	10		5 She Won't Talk To Me.....................................	30	Epic 08513
12/16/89	**3**	33	●	6 **Here And Now**..	6	Epic 73029
4/27/91	**3**	27		7 **Power Of Love/Love Power**...........................	4	Epic 73778
				"Love Power" was a #22 Pop hit for The Sandpebbles in 1968; Cissy Houston, Darlene Love, Lisa Fischer & others (backing vocals)		
8/24/91	**5**	29		8 **Don't Want To Be A Fool**..............................	9	Epic 73879
				Cissy Houston, Tawatha Agee and others (backing vocals)		
3/14/92	**9**	17		9 **Sometimes It's Only Love**.............................		Epic 74226
5/29/93	**30**	9		10 Little Miracles (Happen Every Day).....................	62	Epic 74945
				VAN DYKE, Dick — see ANDREWS, Julie		
				VANGELIS		
				Born Evangelos Papathanassiou on 3/29/43 in Valos, Greece. Keyboardist/composer. Moved to Paris during the late 1960s, then to London in the mid-1970s. Formed rock band Aphrodite's Child in France with Demis Roussos, 1968-early 1970s. Also see Jon & Vangelis.		
12/26/81	**1**⁵	28		Chariots Of Fire - Titles.....................[I]	1¹	Polydor 2189
				from the Academy Award-winning film *Chariots Of Fire*		
				VANITY FARE		
				British pop quintet: Trevor Brice (vocals), Dick Allix, Tony Jarrett, Tony Goulden and Barry Landeman.		
11/15/69	**4**	16		1 **Early In The Morning**..................................	12	Page One 21027
5/2/70	**22**	11	●	2 Hitchin' A Ride...	5	Page One 21029
8/22/70	**22**	5		3 (I Remember) Summer Morning.........................	98	Page One 21033
				VANNELLI, Gino		
				Born on 6/16/52 in Montreal. Pop singer/songwriter. His brother Ross produced Earth, Wind & Fire, Howard Hewett and The California Raisins.		
10/12/74	**17**	8		1 People Gotta Move..	22	A&M 1614
9/23/78	**4**	20		2 I Just Wanna Stop...	4	A&M 2072
2/10/79	**24**	7		3 Wheels Of Life...	78	A&M 2114
4/4/81	**5**	19		4 Living Inside Myself.......................................	6	Arista 0588
9/21/85	**6**	12		5 Hurts To Be In Love.......................................	57	CBS Assoc. 05586
5/2/87	**33**	6		6 Wild Horses..	55	CBS Assoc. 06699
5/18/91	**49**	2		7 If I Should Lose This Love................................		Vie/BMG LP Cut
				from the album *Inconsolable Man* on Vie/BMG 4300		
				VANWARMER, Randy		
				Born Randall Van Wormer on 3/30/55 in Indian Hills, Colorado. Singer/songwriter/guitarist. Moved to England at age 12; returned to U.S. in 1979. Charted two country hits in 1988.		
3/3/79	**1**²	23	●	Just When I Needed You Most.......................	4	Bearsville 0334
				VARTAN, Sylvie — see DENVER, John		
				VAUGHAN, Sarah		
				Born on 3/27/24 in Newark, New Jersey. Jazz singer. Dubbed "The Divine One."		
4/2/66	**5**	8		1 A Lover's Concerto..	63	Mercury 72543

246

DEBUT DATE	PEAK POS	WKS CHR	GOLD	ARTIST — Record Title	POP POS	Label & Number
				VAUGHAN, Sarah — Cont'd		
7/16/66	**33**	3		**2** 1, 2, 3		Mercury 72588
				#2 Pop hit for Len Barry in 1965		
				VAUGHN, Billy		
				Born Richard Vaughn on 4/12/19 in Glasgow, Kentucky; died on 9/26/91 of cancer. Organized the Hilltoppers vocal group in 1952. Music director for Dot Records. Arranger/conductor for Pat Boone, Gale Storm, The Fontane Sisters and many other Dot artists. Billy had more pop hits than any other orchestra leader during the rock era.		
				1)I Love You (And You Love Me) 2)A Swingin' Safari 3)Sweet Maria		
10/30/61	**16**	2		**1** Berlin Melody/ [I]	61	
10/30/61	**18**	3		**2** Come September .... [I]	73	Dot 16262
				movie title song		
3/17/62	**13**	6		**3** Chapel By The Sea .... [I]	69	Dot 16329
7/21/62	**5**	12		**4** A Swingin' Safari .... [I]	13	Dot 16374
				written by Bert Kaempfert		
4/24/65	**23**	1		**5** Mexican Pearls .... [I]	94	Dot 16706
1/1/66	**17**	8		**6** Michelle	77	Dot 16809
				written by John Lennon & Paul McCartney		
1/7/67	**6**	13		**7** Sweet Maria *	105	Dot 16985
5/6/67	**30**	5		**8** Pineapple Market .... [I]		Dot 17000
5/27/67	**4**	15		**9** I Love You (And You Love Me) *		Dot 17021
				*THE BILLY VAUGHN SINGERS		
				same melody as Anthony Quinn's "Sometimes"		
				VEE, Bobby		
				Born Robert Velline on 4/30/43 in Fargo, North Dakota. Formed The Shadows with his brother and a friend in 1959. After Buddy Holly's death in a plane crash, The Shadows filled in on Buddy's next scheduled show in Fargo. First recorded for Soma in 1959. In the films *Swingin' Along, It's Trad, Dad, Play It Cool, C'mon Let's Live A Little* and *Just For Fun*. Still performing on oldies tours.		
1/5/63	**2**³	10		**1** The Night Has A Thousand Eyes	3	Liberty 55521
5/11/63	**5**	4		**2** Charms	13	Liberty 55530
7/13/63	**14**	3		**3** Be True To Yourself	34	Liberty 55581
9/6/75	**37**	6		**4** Loving You		Shady Brook 013
				VEGA, Suzanne		
				Born on 8/12/59 in New York City. Alternative singer/songwriter/guitarist.		
6/27/87	**3**	17		Luka	3	A&M 2937
				VELA, Rosie ❍		
				New York-based fashion model turned singer.		
9/6/86	**29**	5		Magic Smile		A&M 2856
				VELVET, Jimmy		
				Memphis native. Based in Jacksonville, Florida.		
6/5/65	**29**	3		It's Almost Tomorrow	93	Philips 40285
				first released on Velvet Tone 102 in 1964		
				VENTURES, The		
				Guitar-based instrumental rock and roll band formed in the Seattle/Tacoma, Washington area. Consisted of guitarists Nokie Edwards (bass; b: 5/9/39), Bob Bogle (lead; b: 1/16/37) and Don Wilson (rhythm; b: 2/10/37), and drummer Howie Johnson (d: 1988). First recorded for own Blue Horizon label in 1959. Johnson was injured in an auto accident and was replaced by Mel Taylor in 1961. Numerous personnel changes since.		
3/29/69	**8**	11		**1** Hawaii Five-O .... [I]	4	Liberty 56068
				TV series title song		
7/5/69	**17**	7		**2** Theme From "A Summer Place" .... [I]	83	Liberty 56115
7/28/73	**38**	2		**3** Skylab (Passport To The Future) .... [I]		United Art. 277
4/6/74	**47**	3		**4** Main Theme From "The Young And The Restless" .... [I]		United Art. 392
				#8 Pop hit in 1976 for Barry DeVorzon & Perry Botkin, Jr. as "Nadia's Theme"		
				VERA, Billy		
				Born William McCord on 5/28/44 in Riverside, California and raised in Westchester County, New York. Wrote hit songs for many pop, R&B and country artists. In the films *Buckaroo Banzai* and *The Doors*, and the HBO movie *Baja Oklahoma*. Formed The Beaters (an R&B-based, 10-piece band) in Los Angeles in 1979.		
6/29/68	**25**	7		**1** With Pen In Hand	43	Atlantic 2526
				BILLY VERA & THE BEATERS:		
12/13/86	**1**¹	19	●	**2** At This Moment .... [R]	**1**²	Rhino 74403
				popularized by play on TV's *Family Ties*; originally made the *Hot 100* on 9/19/81 (POS 79) on Alfa 7005		
4/30/88	**9**	15		**3** Between Like And Love		Capitol 44149

DEBUT DATE	PEAK POS	WKS CHR	GOLD	ARTIST — Record Title	POP POS	Label & Number
				VIEW FROM THE HILL ✪		
				Trio formed in London in 1983: TV actress/vocalist Angela Wynter with former session musicians Trevor White and Patrick Patterson.		
2/13/88	**26**	11		No Conversation..		Capitol 44095
				VIGRASS & OSBORNE		
				British duo: Paul Vigrass and Gary Osborne.		
6/24/72	**33**	4		1 Men Of Learning..	65	Uni 55330
9/2/72	**39**	3		2 Virginia		Uni 55344
				VILLAGE STOMPERS, The		
				Greenwich Village, New York Dixieland-styled band.		
10/19/63	**1**³	10		1 **Washington Square** ....[I]	2¹	Epic 9617
12/12/64	**19**	1		2 Fiddler On The Roof ....[I]	97	Epic 9740
				Broadway musical title song		
7/17/65	**35**	5		3 Those Magnificent Men In Their Flying Machines............[I]	130	Epic 9824
				movie title song		
★★13★★				**VINTON, Bobby**		
				Born Stanley Robert Vinton on 4/16/35 in Canonsburg, Pennsylvania. Father was a bandleader. Formed own band while in high school; toured as backing band for Dick Clark's "Caravan of Stars" in 1960. Left band for a singing career in 1962. Own musical variety TV series from 1975-78.		
				1)Blue Velvet 2)There! I've Said It Again 3)Roses Are Red (My Love) 4)My Melody Of Love 5)I Love How You Love Me		
7/28/62	**1**⁴	8	●	1 **Roses Are Red (My Love)**	1⁴	Epic 9509
9/1/62	**4**	10		2 **Rain Rain Go Away**	12	Epic 9532
12/15/62	**7**	8		3 **Trouble Is My Middle Name**/	33	
12/15/62	**10**	7		4 Let's Kiss And Make Up..	38	Epic 9561
3/16/63	**8**	9		5 **Over The Mountain (Across The Sea)**	21	Epic 9577
5/25/63	**2**³	11		6 **Blue On Blue**	3	Epic 9593
8/24/63	**1**⁸	13		7 **Blue Velvet**	1³	Epic 9614
11/30/63	**1**⁵	13		8 **There! I've Said It Again**	1⁴	Epic 9638
3/14/64	**2**²	7		9 **My Heart Belongs To Only You**	9	Epic 9662
5/23/64	**3**	8		10 **Tell Me Why**	13	Epic 9687
8/15/64	**2**⁴	7		11 **Clinging Vine**	17	Epic 9705
11/21/64	**3**	1		12 **Mr. Lonely**..	1¹	Epic 9730
3/13/65	**5**	6		13 **Long Lonely Nights**	17	Epic 9768
5/8/65	**7**	4		14 **L-O-N-E-L-Y**	22	Epic 9791
7/10/65	**16**	7		15 Theme From "Harlow" (Lonely Girl)...............................	61	Epic 9814
				from the film *Harlow*		
2/19/66	**27**	4		16 Tears	59	Epic 9894
5/7/66	**24**	5		17 Dum-De-Da	40	Epic 10014
				tune also known as "She Understands Me"		
10/7/67	**39**	3		18 Please Love Me Forever	6	Epic 10228
1/20/68	**10**	8		19 **Just As Much As Ever**	24	Epic 10266
4/20/68	**14**	5		20 Take Good Care Of My Baby	33	Epic 10305
7/20/68	**8**	11		21 **Halfway To Paradise**	23	Epic 10350
11/2/68	**2**⁶	17	●	22 **I Love How You Love Me**	9	Epic 10397
4/12/69	**8**	7		23 **To Know You Is To Love You**	34	Epic 10461
6/21/69	**11**	8		24 **The Days Of Sand And Shovels**	34	Epic 10485
2/14/70	**7**	9		25 **My Elusive Dreams**	46	Epic 10576
7/11/70	**8**	9		26 **No Arms Can Ever Hold You**	93	Epic 10629
9/26/70	**23**	4		27 Why Don't They Understand	109	Epic 10651
4/3/71	**30**	5		28 I'll Make You My Baby	101	Epic 10711
				answer song to "Make Me Your Baby" by Barbara Lewis		
1/22/72	**2**⁴	17		29 **Every Day Of My Life**	24	Epic 10822
6/3/72	**2**¹	13		30 **Sealed With A Kiss**	19	Epic 10861
12/30/72	**27**	6		31 **But I Do**	82	Epic 10936
5/19/73	**40**	2		32 Hurt	106	Epic 10980
9/14/74	**1**¹	16	●	33 **My Melody Of Love**	3	ABC 12022
3/15/75	**5**	10		34 **Beer Barrel Polka**	33	ABC 12056
6/7/75	**23**	7		35 **Wooden Heart**	58	ABC 12100
10/11/75	**23**	6	✓	36 Midnight Show		ABC 12131
4/17/76	**15**	6		37 Moonlight Serenade	97	ABC 12178
12/11/76	**34**	8		38 Nobody But Me		ABC 12229
5/21/77	**44**	7		39 Only Love Can Break A Heart	99	ABC 12265

DEBUT DATE	PEAK POS	WKS CHR	G O L D	ARTIST — Record Title	POP POS	Label & Number
				VINTON, Bobby — Cont'd		
7/30/77	**43**	6		40 Hold Me, Thrill Me, Kiss Me		ABC 12293
7/8/78	**44**	5		41 Summerlove, Sensation..		Elektra 45503
9/1/79	**47**	3	✓	42 Disco Polka (Pennsylvania Polka)...		Tapestry 001
				BOBBY VINTON And His Orchestra		
				#17 hit for the Andrews Sisters in 1942		
11/24/79	**17**	12		43 Make Believe It's Your First Time	78	Tapestry 002
4/18/81	**45**	6		44 Let Me Love You Goodbye	108	Tapestry 006
★★**103**★★				**VOGUES, The**		
				Vocal group formed in Turtle Creek, Pennsylvania in 1960. Consisted of Bill Burkette (lead), Hugh Geyer and Chuck Blasko (tenors) and Don Miller (baritone). Met in high school.		
				1)My Special Angel 2)Turn Around, Look At Me 3)Till		
6/1/68	**3**	20	●	1 **Turn Around, Look At Me**..	7	Reprise 0686
9/7/68	**1**²	12		2 **My Special Angel**	7	Reprise 0766
11/23/68	**5**	11		3 **Till**	27	Reprise 0788
2/1/69	**6**	8		4 **Woman Helping Man/**	47	
3/8/69	**6**	7		5 **No, Not Much**	34	Reprise 0803
4/26/69	**7**	6		6 **Earth Angel (Will You Be Mine)**	42	Reprise 0820
6/21/69	**17**	7		7 Moments To Remember...	47	Reprise 0831
8/23/69	**19**	4		8 Green Fields	92	Reprise 0844
10/18/69	**13**	5		9 See That Girl		Reprise 0856
1/31/70	**21**	6		10 God Only Knows	101	Reprise 0887
5/9/70	**18**	4		11 Hey, That's No Way To Say Goodbye	101	Reprise 0909
				written by Leonard Cohen		
8/1/70	**27**	4		12 The Good Old Songs		Reprise 0931
				medley: Oh Donna/Since I Fell For You/I Miss You So/So This Is Love/Goodnight My Love; theme conceived by Paul Anka		
12/26/70	**8**	9		13 **Since I Don't Have You**		Reprise 0969
				#12 Pop hit for The Skyliners in 1959		
5/22/71	**23**	5		14 Love Song...	118	Bell 991
9/11/71	**38**	2		15 I'll Be With You		Bell 45-127
				above 2 written, produced and arranged by Teddy Randazzo		
8/11/73	**31**	6		16 My Prayer		20th Century 2041
				#1 Pop hit for The Platters in 1956		
11/24/73	**47**	4		17 Wonderful Summer..		20th Century 2060
				#14 Pop hit for Robin Ward in 1963		
4/6/74	**37**	5		18 Prisoner Of Love		20th Century 2085
				#1 hit for Perry Como in 1946		
				VOICES THAT CARE		
				Benefit spearheaded by David Foster and his fiancee Linda Thompson Jenner (ex-wife of Olympian Bruce Jenner) supporting the Persian Gulf allied troops and their families. Among superstar choir: Kevin Costner, Meryl Streep, Billy Crystal, Richard Gere, Gloria Estefan, Wayne Gretzky and many others.		
3/16/91	**6**	19	●	**Voices That Care**	11	Giant 19350
				lead vocals: Ralph Tresvant, Randy Travis, Celine Dion, Peter Cetera, Bobby Brown, Brenda Russell, Warrant, Luther Vandross, Garth Brooks, Kathy Mattea, Nelson, Michael Bolton, Little Richard, Pointer Sisters, Fresh Prince, Mark Knopfler, Kenny G and Warren Wiebe		
				VOLLENWEIDER, Andreas ✪		
				Electro-acoustic harpist from Zurich, Switzerland.		
7/1/89	**25**	11		Dancing With The Lion.. [I]		Columbia 68928
				VOUDOURIS, Roger		
				Born on 12/29/54 in Sacramento, California. Pop singer/songwriter/guitarist.		
4/7/79	**18**	13		Get Used To It	21	Warner 8762

W

WADE, Adam

Born on 3/17/37 in Pittsburgh. Attended Virginia State College and worked as lab assistant with Dr. Jonas Salk team. TV actor/host of the 1976 game show *Musical Chairs*. Worked in *Guys & Dolls* musical in Las Vegas in 1978. TV talkshow host in Los Angeles in the '80s.

7/17/61	**5**	2		1 **The Writing On The Wall**	5	Coed 550

DEBUT DATE	PEAK POS	WKS CHR	GOLD	ARTIST — Record Title	POP POS	Label & Number
				WADE, Adam — Cont'd		
7/24/61	**4**	10		2 As If I Didn't Know	10	Coed 553
9/18/61	**14**	4		3 Tonight I Won't Be There...............................	61	Coed 556
2/6/65	**20**	2		4 Crying In The Chapel	88	Epic 9752
				WADSWORTH MANSION		
				Rock quartet: Steve Jablecki (lead vocals), Wayne Gagnon, John Poole and Mike Jablecki.		
2/20/71	**35**	3		Sweet Mary	7	Sussex 209
				WAGNER, Jack		
				Born on 10/3/59 in Washington, Missouri. Played Frisco Jones on the TV soap opera *General Hospital*; joined the cast of *Santa Barbara* in 1991.		
11/10/84	**1**²	20		1 **All I Need**..	2²	Qwest 29238
5/4/85	**34**	3		2 Lady Of My Heart...	76	Qwest 29085
11/23/85	**15**	10		3 Too Young	52	Qwest 28931
2/22/86	**15**	11		4 Love Can Take Us All The Way..........................		Qwest 28790
				JACK WAGNER With Valerie Carter		
				WAIKIKIS, The		
				Belgian instrumental group.		
12/12/64	**8**	7		1 **Hawaii Tattoo** ....[I]	33	Kapp 30
4/3/65	**22**	3		2 Hawaii Honeymoon ....[I]	91	Kapp 52
				WAITE, John		
				Born on 7/4/55 in Lancashire, England. Lead singer of The Babys and Bad English.		
8/11/84	**7**	14		**Missing You**...	1¹	EMI America 8212
				WALKER, Chris		
				Houston soul singer/jazz bassist. In 1991, 22 years old. Played bass with Ornette Coleman for three years. Worked as musical director for Regina Belle.		
4/25/92	**17**	20		Take Time	29	Pendulum 64813
				WALKER, Jerry Jeff		
				Born Paul Crosby on 3/14/42 in Oneonta, New York. Country-rock singer/songwriter. Wrote "Mr. Bojangles."		
8/3/68	**28**	4		Mr. Bojangles..	77	Atco 6594
				WALLACE, Jerry		
				Born on 12/15/28 in Guilford, Missouri and raised in Glendale, Arizona. Pop-country singer/guitarist. First recorded for Allied in 1951. Appeared on the TV shows *Night Gallery* and *Hec Ramsey*.		
7/25/64	**2**¹	11		1 **In The Misty Moonlight**	19	Challenge 59246
5/6/72	**21**	5		2 To Get To You...	48	Decca 32914
8/12/72	**9**	11		3 **If You Leave Me Tonight I'll Cry**	38	Decca 32989
				from TV's *Night Gallery: The Tune In Dan's Cafe*		
				WANDERLEY, Walter		
				Brazilian organist/pianist/composer. Died of cancer on 9/4/86 (age 55).		
8/13/66	**3**	17		1 **Summer Samba (So Nice)** ....[I]	26	Verve 10421
12/3/66	**20**	7		2 Amanha...[I]		Verve 10456
				WAR		
				Band formed in Long Beach, California in 1969. Consisted of Lonnie Jordan (keyboards), Howard Scott (guitar), Charles Miller (saxophone; murdered in 1980), Morris "B.B." Dickerson (bass), Harold Brown and Thomas "Papa Dee" Allen (percussion) and Lee Oskar (harmonica). Eric Burdon's backup band until 1971. Dickerson was replaced by Luther Rabb. Jordan and Oskar also recorded solo. Alice Tweed Smyth (vocals) added in 1978. Pat Rizzo (horns) and Ron Hammond (former member of Aalon; percussion) added in 1979. Smyth left group in 1982.		
8/14/71	**12**	8		1 All Day Music	35	United Art. 50815
7/17/76	**1**¹	12	●	2 Summer..	7	United Art. 834
4/6/85	**30**	7		3 Groovin		Coco Plum 2002
				#1 Pop hit for The Young Rascals in 1967		
				WARD, Jacky ○		
				Born on 11/18/46 in Groveton, Texas. Supporting act on tours with Ronnie Milsap and Crystal Gayle.		
3/11/78	**32**	9		1 A Lover's Question	106	Mercury 55018
				#6 Pop hit for Clyde McPhatter in 1959		
3/24/79	**49**	1		2 Wisdom Of A Fool..		Mercury 55055
				WARINER, Steve ○		
				Country singer/guitarist. Born on 12/25/54 in Noblesville, Indiana.		
8/13/88	**43**	4		I Should Be With You		MCA 53347

DEBUT DATE	PEAK POS	WKS CHR	G O L D	ARTIST — Record Title	POP POS	Label & Number
	★★93★★			**WARNES, Jennifer** Born in Seattle and raised in Orange County, California. Pop/MOR-styled vocalist. Lead actress in the Los Angeles production of *Hair*.		
				1)*(I've Had) The Time Of My Life* 2)*Right Time Of The Night* 3)*Up Where We Belong*		
2/12/77	**1**[1]	20		1 **Right Time Of The Night**	6	Arista 0223
7/9/77	**9**	14		2 **I'm Dreaming**	50	Arista 0252
6/16/79	**14**	22		3 I Know A Heartache When I See One	19	Arista 0430
12/22/79	**36**	8		4 Don't Make Me Over..	67	Arista 0455
3/22/80	**15**	15		5 When The Feeling Comes Around....................................	45	Arista 0497
12/12/81	**13**	15		6 Could It Be Love	47	Arista 0611
4/3/82	**40**	5		7 Come To Me	107	Arista 0670
8/21/82	**3**	25	▲	8 **Up Where We Belong** .... JOE COCKER and JENNIFER WARNES love theme from the film *An Officer And A Gentleman*	**1**[3]	Island 99996
7/23/83	**8**	16		9 **Nights Are Forever**... from the film *Twilight Zone-The Movie*	105	Warner 29593
11/19/83	**19**	13		10 All The Right Moves .... JENNIFER WARNES/CHRIS THOMPSON movie title song	85	Casablanca 814603
4/25/87	**29**	4		11 First We Take Manhattan .... written by Leonard Cohen		Cypress 661115
8/8/87	**1**[4]	26	●	12 **(I've Had) The Time Of My Life** .... BILL MEDLEY and JENNIFER WARNES love theme from the film *Dirty Dancing*	**1**[1]	RCA 5224
7/18/92	**13**	19		13 Rock You Gently		Private M. LP Cut
12/26/92	**43**	8		14 True Emotion		Private M. LP Cut
5/1/93	**49**	2		15 The Whole Of The Moon .... above 3 from the album *The Hunter* on Private M. 82089		Private M. LP Cut
	★★6★★			**WARWICK, Dionne** Born Marie Dionne Warwick on 12/12/40 in East Orange, New Jersey. In church choir from age six. With the Drinkard Singers gospel group. Formed trio, the Gospelaires, with sister Dee Dee and their aunt Cissy Houston. Attended Hartt College Of Music, Hartford, Connecticut. Much backup studio work in New York during the late '50s. Added an "e" to her last name for a time in the early '70s. She was Burt Bacharach and Hal David's main "voice" for the songs they composed. Co-hosted TV's *Solid Gold* 1980-81, 1985-86.		
				1)*No Night So Long* 2)*I'll Never Fall In Love Again* 3)*That's What Friends Are For* 4)*Heartbreaker* 5)*Deja Vu*		
1/4/64	**2**[3]	10		1 **Anyone Who Had A Heart**..	8	Scepter 1262
5/9/64	**7**	2		2 **Walk On By**...	6	Scepter 1274
7/3/65	**11**	9		3 Here I Am .... from the Broadway musical *What's New Pussycat?*	65	Scepter 12104
4/9/66	**12**	10		4 Message To Michael	8	Scepter 12133
7/30/66	**37**	3		5 Trains And Boats And Planes	22	Scepter 12153
9/2/67	**32**	4		6 The Windows Of The World	32	Scepter 12196
11/25/67	**2**[4]	13		7 (Theme From) Valley Of The Dolls .... from the film *Valley Of The Dolls*; flip side "I Say A Little Prayer" made the *Hot 100* (POS 4)	**2**[4]	Scepter 12203
4/20/68	**4**	13		8 Do You Know The Way To San Jose................................	10	Scepter 12216
8/24/68	**4**	11		9 Who Is Gonna Love Me?	33	Scepter 12226
11/9/68	**7**	11		10 Promises, Promises .... from the Broadway musical of the same title (also #15 below)	19	Scepter 12231
2/8/69	**2**[4]	12		11 This Girl's In Love With You	7	Scepter 12241
5/24/69	**8**	9		12 The April Fools	37	Scepter 12249
7/26/69	**7**	10		13 Odds And Ends	43	Scepter 12256
10/4/69	**10**	8		14 You've Lost That Lovin' Feeling	16	Scepter 12262
1/3/70	**1**[3]	11		15 I'll Never Fall In Love Again	6	Scepter 12273
4/25/70	**5**	8		16 Let Me Go To Him	32	Scepter 12276
7/11/70	**6**	9		17 Paper Mache	43	Scepter 12285
10/10/70	**2**[2]	8		18 Make It Easy On Yourself	37	Scepter 12294
12/12/70	**2**[1]	9		19 The Green Grass Starts To Grow	43	Scepter 12300
3/20/71	**6**	7		20 Who Gets The Guy	57	Scepter 12309
8/14/71	**15**	6		21 Amanda	83	Scepter 12326
3/25/72	**37**	2		22 If We Only Have Love	84	Warner 7560
8/3/74	**3**	16	●	23 Then Came You.. DIONNE WARWICKE AND SPINNERS originally released on Atlantic 3029 earlier in 1974	**1**[1]	Atlantic 3202
12/6/75	**22**	10		24 Once You Hit The Road	79	Warner 8154

DEBUT DATE	PEAK POS	WKS CHR	GOLD	ARTIST — Record Title	POP POS	Label & Number
				WARWICK, Dionne — Cont'd		
4/2/77	**46**	5		25 Only Love Can Break A Heart	109	Musicor 6303
				#2 Pop hit for Gene Pitney in 1962		
5/26/79	**5**	25	●	26 **I'll Never Love This Way Again**	5	Arista 0419
10/27/79	**1**¹	18		27 **Deja Vu**	15	Arista 0459
3/22/80	**10**	18		28 **After You**	65	Arista 0498
				movie title song; above 3 produced by Barry Manilow		
8/2/80	**1**³	24		29 **No Night So Long**	23	Arista 0527
11/8/80	**12**	15		30 Easy Love	62	Arista 0572
6/20/81	**23**	10		31 Some Changes Are For Good	65	Arista 0602
4/24/82	**5**	17		32 **Friends In Love**	38	Arista 0673
				DIONNE WARWICK AND JOHNNY MATHIS		
8/7/82	**14**	13		33 For You		Arista 0701
10/9/82	**1**¹	22		34 **Heartbreaker**	10	Arista 1015
2/26/83	**5**	16		35 **Take The Short Way Home**	41	Arista 1040
6/11/83	**16**	15		36 All The Love In The World	101	Arista 9032
				Barry Gibb (backing vocal, above 3)		
10/8/83	**4**	17		37 **How Many Times Can We Say Goodbye**	27	Arista 9073
				DIONNE WARWICK AND LUTHER VANDROSS		
2/2/85	**12**	10		38 Finder Of Lost Loves		Arista 9281
				DIONNE WARWICK & GLENN JONES		
				TV series title song		
4/13/85	**12**	9		39 Run To Me		Arista 9341
				DIONNE WARWICK with Barry Manilow		
				#16 Pop hit for the Bee Gees in 1972		
11/9/85	**1**²	22	●	40 **That's What Friends Are For**	1⁴	Arista 9422
				DIONNE AND FRIENDS: Elton John, Gladys Knight and Stevie Wonder		
3/8/86	**7**	13		41 Whisper In The Dark	72	Arista 9460
7/4/87	**1**¹	19		42 **Love Power**	12	Arista 9567
				DIONNE WARWICK and JEFFREY OSBORNE		
10/10/87	**7**	16		43 **Reservations For Two**	62	Arista 9638
				DIONNE & KASHIF		
3/19/88	**24**	8		44 Another Chance To Love		Arista 9656
				DIONNE WARWICK & HOWARD HEWETT		
11/4/89	**25**	8		45 Take Good Care Of You And Me		Arista 9901
				DIONNE WARWICK and JEFFREY OSBORNE		
				WASHINGTON, Dinah		
				Born Ruth Lee Jones on 8/29/24 in Tuscaloosa, Alabama; died on 12/14/63 (overdose of alcohol and pills). Jazz-blues vocalist/pianist. Inducted into the Rock and Roll Hall of Fame in 1993 as an early influence.		
10/23/61	**5**	10		1 **September In The Rain**	23	Mercury 71876
				#1 hit for Guy Lombardo in 1937		
2/24/62	**17**	3		2 Tears And Laughter	71	Mercury 71922
5/19/62	**11**	9		3 Where Are You	36	Roulette 4424
				#5 hit for Mildred Bailey in 1937		
				WASHINGTON, Grover Jr.		
				Born on 12/12/43 in Buffalo. Jazz-R&B saxophonist. Own band, the Four Clefs, at age 16. Much session work in Philadelphia, where he now resides.		
2/14/81	**2**²	21		**Just The Two Of Us**	2³	Elektra 47103
				GROVER WASHINGTON, JR./BILL WITHERS		
				WASHINGTON, Keith		
				Detroit native. Supporting vocalist while a teen for The Dramatics. Former backing vocalist for the Jacksons and Miki Howard.		
5/25/91	**31**	13		Kissing You	40	Qwest 19414
				WAS (NOT WAS)		
				Detroit R&B ensemble fronted by composer/bassist Don Fagenson ("Don Was") and lyricist/flutist David Weiss ("David Was"). Includes vocalists Sweet Pea Atkinson and Sir Harry Bowens. Group appeared in the film *The Freshman*.		
6/10/89	**36**	7		Anything Can Happen	75	Chrysalis 43365
				WATANABE, Sadao ✪		
				Pronounced: sah-day-o wah-tah-nob-bee. Jazz saxophonist born in Utsunomiya, Japan, in 1933. To Boston in 1962, attended the Berklee College of Music. Member of the groups of Chico Hamilton and Gary McFarland.		
9/1/84	**31**	7		1 If I'm Still Around Tomorrow		Elektra 69700
				SADAO WATANABE with Roberta Flack		
11/25/89	**6**	31		2 Any Other Fool		Elektra 69254
				SADAO WATANABE (Featuring Patti Austin)		

DEBUT DATE	PEAK POS	WKS CHR	GOLD	ARTIST — Record Title	POP POS	Label & Number
				WATERFRONT Male pop-rock duo of singer Chris Duffy and guitarist Phil Cillia from Cardiff, Wales. Band name derived from the Marlon Brando film *On The Waterfront*.		
4/29/89	**2**[1]	20		**1** Cry..	10	Polydor 871110
9/9/89	**44**	4		**2** Nature Of Love	70	Polydor 871414
11/4/89	**24**	7		**3** Move On..		Polydor 873066
				WATLEY, Jody Born on 1/30/59 in Chicago. Female vocalist of Shalamar (1977-84) and former dancer on TV's *Soul Train*. Her godfather was Jackie Wilson. Won the 1987 Best New Artist Grammy Award.		
10/14/89	**11**	28		**1** Everything	4	MCA 53714
7/18/92	**48**	2		**2** It All Begins With You		MCA 54396
				WAYLON & WILLIE — see JENNINGS, Waylon and/or NELSON, Willie		
				WEATHERLY, Jim Pop-country singer/songwriter born on 3/17/43 in Pontotoc, Mississippi. Wrote Gladys Knight's hits "Neither One Of Us," "Midnight Train To Georgia" and "Best Thing That Ever Happened To Me."		
8/31/74	**6**	13		**1** The Need To Be	11	Buddah 420
1/4/75	**40**	5		**2** High On Love...................................		RCA 10134
1/11/75	**14**	12		**3** I'll Still Love You	87	Buddah 444
8/13/77	**26**	7		**4** All That Keeps Me Going		ABC 12288
11/17/79	**32**	11		**5** Smooth Sailin'		Elektra 46547
				WEBER, Frank ○ Singer/songwriter/pianist.		
5/17/80	**43**	6		You Can Come Home To Me		RCA 11949
				WE FIVE California pop quintet: Beverly Bivens (lead singer), Mike Stewart (brother of John Stewart), Pete Fullerton, Bob Jones and Jerry Burgan.		
7/3/65	**1**[5]	20		You Were On My Mind	3	A&M 770
				WEISBERG, Tim Born in 1943 in Hollywood. Flautist; studied classical music as an adolescent. Performs pop-oriented music with a jazz appeal.		
4/19/75	**34**	8		Dion Blue .... [I]		A&M 1680
				WEISS, Larry ○ Born on 3/25/41 in Newark, New Jersey. Singer/songwriter. Wrote "Rhinestone Cowboy."		
4/13/74	**24**	9		Rhinestone Cowboy .... #1 Pop hit for Glen Campbell in 1975		20th Century 2084
				WEISSBERG, Eric, & Steve Mandell Prominent session musicians. Both had worked with Judy Collins and John Denver.		
1/13/73	**1**[2]	12	●	**Dueling Banjos** .... [I] tune written in 1955; featured in the film *Deliverance*	2[4]	Warner 7659
				WELCH, Bob Born on 7/31/46 in Los Angeles. Guitarist/vocalist with Fleetwood Mac (1971-74). Formed the British rock group Paris in 1976. His father, Robert L. Welch, was a major film/TV producer.		
11/5/77	**10**	15		**1** Sentimental Lady .... Christine McVie and Lindsey Buckingham (backing vocals)	8	Capitol 4479
3/17/79	**42**	9		**2** Precious Love	19	Capitol 4685
				WELCH, Lenny Born on 5/15/38 in Asbury Park, New Jersey. Black pop vocalist.		
11/2/63	**3**	14		**1** Since I Fell For You............................. #20 hit for Paul Gayten in 1947	4	Cadence 1439
4/11/64	**6**	6		**2** Ebb Tide....................................... featured in the film *Sweet Bird Of Youth*; both Frank Chacksfield & Vic Damone had top 10 versions in 1953	25	Cadence 1422
6/26/65	**23**	6		**3** Darling Take Me Back	72	Kapp 662
8/14/65	**6**	10		**4** Two Different Worlds........................	61	Kapp 689
1/10/70	**8**	11		**5** Breaking Up Is Hard To Do................	34	Common. U. 3004
8/5/72	**21**	6		**6** A Sunday Kind Of Love.................... Jo Stafford and Claude Thornhill had top 20 versions in 1947	96	Atco 6894
9/8/73	**25**	5		**7** Since I Don't Have You .... #12 Pop hit for The Skyliners in 1959		Mainstream 5545
				WELCH, Mary ○		
11/18/78	**24**	12		Take It Like A Woman		20th Century 2387

DEBUT DATE	PEAK POS	WKS CHR	G O L D	ARTIST — Record Title	POP POS	Label & Number
				WELK, Lawrence		
				Born on 3/11/03 in Strasburg, North Dakota. Died on 5/17/92 of pneumonia. Accordionist and polka/sweet bandleader since the mid-1920s. Band's style labeled as "champagne music." Own national TV musical variety show began on 7/2/55 and ran on ABC until 9/4/71. New episodes in syndication from 1971 to 1982.		
8/25/62	**10**	5		1 Baby Elephant Walk ....[I]	48	Dot 16364
				from the film *Hatari*		
4/10/65	**17**	4		2 Apples And Bananas ....[I]	75	Dot 16697
3/16/68	**27**	4		3 Green Tambourine ....[I]		Ranwood 801
				#1 Pop hit for The Lemon Pipers in 1968		
2/28/70	**37**	2	√	4 Southtown, U.S.A.		Ranwood 866
				#15 Pop hit for The Dixiebelles in 1964		
				WENDY & LISA		
				Wendy Melvoin (guitar, vocals) and Lisa Coleman (keyboards). Formerly with Prince's band The Revolution. Wendy's father is Mike Melvoin (The Plastic Cow); her sister is Susannah Melvoin (The Family).		
12/26/92	**37**	3		The Closing Of The Year		Geffen 19146
				MUSICAL CAST OF TOYS FEATURING WENDY & LISA		
				from the movie *Toys* starring Robin Williams		
				WEST, Dottie		
				Born Dorothy Marsh on 10/11/32 in McMinnville, Tennessee. Died on 9/4/91 from injuries suffered in a car accident. Country singer.		
10/13/73	**37**	5		1 Country Sunshine	49	RCA 0072
4/8/78	**44**	6		2 Every Time Two Fools Collide	101	United Art. 1137
				KENNY ROGERS & DOTTIE WEST		
4/14/79	**38**	8		3 All I Ever Need Is You	102	United Art. 1276
				KENNY ROGERS with DOTTIE WEST		
				#7 Pop hit for Sonny & Cher in 1971		
1/19/80	**50**	1		4 You Pick Me Up (And Put Me Down)		United Art. 1324
2/23/80	**42**	4		5 A Lesson In Leavin'.	73	United Art. 1339
4/11/81	**7**	20		6 What Are We Doin' In Love	14	Liberty 1404
				DOTTIE WEST with Kenny Rogers		
				WEST, Tommy — see CASHMAN & WEST		
				WET WET WET		
				Pop quartet from Glasgow, Scotland: Graeme Clark, Tom Cunningham, Neil Mitchell and Marti Pellow (vocals). Band name inspired from a line in the Scritti Politti song "Getting, Having, and Holding."		
1/21/89	**44**	2		Angel Eyes (Home And Away)..		Uni 50006
				WHALUM, Kirk		
				Black tenor jazz saxophonist from Memphis. Based in Paris since mid-1992. Prolific backing musician with Whitney Houston, Luther Vandross, Bob James, Al Jarreau, Quincy Jones and others.		
6/5/93	**49**	2		Love Is A Losing Game		Columbia 74956
				KIRK WHALUM Featuring Jevetta Steele		
				WHAM! — see MICHAEL, George		
				WHEN IN ROME		
				U.K.-based trio: Clive Farrington (vocals), Michael Floreale (keyboards) and Andrew Mann (vocals).		
12/10/88	**45**	4		The Promise	11	Virgin 99323
				WHISPERS, The		
				Los Angeles soul group formed in 1964. Consisted of Gordy Harmon, twin brothers Walter and Wallace "Scotty" Scott, Marcus Hutson and Nicholas Caldwell. First recorded for Dore in 1964. Harmon replaced in 1973 by Leaveil Degree who was briefly a member of Friends Of Distinction. The Scotts also recorded as Walter & Scotty since 1993. Group founded the Black Tie record label.		
5/10/80	**40**	4		1 Lady	28	Solar 11928
9/19/87	**49**	3		2 Rock Steady...	7	Solar 70006
				WHITE, Barry		
				Born on 9/12/44 in Galveston, Texas and raised in Los Angeles. Soul singer/songwriter/keyboardist/producer/ arranger. With Upfronts vocal group, recorded for Dore in 1960. A&R man for Mustang/Bronco, 1966-67. Formed Love Unlimited in 1969, which included future wife Glodean James. Leader of 40-piece Love Unlimited Orchestra.		
6/2/73	**27**	6	●	1 I'm Gonna Love You Just A Little More Baby	3	20th Century 2018
9/1/73	**46**	3		2 I've Got So Much To Give	32	20th Century 2042
1/12/74	**40**	5	●	3 Never, Never Gonna Give Ya Up	7	20th Century 2058
8/31/74	**26**	10	●	4 Can't Get Enough Of Your Love, Babe............................	1[1]	20th Century 2120
3/31/90	**26**	10	●	5 The Secret Garden (Sweet Seduction Suite)	31	Qwest 19992
				QUINCY JONES/Al B. Sure!/James Ingram/El DeBarge/Barry White		

DEBUT DATE	PEAK POS	WKS CHR	GOLD	ARTIST — Record Title	POP POS	Label & Number
				WHITE, Bergen ✪		
				Country singer/multi-instrumentalist based in Nashville.		
5/10/75	**45**	5		Come Go With Me		Private S. 45,013
				#4 Pop hit for The Dell-Vikings in 1957		
				WHITE, Karyn		
				Born on 10/14/65. Prominent session singer from Los Angeles. Touring vocalist with O'Bryan in 1984. Recorded with jazz-fusion keyboardist Jeff Lorber in 1986. Married to superproducer Terry Lewis (member of The Time).		
2/4/89	**38**	4	●	**1** The Way You Love Me	7	Warner 27773
3/11/89	**12**	12	●	**2** Superwoman	8	Warner 27783
11/2/91	**37**	4		**3** Romantic	1¹	Warner 19319
1/11/92	**35**	11		**4** The Way I Feel About You	12	Warner 19088
				WHITE, Maurice		
				Born on 12/19/41 in Memphis. Percussionist with Ramsey Lewis from 1966-71. Founder and co-lead vocalist of Earth, Wind & Fire.		
9/21/85	**11**	11		**1** Stand By Me	50	Columbia 05571
12/7/85	**20**	11		**2** I Need You	95	Columbia 05726
				WHITESNAKE		
				Ex-Deep Purple vocalist David Coverdale, who recorded solo as Whitesnake in 1977, formed British heavy-metal band in 1978. Coverdale fronted everchanging lineup.		
12/12/87	**38**	9		Is This Love	2¹	Geffen 28233
★★**167**★★				**WHITING, Margaret**		
				Born on 7/22/24 in Detroit and raised in Hollywood. Daughter of popular composer Richard Whiting ("Till We Meet Again"). Very popular from 1946-54, she had over 40 charted hits.		
				1)The Wheel Of Hurt 2)I Almost Called Your Name 3)Only Love Can Break A Heart		
1/29/66	**29**	8		**1** Somewhere There's Love		London 10815
8/13/66	**1**⁴	24		**2** The Wheel Of Hurt	26	London 101
3/4/67	**29**	3		**3** Just Like A Man	132	London 106
5/6/67	**4**	14		**4** Only Love Can Break A Heart	96	London 108
10/14/67	**4**	16		**5** I Almost Called Your Name	108	London 115
2/17/68	**28**	4		**6** It Keeps Right On A Hurtin'/	115	
2/24/68	**27**	4		**7** I Hate To See Me Go	127	London 119
5/4/68	**19**	7		**8** Faithfully	117	London 122
9/14/68	**11**	8		**9** Can't Get You Out Of My Mind	124	London 124
				written by Paul Anka		
2/1/70	**24**	5	✓	**10** Where Was I		London 126
3/14/70	**14**	4		**11** ("Z" Theme) Life Goes On		London 132
				theme from the film Z		
8/1/70	**32**	3		**12** Until It's Time For You To Go		London 137
				#40 Pop hit for Elvis Presley in 1972		
				WHITTAKER, Roger		
				Born on 3/22/36 in Nairobi, Kenya. British singer.		
				1)The Last Farewell 2)I Don't Believe In If Any More 3)New World In The Morning		
4/4/70	**12**	8		**1** New World In The Morning		RCA 0320
7/25/70	**26**	6		**2** I Don't Believe In If Any More		RCA 0355
3/20/71	**40**	2		**3** Why?	2	RCA 0442
3/8/75	**1**¹	15		**4** The Last Farewell	19	RCA 50030
8/30/75	**10**	11		**5** I Don't Believe In If Any More .... [R]		RCA 10356
1/10/76	**23**	8		**6** Durham Town (The Leavin')		RCA 10447
7/31/76	**16**	11		**7** The First Hello, The Last Goodbye		RCA 10732
2/12/77	**39**	7		**8** Before She Breaks My Heart		RCA 10874
7/22/78	**47**	3		**9** If I Knew Just What To Say		RCA 11300
11/24/79	**35**	13		**10** You Are My Miracle		RCA 11760
				WILCOX, Harlow, and the Oakies		
				Harlow is a top session guitarist from Norman, Oklahoma.		
11/29/69	**18**	6		Groovy Grubworm .... [I]	30	Plantation 28
				WILDE, Kim		
				Born Kim Smith on 11/18/60 in Chiswick, England. Pop-rock singer. Daughter of singer Marty Wilde.		
5/30/87	**30**	7		You Keep Me Hangin' On	1¹	MCA 53024

DEBUT DATE	PEAK POS	WKS CHR	GOLD	ARTIST — Record Title	POP POS	Label & Number
				WILDER, Matthew		
				Born and raised in Manhattan; moved to Los Angeles in the late '70s. Singer/songwriter/keyboardist. Session singer for Rickie Lee Jones and Bette Midler.		
10/2/82	**32**	6		1 Work So Hard		Arista 0703
10/8/83	**4**	22		**2 Break My Stride**..	5	Private I 04113
★★12★★				**WILLIAMS, Andy**		
				Born Howard Andrew Williams on 12/3/28 in Wall Lake, Iowa. Formed quartet with his brothers and eventually moved to Los Angeles. With Bing Crosby on hit "Swingin' On A Star," 1944. With comedienne Kay Thompson in the mid-'40s. Went solo in 1952. On Steve Allen's *Tonight Show* from 1952-55. Own NBC-TV variety series from 1962-67, 1969-71. Appeared in the film *I'd Rather Be Rich* in 1964. Formerly married to singer/actress Claudine Longet. One of America's greatest pop-MOR singers.		
				1)*Can't Get Used To Losing You* 2)*(Where Do I Begin) Love Story* 3)*In The Arms Of Love* 4)*Happy Heart* 5)*More And More*		
11/6/61	**15**	5		1 Danny Boy/	64	
11/13/61	**20**	1		**2** Fly By Night	82	Columbia 42199
6/23/62	**9**	5		**3 Stranger On The Shore**	38	Columbia 42451
10/13/62	**15**	6		**4** Don't You Believe It..	39	Columbia 42523
3/9/63	**1**⁴	14		**5 Can't Get Used To Losing You/**	**2**⁴	
4/13/63	**9**	8		**6 Days Of Wine And Roses**	26	Columbia 42674
				movie title song		
6/29/63	**3**	10		**7 Hopeless**	13	Columbia 42784
1/25/64	**4**	13		**8 A Fool Never Learns**	13	Columbia 42950
4/18/64	**11**	9		**9** Wrong For Each Other	34	Columbia 43015
9/19/64	**3**	8		**10 On The Street Where You Live/**	28	
				from the Broadway musical *My Fair Lady*		
11/14/64	**12**	4		**11** Almost There	67	Columbia 43128
				from the film *I'd Rather Be Rich*		
11/28/64	**2**¹	11		**12 Dear Heart**	24	Columbia 43180
				movie title song		
4/3/65	**4**	7		**13 And Roses And Roses**	36	Columbia 43257
11/27/65	**18**	11		**14** Quiet Nights Of Quiet Stars	92	Columbia 43456
2/12/66	**18**	8	✓	**15** Bye Bye Blues/	127	
				#5 hit for Les Paul & Mary Ford in 1953		
3/5/66	**13**	8		**16** You're Gonna Hear From Me!		Columbia 43519
				from the film *Inside Daisy Clover*		
6/11/66	**17**	6		**17** How Can I Tell Her It's Over......................................	109	Columbia 43650
7/30/66	**1**²	17		**18 In The Arms Of Love**	49	Columbia 43737
4/1/67	**2**¹	13		**19 Music To Watch Girls By**	34	Columbia 44065
7/8/67	**2**⁴	14		**20 More And More**	88	Columbia 44202
10/28/67	**4**	16		**21 Holly**	113	Columbia 44325
5/25/68	**4**	15		**22 Sweet Memories**	75	Columbia 44527
10/26/68	**11**	14		**23** Battle Hymn Of The Republic	33	Columbia 44650
				with the St. Charles Borromeo Choir; recorded at St. Patrick's Cathedral on 6/8/68 as a eulogy to Senator Robert F. Kennedy		
4/5/69	**1**²	14		**24 Happy Heart**	22	Columbia 44818
8/9/69	**12**	7		**25** Live And Learn	119	Columbia 44929
11/1/69	**4**	8		**26 A Woman's Way**	109	Columbia 45003
2/28/70	**28**	3		**27** Can't Help Falling In Love	88	Columbia 45094
6/6/70	**2**²	10		**28 One Day Of Your Life**...	77	Columbia 45175
				written by Neil Sedaka		
10/24/70	**10**	7	✓	**29 Home Lovin' Man**		Columbia 45246
2/6/71	**1**⁴	15		**30 (Where Do I Begin) Love Story**	9	Columbia 45317
				from the film *Love Story*		
8/28/71	**29**	5		**31** A Song For You...	82	Columbia 45434
12/4/71	**29**	4		**32** Love Is All		Columbia 45494
				from the film *T.R. Baskin*		
1/29/72	**30**	4		**33** Music From Across The Way		Columbia 45531
				#84 Pop hit for James Last in 1972		
4/8/72	**7**	12		**34 Love Theme From "The Godfather"** (Speak Softly Love) .	34	Columbia 45579
				from the film *The Godfather*		
8/5/72	**26**	5		**35** MacArthur Park	102	Columbia 45647
				#2 Pop hit for Richard Harris in 1968		
11/4/72	**27**	5		**36** Home Lovin' Man..[R]		Columbia 45716
10/6/73	**23**	9		**37** Solitaire		Columbia 45936
				written by Neil Sedaka; #17 Pop hit for the Carpenters in 1975		

DEBUT DATE	PEAK POS	WKS CHR	G O L D	ARTIST — Record Title	POP POS	Label & Number
				WILLIAMS, Andy — Cont'd		
1/5/74	30	7		38 Remember		Columbia 45985
				ANDY WILLIAMS AND NOELLE (Andy's daughter) #53 Pop hit for Nilsson in 1973		
6/8/74	16	11		39 Love's Theme		Columbia 46049
				#1 Pop hit for Love Unlimited Orchestra in 1974		
9/21/74	29	9		40 Another Lonely Song		Columbia 10029
				#1 Country hit for Tammy Wynette in 1974		
1/11/75	24	7		41 Love Said Goodbye......................................		Columbia 10078
				love theme from the film *The Godfather Part II*		
4/12/75	20	6		42 Cry Softly		Columbia 10113
10/11/75	11	7		43 Sad Eyes..		Columbia 10208
				written by Neil Sedaka		
12/20/75	17	10		44 Tell It Like It Is	72	Columbia 10263
				WILLIAMS, Danny		
				Born on 1/7/42 in Port Elizabeth, South Africa. Moved to England in 1960.		
3/21/64	3	12		**White On White**..	9	United Art. 685
				WILLIAMS, Deniece		
				Born Deniece Chandler on 6/3/51 in Gary, Indiana. Soul vocalist/songwriter. Recorded for Toddlin' Town, early 1960s. Member of Wonderlove, Stevie Wonder's backup group, from 1972-75. Also a popular Inspirational artist.		
3/19/77	38	6		1 Free...	25	Columbia 10429
3/11/78	1¹	19	●	2 **Too Much, Too Little, Too Late** *	1¹	Columbia 10693
7/8/78	16	11		3 You're All I Need To Get By *	47	Columbia 10772
5/1/82	6	19		4 It's Gonna Take A Miracle	10	ARC 02812
3/24/84	14	13		5 Love Won't Let Me Wait *	106	Columbia 04379
				#5 Pop hit for Major Harris in 1975 *****JOHNNY MATHIS & DENIECE WILLIAMS**		
4/21/84	3	19	▲	6 **Let's Hear It For The Boy**..............................	1²	Columbia 04417
				from the film *Footloose*		
				WILLIAMS, Don		
				Born on 5/27/39 in Floydada, Texas. Country singer/songwriter/guitarist. Charted over 15 #1 country hits. Leader of the Pozo-Seco Singers. In films *W.W. & The Dixie Dancekings* and *Smokey & The Bandit 2*.		
10/4/80	8	16		1 **I Believe In You**	24	MCA 41304
3/14/81	39	7		2 Falling Again		MCA 51065
8/15/81	32	7		3 Miracles		MCA 51134
				WILLIAMS, John		
				Born on 2/8/32 in New York City. Noted composer/conductor of many top box-office film hits. Succeeded Arthur Fiedler as conductor of the Boston Pops in 1980. Winner of 15 Grammys. Williams' son, Joseph, became a member of Toto in 1986.		
8/30/75	22	7		1 Main Title (Theme From "Jaws") .... [I]	32	MCA 40439
7/23/77	4	14		2 **Star Wars (Main Title)**.................................. [I]	10	20th Century 2345
				performed by the London Symphony Orchestra		
1/7/78	13	15		3 Theme From "Close Encounters Of The Third Kind" ...... [I]	13	Arista 0300
				all of above from soundtracks composed by Williams		
				WILLIAMS, Mason		
				Born on 8/24/38 in Abilene, Texas. Folk guitarist/songwriter/author/photographer/TV comedy writer (*The Smothers Brothers Comedy Hour*, 1967-69; *Saturday Night Live*, 1980).		
5/25/68	1³	17		1 **Classical Gas** .... [I]	2²	Warner 7190
10/5/68	14	7		2 Baroque-A-Nova .... [I]	96	Warner 7235
12/14/68	13	10		3 Saturday Night At The World	99	Warner 7248
4/5/69	13	8		4 Greensleeves .... [I]	90	Warner 7272
				one of the oldest published songs (from the 16th century)		
7/19/69	33	3		5 A Gift Of Song	118	Warner 7301
7/18/70	31	2		6 Jose's Piece .... [I]		Warner 7402
				WILLIAMS, Paul		
				Born on 9/19/40 in Omaha. Singer/songwriter/actor. Wrote "We've Only Just Begun" and "Rainy Days & Mondays" with partner Roger Nichols, and wrote "Evergreen" with Barbra Streisand. In films *Planet Of The Apes*, *Smokey & The Bandit* and others.		
2/19/72	19	10		1 Waking Up Alone	60	A&M 1325
3/17/73	40	2		2 I Won't Last A Day Without You.........................	106	A&M 1409
				#11 Pop hit for the Carpenters in 1974		
11/24/73	18	13		3 Inspiration...	108	A&M 1479

DEBUT DATE	PEAK POS	WKS CHR	GOLD	ARTIST — Record Title		POP POS	Label & Number

WILLIAMS, Roger

★★102★★

Born Louis Weertz in 1925 in Omaha. Learned to play the piano by age three. Educated at Drake University, Idaho State University, and Juilliard School of Music. Took lessons from Lenny Tristano and Teddy Wilson. Win on the TV show *Arthur Godfrey's Talent Scouts* led to recording contract.

1)Born Free 2)More Than A Miracle 3)Love Me Forever

DEBUT DATE	PEAK POS	WKS CHR	GOLD	ARTIST — Record Title	POP POS	Label & Number
1/13/62	11	4		1 Maria .... [I]	48	Kapp 437
				from the Broadway musical *West Side Story*		
3/10/62	16	3		2 Amor .... [I]	88	Kapp 447
				3 versions hit the top 10 in 1944		
8/14/65	20	6		3 Summer Wind	109	Kapp 55
				ROGER WILLIAMS & The HARRY SIMEONE CHORALE		
				#25 Pop hit for Frank Sinatra in 1966		
10/9/65	10	8		4 Autumn Leaves - 1965 .... [R]	92	Kapp 707
				new version of Williams' #1 Pop hit in 1955 on Kapp 116		
4/30/66	5	19		5 Lara's Theme from "Dr. Zhivago" .... [I]	65	Kapp 738
				from the film *Dr. Zhivago*		
7/30/66	1⁶	24		6 Born Free	7	Kapp 767
				movie title song		
1/21/67	5	14		7 Sunrise, Sunset	84	Kapp 801
				from the Broadway musical *Fiddler On The Roof*		
5/6/67	3	15		8 Love Me Forever	60	Kapp 821
9/16/67	2⁴	19		9 More Than A Miracle	108	Kapp 843
				movie title song		
5/11/68	37	2		10 If You Go (Si Tu Partais)/	[I]	
7/13/68	5	13		11 The Impossible Dream .... [I]	55	Kapp 907
				from the Broadway musical *Man Of La Mancha*		
11/16/68	31	5		12 Only For Lovers .... [I]	119	Kapp 949
5/31/69	21	5		13 Galveston .... [I]	99	Kapp 2007
10/9/76	39	6	✓	14 Cast Your Fate To The Wind * .... [I]		MCA 40625
				#10 Pop hit for Sounds Orchestral in 1965		
1/29/77	32	5		15 Main Theme From "King Kong" * .... [I]		MCA 40669
				from the film *King Kong*;		
				*"MR. PIANO" ROGER WILLIAMS		

WILLIAMS, Terry ☉

5/24/80	30	10		Blame It On The Night		ia 504

WILLIAMS, Vanessa ☉

★★191★★

Born on 3/18/63 in Tarrytown, New York. In 1983, became the first black woman to win Miss America pageant; relinquished crown after *Penthouse* magazine scandal. Married Ramon Hervey (manager of Babyface) in February 1987. Began hosting *Soul of VH-1* on video music TV channel in 1991. Appeared in the film *Harley Davidson & The Marlboro Man* and TV mini-series *The Jacksons: An American Dream*.

DEBUT DATE	PEAK POS	WKS CHR	GOLD	ARTIST — Record Title	POP POS	Label & Number
1/21/89	2¹	25		1 Dreamin'	8	Wing 871078
6/17/89	10	15		2 Darlin' I	88	Wing 871936
1/25/92	1³	33	●	3 Save The Best For Last	1⁵	Wing 865136
5/23/92	2¹	23		4 Just For Tonight	26	Wing 865888
2/6/93	1³	34↑		5 Love Is	3	Giant 18630
				VANESSA WILLIAMS & BRIAN McKNIGHT		

WILLIAMS BROTHERS, The

Andrew and David Williams, the twin nephews of Andy Williams. Hit *Hot 100* in 1974 at age 14 as Andy & David Williams. Re-emerged in the 1980s as The Williams Brothers.

3/7/92	11	21		Can't Cry Hard Enough	42	Warner 19326

WILLIS, Andra ☉

10/10/70	40	2		Knock, Knock Who's There		Paramount 0048
				#92 Pop hit for Mary Hopkin in 1972		

WILLIS, Bruce

Born on 3/19/55 in Penns Grove, New Jersey. Played David Addison on TV's *Moonlighting*. Starred in the *Die Hard* films and others. Child's voice in the *Look Who's Talking* films. Married actress Demi Moore on 11/21/87.

2/7/87	22	9		1 Respect Yourself	5	Motown 1876
				#12 Pop hit for The Staple Singers in 1971		
6/13/87	20	10		2 Under The Boardwalk	59	Motown 1896
				#4 Pop hit for The Drifters in 1964		

WILL TO POWER

Florida-based trio formed and fronted by producer Bob Rosenberg with Dr. J. and Maria Mendez. Rosenberg is the son of singer Gloria Mann. By 1990, reduced to a duo of Rosenberg and Elin Michaels. Group name taken from the work of 19th-century German philosopher Frederich Nietzsche.

10/29/88	2²	20	●	1 Baby, I Love Your Way/Freebird Medley (Free Baby)	1¹	Epic 08034

DEBUT DATE	PEAK POS	WKS CHR	G O L D	ARTIST — Record Title	POP POS	Label & Number
				WILL TO POWER — Cont'd		
12/1/90	4	22		2 I'm Not In Love	7	Epic 73636
				WILSON, Al		
				Born on 6/19/39 in Meridian, Mississippi. Soul singer/drummer. Moved to San Bernadino, California in the late '50s. Member of The Rollers from 1960-62.		
11/17/73	3	18	●	1 Show And Tell	1[1]	Rocky Road 30073
3/30/74	43	4		2 Touch And Go	57	Rocky Road 30076
2/1/75	39	6		3 I Won't Last A Day Without You/Let Me Be The One	70	Rocky Road 30202
5/15/76	38	4		4 I've Got A Feeling (We'll Be Seeing Each Other Again)..	29	Playboy 6062
				WILSON, Ann		
				Born on 6/19/51 in San Diego. Lead singer of the rock group Heart.		
5/19/84	1[1]	22		1 Almost Paradise...Love Theme From Footloose.............	7	Columbia 04418
				MIKE RENO and ANN WILSON		
				from the film *Footloose*		
2/4/89	44	8		2 Surrender To Me	6	Capitol 44288
				ANN WILSON AND ROBIN ZANDER		
				from the film *Tequila Sunrise*; Robin is lead singer of Cheap Trick		
				WILSON, Carl		
				Born on 6/21/46 in Hawthorne, California. Guitarist of The Beach Boys. Married Dean Martin's daughter, Gina, on 11/8/87.		
6/27/81	20	11		1 Heaven.............	107	Caribou 02136
4/16/83	20	11		2 What You Do To Me	72	Caribou 03590
				WILSON, Danny — see DANNY		
				WILSON, Larry Jon ☉		
				Songwriter from Swainsboro, Georgia.		
6/12/76	47	3		Think I Feel A Hitchhike Coming On		Monument 8692
				WILSON, Nancy		
				Born on 2/20/37 in Chillicothe, Ohio and raised in Columbus, Ohio. Jazz stylist with Rusty Bryant's Carolyn Club Band in Columbus. First recorded for Dot in 1956. Moved to New York City in 1959.		
				1)(You Don't Know) How Glad I Am 2)I Wanna Be With You 3)Uptight (Everything's Alright)		
7/4/64	2[1]	7		1 (You Don't Know) How Glad I Am	11	Capitol 5198
10/3/64	9	4		2 I Wanna Be With You	57	Capitol 5254
				from the Broadway musical *Golden Boy*		
8/21/65	30	7		3 Where Does That Leave Me		Capitol 5455
10/23/65	33	7		4 I'll Only Miss Him When I Think Of Him.....................		Capitol 5515
				from the Broadway musical *Skyscraper*		
7/2/66	10	9		5 Uptight (Everything's Alright)/	84	
7/23/66	20	6		6 You've Got Your Troubles		Capitol 5673
				#7 Pop hit for The Fortunes in 1965		
4/13/68	28	13		7 Face It Girl, It's Over.....................	29	Capitol 2136
11/2/68	34	3		8 Peace Of Mind	55	Capitol 2283
12/21/68	31	8		9 In A Long White Room.....................	117	Capitol 2361
12/27/69	28	4		10 Can't Take My Eyes Off You	52	Capitol 2644
6/20/70	32	1	✓	11 This Girl Is A Woman Now.....................		Capitol 2831
				#9 Pop hit for Gary Puckett & The Union Gap in 1969		
				WILSON, Norro ☉		
				Born Norris D. Wilson on 4/4/38 in Scottsville, Kentucky. Outstanding songwriter. Credits include "A Very Special Love Song," "I Love My Friend" and "The Most Beautiful Girl" for Charlie Rich, "I'll See Him Through" for Tammy Wynette, "Baby, Baby (I Know You're A Lady)" for David Houston and "Soul Song" for Joe Stampley.		
11/30/68	24	7		Only You		Smash 2192
				#5 Pop hit for The Platters in 1955		
				WILSON, Robin ☉		
9/21/68	35	3		Where Are They Now?.....................		A&M 959
				WILSON, Shanice		
				Born on 5/14/73. Native of Pittsburgh. To Los Angeles at age seven. Began singing commercial jingles at age eight (appeared in a Kentucky Fried Chicken Commercial with Ella Fitzgerald).		
3/7/92	50	1		I Love Your Smile.....................	2[3]	Motown 2093
				SHANICE		

DEBUT DATE	PEAK POS	WKS CHR	GOLD	ARTIST — Record Title	POP POS	Label & Number
★★120★★				**WILSON PHILLIPS** Vocal/songwriting trio of sisters Carnie and Wendy Wilson, with Chynna Phillips. Carnie and Wendy's father is Brian Wilson (The Beach Boys). Chynna, the daughter of John and Michelle Phillips (The Mamas & The Papas), acted in the film *Caddyshack II*.		
				1)You're In Love 2)Hold On 3)Release Me		
3/24/90	1¹	27	●	1 Hold On	1¹	SBK 07322
6/30/90	1¹	30	●	2 Release Me	1²	SBK 07327
10/13/90	2¹	24		3 Impulsive	4	SBK 07337
2/9/91	1⁴	27		4 You're In Love	1¹	SBK 07343
6/8/91	4	18		5 The Dream Is Still Alive	12	SBK 07356
11/16/91	7	18		6 Daniel..		Polydor LP Cut
				#2 Pop hit for Elton John in 1973; from the album *Two Rooms - Celebrating The Songs Of Elton John & Bernie Taupin* on Polydor 845750		
5/9/92	4	22		7 You Won't See Me Cry.......................................	20	SBK 07385
8/8/92	12	14		8 Give It Up	30	SBK 50398
11/21/92	17	12		9 Flesh & Blood	119	SBK 50415
				WILTON PLACE STREET BAND Los Angeles studio project produced and arranged by Trevor Lawrence (resided on Wilton Place in L.A.).		
2/12/77	9	13		Disco Lucy (I Love Lucy Theme) ....[I] discofied theme from the TV series *I Love Lucy*	24	Island 078
				WINANS, BeBe & CeCe Younger brother and sister of the Detroit gospel-singing family, The Winans: Benjamin "BeBe" and Priscilla "CeCe." They are the seventh and eighth children in a 10-sibling family.		
9/12/87	24	7		I.O.U. Me		Capitol 44009
				WINCHESTER, Jesse Born on 5/17/44 in Shreveport, Louisiana. Pop singer/songwriter/guitarist. Moved to Canada in 1967 to avoid the draft; became a Canadian citizen in 1973.		
5/2/81	12	13		Say What	32	Bearsville 49711
				WINDING, Kai Born on 5/18/22 in Aarhus, Denmark; died on 5/6/83. Jazz trombonist. Moved to U.S. in 1934. With Benny Goodman and Stan Kenton in the mid-1940s.		
7/20/63	2⁴	13		More ....[I] theme from the film *Mondo Cane*	8	Verve 10295
				WING AND A PRAYER FIFE & DRUM CORPS., The Studio group from New York City; vocals by Linda November, Vivian Cherry, Arlene Martell and Helen Miles.		
11/29/75	6	14		Baby Face.. 4 versions hit the top 10 in 1926	14	Wing & Prayer 103
				WINGS — see McCARTNEY, Paul		
				WINSTONS, The Washington, D.C. soul septet: Richard Spencer (lead), Ray Maritano, Quincy Mattison, Phil Tolotta, Sonny Peckrol and G.C. Coleman. Toured as backup band for The Impressions.		
6/14/69	15	9	●	1 Color Him Father	7	Metromedia 117
9/27/69	19	6		2 Love Of The Common People	54	Metromedia 142
				WINTERHALTER, Hugo, and His Orchestra Born on 8/15/09 in Wilkes-Barre, Pennsylvania; died on 9/17/73 (cancer). Conductor/arranger for RCA Records from 1950-63.		
7/19/69	35	4		Theme From "Popi" ....[I] featuring Dick King on harmonica; from the film *Popi*		Musicor 1368
★★82★★				**WINWOOD, Steve** Born on 5/12/48 in Birmingham, England. Rock singer/keyboardist/guitarist. Lead singer of rock bands: Spencer Davis Group, Blind Faith and Traffic.		
				1)The Finer Things 2)Back In The High Life Again 3)Roll With It		
3/14/81	17	12		1 While You See A Chance	7	Island 49656
7/12/86	7	19		2 Higher Love..	1¹	Island 28710
3/7/87	1³	20		3 The Finer Things..	8	Island 28498
6/13/87	1³	21		4 Back In The High Life Again..............................	13	Island 28472
10/17/87	2³	22		5 Valerie..[R] remix of Winwood's 1982 Pop hit (POS 70) on Island 29879	9	Island 28231
3/5/88	7	17		6 Talking Back To The Night	57	Island 28122
6/11/88	1²	20		7 Roll With It	1⁴	Virgin 99326
8/27/88	2³	22		8 Don't You Know What The Night Can Do?.................. tune used in a Michelob TV commercial	6	Virgin 99290

DEBUT DATE	PEAK POS	WKS CHR	GOLD	ARTIST — Record Title	POP POS	Label & Number
				WINWOOD, Steve — Cont'd		
12/3/88	**1**[2]	21		9 **Holding On**	11	Virgin 99261
3/25/89	**22**	8		10 **Hearts On Fire**	53	Virgin 99234
11/3/90	**9**	17		11 **One And Only Man**	18	Virgin 98892
2/16/91	**40**	6		12 **I Will Be Here**		Virgin 98869
				WISNER, Jimmy, Sound ○		
				Jimmy was born on 12/8/31 in Philadelphia. Songwriter/producer. Began career as a pianist for Mel Torme.		
10/4/69	**40**	2		Manhattan Safari .... [I]		Columbia 44959
				WITHERS, Bill		
				Born on 7/4/38 in Slab Fork, West Virginia. Soul vocalist/guitarist/composer. Moved to California in 1967 and made demo records of his songs. First recorded for Sussex in 1970, produced by Booker T. Jones. Married to actress Denise Nicholas.		
				1)Just The Two Of Us 2)Ain't No Sunshine 3)Lean On Me		
8/14/71	**2**[1]	11	●	1 **Ain't No Sunshine**	3	Sussex 219
11/13/71	**16**	6		2 Grandma's Hands	42	Sussex 227
				above 2 produced by Booker T. Jones		
5/27/72	**4**	12	●	3 **Lean On Me**	**1**[3]	Sussex 235
9/9/72	**14**	10	●	4 **Use Me**	**2**[2]	Sussex 241
12/30/72	**33**	3		5 Let Us Love	47	Sussex 247
1/7/78	**25**	8		6 Lovely Day	30	Columbia 10627
2/14/81	**2**[2]	21		7 **Just The Two Of Us**	**2**[3]	Elektra 47103
				GROVER WASHINGTON, JR./BILL WITHERS		
8/25/84	**6**	14		8 **In The Name Of Love**	58	Polydor 881221
				RALPH MacDONALD with Bill Withers		
5/25/85	**40**	2		9 Oh Yeah!	106	Columbia 04841
★★22★★				**WONDER, Stevie**		
				Born Steveland Morris on 5/13/50 in Saginaw, Michigan. Singer/songwriter/multi-instrumentalist/producer. Blind since birth. Signed to Motown in 1960, did backup work. First recorded in 1962, renamed "Little Stevie Wonder" by Berry Gordy, Jr. Married to Syreeta Wright from 1970-72. Near-fatal auto accident on 8/16/73. Winner of 17 Grammy Awards. In the films *Bikini Beach* and *Muscle Beach Party*. Inducted into the Rock and Roll Hall of Fame in 1989.		
				1)Ebony And Ivory 2)Send One Your Love 3)I Just Called To Say I Love You 4)Part-Time Lover		
				5)That's What Friends Are For		
12/17/66	**29**	4		1 A Place In The Sun	9	Tampla 54139
10/5/68	**11**	8		2 Alfie .... [I]	66	Gordy 7076
				EIVETS REDNOW (Stevie Wonder spelled backwards)		
6/14/69	**3**	12		3 **My Cherie Amour**	4	Tamla 54180
11/29/69	**10**	9		4 **Yester-Me, Yester-You, Yesterday**	7	Tamla 54188
3/7/70	**31**	2		5 Never Had A Dream Come True	26	Tamla 54191
9/4/71	**10**	10		6 **If You Really Love Me**	8	Tamla 54208
1/27/73	**38**	3		7 Superstition	**1**[1]	Tamla 54226
3/24/73	**1**[2]	14		8 **You Are The Sunshine Of My Life**	**1**[1]	Tamla 54232
9/1/73	**41**	8		9 Higher Ground	4	Tamla 54235
4/20/74	**9**	11		10 **Don't You Worry 'Bout A Thing**	16	Tamla 54245
1/8/77	**23**	3		11 **I Wish**	**1**[1]	Tamla 54274
1/8/77	**23**	5		12 Isn't She Lovely		Tamla LP Cut
				from the album *Songs In The Key Of Life* on Tamla 340		
4/23/77	**3**	14		13 **Sir Duke**	**1**[3]	Tamla 54281
				a tribute to Duke Ellington		
9/17/77	**29**	7		14 Another Star	32	Tamla 54286
11/5/77	**24**	11		15 As	36	Tamla 54291
11/10/79	**1**[4]	16		16 **Send One Your Love**	4	Tamla 54303
3/22/80	**43**	4		17 Outside My Window	52	Tamla 54308
1/24/81	**20**	9		18 I Ain't Gonna Stand For It	11	Tamla 54320
4/25/81	**33**	6		19 Lately	64	Tamla 54323
				#4 Pop hit for Jodeci in 1993		
2/13/82	**10**	17		20 **That Girl**	4	Tamla 1602
4/10/82	**1**[5]	22	●	21 **Ebony And Ivory**	**1**[7]	Columbia 02860
				PAUL McCARTNEY with Stevie Wonder		
6/12/82	**25**	13		22 Do I Do	13	Tamla 1612
9/11/82	**21**	11		23 Ribbon In The Sky	54	Tamla 1639
11/13/82	**31**	9		24 Used To Be	46	Motown 1650
				CHARLENE & STEVIE WONDER		
8/18/84	**1**[3]	22	●	25 **I Just Called To Say I Love You**	**1**[3]	Motown 1745

261

DEBUT DATE	PEAK POS	WKS CHR	GOLD	ARTIST — Record Title	POP POS	Label & Number
				WONDER, Stevie — Cont'd		
12/1/84	**10**	18		**26 Love Light In Flight**	17	Motown 1769
				above 2 from the film The Woman In Red		
9/7/85	**1**[3]	20		**27 Part-Time Lover**	**1**[1]	Tamla 1808
11/9/85	**1**[2]	22	●	**28 That's What Friends Are For**	**1**[4]	Arista 9422
				DIONNE AND FRIENDS: Elton John, Gladys Knight and Stevie Wonder		
11/30/85	**1**[1]	16		**29 Go Home**	10	Tamla 1817
3/1/86	**1**[2]	15		**30 Overjoyed**	24	Tamla 1832
1/23/88	**16**	12		**31 You Will Know**	77	Motown 1919
5/14/88	**14**	4		**32 My Love**	80	Columbia 07781
				JULIO IGLESIAS Featuring STEVIE WONDER		
11/10/90	**44**	3		**33 Keep Our Love Alive**		Motown 1990
				WOOD, Lauren		
				Pop singer/songwriter/keyboardist; originally from Pittsburgh.		
10/20/79	**5**	8		**1 Please Don't Leave**	24	Warner 49043
				Michael McDonald (harmony vocal)		
11/8/80	**37**	11		**2 Is This The Way Of Love**		20th Century 2470
				CHRIS MONTAN with Lauren Wood		
				WOODS, Stevie		
				R&B vocalist based in Los Angeles. Originally from Columbus, Ohio. Son of jazz great Rusty Bryant.		
9/26/81	**14**	18		**1 Steal The Night**	25	Cotillion 46016
1/30/82	**15**	13		**2 Just Can't Win 'Em All**	38	Cotillion 46030
5/8/82	**23**	10		**3 Fly Away**	84	Cotillion 47006
				WORTH, Marion		
				Born Mary Ann Ward in Birmingham, Alabama. Country singer. Worked on Dallas radio shows in 1947.		
1/5/63	**10**	6		**Shake Me I Rattle (Squeeze Me I Cry)**	42	Columbia 42640
				WRIGHT, Betty — see HUGH, Grayson		
				WRIGHT, Gary		
				Born on 4/26/43 in Creskill, New Jersey. Pop-rock singer/songwriter/keyboardist. Appeared in *Captain Video* TV series at age seven. In the Broadway play *Fanny*. Co-leader of the rock group Spooky Tooth.		
2/7/76	**14**	13	●	**1 Dream Weaver**	**2**[3]	Warner 8167
8/1/81	**32**	9		**2 Really Wanna Know You**	16	Warner 49769
				WYMAN, Karen ☺		
				Born in 1953.		
11/27/71	**40**	2		**Beautiful**		Columbia 45484
				WYNETTE, Tammy		
				Born Virginia Wynette Pugh on 5/5/42 in Itawamba County, Mississippi. With over 15 #1 country hits, dubbed "The First Lady of Country Music." Discovered by producer Billy Sherrill. Married to country star George Jones from 1969-75.		
12/14/68	**11**	11		**1 Stand By Your Man**	19	Epic 10398
9/27/69	**18**	6		**2 The Ways To Love A Man**	81	Epic 10512
6/5/76	**41**	4		**3 'Til I Can Make It On My Own**	84	Epic 50196
9/18/76	**28**	7		**4 You And Me**	101	Epic 50264
				all of above were #1 Country hits		
				WYNONNA — see JUDD, Wynonna		

Y

DEBUT DATE	PEAK POS	WKS CHR	GOLD	ARTIST — Record Title	POP POS	Label & Number
				YANNI ☺		
				Born Yiannis Chryssolmalis in Kalamata, Greece. New Age keyboardist/composer. National champion swimmer of Greece at age 14. Moved to Minneapolis in 1973 to earn psychology degree.		
4/20/91	**38**	7		**Swept Away** ....[I]		Private Music 2084
				YARBROUGH, Glenn		
				Born on 1/12/30 in Milwaukee. Lead singer of The Limeliters (1959-63). Folk singer.		
3/13/65	**2**[3]	14		**1 Baby The Rain Must Fall**	12	RCA 8498
				movie title song		
7/10/65	**9**	9		**2 It's Gonna Be Fine**	54	RCA 8619

DEBUT DATE	PEAK POS	WKS CHR	GOLD	ARTIST — Record Title	POP POS	Label & Number
				YARBROUGH, Glenn — Cont'd		
4/18/70	**35**	4		3 Goodbye Girl		Warner 7382
				written by Laura Nyro		
				YARROW, Peter		
				Born on 5/31/38 in New York City. Folk singer/songwriter/guitarist. Peter of Peter, Paul & Mary. Wrote Mary MacGregor's "Torn Between Two Lovers."		
5/20/72	**25**	4		Weave Me The Sunshine	110	Warner 7587
				YAZ		
				British electronic pop duo: Genevieve Alison Moyet (vocals) and Vince Clarke (formerly of Depeche Mode; keyboards, synthesizers). Duo formerly named Yazoo. Clarke later formed Erasure, and Moyet went solo.		
3/26/83	**38**	4		Only You..	67	Sire 29844
				YOST, Dennis — see CLASSICS IV		
				YOUNG, Barry		
				Pop singer patterned after Dean Martin.		
11/20/65	**3**	12		One Has My Name (The Other Has My Heart)..............	13	Dot 16756
				YOUNG, Faron		
				Born on 2/25/32 in Shreveport, Louisiana. Country singer/guitarist. Charted over 30 top 10 country hits. In films *The Young Sheriff*, *Daniel Boone* and *Hidden Guns*. Founder and one-time publisher of the *Music City News* magazine in Nashville.		
7/17/61	**13**	1		Hello Walls	12	Capitol 4533
				written by Willie Nelson; flip side "Congratulations" made the Country charts (POS 28)		
				YOUNG, John Paul		
				Born in Glasgow, Scotland in 1953 and raised in Australia. Pop singer/songwriter/pianist.		
7/29/78	**1**²	21		1 Love Is In The Air...	7	Scotti Br. 402
12/23/78	**28**	9		2 Lost In Your Love	55	Scotti Br. 405
				YOUNG, Neil		
				Born on 11/12/45 in Toronto. Rock singer/songwriter/guitarist. Formed rock band the Mynah Birds, featuring lead singer Rick James, early '60s. Moved to Los Angeles in 1966 and formed Buffalo Springfield. Went solo in 1969 with backing band Crazy Horse. Joined with Crosby, Stills & Nash, 1970-71. Appeared in the 1987 film *Made In Heaven*. Reunited with Crosby, Stills & Nash in 1988 to record the *American Dream* album.		
3/4/72	**8**	10	●	1 Heart Of Gold	1¹	Reprise 1065
				Linda Ronstadt and James Taylor (backing vocals)		
2/17/79	**43**	5		2 Four Strong Winds...	61	Reprise 1396
				Nicolette Larson (harmony vocal)		
				YOUNG, Paul		
				Born on 1/17/56 in Bedfordshire, England. Pop-rock vocalist/guitarist.		
4/7/84	**40**	5		1 Come Back And Stay	22	Columbia 04313
6/1/85	**1**²	22	●	2 Everytime You Go Away	1¹	Columbia 04867
				written by Daryl Hall		
7/7/90	**1**³	29		3 Oh Girl..	8	Columbia 73377
				#1 pop hit for The Chi-Lites in 1972		
9/28/91	**23**	12		4 Senza Una Donna (Without A Woman)		London LP Cut
				ZUCCHERO with Paul Young		
				from the album *Zucchero* on London 849063		
1/18/92	**1**²	24		5 What Becomes Of The Brokenhearted............................	22	MCA 54331
				#7 Pop hit for Jimmy Ruffin in 1966; from the film *Fried Green Tomatoes*		
				YOUNGBLOODS, The		
				Folk-rock group led by vocalist Jesse Colin Young (born Perry Miller on 11/11/44). Band formed in New York City in late 1965, moved to California in late 1967.		
9/13/69	**37**	3	●	Get Together ....[R]	5	RCA 9752
				originally made the *Hot 100* on 9/2/67 (POS 62) on RCA 9264		
				YOUNG-HOLT UNLIMITED		
				Chicago instrumental soul group: Eldee Young (bass), Isaac "Red" Holt (drums; both of the Ramsey Lewis Trio) and Don Walker (piano). Walker left by 1968.		
2/4/67	**35**	2		1 Wack Wack ....[I]	40	Brunswick 55305
				THE YOUNG HOLT TRIO		
11/23/68	**2**²	15	●	2 Soulful Strut ....[I]	3	Brunswick 55391
8/30/69	**32**	5		3 Straight Ahead ....[I]	110	Brunswick 55417
9/12/70	**18**	6		4 Mellow Dreaming ....[I]	106	Cotillion 44092

DEBUT DATE	PEAK POS	WKS CHR	GOLD	ARTIST — Record Title	POP POS	Label & Number
				YURO, Timi		
				Born Rosemarie Timothy Aurro Yuro on 8/4/40 in Chicago. Moved to Los Angeles in 1952. First recorded for Liberty in 1959. Lost voice in 1980 and underwent three throat operations.		
7/24/61	**2**[1]	12		1 **Hurt/**	4	
10/16/61	**19**	1		2 I Apologize	72	Liberty 55343
				#3 hit for Bing Crosby in 1931		
11/13/61	**9**	5		3 **Smile**	42	Liberty 55375
				#10 hit for Nat King Cole in 1954		
2/17/62	**15**	3		4 Let Me Call You Sweetheart....................	66	Liberty 55410
				#1 hit for The Peerless Quartet in 1911		
8/10/63	**8**	8		5 **Make The World Go Away**	24	Liberty 55587
12/10/66	**37**	4		6 Turn The World Around The Other Way		Mercury 72628

Z

ZAGER & EVANS

Folk-rock duo from Lincoln, Nebraska: Denny Zager and Rick Evans (both sing and play guitar).

7/12/69	**1**[2]	10	●	**In The Year 2525 (Exordium & Terminus)**	**1**[6]	RCA 0174
				released regionally in 1968 on Truth 8082		

ZANDER, Robin — see WILSON, Ann

ZENTNER, Si

Born on 6/13/17 in New York City. Jazz trombone player/bandleader. Played in the 1940s for Jimmy Dorsey, Harry James and Les Brown.

11/20/61	**10**	7		**Up A Lazy River**..[I]	43	Liberty 55374
				#19 hit for Hoagy Carmichael in 1932		

ZUCCHERO ✪

Zucchero "Sugar" Fornaciari — Italian male rock singer.

9/28/91	**23**	12		Senza Una Donna (Without A Woman)................................		London LP Cut
				ZUCCHERO with Paul Young		
				from the album *Zucchero* on London 849063		

TOP 200 ARTISTS

The following section includes a photo display of the *Top 100 Artists*, in rank order, from 1961-1993 followed by a listing of the artists that ranked from #101-200. The photos shown are reproductions of picture sleeves released by these artists. In a few cases, a 7" picture sleeve does not exist for an artist; and, therefore, an album cover photo is used.

Below each name is an accumulated point total. The point system used to create this total is explained on the next page.

POINT SYSTEM

Points are awarded according to the following formula:

1. Each artist's charted singles are given points based on their highest charted position.

$$\#1 = 50 \text{ points for its first week at \#1, plus 5 points for each additional week at \#1}$$
$$\#2 = 45 \text{ points for its first week at \#2, plus 3 points for each additional week at \#2}$$
$$\#3 = 40 \text{ points for its first week at \#3, plus 3 points for each additional week at \#3}$$
$$\#4\text{-}5 = 35 \text{ points}$$
$$\#6\text{-}10 = 30 \text{ points}$$
$$\#11\text{-}20 = 25 \text{ points}$$
$$\#21\text{-}30 = 20 \text{ points}$$
$$\#31\text{-}40 = 15 \text{ points}$$
$$\#41\text{-}50 = 10 \text{ points}$$

2. Total weeks charted are added in.

In the case of a tie, the artist listed first is determined by the following tie-breaker rules:

1) Most charted singles
2) Most Top 40 singles
3) Most Top 10 singles

When two artists combine for a hit record, such as Michael Jackson and Paul McCartney, the full point value is given to both artists. A duo, such as Simon & Garfunkel, Hall & Oates, and Loggins & Messina are considered regular recording teams, and their points are not shared by either artist individually.

ROYAL COURT OF *ADULT CONTEMPORARY* ARTISTS

1. Barbra Streisand
2,637

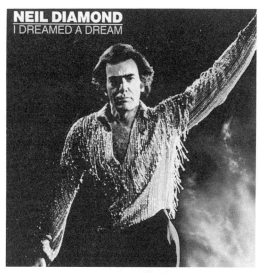

2. Neil Diamond
2,623

3. Elton John
2,350

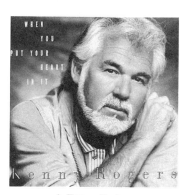

4. Kenny Rogers
2,218

5. Elvis Presley
2,045

6. Dionne Warwick
2,028

7. Barry Manilow
1,941

8. Frank Sinatra
1,904

9. Herb Alpert/Tijuana Brass
1,874

10. Anne Murray
1,820

11. Carpenters
1,802

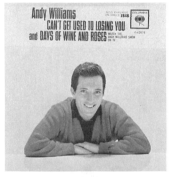

12. Andy Williams
1,765

13. Bobby Vinton
1,741

14. Olivia Newton-John
1,700

15. Glen Campbell
1,667

16. Chicago
1,627

17. Al Martino
1,613

18. Billy Joel
1,612

19. John Denver
1,509

20. Johnny Mathis
1,491

21. Linda Ronstadt
1,408

22. Stevie Wonder
1,393

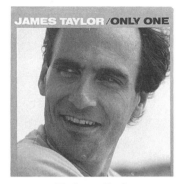

23. James Taylor
1,358

24. Paul McCartney/Wings
1,321

25. Lionel Richie
1,282

26. Engelbert Humperdinck
1,255

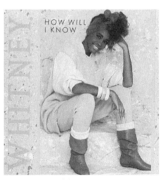

27. Whitney Houston
1,242

28. Dean Martin
1,201

29. Diana Ross
1,181

**30. Gloria Estefan/Miami
Sound Machine**
1,173

31. Jack Jones
1,150

32. Carly Simon
1,147

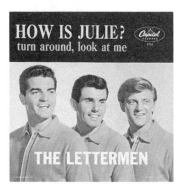

33. The Lettermen
1,146

34. Helen Reddy
1,131

35. Tom Jones
1,114

36. Ray Charles
1,091

37. Phil Collins
1,086

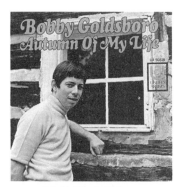

38. Bobby Goldsboro
1,059

39. Sergio Mendes/Brasil '66
1,039

40. Michael Bolton
1,039

41. B.J. Thomas
1,027

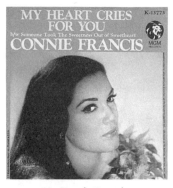

42. Connie Francis
1,020

43. Roberta Flack
1,009

44. Perry Como
1,006

45. Michael Jackson

997

46. George Michael/Wham!

997

47. Petula Clark

964

48. Rod Stewart

942

49. Cher

941

50. The 5th Dimension

940

51. Daryl Hall & John Oates

915

52. Bee Gees

914

53. Tony Bennett

913

54. Dan Fogelberg

900

55. Henry Mancini

890

56. Steve Lawrence

886

57. Madonna
881

58. Fleetwood Mac
862

59. Dolly Parton
850

60. Tony Orlando & Dawn
847

61. Brenda Lee
839

62. Paul Simon
831

63. Paul Anka
823

64. Air Supply
822

65. America
802

66. Ronnie Milsap
796

67. Crystal Gayle
793

68. Carole King
793

69. Bette Midler
781

70. Jerry Vale
772

71. James Ingram
764

72. Eddie Rabbitt
729

73. Wayne Newton
727

74. Peabo Bryson
718

75. Melissa Manchester
714

76. Eydie Gorme
708

77. Genesis
705

78. Richard Marx
702

79. Abba
699

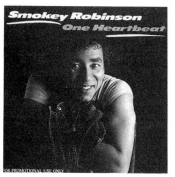

80. Smokey Robinson
697

81. Rita Coolidge
695

82. Steve Winwood
687

83. Brook Benton
685

84. Eddy Arnold
683

85. Natalie Cole
674

86. Amy Grant
671

87. Lobo
668

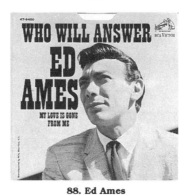

88. Ed Ames
666

89. Peter Cetera
661

90. Captain & Tennille
657

91. Charlie Rich
640

92. Bread
638

93. Jennifer Warnes
637

94. Art Garfunkel
637

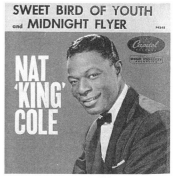

95. Nat "King" Cole
632

96. Peter, Paul & Mary
627

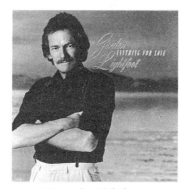

97. Gordon Lightfoot
616

98. Patti Page
611

99. Kenny G
610

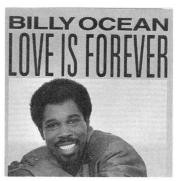

100. Billy Ocean
609

TOP 200 ARTISTS RANKING (#101-#200)

Rank		Points
101.	Kenny Loggins	608
102.	Roger Williams	607
103.	The Vogues	599
104.	Bert Kaempfert And His Orchestra	594
105.	Ray Conniff	583
106.	Roger Miller	580
107.	Mac Davis	579
108.	Gladys Knight & The Pips	579
109.	Vikki Carr	578
110.	Neil Sedaka	577
111.	Huey Lewis & the News	573
112.	Mariah Carey	573
113.	Al Hirt	568
114.	Seals & Crofts	564
115.	Pointer Sisters	558
116.	Christopher Cross	557
117.	Willie Nelson	555
118.	Sheena Easton	555
119.	Celine Dion	554
120.	Wilson Phillips	552
121.	Eagles	545
122.	England Dan & John Ford Coley	545
123.	Sammy Davis, Jr.	539
124.	Commodores	536
125.	George Benson	527
126.	Aretha Franklin	523
127.	Glenn Frey	523
128.	Bruce Hornsby & The Range	516
129.	Trini Lopez	514
130.	Don McLean	514
131.	DeBarge/El DeBarge	512
132.	Vic Dana	511
133.	Frankie Laine	506
134.	The Beach Boys	501
135.	Don Henley	496
136.	Peggy Lee	494
137.	Anita Baker	494
138.	Luther Vandross	493
139.	Kim Carnes	492
140.	Juice Newton	488
141.	Al Jarreau	482
142.	Donna Summer	480
143.	Paul Davis	475
144.	Michael McDonald	468
145.	Aaron Neville	465
146.	Little River Band	464
147.	Eric Carmen	462
148.	Robert Goulet	461
149.	Rick Astley	452
150.	Dusty Springfield	450

Rank		Points
151.	Dan Hill	450
152.	Ray Stevens	448
153.	George Harrison	446
154.	Jimmy Buffett	442
155.	Jimmy Dean	440
156.	Poco	439
157.	Donny Osmond	436
158.	Stephen Bishop	435
159.	Nancy Sinatra	433
160.	Toto	432
161.	Frankie Valli	431
162.	Maureen McGovern	430
163.	Simon & Garfunkel	429
164.	Sade	428
165.	Laura Branigan	426
166.	Bonnie Raitt	426
167.	Margaret Whiting	425
168.	Bob Seger/Silver Bullet Band	422
169.	The Bachelors	421
170.	Jim Croce	421
171.	Cliff Richard	419
172.	Jefferson Starship	417
173.	Dr. Hook	416
174.	Rick Nelson	410
175.	Gilbert O'Sullivan	410
176.	Alabama	408
177.	Andy Gibb	408
178.	The Ray Charles Singers	402
179.	Taylor Dayne	401
180.	Cat Stevens	400
181.	Simply Red	397
182.	Kool & The Gang	392
183.	Judy Collins	388
184.	Jeffrey Osborne	387
185.	George Fischoff	386
186.	The Stylistics	381
187.	Tina Turner	381
188.	Lou Rawls	379
189.	The Sandpipers	377
190.	Spinners	377
191.	Vanessa Williams	370
192.	Johnny Cash	367
193.	Bobby Sherman	366
194.	Crosby, Stills & Nash (& Young)	362
195.	The New Seekers	358
196.	Three Dog Night	356
197.	Johnny Tillotson	355
198.	Ronnie Dove	353
199.	David Gates	353
200.	Roxette	352

A-Z — TOP 200 ARTISTS

A-Z — TOP 200 ARTISTS (cont'd.)

SONG TITLE SECTION

Lists, alphabetically, all titles in the artist section. The artist's name is listed next to each title along with the highest position attained and the year the song debuted on the chart. Some titles show the letter F as a position, indicating that the title was listed as a flip side and did not chart on its own.

A song with more than one charted version is listed once, with the artists' names listed below in chronological order. Many songs that have the same title, but are different tunes, are listed separately, with the most popular title listed first. This will make it easy to determine which songs are the same composition, the number of charted versions of a particular song, and which of these were the most popular.

Cross references have been used throughout to aid in finding a title.

Please keep the following in mind when searching for titles:

Titles beginning with a contraction follow titles that begin with a similar non-contracted word. (Can't follows Can.)

Titles such as "SOS," "I.O.U.," and "P.T. 109" will be found at the beginning of their respective letters; however, titles such as "T-R-O-U-B-L-E" and "R.O.C.K. In The U.S.A.," which are spellings of words, are listed with their regular spellings.

Two-word titles which have the <u>exact</u> same spelling as one-word titles are listed together alphabetically. ("Angel Eyes" is listed directly before "Angeleyes.")

Titles which are <u>identical</u>, except for an apostrophized word in one of the titles, are shown together. ("Lovin' You" appears immediately above "Loving You.")

A

6/66 **"A" Team** *SSgt Barry Sadler*
22/69 **Abergavenny** *Shannon*
4/63 **Abilene** *George Hamilton IV*
19/62 **Above The Stars** *Mr. Acker Bilk*
28/82 **Abracadabra** *Steve Miller Band*
8/68 **Abraham, Martin And John**
    Dion
23/92 **Achy Breaky Heart**
    Billy Ray Cyrus
16/89 **Across The Miles** *Survivor*
8/90 **Across The River**
    Bruce Hornsby & The Range
9/90 **Adios** *Linda Ronstadt*
24/76 **Adios** *Santa Fe*
    Admiral Halsey ..see: Uncle
    Albert
24/90 **Advice For The Young At**
    Heart *Tears For Fears*
5/82 **Africa** *Toto*
40/76 **African Symphony**
    Henry Mancini
10/62 **Afrikaan Beat** *Bert Kaempfert*
1/89 **After All** *Cher & Peter Cetera*
6/84 **After All** *Al Jarreau*
21/65 **After Loving You** *Della Reese*
26/72 **After Midnight** *J.J. Cale*
20/70 **After The Feeling Is Gone** *Lulu*
36/82 **After The Glitter Fades**
    Stevie Nicks
11/74 **After The Goldrush** *Prelude*
3/79 **After The Love Has Gone**
    Earth, Wind & Fire
1/76 **After The Lovin'**
    Engelbert Humperdinck
10/80 **After You** *Dionne Warwick*
5/76 **Afternoon Delight**
    Starland Vocal Band
19/67 **Afterthoughts** *Jack Jones*
46/92 **Again Tonight**
    John Mellencamp
2/84 **Against All Odds (Take A Look**
    At Me Now) *Phil Collins*
8/80 **Against The Wind** *Bob Seger*
6/70 **Ain't No Mountain High**
    Enough *Diana Ross*
    Ain't No Sunshine
2/71   *Bill Withers*
24/72   *Steve Lawrence (medley)*
1/75 **Ain't No Way To Treat A Lady**
    Helen Reddy
14/73 **Ain't No Woman (Like The**
    One I've Got) *Four Tops*
    Ain't Nothing Like The Real
    Thing
17/76   *Donny & Marie Osmond*
21/82   *Chris Christian (medley)*
16/89 **Ain't Too Proud To Beg**
    Rick Astley
    Air That I Breathe
3/74   *Hollies*
42/78   *Mary Travers*
2/70 **Airport Love Theme (Gwen**
    And Vern) *Vincent Bell*
39/70 **Airport Song** *Magna Carta*
    Al Di La'
3/62   *Emilio Pericoli*
4/64   *Ray Charles Singers*
13/65 **Al's Place** *Al Hirt*

    (Aladdin's Theme) ..see:
    Whole New World
    Alfie
9/66   *Joanie Sommers*
29/66   *Carmen McRae*
11/68   *Eivets Rednow (Stevie Wonder)*
5/84 **Alibis** *Sergio Mendes*
34/81 **Alice Doesn't Love Here**
    Anymore *Bobby Goldsboro*
16/81 **Alien** *Atlanta Rhythm Section*
30/79 **Alison** *Linda Ronstadt*
20/72 **Alive** *Bee Gees*
39/78 **Alive Again** *Chicago*
5/66 **All** *James Darren*
1/62 **All Alone Am I** *Brenda Lee*
45/80 **All Around** *America*
7/90 **All Around The World**
    Lisa Stansfield
17/92 **All At Once** *Bonnie Raitt*
37/84 **All Behind Us Now** *Patti Austin*
6/76 **All By Myself** *Eric Carmen*
12/71 **All Day Music** *War*
15/88 **All I Ask Of You**
    Barbra Streisand
    All I Ever Need Is You
1/71   *Sonny & Cher*
38/79   *Kenny Rogers with Dottie West*
12/91 **All I Have**
    Beth Nielsen Chapman
    All I Have To Do Is Dream
6/63   *Richard Chamberlain*
4/70   *Bobbie Gentry & Glen*
        Campbell
30/75   *Nitty Gritty Dirt Band*
25/81   *Andy Gibb & Victoria Principal*
1/73 **All I Know** *Garfunkel*
36/87 **All I Know Is The Way I Feel**
    Pointer Sisters
1/84 **All I Need** *Jack Wagner*
41/81 **All I Need** *Dan Hartman*
7/86 **All I Need Is A Miracle**
    Mike + The Mechanics
32/67 **All I Need Is You** *Brothers Four*
39/83 **All I Need To Know**
    Bette Midler
33/66 **All I See Is You**
    Dusty Springfield
8/78 **All I See Is Your Face** *Dan Hill*
40/75 **All I Wanna Do** *Su Shifrin*
6/90 **All I Wanna Do Is Make Love**
    To You *Heart*
14/92 **All I Want**
    Toad The Wet Sprocket
34/89 **All I Want Is Forever** *James*
    "J.T." Taylor & Regina Belle
7/87 **All I Want Is You** *Carly Simon*
14/86 **All I Wanted** *Kansas*
10/74 **All In Love Is Fair**
    Barbra Streisand
19/89 **All Is Lost** *Southern Pacific*
18/71 **All Kinds Of People**
    Burt Bacharach
1/90 **All My Life**
    Linda Ronstadt/Aaron Neville
2/83 **All My Life** *Kenny Rogers*
48/79 **All My Life** *America*
12/68 **All My Love's Laughter**
    Ed Ames
6/71 **All My Trials** *Ray Stevens*
1/83 **All Night Long (All Night)**
    Lionel Richie

3/65 **(All Of A Sudden) My Heart**
    Sings *Mel Carter*
2/84 **All Of You**
    Julio Iglesias & Diana Ross
40/89 **All Or Nothing At All**
    Al Jarreau
37/75 **All Our Dreams Are Coming**
    True *Gene Page*
40/82 **All Our Tomorrows**
    Eddie Schwartz
5/80 **All Out Of Love** *Air Supply*
33/75 **All Over Me** *Charlie Rich*
17/63 **All Over The World**
    Nat "King" Cole
46/80 **All Over The World**
    Electric Light Orchestra
3/83 **All Right** *Christopher Cross*
15/92 **All Shook Up** *Billy Joel*
35/77 **All Strung Out On You**
    John Travolta
9/66 **All That I Am** *Elvis Presley*
26/77 **All That Keeps Me Going**
    Jim Weatherly
34/68 **All The Brave Young Faces Of**
    The Night *Tommy Leonetti*
16/83 **All The Love In The World**
    Dionne Warwick
    (also see: If You Add)
1/90 **All The Man That I Need**
    Whitney Houston
19/83 **All The Right Moves** *Jennifer*
    Warnes/Chris Thompson
    All The Time
19/67   *Jimmy Roselli*
23/67   *Patti Page*
26/68   *Wayne Newton*
41/79 **All The Time In The World**
    Dr. Hook
42/93 **All These Years** *Sawyer Brown*
6/79 **All Things Are Possible**
    Dan Peek
34/89 **All This I Should Have Known**
    Breathe
1/83 **All This Love** *DeBarge*
9/91 **All This Time** *Sting*
10/88 **All This Time** *Tiffany*
28/83 **All Those Lies** *Glenn Frey*
1/81 **All Those Years Ago**
    George Harrison
4/84 **All Through The Night**
    Cyndi Lauper
1/83 **All Time High** *Rita Coolidge*
21/92 **All Woman** *Lisa Stansfield*
4/77 **All You Get From Love Is A**
    Love Song *Carpenters*
19/83 **Allentown** *Billy Joel*
26/83 **Allergies** *Paul Simon*
2/62 **Alley Cat** *Bent Fabric*
30/79 **Almost Gone** *Barry Mann*
4/78 **Almost Like Being In Love**
    Michael Johnson
4/83 **Almost Over You**
    Sheena Easton
1/84 **Almost Paradise...Love Theme**
    From Footloose
    Mike Reno & Ann Wilson
20/66 **Almost Persuaded** *Patti Page*
12/64 **Almost There** *Andy Williams*
45/93 **Almost Unreal** *Roxette*
2/87 **Alone** *Heart*
1/72 **Alone Again (Naturally)**
    Gilbert O'Sullivan

33/70 **As Far As I'm Concerned**
  Bobby Russell
4/61 **As If I Didn't Know**
  Adam Wade
19/63 **As Long As She Needs Me**
  Sammy Davis, Jr.
7/88 **As Long As We Got Each**
  Other *B.J. Thomas &*
  Dusty Springfield
29/79 **As Long As We Keep Believing**
  Paul Anka
1/88 **As Long As You Follow**
  Fleetwood Mac
45/83 **As My Love For You**
  Perry Como
10/66 **As Tears Go By** *Rolling Stones*
  As Time Goes By
35/73 *Nilsson*
28/76 *Tony Bennett*
5/63 **As Usual** *Brenda Lee*
21/87 **As We Lay** *Shirley Murdock*
28/66 **Ashamed** *Jerry Vale*
46/80 **Ashes By Now** *Rodney Crowell*
7/73 **Ashes To Ashes** *5th Dimension*
4/61 **Astronaut, The** *Jose Jimenez*
39/85 **At Last You're Mine**
  Cheryl Lynn
1/75 **At Seventeen** *Janis Ian*
  (At The Copa) ..see:
  Copacabana
1/86 **At This Moment**
  Billy Vera & The Beaters
11/81 **Atlanta Lady (Something**
  About Your Love)
  Marty Balin
18/75 **Attitude Dancing** *Carly Simon*
4/73 **Aubrey** *Bread*
43/75 **Autobahn** *Kraftwerk*
20/80 **Autograph** *John Denver*
36/84 **Automatic** *Pointer Sisters*
17/72 **Automatically Sunshine**
  Supremes
  Autumn Leaves
10/65 *Roger Williams (1965)*
37/71 *Steve Lawrence & Eydie*
  Gorme (medley)
2/68 **Autumn Of My Life**
  Bobby Goldsboro
1/85 **Axel F** *Harold Faltermeyer*

B

36/84 **B-B-B-Burnin' Up With Love**
  Eddie Rabbitt
9/79 **Babe** *Styx*
1/91 **Baby Baby** *Amy Grant*
16/88 **Baby Boom Baby** *James Taylor*
  Baby Can I Hold You
19/88 *Tracy Chapman*
28/89 *Neil Diamond*
20/77 **Baby Come Back** *Player*
14/84 **Baby Come Back To Me**
  Manhattan Transfer
1/82 **Baby, Come To Me** *Patti*
  Austin with James Ingram
1/72 **Baby Don't Get Hooked On**
  Me *Mac Davis*
35/80 **Baby Don't Go** *Karla Bonoff*

42/75 **(Baby) Don't Let It Mess Your**
  Mind *Donny Gerrard*
27/66 **Baby, Dream Your Dream**
  Tony Bennett
10/62 **Baby Elephant Walk**
  Lawrence Welk
6/75 **Baby Face** *Wing & A Prayer*
  Fife & Drum Corps.
3/87 **Baby Grand**
  Billy Joel Feat. Ray Charles
23/74 **Baby, Hang Up The Phone**
  Carl Graves
10/83 **Baby I Lied** *Deborah Allen*
31/69 **Baby, I Love You** *Andy Kim*
  Baby, I Love Your Way
28/76 *Peter Frampton*
2/88 *Will To Power*
30/79 **Baby, I Need Your Lovin'**
  Eric Carmen
21/70 **Baby, I Need Your Loving**
  O.C. Smith
14/76 **Baby, I'll Give It To You**
  Seals & Crofts
1/71 **Baby I'm-A Want You** *Bread*
11/78 **Baby I'm Burnin'** *Dolly Parton*
  Baby, I'm Yours
21/71 *Jody Miller*
18/78 *Debby Boone*
19/90 **Baby, It's Tonight** *Jude Cole*
25/86 **Baby Please Don't Take It (I**
  Need Your Love)
  Jonathan Butler
17/82 **Baby Step Back**
  Gordon Lightfoot
19/70 **Baby Take Me In Your Arms**
  Jefferson
2/65 **Baby The Rain Must Fall**
  Glenn Yarbrough
8/77 **Baby, What A Big Surprise**
  Chicago
9/83 **Baby, What About You**
  Crystal Gayle
13/76 **Baby, You Look Good To Me**
  Tonight *John Denver*
18/90 **Baby You're Mine** *Basia*
7/61 **Baby's First Christmas**
  Connie Francis
1/74 **Back Home Again** *John Denver*
  Back In My Life Again ..see:
  (Want You)
1/87 **Back In The High Life Again**
  Steve Winwood
30/78 **Back In The U.S.A.**
  Linda Ronstadt
45/76 **Back To The Island**
  Leon Russell
37/73 **Back When My Hair Was Short**
  Gunhill Road
33/87 **Bad** *Michael Jackson*
  Bad, Bad Leroy Brown
9/73 *Jim Croce*
31/74 *Frank Sinatra*
25/75 **Bad Blood** *Neil Sedaka*
8/86 **Bad Boy** *Miami Sound Machine*
4/78 **Baker Street** *Gerry Rafferty*
2/66 **Ballad Of Irving** *Frank Gallop*
14/63 **Ballad Of Jed Clampett**
  Flatt & Scruggs
1/66 **Ballad Of The Green Berets**
  SSgt Barry Sadler
36/66 **Ballad Of The Sad Young Men**
  Steve Lawrence

1/86 **Ballerina Girl** *Lionel Richie*
1/66 **Band Of Gold** *Mel Carter*
22/74 **Band On The Run**
  Paul McCartney & Wings
  Banda, A
1/67 *Herb Alpert*
22/67 *Sue Raney (Parade)*
23/92 **Bang Bang** *David Sanborn*
34/71 **Banks Of The Ohio**
  Olivia Newton-John
37/70 **Barbara, I Love You**
  New Colony Six
39/68 **Barefoot In Baltimore**
  Strawberry Alarm Clock
38/67 **Barefoot In The Park**
  Neal Hefti
  Baretta's Theme ("Keep Your
  Eye On The Sparrow")
14/76 *Rhythm Heritage*
42/76 *Sammy Davis, Jr.*
35/75 **Bargain Store** *Dolly Parton*
14/68 **Baroque-A-Nova**
  Mason Williams
12/66 **Batman Theme** *Neal Hefti*
11/68 **Battle Hymn Of The Republic**
  Andy Williams
21/68 **Battle Of New Orleans**
  Harpers Bizarre
11/73 **Be** *Neil Diamond*
9/64 **Be Anything (But Be Mine)**
  Connie Francis
13/63 **Be Careful Of Stones That**
  You Throw *Dion*
2/82 **Be Mine Tonight** *Neil Diamond*
  Be My Baby
24/70 *Andy Kim*
35/72 *Jody Miller*
18/74 **Be My Day** *Cats*
23/67 **Be My Love** *Mel Carter*
11/85 **Be Near Me** *ABC*
37/88 **Be Still My Beating Heart**
  Sting
31/74 **Be Thankful For What You**
  Got *William DeVaughn*
14/63 **Be True To Yourself** *Bobby Vee*
13/92 **Be Young, Be Foolish, Be**
  Happy *Sonia*
50/78 **Be Your Own Best Friend**
  Ray Stevens
38/74 **Beach Baby** *First Class*
20/81 **Beach Boys Medley**
  Beach Boys
5/64 **Beans In My Ears**
  Serendipity Singers
15/82 **Beatles' Movie Medley** *Beatles*
30/72 **Beautiful** *Gordon Lightfoot*
40/71 **Beautiful** *Karen Wyman*
37/67 **Beautiful Friendship**
  Ahmad Jamal
45/93 **Beautiful Girl** *INXS*
8/76 **Beautiful Noise** *Neil Diamond*
11/71 **Beautiful People** *New Seekers*
6/72 **Beautiful Sunday** *Daniel Boone*
3/91 **Beauty And The Beast**
  Celine Dion & Peabo Bryson
1/90 **Because I Love You (The**
  Postman Song) *Stevie B*
38/90 **Because It's Christmas (For**
  All The Children)
  Barry Manilow
25/67 **Because Of You** *Chris Montez*

290

25/93 **Jessie** *Joshua Kadison*
Jesus Christ Superstar ..see:
   Superstar
27/92 **Jesus He Knows Me** *Genesis*
35/69 **Jet Song (When The**
   Weekend's Over) *Groop*
17/86 **Jimmy Lee** *Aretha Franklin*
16/73 **Jimmy Loves Mary-Anne**
   Looking Glass
13/69 **Jimtown Road** *Mills Brothers*
37/70 **Jingle Jangle** *Archies*
9/75 **Jive Talkin'** *Bee Gees*
29/80 **JoJo** *Boz Scaggs*
2/83 **Joanna** *Kool & The Gang*
6/70 **Joanne** *Michael Nesmith*
42/90 **Joey** *Concrete Blonde*
7/62 **Johnny Loves Me**
   Shelley Fabares
3/69 **Johnny One Time** *Brenda Lee*
10/61 **Johnny Will** *Pat Boone*
44/74 **Jolene** *Dolly Parton*
31/70 **Jose's Piece** *Mason Williams*
44/78 **Josie** *Steely Dan*
2/71 **Joy** *Apollo 100 feat. Tom Parker*
34/74 **Joy** *Isaac Hayes*
35/67 **Joyful Noise**
   Johnny Mann Singers
21/91 **Joyride** *Roxette*
21/69 **Julia** *Ramsey Lewis*
2/70 **Julie, Do Ya Love Me**
   Bobby Sherman
39/70 **July 12, 1939** *Charlie Rich*
23/69 **July You're A Woman**
   Pat Boone
11/84 **Jump (For My Love)**
   Pointer Sisters
33/76 **Junk Food Junkie** *Larry Groce*
44/83 **Just A Little Imagination**
   Patsy
5/77 **Just A Song Before I Go**
   Crosby, Stills & Nash
2/92 **Just Another Day** *Jon Secada*
10/82 **Just Another Day In Paradise**
   Bertie Higgins
7/84 **Just Another Woman In Love**
   Anne Murray
3/85 **Just As I Am** *Air Supply*
10/68 **Just As Much As Ever**
   Bobby Vinton
4/89 **Just Because** *Anita Baker*
4/89 **Just Between You And Me**
   Lou Gramm
15/82 **Just Can't Win 'Em All**
   Stevie Woods
39/65 **Just Dance On By**
   Eydie Gorme
Just Don't Want To Be Lonely
30/73   *Ronnie Dyson*
42/74   *Main Ingredient*
2/92 **Just For Tonight**
   Vanessa Williams
43/90 **Just Having Touched**
   Mark Edwards
33/74 **Just Leave Me Alone**
   Don Potter
29/67 **Just Like A Man**
   Margaret Whiting
9/89 **Just Like Jesse James** *Cher*
47/75 **(Just Like) Romeo And Juliet**
   Sha Na Na
17/80 **(Just Like) Starting Over**
   John Lennon

20/67 **Just Loving You** *Anita Harris*
Just My Imagination
33/71   *Temptations*
40/84   *Modern Romance*
7/81 **Just Once** *Quincy Jones feat.*
   James Ingram
37/72 **Just Once In My Life (medley)**
   Johnny Mathis
Just One Look
50/74   *Anne Murray*
5/79   *Linda Ronstadt*
Just Out Of Reach (Of My Two
   Open Arms)
6/61   *Solomon Burke*
24/75   *Perry Como*
1/77 **Just Remember I Love You**
   Firefall
14/62 **Just Tell Her Jim Said Hello**
   Elvis Presley
2/81 **Just The Two Of Us** *Grover*
   Washington, Jr./Bill Withers
12/91 **Just The Way It Is, Baby**
   Rembrandts
1/77 **Just The Way You Are**
   Billy Joel
1/87 **Just To See Her**
   Smokey Robinson
2/75 **Just Too Many People**
   Melissa Manchester
1/79 **Just When I Needed You Most**
   Randy Vanwarmer
5/65 **Just Yesterday** *Jack Jones*
12/66 **Just Yesterday** *Al Martino*
3/76 **Just You And I**
   Melissa Manchester
7/73 **Just You 'N' Me** *Chicago*
44/74 **Justine** *Kathy Dalton*

K

15/71 **K-Jee** *Nite-Liters*
13/63 **Kansas City** *Trini Lopez*
3/65 **Kansas City Star** *Roger Miller*
3/83 **Karma Chameleon**
   Culture Club
6/69 **Keem-O-Sabe** *Electric Indian*
1/91 **Keep Coming Back**
   Richard Marx
7/89 **Keep Each Other Warm**
   Barry Manilow
36/77 **Keep It Comin' Love**
   KC & The Sunshine Band
32/90 **Keep It Together** *Madonna*
37/89 **Keep On Movin'** *Soul II Soul*
Keep On Singing
22/73   *Austin Roberts*
1/74   *Helen Reddy*
23/75 **Keep On Tryin'** *Poco*
44/90 **Keep Our Love Alive**
   Stevie Wonder
10/68 **Keep The Ball Rollin'** *Al Hirt*
28/71 **Keep The Customer Satisfied**
   Gary Puckett & The Union Gap
40/80 **Keep The Fire** *Kenny Loggins*
(Keep Your Eye On The
   Sparrow) ..see: Baretta's
   Theme
3/85 **Keeping The Faith** *Billy Joel*

26/77 **Kentucky Mornin'** *Al Martino*
3/70 **Kentucky Rain** *Elvis Presley*
1/81 **Key Largo** *Bertie Higgins*
40/88 **Key To You** *David Benoit*
21/66 **Khartoum** *Ferrante & Teicher*
29/70 **Killer Joe** *Quincy Jones*
5/80 **Killin' Time**
   Fred Knoblock & Susan Anton
2/73 **Killing Me Softly With His**
   Song *Roberta Flack*
13/86 **King For A Day**
   Thompson Twins
42/77 **King Is Gone** *Ronnie McDowell*
39/75 **King Kingston** *George Fischoff*
King Kong ..see: Theme From
26/74 **King Of Nothing** *Seals & Crofts*
33/83 **King Of Pain** *Police*
King Of The Road
1/65   *Roger Miller*
35/66   *Mickie Finn*
   (also see: Queen Of The House)
7/90 **King Of Wishful Thinking**
   Go West
7/72 **Kiss An Angel Good Mornin'**
   Charley Pride
12/76 **Kiss And Say Goodbye**
   Manhattans
36/87 **Kiss And Tell** *Breakfast Club*
5/65 **Kiss Away** *Ronnie Dove*
22/68 **Kiss Her Now** *Ed Ames*
10/87 **Kiss Him Goodbye** *Nylons*
2/68 **Kiss Me Goodbye** *Petula Clark*
9/80 **Kiss Me In The Rain**
   Barbra Streisand
20/93 **Kiss Of Life** *Sade*
16/81 **Kiss On My List**
   Daryl Hall & John Oates
Kiss Tomorrow Goodbye
29/66   *Lainie Kazan*
30/66   *Jane Morgan*
19/78 **Kiss You All Over** *Exile*
31/86 **Kisses In The Moonlight**
   George Benson
1/88 **Kissing A Fool** *George Michael*
31/91 **Kissing You** *Keith Washington*
33/67 **Kites Are Fun** *Free Design*
Knock, Knock Who's There
40/70   *Andra Willis*
11/72   *Mary Hopkin*
2/70 **Knock Three Times** *Dawn*
5/73 **Knockin' On Heaven's Door**
   Bob Dylan
7/77 **Knowing Me, Knowing You**
   Abba
32/68 **Knowing When To Leave**
   Michele Lee
29/71 **Ko-Ko Joe** *Jerry Reed*
2/73 **Kodachrome** *Paul Simon*
5/88 **Kokomo** *Beach Boys*
4/68 **Kum Ba Yah** *Tommy Leonetti*
11/86 **Kyrie** *Mr. Mister*

L

9/68 **L. David Sloane** *Michele Lee*
21/68 **L.A. Break Down (And Take**
   Me In) *Jack Jones*
34/84 **L.A. Is My Lady** *Frank Sinatra*

13/71	**Long Ago Tomorrow**	35/71	**Loss Of Love**	19/84	**Love Has A Mind Of Its Own**

310

30/75	**Morning** *Michael Kenny*	39/79	**Much, Much Greater Love**		**My Guy**
2/75	**Mornin' Beautiful** *Dawn*		*Engelbert Humperdinck*	12/72	*Petula Clark*
32/68	**Mornin' Glory** *Bobbie Gentry*	10/69	**Muddy Mississippi Line**	2/82	*Sister Sledge*
	& Glen Campbell		*Bobby Goldsboro*	1/77	**My Heart Belongs To Me**
23/69	**Mornin Mornin**	45/78	**Mull Of Kintyre** *Wings*		*Barbra Streisand*
	Bobby Goldsboro	36/82	**Muscles** *Diana Ross*	2/64	**My Heart Belongs To Only**
6/73	**Morning After**	37/66	**Music And Memories**		**You** *Bobby Vinton*
	Maureen McGovern		*Patti Page*	3/88	**My Heart Can't Tell You No**
1/79	**Morning Dance** *Spyro Gyra*	4/79	**Music Box Dancer** *Frank Mills*		*Rod Stewart*
8/85	**Morning Desire** *Kenny Rogers*	40/74	**Music Eyes** *Heartsfield*		**My Heart Cries For You**
	Morning Girl		**Music From Across The Way**	12/64	*Ray Charles*
39/69	*Neon Philharmonic*	18/71	*James Last*	12/67	*Connie Francis*
34/71	*Lettermen Present Jim Pike*	30/72	*Andy Williams*	42/90	**My Heart Has A Mind Of Its**
1/72	**Morning Has Broken**	22/78	**Music In My Life** *Mac Davis*		**Own** *Sally Moore*
	Cat Stevens	39/71	**Music Lovers (Main Title)**	29/91	**My Heart Is Failing Me** *Riff*
21/80	**Morning Man** *Rupert Holmes*		*Ferrante & Teicher*	31/66	**My Heart Reminds Me**
16/71	**Morning Of Our Lives** *Arkade*	16/86	**Music Of Goodbye** *Melissa*		*Vikki Carr*
1/74	**Morning Side Of The**		*Manchester & Al Jarreau*		**My Heart Sings ..see: (All Of A**
	Mountain	15/68	**Music Played** *Matt Monro*		**Sudden)**
	Donny & Marie Osmond		**Music To Watch Girls By**	11/65	**My Heart Would Know**
43/78	**Morning Sun** *Carole King*	2/66	*Bob Crewe Generation*		*Al Martino*
1/81	**Morning Train (Nine To Five)**	2/67	*Andy Williams*	38/69	**My Heart's Symphony**
	Sheena Easton	31/67	*Al Hirt*		*Four Lads*
13/67	**Morningtown Ride** *Seekers*		**Muskrat Love**	29/80	**My Heroes Have Always Been**
1/73	**Most Beautiful Girl**	11/73	*America*		**Cowboys** *Willie Nelson*
	Charlie Rich	1/76	*Captain & Tennille*	1/85	**My Hometown**
2/70	**Most Of All** *B.J. Thomas*	1/78	**My Angel Baby** *Toby Beau*		*Bruce Springsteen*
8/62	**Most People Get Married**	41/77	**My Best Friend's Wife**	6/61	**My Kind Of Girl** *Matt Monro*
	Patti Page		*Paul Anka*	16/83	**My Kind Of Lady** *Supertramp*
24/71	**Mother** *Barbra Streisand*		**My Boy**	2/78	**My Life** *Billy Joel*
4/72	**Mother And Child Reunion**	13/71	*Richard Harris*	36/71	**My Little Girl (Angel All**
	Paul Simon	1/75	*Elvis Presley*		**A-glow)** *Jerry Vale*
9/65	**Mother Nature, Father Time**	33/83	**My Boyfriend's Back**	31/71	**My Little One** *Marmalade*
	Brook Benton		*Melissa Manchester*	1/75	**My Little Town**
41/91	**Mother's Pride** *George Michael*	4/89	**My Brave Face** *Paul McCartney*		*Simon & Garfunkel*
34/66	**Mothers And Daughters**	26/65	**My Cherie** *Al Martino*	1/73	**My Love** *Paul McCartney*
	Doc Severinsen		**My Cherie Amour**	1/83	**My Love** *Lionel Richie*
12/72	**Motorcycle Mama** *Sailcat*	3/69	*Stevie Wonder*	4/65	**My Love** *Petula Clark*
12/87	**Motortown** *Kane Gang*	32/70	*Ramsey Lewis Trio*	14/88	**My Love** *Julio Iglesias Feat.*
3/91	**Motown Song** *Rod Stewart*	13/61	**My Claire De Lune**		*Stevie Wonder*
11/86	**Move Away** *Culture Club*		*Steve Lawrence*		**My Love, Forgive Me**
34/86	**Move Closer** *Marilyn Martin*		**My Coloring Book**	3/64	*Robert Goulet*
32/69	**Move In A Little Closer, Baby**	7/62	*Kitty Kallen*	17/65	*Ray Charles Singers*
	Mama Cass	8/63	*Sandy Stewart*	25/68	*Jerry Vale*
26/70	**Move Me, O Wondrous Music**	47/76	*Mel Carter*	17/65	**My Man** *Barbra Streisand*
	Ray Charles Singers	38/73	**My Crew** *Rita Coolidge*	1/73	**My Maria** *B.W. Stevenson*
24/89	**Move On** *Waterfront*	1/66	**My Cup Runneth Over**	2/70	**My Marie**
29/91	**Move Right Out** *Rick Astley*		*Ed Ames*		*Engelbert Humperdinck*
40/78	**Movin' Out (Anthony's Song)**	2/62	**My Dad** *Paul Petersen*	1/74	**My Melody Of Love**
	Billy Joel	31/71	**My Days Of Loving You**		*Bobby Vinton*
33/71	**Mozart 40** *Sovereign Collection*		*Perry Como*	34/73	**My Merry-Go-Round**
25/71	**Mozart Symphony No. 40 in G**	7/92	**My Destiny** *Lionel Richie*		*Johnny Nash*
	Minor K.550, 1st Movement		**My Elusive Dreams**	8/80	**My Mother's Eyes** *Bette Midler*
	Waldo De Los Rios	7/70	*Bobby Vinton*	10/73	**My Music** *Loggins & Messina*
	Mr. Bojangles	16/75	*Charlie Rich*	32/90	**My, My, My** *Johnny Gill*
28/68	*Jerry Jeff Walker*	34/84	**My Ever Changing Moods**	30/65	**My Name Is Mud**
38/68	*Bobby Cole*		*Style Council*		*Eddie Rambeau*
10/70	*Nitty Gritty Dirt Band*	2/74	**My Eyes Adored You**	44/91	**My Name Is Not Susan**
29/72	**Mister Can't You See**		*Frankie Valli*		*Whitney Houston*
	Buffy Sainte-Marie	42/77	**My Eyes Get Blurry**	8/89	**My One Temptation** *Mica Paris*
42/90	**Mr. Heartbreak** *Stephen Bishop*		*Kenny Nolan*	2/62	**My Own True Love** *Duprees*
3/64	**Mr. Lonely** *Bobby Vinton*	11/77	**My Fair Share** *Seals & Crofts*		**My Prayer**
25/76	**Mr. Melody** *Natalie Cole*	11/75	**My Father's Song**	31/73	*Vogues*
25/68	**Mister Nico** *Four Jacks & A Jill*		*Barbra Streisand*	19/80	*Ray, Goodman & Brown*
20/61	**Mr. Paganini (You'll Have To**	7/68	**My Favorite Things**	42/79	**My Prayer** *Glen Campbell*
	Swing It) *Ella Fitzgerald*		*Herb Alpert*	38/78	**My Reason To Be Is You**
	Mister Sandman		**My Girl**		*Marilyn McCoo & Billy Davis, Jr.*
12/68	*Bert Kaempfert*	12/85	*Hall & Oates/David Ruffin/*	4/68	**My Shy Violet** *Mills Brothers*
8/81	*Emmylou Harris*		*Eddie Kendrick (medley)*	27/91	**My Side Of The Bed**
	Mrs. Robinson	27/91	*Temptations*		*Susanna Hoffs*
4/68	*Simon & Garfunkel*	9/74	**My Girl Bill** *Jim Stafford*	1/68	**My Special Angel** *Vogues*
20/69	*Booker T. & The M.G.'s*				

23/69	**Play It Again, Sam**	
	Tony Bennett	
3/72	**Play Me** *Neil Diamond*	
20/62	**Play The Thing**	
	Marlowe Morris Quintet	
7/73	**Playground In My Mind**	
	Clint Holmes	
22/82	**Please Be The One**	
	Karla Bonoff	
31/68	**Please Believe Me**	
	Jimmy Roselli	
1/74	**Please Come To Boston**	
	Dave Loggins	
27/79	**Please Don't Go**	
	K.C. & The Sunshine Band	
33/69	**Please Don't Go** *Eddy Arnold*	
5/79	**Please Don't Leave**	
	Lauren Wood	
16/66	**Please Don't Sell My Daddy**	
	No More Wine *Greenwoods*	
30/68	**Please Forgive Me**	
	Frankie Laine	
39/67	**Please Love Me Forever**	
	Bobby Vinton	
1/75	**Please Mr. Please**	
	Olivia Newton-John	
1/74	**Please Mr. Postman**	
	Carpenters	
30/66	**Please Say You're Fooling**	
	Ray Charles	
12/75	**Please Tell Him That I Said**	
	Hello *Debbie Campbell*	
25/69	**Pledge Of Allegiance**	
	Red Skelton	
19/75	**Pledging My Love** *Tom Jones*	
9/62	**Pocketful Of Miracles**	
	Frank Sinatra	
27/72	**Poem For My Little Lady**	
	Bobby Goldsboro	
1/75	**Poetry Man** *Phoebe Snow*	
16/68	**Poor Baby** *Cowsills*	
11/63	**Poor Little Rich Girl**	
	Steve Lawrence	
31/68	**Poor Papa** *Sugar Shoppe*	
27/78	**Poor Poor Pitiful Me**	
	Linda Ronstadt	
17/82	**Pop Goes The Movies** *Meco*	
4/72	**Popcorn** *Hot Butter*	
	Popi ..see: Theme From	
45/76	**Popsicle Toes** *Michael Franks*	
2/63	**Popsicles And Icicles**	
	Murmaids	
38/70	**Poquito Soul** *One G Plus Three*	
15/66	**Portuguese Washerwomen**	
	Baja Marimba Band	
	Poseidon Adventure ..see:	
	Morning After	
42/90	**Possession** *Bad English*	
8/85	**Possession Obsession**	
	Daryl Hall & John Oates	
	(Postman Song) ..see: Because	
	I Love You	
26/73	**Pour Me A Little More Wine**	
	Wayne Newton	
6/85	**Power Of Love**	
	Huey Lewis & the News	
	Power Of Love	
13/85	*Air Supply*	
19/87	*Laura Branigan*	
3/91	**Power Of Love/Love Power**	
	Luther Vandross	

4/90	**Praying For Time**	
	George Michael	
6/72	**Precious And Few** *Climax*	
42/79	**Precious Love** *Bob Welch*	
39/67	**Precious Memories** *Romeos*	
34/81	**Precious To Me** *Phil Seymour*	
26/79	**Pretty Girls**	
	Melissa Manchester	
42/82	**Pretty Kitty** *George Fischoff*	
38/73	**Pretty Lady** *Lighthouse*	
10/63	**Pretty Paper** *Roy Orbison*	
	Pretty Woman ..see: Oh Pretty	
	Woman	
4/69	**Pretty World**	
	Sergio Mendes & Brasil '66	
	(Pretty Young Thing) ..see:	
	P.Y.T.	
38/90	**Price Of Love** *Bad English*	
30/86	**Pride Is Back**	
	Kenny Rogers with Nickie Ryder	
10/84	**Prime Time**	
	Alan Parsons Project	
4/70	**Primrose Lane** *O.C. Smith*	
	(Prisoner) ..see: Love Theme	
	From Eyes Of Laura Mars	
37/74	**Prisoner Of Love** *Vogues*	
30/85	**Private Dancer** *Tina Turner*	
33/81	**Private Eyes**	
	Daryl Hall & John Oates	
35/71	**Problem Child** *Mark Lindsay*	
38/90	**Problem Child** *Beach Boys*	
45/88	**Promise, The** *When In Rome*	
11/66	**Promise Her Anything**	
	Tom Jones	
26/91	**Promise Of A New Day**	
	Paula Abdul	
F/74	**Promised Land** *Elvis Presley*	
6/78	**Promises** *Eric Clapton*	
8/81	**Promises** *Barbra Streisand*	
8/89	**Promises** *Basia*	
39/66	**Promises** *Ray Charles Singers*	
7/68	**Promises, Promises**	
	Dionne Warwick	
19/83	**Promises, Promises**	
	Naked Eyes	
F/71	**Proud Mary** *James Last*	
1/75	**Proud One** *Osmonds*	
1/63	**Puff The Magic Dragon**	
	Peter, Paul & Mary	
31/70	**Puppet Man** *5th Dimension*	
3/65	**Puppet On A String**	
	Elvis Presley	
18/67	**Puppet On A String** *Al Hirt*	
9/68	**(Puppet Song) Whiskey On A**	
	Sunday *Irish Rovers*	
31/90	**Pure** *Lightning Seeds*	
19/71	**Pushbike Song** *Mixtures*	
	Put A Little Love In Your	
	Heart	
2/69	*Jackie DeShannon*	
2/88	*Annie Lennox & Al Green*	
11/90	**Put It There** *Paul McCartney*	
35/72	**Put It Where You Want It**	
	Crusaders	
4/71	**Put Your Hand In The Hand**	
	Ocean	
8/68	**Put Your Head On My**	
	Shoulder *Lettermen*	
24/66	**Put Yourself In My Place**	
	Buddy Greco	
12/83	**Puttin' On The Ritz** *Taco*	

Q

16/68	**Quando M'Innamoro**	
	Sandpipers	
7/70	**Que Sera, Sera (Whatever Will**	
	Be, Will Be) *Mary Hopkin*	
2/81	**Queen Of Hearts** *Juice Newton*	
4/65	**Queen Of The House**	
	Jody Miller	
	(also see: King Of The Road)	
3/69	**Quentin's Theme** *Charles*	
	Randolph Grean Sounde	
	(Quest, The) ..see: Impossible	
	Dream	
34/71	**Questions 67 And 68** *Chicago*	
18/65	**Quiet Nights Of Quiet Stars**	
	Andy Williams	

R

13/77	**Race Among The Ruins**	
	Gordon Lightfoot	
1/65	**Race Is On** *Jack Jones*	
34/75	**Rag Doll** *Sammy Johns*	
3/90	**Rain (medley)** *Dan Fogelberg*	
19/69	**Rain** *Jose Feliciano*	
44/74	**Rain** *Kris Kristofferson &*	
	Rita Coolidge	
3/68	**Rain In My Heart**	
	Frank Sinatra	
38/76	**Rain, Oh Rain** *Fools Gold*	
48/77	**Rain On** *Ray Conniff*	
4/62	**Rain Rain Go Away**	
	Bobby Vinton	
7/70	**Rainbow** *Marmalade*	
16/62	**Rainbow At Midnight**	
	Jimmie Rodgers	
18/79	**Rainbow Connection** *Kermit*	
6/83	**Rainbow's End** *Sergio Mendes*	
1/69	**Raindrops Keep Fallin' On My**	
	Head *B.J. Thomas*	
9/78	**Raining In My Heart** *Leo Sayer*	
1/75	**Rainy Day People**	
	Gordon Lightfoot	
1/71	**Rainy Days And Mondays**	
	Carpenters	
26/71	**Rainy Jane** *Davy Jones*	
2/70	**Rainy Night In Georgia**	
	Brook Benton	
40/74	**Raised On Robbery**	
	Joni Mitchell	
27/73	**Raised On Rock** *Elvis Presley*	
12/73	**Ramblin Man**	
	Allman Brothers Band	
1/62	**Ramblin' Rose** *Nat King Cole*	
37/66	**Rat Race** *Righteous Brothers*	
47/77	**Reach** *New Orleans*	
18/70	**Reach Out And Touch**	
	(Somebody's Hand)	
	Diana Ross	
	Reach Out For Me	
38/67	*Burt Bacharach*	
32/90	*Olivia Newton-John*	
	Reach Out I'll Be There	
16/71	*Diana Ross*	
8/92	*Michael Bolton*	

43/78	**Run For Home** *Lindisfarne*	6/87	**Same Ole Love (365 Days A Year)** *Anita Baker*	15/81	**Say You'll Be Mine** *Christopher Cross*
3/82	**Run For The Roses** *Dan Fogelberg*	3/61	**San Antonio Rose** *Floyd Cramer*	3/77	**Say You'll Stay Until Tomorrow** *Tom Jones*

322

14/65 **Summer Sounds** *Robert Goulet*
30/72 **Summer Sun**
    Jamestown Massacre
Summer Symphony
10/70   *Jack Gold Sound*
34/71   *Jack Gold Sound*
18/73 **Summer (The First Time)**
    Bobby Goldsboro
Summer Wind
9/65   *Wayne Newton*
20/65   *Roger Williams/Harry*
    Simeone Chorale
1/66   *Frank Sinatra*
25/81 **Summer's Here** *James Taylor*
44/78 **Summerlove, Sensation**
    Bobby Vinton
28/71 **Summertime** *Herb Alpert*
31/81 **Sun Ain't Gonna Shine**
    Anymore *Nielsen/Pearson*
34/67 **Sunday For Tea**
    Peter & Gordon
Sunday Kind Of Love
21/72   *Lenny Welch*
28/76   *Kenny Rankin*
Sunday Mornin'
39/68   *Spanky & Our Gang*
14/69   *Oliver*
13/70 **Sunday Morning Coming**
    Down *Johnny Cash*
30/72 **Sunday Morning Sunshine**
    Harry Chapin
42/77 **Sunday School To Broadway**
    Anne Murray
13/75 **Sunday Sunrise** *Anne Murray*
Sunday's Gonna' Come On
    Tuesday ..see: (One Of
    These Days)
1/74 **Sundown** *Gordon Lightfoot*
1/77 **Sunflower** *Glen Campbell*
23/67 **Sunny Day Girl** *Wayne Newton*
16/91 **Sunrise** *Triplets*
33/76 **Sunrise** *Eric Carmen*
Sunrise, Sunset
22/65   *Eddie Fisher*
5/67   *Roger Williams*
18/85 **Sunset Grill** *Don Henley*
17/70 **Sunset Strip** *Ray Stevens*
7/71 **Sunshine** *Jonathan Edwards*
16/73 **Sunshine** *Mickey Newbury*
1/74 **Sunshine On My Shoulders**
    John Denver
30/74 **Sunshine Roses** *Gene Cotton*
25/73 **Sunshine Ship**
    Arthur, Hurley & Gottlieb
18/69 **Sunshine Wine** *Perry Como*
14/65 **Super-cali-fragil-istic-expi-**
    ali-docious *Julie Andrews -*
    Dick Van Dyke
14/81 **Super Trouper** *Abba*
29/79 **Superman** *Barbra Streisand*
35/73 **Superman** *Donna Fargo*
47/79 **Superman** *Herbie Mann*
1/71 **Superstar** *Carpenters*
31/76 **Superstar** *Paul Davis*
17/71 **Superstar - Jesus Christ**
    Superstar
    Assembled Multitude
38/73 **Superstition** *Stevie Wonder*
12/89 **Superwoman** *Karyn White*
37/88 **Surrender** *Swing Out Sister*
44/89 **Surrender To Me**
    Ann Wilson & Robin Zander

45/79 **Surrender To Me**
    McGuinn, Clark & Hillman
20/75 **Susanna's Song (In The**
    California Morning)
    Jerry Cole & Trinity
9/79 **Suspicions** *Eddie Rabbitt*
4/69 **Suspicious Minds** *Elvis Presley*
30/85 **Sussudio** *Phil Collins*
31/73 **Swamp Witch** *Jim Stafford*
S.W.A.T. ..see: Theme From
27/76 **Sway** *Bobby Rydell*
Swayin' To The Music ..see:
    Slow Dancing
9/75 **Swearin' To God** *Frankie Valli*
16/81 **Sweet Baby**
    Stanley Clarke/George Duke
Sweet Caroline (Good Times
    Never Seemed So Good)
3/69   *Neil Diamond*
24/70   *Bert Kaempfert*
24/70 **Sweet Changes** *Jack Jones*
35/74 **Sweet Child** *Johnny Mathis*
5/71 **Sweet City Woman**
    Stampeders
4/81 **Sweet Dreams** *Air Supply*
36/83 **Sweet Dreams (Are Made of**
    This) *Eurythmics*
15/63 **Sweet Dreams (Of You)**
    Patsy Cline
4/86 **Sweet Freedom**
    Michael McDonald
16/70 **Sweet Gingerbread Man**
    Mike Curb Congregation
15/72 **Sweet Inspiration (medley)**
    Barbra Streisand
7/78 **Sweet Life** *Paul Davis*
3/86 **Sweet Love** *Anita Baker*
15/75 **Sweet Loving Man**
    Morris Albert
36/84 **Sweet Magnolia And The**
    Travelling Salesman
    Dan Fogelberg
Sweet Maria
6/67   *Billy Vaughn Singers*
23/67   *Steve Lawrence*
35/71 **Sweet Mary**
    Wadsworth Mansion
4/68 **Sweet Memories** *Andy Williams*
13/67 **Sweet Misery** *Jimmy Dean*
29/77 **Sweet Music Man**
    Kenny Rogers
38/69 **Sweet 'N' Sassy** *Jerry Smith*
37/88 **Sweet Potato Pie** *James Taylor*
2/72 **Sweet Seasons** *Carole King*
24/65 **Sweet September** *Lettermen*
17/62 **Sweet Sixteen Bars** *Earl Grant*
42/81 **Sweet Southern Love**
    Phil Everly
41/79 **Sweet Summer Lovin'**
    Dolly Parton
1/72 **Sweet Surrender** *Bread*
1/74 **Sweet Surrender** *John Denver*
7/78 **Sweet, Sweet Smile** *Carpenters*
41/73 **Sweet Understanding Love**
    Four Tops
1/85 **Sweetest Taboo** *Sade*
1/81 **Sweetest Thing (I've Ever**
    Known) *Juice Newton*
2/70 **Sweetheart**
    Engelbert Humperdinck
40/81 **Sweetheart**
    Franke & The Knockouts

Sweetheart Tree
21/65   *Johnny Mathis*
23/65   *Henry Mancini*
20/79 **Sweets For My Sweet**
    Tony Orlando
38/91 **Swept Away** *Yanni*
38/89 **Swing The Mood (medley)**
    Jive Bunny & The Mastermixers
5/62 **Swingin' Safari** *Billy Vaughn*
19/62 **Swingin' Maid** *Del Shannon*
18/66 **Symphony For Susan** *Arbors*

T

1/74 **TSOP (The Sound Of**
    Philadelphia)
    MFSB feat. The Three Degrees
3/83 **Take A Chance** *Olivia Newton-*
    John & John Travolta
9/78 **Take A Chance On Me** *Abba*
14/61 **Take A Fool's Advice**
    Nat "King" Cole
21/69 **Take A Letter Maria**
    R.B. Greaves
4/80 **Take A Little Rhythm**
    Ali Thomson
35/93 **Take A Look** *Natalie Cole*
18/89 **Take Another Road**
    Jimmy Buffett
5/61 **Take Five**
    Dave Brubeck Quartet
Take Good Care Of Her
40/73   *Johnny Mathis*
27/74   *Elvis Presley*
24/88 **Take Good Care Of Me**
    Jonathan Butler
14/68 **Take Good Care Of My Baby**
    Bobby Vinton
25/89 **Take Good Care Of You And**
    Me *Dionne Warwick &*
    Jeffrey Osborne
24/75 **Take Good Care Of Yourself**
    Three Degrees
6/82 **Take It Away** *Paul McCartney*
12/72 **Take It Easy** *Eagles*
14/82 **Take It Easy On Me**
    Little River Band
24/78 **Take It Like A Woman**
    Mary Welch
4/90 **Take It To Heart**
    Michael McDonald
Take It To The Limit
4/76   *Eagles*
31/83   *Willie Nelson & Waylon*
    Jennings
30/90 **Take Me**
    Everything But The Girl
18/68 **Take Me Back** *Frankie Laine*
39/78 **Take Me Back To Chicago**
    Chicago
5/82 **Take Me Down** *Alabama*
2/86 **Take Me Home** *Phil Collins*
19/79 **Take Me Home** *Cher*
3/71 **Take Me Home, Country**
    Roads *John Denver*
15/81 **Take Me Now** *David Gates*
34/90 **Take Me Through The Night**
    Smokey Robinson

324

34/85 **Tired Of Being Blonde**
  Carly Simon
39/80 **Tired Of Toein' The Line**
  Rocky Burnette
6/62 **To A Sleeping Beauty**
  Jimmy Dean
3/84 **To All The Girls I've Loved
  Before** *Julio Iglesias &
  Willie Nelson*
11/92 **To Be With You** *Mr. Big*
2/68 **To Each His Own**
  Frankie Laine
  **To Everything There Is A
  Season ..see: Turn! Turn!
  Turn!**
21/72 **To Get To You** *Jerry Wallace*
17/68 **To Give (The Reason I Live)**
  Frankie Valli
8/69 **To Know You Is To Love You**
  Bobby Vinton
  To Love Somebody
44/78   *Jackie DeShannon*
1/92   *Michael Bolton*
  **To Love Someone ..see: (What
  A Sad Way)**
31/69 **To Make A Big Man Cry**
  Vic Damone
24/84 **To Me** *Barbara Mandrell/
  Lee Greenwood*
11/67 **To Sir, With Love** *Herbie Mann*
7/74 **To The Door Of The Sun**
  Al Martino
2/68 **To Wait For Love** *Herb Alpert*
10/71 **Toast And Marmalade For Tea**
  Tin Tin
  Today
4/64   *New Christy Minstrels*
19/68   *Jimmie Rodgers*
1/76 **Today's The Day** *America*
1/61 **Together** *Connie Francis*
14/76 **Together** *O.C. Smith*
30/67 **Together** *Trini Lopez*
30/81 **Together** *Tierra*
1/66 **Together Again** *Ray Charles*
36/73 **Together (Body And Soulin')**
  Mission
2/88 **Together Forever** *Rick Astley*
8/72 **Together Let's Find Love**
  5th Dimension
27/68 **Tomboy** *Ronnie Dove*
  Tommy ..see: Overture From
32/71 **Tomorrow** *Bobbi Martin*
39/69 **Tomorrow Is My Friend**
  Jimmie Rodgers
29/69 **Tomorrow Is The First Day Of
  The Rest Of My Life**
  Lana Cantrell
32/93 **Tomorrow's Girls**
  Donald Fagen
  Tonight
2/61   *Ferrante & Teicher*
12/61   *Eddie Fisher*
4/83 **Tonight, I Celebrate My Love**
  Peabo Bryson/Roberta Flack
14/61 **Tonight I Won't Be There**
  Adam Wade
8/69 **Tonight I'll Say A Prayer**
  Eydie Gorme
36/85 **Tonight She Comes** *Cars*
8/87 **Tonight, Tonight, Tonight**
  Genesis

42/76 **Tonight's The Night (Gonna
  Be Alright)** *Rod Stewart*
  **(Too Bad, Too Bad) ..see:
  Dommage, Dommage**
16/72 **Too Beautiful To Last**
  Engelbert Humperdinck
17/90 **Too Cool To Fall In Love**
  Jill Sobule
11/80 **Too Hot** *Kool & The Gang*
1/85 **Too Late For Goodbyes**
  Julian Lennon
47/90 **Too Late To Say Goodbye**
  Richard Marx
6/72 **Too Late To Turn Back Now**
  *Cornelius Brothers & Sister
  Rose*
14/64 **Too Late To Turn Back Now**
  Brook Benton
2/65 **Too Many Rivers** *Brenda Lee*
1/91 **Too Many Walls** *Cathy Dennis*
4/78 **Too Much Heaven** *Bee Gees*
32/92 **Too Much Passion** *Smithereens*
1/78 **Too Much, Too Little, Too
  Late** *Johnny Mathis/Deniece
  Williams*
15/85 **Too Young** *Jack Wagner*
23/72 **Too Young** *Donny Osmond*
7/78 **Took The Last Train**
  David Gates
  Top Of The World
2/73   *Carpenters*
34/73   *Lynn Anderson*
1/76 **Torn Between Two Lovers**
  Mary MacGregor
7/83 **Total Eclipse Of The Heart**
  Bonnie Tyler
36/84 **Touch** *Earth, Wind & Fire*
27/74 **Touch A Hand, Make A Friend**
  Staple Singers
43/74 **Touch And Go** *Al Wilson*
32/91 **Touch Me (All Night Long)**
  Cathy Dennis
  Touch Me In The Morning
1/73   *Diana Ross*
31/74   *Lettermen (medley)*
  Touch Me When We're Dancing
42/79   *Bama*
1/81   *Carpenters*
15/87 **Touch Of Grey** *Grateful Dead*
  Touch The Wind ..see: Eres Tu
37/89 **Toy Soldiers** *Martika*
  Traces
2/69   *Classics IV*
3/69   *Lettermen (medley)*
4/75 **Tracks Of My Tears**
  Linda Ronstadt
5/69 **Tracy** *Cuff Links*
19/79 **Tragedy** *Bee Gees*
9/74 **Train Of Thought** *Cher*
  Trains And Boats And Planes
10/65   *Billy J. Kramer*
37/66   *Dionne Warwick*
31/74 **Travelin' Prayer** *Billy Joel*
30/74 **Traveling Boy** *Garfunkel*
41/79 **Travellin'**
  Jeremy Spencer Band
11/63 **Treat My Baby Good**
  Bobby Darin
14/81 **Trouble** *Lindsey Buckingham*
42/75 **T-R-O-U-B-L-E** *Elvis Presley*
10/83 **Trouble In Paradise** *Jarreau*

7/62 **Trouble Is My Middle Name**
  Bobby Vinton
7/89 **Trouble Me** *10,000 Maniacs*
13/69 **Truck Stop** *Jerry Smith*
1/83 **True** *Spandau Ballet*
5/86 **True Blue** *Madonna*
5/86 **True Colors** *Cyndi Lauper*
24/91 **True Companion** *Marc Cohn*
43/92 **True Emotion** *Jennifer Warnes*
7/69 **True Grit** *Glen Campbell*
2/88 **True Love** *Glenn Frey*
33/70 **True Love Is Greater Than
  Friendship** *Al Martino*
5/63 **True Love Never Runs
  Smooth** *Gene Pitney*
40/80 **True Love Ways** *Mickey Gilley*
27/65 **True Picture** *Jack Jones*
30/66 **Truer Than You Were**
  McGuire Sisters
1/82 **Truly** *Lionel Richie*
9/65 **Truly, Truly, True** *Brenda Lee*
27/66 **Trumpet Pickin'** *Al Hirt*
1/69 **Try A Little Kindness**
  Glen Campbell
30/91 **Try A Little Tenderness**
  Commitments
48/77 **Try A Smile** *Cliff Richard*
6/83 **Try Again** *Champaign*
  Try To Remember
10/65   *Brothers Four*
17/65   *Ed Ames*
2/75   *Gladys Knight & The Pips
  (medley)*
1/76 **Tryin' To Get The Feeling
  Again** *Barry Manilow*
25/77 **Tryin' To Love Two**
  William Bell
  Tubular Bells
15/74   *Mike Oldfield*
47/76   *Champs' Boys Orchestra*
31/82 **Tug Of War** *Paul McCartney*
F/78 **Tumbling Dice** *Linda Ronstadt*
13/87 **Tunnel Of Love**
  Bruce Springsteen
4/84 **Turn Around** *Neil Diamond*
15/63 **Turn Around** *Dick & DeeDee*
  Turn Around, Look At Me
15/62   *Glen Campbell*
3/68   *Vogues*
5/88 **Turn Back The Clock**
  Johnny Hates Jazz
43/76 **Turn The Beat Around**
  Vicki Sue Robinson
3/67 **Turn The World Around**
  Eddy Arnold
37/66 **Turn The World Around The
  Other Way** *Timi Yuro*
28/69 **Turn! Turn! Turn!/To
  Everything There Is A
  Season** *Judy Collins*
9/81 **Turn Your Love Around**
  George Benson
24/71 **Turn Your Radio On**
  Ray Stevens
7/73 **Twelfth Of Never**
  Donny Osmond
15/87 **Twenty Years Ago**
  Kenny Rogers
15/84 **20/20** *George Benson*
6/63 **Twenty Four Hours From
  Tulsa** *Gene Pitney*

327

5/64 **Walk Away** *Matt Monro*
14/88 **Walk Away** *Michael Bolton*
28/67 **Walk Away** *Damita Jo*
43/91 **Walk Away** *Kenny Rogers*
1/65 **Walk In The Black Forest**
    Horst Jankowski
23/68 **Walk In The Park**
    Claudine Longet
14/91 **Walk My Way**
    Beth Nielsen Chapman
4/85 **Walk Of Life** *Dire Straits*
    Walk On By
7/64   *Dionne Warwick*
6/89   *Melissa Manchester*
34/72 **Walk On In** *Lou Rawls*
31/93 **Walk On The Ocean**
    Toad The Wet Sprocket
2/72 **Walk On Water** *Neil Diamond*
15/78 **Walk Right Back** *Anne Murray*
    Walk Right In
1/63   *Rooftop Singers*
39/77   *Dr. Hook*
27/93 **Walk Through The World**
    Marc Cohn
26/66 **Walk With Faith In Your Heart**
    Bachelors
8/69 **Walkin' In The Rain**
    Jay & The Americans
6/67 **Walkin' In The Sunshine**
    Roger Miller
16/67 **Walkin' - Just Walkin'**
    Patti Page
30/80 **Walkin' On A Cloud**
    B.J. Thomas
33/87 **Walking Down Your Street**
    Bangles
14/66 **Walking Happy** *Peggy Lee*
12/91 **Walking In Memphis**
    Marc Cohn
5/75 **Walking In Rhythm**
    Blackbyrds
38/73 **Walking In The Georgia Rain**
    Climax
9/70 **Walking In The Sand**
    Al Martino
26/74 **Walking Man** *James Taylor*
13/89 **Walking On Air** *Stephen Bishop*
6/92 **Walking On Broken Glass**
    Annie Lennox
21/66 **Walking On New Grass**
    Buddy Greco
21/85 **Walking On Sunshine**
    Katrina & The Waves
27/65 **Wanderlust** *Nat "King" Cole*
14/81 **(Want You) Back In My Life
    Again** *Carpenters*
13/73 **Was A Sunny Day** *Josh*
7/89 **Was It Nothing At All**
    Michael Damian
    Washington Square
1/63   *Village Stompers*
22/71   *James Last*
38/73 **Wasn't It Nice In New York
    City** *Tommy Leonetti*
46/81 **Wasn't That A Party** *Rovers*
9/75 **Wasted Days And Wasted
    Nights** *Freddy Fender*
2/82 **Wasted On The Way**
    Crosby, Stills & Nash
1/70 **Watching Scotty Grow**
    Bobby Goldsboro

36/74 **Watching The River Run**
    Loggins & Messina
6/81 **Watching The Wheels**
    John Lennon
10/61 **Water Boy** *Don Shirley Trio*
11/93 **Water From The Moon**
    Celine Dion
21/75 **Waterfall** *Carly Simon*
    Watermelon Man
3/63   *Mongo Santamaria Band*
36/65   *Gloria Lynne*
40/68   *Erroll Garner*
    **(Watermelon Summer) ..see:
    You Made It That Way**
14/77 **Way Down** *Elvis Presley*
1/83 **Way He Makes Me Feel**
    Barbra Streisand
35/92 **Way I Feel About You**
    Karyn White
16/77 **Way I Feel Tonight**
    Bay City Rollers
1/75 **Way I Want To Touch You**
    Captain & Tennille
1/86 **Way It Is**
    Bruce Hornsby & The Range
4/69 **Way It Used To Be**
    Engelbert Humperdinck
    Way Of Love
22/65   *Kathy Kirby*
2/72   *Cher*
33/68 **Way That I Live** *Jack Jones*
5/89 **Way To Your Heart** *Soulsister*
    Way We Were
1/73   *Barbra Streisand*
31/74   *Lettermen (medley)*
2/75   *Gladys Knight & The Pips
    (medley)*
    **Way You Do The Things You
    Do**
9/78   *Rita Coolidge*
12/85   *Hall & Oates / David Ruffin /
    Eddie Kendrick (medley)*
21/90   *UB40*
3/61 **Way You Look Tonight**
    Lettermen
38/89 **Way You Love Me** *Karyn White*
9/87 **Way You Make Me Feel**
    Michael Jackson
18/69 **Ways To Love A Man**
    Tammy Wynette
11/88 **We All Sleep Alone** *Cher*
30/79 **We Are Family** *Sister Sledge*
1/85 **We Are The World**
    USA for Africa
34/84 **We Belong** *Pat Benatar*
37/85 **We Built This City** *Starship*
    We Can Fly
9/68   *Cowsills*
23/68   *Al Hirt (medley)*
12/89 **We Can Last Forever** *Chicago*
7/72 **We Can Make It Together**
    Steve & Eydie/The Osmonds
F/72 **We Can Make The Morning**
    Elvis Presley
26/76 **We Can't Hide It Anymore**
    Larry Santos
6/64 **We Could** *Al Martino*
16/80 **We Could Have It All**
    Maureen McGovern
5/89 **We Didn't Start The Fire**
    Billy Joel

33/81 **We Don't Have To Hold Out**
    Anne Murray
3/85 **We Don't Need Another Hero
    (Thunderdome)** *Tina Turner*
5/79 **We Don't Talk Anymore**
    Cliff Richard
37/71 **We Got A Dream** *Ocean*
19/77 **We Just Disagree** *Dave Mason*
20/75 **We May Never Love Like This
    Again** *Maureen McGovern*
2/73 **We May Never Pass This Way
    (Again)** *Seals & Crofts*
34/88 **We Said Hello Goodbye**
    Phil Collins
17/83 **We Two** *Little River Band*
14/80 **We Were Meant To Be Lovers**
    Photoglo
27/92 **We'll Find The Way**
    Kurt Howell
1/78 **We'll Never Have To Say
    Goodbye Again** *England Dan
    & John Ford Coley*
    We'll Sing In The Sunshine
1/64   *Gale Garnett*
12/78   *Helen Reddy*
23/68 **We're A Home**
    Ray Conniff & The Singers
50/79 **We're A Melody** *Jones Girls*
    We're All Alone
27/76   *Frankie Valli*
1/77   *Rita Coolidge*
46/78 **(We're) Dancin' In The Dark**
    Renee Armand
15/72 **We're Free** *Beverly Bremers*
6/84 **We're Going All The Way**
    Jeffrey Osborne
6/81 **We're In This Love Together**
    Al Jarreau
10/89 **We're Not Makin' Love
    Anymore** *Barbra Streisand*
22/72 **We're Together** *Hillside Singers*
43/79 **We've Got Love**
    Peaches & Herb
10/72 **We've Got To Get It On Again**
    Addrisi Brothers
    We've Got Tonite
29/78   *Bob Seger*
2/83   *Kenny Rogers & Sheena
    Easton*
1/70 **We've Only Just Begun**
    Carpenters
36/87 **We've Only Just Begun (The
    Romance Is Not Over)**
    Glenn Jones
4/89 **We've Saved The Best For
    Last** *Kenny G & Smokey
    Robinson*
36/68 **Weakness In A Man**
    Brook Benton
    Weave Me The Sunshine
25/72   *Peter Yarrow*
5/74   *Perry Como*
1/64 **Wedding, The** *Julie Rogers*
1/69 **Wedding Bell Blues**
    5th Dimension
19/69 **Wedding Cake** *Connie Francis*
    Wedding Song (There Is Love)
3/71   *Paul Stookey*
9/72   *Petula Clark*
23/78   *Mary MacGregor*
29/67 **Wednesday's Child** *Ray Conniff*

11/87	**Why Does It Have To Be (Wrong or Right)** *Restless Heart*	8/77	**Winter Melody** *Donna Summer*		**Woman In Me**
		3/69	**Winter World Of Love** *Engelbert Humperdinck*	17/81	*Crystal Gayle*
39/70	**Why Doesn't Love Make Me Happy** *Lesley Gore*			17/83	*Donna Summer*
		49/79	**Wisdom Of A Fool** *Jacky Ward*	31/83	**Woman In You** *Bee Gees*
23/70	**Why Don't They Understand** *Bobby Vinton*	34/85	**Wise Up** *Amy Grant*	32/88	**Woman Loves A Man** *Joe Cocker*
		2/66	**Wish Me A Rainbow** *Gunter Kallmann Chorus*		
	Why Don't You Believe Me			11/81	**Woman Needs Love (Just Like You Do)** *Ray Parker Jr. & Raydio*
10/63	*Duprees*	40/81	**Wish You Were Here** *Barbara Mandrell*		
25/65	*Vic Damone*			37/86	**Woman Of The World** *Double*
22/78	**Why Have You Left The One You Left Me For** *Crystal Gayle*	12/66	**Wish You Were Here, Buddy** *Pat Boone*	49/78	**Woman To Woman** *Barbara Mandrell*
		4/64	**Wishin' And Hopin'** *Dusty Springfield*	41/75	**Woman Tonight** *America*
28/73	**Why Me** *Kris Kristofferson*			20/76	**Woman's Gotta Have It** *James Taylor*
1/80	**Why Not Me** *Fred Knoblock*	14/65	**Wishing It Was You** *Connie Francis*		
27/68	**Why Say Goodbye** *Connie Francis*	44/88	**Wishing Well** *Terence Trent D'Arby*	4/69	**Woman's Way** *Andy Williams*
				37/71	**Wonder** *Miss Abrams*
	Wichita Lineman	1/74	**Wishing You Were Here** *Chicago*		**Wonder Of You**
1/68	*Glen Campbell*			38/69	*John Davidson*
33/69	*Larry Page Orchestra*	23/73	**With A Child's Heart** *Michael Jackson*	1/70	*Elvis Presley*
34/69	*Sergio Mendes & Brasil '66*			1/75	**Wonderful Baby** *Don McLean*
12/91	**Wicked Game** *Chris Isaak*	31/68	**With A Little Help From My Friends** *Sergio Mendes & Brasil '66*	14/67	**Wonderful Season Of Summer** *Ray Conniff & The Singers*
27/93	**Wide River** *Steve Miller Band*				
3/66	**Wiedersehn** *Al Martino*	5/78	**With A Little Luck** *Wings*	47/73	**Wonderful Summer** *Vogues*
13/70	**Wigwam** *Bob Dylan*	22/89	**With Every Beat Of My Heart** *Taylor Dayne*	39/78	**Wonderful Tonight** *Eric Clapton*
33/87	**Wild Horses** *Gino Vannelli*				
26/83	**Wild Montana Skies** *John Denver & Emmylou Harris*	21/77	**With One More Look At You** *Jack Jones*	2/63	**Wonderful! Wonderful!** *Tymes*
		23/87	**With Or Without You** *U2*		**Wonderful World ..see: (What A)**
	Wild World		**With Pen In Hand**	22/80	**Wondering Where The Lions Are** *Bruce Cockburn*
21/71	*Cat Stevens*	25/68	*Billy Vera*		
28/71	*Gentrys*	30/68	*Jerry Vale*	43/80	**Wonderland** *Commodores*
10/88	*Maxi Priest*	6/69	*Vikki Carr*		**(Woo Woo Song) ..see: You Should Be Mine**
1/75	**Wildfire** *Michael Murphey*	28/72	*Bobby Goldsboro*		
5/73	**Wildflower** *Skylark*	3/65	**With These Hands** *Tom Jones*		**Wooden Heart**
29/74	**Wildwood Weed** *Jim Stafford*	45/91	**With You** *Tony Terry*	1/61	*Joe Dowell*
22/69	**Will You Be Staying After Sunday** *Peppermint Rainbow*	2/79	**With You I'm Born Again** *Billy Preston & Syreeta*	23/75	*Bobby Vinton*
					Woodstock
5/93	**Will You Be There** *Michael Jackson*	6/76	**With Your Love** *Jefferson Starship*	23/70	*Assembled Multitude*
				17/71	*Matthews' Southern Comfort*
	Will You Love Me Tomorrow	15/70	**With Your Love Now** *Bossa Rio*	4/88	**Word In Spanish** *Elton John*
15/72	*Roberta Flack*		**(Without A Woman) ..see: Senza Una Donna**	13/83	**Words** *F.R. David*
42/74	*Melanie*				**Words (Are Impossible)**
17/92	**Will You Marry Me?** *Paula Abdul*	5/69	**Without Her** *Herb Alpert*	25/73	*Drupi (Vado Via)*
		1/70	**Without Love (There Is Nothing)** *Tom Jones*	23/76	*Donny Gerrard*
2/86	**Will You Still Love Me?** *Chicago*			1/86	**Words Get In The Way** *Miami Sound Machine*
			Without You		
28/81	**Willie, Mickey And "The Duke" (Talkin' Baseball)** *Terry Cashman*	1/71	*Nilsson*	32/82	**Work So Hard** *Matthew Wilder*
		41/73	*Pastors (medley)*	2/66	**Work Song** *Herb Alpert*
		48/91	*Air Supply*	9/74	**Workin' At The Car Wash Blues** *Jim Croce*
1/64	**Willow Weep For Me** *Chad & Jeremy*	8/88	**Without You** *Peabo Bryson & Regina Belle*		
				9/69	**Workin' On A Groovy Thing** *5th Dimension*
1/66	**Winchester Cathedral** *New Vaudeville Band*	4/80	**Without Your Love** *Roger Daltrey*	24/68	**Working Man's Prayer** *Arthur Prysock*
	Wind Beneath My Wings	7/87	**Without Your Love** *Toto*		
10/83	*Lou Rawls*	9/63	**Wives And Lovers** *Jack Jones*	5/80	**Working My Way Back To You/Forgive Me, Girl** *Spinners*
23/83	*Gladys Knight & The Pips*		**Wizard Of Oz ..see: Themes From The**		
2/89	*Bette Midler*			9/64	**World I Used To Know** *Jimmie Rodgers*
45/74	**Wind Me Up** *Vikki Carr*	3/62	**Wolverton Mountain** *Claude King*		
43/91	**Wind Of Change** *Scorpions*		(also see: I'm The Girl On)	20/67	**World Of Clowns** *Robert Goulet*
36/68	**Wind Song** *Wes Montgomery*			21/75	**World Of Dreams** *Perry Como*
46/74	**Windfall** *Rick Nelson*	4/81	**Woman** *John Lennon*	17/64	**World Of Lonely People** *Anita Bryant*
3/69	**Windmills Of Your Mind** *Dusty Springfield*	26/68	**Woman, A** *Four Lads*		
		6/69	**Woman Helping Man** *Vogues*	2/65	**World Of Our Own** *Seekers*
32/67	**Windows Of The World** *Dionne Warwick*	37/89	**Woman In Chains** *Tears For Fears*	1/67	**World We Knew (Over And Over)** *Frank Sinatra*
7/68	**Winds Of Change** *Ray Conniff & The Singers*	1/80	**Woman In Love** *Barbra Streisand*	35/85	**World Without Love** *Eddie Rabbitt*
10/67	**Windy** *Wes Montgomery*	50/79	**Woman In Love** *Three Degrees*	37/93	**Worlds Apart** *Jude Cole*
1/80	**Winner Takes It All** *Abba*			20/62	**Worried Mind** *Ray Anthony*
5/75	**Winners And Losers** *Hamilton, Joe Frank & Reynolds*			5/64	**Worry** *Johnny Tillotson*
28/88	**Winter Games** *David Foster*				

15/92 **Would I Lie To You?**
Charles & Eddie
44/75 **Would I Still Have You** Lobo
42/73 **Wouldn't I Be Someone**
Bee Gees
13/84 **Wrapped Around Your Finger**
Police
9/76 **Wreck Of The Edmund**
Fitzgerald Gordon Lightfoot
5/61 **Writing On The Wall**
Adam Wade
49/89 **Writing On The Wall**
One 2 Many
11/64 **Wrong For Each Other**
Andy Williams
31/81 **Wynken, Blynken And Nod**
Doobie Brothers

X

2/80 **Xanadu** Olivia Newton-John/
Electric Light Orchestra

Y

10/84 **Yah Mo B There** James Ingram
(with Michael McDonald)
23/68 **Yard Went On Forever**
Richard Harris
8/77 **Year Of The Cat** Al Stewart
Years
38/80 Barbara Mandrell
40/80 Wayne Newton
17/80 **Years From Now** Dr. Hook
2/61 **Yellow Bird**
Arthur Lyman Group
Yellow Days
13/67 Percy Faith
34/67 Damita Jo
22/70 **Yellow River** Christie
44/76 **Yellow Roses On Her Gown**
Johnny Mathis
49/88 **Yes** Merry Clayton
Yes, I'm Ready
44/76 Tom Sullivan
1/79 Teri DeSario with K.C.
17/68 **Yes Sir, That's My Baby**
Baja Marimba Band
10/69 **Yester-Me, Yester-You,**
Yesterday Stevie Wonder
30/73 **Yesterday And You**
Holly Sherwood
36/75 **Yesterday Can't Hurt Me**
Evie Sands
10/68 **Yesterday I Heard The Rain**
Tony Bennett
Yesterday Once More
1/73 Carpenters
45/81 Spinners (medley)
6/69 **Yesterday, When I Was Young**
Roy Clark
1/81 **Yesterday's Songs**
Neil Diamond
15/64 **Yet...I Know** Steve Lawrence
Yo Yo Man ..see: (I'm A)

3/78 **You** Rita Coolidge
30/80 **You** Earth, Wind & Fire
2/82 **You And I** Eddie Rabbitt with
Crystal Gayle
(also see: You're The Only
Woman)
44/74 **You And I** Johnny Bristol
23/77 **You And Me** Alice Cooper
28/76 **You And Me** Tammy Wynette
1/74 **You And Me Against The**
World Helen Reddy
You And Me (We Wanted It All)
42/80 Frank Sinatra
41/84 Peter Allen
1/83 **You Are** Lionel Richie
22/75 **You Are A Song**
Batdorf & Rodney
26/76 **You Are Beautiful** Stylistics
24/71 **You Are Everything** Stylistics
7/62 **You Are Mine** Frankie Avalon
46/80 **You Are My Heaven** Roberta
Flack with Donny Hathaway
34/92 **You Are My Home**
Linda Eder & Peabo Bryson
3/85 **You Are My Lady**
Freddie Jackson
34/69 **You Are My Life** Herb Alpert
35/79 **You Are My Miracle**
Roger Whittaker
24/72 **You Are My Sunshine**
(medley) Steve Lawrence
28/75 **You Are My Sunshine Girl**
Lettermen
(You Are) My Way Of Life
..see: My Way Of Life
17/77 **You Are On My Mind** Chicago
12/75 **You Are So Beautiful**
Joe Cocker
12/87 **You Are The Girl** Cars
1/73 **You Are The Sunshine Of My**
Life Stevie Wonder
6/76 **You Are The Woman** Firefall
32/73 **You Are What I Am**
Gordon Lightfoot
17/75 **You Are You** Gilbert O'Sullivan
4/78 **You Belong To Me** Carly Simon
2/85 **You Belong To The City**
Glenn Frey
46/90 **You Break It** John Tesh
15/86 **You Can Call Me Al** Paul Simon
34/80 **You Can Call Me Blue**
Michael Johnson
43/80 **You Can Come Home To Me**
Frank Weber
44/79 **You Can Do It** Dobie Gray
5/82 **You Can Do Magic** America
15/74 **You Can Have Her** Sam Neely
4/63 **You Can Never Stop Me**
Loving You Johnny Tillotson
17/74 **You Can Take My Love**
Duncan McDonald
14/74 **You Can't Be A Beacon (If**
Your Light Don't Shine)
Donna Fargo
11/65 **You Can't Be True, Dear**
Patti Page
25/79 **You Can't Change That** Raydio
22/78 **You Can't Dance**
England Dan & John Ford Coley
26/90 **You Can't Deny It**
Lisa Stansfield

13/84 **You Can't Get What You Want**
(Till You Know What You
Want) Joe Jackson
35/65 **You Can't Grow Peaches On A**
Cherry Tree Browns
9/82 **You Can't Hurry Love**
Phil Collins
17/66 **You Can't Roller Skate In A**
Buffalo Herd Roger Miller
2/83 **You Can't Run From Love**
Eddie Rabbitt
11/91 **You Come To My Senses**
Chicago
6/81 **You Could Have Been With Me**
Sheena Easton
2/79 **You Decorated My Life**
Kenny Rogers
3/78 **You Don't Bring Me Flowers**
Barbra Streisand & Neil
Diamond
2/63 **You Don't Have To Be A Baby**
To Cry Caravelles
6/76 **You Don't Have To Be A Star**
(To Be In My Show) Marilyn
McCoo & Billy Davis, Jr.
25/91 **You Don't Have To Go Home**
Tonight Triplets
You Don't Have To Say You
Love Me
8/66 Dusty Springfield
1/70 Elvis Presley
13/88 **You Don't Know**
Scarlett & Black
2/64 **(You Don't Know) How Glad I**
Am Nancy Wilson
You Don't Know Me
1/62 Ray Charles
34/67 Elvis Presley
12/81 Mickey Gilley
18/78 **You Don't Love Me Anymore**
Eddie Rabbitt
9/72 **You Don't Mess Around With**
Jim Jim Croce
32/69 **You Don't Need Me For**
Anything Anymore
Brenda Lee
23/74 **You Foxy Thing, I Love You**
Ronnie & Natalie O'Hara
1/69 **You Gave Me A Mountain**
Frankie Laine
4/85 **You Give Good Love**
Whitney Houston
1/89 **You Got It** Roy Orbison
9/78 **You Got It** Diana Ross
1/86 **You Got It All** Jets
1/90 **You Gotta Love Someone**
Elton John
7/76 **You Gotta Make Your Own**
Sunshine Neil Sedaka
15/83 **You Haven't Heard The Last**
Of Me Peter Allen
34/78 **You Keep Me Dancing**
Samantha Sang
30/87 **You Keep Me Hangin' On**
Kim Wilde
40/67 **You Knew About Her All The**
Time Tommy Leonetti
18/77 **You Know Like I Know**
Ozark Mountain Daredevils
36/83 **You Know What To Do**
Carly Simon

1/77 **You Light Up My Life**
Debby Boone
6/73 **You Light Up My Life**
Carole King
31/74 **You Little Trustmaker** *Tymes*
2/67 **You Made It That Way (Watermelon Summer)**
Perry Como
32/65 **You Made Me Love You**
Aretha Franklin
28/85 **You Make It Feel Like Christmas** *Neil Diamond*
28/77 **You Make Loving Fun**
Fleetwood Mac
6/74 **You Make Me Feel Brand New**
Stylistics
19/76 **You Make Me Feel Like Dancing** *Leo Sayer*
35/68 **You Make Me Think About You** *Johnny Mathis*
48/80 **You May Be Right** *Billy Joel*
38/70 **You, Me And Mexico**
Edward Bear
17/78 **You Need A Woman Tonight**
Captain & Tennille
3/78 **You Needed Me** *Anne Murray*
14/78 **You Never Done It Like That**
Captain & Tennille
32/82 **You Never Gave Up On Me**
Crystal Gayle
6/67 **You, No One But You**
Frankie Laine
23/89 **You On My Mind**
Swing Out Sister
3/67 **You Only Live Twice**
Nancy Sinatra
28/72 **You Ought To Be With Me**
Al Green
50/80 **You Pick Me Up (And Put Me Down)** *Dottie West*
15/83 **You Put The Beat In My Heart**
Eddie Rabbitt
17/93 **You Read Me Wrong**
Lauren Christy
22/81 **You Saved My Soul**
Burton Cummings
8/85 **You Send Me** *Manhattans*
25/76 **You Should Be Dancing**
Bee Gees
2/86 **You Should Be Mine (The Woo Woo Song)** *Jeffrey Osborne*
10/82 **You Should Hear How She Talks About You**
Melissa Manchester
11/79 **You Take My Breath Away**
Rex Smith
38/75 **You Turn Me On**
Nino Tempo & April Stevens
13/72 **You Turn Me On, I'm A Radio**
Joni Mitchell
11/74 **You Turned My World Around**
Frank Sinatra
18/66 **You Wanna Bet**
Barbra Streisand
5/67 **You Wanted Someone To Play With (I Wanted Someone To Love)** *Frankie Laine*
47/73 **You Were Always There**
Donna Fargo
10/84 **You Were Made For Me**
Irene Cara
1/65 **You Were On My Mind** *We Five*

8/65 **You Were Only Fooling (While I Was Falling In Love)**
Vic Damone
39/74 **You Will Be My Music**
Frank Sinatra
16/88 **You Will Know** *Stevie Wonder*
50/87 **You Win Again** *Bee Gees*
18/74 **You Won't Find Another Fool Like Me** *New Seekers*
1/74 **You Won't See Me**
Anne Murray
4/92 **You Won't See Me Cry**
Wilson Phillips
11/66 **You You You** *Mel Carter*
4/65 **You'd Better Come Home**
Petula Clark
17/80 **You'll Accomp'ny Me**
Bob Seger
13/64 **You'll Always Be The One I Love** *Dean Martin*
11/61 **You'll Answer To Me** *Patti Page*
28/76 **You'll Lose A Good Thing**
Freddy Fender
1/76 **You'll Never Find Another Love Like Mine** *Lou Rawls*
4/73 **You'll Never Get To Heaven (If You Break My Heart)**
Stylistics
13/74 **You'll Never Know**
Denny Doherty
16/70 **You'll Remember Me**
Peggy Lee
21/85 **You're A Friend Of Mine**
Clarence Clemons & Jackson Browne
11/72 **You're A Lady** *Peter Skellern*
You're A Part Of Me
18/75 *Susan Jacks*
32/76 *Kim Carnes*
6/78 *Gene Cotton with Kim Carnes*
43/73 **You're A Special Part Of Me**
Diana Ross & Marvin Gaye
You're All I Need To Get By
13/75 *Dawn*
16/78 *Johnny Mathis & Deniece Williams*
21/82 *Chris Christian (medley)*
17/92 **You're All That Matters To Me**
Curtis Stigers
You're Gonna Hear From Me!
13/66 *Andy Williams*
21/66 *Julius LaRosa*
12/74 **You're Gonna Love Yourself In The Morning** *Bonnie Koloc*
44/80 **You're Good For Me** *Exile*
5/74 **(You're) Having My Baby**
Paul Anka with Odia Coates
1/91 **You're In Love** *Wilson Phillips*
17/77 **You're In My Heart (The Final Acclaim)** *Rod Stewart*
25/84 **You're Lookin' Hot Tonight**
Barry Manilow
5/84 **You're Looking Like Love To Me** *Peabo Bryson/Roberta Flack*
11/77 **You're Movin' Out Today**
Bette Midler
6/71 **You're My Man** *Lynn Anderson*

(You're My) Soul And Inspiration
21/70 *Steve Lawrence & Eydie Gorme*
37/72 *Johnny Mathis (medley)*
18/77 *Donny & Marie Osmond*
You're My World
4/64 *Cilla Black*
5/77 *Helen Reddy*
10/75 **You're No Good** *Linda Ronstadt*
1/64 **You're Nobody Till Somebody Loves You** *Dean Martin*
9/89 **You're Not Alone** *Chicago*
32/81 **You're Not Easy To Forget**
Michael Johnson
2/85 **You're Only Human (Second Wind)** *Billy Joel*
1/79 **You're Only Lonely**
J.D. Souther
2/73 **You're Sixteen** *Ringo Starr*
1/72 **You're So Vain** *Carly Simon*
31/84 **You're The Best Thing**
Style Council
(also see: Best Thing)
1/84 **You're The Inspiration**
Chicago
2/78 **You're The Love** *Seals & Crofts*
6/76 **You're The One**
Blood, Sweat & Tears
23/78 **You're The One That I Want**
John Travolta & Olivia Newton-John
14/79 **You're The Only One**
Dolly Parton
48/77 **You're The Only One** *Geils*
5/80 **You're The Only Woman (You & I)** *Ambrosia*
22/65 **You're The Only World I Know**
Sonny James
38/68 **You're The Right One For Me**
Nick Noble
29/91 **You're The Story Of My Life**
Desmond Child
You've Got A Friend
1/71 *James Taylor*
36/71 *Roberta Flack & Donny Hathaway*
7/92 **You've Got A Way**
Kathy Troccoli
7/89 **You've Got It** *Simply Red*
7/76 **You've Got Me Runnin'**
Gene Cotton
36/66 **You've Got Possibilities**
Peggy Lee
20/66 **You've Got Your Troubles**
Nancy Wilson
You've Lost That Lovin' Feeling
10/69 *Dionne Warwick*
15/80 *Daryl Hall & John Oates*
You've Made Me So Very Happy
18/69 *Blood, Sweat & Tears*
31/70 *Lou Rawls*
37/73 **You've Never Been This Far Before** *Conway Twitty*
7/68 **You've Still Got A Place In My Heart** *Dean Martin*
25/65 **Young And Foolish**
Eddie Fisher
6/63 **Young And In Love**
Dick & DeeDee

Z

CHART FACTS & FEATS

A unique compilation of interesting and unusual Adult Contemporary accomplishments.

TOP 20 ARTISTS BY DECADE

SIXTIES ('60-'69)

1.	**Frank Sinatra**	1,399
2.	Herb Alpert/Tijuana Brass	1,244
3.	Al Martino	1,212
4.	Andy Williams	1,156
5.	Dean Martin	1,155
6.	Bobby Vinton	1,110
7.	Connie Francis	999
8.	Jack Jones	981
9.	Elvis Presley	900
10.	Ray Charles	840
11.	Tony Bennett	829
12.	Brenda Lee	823
13.	The Lettermen	817
14.	Petula Clark	763
15.	Jerry Vale	690
16.	Barbra Streisand	685
17.	Eddy Arnold	661
18.	Steve Lawrence	649
19.	Peter, Paul & Mary	627
20.	Ed Ames	608

SEVENTIES ('70-'79)

1.	**Neil Diamond**	1,428
2.	Carpenters	1,427
3.	John Denver	1,186
4.	Olivia Newton-John	1,139
5.	Helen Reddy	1,117
6.	Elvis Presley	1,088
7.	Anne Murray	1,062
8.	Glen Campbell	1,022
9.	Barry Manilow	999
10.	Barbra Streisand	998
11.	Dawn	847
12.	James Taylor	819
13.	Chicago	803
14.	Engelbert Humperdinck	774
15.	Bee Gees	734
16.	Johnny Mathis	732
17.	The 5th Dimension	724
18.	B.J. Thomas	709
19.	Carly Simon	695
20.	Elton John	694

EIGHTIES ('80-'89)

1.	**Kenny Rogers**	1,430
2.	Lionel Richie	1,155
3.	Elton John	1,136
4.	Billy Joel	1,008
5.	Neil Diamond	978
6.	Barbra Streisand	939
7.	Barry Manilow	883
8.	Dionne Warwick	867
9.	Air Supply	799
10.	Dan Fogelberg	786
11.	Stevie Wonder	785
12.	George Michael/Wham!	768
13.	Madonna	767
14.	Anne Murray	758
15.	Phil Collins	758
16.	Whitney Houston	751
17.	Chicago	742
18.	Gloria Estefan/Miami Sound Machine	700
19.	Michael Jackson	656
20.	Daryl Hall & John Oates	637

NINETIES ('90-'93)

1.	**Michael Bolton**	834
2.	Rod Stewart	633
3.	Mariah Carey	573
4.	Gloria Estefan/Miami Sound Machine	570
5.	Wilson Phillips	552
6.	Elton John	520
7.	Celine Dion	511
8.	Whitney Houston	491
9.	Amy Grant	422
10.	Bonnie Raitt	381
11.	Aaron Neville	369
12.	Richard Marx	357
13.	Peabo Bryson	356
14.	Kenny G	333
15.	Phil Collins	328
16.	Genesis	299
17.	Luther Vandross	289
18.	Jon Secada	284
19.	Roxette	280
20.	Don Henley	279

TOP ARTIST ACHIEVEMENTS

MOST CHARTED HITS

1. Barbra Streisand.................60
2. Neil Diamond.....................54
3. Elvis Presley......................52
4. Frank Sinatra 48
5. Johnny Mathis 48
6. Kenny Rogers/First Edition...47
7. Herb Alpert/Tijuana Brass.....46
8. Elton John 45
9. Dionne Warwick 45
10. Andy Williams 44
11. Bobby Vinton....................44
12. Glen Campbell 42
13. Anne Murray.....................41
14. Al Martino 41
15. Barry Manilow...................39
16. Linda Ronstadt..................38
17. Olivia Newton-John 35
18. Chicago.............................34
19. John Denver.......................34
20. Stevie Wonder....................33
21. Englebert Humperdinck 33
22. Carpenters.........................32
23. Billy Joel...........................32
24. Jack Jones 32
25. James Taylor 30
26. Paul McCartney/Wings........30
27. Steve Lawrence 30

MOST TOP 40 HITS

1. Barbra Streisand.................58
2. Neil Diamond.....................53
3. Johnny Mathis 47
4. Elvis Presley......................45
5. Frank Sinatra 45
6. Elton John 44
7. Dionne Warwick 44
8. Herb Alpert/Tijuana Brass.....44
9. Andy Williams 44
10. Kenny Rogers/First Edition...43
11. Bobby Vinton....................39
12. Al Martino 39
13. Barry Manilow...................38
14. Anne Murray.....................38
15. Glen Campbell 38
16. Linda Ronstadt..................34
17. Olivia Newton-John 33
18. Chicago.............................33
19. John Denver.......................33
20. Carpenters.........................32
21. Jack Jones 31
22. Billy Joel...........................30
23. Stevie Wonder....................30
24. James Taylor 30

MOST TOP 10 HITS

1. Neil Diamond 36
2. Barbra Streisand 33
3. Elvis Presley......................31
4. Dionne Warwick 29
5. Kenny Rogers/First Edition...28
6. Barry Manilow...................27
7. Elton John 26
8. Bobby Vinton.....................24
9. Carpenters.........................23
10. Al Martino 23
11. Herb Alpert/Tijuana Brass....22
12. Olivia Newton-John 22
13. Chicago.............................22
14. Frank Sinatra 20
15. Glen Campbell 20
16. Billy Joel...........................20
17. Dean Martin 20
18. Anne Murray.....................19
19. Andy Williams 19
20. James Taylor 19
21. John Denver.......................18
22. Paul McCartney/Wings........18
23. Whitney Houston...............17
24. Lionel Richie 16
25. The Lettermen 16

MOST #1 HITS

1. Carpenters..........................15
2. Elton John 13
3. Barry Manilow....................13
4. Lionel Richie.......................11
5. Olivia Newton-John 10
6. Whitney Houston................10
7. John Denver......................... 9
8. Barbra Streisand 8
9. Neil Diamond..................... 8
10. Kenny Rogers/First Edition.... 8
11. Anne Murray..................... 8
12. Glen Campbell 8
13. Stevie Wonder.................... 8
14. Helen Reddy...................... 8
15. Elvis Presley...................... 7
16. Chicago............................. 7
17. Billy Joel........................... 7
18. Gloria Estefan/Miami
    Sound Machine.................. 7
19. Michael Bolton 7
20. Dionne Warwick 6
21. Frank Sinatra 6
22. Phil Collins........................ 6

MOST WEEKS AT THE #1 POSITION

1. Lionel Richie 47
2. Carpenters.........................38
3. Whitney Houston................31
4. Elton John 29
5. Barbra Streisand 28
6. Barry Manilow...................28
7. Frank Sinatra 26
8. Neil Diamond.....................25
9. Kenny Rogers/First Edition...24
10. Anne Murray.....................24
11. Olivia Newton-John 24
12. Phil Collins........................24
13. Michael Bolton 23
14. Stevie Wonder....................22
15. Elvis Presley......................21
16. Glen Campbell 21
17. Herb Alpert/Tijuana Brass....20
18. Bobby Vinton....................18
19. Peter Cetera.......................17
20. Billy Joel...........................16
21. John Denver.......................15
22. Dean Martin 15
23. Gloria Estefan/Miami
    Sound Machine.................15

MOST NON-*HOT 100* ADULT CONTEMPORARY HITS

1. Johnny Mathis 34
2. Jerry Vale...........................22
3. Eydie Gorme 21
4. Barbra Streisand 20
5. Steve Lawrence 19
6. Andy Williams 18
7. Henry Mancini....................17
8. Frank Sinatra 16
9. Perry Como 16
10. Tony Bennett 16
11. Jack Jones 15
12. Ray Conniff 15
13. Peggy Lee 14

MOST ADULT CONTEMPORARY HITS ONLY

1. Marilyn Maye 8
2. John Davidson ....
3. King Richard's Fluegel
   Knights ....
4. Paul Delicato......................
5. Tony Sandler & Ralph Young ...

The above artists had 5 or more A/C hits but never had a *Hot 100* hit.

Ties are broken according to rank in the *Top 200 Artists* section.

ALL-TIME TOP 50 #1 HITS
1961-1993

PK YR	WKS CHR	WKS T40	WKS T10	WKS @ #1	RANK	TITLE	ARTIST
68	24	24	17	11	1.	Love Is Blue	*Paul Mauriat*
78	19	19	13	10	2.	Time Passages	*Al Stewart*
68	17	17	13	10	3.	This Guy's In Love With You	*Herb Alpert*
61	16	16	12	10	4.	Big Bad John	*Jimmy Dean*
65	13	13	12	10	5.	King Of The Road	*Roger Miller*
64	21	21	18	9	6.	Hello, Dolly!	*Louis Armstrong And The All Stars*
67	17	17	14	9	7.	Somethin' Stupid	*Nancy Sinatra & Frank Sinatra*
91	34	29	15	8	8.	(Everything I Do) I Do It For You	*Bryan Adams*
69	17	17	13	8	9.	Love Theme From Romeo & Juliet	*Henry Mancini*
64	14	14	13	8	10.	Everybody Loves Somebody	*Dean Martin*
63	13	13	11	8	11.	Blue Velvet	*Bobby Vinton*
62	21	21	16	7	12.	Stranger On The Shore	*Mr. Acker Bilk*
79	26	24	15	7	13.	Lead Me On	*Maxine Nightingale*
64	17	17	15	7	14.	We'll Sing In The Sunshine	*Gale Garnett*
93	20 +	20 +	14 +	7	15.	I Don't Wanna Fight	*Tina Turner*
69	20	20	14	7	16.	I've Gotta Be Me	*Sammy Davis, Jr*
77	25	24	13	7	17.	Nobody Does It Better	*Carly Simon*
79	21	20	13	7	18.	Crazy Love	*Poco*
66	20	20	13	7	19.	Strangers In The Night	*Frank Sinatra*
70	16	16	12	7	20.	We've Only Just Begun	*Carpenters*
69	18	18	11	7	21.	Raindrops Keep Fallin' On My Head	*B.J. Thomas*
65	13	13	11	7	22.	Crying In The Chapel	*Elvis Presley*
72	14	14	10	7	23.	Song Sung Blue	*Neil Diamond*
66	24	24	20	6	24.	Born Free	*Roger Williams*
77	22	22	18	6	25.	Love Theme From "A Star Is Born" (Evergreen)	*Barbra Streisand*
93	34	31	17	6	26.	A Whole New World (Aladdin's Theme)	*Peabo Bryson & Regina Belle*
77	26	26	16	6	27.	How Deep Is Your Love	*Bee Gees*
92	30	29	15	6	28.	The One	*Elton John*
85	22	22	14	6	29.	Cherish	*Kool & The Gang*
68	18	18	14	6	30.	Wichita Lineman	*Glen Campbell*
90	28	26	13	6	31.	From A Distance	*Bette Midler*
89	23	22	13	6	32.	Right Here Waiting	*Richard Marx*
89	24	20	12	6	33.	If You Don't Know Me By Now	*Simply Red*
84	24	20	12	6	34.	Hello	*Lionel Richie*
83	20	17	12	6	35.	You Are	*Lionel Richie*
68	15	15	12	6	36.	The Fool On The Hill	*Sergio Mendes & Brasil '66*
62	13	13	12	6	37.	Go Away Little Girl	*Steve Lawrence*
80	22	22	11	6	38.	Lost In Love	*Air Supply*
70	17	17	11	6	39.	Snowbird	*Anne Murray*
70	16	16	11	6	40.	(They Long To Be) Close To You	*Carpenters*
81	19	15	11	6	41.	I Don't Need You	*Kenny Rogers*
81	18	15	11	6	42.	Yesterday's Songs	*Neil Diamond*
83	18	16	10	6	43.	Read 'Em And Weep	*Barry Manilow*
72	16	16	10	6	44.	Alone Again (Naturally)	*Gilbert O'Sullivan*
78	14	14	10	6	45.	We'll Never Have To Say Goodbye Again	*England Dan & John Ford Coley*
71	14	14	10	6	46.	Watching Scotty Grow	*Bobby Goldsboro*
72	14	14	10	6	47.	The First Time Ever I Saw Your Face	*Roberta Flack*
64	10	10	10	6	48.	Ringo	*Lorne Greene*
68	13	13	9	6	49.	Those Were The Days	*Mary Hopkin*
69	13	13	9	6	50.	Galveston	*Glen Campbell*

+: still charted as of 9/25/93

The rankings of the Top 50 #1 Hits are based on the most weeks a record held the No. 1 position. Ties are broken in this order: total weeks in the Top 10, total weeks in the Top 40; and, finally, total weeks charted.

TOP 50 #1 HITS BY DECADE
1961-1969

PK YR	WKS CHR	WKS T40	WKS T10	WKS @ #1	RANK TITLE	ARTIST
68	24	24	17	11	1. Love Is Blue	*Paul Mauriat*
68	17	17	13	10	2. This Guy's In Love With You	*Herb Alpert*
61	16	16	12	10	3. Big Bad John	*Jimmy Dean*
65	13	13	12	10	4. King Of The Road	*Roger Miller*
64	21	21	18	9	5. Hello, Dolly!	*Louis Armstrong*
67	17	17	14	9	6. Somethin' Stupid	*Nancy Sinatra & Frank Sinatra*
69	17	17	13	8	7. Love Theme From Romeo & Juliet	*Henry Mancini*
64	14	14	13	8	8. Everybody Loves Somebody	*Dean Martin*
63	13	13	11	8	9. Blue Velvet	*Bobby Vinton*
62	21	21	16	7	10. Stranger On The Shore	*Mr. Acker Bilk*
64	17	17	15	7	11. We'll Sing In The Sunshine	*Gale Garnett*
69	20	20	14	7	12. I've Gotta Be Me	*Sammy Davis, Jr.*
66	20	20	13	7	13. Strangers In The Night	*Frank Sinatra*
69	18	18	11	7	14. Raindrops Keep Fallin' On My Head	*B.J. Thomas*
65	13	13	11	7	15. Crying In The Chapel	*Elvis Presley*
66	24	24	20	6	16. Born Free	*Roger Williams*
68	18	18	14	6	17. Wichita Lineman	*Glen Campbell*
68	15	15	12	6	18. The Fool On The Hill	*Sergio Mendes & Brasil '66*
62	13	13	12	6	19. Go Away Little Girl	*Steve Lawrence*
64	10	10	10	6	20. Ringo	*Lorne Greene*
68	13	13	9	6	21. Those Were The Days	*Mary Hopkin*
69	13	13	9	6	22. Galveston	*Glen Campbell*
62	9	9	8	6	23. Can't Help Falling In Love	*Elvis Presley*
65	21	21	13	5	24. Taste Of Honey	*Herb Alpert & The Tijuana Brass*
65	20	20	12	5	25. You Were On My Mind	*We Five*
62	15	15	12	5	26. All Alone Am I	*Brenda Lee*
62	14	14	11	5	27. Ramblin' Rose	*Nat "King" Cole*
61	13	13	11	5	28. Michael	*The Highwaymen*
64	13	13	11	5	29. There! I've Said It Again	*Bobby Vinton*
62	13	13	11	5	30. I Can't Stop Loving You	*Ray Charles*
63	13	13	11	5	31. Blowin' In The Wind	*Peter, Paul & Mary*
63	12	12	11	5	32. Sukiyaki	*Kyu Sakamoto*
63	12	12	11	5	33. Walk Right In	*The Rooftop Singers*
67	14	14	10	5	34. The World We Knew (Over And Over)	*Frank Sinatra*
66	12	12	9	5	35. The Ballad Of The Green Berets	*SSgt Barry Sadler*
67	23	23	15	4	36. My Cup Runneth Over	*Ed Ames*
66	24	24	13	4	37. The Wheel Of Hurt	*Margaret Whiting*
67	18	18	13	4	38. Lady	*Jack Jones*
66	18	18	13	4	39. Somewhere, My Love	*Ray Conniff & The Singers*
64	13	13	12	4	40. Love Me With All Your Heart (Cuando Calienta El Sol)	*The Ray Charles Singers*
64	12	12	12	4	41. Java	*Al Hirt*
65	18	18	11	4	42. Make The World Go Away	*Eddy Arnold*
63	16	16	11	4	43. The End Of The World	*Skeeter Davis*
63	14	14	11	4	44. Can't Get Used To Losing You	*Andy Williams*
69	14	14	11	4	45. Jean	*Oliver*
63	13	13	11	4	46. Dominique	*The Singing Nun*
67	17	17	10	4	47. When The Snow Is On The Roses	*Ed Ames*
66	17	17	10	4	48. Spanish Eyes	*Al Martino*
62	13	13	10	4	49. Don't Break The Heart That Loves You	*Connie Francis*
66	13	13	8	4	50. Winchester Cathedral	*The New Vaudeville Band*

TOP 50 #1 HITS BY DECADE
1970-1979

PK YR	WKS CHR	WKS T40	WKS T10	WKS @ #1	RANK	TITLE	ARTIST
78	19	19	13	10	1.	Time Passages	Al Stewart
79	26	24	15	7	2.	Lead Me On	Maxine Nightingale
77	25	24	13	7	3.	Nobody Does It Better	Carly Simon
79	21	20	13	7	4.	Crazy Love	Poco
70	16	16	12	7	5.	We've Only Just Begun	Carpenters
72	14	14	10	7	6.	Song Sung Blue	Neil Diamond
77	22	22	18	6	7.	Love Theme From "A Star Is Born" (Evergreen)	Barbra Streisand
77	26	26	16	6	8.	How Deep Is Your Love	Bee Gees
70	17	17	11	6	9.	Snowbird	Anne Murray
70	16	16	11	6	10.	(They Long To Be) Close To You	Carpenters
72	16	16	10	6	11.	Alone Again (Naturally)	Gilbert O'Sullivan
78	14	14	10	6	12.	We'll Never Have To Say Goodbye Again	England Dan & John Ford Coley
71	14	14	10	6	13.	Watching Scotty Grow	Bobby Goldsboro
72	14	14	10	6	14.	The First Time Ever I Saw Your Face	Roberta Flack
70	10	10	8	6	15.	Bridge Over Troubled Water	Simon & Garfunkel
79	21	20	13	5	16.	You're Only Lonely	J.D. Souther
77	17	17	13	5	17.	It's Sad To Belong	England Dan & John Ford Coley
72	16	16	11	5	18.	Without You	Nilsson
79	18	17	10	5	19.	Broken Hearted Me	Anne Murray
78	14	14	10	5	20.	(What A) Wonderful World	Art Garfunkel/James Taylor/Paul Simon
71	14	14	10	5	21.	It's Too Late	Carole King
71	14	14	10	5	22.	All I Ever Need Is You	Sonny & Cher
71	14	14	8	5	23.	The Night They Drove Old Dixie Down	Joan Baez
77	18	18	14	4	24.	My Heart Belongs To Me	Barbra Streisand
78	23	23	13	4	25.	Just The Way You Are	Billy Joel
77	22	22	13	4	26.	Southern Nights	Glen Campbell
76	19	19	13	4	27.	Muskrat Love	Captain & Tennille
70	19	19	12	4	28.	It's Impossible	Perry Como
78	22	22	11	4	29.	Right Down The Line	Gerry Rafferty
73	16	16	11	4	30.	Leave Me Alone (Ruby Red Dress)	Helen Reddy
79	16	16	11	4	31.	I Just Fall In Love Again	Anne Murray
79	16	15	10	4	32.	Send One Your Love	Stevie Wonder
77	16	15	10	4	33.	Hello Stranger	Yvonne Elliman
73	14	14	10	4	34.	All I Know	Garfunkel
71	15	15	9	4	35.	(Where Do I Begin) Love Story	Andy Williams
71	12	12	9	4	36.	Rainy Days And Mondays	Carpenters
72	15	15	8	4	37.	I Can See Clearly Now	Johnny Nash
70	10	10	6	4	38.	Let It Be	The Beatles
73	23	23	14	3	39.	The Most Beautiful Girl	Charlie Rich
77	20	20	14	3	40.	Looks Like We Made It	Barry Manilow
79	24	23	13	3	41.	Shadows In The Moonlight	Anne Murray
78	18	17	13	3	42.	Fool (If You Think It's Over)	Chris Rea
78	21	20	12	3	43.	Bluer Than Blue	Michael Johnson
74	17	17	11	3	44.	Annie's Song	John Denver
72	21	21	10	3	45.	Baby Don't Get Hooked On Me	Mac Davis
78	16	16	10	3	46.	Even Now	Barry Manilow
78	20	18	9	3	47.	Three Times A Lady	Commodores
74	17	17	9	3	48.	Last Time I Saw Him	Diana Ross
72	15	15	9	3	49.	Clair	Gilbert O'Sullivan
73	13	13	9	3	50.	Say, Has Anybody Seen My Sweet Gypsy Rose	Dawn featuring Tony Orlando

TOP 50 #1 HITS BY DECADE
1980-1989

PK YR	WKS CHR	WKS T40	WKS T10	WKS @ #1	RANK	TITLE	ARTIST
85	22	22	14	6	1.	Cherish	Kool & The Gang
89	23	22	13	6	2.	Right Here Waiting	Richard Marx
89	24	20	12	6	3.	If You Don't Know Me By Now	Simply Red
84	24	20	12	6	4.	Hello	Lionel Richie
83	20	17	12	6	5.	You Are	Lionel Richie
80	22	22	11	6	6.	Lost In Love	Air Supply
81	19	15	11	6	7.	I Don't Need You	Kenny Rogers
81	18	15	11	6	8.	Yesterday's Songs	Neil Diamond
83	18	16	10	6	9.	Read 'Em And Weep	Barry Manilow
89	26	24	14	5	10.	Don't Know Much	Linda Ronstadt/Aaron Neville
89	23	21	13	5	11.	Another Day In Paradise	Phil Collins
84	20	20	13	5	12.	Stuck On You	Lionel Richie
80	21	19	13	5	13.	The Rose	Bette Midler
88	25	22	12	5	14.	Two Hearts	Phil Collins
80	23	22	12	5	15.	Woman In Love	Barbra Streisand
85	20	20	12	5	16.	Say You, Say Me	Lionel Richie
80	20	19	12	5	17.	Magic	Olivia Newton-John
82	21	18	12	5	18.	Any Day Now	Ronnie Milsap
82	28	25	11	5	19.	Chariots Of Fire - Titles	Vangelis
86	20	20	11	5	20.	Greatest Love Of All	Whitney Houston
86	19	19	11	5	21.	Glory Of Love	Peter Cetera
85	22	22	10	5	22.	Careless Whisper	Wham! Featuring George Michael
82	22	18	10	5	23.	Ebony And Ivory	Paul McCarntey with Stevie Wonder
83	27	23	13	4	24.	Never Gonna Let You Go	Sergio Mendes
83	24	20	13	4	25.	Islands In The Stream	Kenny Rogers with Dolly Parton
87	26	24	12	4	26.	(I've Had) The Time Of My Life	Bill Medley & Jennifer Warnes
84	23	23	12	4	27.	If Ever You're In My Arms Again	Peabo Bryson
89	25	22	11	4	28.	After All	Cher & Peter Cetera
85	22	22	11	4	29.	The Search Is Over	Survivor
89	23	21	11	4	30.	The Living Years	Mike + The Mechanics
83	23	20	11	4	31.	All Night Long (All Night)	Lionel Richie
84	19	19	11	4	32.	Penny Lover	Lionel Richie
87	20	20	10	4	33.	Ballerina Girl	Lionel Richie
82	21	19	10	4	34.	Truly	Lionel Richie
80	20	19	10	4	35.	Lady	Kenny Rogers
87	20	18	10	4	36.	Got My Mind Set On You	George Harrison
82	18	18	10	4	37.	The Girl Is Mine	Michael Jackson/Paul McCartney
81	17	15	10	4	38.	What Kind Of Fool	Barbra Streisand & Barry Gibb
88	22	20	9	4	39.	One Good Woman	Peter Cetera
87	22	18	9	4	40.	Little Lies	Fleetwood Mac
81	23	17	9	4	41.	Arthur's Theme (Best That You Can Do)	Christopher Cross
82	19	17	9	4	42.	Even The Nights Are Better	Air Supply
84	20	15	9	4	43.	Got A Hold On Me	Christine McVie
82	21	18	8	4	44.	Heartlight	Neil Diamond
83	19	17	8	4	45.	All Time High	Rita Coolidge
83	18	16	8	4	46.	My Love	Lionel Richie
84	20	15	8	4	47.	Think Of Laura	Christopher Cross
82	24	21	14	3	48.	Hard To Say I'm Sorry	Chicago
80	26	23	13	3	49.	Let Me Love You Tonight	Pure Prairie League
86	22	22	12	3	50.	Love Is Forever	Billy Ocean

TOP 50 #1 HITS BY DECADE
1990-1993

PK YR	WKS CHR	WKS T40	WKS T10	WKS @ #1	RANK	TITLE	ARTIST
91	34	29	15	8	1.	(Everything I Do) I Do It For You	Bryan Adams
93	20 +	20 +	14 +	7	2.	I Don't Wanna Fight	Tina Turner
93	34	31	17	6	3.	A Whole New World (Aladdin's Theme)	Peabo Bryson & Regina Belle
92	30	29	15	6	4.	The One	Elton John
90	28	26	13	6	5.	From A Distance	Bette Midler
92	36	34	14	5	6.	Hold On My Heart	Genesis
92	29	25	14	5	7.	To Love Somebody	Michael Bolton
93	23 +	23 +	14	5	8.	Have I Told You Lately	Rod Stewart
92	28	26	12	5	9.	I Will Always Love You	Whitney Houston
91	27	25	12	5	10.	Rush, Rush	Paula Abdul
90	29	24	12	5	11.	Do You Remember?	Phil Collins
90	27	24	12	5	12.	Here We Are	Gloria Estefan
90	23	21	11	5	13.	You Gotta Love Someone	Elton John
90	24	21	10	5	14.	This Old Heart Of Mine	Rod Stewart (with Ronald Isley)
92	34	32	14	4	15.	Sometimes Love Just Ain't Enough	Patty Smyth with Don Henley
91	27	23	14	4	16.	You're In Love	Wilson Phillips
91	29	28	13	4	17.	Love Is A Wonderful Thing	Michael Bolton
91	33	26	13	4	18.	When A Man Loves A Woman	Michael Bolton
91	29	25	13	4	19.	All The Man That I Need	Whitney Houston
91	22	20	13	4	20.	Keep Coming Back	Richard Marx
90	25	23	11	4	21.	Love Will Lead You Back	Taylor Dayne
93	34 +	33 +	21	3	22.	Love Is	Vanessa Williams & Brian McKnight
92	33	29	16	3	23.	If You Asked Me To	Celine Dion
92	33	29	15	3	24.	Save The Best For Last	Vanessa Williams
91	32	30	14	3	25.	Baby Baby	Amy Grant
91	32	27	14	3	26.	That's What Love Is For	Amy Grant
92	30	27	14	3	27.	Tears In Heaven	Eric Clapton
90	29	27	13	3	28.	Oh Girl	Paul Young
92	29	26	13	3	29.	Can't Let Go	Mariah Carey
92	30	27	12	3	30.	Missing You Now	Michael Bolton Featuring Kenny G
93	27	27	12	3	31.	Simple Life	Elton John
90	24	22	12	3	32.	All My Life	Linda Ronstadt/Aaron Neville
90	28	25	11	3	33.	Vision Of Love	Mariah Carey
90	23	20	9	3	34.	Come Back To Me	Janet Jackson
90	20	19	9	3	35.	When I'm Back On My Feet Again	Michael Bolton
93	34	34	15	2	36.	Forever In Love	Kenny G
92	36	32	14	2	37.	Restless Heart	Peter Cetera
93	25	25	14	2	38.	Tell Me What You Dream	Restless Heart Featuring Warren Hill
90	26	22	14	2	39.	How Am I Supposed To Live Without You	Michael Bolton
91	26	22	13	2	40.	Coming Out Of The Dark	Gloria Estefan
93	21	21	13	2	41.	I Have Nothing	Whitney Houston
91	29	27	11	2	42.	Too Many Walls	Cathy Dennis
92	24	22	11	2	43.	What Becomes Of The Brokenhearted	Paul Young
93	20 +	20 +	11	2	44.	By The Time This Night Is Over	Kenny G & Peabo Bryson
92	21	19	11	2	45.	I'll Be There	Mariah Carey
91	28	24	10	2	46.	The First Time	Surface
92	27	21	10	2	47.	I Will Be Here For You	Michael W. Smith
91	24	21	10	2	48.	Because I Love You (The Postman Song)	Stevie B
91	27	25	9	2	49.	Time, Love And Tenderness	Michael Bolton
92	23	22	9	2	50.	Don't Let The Sun Go Down On Me	George Michael/Elton John

+: still charted as of 9/25/93

RECORDS OF LONGEVITY

Records with 30 or more total weeks charted.

PK YR	PK WKS	PK POS	WKS CHR	RANK	TITLE	ARTIST
90	1	1	38	1.	Love Takes Time	Mariah Carey
90	2	2	38	2.	I Don't Have The Heart	James Ingram
92	2	2	38	3.	Just Another Day	Jon Secada
92	1	3	37	4.	Do You Believe In Us	Jon Secada
92	4	4	37	5.	Take This Heart	Richard Marx
92	5	1	36	6.	Hold On My Heart	Genesis
92	2	1	36	7.	Restless Heart	Peter Cetera
78	3	3	36	8.	You Needed Me	Anne Murray
92	4	6	36	9.	I Can't Make You Love Me	Bonnie Raitt
92	5	4	35	10.	Never A Time	Genesis
88	3	7	35	11.	What A Wonderful World	Louis Armstrong
					(first charted in 1967 for 21 weeks and re-charted in 1988 for 14 weeks)	
91	8	1	34	12.	(Everything I Do) I Do It For You	Bryan Adams
93	6	1	34	13.	A Whole New World (Aladdin's Theme)	Peabo Bryson & Regina Belle
92	4	1	34	14.	Sometimes Love Just Ain't Enough	Patty Smyth with Don Henley
93	3	1	34 +	15.	Love Is	Vanessa Williams & Brian McKnight
93	2	1	34	16.	Forever In Love	Kenny G
92	4	3	34	17.	Beauty And The Beast	Celine Dion & Peabo Bryson
93	1	3	34 +	18.	I See Your Smile	Gloria Estefan
91	3	5	34	19.	Something To Talk About	Bonnie Raitt
92	2	8	34	20.	Stars	Simply Red
91	4	1	33	21.	When A Man Loves A Woman	Michael Bolton
93	3	1	33	22.	If You Asked Me To	Celine Dion
92	3	1	33	23.	Save The Best For Last	Vanessa Williams
92	7	2	33	24.	When She Cries	Restless Heart
91	6	2	33	25.	Every Heartbeat	Amy Grant
92	2	2	33	26.	I Will Remember You	Amy Grant
91	1	2	33	27.	Where Does My Heart Beat Now	Celine Dion
88	1	2	33	28.	Hands To Heaven	Breathe
90	2	3	33	29.	Here And Now	Luther Vandross
93	2	3	33	30.	Faithful	Go West
79	3	6	33	31.	All Things Are Possible	Dan Peek
91	3	1	32	32.	Baby Baby	Amy Grant
91	3	1	32	33.	That's What Love Is For	Amy Grant
92	1	1	32	34.	Hazard	Richard Marx
77	2	2	32	35.	On And On	Stephen Bishop
91	3	5	32	36.	I Wonder Why	Curtis Stigers
91	2	5	32	37.	Place In This World	Michael W. Smith
89	2	1	31	38.	Second Chance	Thirty Eight Special
93	1	1	31 +	39.	I'll Never Get Over You (Getting Over Me)	Expose
91	1	1	31	40.	Everybody Plays The Fool	Aaron Neville
87	1	2	31	41.	The Lady In Red	Chris DeBurgh
91	2	3	31	42.	Show Me The Way	Styx
90	1	6	31	43.	Any Other Fool	Sadao Watanabe Featuring Patti Austin
92	6	1	30	44.	The One	Elton John
92	3	1	30	45.	Tears In Heaven	Eric Clapton
92	3	1	30	46.	Missing You Now	Michael Bolton Featuring Kenny G
91	1	1	30	47.	Cry For Help	Rick Astley
90	1	1	30	48.	Release Me	Wilson Phillips
92	2	2	30	49.	The Last Song	Elton John
88	2	2	30	50.	I'll Always Love You	Taylor Dayne
92	1	2	30	51.	Masterpiece	Atlantic Starr
88	4	5	30	52.	Kokomo	The Beach Boys
93	2	9	30	53.	Heal The World	Michael Jackson
89	1	9	30	54.	Talk It Over	Grayson Hugh
92	1	15	30	55.	Would I Lie To You?	Charles & Eddie

+: still charted as of 9/25/93

f a record charted more than once, the recharted hit must be the original recording and not a remake in order to qualify
see #11 above).

#1 HITS

This section lists in chronological order, by peak date, all 637 singles which hit the #1 position on *Billboard's Easy Listening/Adult Contemporary* chart from July 17, 1961 through July 24, 1993.

Beginning in 1976, *Billboard* ceased publishing a year-end issue. The year's last regular isssue is considered frozen and all chart positions remain the same for the unpublished week.

DATE: Date single first peaked at the #1 position

WKS: Total weeks single held the #1 position

↕: Indicates single hit #1, dropped down, and then returned to the #1 spot

> The <u>top hit</u> of each year is boxed out for quick reference. The top hit is determined by most weeks at the #1 position. If there is a tie, the higher ranked record in our **Billboard Top 1000 x 5** book is selected.

#1 HITS

1961

	DATE	WKS		
1.	7/17	3	**The Boll Weevil Song**	*Brook Benton*
2.	8/7	1	**Together**	*Connie Francis*
3.	8/14	3	**Wooden Heart**	*Joe Dowell*
4.	9/4	5	**Michael**	*The Highwaymen*
5.	10/9	1	**Mexico**	*Bob Moore*
6.	10/16	1	**Sad Movies (Make Me Cry)**	
			Sue Thompson	
7.	10/23	10	**Big Bad John**	*Jimmy Dean*

1962

	DATE	WKS		
1.	1/6	1	**When I Fall In Love**	*The Lettermen*
2.	1/13	6	**Can't Help Falling In Love**	
			Elvis Presley	
3.	2/24	1	**A Little Bitty Tear**	*Burl Ives*
4.	3/3	3	**Midnight In Moscow**	
			Kenny Ball and His Jazzmen	
5.	3/24	4	**Don't Break The Heart That Loves You**	*Connie Francis*
6.	4/21	7	**Stranger On The Shore**	
			Mr. Acker Bilk	
7.	6/9	5↕	**I Can't Stop Loving You**	
			Ray Charles	
8.	7/7	2	**The Stripper**	*David Rose*
9.	7/28	4	**Roses Are Red (My Love)**	
			Bobby Vinton	
10.	8/25	3	**You Don't Know Me**	*Ray Charles*
11.	9/15	5	**Ramblin' Rose**	*Nat "King" Cole*
12.	10/20	1	**I Remember You**	*Frank Ifield*
13.	10/27	2	**Only Love Can Break A Heart**	
			Gene Pitney	
14.	11/10	5	**All Alone Am I**	*Brenda Lee*
15.	12/15	6	**Go Away Little Girl**	*Steve Lawrence*

1963

	DATE	WKS		
1.	1/26	5	**Walk Right In**	*The Rooftop Singers*
2.	3/2	2	**Rhythm Of The Rain**	*The Cascades*
3.	3/16	4	**The End Of The World**	*Skeeter Davis*
4.	4/13	4	**Can't Get Used To Losing You**	
			Andy Williams	
5.	5/11	2	**Puff The Magic Dragon**	
			Peter, Paul & Mary	
6.	5/25	2	**I Love You Because**	*Al Martino*
7.	6/8	5	**Sukiyaki**	*Kyu Sakamoto*
8.	7/13	3	**Tie Me Kangaroo Down, Sport**	
			Rolf Harris	
9.	8/3	5	**Blowin' In The Wind**	
			Peter, Paul & Mary	
10.	9/7	8	**Blue Velvet**	*Bobby Vinton*
11.	11/2	3	**Washington Square**	
			The Village Stompers	
12.	11/23	2	**I'm Leaving It Up To You**	
			Dale & Grace	
13.	12/7	4	**Dominique**	*The Singing Nun*

1964

	DATE	WKS		
1.	1/4	5	**There! I've Said It Again**	
			Bobby Vinton	
2.	2/8	2	**For You**	*Rick Nelson*
3.	2/22	4	**Java**	*Al Hirt*
4.	3/21	1	**Navy Blue**	*Diane Renay*
5.	3/28	9	**Hello, Dolly!**	*Louis Armstrong*
6.	5/30	4	**Love Me With All Your Heart (Cuando Calienta El Sol)**	
			The Ray Charles Singers	
7.	6/27	3	**People**	*Barbra Streisand*
8.	7/18	2	**The Girl From Ipanema**	
			Stan Getz/Astrud Gilberto	
9.	8/1	8	**Everybody Loves Somebody**	
			Dean Martin	
10.	9/26	7	**We'll Sing In The Sunshine**	
			Gale Garnett	
11.	11/14	1	**The Door Is Still Open To My Heart**	
			Dean Martin	
12.	11/21	6	**Ringo**	*Lorne Greene*

1965

	DATE	WKS		
1.	1/2	3	**The Wedding**	*Julie Rogers*
2.	1/23	1	**Willow Weep For Me**	*Chad & Jeremy*
3.	1/30	1	**You're Nobody Till Somebody Loves You**	*Dean Martin*
4.	2/6	1	**Have You Looked Into Your Heart**	
			Jerry Vale	
5.	2/13	10	**King Of The Road**	*Roger Miller*
6.	4/24	1	**The Race Is On**	*Jack Jones*
7.	5/1	3	**Cast Your Fate To The Wind**	
			Sounds Orchestral	
8.	5/22	7	**Crying In The Chapel**	*Elvis Presley*
9.	7/10	2	**A Walk In The Black Forest**	
			Horst Jankowski	
10.	7/24	2	**(Such An) Easy Question**	
			Elvis Presley	
11.	8/7	3	**Save Your Heart For Me**	
			Gary Lewis & The Playboys	
12.	8/28	1	**Hold Me, Thrill Me, Kiss Me**	
			Mel Carter	
13.	9/4	5	**You Were On My Mind**	*We Five*
14.	10/9	3	**I'm Yours**	*Elvis Presley*
15.	10/30	5	**Taste Of Honey**	
			Herb Alpert & The Tijuana Brass	
16.	12/4	4	**Make The World Go Away**	
			Eddy Arnold	

1966

	DATE	WKS		
1.	1/1	1	**England Swings**	*Roger Miller*
2.	1/8	4	**Spanish Eyes**	*Al Martino*
3.	2/5	1	**It Was A Very Good Year**	
			Frank Sinatra	
4.	2/12	3	**Crying Time**	*Ray Charles*
5.	3/5	5	**The Ballad Of The Green Berets**	
			SSgt Barry Sadler	
6.	4/9	3	**I Want To Go With You**	*Eddy Arnold*
7.	4/30	3	**Together Again**	*Ray Charles*

#1 HITS

1966 (cont.)

8.	5/21	2	**Band Of Gold** *Mel Carter*
9.	6/4	7	**Strangers In The Night**
			Frank Sinatra
10.	7/23	1	**The Impossible Dream (The Quest)**
			Jack Jones
11.	7/30	4	**Somewhere, My Love**
			Ray Conniff & The Singers
12.	8/27	1	**I Couldn't Live Without Your Love**
			Petula Clark
13.	9/3	6↕	**Born Free** *Roger Williams*
14.	10/1	2	**In The Arms Of Love** *Andy Williams*
15.	10/15	1	**Summer Wind** *Frank Sinatra*
16.	11/5	4	**The Wheel Of Hurt** *Margaret Whiting*
17.	12/3	4	**Winchester Cathedral**
			The New Vaudeville Band
18.	12/31	3	**That's Life** *Frank Sinatra*

1967

	DATE	WKS	
1.	1/21	2	**Sugar Town** *Nancy Sinatra*
2.	2/4	4	**My Cup Runneth Over** *Ed Ames*
3.	3/4	4	**Lady** *Jack Jones*
4.	4/1	9	**Somethin' Stupid**
			Nancy Sinatra & Frank Sinatra
5.	6/3	2	**Casino Royale**
			Herb Alpert & The Tijuana Brass
6.	6/17	1	**Time, Time** *Ed Ames*
7.	6/24	1	**Stop! And Think It Over** *Perry Como*
8.	7/1	2	**Mary In The Morning** *Al Martino*
9.	7/15	3	**Don't Sleep In The Subway**
			Petula Clark
10.	8/5	1	**It's Such A Pretty World Today**
			Andy Russell
11.	8/12	3	**In The Chapel In The Moonlight**
			Dean Martin
12.	9/2	5	**The World We Knew (Over And Over)** *Frank Sinatra*
13.	10/7	2	**A Banda**
			Herb Alpert & The Tijuana Brass
14.	10/21	3	**It Must Be Him** *Vikki Carr*
15.	11/11	2	**More Than The Eye Can See**
			Al Martino
16.	11/25	4	**When The Snow Is On The Roses**
			Ed Ames
17.	12/23	2	**Cold** *John Gary*

1968

	DATE	WKS	
1.	1/6	2	**Chattanooga Choo Choo**
			Harpers Bizarre
2.	1/20	2	**In The Misty Moonlight** *Dean Martin*
3.	2/3	1	**Am I That Easy To Forget**
			Engelbert Humperdinck
4.	2/10	1	**The Lesson** *Vikki Carr*
5.	2/17	11	**Love Is Blue** *Paul Mauriat*
6.	5/4	2	**Honey** *Bobby Goldsboro*
7.	5/18	3	**The Good, The Bad And The Ugly**
			Hugo Montenegro

1968 (cont.)

8.	6/8	10	**This Guy's In Love With You**
			Herb Alpert
9.	8/17	3	**Classical Gas** *Mason Williams*
10.	9/7	6	**The Fool On The Hill**
			Sergio Mendes & Brasil '66
11.	10/19	2	**My Special Angel** *The Vogues*
12.	11/2	6	**Those Were The Days** *Mary Hopkin*
13.	12/14	6	**Wichita Lineman** *Glen Campbell*

1969

	DATE	WKS	
1.	1/25	7	**I've Gotta Be Me** *Sammy Davis, Jr.*
2.	3/15	2	**You Gave Me A Mountain**
			Frankie Laine
3.	3/29	6	**Galveston** *Glen Campbell*
4.	5/10	2	**Aquarius/Let The Sunshine In**
			The 5th Dimension
5.	5/24	2	**Happy Heart** *Andy Williams*
6.	6/7	8	**Love Theme From Romeo & Juliet**
			Henry Mancini
7.	8/2	2	**Spinning Wheel** *Blood, Sweat & Tears*
8.	8/16	2	**In The Year 2525 (Exordium & Terminus)** *Zager & Evans*
9.	8/30	2	**A Boy Named Sue** *Johnny Cash*
10.	9/13	1	**I'll Never Fall In Love Again**
			Tom Jones
11.	9/20	4	**Jean** *Oliver*
12.	10/18	2	**Is That All There Is** *Peggy Lee*
13.	11/1	2	**Wedding Bell Blues**
			The 5th Dimension
14.	11/15	1	**Try A Little Kindness** *Glen Campbell*
15.	11/22	3	**Leaving On A Jet Plane**
			Peter, Paul & Mary
16.	12/13	7	**Raindrops Keep Fallin' On My Head**
			B.J. Thomas

1970

	DATE	WKS	
1.	1/31	1	**Without Love (There Is Nothing)**
			Tom Jones
2.	2/7	3	**I'll Never Fall In Love Again**
			Dionne Warwick
3.	2/28	6	**Bridge Over Troubled Water**
			Simon & Garfunkel
4.	4/11	4	**Let It Be** *The Beatles*
5.	5/9	2	**For The Love Of Him** *Bobbi Martin*
6.	5/23	3	**Everything Is Beautiful** *Ray Stevens*
7.	6/13	1	**Daughter Of Darkness** *Tom Jones*
8.	6/20	1	**The Wonder Of You** *Elvis Presley*
9.	6/27	2	**A Song Of Joy** *Miguel Rios*
10.	7/11	6	**(They Long To Be) Close To You**
			Carpenters
11.	8/22	1	**I Just Can't Help Believing**
			B.J. Thomas
12.	8/29	6	**Snowbird** *Anne Murray*
13.	10/10	7	**We've Only Just Begun** *Carpenters*
14.	11/28	1	**You Don't Have To Say You Love Me** *Elvis Presley*
15.	12/5	4	**It's Impossible** *Perry Como*

#1 HITS

1971

	DATE	WKS	
1.	1/2	1	**One Less Bell To Answer** *The 5th Dimension*
2.	1/9	6	**Watching Scotty Grow** *Bobby Goldsboro*
3.	2/20	1	**If You Could Read My Mind** *Gordon Lightfoot*
4.	2/27	3	**For All We Know** *Carpenters*
5.	3/20	4↕	**(Where Do I Begin) Love Story** *Andy Williams*
6.	4/3	1	**When There's No You** *Engelbert Humperdinck*
7.	4/24	3	**If** *Bread*
8.	5/15	2	**Me And You And A Dog Named Boo** *Lobo*
9.	5/29	4	**Rainy Days And Mondays** *Carpenters*
10.	6/26	5	**It's Too Late** *Carole King*
11.	7/31	1	**You've Got A Friend** *James Taylor*
12.	8/7	3	**If Not For You** *Olivia Newton-John*
13.	8/28	1	**Beginnings** *Chicago*
14.	9/4	5	**The Night They Drove Old Dixie Down** *Joan Baez*
15.	10/9	2	**Superstar** *Carpenters*
16.	10/23	1	**Never My Love** *The 5th Dimension*
17.	10/30	3	**Peace Train** *Cat Stevens*
18.	11/20	1	**Baby I'm-A Want You** *Bread*
19.	11/27	5	**All I Ever Need Is You** *Sonny & Cher*

1972

	DATE	WKS	
1.	1/1	1	**An Old Fashioned Love Song** *Three Dog Night*
2.	1/8	1	**Cherish** *David Cassidy*
3.	1/15	3	**American Pie - Parts I & II** *Don McLean*
4.	2/5	2	**Hurting Each Other** *Carpenters*
5.	2/19	5	**Without You** *Nilsson*
6.	3/25	1	**Rock And Roll Lullaby** *B.J. Thomas*
7.	4/1	6	**The First Time Ever I Saw Your Face** *Roberta Flack*
8.	5/13	1	**Morning Has Broken** *Cat Stevens*
9.	5/20	2	**The Candy Man** *Sammy Davis, Jr.*
10.	6/3	7	**Song Sung Blue** *Neil Diamond*
11.	7/22	1	**Where Is The Love** *Roberta Flack & Donny Hathaway*
12.	7/29	6	**Alone Again (Naturally)** *Gilbert O'Sullivan*
13.	9/9	1	**The Guitar Man** *Bread*
14.	9/16	3	**Baby Don't Get Hooked On Me** *Mac Davis*
15.	10/7	1	**Black & White** *Three Dog Night*
16.	10/14	2	**Garden Party** *Rick Nelson & The Stone Canyon Band*
17.	10/28	1	**If I Could Reach You** *The 5th Dimension*
18.	11/4	4	**I Can See Clearly Now** *Johnny Nash*
19.	12/2	1	**I'd Love You To Want Me** *Lobo*
20.	12/9	3	**Clair** *Gilbert O'Sullivan*
21.	12/30	2	**Sweet Surrender** *Bread*

1973

	DATE	WKS	
1.	1/13	1	**Been To Canaan** *Carole King*
2.	1/20	2	**You're So Vain** *Carly Simon*
3.	2/3	2	**Don't Expect Me To Be Your Friend** *Lobo*
4.	2/17	2	**Dueling Banjos** *Eric Weissberg & Steve Mandell*
5.	3/3	2	**Last Song** *Edward Bear*
6.	3/17	2	**Danny's Song** *Anne Murray*
7.	3/31	2↕	**Sing** *Carpenters*
8.	4/7	2↕	**Tie A Yellow Ribbon Round The Ole Oak Tree** *Dawn featuring Tony Orlando*
9.	4/28	2	**You Are The Sunshine Of My Life** *Stevie Wonder*
10.	5/12	2	**Daniel** *Elton John*
11.	5/26	1	**And I Love You So** *Perry Como*
12.	6/2	3	**My Love** *Paul McCartney & Wings*
13.	6/23	2	**Boogie Woogie Bugle Boy** *Bette Midler*
14.	7/7	3	**Yesterday Once More** *Carpenters*
15.	7/28	1	**Touch Me In The Morning** *Diana Ross*
16.	8/4	2	**Delta Dawn** *Helen Reddy*
17.	8/18	3	**Say, Has Anybody Seen My Sweet Gypsy Rose** *Dawn featuring Tony Orlando*
18.	9/8	2	**Loves Me Like A Rock** *Paul Simon*
19.	9/22	1	**My Maria** *B.W. Stevenson*
20.	9/29	1	**I'm Coming Home** *Johnny Mathis*
21.	10/6	4	**All I Know** *Garfunkel*
22.	11/3	1	**Paper Roses** *Marie Osmond*
23.	11/10	3	**The Most Beautiful Girl** *Charlie Rich*
24.	12/1	4	**Leave Me Alone (Ruby Red Dress)** *Helen Reddy*
25.	12/29	2	**Time In A Bottle** *Jim Croce*

1974

	DATE	WKS	
1.	1/12	2	**The Way We Were** *Barbra Streisand*
2.	1/26	2	**Love's Theme** *Love Unlimited Orchestra*
3.	2/9	1	**Love Song** *Anne Murray*
4.	2/16	3	**Last Time I Saw Him** *Diana Ross*
5.	3/9	1	**Seasons In The Sun** *Terry Jacks*
6.	3/16	2	**Sunshine On My Shoulders** *John Denver*
7.	3/30	2	**A Very Special Love Song** *Charlie Rich*
8.	4/13	2	**Keep On Singing** *Helen Reddy*
9.	4/27	1	**I'll Have To Say I Love You In A Song** *Jim Croce*
10.	5/4	2	**TSOP (The Sound Of Philadelphia)** *MFSB feat. The Three Degrees*
11.	5/18	1	**The Entertainer** *Marvin Hamlisch*
12.	5/25	1	**Help Me** *Joni Mitchell*
13.	6/1	1	**I Won't Last A Day Without You** *Carpenters*
14.	6/8	2	**Sundown** *Gordon Lightfoot*
15.	6/22	2	**You Won't See Me** *Anne Murray*
16.	7/6	3	**Annie's Song** *John Denver*

#1 HITS

1974 (cont.)

17.	7/27	1	**You And Me Against The World** *Helen Reddy*
18.	8/3	1	**Please Come To Boston** *Dave Loggins*
19.	8/10	2	**Feel Like Makin' Love** *Roberta Flack*
20.	8/24	1	**Call On Me** *Chicago*
21.	8/31	1	**I'm Leaving It (All) Up To You** *Donny & Marie Osmond*
22.	9/7	1	**I Love My Friend** *Charlie Rich*
23.	9/14	3	**I Honestly Love You** *Olivia Newton-John*
24.	10/5	1	**Tin Man** *America*
25.	10/12	1	**Stop And Smell The Roses** *Mac Davis*
26.	10/19	1	**Carefree Highway** *Gordon Lightfoot*
27.	10/26	2	**Back Home Again** *John Denver*
28.	11/9	1	**My Melody Of Love** *Bobby Vinton*
29.	11/16	1	**Longfellow Serenade** *Neil Diamond*
30.	11/23	2	**Laughter In The Rain** *Neil Sedaka*
31.	12/7	1	**Angie Baby** *Helen Reddy*
32.	12/14	1	**When Will I See You Again** *The Three Degrees*
33.	12/21	1	**Wishing You Were Here** *Chicago*
34.	12/28	2	**Mandy** *Barry Manilow*

1975

	DATE	WKS	
1.	1/11	1	**Only You** *Ringo Starr*
2.	1/18	1	**Please Mr. Postman** *Carpenters*
3.	1/25	1	**Morning Side Of The Mountain** *Donny & Marie Osmond*
4.	2/1	1	**Best Of My Love** *Eagles*
5.	2/8	1	**Sweet Surrender** *John Denver*
6.	2/15	1	**Lonely People** *America*
7.	2/22	1	**Nightingale** *Carole King*
8.	3/1	1	**Poetry Man** *Phoebe Snow*
9.	3/8	1	**Have You Never Been Mellow** *Olivia Newton-John*
10.	3/15	1	**I've Been This Way Before** *Neil Diamond*
11.	3/22	1	**(Hey Won't You Play) Another Somebody Done Somebody Wrong Song** *B.J. Thomas*
12.	3/29	1	**Emotion** *Helen Reddy*
13.	4/5	1	**My Boy** *Elvis Presley*
14.	4/12	1	**The Last Farewell** *Roger Whittaker*
15.	4/19	1	**He Don't Love You (Like I Love You)** *Tony Orlando & Dawn*
16.	4/26	1	**It's A Miracle** *Barry Manilow*
17.	5/3	1	**Only Yesterday** *Carpenters*
18.	5/10	1	**The Immigrant** *Neil Sedaka*
19.	5/17	1	**Rainy Day People** *Gordon Lightfoot*
20.	5/24	1	**99 Miles From L.A.** *Albert Hammond*
21.	5/31	1	**Wonderful Baby** *Don McLean*
22.	6/7	1	**Love Will Keep Us Together** *Captain & Tennille*
23.	6/14	1	**Wildfire** *Michael Murphey*
24.	6/21	2	**Midnight Blue** *Melissa Manchester*

1975 (cont.)

25.	7/5	1	**Every Time You Touch Me (I Get High)** *Charlie Rich*
26.	7/12	3	**Please Mr. Please** *Olivia Newton-John*
27.	8/2	1	**Rhinestone Cowboy** *Glen Campbell*
28.	8/9	2	**At Seventeen** *Janis Ian*
29.	8/23	1	**How Sweet It Is (To Be Loved By You)** *James Taylor*
30.	8/30	1	**Fallin' In Love** *Hamilton, Joe Frank & Reynolds*
31.	9/6	1	**Solitaire** *Carpenters*
32.	9/13	1	**The Proud One** *The Osmonds*
33.	9/20	2	**I'm Sorry** *John Denver*
34.	10/4	1	**Ain't No Way To Treat A Lady** *Helen Reddy*
35.	10/11	1	**I Only Have Eyes For You** *Art Garfunkel*
36.	10/18	3	**Something Better To Do** *Olivia Newton-John*
37.	11/8	2	**The Way I Want To Touch You** *Captain & Tennille*
38.	11/22	2	**My Little Town** *Simon & Garfunkel*
39.	12/6	1	**Theme From Mahogany (Do You Know Where You're Going To)** *Diana Ross*
40.	12/13	2	**I Write The Songs** *Barry Manilow*
41.	12/27	1	**Country Boy (You Got Your Feet In L.A.)** *Glen Campbell*

1976

	DATE	WKS	
1.	1/3	1	**Times Of Your Life** *Paul Anka*
2.	1/10	2↕	**Fly Away** *John Denver*
3.	1/17	2	**Let It Shine** *Olivia Newton-John*
4.	2/7	1	**Breaking Up Is Hard To Do** *Neil Sedaka*
5.	2/14	1	**Paloma Blanca** *George Baker Selection*
6.	2/21	1	**Break Away** *Art Garfunkel*
7.	2/28	2	**50 Ways To Leave Your Lover** *Paul Simon*
8.	3/13	1	**Lonely Night (Angel Face)** *Captain & Tennille*
9.	3/20	1	**Venus** *Frankie Avalon*
10.	3/27	1	**Only Love Is Real** *Carole King*
11.	4/3	2	**There's A Kind Of Hush (All Over The World)** *Carpenters*
12.	4/17	1	**Looking For Space** *John Denver*
13.	4/24	1	**Come On Over** *Olivia Newton-John*
14.	5/1	1	**Tryin' To Get The Feeling Again** *Barry Manilow*
15.	5/8	1	**Don't Pull Your Love/Then You Can Tell Me Goodbye** *Glen Campbell*
16.	5/15	2	**Welcome Back** *John Sebastian*
17.	5/29	1	**Silly Love Songs** *Wings*
18.	6/5	1	**Shop Around** *Captain & Tennille*
19.	6/12	1	**Save Your Kisses For Me** *The Brotherhood Of Man*

#1 HITS

1976 (cont.)

	DATE	WKS		
20.	6/19	1	**Never Gonna Fall In Love Again**	
			Eric Carmen	
21.	6/26	2	**Today's The Day** *America*	
22.	7/10	1	**I Need To Be In Love** *Carpenters*	
23.	7/17	2↕	**If You Know What I Mean**	
			Neil Diamond	
24.	7/24	1	**I'm Easy** *Keith Carradine*	
25.	7/31	1	**You'll Never Find Another Love Like Mine** *Lou Rawls*	
26.	8/7	1	**Let 'Em In** *Wings*	
27.	8/21	1	**I'd Really Love To See You Tonight**	
			England Dan & John Ford Coley	
28.	8/28	1	**Shower The People** *James Taylor*	
29.	9/4	1	**Summer** *War*	
30.	9/11	1	**Don't Go Breaking My Heart**	
			Elton John & Kiki Dee	
31.	9/18	1	**Don't Stop Believin'**	
			Olivia Newton-John	
32.	9/25	1	**If You Leave Me Now** *Chicago*	
33.	10/2	1	**I Can't Hear You No More**	
			Helen Reddy	
34.	10/9	1	**Like A Sad Song** *John Denver*	
35.	10/16	2	**Fernando** *Abba*	
36.	10/30	4↕	**Muskrat Love** *Captain & Tennille*	
37.	11/13	1	**This One's For You** *Barry Manilow*	
38.	12/4	2	**After The Lovin'**	
			Engelbert Humperdinck	
39.	12/18	1	**Sorry Seems To Be The Hardest Word** *Elton John*	
40.	12/25	2	**Torn Between Two Lovers**	
			Mary MacGregor	

1977

	DATE	WKS		
1.	1/8	1	**Weekend In New England**	
			Barry Manilow	
2.	1/15	6	**Love Theme From "A Star Is Born" (Evergreen)** *Barbra Streisand*	
3.	2/26	4↕	**Southern Nights** *Glen Campbell*	
4.	3/12	2	**Sam** *Olivia Newton-John*	
5.	4/9	1	**Don't Give Up On Us** *David Soul*	
6.	4/16	1	**Right Time Of The Night**	
			Jennifer Warnes	
7.	4/23	1	**When I Need You** *Leo Sayer*	
8.	4/30	4	**Hello Stranger** *Yvonne Elliman*	
9.	5/28	1	**Margaritaville** *Jimmy Buffett*	
10.	6/4	3	**Looks Like We Made It**	
			Barry Manilow	
11.	6/25	5	**It's Sad To Belong**	
			England Dan & John Ford Coley	
12.	7/30	4	**My Heart Belongs To Me**	
			Barbra Streisand	
13.	8/27	1	**Sunflower** *Glen Campbell*	
14.	9/3	1	**Handy Man** *James Taylor*	
15.	9/10	7	**Nobody Does It Better** *Carly Simon*	
16.	10/29	2	**Just Remember I Love You** *Firefall*	
17.	11/12	1	**We're All Alone** *Rita Coolidge*	
18.	11/19	1	**You Light Up My Life** *Debby Boone*	
19.	11/26	6	**How Deep Is Your Love** *Bee Gees*	

1978

	DATE	WKS		
1.	1/7	4	**Just The Way You Are** *Billy Joel*	
2.	2/4	1	**Desiree** *Neil Diamond*	
3.	2/11	5	**(What A) Wonderful World** *Art Garfunkel/James Taylor/Paul Simon*	
4.	3/18	2↕	**Can't Smile Without You**	
			Barry Manilow	
5.	3/25	6	**We'll Never Have To Say Goodbye Again** *England Dan & John Ford Coley*	
6.	5/13	1	**Feels So Good** *Chuck Mangione*	
7.	5/20	1	**Too Much, Too Little, Too Late**	
			Johnny Mathis/Deniece Williams	
8.	5/27	3	**Even Now** *Barry Manilow*	
9.	6/17	3	**Bluer Than Blue** *Michael Johnson*	
10.	7/8	3	**If Ever I See You Again**	
			Roberta Flack	
11.	7/29	2	**Songbird** *Barbra Streisand*	
12.	8/12	1	**My Angel Baby** *Toby Beau*	
13.	8/19	3	**Three Times A Lady** *Commodores*	
14.	9/9	3	**Fool (If You Think It's Over)**	
			Chris Rea	
15.	9/30	4↕	**Right Down The Line** *Gerry Rafferty*	
16.	10/7	2	**Love Is In The Air** *John Paul Young*	
17.	11/11	10	**Time Passages** *Al Stewart*	

1979

	DATE	WKS		
1.	1/20	2	**This Moment In Time**	
			Engelbert Humperdinck	
2.	2/3	1	**Lotta Love** *Nicolette Larson*	
3.	2/10	4	**I Just Fall In Love Again**	
			Anne Murray	
4.	3/10	7	**Crazy Love** *Poco*	
5.	4/28	1	**I Never Said I Love You** *Orsa Lia*	
6.	5/5	2	**Love Is The Answer**	
			England Dan & John Ford Coley	
7.	5/19	2↕	**Just When I Needed You Most**	
			Randy Vanwarmer	
8.	5/26	2	**She Believes In Me** *Kenny Rogers*	
9.	6/16	3	**Shadows In The Moonlight**	
			Anne Murray	
10.	7/7	7↕	**Lead Me On** *Maxine Nightingale*	
11.	7/28	1	**Morning Dance** *Spyro Gyra*	
12.	8/25	1	**Mama Can't Buy You Love**	
			Elton John	
13.	9/8	2	**Different Worlds** *Maureen McGovern*	
14.	9/22	1	**Rise** *Herb Alpert*	
15.	9/29	2	**Where Were You When I Was Falling In Love** *Lobo*	
16.	10/13	5	**Broken Hearted Me** *Anne Murray*	
17.	11/17	5	**You're Only Lonely** *J.D. Souther*	
18.	12/22	4	**Send One Your Love** *Stevie Wonder*	

1980

	DATE	WKS		
1.	1/19	1	**Deja Vu** *Dionne Warwick*	
2.	1/26	2	**Yes, I'm Ready**	
			Teri DeSario with K.C.	
3.	2/9	1	**Longer** *Dan Fogelberg*	

#1 HITS

1980 (cont.)

4.	2/16	1	**When I Wanted You** *Barry Manilow*
5.	2/23	3↕	**Give It All You Got** *Chuck Mangione*
6.	3/1	1	**Daydream Believer** *Anne Murray*
7.	3/22	6↕	**Lost In Love** *Air Supply*
8.	3/29	1	**Three Times In Love** *Tommy James*
9.	5/10	5	**The Rose** *Bette Midler*
10.	6/14	2	**Little Jeannie** *Elton John*
11.	6/28	3	**Let Me Love You Tonight** *Pure Prairie League*
12.	7/19	5	**Magic** *Olivia Newton-John*
13.	8/23	2	**Why Not Me** *Fred Knoblock*
14.	9/6	2	**Don't Ask Me Why** *Billy Joel*
15.	9/20	3	**No Night So Long** *Dionne Warwick*
16.	10/11	5	**Woman In Love** *Barbra Streisand*
17.	11/15	4	**Lady** *Kenny Rogers*
18.	12/13	2	**Never Be The Same** *Christopher Cross*
19.	12/27	3	**More Than I Can Say** *Leo Sayer*

1981

	DATE	WKS	
1.	1/17	3	**I Love A Rainy Night** *Eddie Rabbitt*
2.	2/7	2	**The Winner Takes It All** *Abba*
3.	2/21	1	**Smoky Mountain Rain** *Ronnie Milsap*
4.	2/28	2	**9 To 5** *Dolly Parton*
5.	3/14	4	**What Kind Of Fool** *Barbra Streisand & Barry Gibb*
6.	4/11	3	**Angel Of The Morning** *Juice Newton*
7.	5/2	2	**Morning Train (Nine To Five)** *Sheena Easton*
8.	5/16	2	**Sukiyaki** *Taste Of Honey*
9.	5/30	2	**How 'Bout Us** *Champaign*
10.	6/13	3	**America** *Neil Diamond*
11.	7/4	1	**All Those Years Ago** *George Harrison*
12.	7/11	6	**I Don't Need You** *Kenny Rogers*
13.	8/22	2	**Touch Me When We're Dancing** *Carpenters*
14.	9/5	3	**Endless Love** *Diana Ross & Lionel Richie*
15.	9/26	4	**Arthur's Theme (Best That You Can Do)** *Christopher Cross*
16.	10/24	2	**Share Your Love With Me** *Kenny Rogers*
17.	11/7	3	**Here I Am (Just When I Thought I Was Over You)** *Air Supply*
18.	11/28	3	**The Old Songs** *Barry Manilow*
19.	12/19	6	**Yesterday's Songs** *Neil Diamond*

1982

	DATE	WKS	
1.	1/30	1	**The Sweetest Thing (I've Ever Known)** *Juice Newton*
2.	2/6	2	**Leader Of The Band** *Dan Fogelberg*
3.	2/20	2	**Somewhere Down The Road** *Barry Manilow*
4.	3/6	2	**Through The Years** *Kenny Rogers*
5.	3/20	2	**Key Largo** *Bertie Higgins*
6.	4/3	5	**Chariots Of Fire - Titles** *Vangelis*

1982 (cont.)

7.	5/8	1	**Shanghai Breezes** *John Denver*
8.	5/15	5	**Ebony And Ivory** *Paul McCartney with Stevie Wonder*
9.	6/19	5	**Any Day Now** *Ronnie Milsap*
10.	7/24	4	**Even The Nights Are Better** *Air Supply*
11.	8/21	3	**Hard To Say I'm Sorry** *Chicago*
12.	9/11	2	**Blue Eyes** *Elton John*
13.	9/25	2	**Love Will Turn You Around** *Kenny Rogers*
14.	10/9	2	**Break It To Me Gently** *Juice Newton*
15.	10/23	4	**Heartlight** *Neil Diamond*
16.	11/20	4	**Truly** *Lionel Richie*
17.	12/18	1	**Heartbreaker** *Dionne Warwick*
18.	12/25	4	**The Girl Is Mine** *Michael Jackson/Paul McCartney*

1983

	DATE	WKS	
1.	1/22	3	**Baby, Come To Me** *Patti Austin with James Ingram*
2.	2/12	2	**Shame On The Moon** *Bob Seger*
3.	2/26	6	**You Are** *Lionel Richie*
4.	4/9	1	**Make Love Stay** *Dan Fogelberg*
5.	4/16	2	**It Might Be You** *Stephen Bishop*
6.	4/30	3	**I Won't Hold You Back** *Toto*
7.	5/21	4	**My Love** *Lionel Richie*
8.	6/18	4	**Never Gonna Let You Go** *Sergio Mendes*
9.	7/16	3	**All This Love** *DeBarge*
10.	8/6	4	**All Time High** *Rita Coolidge*
11.	9/3	3	**How Am I Supposed To Live Without You** *Laura Branigan*
12.	9/24	2	**Tell Her About It** *Billy Joel*
13.	10/8	1	**True** *Spandau Ballet*
14.	10/15	4	**Islands In The Stream** *Kenny Rogers with Dolly Parton*
15.	11/12	4	**All Night Long (All Night)** *Lionel Richie*
16.	12/10	2	**The Way He Makes Me Feel** *Barbra Streisand*
17.	12/24	6	**Read 'Em And Weep** *Barry Manilow*

1984

	DATE	WKS	
1.	2/4	4	**Think Of Laura** *Christopher Cross*
2.	3/3	1	**An Innocent Man** *Billy Joel*
3.	3/10	4	**Got A Hold On Me** *Christine McVie*
4.	4/7	6	**Hello** *Lionel Richie*
5.	5/19	2	**The Longest Time** *Billy Joel*
6.	6/2	3	**Time After Time** *Cyndi Lauper*
7.	6/23	1	**Believe In Me** *Dan Fogelberg*
8.	6/30	1	**Almost Paradise...Love Theme From Footloose** *Mike Reno & Ann Wilson*
9.	7/7	4	**If Ever You're In My Arms Again** *Peabo Bryson*
10.	8/4	5	**Stuck On You** *Lionel Richie*

#1 HITS

1984 (cont.)

11.	9/8	2	**Leave A Tender Moment Alone**
			Billy Joel
12.	9/22	3	**Drive** *The Cars*
13.	10/13	3	**I Just Called To Say I Love You**
			Stevie Wonder
14.	11/3	2	**What About Me?**
			Kenny Rogers with Kim Carnes and
			James Ingram
15.	11/17	4	**Penny Lover** *Lionel Richie*
16.	12/15	1	**Sea Of Love** *The Honeydrippers*
17.	12/22	3	**Do What You Do** *Jermaine Jackson*

1985

	DATE	WKS	
1.	1/12	2	**All I Need** *Jack Wagner*
2.	1/26	2	**You're The Inspiration** *Chicago*
3.	2/9	5	**Careless Whisper**
			Wham! feat. George Michael
4.	3/16	2	**Too Late For Goodbyes**
			Julian Lennon
5.	3/30	3	**One More Night** *Phil Collins*
6.	4/20	2	**We Are The World** *USA for Africa*
7.	5/4	1	**Rhythm Of The Night** *DeBarge*
8.	5/11	2	**Smooth Operator** *Sade*
9.	5/25	2	**Suddenly** *Billy Ocean*
10.	6/8	2	**Axel F** *Harold Faltermeyer*
11.	6/22	4	**The Search Is Over** *Survivor*
12.	7/20	3	**Who's Holding Donna Now** *DeBarge*
13.	8/10	2	**Everytime You Go Away** *Paul Young*
14.	8/24	6	**Cherish** *Kool & The Gang*
15.	10/5	3	**Saving All My Love For You**
			Whitney Houston
16.	10/26	3	**Part-Time Lover** *Stevie Wonder*
17.	11/16	3	**Separate Lives**
			Phil Collins & Marilyn Martin
18.	12/7	5	**Say You, Say Me** *Lionel Richie*

1986

	DATE	WKS	
1.	1/11	2	**That's What Friends Are For**
			Dionne & Friends
2.	1/25	1	**Go Home** *Stevie Wonder*
3.	2/1	1	**My Hometown** *Bruce Springsteen*
4.	2/8	1	**The Sweetest Taboo** *Sade*
5.	2/15	1	**How Will I Know** *Whitney Houston*
6.	2/22	3	**Sara** *Starship*
7.	3/15	3	**These Dreams** *Heart*
8.	4/5	1	**Secret Lovers** *Atlantic Starr*
9.	4/12	2	**Overjoyed** *Stevie Wonder*
10.	4/26	5	**Greatest Love Of All**
			Whitney Houston
11.	5/31	3	**Live To Tell** *Madonna*
12.	6/21	1	**There'll Be Sad Songs (To Make**
			You Cry) *Billy Ocean*
13.	6/28	1	**No One Is To Blame** *Howard Jones*
14.	7/5	2	**Your Wildest Dreams**
			The Moody Blues
15.	7/19	5	**Glory Of Love** *Peter Cetera*

1986 (cont.)

16.	8/23	2	**Words Get In The Way**
			Miami Sound Machine
17.	9/6	2	**Friends And Lovers**
			Gloria Loring & Carl Anderson
18.	9/20	3	**Stuck With You**
			Huey Lewis & the News
19.	10/11	2	**Throwing It All Away** *Genesis*
20.	10/25	2	**I'll Be Over You** *Toto*
21.	11/8	2	**The Next Time I Fall**
			Peter Cetera W/Amy Grant
22.	11/22	2	**Love Will Conquer All** *Lionel Richie*
23.	12/6	2	**The Way It Is**
			Bruce Hornsby & The Range
24.	12/20	3	**Love Is Forever** *Billy Ocean*

1987

	DATE	WKS	
1.	1/10	3	**This Is The Time** *Billy Joel*
2.	1/31	1	**At This Moment**
			Billy Vera & The Beaters
3.	2/7	4	**Ballerina Girl** *Lionel Richie*
4.	3/7	2	**You Got It All** *The Jets*
5.	3/21	3	**Mandolin Rain**
			Bruce Hornsby & The Range
6.	4/11	2	**Nothing's Gonna Stop Us Now**
			Starship
7.	4/25	3	**The Finer Things** *Steve Winwood*
8.	5/16	1	**Just To See Her** *Smokey Robinson*
9.	5/23	1	**La Isla Bonita** *Madonna*
10.	5/30	2	**Always** *Atlantic Starr*
11.	6/13	3	**In Too Deep** *Genesis*
12.	7/4	3	**I Wanna Dance With Somebody**
			(Who Loves Me) *Whitney Houston*
13.	7/25	1	**Moonlighting** *Al Jarreau*
14.	8/1	3	**Back In The High Life Again**
			Steve Winwood
15.	8/22	1	**Love Power**
			Dionne Warwick & Jeffrey Osborne
16.	8/29	3	**I Just Can't Stop Loving You**
			Michael Jackson
17.	9/19	3	**Didn't We Almost Have It All**
			Whitney Houston
18.	10/10	4	**Little Lies** *Fleetwood Mac*
19.	11/7	2	**Breakout** *Swing Out Sister*
20.	11/21	4	**(I've Had) The Time Of My Life**
			Bill Medley & Jennifer Warnes
21.	12/19	4	**Got My Mind Set On You**
			George Harrison

1988

	DATE	WKS	
1.	1/16	3	**Everywhere** *Fleetwood Mac*
2.	2/6	1	**Could've Been** *Tiffany*
3.	2/13	1	**Can't Stay Away From You** *Gloria*
			Estefan & Miami Sound Machine
4.	2/20	1	**Seasons Change** *Expose*
5.	2/27	2	**She's Like The Wind** *Patrick*
			Swayze featuring Wendy Fraser

#1 HITS

1988 (cont.)

6.	3/12	3	**Never Gonna Give You Up** *Rick Astley*
7.	4/2	3	**Where Do Broken Hearts Go** *Whitney Houston*
8.	4/23	3	**Anything For You** *Gloria Estefan & Miami Sound Machine*
9.	5/14	1	**I Don't Want To Live Without You** *Foreigner*
10.	5/21	1	**Shattered Dreams** *Johnny Hates Jazz*
11.	5/28	3	**One More Try** *George Michael*
12.	6/18	1	**The Valley Road** *Bruce Hornsby & The Range*
13.	6/25	3	**Make It Real** *The Jets*
14.	7/16	3	**Make Me Lose Control** *Eric Carmen*
15.	8/6	2	**Roll With It** *Steve Winwood*
16.	8/20	1	**I Don't Wanna Go On With You Like That** *Elton John*
17.	8/27	1	**1-2-3** *Gloria Estefan & Miami Sound Machine*
18.	9/3	4	**One Good Woman** *Peter Cetera*
19.	10/1	1	**It Would Take A Strong Strong Man** *Rick Astley*
20.	10/8	3	**Groovy Kind Of Love** *Phil Collins*
21.	10/29	2	**One Moment In Time** *Whitney Houston*
22.	11/12	2	**How Can I Fall?** *Breathe*
23.	11/26	1	**Kissing A Fool** *George Michael*
24.	12/3	1	**Look Away** *Chicago*
25.	12/10	1	**Giving You The Best That I Got** *Anita Baker*
26.	12/17	1	**Waiting For A Star To Fall** *Boy Meets Girl*
27.	12/24	5	**Two Hearts** *Phil Collins*

1989

	DATE	WKS	
1.	1/28	1	**As Long As You Follow** *Fleetwood Mac*
2.	2/4	2	**Holding On** *Steve Winwood*
3.	2/18	1	**When I'm With You** *Sheriff*
4.	2/25	4	**The Living Years** *Mike & The Mechanics*
5.	3/25	2	**You Got It** *Roy Orbison*
6.	4/8	2	**Eternal Flame** *Bangles*
7.	4/22	4	**After All** *Cher & Peter Cetera*
8.	5/20	2	**Second Chance** *Thirty Eight Special*
9.	6/3	1	**Miss You Like Crazy** *Natalie Cole*
10.	6/10	2	**Everlasting Love** *Howard Jones*
11.	6/24	6	**If You Don't Know Me By Now** *Simply Red*
12.	8/5	6	**Right Here Waiting** *Richard Marx*
13.	9/16	2	**One** *Bee Gees*
14.	9/30	1	**If I Could Turn Back Time** *Cher*
15.	10/7	2	**Cherish** *Madonna*
16.	10/21	1	**Healing Hands** *Elton John*
17.	10/28	5	**Don't Know Much** *Linda Ronstadt/Aaron Neville*
18.	12/2	5	**Another Day In Paradise** *Phil Collins*

1990

	DATE	WKS	
1.	1/6	2	**How Am I Supposed To Live Without You** *Michael Bolton*
2.	1/20	1	**Downtown Train** *Rod Stewart*
3.	1/27	5	**Here We Are** *Gloria Estefan*
4.	3/3	3	**All My Life** *Linda Ronstadt/Aaron Neville*
5.	3/24	4	**Love Will Lead You Back** *Taylor Dayne*
6.	4/21	5	**This Old Heart Of Mine** *Rod Stewart (with Ronald Isley)*
7.	5/26	1	**Hold On** *Wilson Phillips*
8.	6/2	5	**Do You Remember?** *Phil Collins*
9.	7/7	3	**When I'm Back On My Feet Again** *Michael Bolton*
10.	7/28	1	**Cuts Both Ways** *Gloria Estefan*
11.	8/4	3	**Vision Of Love** *Mariah Carey*
12.	8/25	3	**Come Back To Me** *Janet Jackson*
13.	9/15	1	**Release Me** *Wilson Phillips*
14.	9/22	3	**Oh Girl** *Paul Young*
15.	10/13	2	**Unchained Melody** *The Righteous Brothers*
16.	10/27	1	**Love Takes Time** *Mariah Carey*
17.	11/3	6	**From A Distance** *Bette Midler*
18.	12/15	5	**You Gotta Love Someone** *Elton John*

1991

	DATE	WKS	
1.	1/19	2	**Because I Love You (The Postman Song)** *Stevie B*
2.	2/2	2	**The First Time** *Surface*
3.	2/16	4	**All The Man That I Need** *Whitney Houston*
4.	3/16	2	**Coming Out Of The Dark** *Gloria Estefan*
5.	3/30	4	**You're In Love** *Wilson Phillips*
6.	4/27	1	**Cry For Help** *Rick Astley*
7.	5/4	3	**Baby Baby** *Amy Grant*
8.	5/25	4↕	**Love Is A Wonderful Thing** *Michael Bolton*
9.	6/8	1	**I Don't Wanna Cry** *Mariah Carey*
10.	6/29	5	**Rush, Rush** *Paula Abdul*
11.	8/3	8	**(Everything I Do) I Do It For You** *Bryan Adams*
12.	9/28	2	**Time, Love And Tenderness** *Michael Bolton*
13.	10/12	1	**Everybody Plays The Fool** *Aaron Neville*
14.	10/19	2	**Too Many Walls** *Cathy Dennis*
15.	11/2	4	**When A Man Loves A Woman** *Michael Bolton*
16.	11/30	3	**That's What Love Is For** *Amy Grant*
17.	12/21	4	**Keep Coming Back** *Richard Marx*

#1 HITS

LABEL ABBREVIATIONS

ABC-Para. .... ABC-Paramount
Ariola Am. .... Ariola America
Art. of Amer. .... Artists Of America
Atlantic A. .... Atlantic America
Believe .... Believe In A Dream
CBS Assoc. .... CBS Associated
Canadian A. .... Canadian American
Cleve. Int. .... Cleveland International
Common. U. .... Commonwealth United
EMI-Man. .... EMI-Manhattan
Epic Snd. .... Epic Soundtrax
GNP Cresc. .... GNP Crescendo
Midland I. .... Midland International
Motown Yest. .... Motown Yesterday
Music Fac. .... Music Factory
National G. .... National General
Paisley P. .... Paisley Park
Phil. Int. .... Philadelphia International
Private M. .... Private Music
Private S. .... Private Stock
Rolling S. .... Rolling Stones
Scotti Br. .... Scotti Brothers
Sesame St. .... Sesame Street
Stormy F. .... Stormy Forest
Tetragramm. .... Tetragrammaton
Three Bros. .... Three Brothers
United Art. .... United Artists
Verve F. .... Verve Forecast
Wing & Prayer .... Wing And A Prayer
World Art. .... World Artists
World Pac. .... World Pacific

ALL THE HITS THAT

Only Joel Whitburn's Record Research Books List Every

When the talk turns to music, more people turn to Joel Whitburn's Record Research Collection than to any other reference source.

That's because these are the **only** books that get right to the bottom of *Billboard*'s major charts, with **complete, fully accurate chart data on every record ever charted**. So they're quoted with confidence by DJ's, music show hosts, program directors, collectors and other music enthusiasts worldwide.

Each book lists every record's significant chart data, such as peak position, debut date, peak date, weeks charted, label, record number and much more, all conveniently arranged for fast, easy reference. Most books also feature artist biographies, record notes, RIAA Platinum/Gold Record certifications, top artist and record achievements, all-time artist and record rankings, a chronological listing of all #1 hits, and additional in-depth chart information.

Joel Whitburn's Record Research Collection. #1 on **everyone's** hit list.

TOP POP SINGLES 1955-1990
Nearly 20,000 Pop singles - every "Hot 100" hit - arranged by artist. 848 pages. Softcover. $60.

POP SINGLES ANNUAL 1955-1990
A year-by-year ranking, based on chart performance, of the nearly 20,000 Pop hits. 736 pages. $70 Hardcover/$60 Softcover.

TOP POP ALBUMS 1955-1992
An artist-by-artist history of the over 17,000 LPs that ever appeared on *Billboard*'s Pop albums charts, with a complete A-Z listing below each artist of <u>every</u> track from <u>every</u> charted album by that artist. 976 pages. Hardcover. $95.

TOP POP ALBUM TRACKS 1955-1992
An all-inclusive, alphabetical index of every song track from every charted music album, with the artist's name and the album's chart debut year. 544 pages. Hardcover. $55.

BILLBOARD HOT 100/POP SINGLES CHARTS:

THE EIGHTIES 1980-1989
THE SEVENTIES 1970-1979
THE SIXTIES 1960-1969

Three complete collections of the actual weekly "Hot 100" charts from each decade, reproduced in black-and-white at 70% of original size. Over 550 pages each. Deluxe Hardcover. $95 each.

POP CHARTS 1955-1959

Reproductions of every weekly Pop singles chart *Billboard* published from 1955 through 1959 ("Best Sellers," "Jockeys," "Juke Box," "Top 100" and "Hot 100"). 496 pages. Deluxe Hardcover. $95.

BILLBOARD POP ALBUM CHARTS 1965-1969
The greatest of all album eras...straight off the pages of *Billboard*! Every weekly *Billboard* Pop albums chart, shown in its entirety, from 1965 through 1969. All charts reproduced in black-and-white at 70% of original size. 496 pages. Deluxe Hardcover. $95.

EVER CHARTED!

Record To Ever Appear On Every Major Billboard Chart.

POP MEMORIES 1890-1954
The only documented chart history of early American popular music, arranged by artist. 660 pages. Hardcover. $60.

TOP COUNTRY SINGLES 1944-1988
An artist-by-artist listing of every "Country" single ever charted. 564 pages. $60 Hardcover/$50 Softcover.

TOP R&B SINGLES 1942-1988
Every "Soul," "Black," "Urban Contemporary" and "Rhythm & Blues" charted single, listed by artist. 624 pages. $60 Hardcover/$50 Softcover.

TOP ADULT CONTEMPORARY 1961-1993
America's leading listener format is covered hit by hit in this fact-packed volume. Lists, artist by artist, the complete history of *Billboard's* "Easy Listening" and "Adult Contemporary" charts. 368 pages. Hardcover. $50.

BUBBLING UNDER THE HOT 100 1959-1985
Here are 27 years of *Billboard's* unique and intriguing "Bubbling Under" chart, listed by artist. Also features "Bubbling Under" titles that later hit the "Hot 100." 384 pages. Hardcover. $45.

BILLBOARD TOP 1000 x 5
Here for the first time ever, are five complete <u>separate</u> rankings—from #1 right down through #1000—of the all-time top charted hits of Pop Music 1955-1993, Pop Music 1940-1955, Adult Contemporary Music 1961-1993, R&B Music 1942-1993, and Country Music 1944-1993. 272 pages. Softcover. $30.

DAILY #1 HITS 1940-1992
A desktop calendar of a half-century of #1 pop records. Lists one day of the year per page of every record that held the #1 position on the Pop singles charts on that day for each of the past 53+ years. 384 pages. Spiral-bound softcover. $30.

BILLBOARD #1s 1950-1991
A week-by-week listing of every #1 <u>single</u> and <u>album</u> from Billboard's Pop, R&B, Country and Adult Contemporary charts. 336 pages. Softcover. $35.

MUSIC YEARBOOKS 1983/1984/1985/1986
The complete story of each year in music, covering *Billboard's* biggest singles and albums charts. Various page lengths. Softcover. $40 each.

MUSIC & VIDEO YEARBOOKS 1987/1988/1989/1990/1991/1992
Comprehensive, yearly updates on *Billboard's* major singles, albums and videocassettes charts. Various page lengths. Softcover. $40 each.

For complete book descriptions and ordering information, call, write or fax today.

RECORD RESEARCH INC.
P.O. Box 200
Menomonee Falls, WI
53052-0200
U.S.A.
Phone: 414-251-5408
Fax: 414-251-9452

The RECORD RESEARCH *Collection*

Book Title	Quantity	Price	Total
1. Billboard Pop Charts 1955-1959 (Hardcover)	_____	$95	_____
2. Billboard Hot 100 Charts - The Sixties (Hardcover)	_____	$95	_____
3. Billboard Hot 100 Charts - The Seventies (Hardcover)	_____	$95	_____
4. Billboard Hot 100 Charts - The Eighties (Hardcover)	_____	$95	_____
5. Billboard Pop Album Charts 1965-1969 (Hardcover)	_____	$95	_____
6. Top Pop Albums 1955-1992 (Hardcover)	_____	$95	_____
7. Top Pop Album Tracks 1955-1992 (Hardcover)	_____	$55	_____
8. Top Pop Singles 1955-1990 (Softcover)	_____	$60	_____
9. Pop Singles Annual 1955-1990 (Hardcover)	_____	$70	_____
10. Pop Singles Annual 1955-1990 (Softcover)	_____	$60	_____
11. Top Country Singles 1944-1988 (Hardcover)	_____	$60	_____
12. Top Country Singles 1944-1988 (Softcover)	_____	$50	_____
13. Top R&B Singles 1942-1988 (Hardcover)	_____	$60	_____
14. Top R&B Singles 1942-1988 (Softcover)	_____	$50	_____
15. Pop Memories 1890-1954 (Hardcover)	_____	$60	_____
16. Top Adult Contemporary 1961-1993 (Hardcover)	_____	$50	_____
17. Bubbling Under The Hot 100 1959-1985 (Hardcover)	_____	$45	_____
18. Billboard #1s 1950-1991 (Softcover)	_____	$35	_____
19. Billboard Top 1000 x 5 (Softcover)	_____	$30	_____
20. Daily #1 Hits 1940-1992 (Spiral-bound Softcover)	_____	$30	_____
21. Yearbooks (All Softcover)	...$40 each		_____

☐ 1992 ☐ 1991 ☐ 1990 ☐ 1989 ☐ 1988
☐ 1987 ☐ 1986 ☐ 1985 ☐ 1984 ☐ 1983

Shipping & Handling (see below) ..... _____

Total Payment ... $ _____

Shipping & Handling:

All U.S. orders add **$5** for the first book ordered and **$2** for each additional book.

All Canadian and foreign orders add **$6** for the first book ordered and **$3** for each additional book. Canadian and foreign orders are shipped via surface mail and must be paid in U.S. dollars. Call or write for airmail shipping rates.

Payment Method: ☐ Check   ☐ Money Order
  ☐ MasterCard   ☐ VISA

MasterCard or VISA # __ __ __ __ __ __ __ __ __ __ __ __ __ __ __ __

Expiration Date _____ / _____
  Mo.   Yr.

Signature _____

To Charge Your Order By Phone, Call 414-251-5408 or
Fax 414-251-9452 (office hours: 8AM-5PM CST)

Name _____

Company Name _____

Address _____ Apt./Suite # _____

City _____ State/Province_____

ZIP/Postal Code _____ Country_____

Record Research Inc.
P.O. Box 200
Menomonee Falls, WI 53052-0200
U.S.A.

The RECORD RESEARCH *Collection*

Book Title	Quantity	Price	Total
1. Billboard Pop Charts 1955-1959 (Hardcover)		$95	
2. Billboard Hot 100 Charts - The Sixties (Hardcover)		$95	
3. Billboard Hot 100 Charts - The Seventies (Hardcover)		$95	
4. Billboard Hot 100 Charts - The Eighties (Hardcover)		$95	
5. Billboard Pop Album Charts 1965-1969 (Hardcover)		$95	
6. Top Pop Albums 1955-1992 (Hardcover)		$95	
7. Top Pop Album Tracks 1955-1992 (Hardcover)		$55	
8. Top Pop Singles 1955-1990 (Softcover)		$60	
9. Pop Singles Annual 1955-1990 (Hardcover)		$70	
10. Pop Singles Annual 1955-1990 (Softcover)		$60	
11. Top Country Singles 1944-1988 (Hardcover)		$60	
12. Top Country Singles 1944-1988 (Softcover)		$50	
13. Top R&B Singles 1942-1988 (Hardcover)		$60	
14. Top R&B Singles 1942-1988 (Softcover)		$50	
15. Pop Memories 1890-1954 (Hardcover)		$60	
16. Top Adult Contemporary 1961-1993 (Hardcover)		$50	
17. Bubbling Under The Hot 100 1959-1985 (Hardcover)		$45	
18. Billboard #1s 1950-1991 (Softcover)		$35	
19. Billboard Top 1000 x 5 (Softcover)		$30	
20. Daily #1 Hits 1940-1992 (Spiral-bound Softcover)		$30	
21. Yearbooks (All Softcover)		$40 each	

☐ 1992   ☐ 1991   ☐ 1990   ☐ 1989   ☐ 1988
☐ 1987   ☐ 1986   ☐ 1985   ☐ 1984   ☐ 1983

Shipping & Handling (see below) ...._____

Total Payment ...$_____

Shipping & Handling:

All U.S. orders add **$5** for the first book ordered and **$2** for each additional book.

All Canadian and foreign orders add **$6** for the first book ordered and **$3** for each additional book.
Canadian and foreign orders are shipped via surface mail and must be paid in U.S. dollars.
Call or write for airmail shipping rates.

Payment Method: ☐ Check   ☐ Money Order
                      ☐ MasterCard   ☐ VISA

MasterCard or VISA # _ _ _ _   _ _ _ _   _ _ _ _   _ _ _ _

Expiration Date _____ / _____
               Mo.   Yr.

Signature _____

To Charge Your Order By Phone, Call 414-251-5408 or
Fax 414-251-9452 (office hours: 8AM-5PM CST)

Name _____

Company Name _____

Address _____   Apt./Suite # _____

City _____   State/Province _____

ZIP/Postal Code _____   Country _____

Record Research Inc.
P.O. Box 200
Menomonee Falls, WI 53052-0200
U.S.A.